The Interior Urbanism Theory Reader

The Interior Urbanism Theory Reader expands our understanding of urbanism, interiority, and publicness from a global perspective across time and cultures.

From ancient origins to speculative futures, this book explores the rich complexities of interior urbanism as an interstitial socio-spatial condition. Employing an interdisciplinary lens, it examines the intersectional characteristics that define interior urbanism. Fifty chapters investigate the topic in relation to architecture, planning, urban design, interior architecture, interior design, archaeology, engineering, sociology, psychology, and geography. Individual essays reveal the historical, typological, and morphological origins of interior urbanism, as well as its diverse scales, occupancies, and atmospheres.

The Interior Urbanism Theory Reader will appeal to scholars, practitioners, students, and enthusiasts of urbanism, architecture, planning, interiors, and the social sciences.

Gregory Marinic, PhD, is an Associate Professor in the University of Cincinnati College of Design, Architecture, Art, and Planning. He is the Director of URBANIA, a grant-funded research lab that speculates on metropolitan futures with current research focused on housing, urban design, urban morphology, and informal settlements. Prior to academia, he worked in architecture firms in New York and London, including Rafael Viñoly Architects, Gensler, Tsao & McKown Architects, Yoshihara McKee Architects, and ABS Architects. At Viñoly, he contributed to RIBA and AIA award-winning civic, academic, performing arts, residential, aviation, urban design, master planning, and international competition projects. His New York-based multidisciplinary design practice, Arquipelago, has been awarded by the Seoul Metropolitan Government, American Institute of Architects, and Association of Collegiate Schools of Architecture, as well as exhibited in the AIA Center for Architecture in New York, AIA Center for Architecture and Design in Philadelphia, Estonian Architecture Museum in Tallinn, Dongdaemun Design Plaza in Seoul, TSMD Architecture Center in Ankara, and National Building Museum in Washington, DC.

The Interior Urbanism Theory Reader

Edited by
Gregory Marinic

Routledge
Taylor & Francis Group

LONDON AND NEW YORK

Front cover image: Old Arcade (1890) in Cleveland by John Eisenmann and George H. Smith. Photo by Tito Mesias

Back cover image: Interior courtyard of the Cleveland Museum of Art (2013) by Rafael Viñoly. Photo by Gregory Marinic

First published 2024
by Routledge
4 Park Square, Milton Park, Abingdon, Oxon OX14 4RN

and by Routledge
605 Third Avenue, New York, NY 10158

Routledge is an imprint of the Taylor & Francis Group, an informa business

British Library Cataloguing-in-Publication Data
A catalogue record for this book is available from the British Library

Library of Congress Cataloging-in-Publication Data
Names: Marinic, Gregory, editor.
Title: The interior urbanism theory reader / edited by Gregory Marinic.
Description: Abingdon, Oxon: Routledge, 2024. |
Includes bibliographical references and index. |
Identifiers: LCCN 2023018125 (print) | LCCN 2023018126 (ebook) |
ISBN 9781138336308 (hardback) | ISBN 9781138336315 (paperback) |
ISBN 9780429443091 (ebook)
Subjects: LCSH: Space (Architecture)—Social aspects. | Social psychology.
Classification: LCC NA2765 .I57 2024 (print) | LCC NA2765 (ebook) |
DDC 720/.47—dc23/eng/20230801
LC record available at https://lccn.loc.gov/2023018125
LC ebook record available at https://lccn.loc.gov/2023018126

ISBN: 9781138336308 (hbk)
ISBN: 9781138336315 (pbk)
ISBN: 9780429443091 (ebk)

DOI: 10.4324/9780429443091

Typeset in Univers
by codeMantra

Contents

Contents

To Rafael Viñoly (1944–2023)—a colleague, mentor, and friend of so many

Contents

Contributors

Joseph Altshuler is cofounder of Could Be Design, an award-winning Chicago-based design practice, and an Assistant Professor in the School of Architecture. He is also the director of the Architectural Companionship Laboratory, a design research collective that works at the intersection of architecture, public art, creative placemaking, and tactical urbanism. His teaching, practice, and scholarship explore architecture's capacity to build lively audiences, initiate serious play, and amplify participation in civic life. Joseph has authored book chapters and contributed essays to a wide range of international publications, and he is the editor-in-chief of HYPERLINK "https://www.soiledzine.org/" *SOILED*, a periodical of architectural storytelling positioned between a literary journal and a design magazine.

Paramita Atmodiwirjo, PhD, is a professor of architecture at Universitas Indonesia. Her research interests are on the relationship between architecture, interior and the well-being of the users. She obtained her PhD from the University of Sheffield. She received various research grants for the projects that focus on the role of architecture for health and well-being, including the grants from UK Academy of Medical Sciences and Indonesia Ministry of Education. She also works closely with schools and communities in Indonesia in various community engagement projects to improve the quality of spaces for learning and living. She is the recipient of FuturArc Green Leadership Award 2019 and Holcim Award Asia Pacific 2011, and the chief editor of *Interiority* journal.

Suzie Attiwill, PhD, is Professor of Interior Design at RMIT University in Melbourne, Australia. Since 1991, her practice has involved exhibition design, curatorial work, writing and teaching. Research is conducted through a practice of designing with a curatorial inflection attending to arrangements (and re-arrangements) of spatial, temporal, and material relations to intervene in contemporary conditions and experiment with new productions of interior and interiority in relation to modes of living, inhabitation, subjectivity, pedagogy, and creative practice. Collaborative projects include urban + interior, an international publication; beyond building with the Australian Childhood Trauma Group; Abacus Learning Centre for children on the autism spectrum; and a series of curatorial experiments in ecologies of learning – physical, social and mental. From 2018 to 2021, Suzie was Associate Dean Interior Design, RMIT School of Architecture and Urban Design. She also leads the RMIT Interior Design practice research PhD program that is offered in Australia, Europe, and Asia.

Shannon Bassett is Assistant Professor of Architecture and Ecological Urbanism at McEwen School of Architecture, Laurentian University. Her research, teaching, writing and practice operate at the intersection(s) of architecture, urban design and landscape ecology. She holds a Masters of Architecture in Urban Design from the Harvard GSD, and a BArch with Distinction from Carleton University. Her design work and research has been exhibited both nationally, as well as internationally. Her architectural and urban design practice has included designing an urban design masterplan and study for an urban artist colony on a 42-acre site, the Village of the Arts in Bradenton, Florida, as well as a series of speculative design studies for the City of Tampa Riverwalk for the City of Tampa.'

Markus Berger is Associate Professor and Graduate Program Director in the Department of Interior Architecture at the Rhode Island School of Design. He is a registered architect (SBA) in the Netherlands and principal of the Providence based art|design studio InsideOut Design. He co-founded and co-edits Int|AR, the Journal on Interventions and Adaptive Reuse, that encompasses issues of preservation, conservation, alteration and interventions. His work, research, writing and teaching is a critique on modern architecture and focuses on forms of change such as art and design modifications and interventions in the built environment. Berger is widely published.

Graeme Brooker is Professor of Interior Design and Head of Interiors at The Royal College of Art, London. He has published widely on many aspects of the interior and in particular the reuse of existing buildings. His recent publications include *Key Interiors Since 1900* (Laurence King, 2013), *Adaptations* (Bloomsbury 2016), *Brinkworth: So Good So Far* (Lund Humphreys, 2019) and *50 words for Reuse* (Canalside Press, 2022). He has co-authored (with Sally Stone) eight books on the interior, including the highly acclaimed *Rereadings* (RIBA 2005, Volume 2–2018). He has edited numerous volumes such as *The Handbook of Interior Architecture + Design* (with Lois Weinthal, Bloomsbury, 2013) and *Interior Futures* (with Harriet Harries, Kevin Walker, Crucible Press 2019). He is a member of the editorial advisory board of the journals *Interiors: Design: Architecture: Culture* (Bloomsbury) and *IDEA*. In 2015, he was awarded a national teaching fellowship by the HEA, and in 2018 became a principal fellow of the HEA. He is the founder and director of the charity Interior Educators (IE), the national subject association for all interior courses in the UK. He is currently working on his latest book, *The Story of the Interior* (Phaidon, 2022).

Edson G. Cabalfin, PhD, is an educator, architect, designer, researcher, and historian. He is the inaugural Associate Dean for Equity, Diversity, and Inclusion at the School of Architecture at Tulane University, while concurrently serving as the Director of the Social Innovation and Social Entrepreneurship Program. He was the Curator of the Philippine Pavilion at the 16th Venice Architecture Biennale 2018. He received his PhD in the History of Architecture and Urban Development from Cornell University in 2012. Under a Fulbright Fellowship, he obtained his Master of Science in Architecture degree from the University of Cincinnati in 2003. Prior to coming to the USA, he received his professional Bachelor of Science in Architecture and Master of Architecture degrees from the University of the Philippines in 1996 and 2001, respectively.

Stephen Caffey, PhD is an Instructional Associate Professor in the Department of Architecture at Texas A&M University, where he also serves as coordinator for the Master of Science and PhD programs in the department. Caffey's research and teaching focus on visual and spatial cultures of empire, design thinking, and architectural history and theory. Current collaborative projects include the Juneteenth Legacy museum initiative for the Metaverse, applications of artificial intelligence to optimize integration of passive climate-responsive design features into new construction, and the histories and theories of digital architecture and design computation. His interests include visual and spatial literacies, art and architectural history, theory and criticism, virtual heritage, and the history, theory, and practice of design thinking and design processes.

Pablo Martínez Capdevila, ARB, is Senior Lecturer at the University of Portsmouth (UK). Formerly, he taught at the *Bergen Arkitekthøgskole* (Norway) and the *UPSAM* (Madrid). His research is focused on the relation between architecture and politics and on the radical stances that redefine or undermine the discipline. His PhD dissertation on Andrea Branzi's urban models received the *UPM 2014–2015 Extraordinary Prize for Doctoral Dissertations*. As an architect, he worked for leading Madrid offices such as *Abalos & Herreros* and *Carvajal + Casariego* before establishing his own practice *MISC Arquitectos*. His design work and writings have been displayed in exhibitions such as *European Generations* in the *Cité de l'Architecture et du Patrimoine* (Paris) and in the *Intermediae-Matadero Madrid* art center and published in magazines such as *Log, A+T, Plot, L'Arca, Architektur + Wettbewerbe, Arquitectura COAM, Cuadernos de Proyectos Arquitectónicos, TC Cuadernos* and *Future,* and in books by Springer, Routledge and the *Pavillon de l'Arsenal.*

Jodi La Coe is a member of the faculty of the School of Architecture at Marywood University, where she is currently serving as the Associate Director of Undergraduate Studies for their degree programs in architecture, construction management, and interior architecture. In her teaching and research, she explores the reciprocal relationship between perception and representation within the linkages between art and science, in which architecture projects a potentially ethical, meaningful, and healthy future. Her work is published in *Ceilings and Dreams: The Architecture of Levity* (Routledge, 2019) and forthcoming in *Expanding Field: Women in Practice Across the Globe* (Lund Humphries, 2022). She holds a PhD in Architecture and Design Research from the Washington-Alexandria Architecture Center of Virginia Tech and a Master of Architecture in the History and Theory of Architecture from McGill University. La Coe is a registered architect in the Commonwealth of Pennsylvania and SEED-certified by the Public Interest Design Institute.

Reem J. Dashti, PhD, is a Kuwait-based interior architect, educator, and Assistant Professor of Interior Architecture at Kuwait University, Kuwait. Her focus is on environmental psychology, place attachment and the manifestation of cultural identity through architecture and space. Her goal is to offer quality education through innovative & human centered design, highlighting the role of architecture as a mediator to heal the soul, body and mind. Her passion for the human-Interior space relationship aspired her to share design knowledge through projects and public lectures such as "Interior Architecture as human experience" and "Biophilic Design as a healing power" at *Mirzam Design Expo* 2018–2019, Kuwait. In 2021, she became an official lecturer in Kuwait Architecture Academy, an online academic program offering design workshops and lectures such as "elements of atmospheric design" and "Creative Concepts in Sensual Design" to push boundaries, create awareness and connection between community and healthy interior environments.

Judith K. De Jong is an architect, urban designer, and Associate Professor of Architecture at the University of Illinois Chicago, whose work investigates the reciprocating relationships between architecture and the city, and the opportunities for design innovation in architectures and urbanisms of mass culture. Her book, *New SubUrbanisms,* is available at Routledge. De Jong has received support from the Graham Foundation and the Great Cities Institute, where she was a 2011–2012 Faculty Scholar, and has presented her work in the USA and internationally. She has written for *MONU, CITE: The Architecture and Design Review of Houston, Land Forum*, and *The Journal of Architectural Education,* among others, and her proposal "How the Strip Mall Can Save Suburbia" was a finalist in the *Build A Better Burb* competition.

Nerea Feliz is Associate Professor at the School of Architecture at The University of Texas at Austin where she teaches both in the Architecture and in the Interior Design programs. She holds both Masters and Bachelor degrees in Architecture from the Politecnica University of Madrid, Escuela Técnica Superior de Arquitectura (ETSAM). In 2010, she founded Nerea Feliz Studio. Her research encompasses scholarly and creative activities that form a cohesive body of work with a sustained focus on public interiority. Situated at the intersection of architecture, interior design and interior urbanism, her work explores interior design's role as a mediator between us, the public spaces we occupy, and pressing cultural and political questions.

Fiona Fisher, PhD, is a design historian and curator. She is a member of the Modern Interiors Research Centre at Kingston School of Art, Kingston University, London, where she is the curator of Dorich House Museum, the 1930s former studio-home of the Estonian sculptor Dora Gordine (1895–1991) and the writer and art collector Richard Hare (1907–1966). Her research interests include British post-war domestic interiors in relation to suburban modernity, and the design of the modern public house in England with reference to national identity and evolving relationships of public, private and commercial space. Her work has been published in academic journals, including the *London Journal* and *Visual Resources* and her publications include *Designing the British Post-War Home: Kenneth Wood, 1948–1968* (2015) and the co-edited collections *The Routledge Companion to Design Studies* (2016), *British Design: Tradition and Modernity after 1948* (2015) and *Performance, Fashion and the Modern Interior* (2011).

Hessam Ghamari is Associate Professor of Interior Design for the Department of Family & Consumer Sciences at California State University, Northridge (CSUN). Dr. Ghamari has more than 15+ years working as an architect and an interior designer in Iran and the United States. He has experience working on healthcare, hospitality, commercial, and residential projects. Prior to his appointment at CSUN, Dr. Ghamari taught at Appalachian State University for four years. He received his PhD in Environmental Interior Design in 2014 from Texas Tech University. He has published articles in peer-reviewed journals and presented at international conferences on environmental psychology, evidence-based design, and healthcare design. Dr. Ghamari's design philosophy revolves around providing healthy and humanistic environments that can positively impact its users – to improve the quality of life of people in different settings. His design philosophy revolves around providing healthy and humanistic environments that can positively impact the users of those environments.

Michael Grugl is an Austrian innovator and architect. After receiving his first innovation award at age 16, he studied at the Technical University Vienna, from which he holds an MArch (Diplomingenieur für Architektur). He is a former member of Architekturwerkstatt Freistadt, a group focused on the adaptive reuse of historic buildings. Between 2004 and 2012, Google was a partner at Any:time Architects in Linz, Austria and Buenos Aires, Argentina. Grugl has collaborated with the Ars Electronica Future Lab. Works include exhibition designs and pavilions, including digital-interactive installations for Swarovski and the Audioversum Museum of Hearing in Innsbruck, Austria. In 2007 he co-created the Pixel Hotel, a built and operational urban intervention for Linz09 in Europe.

Tasoulla Hadjiyanni, PhD, is Northrop Professor of Interior Design at the University of Minnesota. A refugee from Cyprus, she started to unravel how design, culture, and identity intersect under conditions of displacement with her book *The Making of a Refugee: Children Adopting Refugee Identity in Cyprus* (Praeger, 2002). Hadjiyanni's latest book *The Right to Home: Exploring How Space, Culture, and Identity Intersect with Disparities* (Palgrave Macmillan, 2019) features stories of Hmong, Somalis, Mexicans, Ojibwe, and African Americans in Minnesota to explore how elements of interiors support or suppress meaning-making processes, delineating the production of disparities. As a founder of *Culturally Enriched Communities*, Hadjiyanni's TEDx Minneapolis talk advocates for built environments that eliminate disparities and create communities where everyone can thrive. Hadjiyanni's award-winning teaching pedagogies have been used to decolonize design education and nurture global citizens.

Harriet Harriss, RIBA, FRSA, PFHEA, PhD, is an award-winning educator, qualified architect, and the former Dean of the Pratt School of Architecture in Brooklyn, New York. Her teaching, research, and writing focus upon pioneering pedagogic models for design education and exploring the intersectional edge of social justice and the climate crisis theories and practices.

Jeffrey Johnson, AIA, is Associate Professor and Director of the School of Architecture at the University of Kentucky College of Design and a Principal of SLAB Architecture. Johnson's work and research focuses on the intersection of architecture and the city. His recent research has been investigating the radical transformations of China's urban landscape through the proliferation of superblock development, the basic DNA of large-scale urban growth, which will be included as part of a book he is co-authoring entitled *The China Lab Guide to Megablock Urbanisms* (Actar/GSAPP, 2020). Prior to joining the University of Kentucky, Johnson taught at the Graduate School of Architecture, Planning and Preservation at Columbia University, the Illinois Institute of Technology, and at Tongji University in Shanghai. Johnson was the Curator and Co-Academic Director of the 2013 Bi-City Biennale of Urbanism/Architecture in Shenzhen, China.

Aarati Kanekar, PhD, is Professor of Architecture at DAAP, University of Cincinnati. She has been involved in teaching architecture theory and design studios in the graduate and doctoral program at DAAP where she also served as the MArch thesis coordinator, and the director and coordinator of the MSArch program. Her research focuses on issues of design formulation, more specifically representation and spatial construction of meaning, and morphological studies in inter-media translations. These explorations are reflected in her publications on topics ranging from issues of representation and drawings of Lebbeus Woods, Terragni's Danteum and translations of the Divine Comedy across media, spatiality in Calvino's novels, and game design. Her publications extend from architecture journals such as *Perspecta* and *The Journal of Architecture* to literature and philosophy journals such as *TLE* and *Philosophica*. Her book on translation and representation in architecture *Architecture's Pre-texts: Spaces of Translation* was published by Routledge. She is currently working on spatiality in traditional Indian representations.

Joss Kiely is Assistant Professor at the School of Architecture and Interior Design at the University of Cincinnati, where he teaches courses in architectural history and design studio at the undergraduate and graduate level. He has a BA from Connecticut College in French language and literature and architectural studies and a Master of Architecture, a Master of Science in Architecture, and a PhD in architectural history and theory from the Taubman College of Architecture and Urban Planning at the University of Michigan. His PhD dissertation examined the close relationship between commercial aviation and the rise of the postwar, global architectural practice focusing on the Detroit-based architecture firm of Minoru Yamasaki and Associates. His ongoing research agenda focuses on ideas of soft power and the Cold War master plan as produced by architecture firms after World War II as well as the rise of an "airport modern" style that ushered in a new wave of widespread commercial air travel.

Ji Young Kim, RA, is an architect and educator based in Brooklyn. She focuses on expanding the reach of design through practice, education, and cross-disciplinary collaborations. Ji Young is a principal at Praxes, recognized for interactive interventions in the public realm; her speculative and built projects have been widely published in a number of local and international media. Praxes is grounded in its commitment to expand spatial performance by exploring the social, cultural, and experiential aspects of the built environment. She is a Visiting Assistant Professor of Interior Design at the Pratt Institute and Adjunct Professor of Architecture at the New Jersey Institute of Technology. Her studio focuses on developing meaningful design advocacy through sustainable design strategies. Ji Young received her M. Arch from Columbia University's Graduate

School of Architecture, Planning and Preservation and previously trained as an architect at Korea University in Seoul. Prior to starting praxes, she worked at the New York office of Shigeru Ban Architects.

Patricia Lara-Betancourt is a design historian, researcher, and member of the Modern Interiors Research Centre at Kingston School of Art, Kingston University, London, since 2008. She studied Colombian and Latin American History at the Pontificia Universidad Javeriana and Universidad Nacional de Colombia; and worked as a university lecturer in Colombia from 1990 to 1997. Among her recent publications are two co-edited special issues, *Complex Interior Spaces in London, 1850–1930* (The London Journal, 45 No 2, 2020) and *Locating Design Exchanges in Latin America and the Caribbean* (JDH, 32, No 1, 2019). Other publications include the co-edited volumes *Architectures of Display: Department Stores and Modern Retail* (Routledge, 2017), *Flow: Interior, Landscape and Architecture in the Era of Liquid Modernity* (Bloomsbury, 2018) and her article 'The Quest for Modernity: A Global/National Approach to a History of Design in Latin America', in *Designing Worlds: National Design Histories in the Age of Globalization* (Berghahn, 2016).

Jacopo Leveratto, PhD, is Assistant Professor of Interior Architecture at the School of Architecture, Urban Planning, and Construction Engineering at Politecnico di Milano and a Lecturer in the Department of Architecture and Urban Studies of the same university, where he focuses his researches on the study of architectural habitability. Dr. Leveratto has been a Local Principal Investigator of European Research *en/counter/points* on tactical urbanism and has authored numerous publications in peer-reviewed international journals and edited volumes. He is an Associate Editor of the peer-reviewed journals *Stoà*, *ARK* and *iijournal_International Journal of Interior Architecture and Spatial Design*, and among the others, he has written on *Op.Cit.*, the Italian Review of Art Criticism, *Area*, *Interni*, *Vesper*, *The Journal of Interior Design*, and *Int|AR Journal*. Recently, he has exhibited his work with the collective Walden Architects at the Seoul Biennale of Architecture and Urbanism 2021.

Patrick Lee Lucas, PhD, is Associate Professor in the School of Interiors at the University of Kentucky. He leads seminars, teaches lecture courses, and facilitates studio interactions by engaging in community conversations and encouraging students to think about the place of design in the world. He has presented around the world and published extensively on his research agenda about design and community, including a catalog entitled *Close to Home: Edward Loewenstein's Mid-Century Architectural Innovation in the Civil Rights Era* (2013) and a book, *Athens on the Frontier: Grecian-Style Architecture in the Great Valley of the West, 1820–1860* (2022).

William Mangold is an Assistant Professor and Director of the graduate interiors program at Drexel University. Previously, he taught in the interior design program at Pratt Institute, and worked in the NYC office of Ivan Brice Architecture. He is a PhD candidate in Environmental Psychology at the Graduate Center of the City University of New York, and holds degrees in Fine Arts and Architecture from the Rhode Island School of Design (RISD).

William's work is guided by an interest in the interactions between people and place, underscored by a dedication to social responsibility. Trained as a cabinet maker, he combines practice with theory, integrating hands-on making with ongoing study of interior experiences. His edited volume, *The People, Place, and Space Reader*, brings together scholarship on topics such as home, urban experience, and public space. His current research explores design practices that emphasize engagement, participation, and social justice.

Gregory Marinic, PhD, is an Associate Professor in the University of Cincinnati College of Design, Architecture, Art, and Planning. He is the Director of URBANIA, a grant-funded research lab that speculates on metropolitan futures with current research focused on housing, urban design, urban morphology, and informal settlements. Prior to academia, he worked in architecture firms in New York and London, including Rafael Vinoly Architects, Gensler, Tsao & McKown Architects, Yoshihara McKee Architects, and ABS Architects. At Vinoly, he contributed to RIBA and AIA award-winning civic, academic, performing arts, residential, aviation, urban design, master planning, and international competition projects. His New York-based multidisciplinary design practice, Arquipelago, has been awarded by the Seoul Metropolitan Government, American Institute of Architects, and Association of Collegiate Schools of Architecture, as well as exhibited in the AIA Center for Architecture in New York, AIA Center for Architecture and Design in Philadelphia, Estonian Architecture Museum in Tallinn, Dongdaemun Design Plaza in Seoul, TSMD Architecture Center in Ankara, and National Building Museum in Washington, DC.

Patrizio M. Martinelli, PhD, is an Assistant Professor of Interior Architecture and Architecture at Northumbria University (Newcastle upon Tyne, UK) where his teaching and research focus on modernism, domestic and urban interiors, adaptive reuse, and the concept of theatricality of the interior. He studied and worked at Venice University IUAV where he earned a Master's degree in Architecture and a PhD in Architectural Composition. His research has been published in monographs and journals (such as *Journal of Interior Design, Architecture and Culture, Home Cultures*) and presented at several international conferences and lectures. His creative work on collage and montage techniques has been showcased in galleries and publications throughout Italy, the UK and the United States. From 2017 to 2022, Dr. Martinelli taught at Miami University (Oxford, USA); he is a guest teacher at Münster School of Architecture (Germany) and taught workshops at BTU Cottbus (Germany) and the Escuela de Arquitectura, Toledo (Spain).

Pablo Meninato, PhD, is an architectural critic, and educator. A native of Argentina, Meninato has taught and practiced architecture in Philadelphia, Buenos Aires, and Monterrey, Mexico. Before joining Temple University as an Associate Professor, Meninato taught at various academic institutions, including the University of Pennsylvania, the Universidad de Monterrey, and Universidad de Palermo at Buenos Aires. Meninato's essays have been published in various magazines, journals, and books. He is the author of *Unexpected Affinities* (Routledge, 2018), a book that proposes a historical reassessment of the concept of architectural "type" and its impact on the design process. Meninato is embarked on a multi-year research and publishing project examining how various contemporary architects are developing new and original interventions in informal settlements across Latin America. The first outcome of this project is the co-edited book *Informality and the City—Theories, Actions, Interventions* (Springer Rotterdam, 2022), a multidisciplinary overview of informality in the Global South.

Edward Mitchell is the Director of Architecture and Interior Design at the University of Cincinnati. Prior to his appointment, he was an associate professor at the School of Architecture, Yale University, where he served as the Director of the Post Professional program and coordinated the post-professional and graduate studios in architecture and urbanism. His award-winning practice has been recognized by the Architectural League of New York and the Boston Society of Architects. He has been a member of Vita Nuova, an environmental planning consortium, and the Urban Design Workshop at Yale. He has exhibited, published and lectured internationally. His two latest books, *A Train of Cities* and *Common Wealth* are studies done at Yale on the regional potentials in former industrial centers in Boston and South Coast Massachusetts. He has been the Chair of the National ACSA Annual Meeting and has lectured and exhibited internationally including Yale, Harvard, Princeton, Columbia, University of Illinois, California College of the Arts, Syracuse University, Ohio State University, Parsons, Pratt, University of Kentucky, UCLA, Northeastern University, Aalto University in Helsinki, the Gilbane Development group, and the Salzburg Seminars in Austria.

Diana Nicholas (Dee) established the Design-led Co-strategy 4 Health (DLCS4Health) Lab, an umbrella Lab that houses interdisciplinary research and scholarship, in 2013. She is an Associate Professor and the Founding Director of the MS Design Research Program at Drexel University, in Philadelphia. Dee holds degrees in both Architecture and Fine Arts, and her work as a researcher, teacher, and colleague is primarily concerned with the supportive possibilities within our environments through habit and setting. Her lab takes a socially responsive approach to the research they undertake, and recently she exhibited research works in the Midwest and the East Coast. Dee's work is presented in National and International Journals, including *The Design Journal*, *The Plan Journal*, and *ii Journal: International Journal of Interior Architecture + Spatial Design*.

Ou Ning is a Senior Research Fellow of the Center for Arts, Design, and Social Research in Boston (2019–2021) and the Author of *Utopia in Practice: Bishan Project and Rural Reconstruction* (Palgrave Macmillan, 2020).

Bryan D. Orthel, PhD, NCIDQ, NCARB, is an Associate Professor of Design at Indiana University Bloomington. He believes that designers require interdisciplinary, historically aware, and socially contextualized approaches to solve problems. In teaching, consulting, and professional practice, he has worked with small communities to save and use places as varied as National Historic Landmarks and vernacular structures. His scholarship focuses on the ways people understand and use history in ordinary living (historical consciousness), as well as the teaching and learning of design. His scholarship on heritage and health, design history, preservation, and design thinking has been published in the *International Journal of Heritage Studies*, *Geographical Review*, *Buildings & Landscapes*, *SAGE Open*, *Journal of Interior Design*, *Interiors*, and *Preservation Education & Research*, as well as edited volumes.

Ziad Qureshi is an architect and educator with a decade of experience in the AEC industry. Previously, he was an Associate Professor in the College of Architecture and Design at the University of Houston, a Research One institution where he received Tenure in 2021. He additionally taught architecture and design at Iowa State University, the Universidad de Monterrey in Mexico, and Arizona State University. He currently practices architecture professionally in Minneapolis, where he has participated in multiple award-winning projects, including work with noted American Modernist Ralph Rapson. His research focuses on transnational architecture and urbanism, contextual change and adaptive reuse, and service-based community outreach. Qureshi holds an MDes in History and Theory from Harvard University's GSD and an MArch from Arizona State University. His work has been awarded by the ACSA, IDEC, and AIA and featured in a variety of national and international journals, books, conference proceedings, and exhibitions.

Rebekah Ison Radtke is an Associate Professor in the University of Kentucky College of Design. She earned a Master of Architecture at the School of the Art Institute of Chicago and received a Bachelor of Arts in Interior Design at the University of Kentucky. Professor Radtke investigates how interior design enables social change by applying boundary-spanning pedagogical approaches rather than discipline-specific processes. Since 2011, her transdisciplinary and multi-scalar projects have produced better living and learning environments, as well as healthy communities in national and international venues. Her collaborative work, funded by a range of national entities, include pedagogical projects in China, design-build projects in Brazil, sustainability research in South Africa, community-activated interventions in Appalachia, and experiential learning design initiatives in Lexington, KY. These research endeavors seek to build transformative connections through impactful collaborations and bring spatial design principles to a broader audience.

Hennie Reynders, PhD, is an architect and tenured Full Professor in the Department of Architecture, Interior Architecture and Designed Objects at the School of the Art Institute of Chicago. As an architect and designer, his work crosses disciplinary boundaries and includes art installations, product design, architecture, and landscape urbanism projects. His research and teaching focus on spatial relationships, citizen infrastructure, design theory and interdisciplinary thinking and making at the intersection of art, design and science – more specifically as expressed in the relationship between structure and agency. He has exhibited, lectured and acted as a moderator in Chicago, Barcelona, Edinburgh, Lugano, Melbourne, Tokyo, Johannesburg and other cities internationally. Dr. Reynders earned a first professional degree in Architecture at the University of Pretoria, South Africa, a second professional degree in Urbanism and Activist Practice (MArch) from the University of Illinois *at Chicago* and a PhD from the University of Edinburgh, UK.

Nicky Ryan is the Dean of Design at London College of Communication, University of the Arts London and has over 20 years' experience of teaching, leadership and management in Higher Education. Her undergraduate and postgraduate studies were in the History of Art and Architecture and her PhD thesis examined the relationship between museums and the market. Postdoctoral research has further explored collaborations between business and the arts and the physical spaces in which these relationships are embodied. This interdisciplinary research has resulted in outputs which include book chapters, articles, reviews, and conference papers in relation to contemporary patronage, culture-led regeneration, spatial practices, museums and curating and art and design pedagogies. Nicky is a Trustee on the Board of Age UK Lambeth & Southwark, Chair of the College Climate Action Group and is committed to empowering students to work towards social, racial and climate justice.

Jonathan A. Scelsa is an Associate Professor of Architecture at the Pratt Institute in New York. His research concerns the formal implications of the re-insertion of large scale regional systems, previously expelled by modern planning, into the architectural project of the city. Prior to his time at Pratt, he taught at the University of Pennsylvania, the Rhode Island School of Design, the City College of New York, and the Harvard GSD. Jonathan is a registered architect and founding partner of the New York-based practice, op.AL, which operates at the intersection of Architecture and Landscape. His design work concerning micro-infrastructures has been supported by several institutions, including the American Academy in Rome, the New York State Council of the Arts (NYSCA) and the Architectural League of New York. Jonathan received a Master of Architecture in Urban Design with Distinction from Harvard University and his Bachelor of Architecture from Carnegie Mellon University.

Deborah Schneiderman is a Professor of Interior Design at Pratt Institute and principal/founder of deSc: architecture/design/research. Schneiderman's scholarship and praxis explore the emerging fabricated interior environment and its materiality. Her research includes the books *Inside Prefab: The Ready-Made Interior* (Princeton Architectural Press), *The Prefab Bathroom: An Architectural History* (McFarland), *Textile, Technology and Design: From Interior Space to Outer Space* (co-edited with Alexa Griffith Winton, Bloomsbury) and *Interiors Beyond Architecture* (co-edited with Amy Campos, Routledge). She has published multiple journal articles and chapters in edited volumes, including *The Interior Architecture Theory Reader* (Routledge) and *The Handbook of Design for Sustainability* (Bloomsbury). Schneiderman has lectured internationally in peer-reviewed conferences and invited lectures, including the Storefront for Art and Architecture, The Center for Architecture, and Van Alen Institute Books. Schneiderman earned her Bachelor of Science in Design and Environmental Analysis from Cornell University and MArch from the Southern California Institute of Architecture (SCI-Arc).

Julia Sedlock is a writer, designer, and community advocate based in New York's Hudson Valley. As a founding partner of Cosmo Design Factory, her practice combines residential client work with consultation and facilitation for community development projects. She has co-founded several local organizations and cooperatives that collaborate with neighbors and government to improve access to civic life for all village residents. Julia holds a Master of Architecture and a Master of Arts in Design Criticism from the University of Illinois at Chicago. Julia is the co-author of *Creatures Are Stirring: A Guide to Architectural Companionship* (Applied Research and Design Publishing, 2022). The book prompts readers to develop more intimate friendships with architectural companions through a collection of stories, essays, and case studies that illustrate solidarity among humans, nonhumans, buildings, interiors, and the broader environment.

Alison B. Snyder is an architect, designer, and professor at Pratt Institute in Brooklyn, New York. Her interests, pedagogy and scholarship are informed by how the interior is understood through its integration with architecture, the arts, and locality. Asking socio-cultural questions to consider what propels spatial transformation and adaptability over time, Snyder conducts urban and rural field work, often in Turkey, to analyze and interpret monumental and mundane settings. She is the recipient of a Graham Foundation for Advanced Studies in the Fine Arts grant for her work on light and the Ottoman Mosque, and she has published this and other research on globalizing domestic spaces of Anatolian villages and conditions of interior urbanism found in Istanbul and New York City in a variety of books and journals. Snyder directed the Interior Architecture Program at the University of Oregon, and chaired Pratt's Department of Interior Design.

Penny Sparke is Professor of Design History and the Director of the Modern Interiors Research Centre at Kingston University, London. She graduated from Sussex University in 1971 and completed her PhD in the History of Design at Brighton Polytechnic in 1975. She taught the History of Design at Brighton Polytechnic (1975–1982) and the Royal College of Art (1982–1999). She has given keynote addresses; been a member of journal editorial boards; curated exhibitions; and broadcast and published widely in the field of Design History. Her most important publications include *An Introduction to Design and Culture, 1900 to the Present* (1986, 2004, 2013); *As Long as It's Pink: The Sexual Politics of Taste* (1995, 2010); *Elsie de Wolfe: The Birth of Modern Interior Decoration* (2005); *The Modern Interior* (2008); and *Nature Inside: Plants and Flowers in the Modern Interior* (2021). Her work focuses on modern interiors, gender and identities.

Joori Suh, PhD, is Assistant Professor in the School of Architecture and Interior Design at the University of Cincinnati. As a researcher and educator, Dr. Suh explores the interdisciplinary study of spatial creativity, design theory, and technology integration and strives to seek ways to leverage the understanding and innovation of human interaction with the environment. Her current research primarily focuses on psychological responses to kinetic spatial fractals and embodied generative ideation based on archetypes study. Dr. Suh has published her research in various venues such as *Journal of Interior Design, Design*

Science, Thinking Skills and Creativity, Frontiers in Psychology, and *Encyclopedia of Creativity.* As a licensed interior designer, she practiced in New York and Seoul, Korea for 10 years prior to joining academia. Her educational background includes an MA in Design from Cornell University with a concentration on History, Theory, and Criticisms of Interior Design and a PhD in Human Computer Interaction with a home base in architecture from Iowa State University.

Keena Suh is Associate Professor in the Interior Design Department at Pratt Institute. With an MArch from Columbia University, she has over 20 years of professional practice in architecture and design. Her interest in collaborative design practices complements her pedagogical focus to foster innovative learning and teaching opportunities through cross-disciplinary collaborations and community engagement. She is a co-editor of *Interior Provocations: History, Theory and Practice of Autonomous Interiors* and section editor of *Interior Provocations: Appropriate(d) Interiors.*

Karin Tehve is Associate Professor at Pratt Institute in New York, where she coordinates the theory and undergraduate thesis curriculum in Interior Design. She earned her Master of Architecture degree at the Harvard Graduate School of Design. Her own research and writing concentrates on taste, media and identity, and their intersection with the public realm. Karin founded her practice KT3Dllc in 2001 pursuing projects in architecture, interiors, and site-specific art. Conference presentation includes IDEC, ACSA and *Common Ground.* She has published in the *Journal of Design History, The Journal of Interior Design, The International Journal of Interior Architecture + Spatial Design,* contributed to *Interiors Beyond Architecture,* and is a co-editor for and contributor to *Interior Provocations: History, Theory and Practice of Autonomous Interiors* and *Appropriate(d) Interiors.* Her book, *Taste, Media and Interior Design,* has been published by Routledge in June 2023.

Liz Teston is Associate Professor in the School of Interior Architecture at the University of Tennessee, Knoxville. As the College of Architecture and Design's James Johnson Dudley Faculty Scholar (2017–19) and Fulbright teaching and research grant recipient in Bucharest, Romania (2018), Teston's research focuses on public interiority, design politics and cultural identity. Essays on topics like public interiority, spatial justice, and cultural identity in design can be found in journals such as *Interiority, MONU, ii-journal, The Journal of Interior Design,* and *Int/AR,* as well as book chapters in *Interior Architecture Theory Reader, Interior Futures,* and *A Guide to the Dirty South.*

Jeffrey T. Tilman, PhD, AIA, researches and writes on the history of American architecture between the Civil War and World War II, focusing on the first decades of the twentieth century. A registered architect, Tilman's interest in historic preservation stems from a conviction that preservation is a part of architectural practice and that no work of architecture is fully successful unless it addresses its pre-existing social, political, physical, and historical context. Professor Tilman has taught at the University of Cincinnati since 2000, delivering course work in architectural history, preservation theory, and building conservation. He has also led a number of graduate and undergraduate design studios in adaptive reuse, urbanism, and traditional architectural composition. His biography of Arthur Brown, Jr., remains the standard work on the San Francisco classical architect. He is currently writing on Julia Morgan at the Ecole des Beaux-Arts and on architectural pedagogy at the turn of the twentieth century.

Helen Turner holds an MSArch from the University of Cincinnati and a BS in Interior Architecture from Ohio University. On this foundation, she gained over four years of professional design experience, achieved NCIDQ certification as well as LEED accreditation, and has become an award-winning educator. An Associate Professor and Director of the School of Interiors at the University of Kentucky, her interest in sustainability, materials, theory, and history has informed a unique and synergistic method of research, teaching, and service. Through this lens, she has developed and implemented pedagogy for undergraduate studios as well as undergraduate and graduate support courses. These themes also provide a unique framework for her research, generating scholarship that has been funded by grants, expressed in design-build projects, shared at national and international conferences, as well as published in peer-reviewed journals, including the *Journal of Interior Design* and the *International Journal of Interior Architecture + Spatial Design*.

Vahid Vahdat, PhD, is an Assistant Professor of Architecture and Interior Design at WSU's School of Design and Construction. His primary field of research is spatial mediation, with an emphasis on virtual reality and film. He is the author of "Occidentalist Perceptions of European Architecture in Nineteenth Century Persian Travel Diaries—Travels in Farangi Space." The book has been commended by reviewers for its "compelling and convincing interpretations […] grounded in archival and architectural evidence." Dr. Vahdat has held academic positions in the US and abroad, including at the University of Houston and Texas A&M University. He joined the SDC faculty at Washington State University in 2019. He is the director of WSU's Trimble Technology Lab.

Olivier Vallerand is a community activist, architect, historian, and Assistant Professor at Université de Montréal's School of Design. His research focuses on how to self-intersect with the use and design of the built environment, on queer and feminist approaches to design education, and on alternative design practices. His book *Unplanned Visitors: Queering the Ethics and Aesthetics of Domestic Space*, winner of the 2021 IDEC Book Award, discusses the emergence of queer theory in architectural discourse. His research has been published in the *Journal of Architectural Education, Interiors: Design | Architecture | Culture, Somatechnics, Inter art actuel, The Educational Forum, The Plan, Captures, RACAR*, and in the edited volumes *Whitechapel Documents of Contemporary Art: Sexuality, Contentious Cities: Design and the Gendered Production of Space*, the *Bloomsbury Global Encyclopaedia of Women in Architecture, Queering Architecture: Spaces, Practices, Methods*, and *Making Men, Making History: Canadian Masculinities across Time and Place*. He also regularly writes for *Canadian Architect*.

B.D. Wortham-Galvin is Associate Professor and Director of the Master of Resilient Urban Design Program in the School of Architecture at Clemson

University. She believes that architecture is about people, not buildings. She has spent her distinguished career addressing the complexities and promises of urban design and how it can relate to people and places left out of the traditional design and development decisions. Wortham-Galvin's research confronts the challenges created by humanity's migration into cities. Climate change, for instance, has made the use, containment and placement of water particularly critical. Also, equity issues affect everything from access to housing, schools, parks, libraries, safe streets, and more. Her work on sustainability and stewardship has taken on even greater import in the face of the COVID-19 pandemic and recent national unrest. She works with local and national communities on issues of equity and resilience in managing change in rural, suburban and urban places, emphasizing cultural sustainability and designing cities of the future through an inclusionary process. Wortham-Galvin was named a fellow to the National Society of Collegiate Scholarship, a fellow for the Institute of Small Town Studies, cited in Who's Who in Teaching, and awarded the Martin Fellow for Sustainability and the Alpha Rho Chi Medal. She recently had her course selected as one of five for the 2030 Curriculum Project that honors innovative models for transforming the way sustainable design is taught.

Yandi Andri Yatmo is Professor of Architecture and the Leader of the architectural design research cluster at Universitas Indonesia. He obtained his PhD in Architecture from the University of Sheffield. His research interests are on design theories and methods and their relevance to design practice, including the development of design approaches that are rooted in the society's everyday life and community participation. He is the former head of Indonesian Association of Architecture Higher Education in 2017–2020. He is the recipient of FuturArc Green Leadership Award 2019 and Holcim Award Asia Pacific 2011 for the projects that highlight the important role of architecture for the society.

Shai Yeshayahu is Assistant Professor of Interior Design at Toronto Metropolitan University. He is the co-founder of VerS +, an international research and design practice responsive to how ancient, emerging, and local knowledge and data informs making. The collaborative has designed, fabricated and mounted several complex installations, curated exhibitions, and completed commissioned architectural projects. Shai holds a Bachelor of Science in Architecture Technology (BSAT) from New York Institute of Technology and a Master of Architecture from Ohio State University, Knowlton School of Architecture. Shai previously held an Assistant Professor position and the coordination responsibilities for the development and implementation of an Interdisciplinary Foundation Curriculum at UNLV School of Architecture. Before arriving at UNLV, he held a tenured position at SIUC where he founded and directed the Digital Fabrication Lab, df_Lab, and was leading an initiative to implement a digital culture across the university's curriculum. The df_lab role was to act as a catalyst for applied interdisciplinary research and immersive learning opportunities in the area of digital fabrication. Its goal was to serve as a conduit between students, design professionals, and community stakeholders. Additionally, the Lab supported curricular components related to real-time experimentation and rigorous examination of the logic behind design and making.

Alican Yildiz is a PhD candidate at the School of Planning, University of Cincinnati College of Design, Architecture, Art, and Planning. He received a Bachelor of Urban and Regional Planning (with spatial planning and design focus) from the Istanbul Technical University Faculty of Architecture, and is holding a Master's degree in Community Planning (with spatial planning focus) from School of Planning, University of Cincinnati. He was a spatial research and mapping assistant at UC Niehoff Studio Community Design Center (2016–2017), and at UC Institute for Policy Research (2017–2020), also assisted with Dr. Gregory Marinic's graduate architecture and urban design studio in 2020 Spring at UC SAID, on the informal urbanism of Mexico City. Alican's dissertation aims to understand the uses of contemporary interior environments as public spaces within the Southeast European and Anatolian contexts. His doctoral committee is led by Dr. Vikas Mehta, Dr. Christopher Auffrey, and Dr. Gregory Marinic.

Milagros Zingoni is Associate Professor and the Director of the School of Interior Architecture at the University of Tennessee where she is also the Director of Diversity Relations for the College of Architecture and Design. Milagros, a registered architect from Argentina, has been teaching the next generation of Architects, Interior Designers, Interior Architects and Urban Designers since 2005. Her research explores interiority as ephemeral and spatial experiences in multiple contexts, leveraging design education to develop agency in underrepresented communities and developing pedagogical approaches that can enable design students to develop soft skills with special emphasis in empathy and collaboration, expanding design-build studios in interiors education and cross-disciplinary design-thinking. She has extensive service in the USA and Argentinian communities, profession, and education institutions. Some of her awards include the 2019 IDEC Teaching Excellence Award, 2019 AIA Educator of the Year Award (AZ), 2020 ASU Faculty Mentor Award, and 2022 IIDA Educator Diversity Award.

Preface

The late Rafael Viñoly (1944–2023) was a pioneer of interior urbanism and among the most admired architects of his generation. Born in Uruguay and educated in Argentina, Viñoly founded his New York-based firm in 1983 where he designed a broad and well-respected portfolio of significant civic, cultural, academic, and commercial buildings around the world. On the occasion of his recent death, an obituary written by Fred A. Bernstein for *The New York Times* poignantly captured the importance of his contribution to the development of interior urbanism stating that although Viñoly was not known for a signature style, he had "...a penchant for enclosing large spaces under glass, creating luminous interiors. His addition to the Cleveland Museum of Art, his Kimmel Center for the Performing Arts in Philadelphia, and his Booth School of Business at the University of Chicago all feature dramatic glass-roofed courtyards."

I had the pleasure and privilege of working for Rafael in his New York and London studios where I contributed to several buildings that incorporated impressive interior urban spaces in their designs. These projects, including the Spitzer School of Architecture, 20 Fenchurch Tower, Montevideo Carrasco International Airport, Jazz at Lincoln Center, Booth School of Business, Cleveland Museum of Art, and Curve Theatre, made an indelible impact on my view of architecture, and more specifically on how I perceive publicness, interiority, and urban form. While working with Rafael, I came to understand that he envisioned the vast interior spaces in his buildings as an extension of the city. This book draws inspiration from him. It is dedicated to Rafael, the Viñoly family, and his enduring namesake firm.

Interior courtyard of the
Cleveland Museum of
Art, Rafael Viñoly (2013).
Photo by Gregory Marinic

Introduction

Gregory Marinic

What is interior urbanism? At its core, interior urbanism represents a hybrid spatial condition that mediates indoor and outdoor space through interstitiality. In this book, the terms *interior* and *urban* are the foundational criteria that shape a distinct set of socio-spatial characteristics. While many of the environments examined herein were not intentionally designed to produce this typology, a particular way of making and interpreting space as "interior urbanism" certainly exists. Interior urbanism often transgresses codes of the "outdoor" city by operating in a quasi-public manner or by appropriating space through temporal enclosure. And although different forms of interior urbanism are found worldwide, such spaces are often viewed as merely building interiors despite their significance to the public realm.

The story of interior urbanism begins in ancient times; yet, the phenomenon remains underexplored. Its origins can arguably be traced to city-building in Asia Minor and the multi-level *underground city* of Derinkuyu in Cappadocia during the eighth century BC. Extending to a depth of over 85 meters, the earliest cave systems at Derinkuyu may have been initially carved by the Phyrgians.[1] Derinkuyu is large enough to have sheltered as many as 20,000 people along with their livestock, food storage rooms, and communal spaces, and is one of several underground cities found in Cappadocia.[2] Throughout the broader Mediterranean Basin, colonnades and arcades emerged as the foundational architectural typologies of interior urbanism in territories that were directly influenced by the cultures, languages, governments, and religions of the Greeks and Romans. These built forms are composed of successive arches supported by piers or columns that create monumental spatial configurations. By virtue of their robustness and structural capabilities, ancient colonnades and arcades created environments that blurred boundaries between indoor and outdoor spaces, private domains, and the public realm.

Monumental colonnades, arcades, and temples emerged in the Hellenistic period (323–331 BC) of ancient Greece. These typologies were further refined and built throughout the Roman Empire, taking architectural form in the Colosseum (70–80 AD), Baths of Caracalla (212–216 BC), and Basilica of Maxentius during which time they were incrementally built across the broader Mediterranean Basin in continental Europe, Asia Minor, and North Africa. Historical variants of these colonnade and arcade typologies are embedded into diverse architectures such as the Temple of Horus (57 BC) in Egypt, the Great Colonnade at Apamea (115 AD) in Syria, and the Great Colonnade at Palmyra in Syria,[3] which consists of three sections built separately in the second and third centuries AD.

DOI: 10.4324/9780429443091-1

In North Africa and the Levant, as well as extending deeply through-out the lands of the Ottoman and Persian empires stretching into Central Asia, the spatial conditions of ancient medinas, souks, and bazaars—networks of internal units, nodes, and districts—are composed of arcaded passages and the palimpsests of ancient Egyptian, Greek, Roman, Illyrian, Anatolian, Turkic, Arabic, and Persian cultures. Sitting at a critical geographic hinge between east and west, the urban core of Istanbul holds some of the earliest examples of interior urbanism. Its Grand Bazaar is among the largest and oldest covered markets in the world, extending across a territory of 61 interiorized streets and 4,000 shops.[4] The construction of the Grand Bazaar began in 1455, shortly after the Ottoman conquest of Constantinople and was part of a broader ambition to stimulate economic activity and political influence in the city through monu-mental architectural and infrastructural works.[5]

Further east, interior urban influences emerged in India at the Great Chaitya of the Karla Caves (120 AD) and the Chand Baori, a stepwell in the village of Abhaneri in Rajasthan. The structure, which forms part of a Hindu tem-ple precinct, extends to a depth of 30 meters. In China, pedestrian networks of Beijing developed as interior urban configurations in the form of hutongs. The etymology of the word *hutong* is traced to the Mongolian word for "water well," or "path between tents," or from a Chinese word that described nar-row footpaths that acted as firebreaks for the thirteenth-century capital city of Kublai Khan.[6] These centuries-old neighborhoods were incrementally built during the Yuan dynasty (1279–1368) and expanded in the Ming (1368–1644) and Qing (1644–1911) dynasties.[7] Hutongs share notable spatial qualities with both the Forbidden City and urban parks. Marco Polo (1254–1324) marveled at the metropolitan interiority of Beijing by proclaiming, "...the whole interior of the city is laid out in squares like a chessboard with such masterly precision that no description can do justice to it."[8] These examples identify only a minis-cule fraction of the countless interior urban spaces that have been constructed worldwide from ancient times until today.

In Europe, a critical awareness of interior urbanism within architec-tural and urban theory may be traced to the Italian Renaissance and Leonardo da Vinci's vision for the multi-level *Ideal City* (1487). His design reconfigured the basic organizational principles of urban flows, sanitation, and health to imagine a city composed of layered systems. Inspired by the theoretical speculations of Vitruvius and Leon Battista Alberti, da Vinci proposed a vertically stacked urban-ism through speculative representations consisting of underground, at-grade, and elevated spaces separating various uses and users. Later, Giambattista Nolli envisioned his iconic *Plan of Rome* (1748) as a spatial construct that visu-alized buildings in the urban core as an internal architectural promenade. Unlike conventional urban plans that focused on streets, piazzas, and parks by objec-tifying individual buildings, Nolli opened an entirely new way of seeing and understanding publicness. He achieved this by inversely privileging the interior spatiality of buildings to describe the urban form of Rome.

Embracing ambiguity, Nolli viewed public space as public space, there was no division, no difference between outdoors and indoors. His drawings show space flowing through buildings onto streets, piazzas, and parks whereby interior and exterior spaces are rendered equal. Thus, the Nolli Plan communicates that cities are shaped by countless spaces intended for the public, but that many of these environments are nevertheless privately owned and maintained. Nolli visualizes the potential of these public and semi-public relationships in his figure-ground drawing that poses a trans-scalar urban proposition. His perspective provokes a conversation about rather than a focus on architectural form.

The unprecedented visual complexity of the Nolli Plan compels the viewer to read the envelope of buildings and then to move inward to see the interior. His spatial logic reveals that something "public" also happens within the buildings of Rome, and that it is this interior publicness that draws people across thresholds into an extended perception of the public realm. The Nolli Plan confirms that Giambattista Nolli perceived a shared language of exterior and interior spaces in Rome by proposing a finer grained understanding of how people occupy the city. Nolli articulates the perimeter of buildings to offer a better understanding of urban form as an environmental mixer. Here, individual buildings are not icons, but rather, the city is privileged toward its space.

If Vitruvius (80–15 BC), the Roman military engineer and architect who scribed *De architectura*, is recognized as the preeminent theorist of the foundational principles of architecture, then Walter Benjamin, with his *The Arcades Project* (1927–1940), is the preeminent theorist of interior urbanism. Born in Berlin, German-Jewish philosopher Benjamin cast his lens on Paris and theorized its arcades as an integrated urban system of social, spatial, and architectural conditions. From 1927 to 1940, Benjamin produced a monumental amount of research on the Parisian arcades which remained incomplete due to his death in 1940 during an ill-fated journey across the Pyrenees. Posthumously published and translated into many languages, his unprecedented tome represents one of the greatest works of twentieth-century cultural criticism. Underscoring its importance, *The Arcades Project* is often claimed to be the forerunner of postmodern theory. Widely referenced throughout this book, Benjamin is identified as a pivotal interior urbanist.

Among the most enduring aspects of material culture, the urban built environment crystallizes moments of time into physical form. Identifying the social shifts provoked by modernity in the early twentieth century, Benjamin perceived the Parisian arcades in this way. He cast his lens on the arcade as not only an architecture, but a metropolitan phenomenon by viewing interior spaces as urban spaces and vice versa.

In the early twentieth century, metropolitan complexities and transformative social change gave rise to new visions of urban interiority. A sublime view of future urbanism was captured in cinematic culture by Fritz Lang's *Metropolis* (1927) which characterized cities as increasingly interior and multi-leveled. As noted earlier, the foundational theories of interior urbanism emerged within the research of Walter Benjamin and his seminal *The Arcades Project*. After 1945, master planned interior urbanism rethought cities in Europe and North America from the inside-out. New architectural forms achieved greater autonomy and connectivity in the hermetic environments of cities-within-cities, underground networks, skywalk systems, atria, and megastructures. Responding to climatic, social, psychological, and economic concerns, these large-scale environments were vastly more extensive, complex, and "public" than conventional interiors.

By the late twentieth century, built and unbuilt forms of interior urbanism were primarily assessed by critics in terms of their formal impact on the city. And although such interventions substantially shaped cities and challenged urban norms, modernist variants were often derided as anti-urban and anti-street. In *The Death and Life of Great American Cities* (1961), urban activist Jane Jacobs offered a broad critique of 1950s modernist urban experiments; yet, many of the traditional urban principals that she celebrated also exist within various configurations of interior urbanism. In this sense, indoor conditions often incorporate the five urban elements identified by Kevin Lynch in *The Image of the City* (1961) with paths, edges, districts, nodes, and landmarks providing order, hierarchy, and spatialization. Contrasted with master planned interior urbanism, organic forms have grown in the developing world by incremental, parasitic, and sometimes illegal means through platform circulation networks, appropriated structures, and informal settlements. Together, these systems represent a broad range of parallel urbanisms blending interiority and occupancies that create alternative spatial environments, social experiences, and flexible configurations.

Acknowledging Giambattista Nolli's *Plan of Rome* (1748), Walter Benjamin's *The Arcades Project* (1927–1940), and Archizoom Associati's *No-Stop City* (1969–1972) as triple catalysts, this book casts an early twenty-first-century lens on the histories and theories that intersect with interior urbanism. There is an emerging body of knowledge focusing on the morphologies and socio-spatial transformations of interior urbanism. Responding to such efforts, this book was conceived as a comprehensive and rigorous study of the histories, theories, and interpretations of the phenomenon by scholars who have identified, collected, documented, analyzed, and written on topics surrounding its evolution. Evident in the overlapping importance of Benjamin for many authors in this book, his research serves as a theoretical foundation for understanding the contemporary particularities of urban interiority. Working transdisciplinarily like Nolli, Benjamin, and Archizoom, this book reveals intersectional insights that explain the global evolution of interior urbanism across diverse design characteristics, socio-spatial parameters, and geographic extents. In doing so, it engages the timelessness of Nolli in the streets of Rome, the ponderings of Benjamin in the Parisian arcades, and the speculative vastness of Archizoom, while considering the impact of contemporary consumption, political forces, and identities on interior urbanism.

The Interior Urbanism Theory Reader includes 50 chapters that investigate interior urbanism through theories applied in disciplines, including, but not limited to, architecture, urbanism, urban design, planning, environmental design, interior architecture, interior design, archaeology, engineering, sociology, psychology, and urban geography. This book is structured in two parts that thematically organize individual chapters. *Part I: Histories and Typologies* includes chapters that focus on the historical and typological origins of interior urbanism. *Part II: Theories and Influences* broadens the scope with chapters that explore the various occupancies, auras, atmospheres, and potentialities of the genre in relation to themes of *Inhabitation*, *Threshold*, *Culture*, *Identity*, *Temporality*, *Vastness*, and *Speculation*. Together, these essays explore relations between interiority and urbanity that play a significant role in the interactions of diverse agents in public, semi-public, and quasi-public space.

Each chapter demonstrates that interior urbanism is often a critical nexus that participates in shaping architecture, urban morphology, and the metropolitan experience. Together, the authors herein have crafted a comprehensive array of scholarship about interior urbanism, research that provides an inclusive tome of this spatial type across time, scales, and cultures. Offering unique interpretations of indoor urbanism, their research identifies the urban principles, architectural forms, interior characteristics, socio-spatial occupancies, and latent connections that exist within a condition that sits between urbanism and interiority. From formal-to-informal and ancient-to-speculative—megastructural, incremental, planned, appropriated, organic, or participatory—this book reveals the global scope and speculative potentialities of interior urbanism.

Notes

1 Fitch, Chris, and Matthew Young. *Subterranea: Journey into the Depths of the Earth's Most Extraordinary Underground Spaces*. Portland, OR: Timber Press, 2020.
2 See Pinkowski, Jennifer. "Massive Underground City Found in Cappadocia Region of Turkey." *Adventure. National Geographic*, May 4, 2021. https://www.nationalgeographic.com/adventure/article/150325-underground-city-cappadocia-turkey-archaeology; and An, Jisuk. *Derinkuyu.* Busan: Sanjini, 2019.
3 Butcher, Kevin. *Roman Syria and the Near East*. New York: J. Paul Getty Museum/Getty Publications, 2003.
4 Gülersoy, Çelik. *Story of the Grand Bazaar*. İstanbul: Kitaplığı, 1990.
5 Fleet, Kate, Suraiya Faroqhi, and Kasaba Reşat. *The Cambridge History of Turkey*. New York: Cambridge University Press, 2006.
6 Meyer, Michael. *The Last Days of Old Beijing: Life in the Vanishing Backstreets of a City Transformed*. New York: Bloomsbury, 2010.
7 Meyer, 2010.
8 Wu, Liangyong. *Rehabilitating the Old City of Beijing: A Project in the Ju'er Hutong Neighbourhood*. Vancouver, Canada: UBC Press, 2011.

Part I

Histories and Typologies

Chapter 1

The Arcade

Walter Benjamin in an Era of Ambiguity

Pablo Meninato

On the 26th of September 1940, near the border between Spain and France, German philosopher Walter Benjamin was found dead in the Hotel de Francia, a small hostel located in the Catalan town of Portbou. Fleeing from the Gestapo, Benjamin committed suicide by swallowing pills of morphine. As a Jew, following Germany's invasion of France, Benjamin knew that he would be detained and sent to a concentration camp. Two days later, he was buried in the cemetery of Portbou. At the moment of his death, Benjamin was working on a vast literary project documenting the arcades of Paris. Starting in 1927 and continuing until the moment of his death, Benjamin developed what would become his grand unfinished work, *The Arcades Project*. Thanks to his collaborator and fellow philosopher Georges Bataille, the manuscript was rescued from a closed archive at the Bibliothèque Nationale in Paris where Benjamin left it upon leaving the city. Over the following years, the project was painstakingly reassembled until it was published in German in 1982, while the English version appeared in 1999.

A distinctive feature of modernity is the denial of the notion of "influence" in the realization of the artistic project. A work of art, according to modernism's dogma, should be unique and original, independent from the work of predecessors or contemporaries. This is only one among many subjects that Walter Benjamin's artistic and philosophical approach distinguishes from the modern canon. In direct and unambiguous fashion, Benjamin asserts that the gestation of *The Arcades Project* was sparked by Louis Aragon's surreal novel *Paris Peasant* (1926). Conveying a feverish sense of inspiration and excitement, Benjamin writes to his friend Theodor Adorno about the epiphanic moment after he read Aragon's text. Benjamin writes:

> It opens with Aragon—the *Paysan de Paris*. Evenings, lying in bed, I could never read more than two to three pages by him because my heart started to pound so hard that I had to put the book down.[2]

DOI: 10.4324/9780429443091-3

With a surreal imprint, Benjamin's *The Arcades Project* is a literary collage dedicated to analyzing the history and cultural significance of this technological and urban invention. The structure of his manuscript resembles a mosaic of fragments resulting in an intersection of art, technology, economics, consumption, architecture, urbanism, interiority, and history. Benjamin starts by citing a precise definition of this interior urban space extracted from the *Illustrated Guide of Paris*:

> These arcades, a recent invention of industrial luxury, are glass-roofed, marble-paneled corridors extending through whole blocks of buildings, whose owners have joined together for such enterprises. Lining both sides of these corridors, which get their light from above, are the most elegant shops, so that the passage is a city, a world in miniature.[3]

Benjamin is fascinated by the ambivalence of the arcade: it is covered, though open at both ends, it is simultaneously an interior and exterior space, a public or private setting. While it is part of the city—on rainy days, people use the arcades as protection from the elements and to shorten walks—it is also an autonomous urban construct. The arcades, according to this reasoning, are various places and a singular one. As his literary project unfolds, Benjamin realizes that these same urban forms are replicated throughout Paris: Passage Jouffroy, Galerie Vivienne, Galerie Colbert, and the Passage Choiseul compose a network of arcades that help define the city's urban experience. While no two are alike, they seem uncannily similar. In *The Arcades Project*, Benjamin suggests a common feeling, the notion of encountering a surprisingly familiar place visited for the first time. To visit an arcade—any arcade—is to immerse oneself into an experience replicated many other times in many other spaces; it is the nostalgic feeling of *déjà vu*, the remembrance of a moment not yet lived.

Typological Passages

According to historian Johann Friedrich Geist,[4] the first arcade in Paris was developed within the interiors of the Palais Royal (later referred to as Palais Marchand) and opened in 1786. Soon after, Paris and many European cities were populated with these new kinds of urban spaces, launching what historian Bertrand Lemoine referred to as the "Arcade Era."[5] The arcade, or urban passage, established a new formal, technological, and spatial paradigm; its main features were the blurred distinction between exterior and interior, between public and private, and between architecture and urbanism. As a call to ambiguity, the arcade soon became a source of fascination for poets, writers, historians, and philosophers. For surreal artists, its existence presupposed a challenge to the binary understanding of reality. Diverting from the two most rooted spatial conditions—inside or outside—the arcade rethought seemingly opposed conditions, such as up or down, left or right, male or female (Image 1.1).

Arcades are unusual building creatures. Their presence is marked by ambiguity, places that are neither interior nor exterior; they are not explicitly private, nor technically public spaces. While conveying a strong civic presence, their development and management follow speculative models. Even their

Image 1.1 *Passage du Grand-Cerf*, Paris. Courtesy Marcelo Nougues.

naming suggests a certain ambivalence. Their nomenclature in different languages confirms a cacophonic linguist lineage: they can be referred to as *passages, arcades, covered streets, or galleries* in English, *halle* or *passagem* in German, *galería* or *pasaje* in Spanish, and *galerie* or *passage* in French. This verbal mutability can be interpreted as a key to understanding the uncertain position of the arcade within urban and architectural theory and practice.

In contemporary architectural discourse, the arcade can be understood as a building type. The concept of architectural type can be defined as the formal features shared by a group of buildings or building fragments.[6] Type, consequently, is a mental construct; it is the capacity of identifying and extrapolating formal analogies within various buildings. The "courtyard house," the "rowhouse," or the "skyscraper," for instance, are consolidated building types. In a strict sense, a type can be described but not shown. Therefore, a single example of an arcade does not represent the type; it is after identifying multiple instances that share those formal features how a type is determined. The notion of type blurs the distinction between "high" and "low" architectures. Its spectrum contemplates vernacular and utilitarian constructions, as well as

Image 1.2 *Galleria Vittorio Emanuele II*, Milan. Courtesy Fernando Diez.

buildings designed by the most celebrated architects. Identifying the "arcade type" does not valorize this group of buildings; rather, it simply acknowledges its existence (Image 1.2).

As Benjamin anticipated, the ambivalent condition of the arcade exposed the contradictory impulses of modernism. On the one hand, the arcade can be interpreted as the first typological invention of modernity whereby its novel forms and effects are the result of new materials such as iron and glass, which, in turn, generated new fabrication processes. Modern architecture, according to this idea, is driven by formal and technological innovation, reaffirming the modern project as a *rupture with the past*. On the other hand, the arcade can be seen as a force *contrarian to the modern project*. Like all typologies, the arcade is supported by mechanisms such as imitation and recurrence, notions that were rejected, or disregarded by most modern thinkers and architects.[7]

Death and Resurrection

While at the beginning of the nineteenth century, the emergence of the arcade was seen as a case of typological innovation, by the early twentieth century, the same urban form became an example of decadence and eventual extinction of a building type. Coinciding with the decadence of the arcade, the early twentieth century experienced a crisis of the notion of the city as a collective agency. The origins of this crisis can be associated with the two most influential modern architects and urban thinkers, Le Corbusier and Frank Lloyd Wright. Le Corbusier projected a radical transformation of the traditional city, replacing notions such as urban space and urban fabric, in other words, canceling the city of streets, public squares, and city blocks, for towers scattered amidst generic and undetermined spaces. Wright proposed a "disappearing city,"[8] in which the concept of the traditional town was replaced by an infinite ex-urban checkerboard, dissolving the distinctions between rural, suburban, and urban conditions.

Following the strong criticism of modern planning initially advanced during the 1960s by Aldo Rossi[9] in Italy, and Jane Jacobs in North America,[10] the final decades of the twentieth century witnessed a revalorization of the traditional city, in some cases boosted by state-of-the-art systems of public transportation, as well as the encouragement of walkability and bicycle mobility. At present, many cities around the world are developing new urban paradigms capable of integrating the qualities of traditional towns with contemporary technological developments.

It is, therefore, no surprise that the arcade is experiencing a renaissance. A renewed interest in this architectural form initially coincided with the architectural discourse and practices of the 1960s and 1970s, championed by architects and thinkers such as Giulio Carlo Argan and Aldo Rossi. Projects such as the Derby Town Centre by James Stirling (1970) and Frankfurt Fair Galleria by Oswald Mathias Unger (1979) were the first examples of this tendency. More recently, Norman Foster's Kogod Courtyard, a glass-covered space added to the National Portrait Gallery in Washington, DC (2007), confirms the resurgence of an urban form that until a few decades ago was considered extinct. Merging a traditional spatial concept with high-tech structural innovations, the glazed roof courtyard is an interior space that reflects the seductive qualities of a covered street. Foster's design simultaneously explores the oxymoronic quality of interiority-exteriority while overlapping traditional and new architectural vocabularies and technologies, thus establishing a genealogical line whose origins can be traced to the nineteenth-century urban passage (Image 1.3).

The project that best exemplifies "the return of the arcade" in contemporary architecture is the BCE Place Galleria in Toronto (1992), by Santiago Calatrava. In a heroic integration of architecture, engineering, and technology, Calatrava developed an intervention that uses a traditional type, the urban passage, to create a place that is simultaneously recognizable and exceptional. The Galleria connects various buildings and streets, creating a focal point to enter into Toronto's subterranean pedestrian network. The design process is both evident and effective: the selection of a type which is subjected to alteration mechanisms such as distortion and variation of scale (Image 1.4).[11]

Calatrava's galleria settles two questions. First, it confirms the continual relevance of an interior urban typology that a century ago seemed doomed

Image 1.3 *Kogod Courtyard at the National Portrait Gallery*, Washington DC. Design by Foster and Partners. Courtesy Pablo Meninato.

Image 1.4 *Heritage Square Arcade*, Toronto. Design by Santiago Calatrava Architects & Engineers. Courtesy Eliseo Rabbi-Baldi.

to disappear. What was once cast as a sheer novelty later was rejected and forgotten, only to be rediscovered generations later through fresh and lyrical reinterpretations. Second, the mere fact that an architect so associated with the most formalist branch of "late-modern" architecture uses a conventional typology can only be interpreted as a reconciliation between the concept of type, a concept which, in the 1960s, theoreticians such as Argan[12] and Rossi[13] adopted as an instrument for developing a strong criticism of modern architecture, and contemporary branches of modernism.

The Era of Ambiguity

In his *The Arcades Project*, Walter Benjamin appears sometimes baffled, at times seduced, by modernity's contradictory relations with the urban passage. On the one hand, he interprets those continuous glass vaults as the architectural emblem of modernity. Modern architecture, according to this premise, originated after the development of new construction technologies sparked by the discovery of new materials.[14] The innovative concept of the arcade, adds Benjamin, supports the modern narrative of breaking with the past.[15] Later on, however, Benjamin seems to contradict himself, commenting that those forms do not constitute genuine architectural inventions, but instead derive from an extensive genealogical chain. Their etymological roots can be found in Fourier's nineteenth-century phalanstery, or in ancient types such as the Persian bazaar. The arcade, for Benjamin, can be understood as a paradoxical oscillation between innovation and replication, between tradition and modernity.

What Benjamin introduced is a quality virtually absent in the modern canon: ambiguity. Rather than sidelining or suspending conditions that admit contrarian tendencies, he opts to embrace them.[16] Modern art and architecture, following his logic, could simultaneously break with tradition and be reflected in it. Benjamin revisits the tension between originality and repetition in his essay, "The Work of Art in the Age of Mechanical Reproduction,"[17] where he discusses how authorship and invention are threatened by new artistic practices, such as photography and cinema. If, on the one hand, Benjamin expressed a desire to rescue the significance of traditional work of art—which, he argues, can be distinguished by its "aura"—at the same time, he realizes that the division between conventional artistic categories, such as originality versus duplication, or singularity versus mass-production, appears indeterminate and diluted. It is under the umbrella of these questions that we can better understand Benjamin's obsession with the ambiguous character of urban arcades. It is worth highlighting that the question of ambiguity in the artistic process would become, several decades later, one of the defining attributes of contemporary interior urbanism.

Notes

1   Benjamin, *The Arcades Project*, 8.

2   Quoted in Paris, Vaclav, "Uncreative Influence: Louis Aragon's *Paysan de Paris* and Walter Benjamin's *Passagen-Werk*." *Journal of Modern Literature* 37, no. 1 (2013): 21. doi:10.2979/jmodelite.37.1.21.

3   Benjamin, *The Arcades Project*, 8.

4   Geist, Johann Friedrich, *Arcades. History of a Building Type*. Cambridge & London: The MIT Press, 1983.

5   The expression "Arcade Era" was coined by historian Bertrand Lemoine, author of *Les Passages couverts en France,* Paris: Délégation à l'Action Artistique de la Ville de Paris, 1989.

6 From *Unexpected Affinities, The History of Type in the Architectural Project from Laugier to Duchamp*. New York: Routledge, 2018, 1–9.

7 Alberto Pérez-Gómez argues that the typological project is an "anti-modern" operation. Pérez-Gómez, Alberto, "Architecture Is Not a Convention," in Rockcastle, Garth (ed.), *Type and the (Im)Possibilities of Convention*. New York: Midgard Monograph, 1991, 11–18.

8 See Wright, Frank Lloyd, *The Disappearing City*. New York: W. F. Payson, 1932.

9 Rossi, Aldo, *The Architecture of the City*. Cambridge, MA and London: MIT Press, 1982 (originally published in Italian in 1966).

10 Jacobs, Jane, *The Death and Life of Great American Cities*. New York: Vintage, 1992 (orig. pub. 1961).

11 In my book *Unexpected Affinities*, I discuss the notion of "typological alteration tactics," 95–120.

12 Argan, Giulio Carlo, "On the Typology of Architecture." In Nesbitt, Kate (ed.), *Theorizing a New Agenda for Architecture: An Anthology of Architectural Theory, 1965–1995*. New York: Princeton Architectural, 1996, 243.

13 Rossi, *The Architecture of the City*, 35–45.

14 Benjamin, *The Arcades Project*, 4.

15 Benjamin, *The Arcades Project*, 5.

16 See Löwy, Michael, *Fire Alarm: Reading Walter Benjamin's 'On the Concept of History.'* New York and London: Verso, 2005.

17 Benjamin, Walter, "The Work of Art in the Age of Mechanical Reproduction." In Arendt, Hannah (ed.), *Illuminations*. London: Fontana, 1968, 214–218.

Chapter 2

The Street
Disposition and the Urban Interior

Graeme Brooker

Described as machines, gardens and satellites, throughout history, cities have been portrayed as contrivances that can be organic, gridded and—according to the Situationists—*naked*. In all cities, the street is ascribed a formative and integral role in its planning. In a more complex way, they exemplify the boundaries between private and public, typify conventional as well as aberrant behaviours and epitomize peripheries, margins and edges. As Joseph Rykwert suggests:

> The street is human movement institutionalized.[1]

What transformations occur to the street when it is appropriated through processes of interiorization? This chapter explores the origins of the street in order to discern its essences; then by using a series of exemplars, it examines what happens to them when they are transferred inside. Disposition is used to describe a method of decentralization: one where an element, such as a street, is mobilized and subsequently relocated from its traditionally associated environment. It uses Easterling's summary of disposition, described as

> …an unfolding relationship between potentials….a propensity within a context…. Disposition is immanent, not in the moving parts, but in the relationships between the components.[2]

Origins
Unsurprisingly, the street has a long history. Etymologically derived from the Latin term *strata*, or *sternere*, it denotes a route that is formed from a delimited surface.[3] As a natural phenomenon, it was a path that became discernible through the repeated journeys of numerous travellers. Histories of urbanism often record how cities evolved through the positioning of settlements around natural phenomena and resources, such as shelter from attack and access to

DOI: 10.4324/9780429443091-4

water. Their proximity to trade routes, often near the intersection or confluence of significant paths, roads and streets, was also decisive. Many settlements became important centres of trade because of their associated routes for moving people and goods both internally and externally between them. Boddy notes:

> Widely separated peoples simultaneously invented not only streets – a vastly powerful innovation – but hierarchical patterns of streets.[4]

Early settlements were reliant on their abilities to mobilize their people and their produce in relation to other communities via *the street*.

Militarization

The importance of the protection of mobilized people and products was also critical to the formation of cities. The Roman Republics were founded on the efficient movement of troops, civilians and goods via an extensive network of streets. No fewer than 29 paved military highways radiated out from Rome, with 372 roads connecting the 113 provinces of the empire through 250,000 miles of hard-surfaced streets. These established routes afforded them territorial gains that could be ascertained quickly and supported efficiently with supplies. Streets organized Roman settlements. They would be planned in a grid pattern with a north-south *cardine* and an east-west *decamuni*. Their intersection formed the centre of the city-grid. This rational organization would not only inform the distribution of the various buildings of the municipality, but it would also expedite the quick movement of forces to defend any point of egress such as a gate or wall. This way of organizing communities provided a level of sophisticated urban planning that influenced street patterns across Europe for centuries.[5]

As well as a device to expedite defence, the street could also be used to suppress and temper internal revolt. The *Haussmanization* of the urban fabric of Paris was undertaken partly in response to the unhealthy city but was foremost a riposte to its discontented occupants. The streets were not only designed to bring light and air to some of the squalid cholera-infested districts of the city, but were also designed to expedite the rapid deployment of armed forces to quell any rioting. Their width was both useful for the quick deployment of forces as well as reducing the construction of any robust barricades.

The twentieth century saw Jane Jacobs frame the street as a natural and vibrant place, with neighbours providing a safe context within which people could flourish. This was rationalized in her 'eyes on the street' theory:

> …. there must be eyes upon the street, eyes belonging to those we might call the natural proprietors of the street. Large numbers of people entertain themselves, off and on, by watching street activity.[6]

This very brief overview of the origins of the street documents its formations, but what happens to these dispositions when they are interiorized?

Disposition and the Interior Street

Exterior elements being used in their converse environment form part of the fundamental attributes of interior urbanism. Any element that is placed within an environment within which it is not habitually sited undergoes a transformation where its *dispositions* are transformed. One such way this is manifest is in *climate*.

Climate

Once interiorized, the street renders inclement weather unimportant, maintaining equilibrium through a controlled temperature. Climate control can be political. Recognizing that future European regulation would impact upon the sale of fresh and chilled goods in the open air, Rotterdam council commissioned MVRDV to reconfigure a new enclosed marketplace. Along with extra housing and subsequent parking, the new market would provide a temperate interior climate within which goods could be displayed and sold. The designers configured the new space around the enclosing of a huge internal street. Formed by a huge curved arch, 80 market stalls, with parking below and housing above, were contained inside the huge 120-metre-long, 40-metre-wide and high space. Glazed ends not only offered views into and through the market, but also buffeted external winds, helping to further regulate air flow through the interior (Image 2.1).

The underside of the huge arch was finished with a giant artwork of fresh-market produce that referenced Holland's past and future street markets, requiring the occupants to imagine that they were outside in a bucolic pasture.

The ease by which the outside extremes such as climate can be ameliorated can draw opprobrium, precisely because of its seamless ability to reduce the potency of the external street. Its internal counterpart is arguably denuded of its vibrancy through the loss of contact and tolerance:

> As the glass doors firmly close, the mental realm changes. We are inside, contained, separate, part of the system, a consumer, a peruser, a cruiser…Pleasantly anesthetized …those other older streets, with their troubling smells and winds and unpredictability, swirl into a distant and wispy memory, as vaporous as the smoke and rain outside.[7]

Image 2.1 Markthal. Rotterdam, Netherlands; the new marketplace was formed from an interiorized street, enclosed by a large arched structure containing apartments. Credit: Ossip van Duivenbode & Daria Scagliola/Stijn Brakkee

The predictable climatic dimensions of the internalized street mean that they can advance two other distinct interiorized dimensions: their scenographic and commercial dispositions.

Scenography

When the street is internalized, it becomes a motif. Circulation and surveillance are fundamental external capacities which are emphasized through *scenographication*. An early example of this disposition emerged in the sixteenth century in Vicenza, Northern Italy. In the Teatro Olimpico, Palladio summarized the street as calcified scenography. Placed inside an abandoned fortress, the half-amphitheatre's stage set was embellished with seven, highly stylized receding streetscapes. Replete with trompe-l'oeil cloud ceilings, this confection set the scene for future internalized streets (Image 2.2).

The scenography of the street is implemented emphatically in environments that seek to overtly symbolize its qualities in order to becalm its users into leisure activities. Inside the interiors of Las Vegas, the street is used to intoxicate and seduce its users into undertaking specific leisure activities such as gambling. Replete with gondolas, the Venetian is arranged around its own water-street canal-system. The Pyramidal Luxor, with its 'fictive archaeology' of fabricated obelisks, temple fragments and sarcophagi,[8] claims Egypt as the influence for its interior streets. In Vegas, streets are utilized as organizational but predominantly emblematic components of the urban interior experience. In Caesar's Palace, a place where everyone can 'feel like Caesar', it's obligatory that casino and entertainment complex is one of the world's most valuable real estate complex of shops. The 'Forum', replete with classical statuary, is distributed along an internal street. The scenography of the ancient Roman city is completed by fountains all contained under a vaulted trompe-l'oeil blue sky ceiling. This is evocatively lit in pale lighting for daytime and dusky hues for sunset, effects that change numerous times throughout the day (Image 2.3).

Image 2.2 Teatro Olimpico. Vicenza, Italy; the extended perspectives of each of the streets render them as calcified scenographic stage sets.
Credit: Graeme Brooker

Image 2.3 Caesar's Palace Interior Street; the vaunted tromp' l'oeil sky ceiling changes its colouring numerous times each day.
Credit: Graeme Brooker

In Ceaser's Palace, the street is co-opted as infrastructure and as *motif*. Its fountains, seating, climate control and lighting effects are paraphernalia that fetishize and accentuate the scenographic street configuration. To *passagiata* through them is to engage with the seduction. The street is used for the movement of people but it is primarily a device for commerce via the carefully staged and choreographed flow of people through space.

Commerce

The interior street as commerce became fully formed in the nineteenth century in Paris. The covered street, realized through arcuated constructions, was immortalized in Walter Benjamin's monumental work *The Arcades Project*. It was never completed, but over the 13 years of the work, Benjamin came to realize that the arcades represented modernity and modern life.

Benjamin's fascination with the interiorized streets was emphasized in the evocation of Baudelaire's *flâneur*: the idler or person of leisure, the archetypal urban wanderer. It was in the arcades that Benjamin noted that this meandering could take place only when unfettered by external climatic inclemency. In the process of wandering through the city, the flâneur developed methods of processing the stimuli of the street and its attention-grabbing displays of goods. Benjamin portrayed the arcades as ambiguous spaces of signs, mirrors and displays of goods, placed alongside each other and bathed in a mix of natural and artificial light:

> These arcades, a recent invention of industrial luxury, are glass roofed, marble-panelled corridors, which get their light from above, are the most elegant shops, so that the passage is a city, a world in miniature, in which customers will find everything they need. During sudden rain showers, the arcade is a refuge for the unprepared, to whom they offer a secure if restricted promenade.[9]

The flâneur was the representative of the collective, drifting through these spaces, recognizing their own domestic arrangements:

> The collective is an eternally wakeful, eternally agitated being that – in the space between the building fronts – lives, experiences, understands, and invents as much as individuals do within the privacy of their own four walls…more than anywhere else, the street reveals itself in the arcade as the furnished and familiar interior of the masses.[10]

The twentieth century saw the arcade superseded by their contemporary successors, the mall. The features of the arcade, a street lined with buildings covered by a roof, with the addition of elements such as gardens and places for food, were made accessible and popular with the addition of the affordable motor car.

In 1956, Southdale Center opened in Edina, Minnesota with 800,000 square feet of shopping space contained within a huge shed. Austrian immigrant Victor Gruen designed the centre to remind people of an idyllic arcaded European city centre, with its weather-protected interior maintained at a comfortable 24°C all year round. Gruen envisaged that it would contain not just stores, but also medical facilities, schools and houses, and would essentially depict a small European city brimming with life centred around a series of efficient, climatically controlled streets.

Writer Severini Kowinski has noted that malls are an idealized copy of the external street, a clever instrument deploying motifs and symbols, to reassure its users and commercialize those feelings of security:

> The Gruen strategy builds on peoples longing for a world in which they feel safe. The underlying model is the traditional community and the everyday life of small provincial cities or of European historical towns, enriched by elements of Disneyland'. Nostalgia, filtered by historical and mass media stereotypes, has proved to be a powerful and effective strategy.[11]

In more recent commerce-based environments, the internalized street is utilized as a focused strategically located navigation-device through displays of enticing goods, often traversed in order to proceed towards a further destination. In airport terminals, retail spaces are carefully controlled and focused to ensure '*100% of customers can flow seamlessly past 100% of goods*'.[12] These interior streets are deployed as 'non-linear routes' and 'atomized zones', where the customer can ironically feel '*in control of their route*'.[13] This approach provides a mixture of bewilderment and control, a potent combination in commercial space.

The circulation of passengers through the *duty-free* shop is a street where visitors are led to a store where passengers shopping time is optimized in a highly controlled environment.[14] The ultimate commercialized internal street is found in the IKEA store. Customers are usually brought to an upper-level route, to begin a journey through a series of set-piece rooms. This heightens their desire for goods through the delaying of consumption as they see the products in context before then being finally allowed to obtain a trolley and fill it in the second element of the sequence—'the market' (Image 2.4).

Image 2.4 IKEA store layout. Generic; the internal street of an IKEA store promotes and heightens the desire for goods through the fulfilment of the consumer's need in the finale of the journey in the market hall. Credit: IKEA

As Penn states about this effective sequencing of the internal street:

> Although the sequence is linear, the experience is anything but simple. The role of the showroom is mainly to give the shopper a series of glimpses of aspirational lifestyle settings....However, as you move through the showroom you rapidly become dissociated from everyday life - all views of the external world are obscured and even one's sense of direction is removed by the twists and turns of the route. At the same time, you are shown stage set glimpses of what your life might be like. The effect is more or less subliminal... By the time you arrive at the stairs down to the marketplace ...Now you can buy.[15]

Conclusion

The role of the street in the city has primarily been infrastructural, an instrument that utilized movement. It also contained a moral and political dimension as it was used to condition and temper gathering, community and political response. The street's emergence as an instrument of interior urbanity in the mid-twentieth and early twenty-first centuries has primarily been manifested as a scenographic and commercial project: as an interior route through a shopping mall, as a journey through an airport terminal or as a determined route through a store. It has been appropriated, essentially for financial gain through the commercialization of infrastructure and public space. Its interiorization into places that are, or have become, overtly commercialized, secured, surveilled and highly controlled, has allowed the user to resist exterior distractions such as the weather, and thus become distracted, potentially disinhibited, to then be tempted to consume. The seamlessness with which the internal street encompasses its occupants has been enhanced by subjectivity manifested as scenography: gardens, fountains, shop windows and so on. Emblems of its external counterpart transported inside in order to set the scene. Arguably, it is precisely this choreography that endows it with the emblematic or motif-like qualities as it becomes an instrument of explicit consumption, a significant counterpart to its external relative.

Notes

1 Rykwert, Joseph. The Street: The Use of its History. In Anderson, Stanford (Ed). *On Streets*. The MIT Press, 1978, p. 15.

2 Easterling, Keller. *Extrastatecraft. The Power of Infrastructure Space*. Verso, 2014, p. 72.

3 Barnhart, Robert. *Dictionary of Etymology*. Chambers, 1988, p. 1075

4 Boddy, Trevor. Underground and Overhead: Building the Analogous City. In Sorkin, Michael (Ed). *Variations on a Theme Park. The New American City and the End of Public Space*. Hill and Wang, 1992, p. 127.

5 Where I write this essay in London, many roads are of Roman origin. See http://mappinglondon. co.uk/2013/londons-roman-roads/ for the main ones.

6 Jacobs, Jane. *The Death and Life of Great American Cities*. The Modern Library, 1993 edition, p. 44

7 Boddy, Trevor. Underground and Overhead: Building the Analogous City. In Sorkin, Michael (Ed). *Variations on a Theme Park. The New American City and the End of Public Space*. Hill and Wang, 1992, p. 124.

8   Cass, Jeffrey. Egypt on Steroids: Luxor Las Vegas and Postmodern Orientalism. In Lasansky, D. Medina and McLaren, Brian (Eds). *Architecture and Tourism*. BERG, 2004, p. 250.

9   Illustrated guide to Paris, 1852 – quoted by Benjamin, Walter. *Paris Capital of the Nineteenth Century. The Arcades Project,* translated by Howard Eiland and Kevin McLaughlin. Belknap Press, 2002, p. 3

10   Ibid., p. 879

11   ibid., p. 59

12   Morrell, Liz. Better by Design. *Retail Masterplanning – Passenger Terminal World.* January 2016, p. 31–35. Found at http://viewer.zmags.com/publication/5b7a9b68#/5b7a9b68/34, accessed 12th October 2018.

13   Ibid., p. 32

14   ibid., p. 33

15   Penn, Alan. *The Complexity of the Elementary Interface: Shopping Space.* Fifth International Space Syntax Symposium Proceedings. A. Van Nes (Ed). Delft, 2005, 25–42, p. 15

Chapter 3

The Megablock
Beijing under One Roof

Jeffrey Johnson

Large-scale superblock development in China has been a focus of my research for over 12 years.[1] My research is driven by an interest in how emerging urbanisms operating at a large scale can be adapted, reinterpreted, and deployed in other rapidly urbanizing contexts. This research redefines the 'superblock', the typical urban unit in China, into the 'Megablock', an urban prototype that holds the promise of fulfilling the social, economic, spatial, and ecological challenges faced by the city in the future. Parkview Green is an example of a Megablock. This chapter elaborates how a sustainable, forward-looking, self-contained urban microcosm is contained within a single enclosure—the Beijing megablock.

Over the past two decades, China has constructed countless awe-inspiring structures. The economic boom following Deng Xiaoping's Open and Reform in 1979 fueled a massive urban expansion, while the 2008 Beijing Olympics catapulted China onto the global stage with impressive new architecture as the backdrop. Parkview Green, completed in 2009 and designed by Hong Kong-based Integrated Design Associates in collaboration with Arup, is a project that was realized in the wake of these ambitions. It was also conceived within the context of contemporary Beijing where urban planning and economic factors encourage large-scale development. While many of the ambitious projects in China that came before it placed emphasis on iconic and monumental forms, Parkview Green's originality is found in its voluminous urban interior that is encased within an innovative high-tech shell. It is a miniature city under a single roof—a project that points both toward the future and one that harkens back to numerous visionary examples that proposed alternative urban futures.

Superblock Development

In China today, the default solution for accommodating rapid urban growth is large-scale superblock development, a carryover from the Soviet-influenced communist-era planning. With site areas that can exceed 40 hectares, and

DOI: 10.4324/9780429443091-5

populations reaching over 100,000, these autonomous blocks, often surrounded by walls, have been radically transforming cities in China. Operating between the scales of architecture and the city, they act as spatial instruments with social, cultural, environmental, and economic implications. The majority are designed in isolation as autonomous enclaves enclosed by walls and consisting of a collection of repetitive structures that encourage and reinforce an inward-focused lifestyle. Access is controlled, with minimal connectivity to adjacent sites and the general urban context. Public accessibility is either discouraged or outright prohibited. The superblock is essentially a city within a city, with its own internal organization and infrastructure. Each one is an urban island that takes no part in an overall social or spatial narrative. As a result, vast areas in Chinese cities have been transformed into territories of disconnected urban fragments.

Parkview Green, with its multiple functions and public interior, challenges the convention of exclusive and private large-scale development by shifting the emphasis toward connectivity to the city and providing more spaces dedicated to the public. It exemplifies a shift toward mixed-use development as the model of choice for many new urban projects.

Urban Context

Parkview Green is located in Beijing, a city of over 21 million, between the second and third Ring Roads in the Chaoyang district, east of the city center and the historical Forbidden City, and not far from the OMA/Rem Koolhaas-designed CCTV Headquarters. In anticipation for the 2008 Beijing Olympics and the plan to locate the Beijing Capital International Airport to the northeast (Beijing has already built a new larger international airport to the south in 2019), this area, easily accessible to the airport and the Ring Roads, was master planned as a new Central Business District (CBD) with over 250 new towers. Up until the 2000s, this area was predominantly made up of social housing estates built in the 1970s and later, some of which still exist today.

Parkview Green's site is a rectilinear-shaped, 200-meter by 180-meter block adjacent to socialist-era housing blocks from a half-century ago and contemporary commercial mixed-use developments such as SOHO Shangdu and The Place, with its extravagant LED screen canopy extending 250 meters by 30 meters across a shopping plaza. Because of its location within the CBD, the site is conveniently located within walking distance of the Beijing Subway and multiple municipal bus stops. Similar to almost every new project constructed within Beijing's Ring Roads, the site for Parkview Green was cleared—*tabula rasa*—for the new construction with no traces of what existed before it. With commercial investment within the Ring Roads expected to continue for some time into the future, it will play an influential role in the transformation of the district (Image 3.1).

Connection to the City

The success of Parkview Green will be measured in various ways. Because it is a commercial development first and foremost, its ability to attract and maintain tenants and hotel guests, as well its ability to entice consumers into its interior retail spaces, is paramount for its financial success and sustainability. However, perhaps more importantly for the city and its inhabitants would be its ability to

Image 3.1 Parkview Green from the street. Credit: Jeffrey Johnson

engage with the surrounding neighborhood and provide spaces for interaction and gathering. As noted above, the majority of large-scale superblock projects that are constructed in China are exclusive and neither connect to the urban fabric nor welcome the general public.

Parkview Green is simultaneously opened and connected to the public as well as closed off from it. From a distance, its sharp and planar glass façades address the street edge abruptly. However, as the building is approached, the glass façades rise not from the urban ground plane but emerge from sunken gardens carved into the ground, thus setting the building back from the street's edge. The building is connected to the public by a series of bridges that extend from the sidewalk across the sunken gardens that penetrate through the exterior envelope into the interior. The pathways become a dynamic network of interior streets and bridges that organize circulation within the interior. While the exterior sunken gardens provide a dramatic transition between the chaotic urban surroundings and the controlled environment of the interior, they could also seem to reflect an attitude that is more exclusive and unwelcoming. Moreover, the bridges might entice and spark one's curiosity of what lies inside the building, but they can also represent a foreboding obstacle. Not unlike the walls that bound and separate the superblock housing estates found throughout the city, the sunken gardens symbolize a barrier complicating the project's intentions of being connected, open, and welcoming (Image 3.2).

Four Towers under One Roof

Parkview Green is a 200,000-square meter mixed-use project which includes class-A offices, a six-star hotel, four stories of retail, and underground parking.[2] The project was designed as an agglomeration of four discrete towers, two nine-story and two 18-story, each located at one of the four corners of the site

Image 3.2 Bridges spanning across the sunken garden.
Credit: Jeffrey Johnson

and wrapped in an 'environmental envelope'[3] While the four towers are legible from within, from the exterior, they are concealed behind a massive glass envelope. Since I saw the initial proposal for Parkview Green, with its massive pyramid-shaped all-glass form and its voluminous public interior, I have been fascinated with its position within an architectural history of visionary urban structures and vast public interiors.

Beginning with its overall exterior appearance, Parkview Green's crystalline form is constructed out of a glass and ethylene tetrafluoroethylene (ETFE) envelope. The pyramid-like form, partly shaped by zoning regulations, sits on the site as an almost scale-less object with sharp knife-like edges. Its glass façades, with their visible diagonal steel structure, are highly reflective surfaces during the day concealing what lies inside. At night, the surfaces become transparent revealing the vibrant interior and allowing the object to glow and appear to hover above the ground. Set against the backdrop of Beijing, often gray and dusty, its overall high-tech appearance is unique and alien. Similar to the ambitions of Joseph Paxton's Crystal Palace for The Great Exposition in London in 1851 where he utilized the most current technologies to construct a huge greenhouse-like structure that housed a voluminous interior public space, Parkview Green's steel, glass, and ETFE envelope capitalizes on the most current building technologies to project an aesthetic of progress and the future.

Parkview Green's massive urban interior, enveloped by a single skin, also finds precedent and inspiration from many architectural and urban visionaries of the twentieth century. Some of their ideas were intended as realizable propositions, while others were conceived as provocations and speculations on the future. Perhaps one of the most well-known and relevant propositions was conceived by Buckminster Fuller in 1960 where he imagined a two-mile diameter steel and glass geodesic dome that would envelope

Midtown Manhattan. *Dome over Manhattan* was a completely interiorized city with a controlled environment. Since Fuller proposed this, numerous other proposals have been conceived, perhaps most famously Fuller's own Biosphere designed for the World's Expo in 1967 and its offspring Biosphere 2 engineered by Pearce Structures, Inc. (Peter John Pearce was an associate of Buckminster Fuller) and built in 1987 in the Arizona desert. The recent Eden Project in Great Britain designed by Grimshaw Architects and completed in 2001 is a contemporary example. While these projects are not urban interiors, they are cogent examples of enveloping vast interiors to create controlled environments and microclimates.

Parkview Green's vast interior is defined by the space between the four towers that sit at the corners of the site. Covered by a diagrid of operable translucent ETFE roof panels, the large void between the towers is an impressive public atrium-like space that is crisscrossed by elevated walkways and bridges. Immediately upon entering the building for the first time, you are struck by its dynamism created by the multi-layered and three-dimensional system of escalators, glass elevators, walkways, sky gardens, bridges, and suspended sculptures. It is as if you walked into a dense three-dimensional city reminiscent of Piranesi's labyrinthine spaces envisioned in his *The Prisons* (circa 1745, 1761) etchings. The grandness of the interior space can also evoke a sense of the sublime. Its monumental scale is reminiscent of Boullées' visionary civic interiors such as those depicted for the Cenotaph for Sir Isaac Newton (1784) and Bibliothéque du Roi (1785) (Image 3.3).

In addition to the more futuristic and even utopian historical precedents noted above, Parkview Green's interior is perhaps most directly aligned pragmatically with the shopping mall. There are no allusions that Parkview Green is anything but a commercial development and retail plays a fundamental role in its economics. The shops and restaurants, which are located at the first four floors of the four towers, serve the offices and hotels, but are also what draws the general public into the building generating its vitality and energy. Perhaps the most applicable historical antecedent that still exists today is the Galleria Vittoria Emanuele II in Milan, which is a grand, four-story double arcade with glass and iron vaults and an octagon-shaped dome at its center.[4] Sited in the center of Milan near the Duomo in the Piazza del Duomo, the public flows freely from the public piazza and surrounding city into the Galleria's interior arcades lined with shops and cafes. Like the Galleria, Parkview Green provides an interior urban nexus within an iconic architectural form.

During the decades-long success of the suburban shopping mall in the twentieth century, predominantly in North America, but also in other parts of the world, commercial developers began to incorporate the interior shopping street model into their urban development projects. The shopping street returned to urban centers in novel forms. The influence of the pedways that created a network of elevated pedestrian streets in, for example, Minneapolis and Atlanta, and perhaps most extensively and successfully in Hong Kong's Central district, can be seen in Parkview Green's interior network of suspended walkways and bridges that connect visitors to the shops and restaurants. Additionally, the influence of the adaptation of the atrium in large-scale commercial urban projects by architects such as John Portman is clearly apparent in Parkview Green's voluminous central public interior space.

Image 3.3 Interior atrium.
Credit: Jeffrey Johnson

Today, even as we continue to witness the demise of the suburban shopping mall, and dedicated retail spaces in general, we still see new forms of urban interiors and commercial shopping strategies arise. In numerous cities across the globe, the economic climate encourages increasingly larger urban developments. In cities such as New York, Hong Kong, Singapore, Shanghai, and Beijing, entire city blocks are constructed that incorporate a network of interior streets within multi-story podiums. Many of these podiums provide an elevated artificial ground from which towers arise. Perhaps one of the most extreme being Kowloon Station master planned by TFP Farrells in Hong Kong's West Kowloon district and connected directly to mass transit and elevated highways. Tower and podium projects are radically reshaping the city and the street, even in some cases like Kowloon Station, almost completely closed off to the street. While Parkview Green's program matches many contemporary mixed-use developments, its design rejects the predominate tower and podium model by completely reconceptualizing it by sinking the towers into the ground and encasing them within a single envelope (Image 3.4).

Image 3.4 Interior atrium.
Credit: Jeffrey Johnson

Urban Microclimate

While the building's striking glass pyramidal form, its exterior sunken gardens and bridges, and its voluminous interior atrium with its crisscrossing suspended walkways are impressive, perhaps Parkview Green's real innovation is found in the Arup-designed building technologies utilized to create its interior microclimate. Like Buckminster Fuller's visions for a controlled interior urban microclimate before it, Parkview Green is a radical, forward-looking project that sets a standard for future large-scale urban development. Not only is it one of the first structures in Beijing to be designed environmentally sustainable (LEED Platinum), but it is also the first to make use of a microclimate as a means of minimizing energy consumption throughout the building's lifetime.

The project's iconic pyramidal form is wrapped in a high-tech transparent 'environmental envelope' constructed of glass and ETFE panels. The envelope encapsulates the four towers and atrium functioning as a filter between the interior and exterior environments. In the extreme seasonal temperature variations in Beijing, the envelope reduces heat loss during frigid winters and minimizes the need for air conditioning in the warm summers. To assist in cooling in the summer, the Arup team designed ventilation louvers at the top of the enclosure allowing the warmest air to discharge and drawing the cooler air up from the bottom creating air movement and natural ventilation.[5] This hybrid system contributes to 60% energy saving in summer when compared to a conventional office air conditioning system. In winter, the highly insulated collective façades can offer up to 80% energy savings over the conventional office designs.[6] In addition to the high-tech envelope, the building uses a hybrid heating and cooling system that utilizes passive and active green technologies, including a pre-cooling system that utilizes underground air, ceiling radiant cooling, and under-floor air conditioning. Rainwater is collected from the roof and paved areas and used for landscape irrigation. Wastewater from sinks, showers, and washing faucets is also treated for use in sanitation and irrigation.[7]

Megablock Futures

With China's ambitious plans to move another 200–250 million people into cities from the countryside by 2025, the superblock and large-scale urban development will undoubtedly play a significant role in the growth of the city. With the positive shift toward more sustainable low-carbon planning strategies, a more open and porous perimeter to encourage connectivity, an emphasis on providing and maintaining public spaces, and a turn toward more mixed-use programming, the Megablock in its variety of hybrid forms holds the promise of an adaptable model for future urbanization. Parkview Green, even with its faults, is an ambitious and forward-looking example of how a Megablock might positively impact the city in the future.

Notes

1 See my book project: Jeffrey Johnson, Cressica Brazier, and Tat Lam, *China Lab Guide to Megablock Urbanisms* (New York, Barcelona: Actar Publishers and New York: Columbia University Graduate School of Architecture, Planning and Preservation, 2020).

2 http://www.parkviewgreen.com/eng.

3 http://www.parkviewgreen.com/eng/news-and-events/from-the-press/a-microclimate-of-vibrancy.

4 For a detailed history, see Chuihua Judy Chung, Jeffrey Inaba, Rem Koolhaas, and Sze Tsung Leong (eds.), *The Harvard Design School Guide to Shopping* (Cologne: Taschen, 2001).

5 https://www.arup.com/projects/beijing-parkview-green.

6 http://www.parkviewgreen.com/eng/news-and-events/from-the-press/a-microclimate-of-vibrancy.

7 Ibid.

Chapter 4

The Laneway

Urbanism through the Lens of Interiority and Heterotopia

Rebekah Ison Radtke

The laneway is an intimate form of functional space central to the historic evolution of cities. A balance of public and private, fast and slow, interior and exterior, laneways (or alleys) connect the past to the present in seemingly dichotomous ways. Underutilized and often understood as purely service zones, the laneway is often characterized as undesirable or deviant; however, laneways offer opportunities for incremental expansion and revitalization. Accommodating internal and incremental growth, recent socio-spatial adaptations of laneways reflect the history and site-specific nuances of communities.

The very expression of the laneway is temporal and creates "other spaces" within the urban environment. Here, the character of the city reflects a microcosm of urban life manifested as a quasi-interior condition. Serving as exterior skins but operating as interior spaces—deeply personal and intimate in scale, laneways express interiority, yet remain undeniably exterior domains. This chapter argues that laneways can be interpreted as interior spaces within the urban context, applying Michel Foucault's theory of heterotopia to reveal their interior urbanity. As heterotopic spaces, laneways connect old and new, public and private, practical and cultural, interior and exterior.

Origins

Laneways trace their earliest form to China with narrow alleys bridging courtyards called *hutongs*, or close-knit residential courtyard communities.[1] Laneways have existed in early civilizations in various forms throughout the Indus Valley Civilization.[2] In Greek and Roman cities, laneways were integral to city design and synonymous with functionality in the built environment across cultures. From east to west, laneways spread as civilizations built cities. In the Middle Ages, laneways were narrow footpaths providing movement corridors within settlements. These connective spaces were refined over time into formalized avenues during the Renaissance.[3] After the Great

DOI: 10.4324/9780429443091-6

Fire in London (1666), formalized standards created the mew which allowed for rear access to the city's grand estates for coal-burning furnaces and servant routines. The mews of London were typically articulated as a two-story carriage house with storage below and servant quarters above sited along a double-loaded and narrow cobblestone right-of-way.

Through English colonization, the laneway migrated around the globe so that this typology functions quite similarly in the United States, Canada, Australia, New Zealand, Caribbean, and elsewhere across the Anglosphere. In North America, the Land Survey of 1785 established that new cities would apply a gridiron to create blocks and lots, building on the formal qualities of early alleys dating from fifth century BC in ancient Greece (Clay 1978).[4] In the Southern United States, alleys reflect the history of slavery as they provided a way for owners to keep a watchful eye over enslaved people housed in accessory buildings near the alley.[5] In the Northern United States, alleys provided frontages for tenement housing during the late nineteenth and early twentieth centuries when immigrants were flowing into the densely populated neighborhoods of Boston, New York, Philadelphia, Chicago, Cincinnati, and elsewhere.[6] In later years, laneways remained service-oriented but also provided space for the homeless, recently migrated populations, and displaced persons.[7]

In Washington, DC, Roosevelt sought to eliminate alleys from the capital city with the Alley Dwelling Authority in 1934; however, he was unable to completely implement these changes because of the work of citizens and preservationists alike. With the advent and widespread use of the automobile after World War II, most city planning was oriented toward the street as laneways fell out of use. With increased concern for cleanliness, Garden City planning principles and super blocks prevailed, while the Federal Housing Administration approved loans and incentivized community development designed to eliminate alleys.[8] As American cities expanded further beyond urban cores, suburbia was defined by single-family houses on large lots with garages fronting the street.

Despite such lack of interest in laneways, Jane Jacobs advocated for close-knit older communities, prioritizing the alley and how it connected people in the urban environment.[9] Acknowledging "eyes on the street", her book, *The Life and Death of Great American Cities,* encouraged social mixing and diversity to increase neighborliness. She envisioned neighborhoods that moved away from the mass construction and income segregation that emerged during the City Beautiful movement. New Urbanists widely embraced her ideas in the 1980s, emphasizing the importance of walkability, accessibility, and proximity in the urban environment.[10] In the United States, greater priority was placed on the street. Heeding the call of preservationists, planners and architects began valuing neighborhoods that were older while discouraging suburban sprawl. These ideas have subsequently led to downtown revitalization and community growth focused on density, diversity, and alternative transit such as walking or biking. These approaches highlight the value and importance of the laneway in the widespread reassessment of the contemporary city.[11]

Laneways and Heterotopia

Laneways represent the back porch of the city, an authentic expression of civic values and the true interior of the city. Stewart Brand speaks of how buildings evolve over time as they adapt to their occupants. This is also true for laneways whose spaces have continually adapted to serve the city as an interior environ-ment; low-cost adaptations allow laneways to reinvent their purpose from ser-vice spaces into civic spaces serving the community.[12] The spatial qualities of the laneway can be thought of abstractly as Frank Duffy describes shearing layers, as components of layers that have different lifespans. The time scales of the urban realm are eternal in the site form, but the interior "stuff" is rapidly evolving, which transitions laneways into an interior environment, or as spatial layers.[13]

Furthermore, laneways can be interpreted as spaces of otherness. Otherspaces operate simultaneously as an interior and exterior across time and scales to house parallel forms of inhabitation.[14] Michel Foucault discusses heterotopia as "other" spaces that are seemingly unrelated, contradictory, or contrasting. He states that we have not reached practical desanctification of space and that "oppositions remain inviolable".[15] In regard to laneways, such contradictions are accepted as givens, old and new, public and private, family and social, useful and cultural. Thus, in addition to the contradictions proposed by Foucault, a laneway can be viewed as equally urban and interior.

Henri Lefebvre extends the concept of heterotopia in *The Production of Space* where he characterizes space as a product of social values. In the lan-eway, otherness exists through interactions between interiority and changing occupancies over time.[16] Building on ideas established by Foucault and Lefeb-vre about the importance of social space and "spaces of representation", inde-terminate spaces in the public realm are not limited to the group that created them. In this theory, space is defined relationally to describe how it coexists with its adjacencies. The principles outlined below will argue that heterotopia is a lens to analyze laneways as a form of urban interiority (Image 4.1).

In the first principle, the heterotopia of deviation contextualizes the place of laneways within this theory. Foucault describes deviance as behaviors that cannot exist within the mean or standard of the city. Behaviors that have been characterized in the history of laneways are viewed as unseemly, but also organic, unorganized, and ripe for renewal. Deviance is allowed, accepted, and embraced within laneways, such as the Graffiti Alley in Toronto. Here, the artistic expression of street art is deviant in and of itself—it represents high art. Such actions are too discursive for the boulevards and central squares of the city. Temporary and outsider art must exist in unregulated spaces that are less patrolled and precious. Laneways encourage and create space for behaviors that cannot occur in the public eye, yet still exist in public space. In some cities, laneways have become appropriated by citizens to act more like interior spaces within the urban context. Building on the notion of the private spaces of an urban back porch, laneways are intrinsically personal expressions of the local community. Cenzatti describes this concept as "invisibility and recognition".[17]

The second principle of heterotopia refers to transformation over time. A space once intended to serve in a specific way can move beyond that purpose as cultural values shift. Laneways are responsive to the culture of the time and are not fixed in space. Their structure remains the same but the skin evolves and responds to the culture of the city. In some contexts, transforma-tion of laneways is often manifested through housing. Responding to popula-tion growth in the city, infill housing with granny quarters, Airbnb, and other residential projects address stress and result in policy changes. In Detroit, The Alley Project has become a community ownership project with grassroots

Image 4.1 Graffiti Alley, Toronto, Ontario, Canada. Credit: Rebekah Radtke

initiatives that create social spaces responding to communal needs. In Melbourne, the public realm of laneways has allowed a new market for bistros, bars, and restaurants offering a vibrant new subculture. In Toronto, shifting laneway use is reflected in graffiti art, but the space still functions as a conventional alley. Greening the alleyway to discourage surface runoff and water retention is a priority in Chicago. In other cities, less significant adaptations maintain the historic function of alleys by providing enhanced circulation and services to residences with no additional enhancements. In all cases, alleys have adapted over time to respond to contemporary needs. This fluidity has made alleys responsive to expanding rights-to-the-city (Image 4.2).

The third principle of heterotopia addresses the incompatibility of emergent functions of the site, juxtaposing real spaces with perceived ones and superimposing alternative meanings. In relation to the laneway, this can be interpreted through shifting public space. In an alley where garbage and services

Image 4.2 Ruth Lyons Lane, Cincinnati, Ohio, USA.
Credit: Rebekah Radtke

might occur, a party for a toddler and a pop-up bar directly adjacent to a recycling bin superimpose new occupancies. In Cincinnati, certain alleyways have been reconceived through materials and surface articulations, yet still provide access and mobility. These juxtaposed uses and activities keep the space adaptable and useful. In the practice of interior design, temporary fixes are often centered on addressing the daily needs of people. Although laneways are not enclosed interiors, urban dwellers are increasingly appropriating and adapting these spaces to serve their private, more typically interiorized daily needs.

The fourth principle of heterotopia explores the slices of time where there are two heterotopias: one of the festival and one of eternity. These are seen in the built environment as a museum to represent eternity and a carnival to represent the festival. Joining these two ideas together is achieved in the huts of Djerba, encapsulating ancient history in a temporal manner. In this principle of eternity, time can exist in one place like libraries and museums, building on each other and continually expanding. In the same way, laneways are always the same, and yet always adding to the skins of buildings, layers of history; grit, paint, and stories tell the narrative of these places. They are less curated than

Image 4.3 Degraves Street, Melbourne, Victoria, Australia. Credit: Rebekah Radtke

street frontages that express an outward focus for desired perceptions in the public gaze (Image 4.3).

On the one hand, the immobile space and indefinite time of the city grid were designed by Western civilization for order and structure. On the other, laneways are responsive to the immobile organizing grid, bound in time and space. But in the same space, a temporal nature exists in the laneways as well, providing pop-up spaces and street fairs. The streets parks that represent playscapes for neighborhoods that do not have this permanent infrastructure can be seen in the work of Better Block, using public space to reactivate neighborhoods in communities such as Dallas, as well as the work of Gehl Architects in Sydney and Melbourne.

The fifth principle of heterotopia investigates the notion of being both open and closed and how space can be private yet open. Penetrable but still isolated, space cannot be a public space without open access; intermittent publicness must be accessed through permission. This principle can be seen in the alley as they often serve as a home for transient populations. People can reside in the space, take ownership, and form identity within this space, but also the transient dweller is typically not welcome to loiter. These occupancies, in turn, discourage other populations from using the spaces for fear of safety. In response to such issues, Melbourne seeks to make laneways accessible and welcoming to all.

In the last sixth principle, and perhaps the most esoteric and elusive trait of the theory, Foucault speaks of how heterotopias function in all spaces that remain. In the space of illusion, similar to a brothel, heterotopia creates an experience of illusion in contrast to utopian space like Jesuit or American colonies juxtaposed against our quotidian world. Order occurs through colonization and religious ideas made manifest in design; thus, it can be applied to the creation of alleyways. Foucault discussed Jesuit communities and Puritan settlements as examples of this spatial order constructed to symbolically represent predetermined perfection through the plan of their settlements. In the same way, David Harvey sees the street or urban square as public space for riots and private lived moments.[18] The alley supports activities that represent a simultaneous publicness and intimacy of the interior (Image 4.4).

The multiplicity of one space over time to serve various activities and movements in heterotopia further parallels how an alley serves many activities over time, and thus responds to the culture and climate of its context. An alley creates a socially activated zone that reflects its current community. It is an

Image 4.4 The Belt Alley, Detroit, Michigan, USA. Credit: Rebekah Radtke

adaptable otherspace, and because of its scale, it is personal and limited to specific yet infinite behaviors addressing the needs of its occupants. Heterotopia encourages behaviors and activities that do not conform to societal norms. This is true of alleys. Public squares host parades and sanctioned activities that have been institutionalized and ordained. In alleys, the activities are private and responsive actions of ground-up micro-communities. Against the notion that bigger is better, publicness at an intimate and interior scale is an important aspect of the resilient and livable city.

Conclusion

Cities evolve with faded building typologies and spatial memories of past occupants and their artifacts. Infrastructure tells the history of a place because it is old and slow to change; however, people quickly adapt. Technology and the movement of workers, residents, and tourists quickly change, while the longstanding urban infrastructure remains. Scarcity of land intersects with the ever-evolving needs of city dwellers.

Typically unseen and ignored, laneways are a rich commodity in urbanism. As demands on space have increased, creative adaptations of the city focus on the importance of historic neighborhoods and latent spaces. The human scale of the city creates diverse experiences that connect our humanity. Small details remind us of who we are as individuals, but also bridge us into a larger network of interwoven communities. Insignificant details of a shop display or a cobblestone street seen along a daily commute can have a profound impact on an urban dweller. The repetition of experiences allows us to deeply know the intricacies of the built environment and to collect memories of form, materiality, and scale as it relates to our own lived experiences.

At a time when cities are densifying, the everyday need for gathering spaces remains paramount. In a socially divisive time in history, there is a rising need for accessible and adaptive public space that brings together diverse communities. This chapter proposed that urban dwellers need opportunities to express personalization of public space. This research demonstrates that such expression increasingly occurs in the urban realm of laneways. Laneways provide territories to address communal needs through negotiation and activism. An interior lens can be used to resituate laneways within the practice of city planning to envision more participatory approaches to urban design.

Notes

1 Meyer, Michael, *The Last Days of Old beijing: Life in the vanishing backstreets of a city transformed* (New York: Bloomsbury Publishing, 2009).
2 Gerald Hodge and David L.A. Gordon, *Planning Canadian Communities: An Introduction to the Principles, Practices and Participants* (Toronto: Nelson Thomson 5th ed., 2007).
3 A.E.J. Morris, *The History of Urban Form before the Industrial Revolutions* (New York: John Wiley & Sons, 1993).
4 Grady Clay, *Being a Disquisition upon the Origins, Natural Disposition and Occurrences in the American Scene of Alleys: A Hidden Resource* (Louisville, KY: G. Clay & Co., 1978).
5 James Borchert, Urban Neighborhood and Community: Informal Group Life, 1850–1970. *Journal of Interdisciplinary History* XI(4): 607–631, 1981. Ellen Beasley, *The Alleys and Back Buildings of Galveston* (Houston: Rice University Press,1996).

6   Jacob Riis, *How the Other Half Lives: Studies Among the Tenements of New York* (New York: Charles Scribner's Sons, 1890).

7   Paul M. Hess, Fronts and Backs: The Use of Streets, Yards, and Alleys in Toronto-Area New Urbanist Neighborhoods. *Journal of Planning Education and Research* 28(2): 196–212, 2008.

8   Sara A. Hage, *Alley: Negotiating Identity in Traditional, Urban, and New Urban Communities* (2008). Masters Theses 1911 - February 2014. 110. https://doi.org/10.7275/441438.

9   Jane Jacobs, *The Death and Life of Great American Cities* (New York: Modern Library, 1961)

10 Congress and Emily Talen, *Charter of the New Urbanism, 2nd Edition* (New York: McGraw Hill Professional, 2013).

11 Alex Krieger, The Virtues of Cities. *Places* 10(2): 64–71, 1996.

12 Stewart Brand, *How Buildings Learn: What Happens after They're Built* (New York: Penguin Book, 1994).

13 Stewart Brand, *How Buildings Learn: What Happens after They're Built.* (New York: Penguin Book, 1999).

14 Kevin Lynch, *The Image of the City* (Cambridge: Massachusetts Institute of Technology, 1960).

15 Michel Foucault, Of Other Spaces, Heterotopias. Translate from *Architecture, Mouvement, Countinuité* (5): 46–49, 1984.

16 Henri Lefebvre, *The Production of Space* (Hoboken, New Jersey: Blackwell Publishers Inc, 1999).

17 M. Dehaene and L. De Cauter (Eds.) *Heterotopia and the City – Urban Theory and the Transformations of Public Space*, Oxford, UK and Cambridge, MA: Blackwell, 2008.

18 David Harvey, *Flexible Accumulation through Urbanization: Reflections on Post-Modernism in the American City* (Antipode 19, 1987).

Chapter 5

The Bazaar

Public Interior Environments as Integrated Socio-Spatial Systems

Hessam Ghamari

Bazaars are among the most significant socio-spatial systems in Near Eastern cities, central places in which economic, commercial, social, and cultural activities occur. In his book "The City Square," Michael Webb highlights the importance of the public square as a microcosm of urban life.[1] He posits that these spaces emerged in response to political, cultural, climatic, commercial, topographic, and defense conditions. Traditional Persian bazaars interconnect residential areas, socio-political zones, and commercial districts. In Iranian traditional cities, the bazaar has historically embodied an interior urban system supporting the economic, social, political, cultural, and civic activities of people.[2] Bazaars form the backbone and commercial heart of Iranian cities. They are characterized by their public interiority, while being defined by primary and secondary linear circulation spaces called *rasteh,* open-closed spaces, and indoor-outdoor spaces featuring ornate arches, skylights, and domes (karbandis) along a fixed axis or multiple axes (Image 5.1).[3]

   The study of Isfahan, a historic city in Iran whose bazaar has incrementally developed over the years, demonstrates the structural principles of the Persian bazaar. This socio-spatial typology represents a timeless aspect of urban form across different periods of Iranian history. The bazaar is an indispensable organ of the city, constituted by hierarchical layers of religious, social, and economic functions. Its urban form promotes community and metropolitan coherence. This chapter discusses the architectural features of the bazaar as an urban interior space, as well as its impact on the broader civic and economic life of the city. This discussion reveals how socio-cultural and architectural features of the bazaar play a central role in creating publicness and interior urbanism.

DOI: 10.4324/9780429443091-7

Image 5.1 Mirza Shafiee Timcheh. Credit: Mirza Shafie

It applies the urban criteria of theorist Kevin Lynch and sustainable practices to the Bazaar of Tabriz to assess such principles vis-à-vis publicness, interior urban spatiality, and inherent sustainability

Origins and Evolution

The term "bazaar" is an ancient Persian term that is an essential part of Middle Eastern culture. There is a long history behind the evolution of the bazaar and historic records demonstrate that the typology dates to 3000 BC in Iranian towns and cities. The bazaar initially emerged as an economic urban establishment during the Sasanian era. The main cores of most bazaars were created near city gates with the highest traffic volumes. The incremental formation of bazaars was dependent on population growth and economic activity. For instance, there were only two *caravansaries* (roadside inns) in the Bazaar of Naeen. In thriving smaller cities, local bazaars often provided for the daily needs of inhabitants, while the main part of the bazaar served foreign traders. In the tenth century AD, Persian philosopher Naser Khusraw noted that there were 50 caravansaries in the valleys near Isfahan and 1,802 caravansaries in Isfahan itself (Image 5.2).[4]

Urban history reveals that various factors have influenced the development of ancient bazaars. Production and consumption have always been among the most essential factors in urban growth. In traditional cities, the bazaar served as the primary place for economic, social, political, cultural, and civic activities. Transcending their physical attributes, bazaars created a sense of community, unity, and identity.[5] The traditional bazaar is a unified, self-contained building, a primarily enclosed complex of shops, passageways, and caravansaries, interspersed with enclosed public squares (meydan), religious buildings, bathhouses (hammam), and other public institutions.

Image 5.2 Raasteh, Tabriz Bazaar. Credit: Kaveh Mansoori

Socio-spatial and Cultural Impact

The built environment has always reflected connections between people and culture throughout history.[6] A city reflects culture, while each culture represents social structures as well as behavioral interactions shaped by connections and communications among individuals, classes, communities, and environments in the larger metropolitan system.[7] In the bazaar, these interactions are facilitated by the socio-spatial organization of public interior space. As the most privileged urban typology in Near Eastern cities, the bazaar is an integral component of the Iranian historical urban context, acting as not only public space but as a vertebral metropolitan spine and place of consumption.[8]

The Iranian bazaar reveals that its formation and evolution have been linked to various factors. Economics, politics, and religion have played important roles in both prosperity and repression of the bazaar throughout history. Yet, the Iranian bazaar is a significant urban system because it is embedded into urban life. Iranian bazaars have always offered socio-cultural performative qualities alongside commercial functions.[9] Bazaars have maintained their important public role throughout history across continual shifts in lifestyle. Forming the heart of cities, the bazaar plays a similar role to the European "piazza" in the Middle Ages or "hiruba" in Japanese cities during their modern industrialization.[10] To summarize, bazaars offer important spaces for manifold uses beyond commercial activities.[11]

As essential aspects of urban form, bazaars define the skeletal framework of Iranian cities. In many traditional cities, the bazaar establishes the main urban axis and plays a primary role in the general layout.[12] The bazaar is typically located at the center of the city where it connects different parts of the urban context. In most Iranian cities, the main infrastructure of the city was formed by the bazaars. As an indoor urban public space, its architecture creates an artistically and technically rich environment with a mysterious atmosphere. Although bazaars were initially built for commercial purposes, its interior spaces support diverse activities, interactions, and urban events.

The bazaar is not only the primary commercial center, but also the main public space of Iranian cities. Unlike cities in the West, this, in an interior urban typology, used not only space for global interaction, but also an urban-scale system that organizes public, religious, and commercial zones of the larger city. The bazaar reflects architectural styles, urban principles, and cultural sensibilities of different historical periods. Hence, a survey of Iranian bazaars shows the incremental expansion and layering of their urban morphology. Notable among Iranian bazaars, the Bazaar of Tabriz provides an outstanding case of incrementality in design characteristics that transcend various historical periods.[13]

Bazaars are formed as a network of retail spaces with a central flow organizing shops in parallel with connections to other programs, including mosques, holy places, schools, inns, and bathrooms, as well as secondary connections to residential passages.[14] For instance, the Friday mosque—the mosque that hosts Friday noon prayers known as the jumu'ah—is the main religious and political center in the city; this mosque is typically an integral part of the bazaar. Moreover, bazaars offer a public space in which to celebrate important political events, or to refuse celebrating such events, while expressing political disagreement. Moreover, the interior lanes of the bazaar provide the primary urban space for important religious functions connected to social and public issues. For instance, the Ashura ritual is the most important social and religious event for Iranian society, at which time commercial spaces in the bazaar temporarily accommodate holiday festivities.

Social Importance of Iranian Bazaars

Iranian bazaars represent a criterion for understanding the quality of urban life in different periods throughout Iranian history. The political and consumptive aspects of Iranian bazaars are derived from the crucial impact of Iranian bazaars at the scale of the city. Like the ancient agora, Middle Eastern souq, and Western marketplaces, Iranian traditional bazaars became the most important factor in fostering the growth of governmental jurisdiction and economic activities in urban life.[15] The Iranian bazaar is a symbolic institution that shows a sense of solidarity, cohesion, and cooperation, an interior place that generates social capital and public interactions between different stratums. It provides for social equity by linking vulnerable and affluent classes, while offering all citizens rights-to-the-city.[16] The literature surrounding bazaars demonstrates that their multifunctional offerings have had a crucial impact on the urban development of Iranian cities (Image 5.3).

Interior Urban Typologies in the Bazaar of Tabriz

As a case study, the Bazaar of Tabriz demonstrates how this urban-scale interior space offers significant contributions to the broader character of the city. Elements of the Bazaar of Tabriz can be correlated with the five urban elements (paths, nodes, edges, districts, and landmarks) defined by Kevin Lynch in his seminal book, *The Image of the City* (1960).[17]

Paths

Rasteh, or covered streets, in the bazaar represent paths that determine the interior urban form of the entire network.

Image 5.3 Mozaffarieh Timcheh.
Credit: Kaveh Mansoori

Nodes

Intersections of the *rasteh* paths create nodes in the bazaar. These nodes specify focal points within the larger urban layout of the city. They shape junctions with open urban spaces, defined by ornaments and shapes called "*mogharnas* and *karbandi.*"

Landmarks

Several elements act as landmarks in the bazaar to allow people to locate themselves within the broader urban environment. Open courtyards in the bazaar contrast with covered spaces and serve as wayfinding elements. Interior open spaces, such as the Amir Dome, create interior landmarks and visual cues for navigation.

Edges

Edges in the bazaar are identified as boundaries between interior and exterior spaces. These boundaries define interstitial zones between the bazaar itself and adjacent outdoor spaces to create thresholds, while marking a sequential path into the broader urban context.

Districts

Districts in the bazaar are composed of pathways and trading shops. These districts consist of "*sara*" (large districts) and "*timcheh*" (small districts) that surround interior courtyards to produce larger interior urban configurations.

Sustainable Impact of the Bazaar

Over time, bazaars gradually formed into multifunctional environments addressing the needs of their users. They established places to gather and connect the interests of different types of people. Today, at the metropolitan scale, these places support social interactions that contribute to socio-economic sustainability.[18] Walking through the bazaar engages the five senses and creates an enjoyable shopping, meeting, and interactive environment to explore interconnected passageways. This creates a vibrant and dynamic environment in which various activities occur. The unique image of the bazaar, with its architectural features and ornamental elements, offers public common areas for social interactions, conversations, and daily activities. The bazaar is an organic, spontaneous, and flexible typology. It represents a sense of place which generates community cohesion, and at the same time, an environmentally friendly urban form supporting economic and social sustainability.

Bazaars have adopted various shapes over time; the impact of climatic and geographic conditions on their architecture is clear. Traditional bazaars are sited to address heliotropic and climatic conditions. Moreover, the selection of materials, shading devices, natural ventilation features, and daylighted courtyards have contributed to the inherent energy efficiency and environmental sustainability of bazaars.[19] The following characteristics contribute to the environmental sustainability of bazaars:

Climate Responsible Design

Most traditional bazaars have been constructed in accordance with climatic conditions. For instance, the passive thermal heating system for the Bazaar of Tabriz uses brick as the main construction material. The roof domes provide natural ventilation in hot summer months.[20]

Sustainable and Local Materials

Traditional bazaars in Iran are generally made of masonry local materials such as brick and stone. The benefit of using these materials is their thermal capacity which helps to naturally control the interior temperature.

Roofs

Most traditional Iranian bazaars are covered with domed roofs. For instance, the Bazaar of Tabriz is decorated with magnificent stuccos and high brick arched (e.g. dome and vault) roofs. The domed roofs are primarily used to protect the building against windstorms and severe sunshine, as well as to lower heat transfer into the building. These roofs have a great impact on reducing structural load; the holes in the crowns enhance the natural ventilation of interior spaces in summer.[21]

Daylighting

Daylighting as a symbolic traditional element has been extensively used in traditional Iranian bazaars. The daylighting in indoor bazaar environments provides for comfort, health, efficiency, safety, and security. In most traditional bazaars, daylighting was based on factors such as the spiritual dimension of holiness, light adjustment and uniformity, temperature regulation, and energy storage in relation to shifting climatic conditions (Image 5.4).

Courtyards

Courtyards are used as climate modifiers in traditional bazaars. These architectural elements allow outdoor activities with protection from wind, dust, and sunlight. They also provide daylighting of indoor environments and enhance natural ventilation. These in-between, semi-open spaces create areas for public social interactions and activities.

Conclusion

Bazaars are an interior urban form that interrelates the economic, social, religious, and cultural complexities of cites. The emergence of bazaars was a key factor in establishing transnational social, cultural, and economic exchanges between different peoples. Bazaars continuously have served as the main backbone of cities and as a dominant, cohesive aspect of the urban context. The bazaar is a self-determined organization that shapes a decentralized network in which different mahallehs (communities) are interrelated. Bazaars not only unify the mahallehs, but also create a symbol of identity and cohesion for citizens. Their public interiority offers a unifying model for the broader body of the city.

Although Iranian bazaars have influenced different political and economic factors, the main image of Iranian bazaars is represented in their socio-cultural structure. These interior urban worlds create a sense of place

Image 5.4 Mirza Shafiee Timcheh.
Credit: Mirza Shafie

attachment, while generating connections between residential and socio-commercial activities, between private and public realms. Throughout time, they have continually served as transnational interior public places that nurture people, convey culture, promote commerce, and foster dialogue among diverse local and global communities.

Notes

1 Michael, Webb. *The City Square*. London: Thames and Hudson, 1980.
2 Mohammad Saeed, Moosavi. "Bazaars and Its Role in the Development of Iranian Traditional Cities." In *IRCICA, International Conference on Islamic Archeology*, 2005.
3 Reza, Mohammad, Pourjafar, and Ahmad Pourjafar. "The Role of Social Capital in the Traditional Markets of the Economic Situation in Iran." *Urban Management* 27, no. 203 (2011): 22.
4 Ali, Ashraf. "Historical Features of Urbanization in Iran; Social Science Letters." Paper presented at the Social Science Faculty, Tehran, 1974.
5 Amin, Adelzadeh. "Social Dimensions of Bazaar in Historical Cities of Iran: The Tabriz Bazaar." *The International Journal of Engineering and Science* 5, no. 5 (2016): 36–44.

6   Bodart, Magali, and Arnaud Evrard, eds. Architecture & Sustainable Development, Vol. 2: 27th International Conference on Passive and Low Energy Architecture. Louvain: Presses univ. de Louvain, 2011.
    Iranica, Encyclopedia. 1989.

7   Jorg, Kurt Groter. *Aesthetics in Architecture.* 5th ed. Tehran: Shahid Beheshti University Publication, 2009.

8   Reza, Masoudi Nejad. *Social Bazaar and Commercial Bazaar; Comparative Study of Spatial Role of Iranian Bazaar in theHistoric Cities in Different Social- Economical Context.* London, 2005.

9   Reza, Mohammard, Pourjafar, Masoome Amini, Elham Hatami-Varzaneh, and Mohammadjavad Mahdavinejad. "Role of Bazaars as a Unifying Factor in Traditional Cities of Iran: The Isfahan Bazaar." *Frontiers of Architectural Research* 3, no. 1 (2014): 10–19.

10 Mansour, Falamaki. Mohammad. *Formation of Architecture in the Experiences of the Iran and West.* Tehran: Faza, 2006.

11 Shokooh, Velshani, Iman Madani, Amir Reza Karimi Azar, and Seyed Bagher Hosseini. "Effect of Physical Factors on the Sense of Security of the People in Isfahan's Traditional Bazaar." Paper presented at the Asian Conference on Environment-Behaviour Studies, Tehran, Iran, 2015.

12 Reza, Mohammard, Pourjafar, Masoome Amini, Elham Hatami-Varzaneh, and Mohammadjavad Mahdavinejad. "Role of Bazaars as a Unifying Factor in Traditional Cities of Iran: The Isfahan Bazaar." *Frontiers of Architectural Research* 3, no. 1 (2014): 10–19.

13 Amin, Adelzadeh. "Social Dimensions of Bazaar in Historical Cities of Iran: The Tabriz Bazaar." *The International Journal of Engineering and Science* 5, no. 5 (2016): 36–44.

14 Nader, Ardalan. *The Sense of Unity: The Sufi Traditional in Persian Architecture.* Tehran: Elme-E-Memar, 2011.

15 Kaylee, Harris. "The Bazaar." *The Iran Premier* (2010).

16 Nadim, Azeri. *The Experience of Modernity; The Story Commercial Spaces in Tehran.* Tehran: Tissa Publication, 2012.

17 Kevin, Lynch. *The Image of the City.* United States: The MIT Press, 1960.

18 Ahmad, Mohammadi Kalan, and Edward Oliveira. "Sustainable Architecture of the Bazaar of Tabriz and Its Relation with the Social and Cultural Aspects." *International Research Journal* 4, no. 1 (2014): 5–12.

19 Hossein, Soltanzadeh. "From Saras to Shopping Centers." *Architecture and Culture* 9, no. 30 (2008): 26–40.

20 Saeed, Nassehzadeh, Farid Mahdavi, and Javad Mahdavi. "Analyzing the Sustainable Architecture of Tabriz Bazaar in Iranian Tradition Area." *Cutting Edge Technologies and Concepts for Future Buildings,* University of Applied Sciences, (2011): 17–28.

21 Ali, Faghih, and Mohammad Bahadori. "Experimental Investigation of Air Flow over Domed Roof." *Iranian Journal of Science and Technology, Transaction B- Engineering* 33, no. 3 (2009): 207–216.

Chapter 6

The Platform City
Skywalking in Metro Manila

Edson G. Cabalfin

Urbanization, as one of the concurrent effects of industrialization of the eighteenth and nineteenth centuries, brought about new challenges in dense cities: pollution, traffic congestion, overcrowding, crime, poverty, security, and other social inequalities. Architects, planners, and designers in the last 400 years sought to respond to the environmental, political, economic, and social-cultural changes brought about urbanization through the reimagining of the city as utopia or dystopia. Among the many responses, self-contained cities have become a popular trope in re-imagining urbanism. The platform city, or the interior-oriented, elevated pedestrian circulation passageways connecting buildings, embodies various forms and permutations, including elevated walkways, glass tubes, cantilevered space frames, skybridges, catwalks, and multi-level bridges. It provides many functions in response to the city: as an interiorized pedestrian circulation system; as separation of pedestrians from vehicular traffic; as providing safety and security to people; as ensuring unimpeded and free-flowing mobility of people, service, and goods; as a means of access to isolated and remote areas; as respite above or separated from the density, pollution, and congested traffic; and as an escape from the chaos of the everyday especially on the ground level.

Elevated walkways, as part of the urban circulation network, also become part of the interiorization of the city. By this, we mean how urbanism is not only an exterior phenomenon but is also an interior experience. In a lot of cases, these elevated walkway systems were precisely built in downtown city areas to create a separate world from the public spaces outside the building into an inward-looking almost hermetically sealed interior space. While still in other situations, the expansion of this interior space throughout the city is akin to a complex web of pathways, hallways, and internal corridors that creates a labyrinthine experience.

DOI: 10.4324/9780429443091-8

Similar to streets, skywalks are also under the purview of public or private regulation. Funding can come from public, private, or a combination of funding sources. Whether public or private, the walkways, much like exterior streets, are susceptible to the politics of control: Who determines who is allowed to inhabit the space? What activities are allowed in the space? What kinds of policies are being instituted and for whom are these policies most beneficial? Panoptic control is now manifested through the ubiquitous surveillance cameras and ever-present security guards in these areas, part of the phenomenon of militarizing the city.[1] One cannot truly escape being watched in any of these walkways. Are these spaces, therefore, truly private or public?

Case Study: Platforming Metro Manila

Metro Manila, as the National Capital Region, is the economic and political capital of the Republic of the Philippines.[2] Located on Luzon, the largest island in the Philippine Archipelago, Metro Manila emerged from its origins as a Spanish colonial capital city from the sixteenth to the nineteenth century and later as a "City Beautiful" city under American colonial control during the first half of the twentieth century.[3] Metro Manila as an administrative region was created in 1975 through Presidential Decree No. 824 during the dictatorship of President Ferdinand E. Marcos as a way to consolidate the capital city and seat of government.[4]

The population of Metro Manila was almost 13 million in the 2015 census, which accounted for about 13% of the population of the country.[5] Metro Manila covers a land area of 619.57 square kilometers constituting about 2% of the country's land area. The region accounts for 33% of the Gross Domestic Product (GDP) of the nation, and when taken together with the surrounding areas as part of Mega Manila, the region accounts to 50% of the country's GDP.[6] The region is densely packed and expansive, ranking in the top 15th among the largest urban agglomerations in the world.

This case study on elevated walkways looks at three areas of Metro Manila: Araneta Center (Cubao, Quezon City); Ortigas Central Business District (Pasig City); and Makati Central Business District (Makati City). These business districts exemplify the earliest and most extensive system of pedestrian walkways in the National Capital Region of the Philippines. Each example varies in size, scope, type, and approach, but all share the intent of creating a walkable pedestrian system that supports commercial activity within the business district.

Araneta Center in Cubao, Quezon City

Cubao was one of the earliest commercial districts in Quezon City emerging during the construction boom of the 1950s and 1960s.[7] The center of commercial activity in the new city was Araneta Center, a 35-hectare enclave business district privately owned by the Araneta Group. Its commercial district is bounded by the major thoroughfares of Epifanio Delos Santos Avenue (EDSA) and Aurora Boulevard. The building of the Araneta Coliseum in the 1960s, a 25,000-capacity domed coliseum, preceded the expansion of the surrounding business district in the 1970s with the construction of several commercial developments serving the middle and upper-class residents of Quezon City.[8]

In the early 2000s, the district underwent a US$ 600 million (30-Billion Peso) redevelopment beginning with the construction of Gateway Mall, Manhattan Garden City, Novotel Manila, and other projects as part of a 20-year development and expansion plan.[9] These projects added new condominiums, commercial space, and offices, while attracting several Information Technology-Business Process Outsourcing (IT-BPO) companies. Throughout the redevelopment, one of the key features was a pedestrian network that connected various commercial and residential buildings with existing public transportation nodes.[10]

Araneta Center is strategically located within a station that connects two lines of the light rail system: Manila Light Rail Transit (LRT) Line 2 along Aurora Boulevard and Metro Rail Transit (MRT) Line 3 along EDSA. Araneta Center facilitates pedestrian movement between these two important transit lines with a network of elevated bridges, passageways, and walking paths linking individual buildings. From the MRT and LRT Cubao Araneta stations, customers can go through Farmer's Plaza and Gateway Mall to access bus depots, jeepneys, and tricycle stops that service other areas of the city.

The elevated walkways in Araneta City are primarily covered but are open to natural ventilation. The other skybridges are completely enclosed and air-conditioned, such as the bridge connecting Gateway to New Frontier Theater. Landscape plantings usually line the covered walkways open on both sides. Sun-shading devices typically line the edges of the walkways or have extended overhangs that protect pedestrians from the intense tropical heat or rain showers. Most of the bridges are flat or ramped to allow for wheelchair access. The transitions, however, from one level to another

Image 6.1 Skybridge in Araneta Center, Cubao, Quezon City.
Credit: Edson Cabalfin

Image 6.2 Skybridge entering SM Shoemart Mall in Araneta Center, Cubao, Quezon City. Credit: Edson Cabalfin

between buildings do not allow easy wheelchair access, although there are escalators and ramps in some areas. Elevators are not available in all areas (Images 6.1 and 6.2).

Ortigas Center (Pasig City)

Ortigas Center is another important business district that emerged in the 1980s and 1990s. With an area of 100 hectares, the business district is the second largest commercial area in Metro Manila. The district is located within the jurisdictions of three cities: Quezon City, Pasig City, and Mandaluyong City. Efforts to improve the pedestrian network have been proposed and constructed over the years. One such program was the "Ortigas Greenways" project funded by ADB to study the pedestrianization of the Ortigas Central Business District. Designed by Paulo Alcazaren of PGAA Creative Design, the project includes a series of interconnected elevated walkways, covered on-grade sidewalks, pocket parks, and other sidewalk improvements that aim to enhance the pedestrian and cycling experience of the business district.[11]

Opened in 2018, the Pasig City Central Business District Redevelopment Project followed the principles of the Ortigas Greenways project through the implementation of interconnected elevated walkways, covered on-grade sidewalks, and landscaping improvements.[12] The project was funded by the local government of Pasig City and included only areas under the jurisdiction of the city. An elevated pedestrian plaza with seating, landscaping, and covered areas was built at the intersection of Julia Vargas and F. Ortigas avenues.[13]

Makati Central Business District (Makati City)

The most extensive elevated pedestrian network system within a business district can be found at the Makati Central Business District (MCBD). About 30% of the country's top 1,000 companies are located within its CBD area. The

MCBD has the highest daytime population in the Philippines at 1.3 million during the weekdays; it is a bustling commercial district throughout the day and night.[14]

In the last two decades, infrastructural improvements were introduced to create a more comfortable and convenient pedestrian experience throughout the business district. The Makati pedestrian network is an interconnected series of pedestrian elevated walkways, underground connectors, and on-grade walkways that run through the MCBD. The infrastructural improvements were privately funded by the Makati Commercial Estates Association (MACEA), the association of property owners in the Makati CBD. As of 2019, an average of 1.9 million pedestrian users daily were affected by improvements in the CBD.[15]

Considered the country's longest covered elevated walkway, the pedestrian network is connected on one end to the Manila Metro Rail Transit System (MRT) Line 3 which runs along EDSA, the major thoroughfare connecting the southern and northern areas of Metro Manila. The other end of the elevated walkway connects to the northern part of the Makati CBD, in the vicinity of the Makati Medical Center close to the major intersection of Ayala Avenue and Senator Gil Puyat Avenue.

Along the 1,100-meter pedestrian network, an elevated walkway weaves in and out of buildings connecting major points along Dela Rosa Street, running parallel to the major connector street of Ayala Avenue. From the Makati Medical Center terminus on the intersection of Salcedo Avenue and Dela Rosa Avenue, the elevated walkway hovers above Dela Rosa Street with intermittent breaks of vertical circulation. Stairs, escalators, and elevators bring pedestrians from the street level onto the elevated street. The external walkways are mostly open-air passageways with curved roofing and wide overhangs. Similar to the walkways in Araneta Center and Ortigas Center, the skywalks in Makati are also planted with vegetation along the edges (Images 6.3 and 6.4).

The elevated walkways weave in and out of carpark buildings along Dela Rosa. Within the carparks, rentable commercial stalls line the pedestrian walkways. As interior spaces, the walkway transitions from an external space to an interiorized arcade-type structure with shops. In recent years, artists have

Image 6.3 Elevated walkway along Dela Rosa Street in Makati Central Business District, Makati City.
Credit: Edson Cabalfin

Image 6.4 Skybridge crossing Makati Avenue in Makati Central Business District, Makati City. Credit: Edson Cabalfin

been commissioned to create murals on the ceilings and walls of the carpark building, creating a sense of place for an otherwise mundane walkway.

This walkway turns on to Legaspi Street to connect with the Greenbelt 5 shopping mall, then snakes to the side of Ayala Museum, eventually linking Greenbelt 4 and entering Landmark Mall at the beginning of the interiorized pedestrian experience. The start of the interiorization of the walkways also signals a change from naturally ventilated paths to the air-conditioned environments within the malls. From Landmark, through its department store, the hallways of the mall connect to Glorietta Ayala Center and eventually to SM Makati. The pathway shifts to accommodate different levels between Glorietta and SM Makati via escalators within the malls. Going through SM Makati, one can directly connect with the MRT Ayala Station along EDSA, the other major terminus of the elevated walkway system.

Convergence and Divergences

The three case studies of Araneta Center in Quezon City, Ortigas Center in Pasig City, and the Makati CBD in Makati City have similarities and differences. For one, all are located within the tropical environment of Metro Manila, and therefore, must contend with abundant sunlight, humid air, and heavy rain showers throughout the year. In some cases, such as in Araneta Center and Makati CBD, the elevated walkways transition from exterior to interior spaces and vice versa, varying the pedestrian experience along the circulation path. The city is spatially inverted from the exterior to the interior at varying moments. The change of air quality is also made evident as one moves from the open-air exterior walkways to the interiorized air-conditioned spaces of the pathways. The pedestrian network, therefore, is not consistent in terms of spatial experience and atmosphere along the entire route.

The elevated walkways in these Metro Manila cases all support commercial activity under neoliberal urbanism, which refers to the ways cities are made competitive and profitable following neoliberal policies of free trade, free market commerce, deregulation, privatization, and minimal state intervention.[16] These elevated pathways facilitate the seamless movement of people, goods, and services throughout the commercial establishments. Window-shopping is not only present in the mall itself as the walkways become modalities of displaying and showcasing products. The free flow of pedestrians along this pathway ensures steady traffic of potential consumers to the stores. These pathways connect to major public transportation nodes, linking not just shopping malls but also commercial offices and residential condominiums, guaranteeing that access and convenience becomes commodities in themselves. The uninterrupted interior and exterior pedestrian networks are both a product and a process of neoliberal urbanism.

Still connected to neoliberal urbanism is the issue of private-public ownership of the elevated walkways. While the walkways in Araneta Center, Ortigas Center, and Makati CBD are all privately owned, they are funded differently: Araneta and Makati are privately funded, while Ortigas Center is publicly funded. While the elevated walkways function as quasi-public spaces, which can be used by anybody, they are not really public spaces in the true sense. Though these spaces provide important public functions, they are, nonetheless, under private property and control oftentimes outside the jurisdiction of local governments.

As the examples of efforts by the Philippine government and ADB testify, the skybridges and elevated walkways as urban spaces can potentially be the result of private and public partnerships. There needs to be a reconsideration, however, as to how these walkways become integrated into the city, whether as public and/or private interior-exterior spaces. Would it be possible to reimagine the skywalks as simply a separation of pedestrian and vehicular circulation? Is it possible that skywalks evolve from mere circulation pathways to continuously interiorized inhabited spaces? As interior spaces, would elevated walkways evolve to become transformative and empowering for city dwellers? It will be fascinating to imagine the transformation of the Asian city through elevated pedestrian walkways and its radical effect on the lives of urban dwellers of the future.

Notes

1   Stephen Graham, *Cities Under Siege: The New Military Urbanism* (London: Verso Books, 2011)

2   Manuel Caoili, *The Origins of Metropolitan Manila: A Political and Social Analysis* (Quezon City: University of the Philippines Press, 1999), pp. 22–63

3   Robert Reed, "From Suprabarangay to Colonial Capital", in *Forms of Dominance: On the Architecture and Urbanism of the Colonial Enterprise*, edited by Nezar AlSayyad (Brookfield: Avebury, 1992), pp. 45–82; Robert Reed, *Colonial Manila: The Context of Hispanic Urbanism and Process of Morphogenesis* (Berkeley: University of California Press, 1978)

4   Caoili, *The Origins of Metropolitan Manila: A Political and Social Analysis*, pp. 150, 180

5   National Capital Region, Population, *Philippine Statistics Authority*, https://psa.gov.ph/population-and-housing/title/Population%20of%20the%20National%20Capital%20Region%20%28Based%20on%20the%202015%20Census%20of%20Population%29, accessed April 5, 2020

6   Ibid., p. 3

7   Michael D. Pante, *A Capital City at the Margins: Quezon City and Urbanization in the Twentieth-Century Philippines* (Quezon City: Ateneo de Manila University Press, 2019), pp. 173–175

8   Ibid., p. 175.

9 "Araneta Center Redevelopment On Track", *Philippine Star*, November 28, 2015, https://www.philstar.com/business/2015/11/28/1526955/araneta-center-redevelopment-track, accessed April 3, 2020

10 "Araneta Group Earmarks At Least P30-b to Transform Araneta Center in Cubao", *GMA News Online*, July 29, 2014, https://www.gmanetwork.com/news/money/companies/372432/araneta-group-earmarks-at-least-p30-b-to-transform-araneta-center-in-cubao/story/?amp, accessed April 2, 2020

11 "Imagining Metro Manila as a 'Green Capital'", *ABS-CBN News*, May 09, 2019, https://news.abs-cbn.com/news/05/09/19/imagining-metro-manila-as-a-green-capital, accessed April 1, 2020; "Ortigas Greenways", *PGAA Creative Design*, https://pgaacreativedesign.com/projects/urban-design/ortigas-greenways, accessed April 02, 2020

12 "Pasig City Central Business District Redevelopment", *PGAA Creative Design*, https://pgaacreativedesign.com/projects/urban-design/pasig-city-central-business-district-redevelopment, accessed April 02, 2020.

13 Metro Manila Growing More Walkable, One Footbridge at a Time", *ABS-CBN News*, November 21, 2017, https://news.abs-cbn.com/business/11/21/17/metro-manila-growing-more-walkable-one-footbridge-at-a-time accessed April 01, 2020.

14 Salvador Tan, "Transforming a Business District into Walkable Space with Private Financing", *Development Asia Website*, https://development.asia/case-study/transforming-business-district-walkable-space-private-financing, accessed March 25, 2020

15 *Co-creating Sustainable Communities: 2018 Annual Report*. Ayala Land, 2019, p. 79, https://ir.ayalaland.com.ph/category/sustainability/sustainability-reports/, accessed March 25, 2020

16 David Harvey, *A Brief History of Neoliberalism* (Oxford: Oxford University Press, 2007), p. 2; Jamie Peck, Nik Theodore, and Neil Brenner, "Neoliberal Urbanism: Models, Moments, Mutations", *SAIS Review of International Affairs 29*(1), Winter-Spring 2009: 49–66.

Chapter 7

The Skywalk
Interior Urban Pedestrian Infrastructures

Ziad Qureshi

The enclosed environments of elevated walkways provide a valuable reference to urban history and development. While urban downtowns historically were the core of civic life, growing pressures in the mid-twentieth century from suburbanization and new regional shopping malls led to the social, economic, and spatial decline of cities. From the early 1960s, the advent of "skyway" systems in the urban centers attempted to regain this lost primacy, creating continuous interior environments that joined disparate spaces together into a singular infrastructure that transformed the pedestrian urban experience from the street to the sky.

From social fragmentation to environmentalism, the creation of skyway systems echoes broader design trends. Shifting human activity away from the public urban streetscape, the development of mainly private skyways offers insight into the changing status of public space in the city, responding to a desire for control and safety in the face of social upheaval, as well as the associated impact on ordered urban life. A renewed interest in the civic experience of the city and the reactivation of the urban realm has often focused once again on a return to street life. With many interstitial and residual spaces in skyway networks occupied by retail activities, additional pressures are being placed on such infrastructures as traditional retail declines. These conditions are creating questions regarding the future of pedestrian interior urban infrastructures. This chapter surveys the growth, design, and occupancy of skyway systems in North American cities, offering comparative and contrasting historical and contextual understandings, as well as illumination of their potential futures.

The Origins of the Idea
The development of urban interior infrastructures reflected broader developments in the social, economic, and spatial realms. From the Greek agora to Baron Haussmann's Plan for Paris in the nineteenth century, the commercial

DOI: 10.4324/9780429443091-9

and social motivations for new urban forms have been fundamental in the emergence of the city, underpinned by new urban theories. The transformative impact of the Industrial Revolution on urbanism, including concentrations of capital and populations, new means of rapid transportation, and the emergence of the consumerist and leisure capabilities of the social middle class, reshaped the configuration of cities, creating new pressures and new innovations. Social, economic, technological, and spatial developments in the city led to the creation of innovative new interior urban design solutions.

In the post-World War II period, large-scale and unprecedented change arrived that fundamentally impacted the city. The process of postwar suburbanization, combined with the rising primacy of the automobile as the essential means of transportation, created new pressures that demanded responses in urban form, and led to the establishment of a multitude of new infrastructures. As early as 1929, noted urban designer Hugh Ferriss proposed a version of the skyway as a means of addressing congestion by elevating pedestrians above vehicular traffic.[1] The economic and demographic boom, coupled with the rise of a new consumer culture and the support of powerful new Federal legislation in the United States, drove an exodus of population, capital, and power to the new suburbs. This evacuation of metropolises left behind a vacuum of neglect and abandonment in the core of the city, leading to the acceleration of urban decay. Subsequent urban renewal in the 1960s created an atmosphere of rapid and often radical change in the social and spatial realms. It is within this unique historical context that new theoretical, urban, architectural, and interior responses were fomented.

Concerned with the decline of civic and social life resulting from suburbanization and automobile transport, socialist Austrian émigré and architect Victor Gruen famously established the shopping mall as a new solution for an urban re-gravitation, prioritizing the pedestrian.[2] Realizing the loss of the traditional functions of the city to suburbia Gruen's innovative Southdale Center in Minneapolis (1956), the world's first fully enclosed shopping mall intended to provide a new "crystallization point" around which suburban life could center and thrive. Often stripped of Gruen's original strong social and civic intentions, the subsequent shopping malls nonetheless became new interior-oriented infrastructures that were reproduced throughout the world.

Further discourse during this period established the framework for responsive and innovative urban infrastructural development. The decline of downtown cores precipitated both large-scale urban renewal and more individual architectural responses. Affected by perceptions of safety, perceived or otherwise, that were environmental, social, and vehicular in nature, a variety of internally focused design solutions intended to re-focus human activity back to the urban core. These economic, social, and interior motivations are illustrated in the prominent work of American architect John Portman. His designs for projects such as Peachtree Center in Atlanta (1965) and Renaissance Center in Detroit (1977) were inward and interior-focused during a time of urban decay.

Such environments offered a "city within a city" urban autonomy with programmatic diversification which isolated and insulated occupants from broader urban malaise. Architect and theorist Rem Koolhaas has commented on the nature of commercial spaces in the city being an emulation of urbanism that they provide urban effects that are artificially created but are removed from the actual problems of the city.[3] Skyways, as interior and urban networks, offered a means of traversing the city above the streetscape, enabling users to bypass the context and concerns of the broader environment.

Twin Cities: Histories and Origins

Illustrating the origins of skyway urban infrastructural systems, the Twin Cities of Minneapolis and St. Paul in Minnesota offer a narrative of both common motivations and different approaches, illuminating a comparative framework for understanding. The Minneapolis Skyway System opened in August 1962, eventually growing into the longest and largest continuous system in the world. The 11 miles/18 km of enclosed and climate-controlled interior space connects a multitude of various buildings and environments at the second or third levels above the street. Connected spaces include retail, commercial, corporate, government, hospitality, financial, sport, and residential buildings allowing varied activities to occur in the downtown area independent from the street. Originally driven by real estate developer and businessman Leslie C. Park and architect Ed Baker, the development of the Minneapolis Skyway was accelerated by the significant suburban exodus of the General Mills headquarters to neighboring Golden Valley in 1955, as well as the opening of Gruen's Southdale Center in Edina with its extensive parking in 1956. The loss of capital and population to suburbia continued throughout the 1950s, leaving city and business leaders to entertain Park's concept for a new pedestrian infrastructure. The difficult climate of Minnesota, especially the hard winters, also encouraged the exploration of new solutions to ensure that users would be protected from both environmental and vehicular impacts (Figure 7.1).

Specific to the Minneapolis Skyway solution was a decentralized approach. The development of the system pursued private and independently implemented processes that were ad-hoc in nature. Additionally, the original sections of the network were retrofitted to existing buildings in agreement with adjacent private developers; it was not until later additions to the system that designs were implemented and integrated into new building construction.

Figure 7.1 South view over Nicollet Mall connecting Minneapolis City Center and Gaviidae common.
Credit: Ziad Qureshi

The incentive for developers to integrate their buildings came from an interest in increasing second floor rents. This prompted local newspaper the *Minneapolis Tribune* to designate a new nickname for Minneapolis: the "Second Story City."[4] The opening of the IDS Center in 1974 designed by Philip Johnson finally served as a new nexus for the urban infrastructure system, culminating in its Crystal Court as a primary node where skyways extended in all four directions. While real estate and commercial considerations were the primary driver for building owners to participate, the social, environmental, and safety perspectives were also integral to the interior system's expansion. Minneapolis also furthered the redevelopment of its downtown core at the street and exterior levels, with the construction of the pioneering transit-oriented pedestrian space of Nicollet Mall (1968) designed by landscape architects Lawrence Halprin and Associates. Urban revitalization, a means of competing with ongoing suburbanization and the co-existence of multiple forms of transportation, became the hallmark of such infrastructural ventures (Figure 7.2).

While these motivations were shared by the neighboring and rival city of St. Paul, the pursuit was differentiated. Originally proposed by private real estate developer Watson Davidson, the opening of the St. Paul Skyway in 1967 surpassed the ad-hoc and privatized approach of Minneapolis. St. Paul pursued a compact and smaller system of approximately 40 skyway connections with a total length of 5 miles/8 km. The system was publicly developed with universal access as a core goal and uniform design standards.[5] The system is partially funded by public dollars with private administration of each individual bridge. The semi-public nature of the spaces has ensured consistent access hours and an aesthetic clarity to its identity despite the public/private overlap. However, the standardization of the skyways in St. Paul produced homogenization and introversion, exacerbating the detrimental effect of such airborne infrastructures on the street level. This effect, evident at the national level, was criticized by urbanist William H. Whyte who illustrated its impact by dubbing St. Paul "the blank-wall capital of the United States" in 1988.[6] The issues of the legal framework and management responsibilities, as well as the detrimental effects to the streetscape level, have continued to be problematic in the skyway systems of St. Paul, Minneapolis, and elsewhere.[7]

Figure 7.2 West view along 4th St. from the Skyway connecting the Pioneer Press building and Burger Federal building.
Credit: Ziad Qureshi

Contemporary Questions and the Future

In the twenty-first century, a renewed interest in the civic experience of the city has led to the reactivation of the urban realm. The resulting focus has shifted focus on a return to street life, placing new pressures on the continuing growth and investment into skyway interior infrastructural systems. Recent design work, such as landscape architect James Corner's Field Operations reinvention of Nicollet Avenue in Minneapolis (2018), represents a re-gravitation of occupancy to the open street. As most interstitial and residual spaces in skyway networks are occupied by retail activities, additional concerns are emerging about infrastructures such as traditional retail experiences decline. The contemporary condition of skyways is one of an uncertain status and future.

The history and trajectory of the Cincinnati Skywalk are evident in both typical origins and contemporary concerns about the future relevance of skyway infrastructures. Beginning in 1971 with the connection of the convention center to Fountain Square, its elevated downtown pedestrian system underwent ongoing expansion, and finally, was completed in 1997. At its peak, the Cincinnati Skywalk reached a total length of 1.3 miles/2.1 km and extended across seven urban blocks. Significant to the future of such interior urban infrastructures, the city has rethought the relevance of its skywalk. Following the 2002 Center City Plan, which proposed the reconfiguration and removal of the system, Cincinnati realigned its urban priorities toward street-level activation. Later that year, segments of the Skywalk began to be demolished. Similar questions have arisen in cities such as Hartford, Charlotte, and Dallas regarding above- and below-ground pedestrian-oriented urban interior infrastructures.[8] Baltimore has demolished seven of its skyways and Spokane has opted to restrict any further expansion of its network, while Minneapolis has engaged in spatial debate with street-level projects like the aforementioned Nicollet Mall (Figures 7.3 and 7.4).[9]

Figure 7.3 Winnipeg Walkway, a skyway section wrapping the Delta Hotel.
Credit: Ccyyrree

Figure 7.4 Kyle, A street performer in the Des Moines Skywalk. Credit: Mark Hesseltine

Questions about the future role of skyways are being raised in Des Moines from the perspective of their adaptation to contemporary urban growth. In many American cities, residential population growth in the core downtown areas in the twenty-first century has placed new pressures on skyway systems. Comprising 4.2 miles/6.75 km of climate-controlled space linking 55 buildings and 12 parking ramps, the Des Moines Skywalk system first opened in 1982. As a public/private partnership, the city provides oversight and coordination of maintenance as well as coordination between various Skywalk Association members. In Des Moines, as elsewhere, the original design intent was to serve workday commercial life. As residential occupancy in the downtown core has significantly increased in recent years, the skywalk system has strained to adapt to this change. In an irony to the original historical motivations for the advent of many skyway systems, new safety concerns have arisen resulting from the new 24-hour presence of users. An increase in violent incidents outside of working hours has paralleled the growth of the downtown residential population in Des Moines, raising new questions about safety, security, and resource allocation.[10] The needs of existing skyway systems to adapt to contemporary urban developments are a challenge to their future viability and vitality. The semi-public nature of urban interiors has challenged the notion of what civic space entails. Fundamental unresolved questions regarding this blurred territory have been raised as they affect public activities and civil liberties to minorities and populations that are not defined by the homogenous and traditional makeup of earlier skywalk users.[11]

These conditions are creating questions regarding the future of North America's interiorized urban pedestrian infrastructures, as well as their ability to remain viable in the dynamic urban fabric of changing cities. Despite these challenges, the enclosed environments of many elevated walkways provide valuable insight on urban history and development. From the early 1960s to the current moment, these spaces have attempted to mitigate the social, economic, and spatial decline of cities via their service. The continuous interior environments of skyway systems joined disparate spaces together into singular infrastructures that networked downtowns. As our urban environments continue to diversify, skyway infrastructures offer a unique ability to offer spatial integration. They may still find new opportunities allowing pedestrians to continue to *walk in the sky*.

Notes

1   Millett, Larry. *Lost Twin Cities*. Saint Paul: Minnesota Historical Society Press, 1992, p. 272.

2   Gruen, Victor. *The Heart of Our Cities: The Urban Crisis - Diagnoses and Cure*. London: Thames and Hudson, 1965.

3   Koolhaas, Rem (ed.). *The Harvard Design School Guide to Shopping: Project on the City Volume 2*. Cologne: Taschen, 2002.

4   Nathanson, Iric. "Minneapolis' Oldest Skyway Still in Use Turns 50." *Minnpost*, 03 July 2013. Accessed 20 March 2020 https://www.minnpost.com/minnesota-history/2013/07/minneapolis-oldest-skyway-still-use-turns-50/.

5   *General Policy Statement for the Construction of the Saint Paul Skyway System*. Department of Planning and Economic Development of the City of Saint Paul, Minnesota. 08 January 1980, Amended 24 February 2006. Accessed 20 March 2020 https://www.stpaul.gov/DocumentCenter/View7/Skywaygeneralpolicy2006.pdf.

6   Whyte, William H. *City: Rediscovering the Center*. Philadelphia: University of Pennsylvania Press, 1988, pp. 222–228.

7   Lindeke, Bill. "St. Paul's Skyway Issues Are Ongoing and Unsolved." *Minnpost*, 03 February 2017. Accessed 06 April 2020 https://www.minnpost.com/cityscape/2017/02/st-pauls-skyway-issues-are-ongoing-and-unsolved/.

8   Healy, Patrick O'Gilfoil. "Rethinking Skyways and Tunnels." *The New York Times*, 03 August 2005. Accessed 06 April 2020 https://www.nytimes.com/2005/08/03/realestate/rethinking-skyways-and-tunnels.html.

9   "Vexed by Skywalk Success? Des Moines Isn't Alone." *Associated Press*, 21 June 2016. Accessed 20 March 2020 https://www.desmoinesregister.com/story/money/business/2016/06/21/skywalks-des-moines-urban-problem/86178078/.

10 Joens, Philip. "Skywalk Security Contractor Says Resources Haven't Kept Up With Downtown Des Moines Changes." *The Des Moines Register*, 15 October 2019. Accessed 20 March 2020 https://www.desmoinesregister.com/story/news/crime-and-courts/2019/10/15/des-moines-skywalk-safety-contractor-says-hes-long-had-concerns/3986140002/.

11 Robertson, Kent A. "Pedestrian Skywalk Systems: Downtown's Great Hope or Pathways to Ruin?" *Transportation Quarterly* v. 42, i. 3, pp. 457–484, July 1988, p. 469.

Chapter 8

The Atrium
An Indoor Public Space

Milagros Zingoni

Plato and Aristotle would argue that we organize and classify the world in an effort to achieve a better understanding of it.[1] Atria, galleries, and lobbies represent public space classifications, referred to as typologies that, when applied in real time, inform new taxonomies. These indoor spaces have social and physical structures much like urban form which situates interior urbanism as a taxonomy of public space. In this sense, the atrium performs as an interstitial space that originally intended to blur the boundary between the indoors and outdoors, yet now blurs the boundary between the public and the private. This is accomplished by creating a threshold with a system of layers among the public, semi-public, semi-private, and private dimensions of the city. In this sense, the atrium allows for a relationship between its social and spatial facets. When these two facets intertwine, they define a particular setting that distinguishes it from all other categories of built environments.[2] Because of its intrinsically public nature, the atrium acts as a vessel that holds a range of content, including learning, cultural norms, and social rules. In recent decades, such social aspects are often discussed as important parameters of social responsibility and a vital component of social sustainability. It is a clear manifestation of the symbiotic relationship between people and space. As such, it is an interior typology that adeptly represents the notion of interior urbanism.

The atrium is perceived as a well-defined exterior room within the interior and, because of its relationship to all subservient spaces, it functions as an interior public space. It proposes notions of "vulnerable urbanism," an urban design strategy that allows things to occur by highlighting the role of the user to activate spaces.[3] This notion of vulnerable urbanism, combined with Marinic's definition of interior urbanism in this book, proposes a "vulnerable interiority." Marinic primarily describes interior urbanism by the "interconnectivity, materiality, and civic character of interior spaces at an urban scale." Within this context, atria are interior public spaces similar to those found outdoors or in connection with the outdoors. The intersection of these two concepts, interior urbanism and vulnerable urbanism, results in a "vulnerable interiority"

DOI: 10.4324/9780429443091-10

and an interior space that is in constant flux with its public character: without people, there is no architecture; without interaction within the building, there is no interiority; and without urban context, there is neither architecture nor interiority.

The public character of an atrium responds to vulnerable interiority by producing more inclusive, place-based experiences incorporating a theoretical framework addressing issues of equity, culture, and belonging through inhabitation. For example, everyone who has access to a building has access to its atrium in a nonhierarchical manner, reconciling people with each other. At the same time, such control inherently embodies exclusion writ large. They define and enable notions of publicness to their maximum expression. This idea of vulnerable interiority, as opposed to a finished controlled product, engages users as the main drivers of the spatial atmosphere. It allows for and encourages transformable experiences within the public interior realm. Atria are manifested as resilient spaces because they are in permanent flux operating within the physical context, social relations, and nearly constant re-arrangement of furniture. Peoples' interactions create these ephemeral and intangible experiences. Their behaviors and appropriation of the public space are influenced by many designed factors such as thermal comfort, daylighting, branding, wayfinding, interior finishes, acoustics, and artwork. Organic factors such as the space resiliency, sense of crowd, and diverse programming also play a vital role in creating successful atrium environments.

Over the last 2,000 years, buildings have been built with an assortment of atrium types. The popularity of this type has come, gone, and come around again throughout history. Originally created as a translation of the courtyard, the Roman house first employed the atrium as a large central space open to the sky. Originally created as grand entrance spaces, it had a focal courtyard, a sheltered semi-public area, and a defined horizontal emphasis. The architectural, environmental, and economic benefits associated with the atrium typology enabled their evolution across history. Throughout the atrium's evolution, it has developed and morphed into a mediator between the interior and the exterior in multiple contexts, as a source of daylighting for deep buildings, and, in some cases, these spaces reduce energy loss and support natural ventilation.[4] Furthermore, atria provide the added value of facilitating social interaction and promote a sense of belonging. In recent decades, such social aspects are often discussed as important parameters of social responsibility and a vital component of social sustainability.

In today's fast-paced lifestyle, atria enable users to recover from the effects of technology-induced stress and isolation by creating a space for gathering or restoring. They are designed to be experienced alone or as the most publicly used space of a building. It is a place to enjoy spatial quality and it frames opportunities for unexpected or informal activities. The atrium is now considered an applied taxonomy of public space juxtaposed as an interior agora with public character. This is emphasized by Pimplott's[5] notion of the "public interior" as a cultural space in which people continuously negotiate.

The progress of construction techniques and technology enabled glass roofs to cover existing courtyards or service courts, converting these outdoor spaces into atria, also improving possibilities for air quality control. This created a type of space not previously available in most cities, an all-weather public gathering space. Saxon[6] echoes this sentiment in his description of the atrium's power: "The atrium can bring light, but keep wind, rain, solar gain and extreme temperatures away from overlooking the space, reducing costs and increasing comfort." The typology of the skyscraper combined with the evolution in climate control and the need to bring the public realm back to the people are the basis for adapting atrium typology as a norm.

From a formal composition point of view, an atrium contributes to an array of possibilities to urban design. It can handle awkwardly shaped sites. This is due to the atrium's inherent ability to organize and create formal and spatial relationships within its interior and exterior contexts. Paraphrasing Ellin's[7] definition of vulnerable urbanism, it is the idea that both spaces are better because of the other: no light without darkness, no interior without exterior, no silence without sound—both spaces embrace and allow the other. The atrium is also a tactical spatial typology used to address aged buildings to enable adaptive reuse projects in which the program drastically shifts. It can address new requirements without affecting the historic character of the building, or change the character of the space by covering an existing courtyard and transforming the space into an atrium.

The roots of the contemporary atrium derive from a creative synthesis of the democratic Greek agora, the living room, and the garden. Defined by a three-dimensional space, atria often provide a variety of sensory stimuli. The quality of the atmosphere is also conferred by the quality of natural lighting, either direct or indirect, which differentiates the public room from all other spaces in the building. Distinctively, the atrium is not subservient to its adjacencies nor to the relationship with the entrance. Rather, it acts as a protagonist among all spaces because of its public quality, as well as the message it conveys symbiotically between the programming of the building in relation to its interior and exterior.

As the typology of the atrium continued evolving during the postwar period, it became primarily a building-based exterior experience. In the last 50 years, we have seen a considerable increase of atria in commercial buildings across the world as a means to showcase corporate branding in a notable interior semi-public space. It evolved from the notion of an internal exteriority to an interior experience often found in the garden atria. These are the precedents of what is presently discussed as biophilic design—the belief that people feel better and perform more efficiently when they are in direct contact with nature.

Atrium as a Garden

One of the first examples of the atrium as a garden is found in the Ford Foundation Building (1967) in New York designed by Roche and Dinkeloo.[8] This building is organized around an interior garden within a greenhouse-like atrium. The project's parti is based upon the architects' intent to respond to energy efficiency and environmental experience, allowing its users to inhabit an indoor garden as part of the workplace environment. The atrium occupies almost half of the footprint of the building for the purpose of providing greenery, light, and air. This allows for visual connections across different sides of the atrium and across levels. Planters with large plants are located at the perimeter of each level facing the atrium, intentionally creating a continuum between the ground garden and the vertical surfaces that surround the atrium. The Ford Foundation atrium is the precedent for more recent approaches that integrate landscaping within atria and which has become a popular method in promoting wellness. Hence, they received the designation as an interior landmark in Manhattan.

Atrium as an Interior-Exterior Threshold

Atria can also act as a threshold between an interior and an exterior space. Within this context, atria often extend beyond the interiority of the building such as in the Ford Foundation atrium. For instance, the recently renovated "Banco de Londres" (1959–1966), now the headquarters of the "Banco Hipotecario Nacional," in Buenos Aires is spatially organized around two atria. In essence, the building envelope façade defines an exterior atrium by a system of layers extending from the very public (the sidewalk and two narrow streets), through the quasi-public (the exterior atrium), to the quasi-private (the interior entry sequence atrium), and finally to the private spaces (the second atrium that organizes the offices). Testa's clear design intent creates continuity between both areas, making a sort of roofed plaza that is completely public. Indeed, he intended to articulate the building with the street by essentially forming a covered square, as an atrium. Architect Testa leveraged the corner lot creating an experience akin to being inside an exterior space or outside an interior space within the city through a system of hung brutalist concrete surfaces that define this first atrium. This conforms the urban fabric from the exterior, while providing a duality on the interior side of the threshold through the large void. These concrete surfaces are considered as simultaneously belonging to both the interior and the exterior, changing the perception of the scale and its role depending on where one stands. This creates continuity between the well-lit and expansive interior and its narrow exterior context. This is interior urbanism (Images 8.1–8.4).

This first atrium still retains its original finishes and defines the contrast between the brutalism of the concrete and its blue flooring, being one of the most noteworthy characteristics of the interior building. Like the Ford Foundation's atrium, a system of horizontal floating slabs defines the Banco de Londres' second atrium. It recreates an interior urban experience by organizing all other interior spaces around it to provide multiple spatial qualities. The handrails are composed as a continuation of the band; they are painted with the same hue as the flooring to emphasize the envelope of the atrium. Natural light bounces off the hard-concrete surfaces and slabs, and filters across the served spaces and interconnects the interior atrium.

Testa was both a sculptor and an architect; the interior space of the Banco de Londres is a singular product of both art and architecture. Two clear examples are the sculptural concrete pieces and the integration of color in the flooring as a main component that defines the space, an atypical approach at that time in Argentina.

Atrium as a Public Space (a Covered Agora)

The architectural typology of the atrium as a building type often addresses the owner's intention and sensitivity toward the public good; it is the manifestation of an interior-oriented, democratically inclusive public space. The atrium interiority responds to the identity and/or values of the brand that also propose

Image 8.1 Left: Exterior Atrium Formal Banco de Londres, now Banco Hipotecario Nacional. Buenos Aires, Argentina, by Architect Clorindo Testa.
Credit: Juan Vega

Image 8.2 Recently remodeled Entry Sequence. First interior atrium. Formal Banco de Londres, now Banco Hipotecario Nacional. Buenos Aires, Argentina by architect Clorindo Testa.
Credit: Juan Vega

a space in constant flux, enabling spontaneous-non-prescribed activities. An example of this is the A+A Building at the University of Tennessee, Knoxville. This atrium not only defines the formal composition of the College of Architecture and Design, but it represents the value of a communal space in constant flux. Lately, there has been a new type of atrium that incorporates vertical circulation as an inhabitable component of the atrium. Often named "democratic stairs," "social stairs," or "learning stairs," this vertical element connects the circulation of the atrium with other levels that face the atrium itself.

Image 8.3 Recently remodeled Central Atrium. Formal Banco de Londres, now Banco Hipotecario Nacional. Buenos Aires, Argentina by architect Clorindo Testa.
Credit: Juan Vega

In this sense, atria are an interior urbanism typology that addresses value through a different lens. They encourage exchange of knowledge and collaboration, while also showcasing the identity and branding of the company through limited finishes, materials, and semiotics. Regardless of intent, these are examples in which social content and spatial conditions interweave a system of layers of publicness and privateness within the built environment. In this way, atria improve the sense of community within the building.

Conclusion

In the introduction of this chapter, atria are referred to as a hybrid between two concepts: interior urbanism and vulnerable urbanism. In this essence, the public realm is part of the entire urban fabric to which the public has physical and visual

Image 8.4 A+A Building-College of Architecture and Design, University of Tennessee, Knoxville. Credit: Milagros Zingoni

access,[9] thus supporting the notion that city space serves three vital functions: as a meeting place, marketplace, and connective space.[10] Yet, the city is also "the common ground where people carry out the functional and ritual activities that bind a community, whether in the normal routines of life or in periodic festivities."[11] Public space is inclusive; it is "a space that allows all people to have access to it and activities within it."[12] Tangible and intangible borders define the atrium space. Experiences within the atrium not only depend on the physical characteristics of the space but also on the flux of its ephemeral qualities. At its core, the atrium is the interior public space within the building envelope.

Akin to urban design strategies, atria address relationships in the public realm, built form, and transportation; they demonstrate how these seamlessly work together in a "people first" design philosophy.[13] Both the urban public realm and the atrium provide diverse options for programming spaces and form: the character of a town or spatial branding the notion of being both in constant flux, to address constant short- and long-term changes, their wayfinding aspects, and how the latter enable visitors to meander through the space. Both the city and the atrium draw on the speculation that these characteristics influence users' perceptions and cognition within public space.

Differing approaches demonstrate that atria can serve as vital elements. For the user, the atrium provides an experience in terms of scale, proportion, light, and programming. For architects, the atrium allows them to create a blurred threshold between inside and the immediate exterior context, while providing a voluminous interior space that raises the overall experience inside the building. For owners, it is a clear manifestation of their identity, as well as their values and the importance that they place on providing a democratic space that is inclusive.

Unlike Roman atria, contemporary atria are often a component of the entry sequence, predisposing the user to grandeur experiences, similar to entering a palace. But unlike other typologies that are becoming obsolete, the atrium has proven to be a resilient typology that continues to change and adapt in response to the needs of people, the architectural envelope, and the urban context. Urbanistically, the atrium is a semi-public space; climatically, it organizes the building envelope and inner fabric to modify the site climate passively by reducing energy consumption; kinetically, it allows people to move through and into the building; and socially, it gathers people and enables them to appropriate it in informal ways. Throughout the evolution of the atrium, it has maintained its character as a sociopetal environment that connects people, creating opportunities for informal and formal interactions perceived by the user as nonhierarchical and unassigned. These characteristics define atria as symbiotic spaces that mutually benefit from the coexistence of unlike organisms. In the twentieth century, atrium-oriented buildings have spread more than any other building form since the skyscraper.[14] Since then, atria have served as a symbol of its owner's care for people inhabiting the building envelope, as a stage for entertainment and display, or as a symbol of status and power. Today, most atria function as communal living rooms. They supply a variety of opportunities for informal social interaction. As noted, this was not always the case. During its evolution as an enclosed courtyard, this newer atrium design and experience morphed from conveying a public quality to a private character. Although the atrium has been through many iterations, in this day and age, its public character has endured.

"In an information society, cities are a place where information is produced, exchanged and processed."[15] The taxonomy of today's atrium is, at its essence, a covered public space. It provides a public character in which people can gather to produce or exchange information, but it is also a place which enables people to disconnect from the daily stress and connect at a human level with others. Both a complex and contradictory concept, the atrium connotes a public character and democratic experience.

Notes

1   Plato. *The Complete Works*. Cambridge: Hacking Publishing Company, 1997. Aristotle. *The Complete Works*. Princeton: Princeton University Press, 1984.

2   Zingoni, M. A Matter of Scale or Social Content? Infilling Voids for Social Action, Learning from and in the Neighborhood. *Spaces and Flow: An International Journal of Urban and ExtraUrban Studies*, 7 (4) (2016): 1–21

3   Ellin, Nan. *Integral Urbanism*. New York: Routledge, 2006

4   Sharples, S. & D. Lash. Daylight in Atrium Buildings: A Critical Review. *Architectural Science Review*, 50 (4) (2007): 301–312. DOI: 10.3763/asre.2007.5037.

5   Pimlott, M. *The Public Interior as an Idea and Project*. Heijningen: Jap Sam Books, 2016.

6   Saxon, Richard. *Atrium Buildings: Development and Design*. London: Architectural Press, 1983.

7   Ellin, Nan. *Integral Urbanism*. New York: Routledge, 2006.

8   AD Classics: The Ford Foundation/Kevin Roche John Dinkeloo and Associates. *Archdaily*. https://www.archdaily.com/436653/ad-classics-the-ford-foundation-kevin-roche-john-dinkeloo-and-associates

9   Tibbalds, Francis. Making People-Friendly Towns Improving the Public Environment in Towns and Cities. London: E & FN Spon, 2001.

10 Gehl, Jan. In Ward Thompson, Catharine., and Penny. Travlou. Open Space : People Space. London ;: Taylor and Francis, 2007.

11 Ward, Colin. "People and Place -- Public Space by Stephen Carr, Mark Francis, Leanne G. Rivlin and Andrew M. Stone." The Architectural Review. London: Emap Limited, 1993.

12 Madanipour, Ali. *Public and Private Spaces of the City*. London; New York: Routledge, 2003, p. 144.

13 Zingoni, M. A Matter of Scale or Social Content? Infilling Voids for Social Action, Learning from and in the Neighborhood. *Spaces and Flow: An International Journal of Urban and ExtraUrban Studies*, 7 (4) (2016): 1–21.

14 Saxon, Richard. *Atrium Buildings: Development and Design*. London: Architectural Press, 1983, p. 6.

15 Hung, W. Y. & W. K. Chow. A Review on Architectural Aspects of Atrium Buildings. *Architectural Science Review*, 44 (3) (2001): 285–295, 286. DOI: 10.1080/00038628.2001.9697484.

Chapter 9

The Subway

Interior Urbanism at the Metropolitan Scale

Alican Yildiz

From the utilitarian perspective of urbanism, subways merely embody a technological imperative of contemporary urban life in which city residents require mass transit to travel—from *point A* to *point B*—in a rapid, affordable, and planned fashion. In urban settings, participating in public life often requires using subway infrastructures, including stations, carriages, tunnels, and so on. However, the socio-spatial significance of subways in our collective urban imagination is, perhaps, somewhat less connected to the iconic plazas, libraries, and other civic spaces—the most dominant spatial figures that shape publicness in the city. Nevertheless, our daily lives in the largest global cities increasingly rely on and are being shaped by subways and their relationship with the urban built form. Structural components shape the subway into a linear and amorphous contemporary urbanism. These components create interior public spaces that mix people of diverse socio-economic and demographic characteristics to shape the everyday. The transformative role of the subways on people and the city can be traced back to the development of modern cities, when the first subways emerged as a pragmatic response to high-density urbanization.

Origins

Industrial development-led urbanization approached its peak toward the end of the nineteenth century. At the same time, the subway typology was beginning to take form with the opening of London's first electrified subways in 1890. Britain's pioneering position in subway development was due to J.H. Greathead's invention of the tunneling shield technique that allowed developers to tunnel under adequate depth to prevent disruption to building foundations. The London Tube was innovative in its time and influenced other major cities in the decades that followed. On the European mainland, Budapest was the first city to construct an electric subway (1896) with its 4-km rail line. In 1900, the métro in Paris surpassed Budapest by inaugurating subway operations with a 10-km

DOI: 10.4324/9780429443091-11

central line. Germany finished the construction of the Berlin U-Bahn in 1902, and opened the Hamburg U-Bahn in 1904. By then, subways had expanded into the other industrialized countries across Europe with different levels of techno-logical capacity, spatial vastness, and structural complexity.

This historical emergence of subways in Europe also allows us to rationalize the structural evolution of the typology, as well as the relationship between the spatial transformation and political economies of cities after the Industrial Revolution. Expanding industrial, residential, and mixed-use commer-cial districts were in the process of encircling most urban centers of Europe and North America by the early twentieth century. The automobile sector and Fordism did not yet reach the economies of scale needed to equip the growing size of urban workers and petit-bourgeois; distances between the workplace, dwelling, shopping, and leisure were rapidly increasing. Thus, developing intra-city mass transit systems became de rigeur.

Nevertheless, this necessity faced spatial barriers within high-density urbanism. Cities had limited land to build such mass transit even though they had the economic and technological means to do so. The developers, public or private, had no choice but to go underground. Otherwise, they would have needed to demolish the enormous swaths of urban districts, as decades prior the Haussmann Plan imposed such destruction on Paris to achieve its mon-umental boulevards. Thus, investing the surplus financial capital in expensive subway projects arguably became the most profitable option for city adminis-trators and developers (Figure 9.1).

The first subway in the United States opened in Boston in 1897 with a 2.4-km underground rail line. In New York, the private Interborough Rapid

Figure 9.1 Boston Subway Station: The first underground rail line in the United States. Credit: Alican Yildiz, 2018

Transit Company finished the construction of its first subway line in 1904. Philadelphia also followed its northern counterparts in 1907. Even though the New York City Subway soon became the largest public transit system in the world with new lines connecting The Bronx to Brooklyn by linking all of the Manhattan lines, these early US developments eventually stagnated.[1] It was 1943 when Chicago opened its first subway. The national capital, Washington, DC, which has one of the most architecturally monumental rail systems in the United States,[2] did not have any subway lines in operation until 1976. New York City opened its first new line (first phase of the Second Avenue Subway) since 1940 in 2017.[3] However, the conditions of the New York City Subway still remain far away from having the recognition and utility enjoyed by the Washington Metro and other major cities around the world. It is infamous for ongoing delays, failing technological infrastructure, and poor station qualities due to lack of public investment and maintenance over many decades.

The sequence and current fate of the subways in the United States also point to how different development trajectories create spatial, material, and immaterial conditions, while the subway typology shapes urban experience of contemporary cities. New York and Washington, DC offer a significant opportunity to speak about the impact of structural components on publicness and interiority at the scale of subways. To do so, we ought to formalize structural components of the subway typology. This research uses three concepts—system, ecology, and temporality—to articulate the interrelated and multi-dimensional socio-spatial complexities of subways through comparing systems in New York and Washington, DC.

Components of Subways: System, Ecology, and Temporality

Publicness and interiority of the subway typology at an urban scale could be articulated by multiple structural components. Publicness here does not merely seek public ownership of the subways, but implies public use and access of subway stations and their adjacent service spaces such as platforms, stairs, elevators, and passenger tunnels, as well as entrances, waiting areas, and ticketing foyers.[4] A gradient of public use and access along the connected interior spatial environments of subway stations relies on many factors, including connectivity, wayfinding, spatial design qualities, and climate conditions, as well as societal and institutional constructs such as security measures, ticket prices, discriminatory behaviors, standards, and rules.

Although strongly tied to publicness, the interiority of the subway typology forms an ambiguous mix of material and immaterial conditions since the interior condition itself requires an avid spatial distinction (e.g. enclosed spaces and architectural envelopes) in addition to the perception and sensibilities of individuals (e.g. insideness through feeling at-home and safe).[5] Thus, the overarching framework of this chapter will emphasize system, ecology, and temporality concepts to explain spatial, material, and immaterial conditions that ultimately become a definitive force that shapes our experience in subways.

System

A *system* refers to horizontal spatial conditions and network extensions of subways at the urban scale. Linear or circular expansion of subway lines and station location frequencies, as well as configurations and accessibility of subway stations relative to the urban built form (e.g. plazas, parks, sidewalks, streets, various land use districts, and amenities) impart impacts on the publicness and interiority of subways. In regard to the spatial reach of the system and its relationship with the urban built form, 36 lines and 424 stations of the New York City Subway accommodate 1,757-billion ridership annually, a significant contrast to the Washington Metro's 9 lines, 91 stations, and 182 million annual riders.[6] The different trajectory of their developments could yield these systematic differences; nevertheless, rather than quantitative grandiosity, the performative quality of the subway system demands a strategic spatial organization and configuration at the scales of cities. In doing so, the connectivity to urban neighborhoods, amenities, and institutions where everyday life occurs creates necessary spatial conditions that increase use and access to subways. This could also support interiority at an urban scale when other material and immaterial conditions are provided and sustained (Figure 9.2).

New York City, for instance, reveals a critical place in which to frame this argument. Manhattan, where stations have walkable spatial relationships with urban nodes, districts, and landmarks, allows us to assume significant publicness through shorter distances to stations and more frequent use of subway stations. Yet, the Manhattan context also points to an overt underestimation of the station's own internal spatial structure which could contradict affordances in publicly accessible interiors.[7] Derelict subway stations and carriages are not perceived as desirable places or urban living rooms by regular subway users. They can, however, represent just another drudgery of everyday urban life, even if a station sits only a few blocks away. This argument subsequently directs us to the importance of interior spatial environments with better quality material and immaterial conditions.

Figure 9.2 NYC Subway, Wall Street Station Platform.
Credit: Alican Yildiz, 2016

Ecology

In the context of subways, ecology articulates a vertical, multi-layered, and three-dimensional interior environment of stations. From street-level entrances to mezzanines and multi-story circulation spaces (e.g. stairs and elevators), and from passenger platforms to mass-produced train carriers, subway stations spatially compose an ecology of internalized urban fauna of humans, subway species (e.g. rats, flies, and insects), atmospheres, machines, and other man-made and natural sensibilities. These elements come together to form a spatial interrelationship with each other, and ultimately, enhance or contradict publicness and interiority within the subways.

Particularly, the design of stations and carriages, as well as the moderation of interior sensorial and atmospheric conditions, can produce direct influences on how people use and access subways. Facilitating spaces, pathways, and co-presences through signs, lights, furniture, interior facades, and gates are most significant examples of these spatial and material design impacts; they affect subway users' voluntary or involuntary interaction with each other. Thus, the interconnected and multi-layered components of publicness and interiority become a subsequential force to restructure and shape the experience of everyday urban mobility. A comparison between the New York City Subway and the Washington Metro supports that argument.

Apart from the first phase of the Second Avenue Subway, the Oculus, and the Fulton Center Transit Hub, most subway lines and their adjacent stations in New York were built before the 1940s. These stations lack the comprehensive renovation and material uplift across their architectures, envelopes, and infrastructural spaces. This also creates accessibility problems since the circulation path from subway station entrances to platforms does not always provide elevators, but relies solely on multi-level stairs. Wear and tear, therefore, is an everyday condition that ultimately reduces the utility and experience of uses. Heat and noise extremes on station platforms often reach the level of severe public health impact, revealing the systematic disadvantages of the New York City Subway (Figure 9.3).

On the one hand, the proximity and frequency of station locations cannot yield an attractive publicness for users because the system lacks basic spatial, material, and immaterial qualities.[8] On the other hand, the Washington Metro delivers distinct spatial and material advantages, given its federal government-led development trajectory, its symbolic importance as the mass transit system of the capital, and most importantly, the architectural monumentality of its underground stations. These conditions are spatially manifested in circulation and accessibility since many stations have large-scale stairways and platforms, as well as elevators. Along with unique spatial dynamics, the Washington Metro offers well-maintained material conditions and positive visual qualities of interiority.[9] The stations do not feel like outdoor spaces. The coffered ceiling vaults of Washington's Federalist architecture, exposed concrete, and bold design motifs create visual continuity. The aural atmosphere of the platforms, which is lacking in New York City, is probably the most significant outcome of the formal and stylistic interior architectural elements that shape the spatial experience and monumentality of the Washington Metro.

Figure 9.3 The coffered ceiling vaults and the repetitive design motifs on the expose concrete, Washington Metro. Credit: Alican Yildiz, 2018

Temporality

Tied to both the system and ecology components, temporality underscores two similar conceptualizations. The first points to the *operational schedule*, in other words, *the service frequency* of the subways at the scale of the system. Twenty-four-hour underground services objectively yield supreme advantages compared to subways that operate on less comprehensive schedules. A privilege of using the subways after midnight allows urban residents to fully participate in public life without facing the possible concerns of night-time mobility and security. This ultimately can increase public use and accessibility of subways where the high frequency and reliability of subway services are available and maintained. For instance, the New York City Subway works 24 hours a day; however, between midnight and 6 am, wait times increase and services stop on particular lines. Washington Metro services do not run after 11:30 p.m. Monday through Thursday; 1 a.m. on Friday and Saturday, and 11 p.m. on Sunday.[10]

These daily differences in operational hours bring us to the second aspect of temporality which relates to *duration*, in other words, *the time spent within the subways* including its service and technological spaces as passengers. Accordingly, the system and ecology components become the spatial and material parameters of the duration. The larger system extent impacts scheduling and frequency by increasing or decreasing people's time (duration) in the subways. In addition, the quality and characteristics of the subway ecology might require specific operational schedules that can encourage people to spend more time in subway stations by facilitating attractive public amenities and programs. On the one hand, the subway ecology can diminish interior conditions by creating physically hostile and atmospherically unwelcoming spaces

Figure 9.4 A departure of the train from the Washington Metro platform.
Credit: Alican Yildiz, 2018

as documented in the New York City Subway. On the other hand, the monumental architecture and pleasant aural experience of the Washington Metro stations arguably create positive outcomes on duration (Figure 9.4).

Temporality, therefore, has an ambiguous relationship with publicness and interiority. Twenty-four-hour and high-frequency service are definitely positive immaterial conditions. A larger and more accessible system spatially reaches all residential, mixed-use, and commercial districts. Yet, passenger movement within and along the subways still could be a spatially disorienting experience for users. As longer distance increases occupancy duration, the temporality component could turn subway tunnels, platforms, and carriages into spaces of temporal alienation in which time spent is not an intuitively chosen activity. Instead, it is viewed as an unavoidable aspect of contemporary urban life.

Conclusion: Subways as Public Interiors

The subway typology as conceptualized above delivers us an analytical framework suggesting that contemporary cities are ultimately shaped by the structural components of subways. Yet, the social-spatial manifestation of subway systems as public interiors still must confront the very nature of the subway typology itself. The comparison of the subway systems of New York City and Washington, DC reveals that the availability and appropriation of subways at an urban scale can improve publicness and interiority. It does so by structuring systematic and ecological qualities in spatial and material contexts. However, the potential conditions of the temporality aspect continue to result in various physical, sensorial, and psychological barriers for subway users. We should not underestimate the possibilities and potentialities of recognizing subways as interior public spaces. Interior urbanism is not a finished urban project after all, but rather, an ongoing rethinking of various spatial, material, and immaterial layers and dynamics of the city. The subways, therefore, demonstrate an optimistic and transformative vision of contemporary interior publicness.

Notes

1 Most, Doug. *The Race Underground: Boston, New York, and the Incredible Rivalry That Built America's First Subway*. St. Martin's Press, 2014.

2 Schrag, Zachary M. *The Great Society Subway: A History of the Washington Metro*. JHU Press, 2014.

3 English, Jonathan. "Why New York City stopped building subways", accessed February 6, 2020, https://www.citylab.com/transportation/2018/04/why-new-york-city-stopped-building-subways/557567/.

4 Carmona, Matthew. "Contemporary public space: Critique and classification, part one: Critique." *Journal of Urban Design* 15, no. 1 (2010): 123–148.

5 Stafford, Lisa. "Contested interiority: Sense of outsideness/insideness conveyed through everyday interactions with university campus doors." *Interiority* 2, no. 1 (2019): 25–41.

6 "Subways: MTA annual subway ridership." *MTA*, accessed February 4, 2020, http://web.mta.info/nyct/facts/ffsubway.htm, and "Metrorail ridership grew by 20,000 trips per weekday in 2019". *WMATA*, accessed February 4, 2020, https://www.wmata.com/about/news/2019-Metrorail-ridership.cfm#main-content.

7 Maier, Jonathan H.A., Georges M. Fadel, and Dina G. Battisto. "An affordance-based approach to architectural theory, design, and practice." *Design Studies* 30, no. 4 (2009): 393–414.

8 Bliss, Laura. "It's way too hot on the New York City subway", accessed February 6, 2020, https://www.citylab.com/transportation/2018/08/its-way-too-hot-on-the-new-york-city-subway/567278/.

9 Ibid.

10 Ibid.

Chapter 10

The Railway Station

An Interior Urban Connection

Bryan D. Orthel

The railway station is a unique urban interior that is not a destination, but a connection. Railway stations invite people in and let them emerge somewhere else. The scalar realities of the station (e.g., small wayside, large centralized station, and inter-urban connection) are transformative for how people understand and interact across the city. A railway passenger enters one interior space to be transported to a different interior space. The experience is uniquely the result of being inside. As a result, the interiority of the railway station challenges our perception of place and social relationships.

Railway Stations as an Archetype

The development of the passenger railway station between 1830 and 1930 reflected the creation of a new building type shaped to a disruptive technology and new culture. Passenger service on railways changed how people moved between places. The process of entering this system—ticketing, waiting, loading, riding, and exiting—shapes an urban (and often inter-urban) interiority that is now shared by air and space transportation hubs. In the United States, the buildings passengers used in waiting and transferring along railway lines were originally repurposed from other uses.[1] Like stagecoach systems, early railway companies relied on hotels and taverns near the rail lines to service passenger needs for food and cover. Houses, barns, and unused railway cars were adapted where existing services were not available. Purpose-built stations became the emergent interface between existing cities, suburbs, and the continent-wide expanse of soon-to-be-connected rural places. Most stations were small, one- or two-story structures built alongside the tracks to allow rapid loading and unloading of passengers and cargo into rail cars that paused briefly (i.e., through stations). These early stations had interiors, but were not the same as the uniquely urban interiors that emerged in central and terminal stations.

Intra-urban passenger railway service in the United States started in May 1830 in Baltimore, Maryland. The world's first inter-urban railway service began in September 1830 (Liverpool to Manchester, Great Britain).[2] The Manchester

DOI: 10.4324/9780429443091-12

Station (Liverpool Road) already featured the core pieces of the railway station typology: passengers arrived and purchased a ticket, were directed to a dedicated waiting room, and were called to a platform to load into a railway car. Within a year of opening, the Liverpool Road Station also had space for shops and offices. Passenger loading and unloading occurred on a covered platform. These parts would become standard in railway stations worldwide. As the station type developed over 100 years, stations were cast as semi-public (owned) spaces mixing commercial and communal interests (Image 10.1).

The multiple rail lines servicing a station were often located below or above the grade level, necessitating stairs and ramps to move passengers from the ticketing and waiting areas to the loading platforms. Stations in urban areas were commonly served by tracks that terminated at the station (a head or stub station, rather than a through station with tracks traveling past) (Images 10.2 and 10.3).

Station support spaces for baggage and cargo were located near the passenger spaces, but also commonly relegated to basements or separate buildings. Servicing of locomotives and railcars occurred in the station or in a nearby railyard. The basic services were grouped into a two-part building: a station or headhouse and an attached platform or train shed. This distribution of functions remains the primary organization of stations today.

Image 10.1 "Plan of the Pennsylvania Railroad's new station on Manhattan Island" published in the *New-York Tribune*, Sunday, July 17, 1904 (designed by McKim, Mead, & White; New York, NY; opened 1910, demolished 1963). The railway station is a complicated intersection of multiple parts. In this view, people enter the station from the urban street. As they traverse the horizontal and vertical layers of the station, people engage with a vast set of spaces designed for trains, large numbers of passengers, and commerce. Image from the Library of Congress, https://chroniclingamerica. loc.gov/lccn/ sn83030214/1904-07- 17/ed-1/seq-47/, public domain.

New-York Tribune.
ILLUSTRATED SUPPLEMENT.
SUNDAY, JULY 17, 1904.

PLAN OF THE PENNSYLVANIA RAILROAD'S NEW STATION ON MANHATTAN ISLAND.

THE THIRTY-FIRST-ST. FRONT OF THE GREAT STATION, SHOWING CAR TRACKS UNDER THE STREET LEVEL.

AN INTERIOR VIEW OF THE GREAT STATION, SHOWING CARS UNDER THE PASSENGERS' WAITING ROOM.

The larger, urban stations provided for the rail lines—sheltering trains, people, cargo, and auxiliary services inside large connected volumes of waiting rooms, halls, and train sheds. The growth in popularity of inter-urban railway travel—and competition between railway companies—resulted in competing union and central stations. Railway companies built increasingly elaborate stations to mark their service, often expanding or rebuilding on the same site multiple times. In the United States, these buildings included Chicago Union Station (Chicago, 1874, 1881, 1925), Reading Terminal (Philadelphia, 1893), Union Station (St. Louis, 1894), Washington Union Station (Washington, DC, 1907), Grand Central Terminal (New York, 1871, 1913), Kansas City Union Station (Kansas City, 1914), and Union Passenger Terminal (Los Angeles, 1939). Globally, influential stations included Madrid Atocha Station (Madrid, 1851, 1892, 1985–1992), Kings Cross and St. Pancras Stations (London, 1852, 1868–1887), Gare du Nord (Paris, 1864), Haydarpaşa Station (Istanbul, 1872), Gare d'Orsay (Paris, 1900), and Gare de Lyon (Paris, 1900). Stations were constructed in aesthetic styles ranging from Greek and Renaissance Revival to Art Deco and Arts and Crafts.

Railway stations provided transportation for travelers going long distances and daily commuters arriving in the city from suburban areas. The stations

Image 10.3 Stairway access from track level to the Waiting Room and street, Pennsylvania Railroad Station (New York, NY) image circa 1910-1915. A railway station's track-level platforms (or trainshed) interface between the movement of people and train cars. The interaction combines infrastructure (i.e., tracks and platforms) with the functional practicalities of pedestrian routes to and from the station. Again, the space is an interior, but the scale and function reference urbanity. Image from the Library of Congress, LC-DIG-det-4a19910, public domain.

were a node in any city's larger transportation network. Buses, ferries, taxis, and private cars moved passengers from the terminal to other points in the city. Eventually, the co location of subway and other mass transit systems allowed commuters to arrive at the station via train and seamlessly transfer to a subway or transit line connecting outward into the city. Subway stations are a related type of railway system also identified as an urban interior. The systems in cities as diverse as Moscow, Paris, Seoul, and Washington, DC are notable for their organization and aesthetic development as notable examples of interior urbanism.

Railway stations included the amenities a traveler or commuter needed, such as restaurants, newspaper stands, drug stores, and barber shops.[3] Stations also featured medical facilities, art galleries, mortuaries, public baths, pools, and professional office space.[4] The stations were finished using durable materials (e.g., marble, terrazzo, quality woods, and tilework) and the latest in electrical technologies. Concourses and public waiting rooms of the stations were often used for more than the required practicalities. For example, the concourse at New York's Grand Central Station is recognized as a public assembly room for events as varied as casual socialization and political speeches.[5]

The railway station's effect as a new building type was closely linked to the technology of steam, diesel, and electric engines that powered trains between cities. The stations' construction relied on new engineering feats to tunnel, bridge, or elevate railway tracks across urban environments and past natural obstacles. Further, the scale of buildings interacting with trains required vast train sheds and platforms to accommodate movement, air quality, and weather. The stations provided a distinct place of departure and arrival for passengers (and cargo). They were much more than points of intersection between the urban fabric and inter-urban rail lines. Railway stations became important semi-public and public spaces linked to hope, despair, class, race, leisure, and work.

Railway Stations in Culture

The cultural importance of the railway station requires examining how these spaces were part of the larger urban interaction related to labor, race, and society. In the United States, railway travel replaced horses or ships for long-distance travel along the US Eastern seaboard and along rivers into the American frontier. The transcontinental North American railway (realized in 1869) expanded the possibilities for moving people and cargo. Railway travel became safe, fast, more economical, and more direct.

Railway systems also redefined the spatial environment by changing the speed and extension of information movement. Telegraph service was often commingled with the railway system. Stationmasters relied on the telegraph to manage traffic on rail lines. Telegraph service also enabled the speedy transmission of private messages across vast distances. Postal mail was often delivered via train. Post and telegraph offices, possibly co-located with railway stations, drew people to these places for reasons other than traveling on the line.[6] As a result, the railway station (big or small) was a hub for information and social exchange.

Station as Experience

Railway stations were and are both everyday experience and extraordinary moments. Millions of passengers still move through railway stations daily. For some, the experience is transactional—a part of the system that moves them from one part of the city to another. For them, entering the station is stepping into an urban interior that functions as a means. For others, the experience can be awe-inspiring. Vincent Scully famously described arriving in New York via the circa-1910 Penn Station as entering the city like a god.[7] Station patrons experience these urban-scale interiors with excitement and mundanity.

The railway station is an exciting part of an urban experience. Charles Eames described his interest in the St. Louis Central Train Station as an exploration of a trainscape defined by the "interplay of color and movements, and a complexity of a track and switching system."[8] The use, connection, and mixing were most interesting as part of "rich associations" rather than stolid examination of the buildings. In similar ways, people use railway stations as places for informal social gathering and entertainment. The railway waiting room has been described as "human theater."[9] In the 1930s, Thomas Wolfe wrote about the crowd in Penn Station's original General Waiting Room:

> There were people who saw everything, and people who saw nothing, people who were weary, sullen, sour, and people who laughed, shouted, and were exultant with the thrill of the voyage, people who thrust and jostled, and people who stood quietly and watched and waited…they were all there harmonized and given a moment of intense and somber meaning as they gathered.[10]

These gatherings of people—travelers and observers—occur at railway stations and depots in cities and small towns.[11] People gather in anticipation of a train's arrival and departure, to collect mail or packages, to talk and make social connections, and to simply watch the flow of humanity. Restaurants and shopping were once strong parts of a station's vibrant scene. Tourists often pause to marvel at the scale and detail of a historic station.

Railway stations also become a sanctuary from life. In his travel journals, Ryszard Kapuściński, a Polish poet, wrote about arriving by train at the Sealdah Station (Kolkata, India) a few years after India's independence in 1947:

> On every square inch of the enormous terminal, on its long platforms, its dead-end tracks, the swampy fields nearby, sat or lay tens of thousands of emaciated people....They seemed a lifeless component of this dismal landscape...this was the end of their road.[12]

These people were refugees displaced by India's civil war. They used the space to simply exist. The station was a common shelter. Kapuściński's travel writing presents the railway station as an architectural counterpoint to the palatial and exclusive spaces in the urban environment that are reserved for few. Describing his trip across India, he noted the anonymizing and de-humanizing experiences of being within train stations teaming with occupants who are highly segregated and seemingly unconcerned with each other. Inside, yet isolated.

Unequal Experience

Similar to other aspects of urbanity, the railway station reified inequality. Railways depend on people's economic need and social desire to travel. At first, rail travel was unavailable to most of the population. Further, stations built around the United States featured separate waiting and toilet rooms for people of different races and genders. Some stations provided separate facilities for immigrants (for the practicalities of either processing travel documents or maintaining clear separations with others). Black travelers were often denied equal access to station amenities, like restaurants, and rail services by design and social practice.

Railway stations also often relied on the labor of socially and economically marginalized people, specifically people of color.[13] The ubiquitous Pullman sleeper car and the attending African-American Pullman porters are both evidence of this discriminatory behavior and the conflict between monopolistic corporate power and labor. The Pullman Strike (1894) and unionization of the porters in the 1920s are only two points in this long-standing racial and economic conflict. While the Pullman porter worked the eponymous sleeper cars, thousands more coach porters provided service to passengers riding in standard coaches. Once passengers arrived at a station, omnipresent Red Cap attendants moved luggage, provided local guidance to out-of-town visitors, and performed other maintenance duties. The Red Cap attendants were predominantly black men who were not paid a wage. They relied on tips and often paid for the opportunity to work at the station. Men and women of color also worked in the kitchens, hotels, and maintenance departments within railway stations. The people who held these positions were subjected to discriminatory treatment by passengers, railway managers, and station officials.[14]

In many places, the railway lines into a city and new stations were built on land the railway companies or city officials deemed slums or otherwise blighted. For example, the construction of Penn Station in New York City involved clearing an eight-acre area in the Tenderloin district that had been home to lower economic class residents reflecting the racial and social separations in society.[15] The residents were forced out of their neighborhoods in a process we now recognize destroys communities, social capital, and the long-term prosperity of the affected people. The railway station as an urban interior—a microcosm of conditions of the larger city—was created through these oppressive, discriminatory interactions.

Stations Now

The railway station continues to be an active part of some cities' urban life. Where railway service remains a viable connection (e.g., along the East Coast of the United States and between many European cities), railway stations are being renovated and built new (e.g., New York's redevelopment of Penn and Moynihan Station, London's redevelopment of King's Cross Station or Crossrail line, Belgium's renovation of Antwerp Central station and construction of Liège-Guilleminis, and China's high-speed railway system). These projects are often discussed in terms of scale and efficiency.

In the twenty-first century, the railway station remains a vibrant archetype. Notable new stations follow the basic structure of nineteenth-century stations but, like the original stations, reflect the cultural and aesthetic choices of the time. Whereas the original railway stations worked with Victorian and Neoclassical motifs then ascendant, current stations use forms and aesthetics drawn from the digitalization of design and construction such as Gare de Strasbourg-Ville, West Kowloon station in Hong Kong, and Delft Municipal Station, among others (Image 10.4).

Beyond form, the design of contemporary railway stations relies on analysis and research to correct past problems as varied as air quality, acoustic control, thermal comfort, and crowd movement during peak use.[16] Further, railway stations are recognized as factors in urban planning issues related to gentrification, housing density, public health, road capacity, and environmental quality.

Image 10.4 Interior view, Delft municipal train station (designed by Mecanoo; Delft, Netherlands; opened 2015), image circa 2017. The station continues to follow the two-part structure and user sequence of historic stations. In this image, the entrance and access to ticketing and waiting areas are visible from the left rising to the upper level. Access to platforms is visible on the lower level (lower right corner). The form of the station reflects the scale of the surrounding urban area but introduces new plasticity of space derived from contemporary culture. Image from WeeJeeVeevia Wikimedia, CC BY-SA 4.0, https://commons.wikimedia.org/wiki/File:20170720_Delft_station_04.jpg.

The contemporary railway station remains grand and mundane. While prominent stations are built to emphasize location and ambition, the majority of railway stations serve a more everyday audience. Stations along mass transit lines (e.g., subways and light rail systems) are the entry and exit points for millions of commuters daily. These stations, less grand than their predecessors like the original Penn Station, are nonetheless portals into a vast urban interior linking place to place. Most such stations are primarily functional and shaped as egalitarian places. The cost of entry is still beyond some individuals' means, but is accessible to a greater percentage of the population than the original railway systems. As a result, these spaces are arguably more important in the life of the city.

The railway station's role as urban interior connects people across space and interaction. The building type's function relies on the inherent interior realities of entering one place and exiting another. The station becomes a portal accessing spaces far away from within. At the same time, the cultural power of the railway station has diversified. Once defined by the unknown possibility of who and what could arrive with the train, the railway station is now a more egalitarian way for millions of people to travel daily around and between their cities. The railway station is an interior urban connection.

Notes

1   H. Roger Grant, *Living in the Depot: The Two-Story Railroad Station*, Iowa City, University of Iowa Press, 1993.

2   The earliest passenger railway service started in Wales (1807).

3   John Bell and Maxine R. Leighton, *Grand Central: Gateway to a Million Lives*, New York City, W.W. Norton, 2000.

4   John A. Droege, *Passenger Terminals and Trains*, New York City, McGraw-Hill, 1916.

5   Bell and Leighton, 2000.

6   H. Roger Grant, *Railroads and the American People*, Bloomington, Indiana University Press, 2012; Jill Jonnes, *Conquering Gotham: The Construction of Penn Station and Its Tunnels*, New York City, Viking, 2007.

7   His description continued to define the current Penn Station as entering the city like a rat.

8   Charles Eames, "St. Louis Train Station 1957," in *An Eames Anthology: Articles, Film Scripts, Interviews, Letters, Notes, Speeches by Charles and Ray Eames*, edited by Daniel Ostroff, New Haven, CT, Yale University Press, 2015, volume 2, p. 162.

9   Jonnes, 2007, p. 300.

10 Quoted in Jonnes, 2007, p. 300.

11 Grant, 1983.

12 Ryszard Kapuściński, *Travels with Herodotus*, translated by Klara Glowszewska, New York City, Knopf, 2007/2004, p. 28.

13 Theodore Kornweibel, Jr., *Railroads in the African American Experience*, Baltimore, MD, Johns Hopkins University Press, 2010.

14 Grant, 2012; Kornweibel, 2010.

15 Jonnes, 2007.

16 Yingying Cha, Minghui Tu, Max Elmgren, Sanna Silvergren, and Ulf Olofsson, "Factors Affecting the Exposure of Passengers, Service Staff and Train Drivers Inside Trains to Airbourne Particles," *Environmental Research* 166 (2018): 16–24.

Chapter 11

The Government Center

An Interface between Power and the People

Jeffrey T. Tilman

Democratic societies require spaces in which the public may assemble to address their elected leadership. In architecture and urban design, much attention has been given to the outdoor places of assembly, from massive formal public squares, like the Mall in Washington, DC to less imposing urban moments, like London's Speaker's Corner, to much smaller appropriated spaces, such as People's Park in Berkeley. Champions of these spaces assert that they are essential to creating a forum for ideas, a necessary ingredient for a healthy democratic society; this view is sometimes challenged by those who believe that modern communications technology has obviated the need for physical assembly. Recent non-violent protests around the globe, from Hong Kong to Paris, would suggest that the desire to confront power with thousands of others, to visually demonstrate one's numbers, is still an essential human need. The Center for Public Space Design finds that "[civic] design can create an important foundation for improving local democracy and opening the lines of communication between citizens and local government."[1]

The places of public assembly and redress most often discussed in the literature are urban squares or plazas. The analogous interior urban spaces of civic engagement have been much less discussed. Charles T. Goodsell, in his *The Social Meaning of Civic Space*, is one of the few authors to address the interior setting of political discourse. He defines civic space as being well-enclosed interior rooms, accessible to the general public, that are dedicated to the execution of governmental functions or other defined public activities.[2] The notion of civic space is hardly new; audience halls have their roots in royal palaces, and legislative chambers have their ultimate origins in the *Bouletrion* of ancient Athens. However, these spaces are not necessarily accessible to the entire polity—one is invited into the presence of a sovereign, where one's inferiority to the king or queen is constantly referenced. Access to a legislative house is highly controlled, and only those members of the body recognized by

DOI: 10.4324/9780429443091-13

the chair may speak. Spaces used for a truly democratic discussion of issues, or an appeal to elected authority, are rarely found within the halls of power, but are instead in the corridors and lobbies immediately adjacent. For a time, they were designated places, essential to the program of any seat of local, regional, or even national authority, and given a formal name, the *salle des pas-perdus*, the "hall of lost steps." These interior urban spaces, within the seat of power but fully public, are the subject of this chapter.

In the English colonial period of the United States, places of governance were nearly always borrowed from the local church or tavern. In the seventeenth century, very few towns had fixed places of governance and judges presided over circuits, moving from place to place so that court days (and the markets that so often accompanied them) were held once or twice a month, or, in larger towns, perhaps once a week. Thus, courts and other events of governance were held in makeshift quarters until the population warranted a market hall or a courthouse. In Virginia, for example, a whole slate of courthouses was built under the reign of George II, as county administrative bodies reached well into the interior of the colony and to the Appalachian Mountains. At about the same time, the statehouse at Williamsburg burned, and a new edifice, described by Jefferson in his *Notes on the State of Virginia*, was constructed in the early 1750s.[3] This building offered an assembly hall for the House of Burgesses, and several courtrooms on the ground floor, but not much more than a stair hall as accommodation to the general public. Jefferson's own replacement for this building, the present Statehouse at Richmond, offers gracious public space on its grounds and within its porticos, but just the relatively tight rotunda at its center, dominated by the Houdon statue of Washington. Of course, Jefferson was attempting to shoehorn all the functions of state government into a relatively modest Roman temple, and he had no modern precedent to draw upon.

Public buildings constructed after the Civil War tended to prioritize public gathering space. French architectural theory, as promulgated by the Ecole des Beaux-Arts, required that the public be led from a building's entrance to the primary function spaces by a commodious and clearly defined circulation route—this was termed the *marche*. For civic buildings, this often meant that there was a series of public spaces before one arrived at the legislative chamber or governor's office. One great example of this is San Francisco City Hall. Designed by Bakewell & Brown in 1912, and constructed over the ensuing four years, the building skillfully realizes in steel and stone the power structure implemented by a new city charter passed by the citizenry just a year earlier. A visitor entering from the Civic Center Plaza moves from the entrance lobby into a great Rotunda, and up a monumental stair that takes the visitor directly to the Supervisor's Chamber. To the left and right, a gallery rings the Rotunda and leads one to the mayor' suite, which is directly opposite. To either side, one finds large light courts, which serve on the ground floor as large, light-filled transaction lobbies (where you pay your water bill, etc.) and on the upper three floors light double-loaded corridors of offices (and formerly court rooms). Arthur Brown, Jr., the firm's designer, split a functional four-story office building in half, and inserted between those halves one of the most inspirational spaces in the City, lit by the fourth-largest dome in the Western world (in fact, a few feet higher than that of the United States Capitol) (Image 11.1).

Image 11.1 Rotunda and ceremonial stair within San Francisco City Hall. Credit: Jeffrey Tilman

Were San Francisco City Hall built today, the Rotunda would have been value-engineered out of existence because the square footage it occupies was not enumerated in the very detailed program brief. Fortunately, no one questioned such a grand architectural gesture in 1912, and the space has contributed immensely to the civic life of the City. A complement to the two-block expanse of Civic Center Plaza and the Civic Auditorium next door (and later the War Memorial complex across Van Ness Avenue), the Rotunda is where the mayor makes her proclamations, where significant moments in the life of the community are commemorated, and where important events like naturalization ceremonies and marriages take place. Weddings have become, in fact, a particularly important part of San Francisco City Hall's identity. The first bride to be wed on the steps of City Hall was the architect's own daughter, Sylvia Brown Jensen, and thousands of couples have followed suit. When then-mayor Gavin Newsom ordered city officials to grant marriage licenses to thousands of gay and lesbian couples in 2004, the Rotunda became the site of both joy and later protest, as those licenses were deemed void by the California Supreme Court. Today, weddings of all types are held in the Rotunda, and indeed it is the single most popular location for a wedding in the entire city. Whether San Franciscans are commemorating an important historic milestone in the life of the City, celebrating a victory of the local sports teams, or protesting an act of government, local or state, foreign or domestic, City Hall is the genus loci of the event—it is seen by all in the City as the center of collective civic life.

The architectural theory of the Beaux-Arts was challenged and eventually superseded by the Modern Movement, which celebrated construction for its own sake, and valued efficiency and seriousness of purpose above all else. In Europe, the tradition of the city hall as a social as well as political center remained, and some landmark buildings in the Modern form were built even as many older structures were rebuilt after the damage of the Second World War. Many of these retained the salle des pas-perdus, transformed into a gallery or public concourse. A good example of this is Richard Meier and Partners' City Hall and Library in The Hague, The Netherlands. The entire core of the building is an enormous trapezoidal, ten-story atrium. Meier intended this space to become the city's *res publica*, the emotional collective home of the city's inhabitants.[4] Now filled out with retail at its periphery, and much less furniture than one might expect, the vast expanse of space is certainly sublime, but in no way does it foster a collective spirit among the citizens, as they are simply too far apart from one another; lost is a sea of white steel and stone.

In the United States, civic structures of the post-War period tended to separate purely functional uses from the communal or ceremonial, much to the detriment of all. Without the association of collective experience, these newer buildings did not develop an emotional resonance with the community—they remained functional locations where one did business with government, but they did not represent the body politic.

One of the less successful of these city halls, but beloved by architects, is Boston City Hall. Designed in competition by a trio of architects in association (Gerhard Kallmann, lead, with Michael McKinnell and Edward Knowles), the building was to be the focal point of a new governmental district that replaced the "disreputable" Scollay Square. The architect's stated intention was to create a contrast between the glassy curtain walls of the corporate architecture of the time with something solid, rough, and vaguely reminiscent of the brick and stone architecture of the nineteenth-century city. There is no doubt that the building, one of the preeminent examples of Brutalism in the United States, exudes mass and permanence. It also housed the various city departments effectively, if not lavishly, until the growth of the city bureaucracy outstripped the building's capacity. However, the building offers the public little in the way of community space, other than the stair atrium, which has been difficult to comfortably condition and to maintain accessibility. The security regime required after the attacks of 2001 have reduced public accessibility even further, as often only one entrance to the building is available to the public. While a major renovation by Utile Architecture promises to address some of the shortcomings of the building, and improve accessibility for those with limited mobility, the scheme will split the entry stair hall in two (non-secure and secure zones), limiting its use for public events. In fact, the amount of public space in the lower floors will actually be reduced to accommodate new hearing rooms and meeting spaces that are being moved from the upper floors (Image 11.2).[5]

Image 11.2 Main Lobby and Stair at Boston City Hall.
Credit: Bill Lebovich for the Historic American Building Survey Library of Congress, Prints and Photographs Division

Boston City Hall has never developed a following with its public. Its primary defenders have been architects, who rightly see it as one of the most influential buildings of the 1960s, and as a primary training ground for an entire generation of Boston architects. Nevertheless, the building has been so loathed in Boston that several city administrations have explored means by which a new city hall might be constructed so that the old one might be demolished, or at least used for some other purpose.[6] Now eligible for the National Register of Historic Places, and likely protected from demolition, it is hoped that a renovation of City Hall and Government Square will give to the city the community amenities that the city hall itself struggles to provide.

More recent city halls have often incorporated an unstructured "event space" meant to serve the purpose of the *salle des pas-perdus*. In San Jose's new City Hall, designed by Richard Meier and Partners and completed in 2007, a completely separate building, a four-story domed structure termed the Rotunda, sits in a hardscaped plaza set alongside curving colonnades, looking more like an astronomical observatory than a civic building. The vision of former mayor Ron Gonzales, the Rotunda is a cavernous space, with staircases that fly along the curved walls reaching up to the upper floors and out to the adjacent buildings. Conceptually, Meier envisioned the Rotunda to be the entry to the entire complex. Unfortunately, it doesn't really serve this purpose, as the council chambers are in a three-story building to the west, and the majority of the city's bureaucratic functions are housed in an 18-story slab to the east.[7] Visitors simply enter directly into these buildings, and the Rotunda itself is very often locked due to security concerns. While the building earns its keep on many weekends as an event center, the Rotunda's intended role as the heart of civic life in San Jose has never materialized. Indeed, instead of unifying the city with a vibrant cultural space, San Jose's City Hall has instead symbolically divided the city, the administrative slab visually separating the city's prosperous downtown and Silicon-Valley fueled west side from the less well-off, working-class east (Image 11.3).

Image 11.3 Rotunda at San Jose City Hall. Credit: Jeffrey Tilman

Statehouses and national capitols do not have a responsibility to be representative of the immediate community in which they are located. They must instead represent the entire population of the territory governed. Thus, most of them do not have a host of community meeting spaces, and their circulation spaces tend to be tightly controlled behind a security cordon. As you might imagine, this was not always the case. The United States Capitol, for example, required Members of Congress to move through the Rotunda or the crypt below to move from the House side to the Senate side. Petitioners and agents would buttonhole Members as they moved about the building, waiting for them in the lobbies of the chambers, this said to give rise to the term "lobbyist," at least in America. Thomas U. Walter's addition in the 1860s did not do anything to alleviate this situation, as the stone that supported the Rotunda was deemed to be too weak to support additional spaces to the east or the west.

In the mid-1950s, Speaker of the House Sam Rayburn believed that the situation had become intolerable—the capitol needed a significant expansion, and it was necessary to create some sort of "backstairs" communication between the two halves of the building so Members could avoid the general public when moving from the chambers to their offices, by now located in large buildings to the north and south of the Capitol. The Architect of the Capitol at the time was George Stewart, who was not, in fact, an architect. To study the possibility of enlarging the Capitol, Stewart created a three-member commission, which comprised the leading classically trained architects of the day, Arthur Brown, Jr., John Harbeson, and Henry R. Shepley. The commission was charged to look at the possibility of moving the East Portico of the Capitol further east, as much as 50 feet, to correct a design anomaly arising from Walter's cast-iron dome (namely, that the dome was cantilevered over the East Portico). The Commission refused to endorse these plans, but Reyburn used the occasion of Brown's unexpected death to override its findings and to issue legislation demanding that Stewart proceed with an extension that would move the East Portico, the East Façade, and the linking bays on either side 23 feet 6 inches further east.[8] This new space was used to add offices, a Member's dining room, and most importantly, a passage behind the Rotunda that allowed secure movement between the two chambers. Since the completion of the massive underground Capitol Visitor's Center in 2008, the whole of the Capitol has been made the preserve of the Members and their staffs, with visits by the public carefully orchestrated and controlled (Image 11.4).[9]

The question remains as to the purpose of the *salle des pas-perdus* in the twenty-first century. As digital communication becomes ever more universal and immediate, the challenge isn't necessarily to be seen and heard, but to be differentiated from literally thousands of others whose messages are vying for the same attention, whether it be that of a mayor, a governor, a legislator, or a prime minister or president. Security concerns have brought the unprogrammed civic space to its near-obsolescence. Will future generations feel that a physical presence at the seat of power is of little impact? Or will a show of numbers, unified behind a cause, still be capable of influencing our elected decision-makers?

Architects seem to agree that these interior spaces do matter. The collective physical presence of the masses chanting in righteous anger or in joyous celebration may or may not sway an elected politician, but it has always played well in the media, whether that be on a newsreel, on a television broadcast, or on Instagram. The energy of the people, assembled with steely purpose at the portals of power, cannot be repudiated with a tweetstorm. Architecture has the capacity to aggrandize the purpose of those who inhabit it, but only if it presents space at a scale that suggests no one person is greater than the collective, and that the present owes a debt to the past and a responsibility to the future. The corridors of power should be a place where those in authority are held accountable to their public; not accosted or intimidated, but reminded of the people and the institutions they have sworn to serve.

PHOTO RELEASED BY THE ARCHITECT OF THE CAPITOL ILLUSTRATES CURRENT PLAN (OUTLINED IN BLACK) FOR EAST FRONT EXTENSION. BY ACT OF CONGRESS, THE PROPOSAL IS SUBSTANTIALLY IN ACCORDANCE WITH "SCHEME B" AS SUBMITTED—BUT DEFINITELY NOT RECOMMENDED BY CARRERE & HASTINGS IN 1904. PENDING LEGISLATION WOULD RESCIND "SCHEME B" REQUIREMENT AND PERMIT STUDY.

Image 11.4 Image board illustrating extension of the United States Capitol, c. 1957.
Credit: Office of the Architect of the Capitol

Notes

1 Center for Active Design, *Assembly: Civic Design Guidelines* (New York: CfAD, 2018), 90.

2 Charles T. Goodsell, *The Social Meaning of Civic Space: Studying Political Authority Through Architecture* (Lawrence: University Press of Kansas, 1988), 10–13.

3 The first Capitol at Williamsburg burned in 1747. Jefferson's description of the successor (not reconstructed at Colonial Williamsburg) is found in Thomas Jefferson, *Notes on the State of Virginia*, 1787, 200–205.

4 "The Hague City Hall and Central Library," Richard Meier and Partners Architects, *LLC, Digital Portfolio*. https://www.richardmeier.com/?projects=the-hague-city-hall-central-library-2. Accessed April 2, 2020.

5 Eric Baldwin, "Boston City Hall Celebrates 50th Anniversary, Prepares for Major Renovation," *Arch Daily*, January 14, 2019. https://www.archdaily.com/909401/boston-city-hall-celebrates-50th-anniversary-prepares-for-major-renovation?ad_medium=gallery. Accessed February 29, 2020.

6 Paul McMorrow, "Boston City Hall Should be Torn Down," *Boston Globe*, September 24, 2013.

7 "San Jose City Hall: Large Rotunda Embraces a City's Residents," *Architectural Record*, March 2007. Online Ed.

8 "Chronology of Plans to Extend the East Front of the Capitol," *Journal of the AIA*, June 1958, 271 and "News," *Architectural Forum* 107: 10 (October 1957), 5.

9 For a more detailed discussion of the Capitol Visitor's Center project, see the website for the *Architect of the Capitol*, https://www.aoc.gov/capitol-buildings/construction-capitol-visitor-center. Accessed March 15, 2020.

Chapter 12

The Library

Interior Urbanism as a Layered Experience of Public Space

William Mangold

Public space is often represented and interpreted in a binary way: solid/void, public/private, and so on. However, libraries are often experienced as environments encoded with varying degrees, expressions, and feelings of "publicness." This chapter discusses the material and historical conditions that contributed to the unique spatial character of libraries, and then looks at the New York Public Library to develop an argument that interior urbanism is characterized by a layered experience of public space.

Drawing upon library examples, the layered character of interior urban space is theorized in three related registers. Iain Borden's conception of the urban landscape, understood through skateboarding as "a constant layer through the city," suggests interior urbanism be considered as a boundary-less condition. The work of William Whyte and ideas of "place" help frame interior urbanism at the scale of human interaction. The idea of "mapping as a generative process," articulated by both James Corner and Denise Scott Brown, allows us to understand interior urbanism as a way to conceive (or reconceive) spaces as public.

Library Histories

The history of libraries[1] is marked by the innovation of various writing mediums and social developments. Libraries in the Western world date from antiquity when information was written on clay tablets and papyrus scrolls, and collected and stored by rulers to display their power and promote their culture.[2] However, these early buildings and artifacts have largely been lost.[3] The library as a repository for books traces its history to the development of parchment as a medium for writing, and its subsequent assembly into bound volumes around 50 AD.[4]

Around 400 AD, Christian monasteries began efforts to preserve and copy sacred texts, including Saint Catherine's Monastery in Egypt which is the oldest library still in existence. These monasteries would typically include

DOI: 10.4324/9780429443091-14

a workroom (scriptorium) for monk copyists, a cupboard (armarium) to store books, and lectern desks upon which the large volumes could be read. By 1200 AD, Europeans learned papermaking which replaced parchment because paper was cheaper and could be bound into thinner and lighter volumes. Around the same time, universities began to replace monasteries as centers for learning and culture in European cities, and books were produced (by hand) that advanced secular knowledge of law, history, and commerce.[5]

The expansion of knowledge during the Renaissance, fueled by the invention of the printing press in 1440, greatly increased the number and size of book collections. Universities, the church, and individual patrons commissioned and collected books. The expanded availability of books led to changes in the way they were stored and used. While the previous hand-copied codices were heavy, rare, and expensive—stored flat, with metal clasps to keep them closed, and frequently chained to the casework—the new press-printed books were comparatively light, common, affordable, and could be stored on open shelves. If the old lectern system could store approximately three books per yard, in examples such as the Biblioteca Malatestiana (1452) in Cesena, Italy, and the Library of St. Peter and St. Walburga (1555) in Zutphen, Netherlands, the new layout with books on stacked shelves could hold 200 or more volumes in the same space in libraries such as the Escorial Library (1585) in San Lorenzo de El Escorial, Spain and the Trinity Hall Library (1600) in Cambridge, England. Despite growing collections, these places were virtually private and accessible only to their owners or select scholars.

Collections continued to expand, and many libraries were founded during the Enlightenment, but the next major shift came during the Industrial Revolution and late nineteenth century. Advancing production techniques made books cheaper and plentiful, but the more significant developments for libraries were due to changing social attitudes. Victorian values and social reform efforts, coupled with wealthy benefactors, led to the widespread establishment of *public* libraries. The public library system in Britain began with the Public Libraries Act of 1850 (following the Museums Act of 1845), and by 1900, there were 300 British cities with public libraries. Public libraries represented a major shift in who had access to books, and grew out of three previous trends in libraries: (1) social libraries initiated the sharing of books and quality content, (2) circulating libraries introduced novels and popular materials, and (3) school district libraries were publicly funded.[6] The Boston Public Library, considered the first American library founded on the principles of public funding and educating the general public, opened in 1854. Between 1880 and 1930, Andrew Carnegie funded over 2,500 public libraries throughout the English-speaking world,[7] most of which remain in use.[8] Public libraries in general, and Carnegie libraries specifically, established the spaces and functions that are familiar today—open stacks, reading rooms, children's collections—transforming libraries into centers for community life, in examples including the Bibliothèque Nationale (1867) in Paris, Boston Public Library (1895), New York Public Library (1911), and the Stockholm City Library (1928).

This trend of libraries as social hubs continued into the late twentieth century and accelerated with the internet and social media, reducing space needed for collections but increasing the demand for connection: "connections between different groups of library users, connections between library users and library staff, connections between library users and resources."[9] Libraries emphasizing these new connective aims used architectural strategies of dislocating book stacks from the main library functions, while creating spaces for interaction in libraries, including the Berlin Staatsbibliothek (1978), Bibliothèque Nationale (1996) in Paris, Utrecht University Library (2004), and the Seattle Public Library (2004).

Libraries are now debating about what their role will be in the coming decades as knowledge changes in the information age. Current discourse centers around libraries as "anchor institutions" that are "enduring organizations that remain in their geographic locations and play a vital role in their local communities and economies…and align institutional objectives with place-based, economic, human, and intellectual resources to better the welfare of the community in which the anchor resides."[10]

Libraries have always played this role, but with their transition into public institutions and the Carnegie program, libraries rose in prominence as hubs of social and cultural activity. Today, libraries are designed as places for people, and even as information technology makes their role as repositories obsolete, libraries seek opportunities to draw new patrons who use libraries in innovative ways, including the Seattle Public Library (2004) and the Helsinki Central Library (2018).

Library Spaces

Several notable features that characterize the varied history and use of libraries are worth considering. While libraries may serve any number of grandiose aims—repository of knowledge, marker of status, uplifter of masses—these buildings basically conjoin two functions: storage and study space. Most of the earliest libraries, and many small or recent libraries, integrate these functions in libraries, including the Biblioteca Malatestiana, the Library of St. Peter and St. Walburga, and the Seattle Public Library. Some libraries with very large collections do not allow patrons to access the books directly; their public areas are mainly study spaces as exemplified by the Bibliotheque Nationale and the New York Public Library. Conversely, some libraries make stacks available to patrons; these spaces tend to emphasize the storage of books as demonstrated in the Bodleian Library (1612) in Oxford, England, the Biblioteca Angelica (1765) in Rome, and the Peabody Library (1866) in Baltimore. The specific furniture and fittings designed to serve the functions of storage and study make libraries distinct.

Perhaps the most recognizable feature of libraries, especially compared to virtually every other building type, is their quietness. Between social cues, supervising librarians, and an abundance of books to mitigate sound, libraries have historically been quiet spaces that encourage solitary activity and contemplation. Further emphasizing the quiet, contemplative aspects of libraries, lending them an almost sacred quality, is the processional movement through space. The process of finding a book typically entails a sequence of actions that move a visitor through the library. Furthermore, the architectural spaces of early libraries were arranged in a way to lift them off the ground to avoid dampness. Structural support that was required for later collections meant that reading spaces were located above storage spaces. As a result, a visitor experiences moving through a series of spaces that take them progressively upward. This sequence was codified in a number of large public libraries through the idea that visiting a library should give one the sense of being uplifted and enlightened in buildings such as the Bibliothèque Sainte-Geneviève (1850), Bibliothèque Nationale (1867), Boston Public Library, (1895), and New York Public Library (1911).

Quality of light is another notable aspect of library spaces. While the storage stacks don't require much lighting—and some libraries leave them dark until a visitor approaches—the reading spaces require good quality and carefully controlled lighting. Early libraries insisted that no candles be used in library spaces and often had the best windows available to allow light for reading. Later libraries used clerestory windows, sunken courtyards, or other ways to bring natural light into reading spaces indirectly as evidenced in the Stockholm City Library (1928), Beinecke Library (1963), and the Bibliothèque Nationale (1996).

The qualities of light and quietness contribute to another main feature of library spaces, that of vastness. The reading rooms of large public libraries are among the largest urban interior spaces. The size of these rooms is a reflection of the grandiose attitudes of the benefactors, but also a consequence of serving a large number of visitors. It is somewhat startling to walk into these vast rooms and observe so many people quietly working.[11] Some libraries are also designed to show off the vastness of their collections. Libraries of the Rococo period often aimed to compose a room to embody the full collection in one space to demonstrate the breadth of knowledge of the owner, as well as the fantasy that everything could be known and collected in one place. Later, larger libraries were sometimes arranged on the principle of surveillance that all books should be visible to the librarian. In any case, the experience of library spaces is one that promotes a sense of one's place in the vastness of history and knowledge in examples such as the Bodleian Library (1612), Biblioteca Angelica (1765), and the Peabody Library (1866).

Spatial Study of the New York Public Library

The New York Public Library, designed by Carrere and Hastings, is a principal example of many of the spatial experiences described herein. The configuration

ROTUNDA
ASTOR HALL
ENTRY DOOR
PORTICO

MAIN READING ROOM
CATALOG ROOM
MEZZANINE
FLANKING STAIR

MAIN TERRACE
LIBRARY SIDEWALK
5TH AVENUE SIDEWALK

LAYERS OF PUBLIC SPACE AT NEW YORK PUBLIC LIBRARY

Image 12.1 Layers of exterior and interior public spaces at New York Public Library. Credit: William Mangold

Image 12.2 View of exterior public space at New York Public Library. Credit: William Mangold

Image 12.3 View of Astor Hall from mezzanine at New York Public Library. Credit: William Mangold

Image 12.4 View of main reading room at New York Public Library. Credit: William Mangold

and layout of spaces, with the reading room on the top, were determined by the librarian John Shaw Billings who sought an efficient system for storing, retrieving, and reshelving books. Thus, the architects designed a highly refined and orchestrated sequence of spaces leading up to the main reading room.

Image 12.1 diagrams the main public spaces within and around the New York Public Library produced through an architectural field survey and observations of activity.[12] Visitors to the exterior terraces and interior rooms of the library traverse a series of thresholds, bringing them into spaces that, though still very large and fully public, are experienced as increasingly more quiet, private, and intimate.[13] This experiential conflation of public and private leads to further consideration of how space is experienced as layered, and how specific social and architectural thresholds create boundaries that provide definition for these experiences.

With its Beaux-Arts symmetry and hierarchical arrangement of spaces, the New York Public Library reveals its distinctive thresholds and spatial layers. Three short steps distinguish the library precinct from the main sidewalk on 5th Avenue. Moving through this threshold brings a visitor to a level barely removed from the sidewalk, yet separated from the busy flow of pedestrian traffic. Another layer of space is identifiable in the main terrace area, five steps up, covered by trees, and surrounded by a stone balustrade. Here, tables and chairs host various activities—sitting, eating, reading, talking—that define the community function of the library. From here, a visitor ascends three segments of stairs leading to a portico and the doors of the library.

After moving through the small entry door, a visitor finds themselves in the expansive marble space of Astor Hall. Flanking sets of stairs, a mezzanine level affords views into Astor Hall and gives the visitor symmetrical opportunities to move upward toward the main reading room. Once on the upper level, a visitor passes through the wood-paneled Rotunda into the Catalog Room before arriving in the Rose Main Reading Room. This space is characterized by its quietness, lightness, and vastness, a sensation enhanced by the processional experience. The layered quality of space is articulated through changes in elevation and direction, compression at doorways and thresholds, and a gradual quieting of activity. It is worth noting the ways that we understand this space as public, and how it relates to the questions of interior urbanism as articulated by Denise Scott Brown:

> As 'interior urbanists', we find we must work with categories of function beyond those of the brief. These relate to the building's role in the community and may concern the size and volume of movement or activity. Particularly important are categories that differentiate between public and private activities or spaces and help to define the character of each and the relations between them.[14]

Making and Remaking "Publicness" in Interior Urbanism

A type of radical reworking of "function beyond the brief" happens every day by skateboarders. In his 2003 book, *Skateboarding, Space and the City: Architecture and the Body*, Iain Borden builds upon ideas of Henri Lefebvre, suggesting,

> Space becomes a uniform entity, a constant layer through the city that can be utilized, in this case, as a surface on which to skate… Skaters follow the homogeneity-fragmentation contradiction of abstract space by oscillating from this macro conception of space to the micro one of the architectural element; they move from the open canvas of the urban realm to the close focus of a specific wall, bench, fire hydrant, curb, or rail.[15]

The shift from macro to micro—from the large-scale surfaces of streets and sidewalks to small-scale furniture and railings—is an important reference in considering how the continuous landscape of urban exterior and interior spaces is experienced and navigated.

Another important reference in theorizing the experience of interior urbanism is the work of William H. Whyte and other advocates of place. Whyte studied the character and amenities of public spaces, especially at the immediate scale of human experience. His work, *The Social Life of Small Urban Spaces* (1980), continues to guide design efforts toward making actively used places that provide elements for seating, shade, and access. Curb cuts, trees, and street furniture contribute to a layered experience of urban space that allows people to find themselves comfortable and at home within the public realm. This sense of place conflated a feeling of public and private experiences in the library and other spaces of interior urbanism.

Theorizing interior urbanism as characteristically *public* relies upon (1) the idea of space as a continuous landscape, and (2) recognition of places that are comfortable for social interaction. Addressing the political aspect of public space draws upon a third point of reference: generative mapping. In *The Agency of Mapping* (1999), James Corner declares, "the function of mapping is less to mirror reality than to engender the re-shaping of the worlds in which people live… Mapping unfolds potential; it remakes territory over and over again, each time with new and diverse consequences." Later, he continues:

> Reality then, as in concepts such as 'landscape' or 'space', is not something external and 'given' for our apprehension; rather, it is constituted, or 'formed', through our participation with things: material objects, images, values, cultural codes, places, cognitive schema, events, and maps.[16]

This technique of mapping as a way of remaking territory suggests how it is possible to consider library spaces and the various terrains of interior urbanism to be part of the public realm.

Conclusion

Considered within the context of interior urbanism, libraries exhibit characteristic features, including an integration of functional spaces, vastness of scale, and sequential experience of space. For the New York Public Library, the sequencing of space begins at the sidewalk (if not before) and continues from exterior to interior into the reading room. This continuous landscape exemplifies the condition of interior urbanism in the micro-experiences of place afforded by various rooms, niches, and perches. What is implicit in the surface and detail encountered by the skateboarder (or pedestrian) moving through space becomes explicit in the designed sequence of the library. The nuance and refinement of materials, details, and views make every step unique, continuously framing and reframing a sense of space.

Mapping this experience allows for insight into the meaning and conditions of library space as public space. In this case, the method of mapping and analysis was intentionally simple: demarcation of the architectural thresholds and boundaries of social activity. But in so doing, the layered character of the spaces reveals that "public" is a varied experience and does not exist as a binary condition with "private." This allows agency. Spatial boundaries can be created to differentiate areas of use and access. Thresholds can be employed to create specific transitions (smooth, disjunctive, etc.) between layers of space. Features can be designed to afford opportunities to rest, change pace, or take a seat in spaces designed for public use. Mapping can be employed to understand and remake these conditions.

Notes

1   See *The Library: A World History* (2013) by James W.P. Campbell and Will Pryce, and *History of Libraries of the Western World* (1999) by Michael Harris.

2   The earliest archive of written materials was in the ancient Sumerian city-state of Uruk around 3400 BC.

3   The survival of books and libraries (even today) was impacted by political battles and ideologies, which sometimes entailed massive destruction of books.

4   For more information, see *Parchment and the History of Books*. By K.E. Carr, Quatr.us Study Guides, 2017.

5   Most monastic collections up to the thirteenth century had fewer than 100 volumes. By 1338, the Sorbonne had the largest collection in Europe with 338 books for consultation and 1,728 books in its register, of which 300 were marked as lost.

6   Harris, Michael H. 1999. *History of Libraries of the Western World*. 4th edition. Lanham, MD: The Scarecrow Press, Inc.

7   The funding of these libraries typically covered the cost of construction of the building and acquisition of books, but required municipalities to provide the land and guarantee a revenue stream (taxes) for staffing and maintenance of the library and the collection.

8   A 1992 *New York Times* report noted that 1,554 of the 1,681 original buildings in the United States still existed.

9   Latimer, Karen. 2011. "Collections to Connections: Changing Spaces and New Challenges in Academic Library Buildings," *Library Design: From Past to Present, Library Trends* Vol. 60, No. 1, pp. 112–133.

10 Hopkins, *Karen Brooks*, 2018. "Anchor Arts Institutions: What Are They and How Can They Enrich Communities?"

11 The main reading room of the NYPL, at 78 ft wide by 297 ft long and 51 ft high, is one of the largest rooms in the United States, and seats 624 patrons.

12 Further diagrams and documentation of the observations are available at wmangold.org

13 In *The Library*, Campbell and Pryce write, "When the doors of the New York Public Library open, the readers have to climb huge sets of staircases and pass through a series of grand marble-lined halls to reach the reading rooms above."

14 Scott Brown, Denise, and Maurice Hartveld. 2007. "On Public Interior Space," in *AA Files 56*. London: Architectural Association Publications.

15 Borden, Iain. 2003. *Skateboarding, Space and the City: Architecture and the Body*. London: Bloomsbury.

16 Corner, James. 1999. "The Agency of Mapping: Speculation, Critique and Invention," in Denis Cosgrove, ed. *Mappings*. London: Reaktion Books, pp. 231–252, 213, 223.

Chapter 13

The Museum
An Urban Threshold

Jonathan A. Scelsa

The evolution of the museum is a story of the functional problems of designing spaces for display within a larger framework. The museum has been identified by Michel Foucault as an 'otherspace,' a world outside of our own. Foucault described this condition in 'the collection museum,' as an example of hetero-topia, a place of reflection on our own society's preferences and ideals with the arrangement of objects in our own world.[1] The agency of the architect is to create an architectural envelope that binds these worlds together, while simultaneously allowing for their autonomy as rooms nested within a larger whole. This condition of nesting, considered in conjunction with the growth in square footage of our museum's in the modern city, might encourage us as designers to reconsider the interior museum as a city within a city.

Arguably, the history of the architecture of the museum is less about the morphology of its geometry and more about its use of elements such as the wall and door as a technology of power.[2] The art gallery began as an outgrowth of the manor or palace, as an aristocratic space for collecting artifacts. This form of residential nineteenth-century architecture was most typically arranged in what would be referred to as an 'enfilade' or a configuration in which rooms are aligned along a linear axis through their thresholds. The enfilade gained traction in the late baroque European palace as a series of rooms each in a hierarchy, often festooned with art of higher value and scale as one reached the place of greatest privacy within the manor. A notable example of this linear type is the Louvre in Paris erected by Louis XIII and later converted into an art museum. The three-story palace features two- and sometimes one-room wide enfilade configurations that define two centralized courtyards. This linear typology, illuminated from windows, became synchronously known and understood for its display of two-dimensional artworks. Soon thereafter, this formal type would be perfected in terms of its lighting conditions.

An early prototype of this arrangement could be seen in the Dulwich Picture Gallery (1817) in South London by Sir John Soane. This early example of a public art gallery on a college campus features five rooms, each lit from above

DOI: 10.4324/9780429443091-15

from a dedicated sky portal and abutted with axially aligned thresholds, demonstrating an early typological tendency to organize content sequentially along a linear spine by artist topic or region. The picture gallery demarcates the moment when art display moved from rooms lit horizontally from windows to vertically to vertical illumination from apertures above, leaving the only aperture on the vertical wall surface to be the threshold between rooms. The Dulwich Picture Gallery represents an indicative moment when the museum was defining itself away from the private collection for aristocracy toward an educational device for the masses. Dulwich was somewhere in between, a private collection on a campus. In Western Europe, the nineteenth century saw a rise in state-sponsored architectural competitions that switched from spaces for the display of private wealth serving aristocrats to spaces oriented as critical public infrastructure.[3]

The turn of the twentieth century witnessed the museum migrate from private collections held in well-off homes and colleges into the center of the modern city as a public amenity. The museum brought both the enfilade and domestic scaled rooms now decoupled from its former linear arrangement in favor of a spread 'mat configuration' afforded by its new roof illumination strategy. Examples include the Metropolitan Museum of Art (1874) by Richard Morris Hunt in New York and the Stedelijk Museum (1895) by Adriaan Willem Weissman in Amsterdam. This arrangement of rooms at the domestic scale provided ample wall space required for the display for painting. Meanwhile, the space between the adorned walls housed cases for small sculpture, fine crafts, and textiles. Curators became accustomed to using rooms thematically, whereby each work was linked by a time-period or concept. Viewers followed the walls, while thresholds served as breaks between each thematic world of art.

The Intermezzo Corridor

The domestic scale enfilade extended its typology successfully through much of the twentieth century, through the periods of Modernity, Objet d'art, and post-modernity. The latter half of the twentieth century, by contrast, saw a change to the very spatial premise of art as Object that had been upheld in the previous centuries. Artists began to challenge the medium and practice of art as a commodified piece of the physical world—questioning its scale, tangibility, temporality, and procedure. These efforts resulted in installation-based work that would engage more than the wall and floor, but would encompass an immersive architectural experience. The resulting spatial experience between artists could result in one room requiring total darkness for the curation of light, while the next room would require an immersive walk-through sculpture. This immersivity of the experience saw real consequence in the typological space of the museum. This differentiated nature of the contemporary field of art demanded a new space to emerge, what we might call an 'intermezzo,' like a sorbet in between luxuriant courses, a space for returning to a neutral state after an all-encompassing experience within an individual artist's work. An early example of this corridor can be noted in the Museum of Modern Art in Manhattan and the Contemporary Art Annex in Queens. The Annex, known as PS1, opened its doors in 1997 as a reuse of an existing public-school building featuring a series of classrooms flanking a centralized corridor. This double-loaded corridor provided an intermezzo between art interventions curated by artists within a larger framework (Image 13.1).

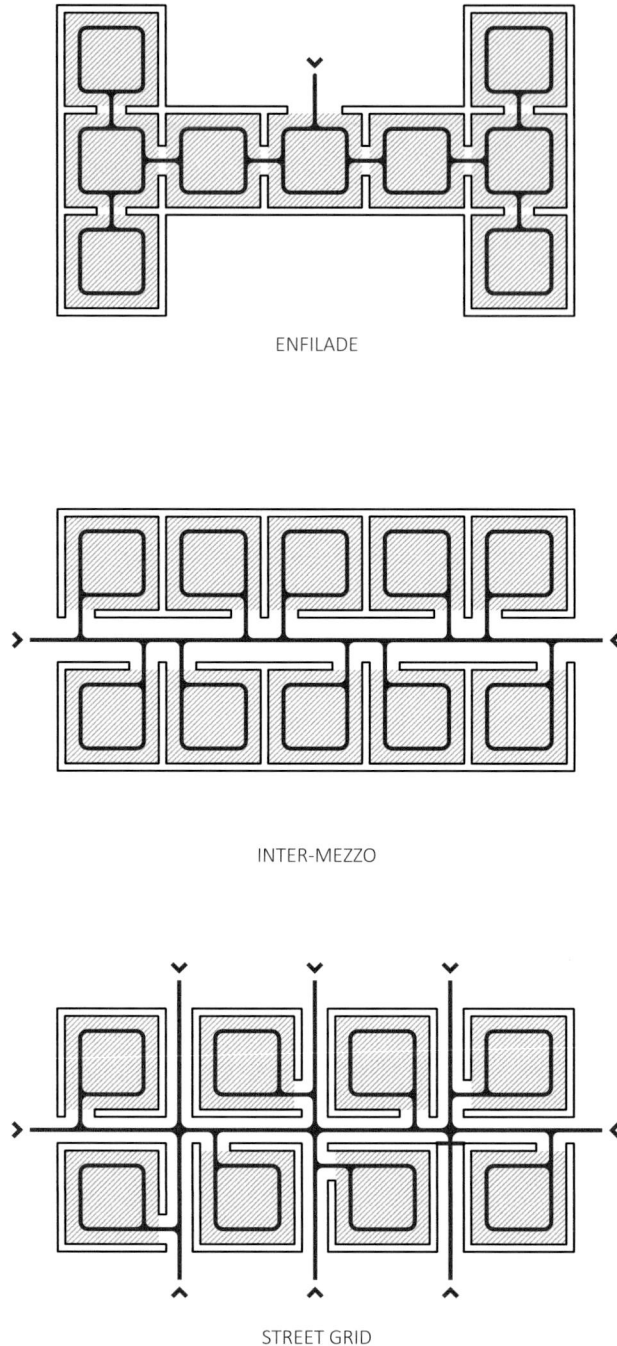

ENFILADE

INTER-MEZZO

STREET GRID

Image 13.1 The development of the museum is synchronous with the type and quality of artwork. This chicken and egg dilemma can best be described in the form of three paradigms. The enfilade, or a collection of rooms aligned via doors, situated in the nineteenth century with artwork for painting and small objects. The corridor model situates work that can be grouped thematically in clusters, based on its zone that may or may not feature room-to-room access but is notably divided thematically by the main building circulation. Finally and most recently, the pavilion or intermezzo approach wherein each room is further separated by the building circulation, resembling a figure—ground street situation. Herein each room acts as an autonomous space. Jonathan A. Scelsa (2013), Image Courtesy of the Author.

Corridor as an Internal Road

This break between worlds, provided by the intermezzo, seems to have emerged at a time when these institutions are expanding in scale. There were changes in typology from collections or storage complexes to Foucauldian heterotopias, or spaces more like exposition spaces, fairgrounds, or markets. This corridor space, framed as an internal street, has more clear typological relationships to the Crystal Palace, as part of an 'exhibition complex' with typological links to the department store and nineteenth-century arcade. This formal kinship with a centralizing road network underscores the museum's genealogical relationship to the contemporary shopping mall and airport—territories of the urban flâneur. Contemporary museum briefs call on architects to design projects that house space in ways much like the great expositions of the mid-twentieth century. These expos, such as the 1964 New York World's fair, were designed and planned as micro-cities with towers where the public could witness their encompassing urbanism across many acres.[4]

The contemporary museum, not unlike the fairground and expo, includes dining facilities, retail, event halls, and educational facilities in addition to increasingly large exhibition spaces. Much like these other types, as museums grew in size, they demanded systems of wayfinding and circulation hierarchy. While this networked road strategy has clear organizational benefits, it also embodies other city-like notions and ideas of urbanization. The twenty-first-century museum, much like its oversized cousins, is predicated on a financial model of continual adaptive growth rather than finite construction. As such, the museum is an aggregate-based system like the arcades of the nineteenth century, representing a series of arterial infrastructure links around which new connections and expansions can be linked.

Possible Grids

This tendency toward road-based organization is demonstrated in several museum proposals and built work that employ the internalized corridor, aggregating the double-loaded corridor into something more akin to the urban grid of a city. This new interior 'figure-ground' includes rooms of art floating within an archipelago of corridors. When is an elongated Manhattan grid relevant versus the informality of the medieval Camillo Sitte grid? Would the ramifications of L'Enfant's concept of Washington, DC suggest placing iconic art along boulevards? Would Cerda's Barcelona create more of a continuum of modular, public interior spaces akin to Catalan courtyards? This new approach to museum layout echoes the development of the nineteenth-century city itself. It packs artwork into a sprawling model aimed at giving the viewer more time to walk. This new field of dedicated circulation more closely resembles urbanism (Image 13.2).

As an example of seventeenth-century baroque planning, OMA's 2012 proposal for the National Museum of China includes spaces akin to avenues with long, uninterrupted vistas flanked on either sides by comparably sized edifices. The concept shows a clear likeness to Charles L'Enfant's Plan for Washington, DC of 1791. The main axes configure the plan into five discrete zones with varying scales of enfilade focusing movement toward a central polis or plaza. This model, similar to the more recent work of OMA, offers an image of metropolitanism and provides rapid access to a central space. Furthermore, this plan affords the flâneur walking possibilities and direct movement across the whole. Similar to the Baroque city, the main corridors shape a vista to a prominent monument, combining a new museum typology with an older cellular model (Image 13.3).

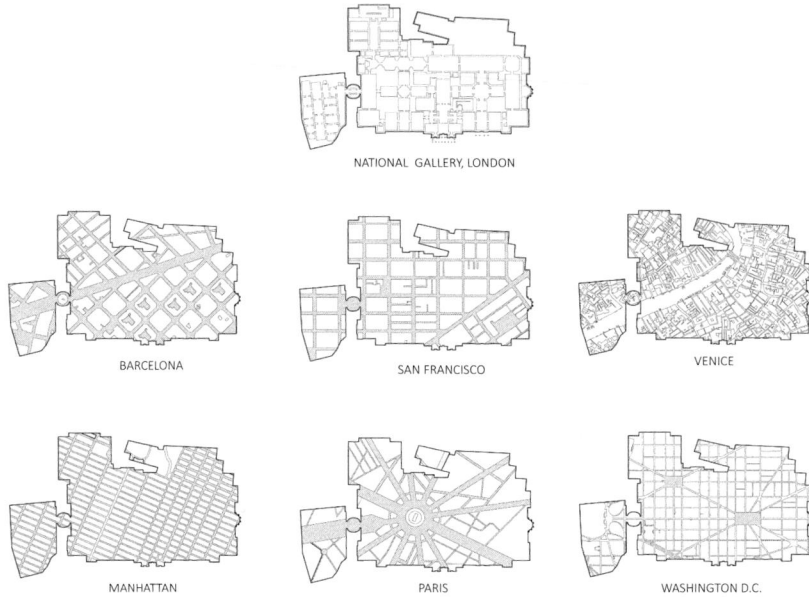

NATIONAL GALLERY, LONDON

BARCELONA

SAN FRANCISCO

VENICE

MANHATTAN

PARIS

WASHINGTON D.C.

Image 13.2 We have witnessed as of late several models of street circulation that can be adapted from urban grids to the museum. We have seen ideas of radial city grids from baroque urban planning featuring large objects and monuments at the center with smaller more antique cities at the periphery. Other models suggest the ring-road, a major access that surrounds and binds the different sectors of the museum. More recently, the pavilion or archipelagic approach has been seen in two forms. One resembling an informal aggregate of like-sized and shaped elements, and another where the spacing and scale of the road resemble a methodical equity-based planning. Jonathan A. Scelsa (2013), Image Courtesy of the Author.

The peripheral ring-road is another form of arterial planning for museums at another scale of urbanism. The peripheral ring strategy allows circumnavigation of a city center along its periphery from various districts from outside the core. The REX Architects second place proposal for the Munch Museum (2009) in Oslo features a plan of nine diversely organized galleries. These unique conditions, each with variations in spatial, light, and formal parameters, are circumscribed by a peripheral ring corridor. Its internal ring-road offers museum visitors a promenade or vista of the bay surrounding the museum. This panorama would be observed, while a user is circulating and choosing the specific museum district to enter. The museum's exhibition core is structured as a nine-square grid with eight gallery districts surrounding a central utility core, representing an infrastructural or political zone.

Looking beyond European models of urbanism lets us consider the twentieth-century grid of New York, a model of urban planning wherein difference is afforded at the scale of the block. SANAA Architects have explored this notion of corridor and road redundancy in their twenty-first-century Museum of Contemporary Art in Kanazawa, Japan. Built in 2004, the museum features galleries designed as individual boxes varying in size and shape, and then gathered together like an archipelago within a larger cylindrical volume. The galleries are separated by a three-meter corridor allowing for circulation that flows between and around each. Each gallery offers different possibilities for artist interventions varying in height, size, and even interior or exterior enclosure; some galleries are completely exteriorized into courtyards. Like the Munch Museum proposal by REX, a circular path provides both a ring-road condition and milieu for the volumes. In the case of the Kanazawa museum, the grid acts as the intensifier—an element that defines its metropolitan density allowing each part to be both discrete and unified.[5]

Like the universal grid and metropolitan principles of Manhattan, the grid model acts like urban planning to express a visible order. We see other

Image 13.3 As designers move forward, we can examine multiple types of museum organizations through the simple comparison of outer form to urban grid sampling. This method suggests that perhaps each gallery can exhibit a micro-differentiation within a larger framework. Imbuing the overall museum with identity while individual choice is provided to curators for each artist. Jonathan A. Scelsa (2013), Image Courtesy of the Author.

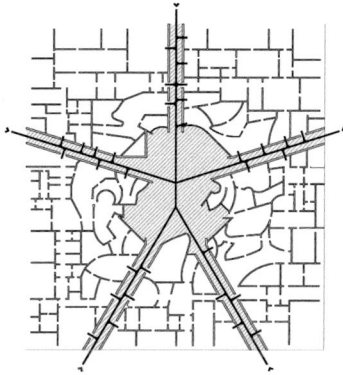

OMA / NATIONAL MUSEUM OF CHINA

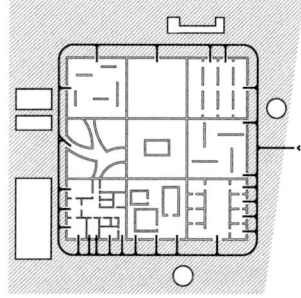

REX / MUNCH MUSEUM

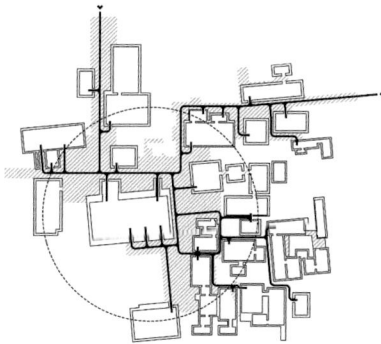

NOUVEL / LOUVRE ABU DHABI

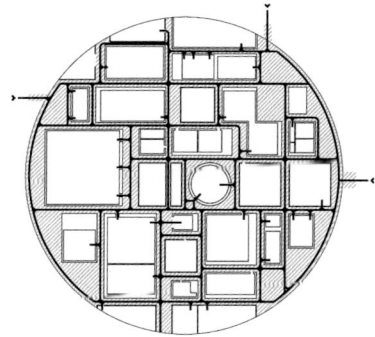

SANAA / 21ST CENTURY MUSEUM

architects borrow from urban planning in the recently completed Louvre expansion in Abu Dhabi. Designed by architect Jean Nouvel, this new museum sits on the shores of Saadiyat Island and employs the archipelago-like planning of the Kanazawa project. Nouvel collects volumes of differing scale and size within a larger form, in this case, an oversized umbrella roof. Beneath its frame, galleries differentiate in size and form; they are organized in a different fashion than the SANAA example, eschewing the grid for an apparent dis-ordered strategy. The gallery boxes, ordered like clusters, are terraced in both plan and section to create an urbanism that looks like vernacular, self-built dwellings. In this case, the ordering principle is not evidenced in the space in between, but rather in the similarly scaled size of individual elements; they share an infrastructural roof and flank a road that amorphously defines circulation paths. The space within and outside of the galleries demonstrates a stark juxtaposition in visible quality and light. The internal atmospheres are curated and controlled; the negotiating space is controlled and suggested by the architectural form of the planner, master architect Nouvel.

Scaling Benefits

These new paradigmatic museums could be perceived as inefficient as they display a large redundancy of non-programmed circulatory space that increases their size and overall cost. This redundancy, however, has many functional positives beyond the architectural experience. One of the unique challenges in contemporary museum design is balancing the contradictory needs for both architectural ingenuity and curatorial flexibility. The use of the urban street grid for the museum plan presents a unique solution to free-standing galleries. The architect retains design agency over the infrastructural space of the organization while removing the art spaces themselves from the scope. This relationship resembles that of the urban designer to the architect as well, in which the role of the planner is to create the massing and zoning, while the architect shapes differentiation within that framework. This paradigm offers each contributing agent a space in which to operate without restraining or adversely affecting the others domain. Furthermore, given the nature of rotating exhibitions, redundancy in circulation can absorb the installation and de-installation process without total closure of the system. Thus, it acts like a street grid during times of construction.

As a consequence of separating art into objects and circulation by zone, several of these prototypes suggest the possibility of a wall-less museum curated as individual buildings within the framework of the city. One new movement was initiated by Chicago-based artist Theaster Gates and the Rebuild Foundation whose mission is 'neighborhood transformation' by acquiring properties in shrinking cities for cultural and community programming.[6] Other examples include the recent reuse of the Colonels Row residences on Governors Island in New York Harbor into a set of galleries comprising a larger public museum. These projects create the effect of a single art complex composed of individual spaces. They use the public infrastructure of streets as the connective tissue for a larger museum. This twenty-first-century phenomenon aligns with the actions of municipal governments. At some level, this questions both the meaning and necessity of the museum as a building, perhaps reducing the edifice as a space of legitimacy within the art world. Counter to that argument may be a sense that the urban scale is where art truly becomes political and contested. It is here where the display and communicative power of art becomes insidious between the planned and unplanned.[7]

Such issues are clearly at play in certain historical settings such as Florence and Venice, medieval cities that have leveraged the urban space of tourism for events like the Venice Biennale. The urbanized islands in the Venetian Lagoon are undeniably an 'otherspace' due to their distinctive vernacular and isolation from the larger municipal world. During this biannual festival which centers on the easternmost island of Castello, several countries have historically occupied a series of discrete pavilions within a bounded garden to celebrate the contemporary state of the avant-garde. This arrangement suggests a campus museum much like the prior example of Governors Island. As the Biennale has increased in scale with more participating countries each year, those nations without pavilions occupy and rent spaces on adjacent islands, thus expanding the exhibition's footprint to the outer limits of the archipelago. Given this elasticity of scale, the museum as a typology might be considered metropolitan in its programming, intensified by the boundaries of walls and urban limits. Through this lens, the museum is scalable from the house, to the building, to the city and perhaps one day—to the planetary.

Notes

1   Anthony Giddens, *The Constitution of Society; Outline of a Theory of Structuration* (Berkeley and Los Angeles: University of California Press, 1986), p. 129.

2   Ibid.

3   Tony Bennet, 1995. *The Birth of the Museum: History, Theory, Politics* (Routledge: New York, 1995), p. 68.

4   Ibid., p. 84.

5   Pier Vittorio Aureli, *The Possibility of an Absolute Architecture* (MIT Press: Cambridge, MA, 2011), p. 225.

6   Rebuild Foundation, "About." https://rebuild-foundation.org/our-story/ (accessed October 27, 2018).

7   Walter Benjamin and J. A. Underwood, *The Work of Art in the Age of Mechanical Reproduction* (Penguin: London, 2008), p. 54.

Chapter 14

The Department Store
A Moment before the Mall

Patrick Lee Lucas

As the shopping mall began to dominate the suburban landscape in the middle of the twentieth century, urban retailers attempted to attract and retain customers on Main Street by updating shops and storefronts in the Moderne or International Style. Behind the slick facades, the ever more transparent storefronts brightly lit by changes in lighting and display, the nineteenth-century mercantile building type and its attendant interior remained virtually unchanged. In this case study of a mid-century urban department store in a moderately sized Southern town, the building stands as a vestigial remnant of the nineteenth-century mercantile landscape.

Places to Shop
Since its initial introduction in the 1840s, the primary building program of the department store has included open interior space uncluttered by structural columns, an articulated facade with elaborate storefront to attract passersby, convenient delivery access, and adjacency to public transportation and, later, large areas of parking for patrons. For nearly two centuries, the counterculture within the stores and the stage-like settings in mocked-up rooms and in shop windows offered the newest products and glamorous fashions available to passersby. As the nineteenth century yielded to the twentieth, the urban interiors of these retail giants increasingly became ever more the domain of the middle class, particularly with the robust consumer economy mass-marketing strategies, styled goods, and planned obsolescence of the 1920s. The commercial optimism that followed World War II was characterized by plentiful and inexpensive goods for suburban homes, a time when promoters primed consumers to consume fueled by new credit schemes. Though the pent-up demand for things embodied consumer habits of the mid-twentieth century, not much had changed in the interior organization of the department store; yet, these spaces became increasingly more "self-service" than ever before. In the moment before the mall and the massive transformation of a suburban space as the center of the retail experience, downtown shop owners struggled to

DOI: 10.4324/9780429443091-16

stay abreast of retail trends, including the architectural presence of the store on the street.

In the mid-twentieth century, consumers and corporate culture adopted for these buildings what some have called the 1950s "department store modern," a style "predicated on making fashionable consumables irresistibly modern" as "tools of capitalism."[1] Expressed architecturally, the visual materials of desire – color, glass, and light – used for centuries by royal courts and the military as signs to others of power and prestige were adopted by department stores, as well as with a host of other retail establishments, institutions of higher education, and museums as they coalesced into a broader consumer culture.[2] As store ownership moved from founders to grandsons by the mid-twentieth century, the department store assumed "normative social and cultural roles...as a distributor of goods" through self-service sales schemes, evocative displays, exhibits, demonstrations, and lectures.[3] Even national cultural institutions, such as the Museum of Modern Art, used department stores as places for events and displays in the twentieth century, a practice echoing the two previous centuries where mercantile spaces provided the stage for bringing high culture to the everyday.

Though many survived the depression in the 1930s, department stores ceased to be economic powerhouses as owners faced daunting challenges with competitor businesses, increased infrastructure costs, the shift to suburban living, and the presence of traffic congestion in downtowns, along with the fallout from urban renewal programs. The interwar years saw "modernization and enlargement and extension of the individual store to other cities, alongside the phenomenal growth of chain stores operated by Sears, Roebuck; Montgomery Ward, and J.C. Penney Co." Writing in the mid-century, John William Ferry characterized the deterioration of properties in downtowns and the mass production of cars for private use as key conditions that shifted retail focus to the suburbs. Despite these challenges, he speculated on a positive future for downtown retail, noting that "the present difficulties of the downtown stores...will be overcome with the same ingenuity and enterprise that have been shown through a hundred years of coping with problems of finance, business depressions, and the impact of war."[4] Looking back from the twenty-first century, we now know that what Ferry characterized as a prosperous vision for center city mercantile concerns did not come to pass.

Mid-Century Design Influences

A writer in *Architectural Forum* in 1950 suggested that air-conditioning, modern lighting, low-cost acoustic materials, lightweight curtain walls, flexible ceiling, and partitioning all shaped retail space, resulting in the characterization that "in the last ten years more has happened to downtown store design than happened in the previous hundred." The reviewer indicated that not all designs lived up to their promise, "Merely to hold their own in the sharpening fight for the shopping dollar, downtown merchants were now obliged to re-plan and modernize as they never had before," resulting in "many stores that look contemporary really have nothing but a skin-deep coating of 'modernistic' design."[5] All of these architectural innovations contributed to the fluid language of stores in the mid-century, and the aesthetic changes to window display, interior layout, and overall form gave insight into the motivations of both designers and owners as they continued to try to attract customers.

The "visual front" storefront style presented a picture within a picture, a frame for consumerism. Both the frame and the images and artifacts within represented "an übergallery in which the picture hangs" at the scale of the street to capture the "hearts, minds, and pocketbooks" of consumers, a platform and space where patrons come onstage or backstage "instead of ovations, the audience was to consume." As selling required novel, eye-catching approaches that linked to desire, not need, the store windows and the displays within had to be styled as "chic dioramas," wherein stylish mannequins modeled the latest couture and showcased the finest products. By transforming the ordinary and everyday into the spectacle and unparalleled, "architects and interior designers collaborated on strategies to manipulate the average consumer's behavior by guiding her to that streamlined cash register in the back of the store." In the process, "The barrier between sidewalk and the store practically disappeared – the only thing between the shopper and the product was glass." Advanced technology made non-glare transparent glass possible and glass companies responded by publishing lush catalogs to standardize storefront design. The 1945 Libbey's catalog assured architects, designers, and owners that "a Visual Front (brand name) contains no 'gingerbread' to distract the attention of a passer-by away from the goods for sale" so that "each enticingly designed window on the world has a curiously irresistible hypnotic pull…which makes sales almost automatic."[6]

In order to lay out the interior to maximum advantage, architect Morris Ketchum suggested categorizing merchandise into three groups – impulse, convenience, and demand merchandise – locating impulse merchandise near the door, convenience merchandise midway on the circulation path and demand merchandise at the far end of the "shopping street" on the interior.[7] This panoramic view of interior display installation activates all elements in a space (ledges, floor displays, wall trims, counter tops, showcases, and tables) and provides a design language that focuses on customer experience and direct interaction with wares. Two years later, Ketchum described the "great vanishing act in store design" where, one after the other, "traditional elements of the store interior have literally disappeared in favor of maximum visibility for the merchandise itself," including a recessed storefront to pull the customer directly into the store, greater visibility to the urban interior by drivers being able to take in sweeping interior images, reduced sales counter frequency and size, greater emphasis on moveable fixture designs, recessed lighting, and easily demountable walls and ceiling panels with the "happy result of putting as few obstacles between [the customer] and the merchandise as possible," and reducing overall costs in initial construction as well as demolition of more permanent displays over time.[8]

Not only did the design of stores impact consumer behavior, but customer experience also deeply informed the success of the department store. Fred Lazarus, Jr., president of the Federated Department Stores, indicated that "a department store must have certain aspects of a circus…it has to create a sense of excitement and activity for the shopper. It's got to look busy, feel busy, be busy. Customers just won't shop in a dead atmosphere."[9] In the moment before the mall, downtown department store owners struggled to chase and retain their chief customers. As middle-class women continued to shop for their husbands and children and made "lifetime purchases" of home furnishings or major household appliances, stores began to revise their methods for the suburban customer who came to town. Store owners located or relocated their retail emporia near rail and bus stations, offered lunch hour promotions, provided exemplary and efficient customer service, installed luxurious restaurants, built auditoriums, and provided other kinds of spaces to make downtown stores a destination.

Wolf Wile Department Store

The Wolf Wile Department Store Building, a well-known architectural mid-twentieth-century landmark in Lexington, Kentucky, is a four-story commercial structure at the corner of Quality Street and the major east-west thoroughfare in town, East Main Street. From the time of the construction of the building in 1949–1950 until the closing of the firm in 1992, the Wolf Wile Building housed one of Lexington's most prominent commercial concerns. Its upscale clothing and household goods served a prosperous community with its diverse economy based in agriculture, manufacturing, higher education, and government. Designed in the International Style by the New York firm of Amos Parrish & Co. in collaboration with the Lexington architectural firm of Frankel & Curtis, the structure stands as a significant example of the last gasp efforts to anchor department stores in the city center. Consequently, the structure features both urban and suburban design features, tempered by regional variants and materials. Fundamentally, an East Coast building that found its way to Main Street Lexington modified in form and execution by owner, designer, and architect. Wolf Wile's unique architecture embodies features developed both by the owners and by the designers to make it more contextual with its surroundings and local commercial building forms (Image 14.1).

Figure 14.1 Wolf Wile company department store facade rendering designed by Amos Parrish & Co., New York. Credit: Patrick Lee Lucas

The Wolf Wile Department Store Building offered an exciting departure in appearance and form for a retail presence in Lexington. At the project's completion, the local press characterized the building as "futuristic," "modernistic," and "swanky." These exuberant expressions recognized boldly unusual design characteristics that contrasted with the existing built environment. Because of these, Wolf Wile's remained significant as the only building of its type in the community; moreover, there were very few examples in the broader region of Kentucky. Appearing perfectly at mid-century, the Wolf Wile structure witnessed first the post-World War II expansion of commerce in Lexington, and afterward, the growing emergence of retail activity in suburban shopping malls. The burgeoning of the malls resulted in a gradual disappearance of Main Street retail businesses. Remarkably viable through its expert management and devoted clientele, Wolf Wile was, in fact, Lexington's sole remaining family owned department store when it closed in 1992. The Wolf Wile Department Store Building and the enterprising commercial initiative it long represented typify the struggle of a community to reconcile the dynamics of expanding commercial growth with the traditional concept of downtown as a center of community. The building embodies an exuberant and optimistic part of American history and culture that is associated with the boom following World War II – an outlook that celebrated streamlined design, consumer convenience, the automobile, and above all, an optimistic anticipation of the future.

For the scheme, the architects and designers abandoned the idea of a highly decorated front facade oriented to Main Street in favor of a display window/entrance system which connected outside with inside. It shaped a free-flowing view and path into and out of the building, and thus, created an urban interior to be occupied by passersby. To achieve this design concept, store designers placed three pairs of double herculite doors side by side and concentrated the location of large display windows adjacent to the entry. The result of this design choice – a display area and vestibule where customers observed a mercantile vista through the front entrance and display areas – sits beneath an overhanging canopy that unites the entryway and display windows and serves as a sort of porch to cover this occupiable thickened front facade. In contrast, the remainder of the building, clad in a tight stone and brick veneer, provides a planar skin for the large volume in the four-floor building. A pylon stands as a bookend on the northwest corner of the front facade, separating the Wolf Wile Department Store Building from the neighboring building to its west. While somewhat reminiscent of vertical sign systems from earlier twentieth-century buildings, this pylon physically separates this International Style building from its neighbors along Main Street. Three stainless-steel-tapered columns support the overhang above the first-floor entrance to this building away from the plane of the front facade and in the public space of the sidewalk. Free from decoration and articulation, the stainless-steel columns serve as an additional means of articulating the fluid public/private space in the front wall system and of the street.

In the Moment before the Mall

The Wolf Wile Department Store Building, constructed in a time of great change in American culture, asserted a new presence on Main Street in a way that no building had prior, or no building has since. In 1949–1950, the owners of this department store structure recognized the value of remaining on Main Street in downtown Lexington. Moreover, the owners recognized the need for something different along Main Street to catch customers' attention and provide a marketing mechanism to draw customers into the store. This building respects Main Street traditions of design and expands them in suburban ways, cladding these traditions in an International Style language unparalleled in the community. The owners and designers of the building carefully draw this building to its predecessor neighbors through materials and use in the design. The vision for the Wolf Wile Department Store Building, a model building that would represent downtown Lexington of the future, suggested a new form of urban interior that never quite took hold, the downtown department store of the later twentieth century. Joseph S. Wile, Sr., noted the design schematic laid out by Amos Parrish as one which was intended for the remainder of the same block on East Main Street – a series of stores in a modern style united by a common covered walkway, thus creating a semi-public occupiable space on Main Street.[10] The architect's and designer's collective efforts to initiate a new, more suburban vision for downtown Lexington never came to pass. Though the as-designed Wolf Wile Department Store Building served as a cornerstone of a new suburban model for downtown, by the time the community was ready to fully embrace this strategic direction, suburban development overwhelmed any attempt to concentrate retail in the commercial downtown. The Wolf Wile Department Store Building, a richly detailed, simply designed modern structure embodying this new type of urban interior, combined important tradition with a forward-thinking image for Main Street. It remains an invaluable resource in understanding this critical juncture in the community's development history and as a building that captures a type of urban interior that rarely exists outside of the mid-twentieth century.

Notes

1   Steven Heller, "Department Store Modern," in Jim Heimann, ed. *Shop America: Mid-century Storefront Design, 1938–1950* (New York, Taschen, 2007), 8, 11.

2   William Leach, *Land of Desire: Merchants, Power, and the Rise of the New American Culture* (New York, Vintage, 1993).

3   Jan Whitaker, *Service and Style* (London, St. Martin's Press, 2006), 4.

4   John William Ferry, *A History of the Department Store* (New York, Macmillan, 1960), 183.

5   *Architectural Forum*. "What Makes a 1940 Store Obsolete?" (July 1950), 62–79 (62).

6   Jim Heimann, ed. *Shop America: Mid-century Storefront Design, 1938–1950* (New York, Taschen, 2007), 7–13.

7   E.B. Weiss, *Selling to and Through the New Department Store* (New York, Funk & Wagnalls, 1948), 175–177, 181.

8   *Architectural Forum*. "What Makes a 1940 Store Obsolete?" (July 1950), 63.

9   *Business Week*. "Stores Go Into Show Business" (October 23, 1954), 46–49.

10 Ibid.

Chapter 15

The Shopping Mall

City within a Suburb

Judith K. De Jong

Free time is not an inherently modern idea; public events in the public spaces of the historical city make this clear, and the wealthy, once primarily aristocrats, certainly had plenty of leisure time. One of modernism's effects, however, was an expansion of free time for a wider range of people, including an emerging middle class with a higher standard of living, which resulted from improving transportation, communication, and production technologies, among other things. More free time encouraged new forms of leisure, which generated new kinds of space. The transformation of shopping from a chore to a choice was particularly impactful, famously spawning the world's most effective machine for consumption: the suburban shopping mall in mid-twentieth century America. But the cultural and economic conditions that produced the mall have fundamentally changed, contributing to a proliferation of "dead malls," and many remaining retail-only malls are struggling. Instead, the future of the mall may depend on an alternative understanding and projection of its origins. Situated by Walter Benjamin's arcades, Victor Gruen's suburban centers, and Gerald Hines' "new downtown," this trajectory understands the interiorized center of collective life as a *City within a Suburb*.[1]

Organization and Anchor

The linear shopping streets called "arcades" that appeared in urban Europe in the nineteenth century created a distinct feeling of interiorization, even as they remained open to, and contiguous with, adjacent public sidewalks. Whether small (the Passage de Panorama in Paris, 1799), medium (the Burlington Arcade in London, 1819), or large (the Galleria Vittorio Emmanuelle in Milan, 1867), the distinctive entryways, glass roofs, special lighting, and pedestrian-only status combined to produce an "inner space" along its length.[2] In contrast, the center-city department stores that emerged simultaneous to the arcades, such as Le Bon Marche in Paris (1852), centered circulation and assembly in soaring atria, bringing shoppers together under one glass and cast-iron roof. This model, which proliferated through Europe and the United States, included Marshall Field's in Chicago and Selfridge's in London.

DOI: 10.4324/9780429443091-17

The downtown department store remained the dominant site of shopping as leisure until the end of World War II. But as residential decentralization accelerated in America after the war, so too did retail decentralization, led by the companies that owned the downtown department stores, including Bon Marche in Seattle, Hudson's in Detroit, and Dayton's in Minneapolis. As a result, shopping produced another collective interior in the shopping mall, a new typology that combined the linear organization of the arcades with the centralizing actions of the department store to remarkable effect. At the same time, it did so in a radically different place. In 1950, historic images show architects John Graham and Company located a pedestrianized, linear shopping "street" in the middle of a big parking lot north of downtown Seattle. While roofless, and therefore technically outside, the Northgate Shopping Center's limited fenestration along the surrounding parking clearly conveyed the inward orientation of the project. That interiority was reinforced by the location of a branch of Bon Marche, the downtown department store, at the midpoint of the shopping street, where it became the "anchor," or primary attraction. A few years later, at the Northland Shopping Center (1954) outside of Detroit, designed by Victor Gruen and Associates, Hudson's Department Store was the central anchor of an inward-facing pinwheel plan with short, radiating "streets" lined with stores.

The location of the anchor fundamentally shifted when Gruen and Associates designed the Southdale Shopping Center (1956), outside of Minneapolis. Southdale was the first to have two department stores—Dayton's and Donaldson's—located at opposite ends of the mall and connected by a linear shopping street, thus introducing the "dumb-bell" organization of anchor/street/anchor.[3] The dumb-bell proved so effective at moving shoppers along the full length of the infill retail lining the streets and connecting the anchors—thereby advancing economic gains—that it became the primary organizational technique of many subsequent malls. Moreover, the dumb-bell was surprisingly extendable and flexible. Streets could be of various widths, and as they grew, malls could sprout multiple arms, each with a department store as its anchor, and those arms could extend in many directions.

However, the department store's struggle to remain viable in the face of consolidation, discount retailing, over-retailing, and online retailing necessitated a reimagination of the nature of the anchor. At malls such as the Memorial City Mall in Houston and Broadway Commons in Hicksville, Long Island, the retailer Target replaced a department store as a primary anchor.[4] But at many malls, the anchor is no longer focused on retail, but on experience. This is primarily about entertainment, most typically by adding multiplex movie theaters, and most notoriously by encompassing an entire amusement park, such as at the Edmonton Mall in Ottawa, Canada, or the Mall of America in Bloomington, Minnesota. Increasingly, however, experience encompasses more everyday recreational facilities such as gyms, bowling alleys, and rock climbing facilities. The ice rink is a surprisingly resilient recreational favorite: pioneered by the Houston Galleria when it opened in 1970, ice rinks are currently found at malls such as the Lloyd Center in Portland, Oregon; the Memorial City Mall in Houston; and the Westfield Countryside Mall in Clearwater, Florida. In late 2006, a professional ice rink was built on top of an existing seven-story parking garage as a new anchor for the Ballston Commons Mall in Arlington, Virginia; the MedStar Capitals IcePlex serves as the training facility of the National Hockey League's Washington Capitals, and provides public skating through open skates, lessons, and amateur hockey leagues.

But a more radical re-imagining of the experience anchor is also underway. At the One Hundred Oaks Mall in Nashville, Tennessee, the primary attraction is a branch of the Vanderbilt University Medical Center, which occupies almost half of the 880,000 square feet mall, including the entirety of the second and third floors, as well as a former department store;[5] the rest of the mall remains retail. At the Global Mall at the Crossings in Nashville, the primary anchors, all former department stores, include the Nashville State Community College Southeast campus, the Southeast Community Center, a branch of the Nashville Public Library, and Bridgestone offices; the rest of the mall is retail.[6] The former Roses Department Store at the University Mall in Blacksburg, Virginia, is now the Math Emporium of Virginia Tech University, which contains 60,000 square feet of computer-based teaching space available 24 hours a day/ seven days a week.[7] The remainder of the mall is primarily retail, including a branch of the University's bookstore.

Mix and Audience

Some arcades were almost exclusively retail-focused, such as the Burlington Arcade, which was and remains high-end retail. Others, however, comprised mixed programs, including cafes, services such as hair salons, and apartments found upstairs. Walter Benjamin included a description of the arcade as "a city, a world in miniature, in which customers will find everything they need."[8] In the early department stores, "mix" was more so a condition of merchandise rather than program. Taking advantage of new forms of transportation such as the railroad, owners could import a wide range of goods from further afield, creating a new world of desire for mostly female customers; Le Bon Marche in particular is credited with "pioneer[ing] the idea of the department store as a building purposefully designed for fashionable public assembly."[9]

At the Southdale Center, mix and audience came together in an inventive new way when the centralizing atrium of the department store was shifted to the interior of the mall, creating an even more explicit form of interior collective space (Image 15.1). For Gruen, an Austrian immigrant whose reference was historic European public spaces, the emphasis on a well-designed collective realm—whether indoors or outdoors—was key to his idea that the mall could be an "introverted" center for suburban life.[10] At Southdale, the design of the central atrium included a café, exhibition space, and stage; social life in the space was enhanced through event programming, including fancy dances and concerts.[11] The collective space of the atrium contributed to the programmatic mix that Gruen thought critical to the success of these centers, which at Southdale also included a post office, a supermarket, and, somewhat inexplicably, a petting zoo. And as Gruen hoped, the mall became an important place for "suburbanites…to congregate for many hours."[12]

Gruen further believed that malls could be "satellite downtown areas, offering much of what metropolitan centers give,"[13] but his projects achieved a limited version of this. Rather, it was the Houston Galleria (Phase 1, 1970), designed by Gyo Obata of HOK, which established the real potential of the mall as a City within a Suburb (Image 15.2).[14] Inspired by the Galleria Vittorio Emmanuele in Milan and Rockefeller Center in New York City,[15]

Image 15.1 View of Southdale Shopping Center's central collective space. Image courtesy of A Century of Minnesota Architecture (N1) Northwest Architectural Archives, University of Minnesota Libraries, Minneapolis, Minnesota, United States of America.

the 600,000 square feet Houston Galleria evolved into a classic dumb-bell organization. The large department store anchoring its first end was connected to a wide interior street lined with three floors of retail and covered with a glass barrel-vault. At its "center" was the aforementioned first-of-its-kind ice rink. But other urban components designed by HOK were also integral to the mall, including a 22-story office building (1969); a 400-room hotel (1971); and another 25-story office building (1973). Upon the Galleria's opening in November 1970, Gerald Hines asserted, "(a) shopping center it is not. It will be a new downtown."[16] (Image 15.3)

Subsequent additions reinforced this downtown idea. In July of 1971, an enclosed tennis center, then-called the University Club (now Life Time Galleria Houston), opened on the fourth level of the Galleria; its jogging track encircled the exterior of the barrel-vault, allowing shoppers inside the mall to watch runners passing by. Galleria II, which opened in 1977, not only extended the interior retail street and added another department store anchor, but also added a 7-story office building and a 500-room hotel. A third department store anchor opened in 1979. Galleria III (1986), Galleria IV (2003), and Galleria V (2006) together added another 1,160,000 square feet of retail,[17] extending linear street and anchor in new directions. In 2016, a 30-story residential tower

Image 15.2 View of Galleria Vittorio Emaneule from interior street. Image courtesy of Dora Dragoni [CC BY 3.0 (https://creativecommons.org/licenses/by/3.0)]. https://upload.wikimedia.org/wikipedia/commons/d/d1/Galleria_Vittorio_Emanuele_II_-_panoramio_%286%29.jpg (Accessed January 21, 2019). Original image in color.

of 225 hotel rooms and 75–100 condominiums was proposed for the southwest corner of the mall.[18] With the exception of a few small surface lots, parking is housed in massive, multi-story garages. Thus, while the Galleria's overall square footage is extremely large, its limited site and subsequent verticality produced a footprint that is surprisingly "compact."

For Hines, the mix of programs was about developing multiple audiences across different times: the hotel would provide evening traffic, the office buildings would provide weekday traffic, and the shopping would provide weekend traffic.[19] Amenities would further this mix, which at first included the ice rink, bowling rink, and movie theaters. While only the ice rink remains, food has emerged as a primary experience. A wide range of food options line the ice rink on both sides, many of which have café-style "outdoor" seating, producing particularly lively edges to the rink. At its best, the mall hosts daily life for a variety of not-just-suburban audiences, including office, hotel, and mall workers; ice skaters; morning mall walkers; evening joggers on the track above; and others. (Image 15.4)

If the Galleria's organization, size, mix, and range of audiences produced a "compact," vertical City within a Suburb, the Memorial City Mall,

Image 15.3 View of Galleria Mall from interior ice rink. Image courtesy of Postoak [CC BY 3.0 (https://creativecommons.org/licenses/by/3.0)]. https://commons.wikimedia.org/wiki/File:Galleria-PolarIce.jpg (Accessed September 14, 2022). Original image in color.

approximately eight miles north and west of the Galleria, is a sprawling, horizontal City within a Suburb. Like Northgate, the Memorial City Shopping Center was launched in 1966 as a pedestrian "street," although here completely enclosed, with a single department store anchoring one end; its stores served a rapidly suburbanizing, mostly residential area of west Houston. In the 1970s, however, Conoco Inc. and Shell Oil Company built corporate campuses nearby, subsequently attracting other energy companies. Three additional department store anchors were added to the mall, extending the classic dumb-bell organizational logic, and by 1978, Memorial City Mall was a very large mall of almost entirely retail space. In 2001, owners MetroNational announced redevelopment plans, which included the addition of a professionally sized ice rink for hockey and recreational skating (2003), and later, family focused amenities such as Frolic's Castle, a free indoor playground for kids under 48" tall (2014).[20] Collectively, these reflected the ongoing shift toward experience, although at Memorial City, they complemented rather than replaced traditional department store anchors. Unlike Southdale and the Galleria, the Memorial City Mall has no centralizing atrium in which interior collective space is found. Rather, its primary collective space is an anchor; "the Square," an Astroturf event lawn designed by Kudela & Weinheimer Landscape Architects, opened in 2016 at the western edge of the Mall. While technically outside, it is lined on two sides by restaurants and contiguous to mall circulation such that it connects seamlessly to the interior of the mall. As the main social space, it is heavily programmed with events, including movies, concerts, and Circus Night.[21]

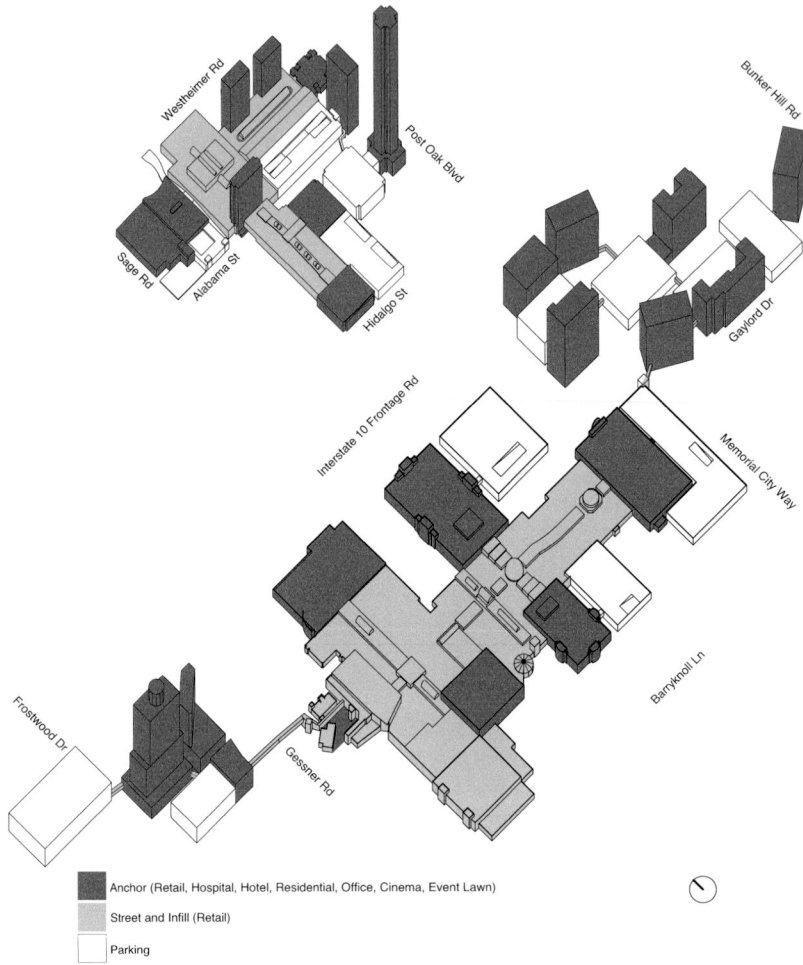

Image 15.4 Comparison of organization and anchors between Galleria Mall (*top*) and Memorial City Mall (*bottom*). Image courtesy of Judith K. De Jong and Rachel Birdsell.

Additional initiatives, however, were more transformative. In 2006, the Memorial Hermann Memorial City Medical Center, located west across a ten-lane road from the Mall, embarked on a massive expansion, including a 33-story tower with a pineapple-like crown that has become the iconic symbol of the area. Soon thereafter, the Mall built a pedestrian skybridge that connected the medical complex and an adjacent hotel (2011) directly into the linear street of the Mall, effectively making them the Mall's western anchor. In 2012, the Mall owners extended the skybridge to the eastern edge, connecting to a series of new office towers, a new residential tower, and another new hotel (2017), all of which effectively become the Mall's eastern anchors.[22] While parking is increasingly found in multi-story garages, the Mall sits within a large surface lot, and thus it still feels suburban. But like the Galleria, the mix of programs enables a range of audiences for whom the mall is an important part of everyday life, including medical center personnel; office, hotel, and mall workers; families, particularly with children; mall walkers; residents of the adjacent apartment buildings; and others.

The Future of the City within a Suburb

The transformation of the Memorial City Mall is typical insofar as it began as a relatively small, almost exclusively retail-focused place, and evolved over 50 years into a City within a Suburb; this process is fundamentally one of urbanizing. Also common is that the Memorial City Mall urbanized in tandem with the surrounding Energy Corridor area, which evolved from a largely residential suburb with two corporate campuses to the third largest employment area in the Houston region in 2018.[23] The parallel, often symbiotic, transformation of urbanizing malls and urbanizing suburbs is occurring elsewhere as well, including Tysons Center in Tysons Corner, Virginia, and the Old Orchard Mall in Skokie, Illinois, among others. The apotheosis of this interconnected urbanization is, not surprisingly, the Galleria. While designed more unusually from the outset as a City within a Suburb, the surrounding Uptown area has urbanized so rapidly and dramatically—and has thereby influenced the further urbanization of the mall—that the Galleria might even have become a City within a City. Might others follow? Regardless, while their origin, scale, and degree and speed of transformation may differ, the sprawling, horizontal Memorial City Mall, the "compact," vertical Houston Galleria—and all the City within a Suburb versions in-between—combine organization, anchor, mix, and audience to important collective effect. The future of the mall does indeed depend on it.

Notes

1 This essay develops from Judith K. De Jong, "Mall Futures," in *MONU: Interior Urbanism*, #21, Autumn 2014 (www.monu-magazine.com) and *New SubUrbanisms* (New York: Routledge, 2014).
2 Walter Benjamin, *The Arcades Project* (Cambridge, MA: Harvard University Press, 1999), 871.
3 Alex Wall, *Victor Gruen: From Urban Shop to New City* (Barcelona: Actar, 2005), 102.
4 Ironically, Target was founded by the Dayton Company in Minneapolis.
5 https://www.greshamsmith.com/project/vanderbilt-medical-center-one-hundred-oaks-mall/ Accessed October 21, 2018.
6 Wood S. Caldwell, "Hickory Hollow, Nashville's Next Big Comeback," *The Tennessean*, May 25, 2015. https://www.tennessean.com/story/money/real-estate/2015/05/22/hickory-hollow-nashvilles-next-big-comeback/27816909/ Accessed October 5, 2018.
7 Daniel de Vise, "At Virginia Tech, Computers Help Solve a Math Class Problem," *The Washington Post*, April 22, 2012. https://www.washingtonpost.com/local/education/at-virginia-tech-computers-help-solve-a-math-class-problem/2012/04/22/gIQAmAOmaT_story.html Accessed September 10, 2018.
8 *Illustrated Guide to Paris*, in Benjamin, *The Arcades Project*, 873.
9 Brian Nelson, "Introduction," in *The Ladies Paradise by Emile Zola,* translated with an Introduction and Notes by Brian Nelson (Oxford: Oxford University Press, 1995), xi–xii.
10 Victor Gruen and Lawrence P. Smith, "Shopping Centers: The New Building Type," *Progressive Architecture*, June 1952, 68–69.
11 Wall, *Victor Gruen*, 97–99.
12 Gruen and Smith, "Shopping Centers: The New Building Type," 68.
13 Gruen and Smith, "Shopping Centers: The New Building Type," 68.
14 "City within a suburb" is often used in real estate materials and articles regarding "lifestyle centers" and denser development.
15 Stephen Fox, "5015 Westheimer Road," in *Houston Architectural Guide*, 2nd ed., ed. Gerald Moorhead and Yolita Schmidt (Houston, TX: American Institute of Architects/Houston Chapter and Herring Press, 1999), 243.
16 Fox, "5015 Westheimer Road," 243.

17 Flori Meeks, "A Look Back: Galleria's Opening Caught World's Eye," *The Houston Chronicle*, September 4, 2012. https://www.chron.com/memorial/news/article/A-look-back-Galleria-s-opening-caught-world-s-eye-3838796.php#item-85307-tbla-3 Accessed October 26, 2018.

18 Erin Mulvaney, "Galleria Plans a Tall Addition with New 30-Story Hotel, Residential Tower," https://www.chron.com/business/real-estate/article/Galleria-plans-a-tall-addition 7233265.php%20%20 Accessed%20October%2026 Accessed November 4, 2018.

19 Lisa Gray, "The Galleria," in *Hines: A Legacy of Quality in the Built Environment*, Mark Seal (Bainbridge Island, WA: Fenwick Publishing Group, 2007), 70.

20 Joy Sewing, "Houston Kids to Frolic at World's Largest Mall Playground," *Houston Chronicle*, October 9, 2014. https://www.houstonchronicle.com/life/article/Houston-kids-to-frolic-at-world-s-largest-mall-5812735.php Accessed January 3, 2016; Mike Sheridan, "Metronational Undertakes $500 Million Urban Community Project in Houston," *NREI*, August 23, 2001. https://www.nreionline.com/news/metronational-undertakes-500-million-urban-community-project-houston Accessed January 3, 2016.

21 http://www.memorialcity.com/venue/the-square-at-memorial-city/ Accessed November 4, 2018.

22 "MemorialCityWelcomeKit," http://www.memorialcity.com/ Accessed November 4, 2018.

23 "Where Energy Moves," http://www.energycorridor.org/about Accessed November 4, 2018.

Chapter 16

The Supermarket
An Edible Urban Interior

Nerea Feliz

Archizoom Associati's 1970s dystopian "No-Stop City" manifesto affirmed, *The city no longer "represents" the system, but becomes the system itself, programmed and isotropic... Production and Consumption possess* (sic) *one and the same ideology, which is that of Programming.*[3] No-Stop City portrayed the future of the capitalist metropolis as an endless supermarket, an infinite urban interior. This dystopian project was not an alternative to reality but an amplification of existing conditions, an endless multiplication of a standard 15′ × 15′ supermarket interior with a grid of columns that they referred to as a "quantitative utopia"[4]—an inescapable isotropic field. Today, the supermarket is a global typology and a quintessential part of the contemporary *quotidian*. The ubiquity of the supermarket has saturated the global environment with self-similar, large-scale urban and suburban interiors. This chapter analyzes the supermarket as an interior urbanism embodying more than an enclosed environment concealed within architecture. Rather, it is an intersectional entity where the relationships between micro conditions (data, goods, furnishings, and fixtures) and macro flows (logistics, global infrastructures, societal aspirations, and consumption patterns) are inextricably linked (Image 16.1).

From the Circulation of Products to the Creation of Global Networks

Archizoom Associati identified the "programming" nature of the urban interiority of consumption. The design of contemporary supermarkets is determined by logistics, data collection, computational technology, and neoliberal economic imperatives. In his book "The Rule of Logistics: Walmart and the Architecture of Fulfillment," Jesse LeCavalier describes logistics as "*the science of managing things in space and time,*" and Walmart's supermarkets as "*valves*" controlling the circulation of people and goods.[5] Although not new, markets have always involved logistics to some extent. The ancient market was located at the lowest point of the city as if to imply that everything should naturally flow toward it. Trade routes determined the location of cities and vice versa; the urban core

DOI: 10.4324/9780429443091-18

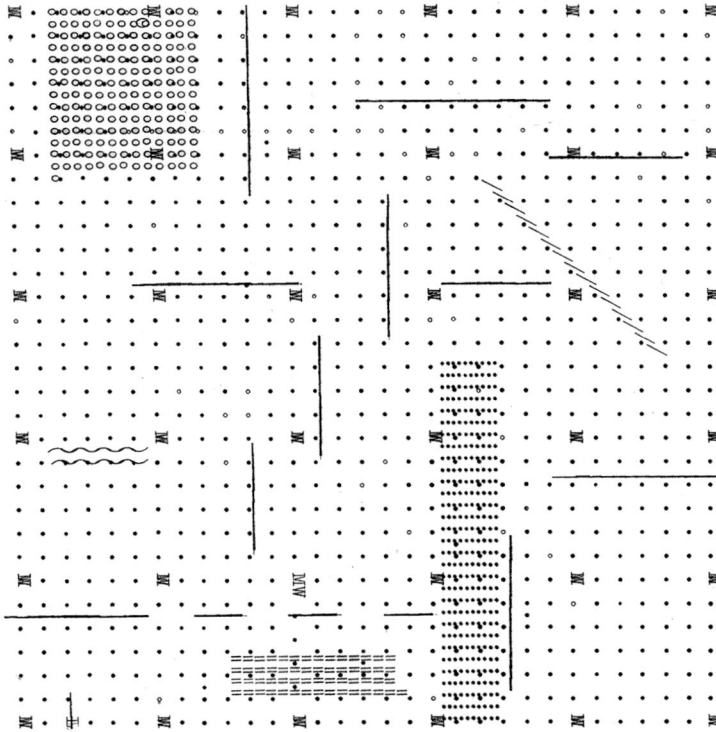

Image 16.1 "Diagrama Abitativo Omogeneo, Ipotesi di Linguaggio Architettonico non Figurativo" by Archizoom Associati.
Credit: Andrea Branzi

was embodied by the market. Max Weber explains how the city originates in economic terms as a market center where locals and rural inhabitants exchange goods.[6] Markets have always worked as "valves"; however, today the extent and the speed of the flow of commodities are unprecedented.

Contemporary food networks constitute a worldwide pulsating organism; the "No-Stop City" appellation could be reinterpreted to designate the permanent state of flux in merchandise. If the ancient market constituted a bottom-up system defined by local connections among multiple vendors and citizens, contemporary consumption is defined by international corporations that dominate the food industry by perfecting top-down logistics. The central task of commerce logistics is designing the flow and circulation of products, including wholesale, distribution, and merchandising of goods at a global scale. Mass consumption, technological innovation, transportation advances, and globalization have deeply transformed the market from its original form as a regional, bottom-up system into the contemporary supermarket and hypermarket—a spatial product of global logistics.

From the Domestic Fridge to the Origin of a New Architectural Typology

The birth of the supermarket as a typology also reflects the recursive relationship between the "micro" and the "macro." Americans' early use of domestic refrigerators in the 1920s fundamentally disrupted consumption patterns.

New domestic appliances allowed them to significantly increase the quantity of food that could be stored at home. Additionally, private automobiles facilitated the transport of a greater volume of groceries, and less trips to the market were necessary. Shifting patterns of consumption created a growing demand for larger stores. Richard Longstreth identifies Los Angeles' drive-in stores, grocery stores connected to gas stations, as the embryo of the supermarket.[7] With the proliferation of automobiles, the drive-in format became increasingly convenient. Rising care ownership and the use of air conditioning further contributed to the proliferation of grocery stores. In 1928, Ralph's Grocery Company opened its first self-service store in Southern California.[8] The new self-service store format broke from conventional retail practices while reducing the number of employees. Consumers enjoyed roaming freely within the novel, neutral, diaphanous, and non-hierarchical space. A new retail typology of standalone buildings with abundant parking for automobile owners emerged. These complexes were privately owned and managed; the assortment of products was devised to enhance the desirability of the others. Stores targeted a newly identified audience, the middle-class suburban household.

World War II depleted the workforce, motivating an increase in the number of self-service stores.[9] The car, refrigerator, and air conditioning enabled the birth of a new type of retail space. In 1948, Morris Ketchum declared in *Progressive Architecture* that

> no modern store can function properly without provision for up-to-date heating, ventilating, and air conditioning ... public demand has made air-conditioning ... one of the most important factors in store planning.... Air conditioning helps to prevent merchandise spoilage, reduces cleaning bills, and increases personnel efficiency ... larger stores cannot operate efficiently without it.[10]

Mechanically engineered climates enabled the autonomy of interior space from exterior climate, and therefore, the progressive enlargement of interior spaces. By 1950, the new retail model pioneered by California's retailers had sprawled across the United States.[11]

From Data to Built Form

Universal and extraordinarily familiar, an average contemporary supermarket is 41,300 square feet.[12] Infrastructural in nature, the logistical character of supermarkets made them an early product of Mario Carpo's paradigm change from the architecture of objects to the iterative character of the architecture of "objectiles."[13] Jesse LeCavalier explains that each of Walmart's individual supermarkets is a locally adapted version of generic prototype stores. Regional demands, such as demand for particular produce and goods, building codes, and zoning ordinances, determine their final square footage and layout.[14] Under the supermarket's universal appearance, each store has highly customized goods tailored to localized needs identified by computing technology through data collection.[15] Walmart's data centers keep record of all individual purchases for two years; its inventory software allows Walmart to react to customer behaviors dictating the supply of goods, allocation of items in the store, etc.[16] A product's top-up protocol is digitally activated when an article's quantity decreases to a critical predetermined number.[17] The latest technologies help expedite the global supply of products from producers to retailers and consumers, while cutting costs and maximizing sales. There is a constant feedback loop of data and product circulation. Supermarkets and hypermarkets operate within vast infrastructural networks as "*containers*" and "*conduits*" of both people and merchandise.[18]

From Edible Bricks to an Urban Scale Biological Microcosm

Contemporary supermarkets host an exceptional array of biodiversity that cannot be paralleled by any natural ecosystem. A typical supermarket carries around 42,000 products.[19] The biological microcosm of the supermarket is an encapsulated, intensified version of the natural world that establishes an almost indexical relationship between its internal selection of produce and the agrarian world outside. Avocados from Mexico, pineapples from Costa Rica, tomatoes from the Netherlands, rib-eye steak from South Dakota fed with Iowa grain, salmon from Alaska—most products at the supermarket have traveled more than their average consumer. Within this engineered interior landscape of perishable goods, everything seems to be fresh, sprayed, burnished; nature is exuberant, imperishable, harmless, generous, and inexhaustible.

The correlation between the micro (goods) and the macro (logistics) has governed the evolution of the supermarket typology. Engaging all senses, the interior of the supermarket is built of food items, or consumable "bricks," competing for the manipulation of desire by stimulating unconscious physical and psychological reactions. Supermarkets share a sensory layout. First, sight is engaged; the bountiful section of produce is always located at the entrance. Smell is next; customers need to cross the bakery that is strategically positioned adjacent to the central aisles. Music plays; promotional tastings complete this multisensory experience. LED lighting intensifies the persuasive messages on the bright-colored packaging. Spatially, content becomes the container of space. Food items adopt traditionally architectural functions. The piles of goods take on an intermediate dimension between the urban (space) and the architectural (form), conforming into edible walls, streets suitable for cart traffic, and gardens of fresh produce.

The design of supermarkets defies conventional disciplinary hierarchies, interior layout and the display of salable contents is primary and architecture is secondary. Here, the conventional design process has been reversed. Inventory management and display protocols inform the layout of the shopping floor.[20] The display of goods and the circulation of contents dictate the design of each store. The architectural envelope supports and is contingent on its inner layout. The absence of expression and semantic meaning of the big-box shed contrasts with the hyper-coded packaging of the products for sale. Iconographic and cultural signifiers shift from architecture to the world of merchandising. The supermarket's interior consists of smooth and shiny surfaces and polished concrete floors, it disappears as an indeterminate backdrop behind a mesmerizing exuberance of food illuminated by fluorescent light. The dazzling aesthetics of packaging design dominate the space. Merchandise graphics compete to attract and sustain the viewers' attention. The illusion of infinite availability of goods and produce emerges when walking through endless aisles of self-similar items. The interior of the supermarket evokes an inhabitable still-life composition, a celebration of perishable material pleasures curated by logistical optimization and economic forces. Pop artists such as Andy Warhol fetishized merchandising graphics and their role in culture and consumerism. The spectacle of consumption and the still-life "on steroids" nature of the supermarket interior fascinated the avant-garde movement that elevated the supermarket and commonplace products to an art form that started to merge art and everyday life.[21]

From Minor Technical Adjustments to Radical Economic Savings and Labor Transformations

How are logistics manifested in the interior design of the supermarket? LeCavalier describes the way interior design in the supermarket is dictated by technology, management systems, and economic performance criteria, that is, by commerce logistics instead of design.[22] The standardization of components saves costs in materials, assembly, and maintenance. When it comes to incrementing sales, speed of supply, and profits, minor adjustments can generate huge economic gains. Walmart's initiative to change their refrigerator's vitrine lighting system from fluorescent fixtures to optimized LEDs resulted in an open call to lighting manufacturers requesting the design of cutting-edge fixtures that were not available yet in the market.[23] With this example, Le Cavalier explains how the extensive size and scale of international food corporations allows them to drive and challenge technology manufacturers, in a context where every interior design feature has been carefully calibrated to maximize sales and productivity.

If self-service revolutionized the market typology at the beginning of the twentieth century by making customers perform vendor's tasks, the current automation and digitization of labor could render in-store human employees completely unnecessary. In 2017, Walmart filed a patent to create a system of assistant drones to check prices and find products for shoppers.[24] Another patent would equip shopping carts with sensors to report on their contents and their location.[25] Walmart has investigated using cameras and electrical transmitters to monitor shelves, ensuring that they remain stocked.[26] Amazon's first physical grocery store, Amazon Go, eliminated check-out desks. Exhaustive camera surveillance, monitoring systems, and a new app allow Amazon to accurately bill its customers.[27] Human workers may be cheaper than AI for now, but as technology advances, the situation could look very different.

From Iconographic Packaging to an Ethnographic Taxonomy

Commerce engages a network of information and capital involving profound social and cultural desires. These complex relationships constitute a variable organic system hosted at the market. Behind the supermarket's layout and shelving distribution, there is what food marketing specialist Michael Moss describes as a fiercely competitive industry, fighting for "stomach share."[28] Consumption is not merely passive; the orderliness and quasi-clinical neatness of the supermarket interior disguises its relationship to fundamental desire, as well as to complex social and psychological aspirations. The fetishization of goods enhances salability. Semiotically charged packaging is both the container of products and the vessel for cultural and sociological messages. Tracking the plurality of shifting and emerging notions of lifestyle, the consumable character of goods on display turns the interior of the supermarket into a snapshot of society. The items for sale define an ethnographic taxonomy mirroring the plurality of cultural and socioeconomic forces. In this respect, the supermarket can be understood as a commercial manifestation of the collective unconscious. An accurate commercial portrait of society emerges from this interior revealing tangible qualities—what we eat and consume, as well as intangible aspects such as shifting societal beliefs and aspirations.

From Physical to Virtual and a New Hybrid Market Space

Archizoom Associati anticipated the pervasive expansion of the project of consumption. With the globalization of online shopping, Archizoom's dystopian overlap of production and consumption has become a reality. E-commerce has made consumption ubiquitous; shopping has become a state of mind that takes place anywhere with an internet connection. Retail's perpetual desire to increase consumer activity has invaded our personal phones and computers. This never-ending shopping space is being created by the digitized economy of the twenty-first century. Walter Benjamin described strolling, selecting, purchasing, and consuming as activities that defined modern life. Today, those same activities take place online. The contemporary flâneur strolls through social media, encounters commodities, compares product reviews, analyzes prices, selects, purchases, and consumes online. Indulging in this form of consumption is a substantial part of contemporary "leisure" time.[29]

Many retailers operate both online and offline; it is not an online versus offline battle, while Amazon started opening physical stores; Walmart continues to increase their online presence. Tracking our shopping habits and using targeted advertising to influence our behavior, contemporary retailers are beginning to shape an emerging "hybrid marketplace" that combines physical and virtual spaces. Augmented shopping makes consumerism more persuasive by communicating directly to customers through their mobile phones to influence behavior inside the store. Using Bluetooth-enabled "beacons" that communicate with installed apps, sellers can trigger alerts on shopper's smartphones as they pass certain locations.[30] Purchase history records can be used to make live shopping suggestions. The power of these "beacons" to impact consumers' conduct in real time can affect the way customers move through a store, interact with products, and eventually will modify both retailers' and customers' understanding of the conventional sensory experience and overall perception of retail space. Using information about real-time consumer interactions might redefine the interface of shopping technology. We can assume that online and offline shopping activities will be further entangled in the new hybrid marketplace, simultaneously physical and virtual.

Conclusion

Across history, urban interiors have often been associated with vast interior commercial spaces. From souks and bazaars to arcades and the contemporary mall, retail has often provided a space for informal assembly and congregation.

Despite their commercial character, the souk and the bazaar provided citizens with privileged nodes of socialization and a strong sense of communal identity and ownership of public space. In contrast, contemporary supermarkets and hypermarkets are plain food supply infrastructures where people move through even faster than the merchandise. In opposition to the generic, unappealing, and logistical nature of the supermarket, the personal customization of the emerging "hybrid market space" can trap consumers in an infinite loop of shopping desire. A "No-Stop E-Shopping City" that is individual, insular, and solitary (Image 16.2).

In 1985, Andy Warhol famously said: *"Lock up a department store today, open the door after a hundred years and you will have a Museum of Modern Art"*[31]. A hundred years from now, a supermarket may not be a museum of art, but it will be a relic due to the pace of technological transformation in commerce fueled by neoliberal economics. The technologies operating today will undoubtedly change and even disappear in favor of new ones. The prospects of online and augmented shopping and new forms of delivery will further determine the physical evolution of the supermarket interior. Robotic technology and

Image 16.2 Andy Warhol shops at Gristede's market in New York, 1964. Photographer: Bob Adelman. ©Bob Adelman Estate

digital monitoring systems continue to accelerate and automatize traditionally human tasks. Challenging privacy through surveillance and data mining, the contemporary conflict among public indoor life, corporate territorial control, and social manipulation is essential in the urban interior. Supermarkets are the spatial manifestation of data manipulated by corporate interests. Algorithms, data management, and virtuality are increasingly universal design tools, and the urban interior of the supermarket sits at the forefront of a novel spatial understanding often neglected by interior design discourse.

Interior design that begins with the display of a can of soup has profound societal implications, including changes in transportation networks, agricultural production, labor dynamics, cultural trends, etc. The supermarket epitomizes a kind of interior urbanism that in its territorial implications, infrastructural nature, and virtual extent cannot be solely understood in traditional disciplinary terms as a manufactured and heavily engineered microcosm concealed within architecture; it is the dynamic and pervading intersection of micro conditions and macro flows.

Acknowledgment

Portions of this chapter were presented in the ACSA 2018 International Conference and published in its proceedings.

Notes

1 Andrea Branzi, *No-Stop City, Archizoom Associati* (Paris: HYX, Librarie de L'Architecture de la ville, 2006), 178.
2 Ibid., 179.
3 Ibid., 178.
4 Ibid., 179.
5 Jesse LeCavalier, *The Rule of Logistics: Walmart and the Architecture of Fulfillment* (Minneapolis, MN: University of Minnesota Press, 2016), Kindle edition.
6 Max Weber, "The nature of the city," in *Classic Essays on the Culture of Cities,* ed. Richard Sennet (Appleton-Century-Crofts, NJ: Prentice Hall, 1969).
7 Richard Longstreth, *The Drive-In, the Supermarket, and the Transformation of Commercial Space in Los Angeles 1914–1941* (London: MIT Press, 2000).
8 Ibid., 82.
9 Ibid., 163.
10 Morris Ketchum, *Shops and Stores* (New York: Reinhold, 1948), 90, 92, in Sze Tsung Leong and Srdjan Jovanovich Weiss, "Air conditioning," in *Project on the City 2, Harvard Design School Guide to Shopping*, ed. Chuihua Judy Chung, Jeffrey Inaba, Rem Koolhaas, Sze Tsung Leong (Germany: Taschen, 2001) 114.
11 Richard Longstreth, *The Drive-In, the Supermarket, and the Transformation of Commercial Space in Los Angeles 1914–1941* (London: MIT Press, 2000) 163.
12 "*Supermarket Facts*" Food Marketing Institute, accessed July 14, 2018, https://www.fmi.org/our-research/supermarket-facts
13 Mario Carpo, *The Alphabet and the Algorithm* (Cambridge, MA and London: The MIT Press 2011), 126.
14 LeCavalier. Kindle edition.
15 Ibid.
16 Ibid.
17 Ibid.
18 Ibid.
19 "Supermarket facts" Food Marketing Institute.
20 LeCavalier. Kindle edition.

21 Cristoph Grunenberg, "The American supermarket," in *Shopping*, ed. Cristoph Grunenberg and Max Hollein (Ostfildern-Ruit, Germany: Hatje Cantz Publishers, 2002), 171.

22 LeCavalier. Kindle edition.

23 Ibid.

24 Eleanor Gibson, "Walmart files patent for drone shopping assistants." *Dezeen*, March 27, 2018. https://www.dezeen.com/2018/03/27/walmart-patent-drone-shopping-assistant-robot-wearable-technology/

25 Ibid.

26 Ibid.

27 Laura Bliss, "Amazon go might kill more than just supermarkets." *CITYLAB*, March 14, 2018. https://www.citylab.com/life/2018/03/the-unbearable-sadness-of-amazon-go/555254/

28 Michael Moss, "Navigating the supermarket aisles" video found in: Emily Weinstein, "Pots and pans, but little pain." *The New York Times*, April 30, 2013. https://www.nytimes.com/2013/05/01/dining/making-lunch-with-michael-pollan-and-michael-moss.html

29 Nerea Feliz, "No-stop shopping city, supermarkets, hybrid space, and the logistics of the quotidien." *New Instrumentalities*, Proceedings of the 2018 ACSA International Conference.

30 Sabrina Korber, "Retail's "beacon" of hope: shopping that's personal." *CNBC*, May 26, 2015. https://www.cnbc.com/2015/05/26/retails-newest-brick-and-mortar-bet.html

31 Cristoph Grunenberg and Max Hollein, *Shopping* (Ostfildern-Ruit, Germany: Hatje Cantz Publishers, 2002), 91.

Chapter 17

The Hotel
Revisiting the Bonaventure

Gregory Marinic

Throughout the 1960s and 1970s, architect John Portman designed and developed several unprecedented projects in the United States that blended consumer culture and architecture. Massive in scope, these works responded to shifting socio-economic conditions with a groundbreaking approach to urban redevelopment. One of these projects, the Bonaventure hotel and retail complex, sprawls across an urban renewal district in downtown Los Angeles. Like a time capsule of late twentieth-century aesthetics with its Brutalist concrete podium and towers wrapped in mirrored-glass curtain walls, the Bonaventure aspired to be a city in miniature.[1] In his seminal critique of 1984, Fredric Jameson proclaimed that Portman actually had designed a hyperspace—a mini-city—an entirely hermetic urban experience that embodied a unique postmodern socio-spatiality.[2]

Portman's work demonstrates only one approach that integrated the outdoors into hotel interior spaces of its time. Throughout the 1960s and 1970s, a global array of projects, including the El Conquistador Hotel (1965) in Puerto Rico by Morris Lapidus, Camino Real Polanco Hotel (1968) in Mexico City by Ricard Legorreta, Hôtel La Grande Motte (1970) in France by Jean Balladur, and the Haludovo Palace Hotel (1972) in Croatia by Boris Magaš, expressed interiorized urban characteristics; however, the Bonaventure stood apart for its unique postmodern spatiality. Since opening in 1976, it has been roundly criticized for its fortress-like architecture but continues to assert a long-term influence on popular culture. This chapter revisits the Bonaventure to examine hotel complexities and social dynamics of the late modern era. It focuses on the 1980s critiques of Fredric Jameson and Jean Baudrillard to reassess the Bonaventure within postmodern discourse, more recent scholarship, and our current age of disinformation, global pandemics, social fragmentation, and retail decline.

Interior Streets

Portman's monumental Los Angeles Bonaventure, San Francisco Embarcadero Center, and Detroit Renaissance Center may be traced to principles initially

DOI: 10.4324/9780429443091-19

tested in the 1960s Atlanta Peachtree Center master plan. Opening in 1967, the Hyatt Regency Atlanta, the first Portman atrium hotel, radically transformed the hotel typology into a microcosm of the city.[3] Portman borrowed many outdoor functions associated with the Copenhagen Tivoli precedent that he favored—window-shopping, café-sitting, and people-watching—and employed these activities as interior programs.[4] Portman drew from the faded memory of a bustling downtown to create a parallel experience at a massive scale—a spectacular, utopian, and autonomous interiorized environment.

In the decade before the Hyatt Regency Atlanta opened, the convergence of mall culture, fantasy entertainment, and thematic design began shifting expectations for building interiors at a civic scale. During this time, "outdoor translated into indoor" concepts were integrated into suburban shopping malls in cities across North America, as well as within theme parks and world's fair architecture across the globe. In suburban Minneapolis, Southdale Center (1956) was the first indoor, multi-story shopping center in the United States. Southdale was developed by the Dayton Company department store and designed by Victor Gruen, an Austrian-born architect and pioneer of American shopping mall design. As a European socialist, Gruen was critical of the suburban lifestyle of 1950s America and sought through his work to transform suburban retail environments into communal gathering places where people would shop and socialize.[5] Gruen modeled Southdale on the arcades and café culture of Central European cities by hybridizing retail with entertainment while introducing perceived "public" social space into a suburban context. As a new model for communal space, a climate-controlled and privately owned suburban interior space, Southdale impacted the aesthetics of an entire generation of suburban shopping malls. Setting the standard for the modern, climate-controlled, and ideal shopping experience, it fundamentally addressed emerging pressures and reactions within the urban core.

In the 1960s, Portman employed design tactics in American city centers much like those used by Gruen in American suburbs during the previous decade. *The New York Times* architecture critic Herbert Muschamp began referring to his Portman's Peachtree Center in downtown Atlanta as "architecture at happy hour."[6] Upon opening in 1967, the Hyatt Regency Atlanta was wildly popular in the mainstream and academic media. Paul Goldberger stated that it was the first contemporary concept that brought an urban experience into a building, and that Portman was "…the only architect of his era to create not only a series of significant buildings, but a new urban type."[7] The observations of both Muschamp and Goldberger embraced this very different vision for vast interior spaces in the urban core.

By the 1970s, the increasingly large scale of Portman projects, culminating in the Detroit Renaissance Center, revealed the notable suspicion of central cities by white Americans in the suburbs, as well as Portman's personal ambitions as both an architect and a developer.[8] While American cities sought a bold rebound from the turbulent social divisions of the previous decade, city centers remained largely avoided by white middle-class suburbanites. With their fantastical hyperspaces, Portman projects in Atlanta, Los Angeles, and Detroit sought to lure the "white flight" generation back downtown with interiorized urbanism.[9]

Sheathed in an otherworldly late modern 1970s aesthetic, Portman projects in Detroit and Los Angeles reflected the cinematic world of Fritz Lang's *Metropolis* by blending a normative suburban shopping mall with glass towers and a convention hotel to create an autonomous urbanism. As Muschamp famously noted, Portman translated exterior functions into the interior to replace the conventional downtown with a parallel experience that was separate, controllable, and thus, utopian.[10] Portman recomposed cinematic visions and Space Age fantasies into physical form as placeholders for the real city.

By the early 1980s, the tide had turned on Portman with increasing criticism that drew attention to how his projects had rejected the city. Theorist Fredric Jameson was famously confused by the "postmodern hyperspace" of the Bonaventure, an observation that would figure prominently in his 1984 essay and later book, *Postmodernism, or the Cultural Logic of Late Capitalism*. Jameson's reading of the building provoked the memorable "Bonaventure Debates" of the late 1980s. By the early 2000s, a new generation of critics, including Reinhold Martin, Edward Soja, Peter Brooker, Mohsen Mostafavi, K. Michael Hayes, Alexander Porter, Charles Rice, Preston Scott Cohen, Jennifer Bonner, and others, took renewed interest in Portman and the urbanity of his interior spaces. Their intersecting insights underscore the importance of Portman projects within late twentieth-century urban morphology.[11]

Late Modernism Meets Postmodernism

The 1965 and 1992 Los Angeles riots were sparked by police brutality in neighborhoods besieged with multigenerational poverty and racial segregation. As an architecture of monumental scale, the Bonaventure was designed to ignore such realities and create an aspirational city-within-a-city. Confusing and difficult to navigate, how does the Bonaventure reflect Jameson's postmodern spatiality? Jameson points to the spatial narrative as a primary structure for his claim.[12] He asserts that Portman reveals postmodernity through an alternative engagement of the human body in an existential and interpretive relationship with space. Jameson says, "…(Portman) attempts to see our physical trajectories through such buildings as virtual narratives or stories, as dynamic paths and narrative paradigms which we as visitors are asked to fulfill and complete with our own bodies and movements."[13]

In the early 1960s, late Modernism began challenging the singularity of the International Style by migrating away from pure functionalism, while retaining many of its formal impulses. In the Bonaventure, Portman paired the aesthetics of curtain-wall lightness espoused by Mies van der Rohe with a monolithic, Brutalist concrete podium that visually responded to social uncertainties. This marriage of the International Style's transparency and Brutalism's formidable impermeability illustrates one of the most salient legacies of Portman's 1970s mega-hotels. His second generation of hotel hyperspaces, including the Peachtree Plaza in Atlanta, The Bonaventure in Los Angeles, and Renaissance Center in Detroit, extended and transformed the principles of the Hyatt Regency Atlanta atrium hotel prototype by pairing a Brutalist base with the formal purity of mirrored glass towers (Image 17.1).

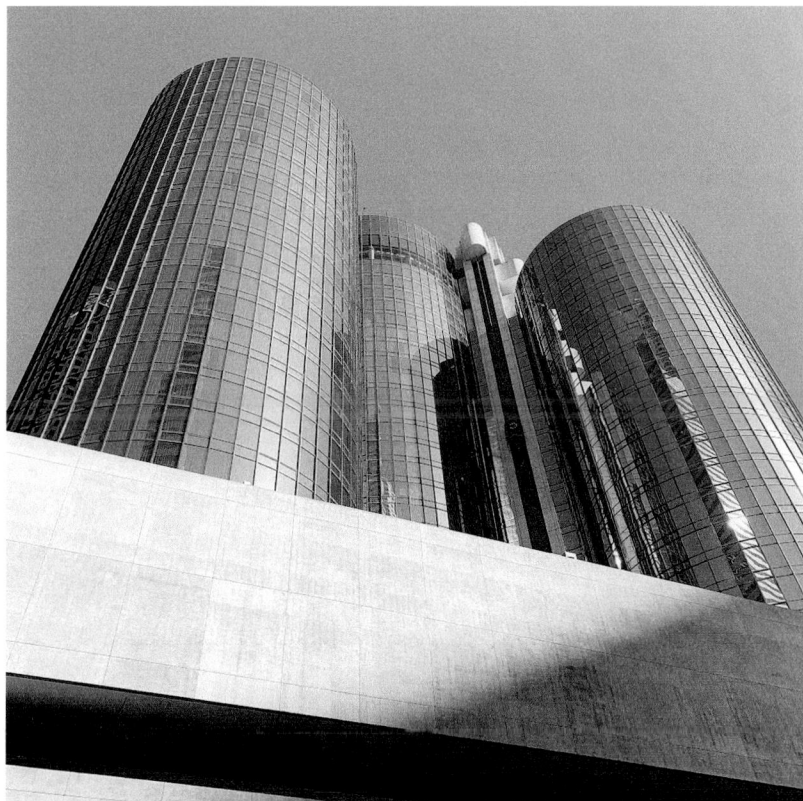

Image 17.1 Exterior view of the Los Angeles Bonaventure.
Credit: Gregory Marinc

Among the greatest ironies of using a hybrid Brutalist-High Tech architectural aesthetic for the Los Angeles Bonaventure podium is the mixed message that it conveyed to the public. Thus, the style was viewed by the American middle class as an architecture of socialism and urban decay rather than comfort and luxury. These perceptions undergirded the widespread unpopularity of Brutalism in the United States as both an ideology and an architectural style. Nevertheless, the Bonaventure podium is Brutalist, while its sleek, mirrored-glass towers are coded as late Modernism, resulting in an external aura that is neither purely Brutalist nor high-tech. Its postmodernity, Jameson asserts, is expressed in an interior spatial language, through its confounding interiority. Unlike the visual clarity of Modernism with its intentional connections between interior and exterior, relationships that were intentionally continuous, the Bonaventure subverts such connectivity. Like a suburban metaphor for living and consuming, the outdoors are made indoors, while the rest of downtown is deemed peripheral or non-existent (Image 17.2).

For Jameson, understanding the Bonaventure must be tied to acknowledging its postmodern spatiality. Here, the postmodern is not mere symbolism, historicism, or kitsch; postmodernity is embodied by an avant-garde interior-exterior complexity and chaotic signifiers. This "misunderstood postmodernity" of the Bonaventure has been widely criticized as unclear and anti-urban. This argument reflects nineteenth-century expectations

Image 17.2 Looking up toward the exterior of the Los Angeles Bonaventure. Credit: Gregory Marinic

that endure in our contemporary age for an expressly exterior-oriented urbanism. Nevertheless, to fully appreciate the Jameson's reading of the Bonaventure's unique hyperspatiality, one must embrace the notion of an indoor city (Image 17.3).

Building on Jean Baudrillard's perspective on the death of the subject through an enslavement to mass-media, as well as Foucault's critique of subjectivity, the spatial freedom of the Bonaventure demonstrates the death of a defined style in the late twentieth century and the return to something more personal and intuitive.[14] Jameson claims that pastiche thrives in societies where the "media-enslaved" are uncritical. This postmodern spatial pastiche reflects a media-dominated culture, as well as a public who lack subjectivity and a desire for high art. His observations can be applied to our contemporary moment to the visual cultures and pathologies of current social media—Facebook, Instagram, Twitter, and so on—spaces of profound misinformation, confusion, displacement, and narcissism.

Claiming that capitalism and consumer commodification have destroyed the ability for contemporary culture to produce something authentically new, Jameson further rationalizes that postmodern pastiche reveals

Image 17.3 Interior view of concrete ramps and stairs within the podium base of the Los Angeles Bonaventure.
Credit: Gregory Marinic

an inability to create new "styles" as they are thought to have already been invented. Thus, art and the past are endlessly recycled, and Modernism becomes merely a postmodern code. As discussed herein, Portman coded the building envelope of his Bonaventure as "modern" while simultaneously exploring postmodern interiority. Jameson explains the appeal of nostalgia and reinterpreting the past in postmodern art and architecture. The commodification of culture and a recycled past created what he terms a "schizophrenic disposition" within postmodern space.[15] For Jameson, postmodern schizophrenia derives from a lack of historicity, or rather, the disappearance of history as society endlessly revisits its past (Image 17.4).

Jameson, Aureli, and Baudrillard in the Bonaventure

The ponderings of Fredric Jameson, Pier Vittorio Aureli, and Jean Baudrillard provide overlapping theoretical insights into postmodern spatial complexity based on divergent rationales. Considered in relation to the Bonaventure, each theorist's ideas may be applied to interrogate urban-scale interiors. Confusion, infinity, and anonymity operate in similar yet different ways when applied to indoor urbanism. Each aspect impacts the spatial understandings and

Image 17.4 Interior view of podium base with lobby lake, shopping gallery, and elevators in the Los Angeles Bonaventure.
Credit: Gregory Marinic

parameters of an urban interior hyperspace, and to shift its perceived effects. Jameson's notion of confusion within the unmappable Bonaventure engages with Archizoom's parallel urban investigations of the same era. In his book *The Possibility of an Absolute Architecture*, Aureli examines lateral infinities operating within the work of Archizoom and Hilberseimer as total spaces of popular culture, capitalism, and consumption.[16] Both operate similarly at the hyperscale of Portman's interior urbanism. Finally, Baudrillard's insights on urban anonymity apply to the spatial complexity, sublime materiality, monumental massing, and conventionally "exterior" internal qualities of the Bonaventure.

As an embodiment of postmodernity, Jameson spoke pointedly of spatial confusion within the Bonaventure:

> So, I come finally to my principal point here, that this latest mutation in space—postmodern hyperspace—has finally succeeded on transcending the capacities of the individual human body to locate itself, to organize its immediate surroundings perceptually, and cognitively map its position in a mappable external world.[17]

Like the Bonaventure, Archizoom's *No-stop City* (1968–1972) proposal embodied the perception of an infinite urbanism[18] inspired by the 1960s theoretical discourse known as *Operaismo*, or an autonomist Marxism.[19] Archizoom assumed an infinite and continuous process of urbanization based on an endless expansion of population, industrial production, and consumption. It modeled a totalitarian vision of the urban future, whereby centralized primacy as a source of financial, political, and industrial capital would be superseded by a more powerful and decentralized periphery. Inspired by Hilberseimer's urban plans, *No-Stop City* proposes a uniform density as a continuous periphery fostering production, accumulation, consumption, and lateral sprawl.[20]

The Bonaventure's layered interiors operate much like the vast, horizontal expanses of *No-Stop City*, fields of urbanization with protected, climate-controlled, and artificially illuminated space.[21] With its centralized and quadrilaterally symmetrical plan, the Bonaventure confounds users who perceive endlessness as they attempt to navigate the internal circulation ring of the complex. Entrances and exits, ramps, elevators, and escalators decouple the visitor from conventional formal, functional, spatial, and indeed, directional expectations. Both projects illustrate a continual migration toward megastructural interior urbanism. While the 1967 Hyatt Regency Atlanta was a component of the larger Peachtree Center master plan, Portman's 1970s projects—the Embarcadero Center, the Bonaventure, and the Renaissance Center—were designed as lateral, interiorized platform cities with plug-in components.

Baudrillard identified the World Trade Center, the Beaubourg, and the Bonaventure as buildings that embodied the cultural logic of modernity and postmodernity.[22] Baudrillard remarked, "Blocks like the Bonaventure building claim to be perfect, self-sufficient miniature cities. But they cut themselves off from the city more than they interact with it. They stop seeing it. They refract it like a dark surface."[23] He expanded on its disorientation by claiming:

> All around, the tinted glass facades of the buildings are like faces: frosted surfaces. It is as though there were no one inside the buildings, as if there were no one behind the faces. And there really is no one. This is what the ideal city is like.[24]

His observations, rooted in the post-structuralist conviction that meaning emerges from systems of signs working together, are underscored by an analysis and critique of shifts operating simultaneously within global architecture and popular culture. Baudrillard viewed the hyperspaces of the Bonaventure as an unintentional parody of Modernism with their arbitrary and misleading spatial language.[25] Both Jameson and Baudrillard conclude that it is the subversive notion of modern parody which places the Bonaventure within the postmodern.[26] Today, such social alienation takes on even deeper meaning in our cyberspace-oriented contemporary moment.

For Baudrillard, the Modernist parody represents a dialectic relationship between what is considered acceptable and related to universal norms, while being influenced by subjective aesthetic preferences. Even so, he applauds Portman's ability to create a utopian interior world which replicates the city within a building.[27] The anonymity of the Bonaventure in its podium base is underscored by the lack of a central and hierarchically significant entrance. Its five towers emerge from a hulking concrete podium; yet, pedestrians experience this interior world as both under-scaled and discrete. Its modernity is based on hegemony within the city, its difference (or indifference) codes its superiority to the surrounding context. Nevertheless, such indifference guides how Portman connects his interior world to the city beyond, isolating itself to create an autonomous interior world, a postmodern micro-world. This isolation heightens the obscurity and insignificance of its entrances as if the space within aspires to be inaccessible. At the same time, the reflective glass skin mirrors its context—further blurring the Bonaventure within the city to dematerialize it. Once inside, disorientation overcomes those navigating spatial vastness; minimal visual connectivity to the outdoors further reinforces the primacy of the interior (Image 17.5).

Image 17.5 Interior view of cocktail pods and lobby lake in the Los Angeles Bonaventure.
Credit: Gregory Marinic

Reflecting on the Bonaventure

Portman conceived the Bonaventure as a seductive image of a future society, as an architectural icon, a hedonistic place of consumption and desire. Since childhood, I have been fascinated by the Bonaventure for its monumental interiority, and later, for its influence on a generation of theorists, particularly Fredric Jameson. Revisiting the Bonaventure to reassess the Portman-effect, the American cities of Atlanta, Detroit, and Los Angeles share significant common denominators. Each experienced mid-1960s racial riots, followed by white flight, and long-term suburbanization well into the 1980s and 1990s. These cities responded similarly by rejecting the uncontrollable aspects of city life in favor of an alternative urbanism achieved by a John Portman-designed hotel-retail-commercial-entertainment hyperspace. These enclosed "streetscapes" may be viewed as a late twentieth-century postmodern American translation of the speculative Parisian arcade. Like the world of the flâneur, desire and modernity were embedded within Portman's new interior realms as a cornucopia of consumption. Like the Parisian arcades, Portman's work and its progeny reveal the impact of social shifts, popular culture, and technological advances in reshaping cities and societies as consumptive utopias. Marginally successful and continually adapted, Portman's hotel-oriented interpretation of the arcade has, in fact, proven to be too large to entirely collapse, yet shares with the arcade similar aspects of obsolescence, abandonment, and neglect.

As a point of discussion in relation to postmodernism, the discourse surrounding the Bonaventure's postmodernity contradicts the most obvious, stylized, and symbolic notions of the genre, or rather, the most common interpretation of what postmodernism "is," and ultimately, of its potential as a critical architecture. Its postmodern spatiality is clearly defined in Jameson's argument that the cultural logic of the 1970s reinforced capitalistic impulses within the popular consciousness. He argued that the Bonaventure hyperspace resisted late capitalism through spatial de-territorialization. Postmodernism is most often paired with capitalism and production as a form of consumer kitsch tied to bourgeois vulgarity. Jameson believed that it is within architecture that modifications to aesthetic production are most clearly manifested. Through the slow yet rigorous practice of architecture, society expresses its most significant social and aesthetic preferences. In the Bonaventure, a new preference for controllable and internalized urbanism "meeting the needs" of wary suburbanites was realized by architect-developer John Portman.

While the most obvious postmodern examples of architecture at the time, such as the Portland Building (Michael Graves, 1982) and the AT+T Building (Philip Johnson, 1984), displayed a superficial postmodern aesthetic, the Bonaventure achieved a more sophisticated postmodernism that performed spatially rather than formally. The space and the subject have switched places. Thus, the space and its interior urbanism represent the milieu in which the Bonaventure operates. The Bonaventure can be interpreted as a postmodern spatial critique of the *Ville Radieuse* and other modernist urbanisms, while the subject is the white American suburbanite. Postmodern hyperspace and white suburbanites rejected the city, both rejected modernist urban planning in favor of an interiorized, controllable, and capitalist environment tuned to consumption. Portman accommodated their preferences and soothed their prejudices. Bowing to visceral rather than visual appeal, the postmodern complexities of the Bonaventure rejected the symbolic depthless and historicity of mainstream postmodernism. Portman achieved, knowingly or not, something far more subversive and sublime.

Although often viewed as existing at opposite ends of the scale of architecture, interior spaces and urbanism share common principles. Jameson articulated the spatial essence of the Bonaventure vis-à-vis three spatially based postmodern influences, including a temporal spatial logic, a new approach to the sublime, and re-envisioning urbanism as an interiorized hyperspace. In the words of both Jameson and Baudrillard, the Bonaventure represented the spatial confusion of late twentieth-century society. Its vast interior spaces presaged a next generation of increasingly monumental and capitalistic urban-scale interventions worldwide. Its more recent appropriation as a "selfie" backdrop for social media has reconfirmed its place in popular culture. Today, as social disorientation has metastasized in cyberspace, the Bonaventure's postmodern interior acts as a globalized canvas onto which the masses project their fantasies, anxieties, and desires.

Notes

1   See Jameson, Fredric, "Postmodernism, or the Cultural Logic of Late Modernism", *New Left Review*, vol. 2, no. 146, July–August 1984, pp. 53–92.

2   Ibid.

3   Goldberger, Paul, "John Portman: Imagined Cities", in *Global Architecture*. Tokyo: ADA Edita, 1981.

4   Ibid.

5   "Retailing Birth, Death, and Shopping", *The Economist*, December 19, 2007.

6   Kurutz, Steven, "John Portman: Symphonic Architect", *The New York Times*, October 19, 2011.

7   Portman, John, Riani, Paolo, Goldberger, Paul, and Portman, John, *Italy: L'Arca*, 1990, and "The Portman Archives", https://www.portmanarchives.com/groundbreaker

8   Avila, Eric, Popular Culture in the Age of White Flight: Fear and Fantasy in Suburban Los Angeles. London: University of California Press, 2006.

9   Rutheiser, Charles, Imagineering Atlanta: The Politics of Place in the City of Dreams. London: Verso Books, 1996.

10 Muschamp, Herbert, *Hearts of the City*. London: Knopf Doubleday Publishing Group, 2013.

11 More recent assessments of John Portman's work include *John Portman: Art and Architecture* (High Museum of Art, 2009), *John Portman: A Life of Building* (Ben Loeterman, 2013), *Modernism/Postmodernism* (Peter Brooker, 2014), *Interior Urbanism: John Portman and Downtown America* (Charles Rice, 2016), *Portman's America and Other Speculations* (Mohsen Mostafavi, 2017), among others.

12 Martin, Reinhold, *Utopia's Ghost: Architecture and Postmodernism, Again*. London: University of Minnesota Press, 2010.

13 See essay by Jameson, 'Bonaventure Hotel', in The Postmodern Presence: Readings on Postmodernism in American Culture and Society. India: AltaMira Press, 1998.

14 Baudrillard, Jean, *Simulacra et Simulation*. Paris: Editions Galilee, 1981.

15 Jameson, Fredric, "Culture and Finance Capital." 1996 ed. *The Cultural Turn*. London: Verso, 1998.

16 Aureli, Pier Vittorio, *The Possibility of an Absolute Architecture*. Cambridge, MA: The MIT Press, 2011.

17 Jameson, 1991.

18 Archizoom's No-Stop City was published in several venues during the early 1970s, including *Casabella* (no. 350–351, 1970) as 'Citta, catena di montagio del soiale' (City, Assembly Line of the Social), and in *Domus* (no. 496, 1971) as "No-Stop City: Residential Parking, Climatic Universal System".

19 The Italian theoretical and political movement, *Operaismo*, was active in the 1960s and early 1970s.

20 Aureli, 2011.

21 Aureli, 2011.

22 Gane, Mike, Baudrillard's Beastiary: Baudrillard and Culture. New York: Routledge, 2002.

23 Baudrillard, Jean, and Chris Turner, *America*. London: Verso, 2010.

24 Ibid.

25 See *The Anti-Aesthetic: Essays on Postmodern Culture,* edited by Hal Foster. Port Townsend, 1985; republished as "Postmodern Culture" London, 1985.

26 See Jameson, Marxism and Form: Twentieth-Century Dialectical Theories of Literature. Princeton, 1974, p. 34.

27 Baudrillard, 1981.

Chapter 18

The Cruise Ship
Urbanism at Sea

Joss Kiely and Gregory Marinic

When the first transatlantic steamships set sail from Europe to North America in the mid-nineteenth century, people from around the world marveled at their remarkable technology. The new ships represented an important shift in intercontinental trade and the movement of people, serving as the forerunners of ocean liners that would captivate public imagination in the next century. Between 1850 and 1900, three British companies—Cunard, White Star, and Inman—dominated steamship passenger travel in the North Atlantic.[1] By the turn of the twentieth century, growing numbers of emigrants sought passage to the United States while an emerging class of Gilded Age travelers demanded greater safety, comfort, speed, and luxury. Increasing competition from continental European ships forced the British lines to add amenities such as bars, lounges, restaurants, and swimming pools. Serving dual purposes of migration and leisure, the socio-spatial conditions of ships became highly stratified.

In many ways, the ocean liner existed as a kind of both/and condition. It was at once a playground for the elite and functional transport for immigrants seeking new lives in America. Few ships captured the attention of the world more than the *R.M.S. Titanic*. On the one hand, its staterooms set the standard for the era with their spatial and material opulence, while on the other, its steerage accommodations ironically foreshadowed the tenement housing where many immigrants would ultimately live upon arriving in America. Thus, the ocean liner can be understood as a kind of floating city whose socio-spatial conditions closely mimicked the demographic divisions found in European and American cities at the time. While these layers of the city appear laterally, those of the ship unfolded vertically. Here, the inherent exploitation by the elite of those traveling in the lower decks remained intact. The interiority of the steamship was a metaphor for the city (Image 18.1).

The Leisure Cruise
In the pre-WWII years, there was an implicit hierarchy within the ocean liners plying the North Atlantic. Mirroring the urban conditions of the cities that they

DOI: 10.4324/9780429443091-20

Image 18.1 Aquitania from 1913 showing a section of the Cunard Line's huge emigration steamship *aquitania*. Credit: Wikimedia Commons

navigated between, their accommodations, decks, and passageways were stratified. Diverse lived experiences were seen on every level on the ship that created a kind of interior urban condition. Each class of travel had a designated space, and yet all passengers would bump elbows throughout the ship much like the sidewalks of London or New York. Passengers took their meals on board in spaces ranging from the basic to the opulent. Music performances were held for those on the upper decks, whereas music would be informally played by fellow passengers traveling in steerage. The exterior decks and walkways were more internally oriented than not, controlled zones and privatized spaces set within the watchful view of passengers, captain, and crew.

In the early postwar years, large ships plied the seas not only to transport people and goods, but increasingly as a sort of leisure cruise offering an escape from everyday life. This phenomenon led the ship itself to evolve into a holiday destination for people of all ages and backgrounds. The cruise ship as a destination was borne from a desire to escape which instilled a certain kind of performance in both passengers and crew. Although one might think that the real pleasure of cruising would lay beyond the horizon—in an expansive ocean or distant port-of-call—in most cases, cruise lines aimed to create entirely autonomous worlds more captivating than those outside. Royal Caribbean once described the experience, "...it is only by stepping away from the railing and gazing inwardly that one discovers the true and essential beauty of these ships."[2] This understanding of the cruise ship underscores how the vessel itself was perceived as an iconic place. As a result, the companies that owned and operated cruise ships, as well as the designers of the interiors, were incentivized to shape them into ever-larger landscapes of consumption.

The origins of contemporary cruise ship culture may be traced to innovations of the 1960s when shopping, entertainment, and contemporary consumer culture became increasingly blended activities. As evidenced in elaborate world expositions of the time, the 1964 New York World's Fair was a hybrid collaboration of the film industry, corporate America, and a development authority that merged aspects of high culture consumption and spatial design to construct novel visual and sensorial experiences. Created by Walt Disney Enterprises as the UNICEF Pavilion and sponsored by the Pepsi Corporation, the *It's a Small World* attraction translated full-scale exterior experiences into an entirely internalized and controlled environment. Space, time, and ambient effects were choreographed to present interiorized cityscapes that simulated outdoor environments at a grand scale.

It's a Small World was a groundbreaking success that was eventually transferred and rebuilt at Disneyland in Anaheim, California in 1966, and then renovated in 1971. The building interior is surprisingly larger than its exterior massing suggests. Visitors travel in small boats through multi-story spatial environments to visit various regions of the world within what is perceived as an outdoor experience. Boats float past animatronic dolls dressed in folk costumes singing "It's a Small World" together in various languages. Disney also revealed other key people behind the ride's development. Artist Mary Blair was a key design team member who developed significant two-dimensional artworks and conceptual designs for the project, while animator and designer Rolly Crump shaped a fantastical three-dimensional world from her visions. Disney film animator Marc Davis created many of the character vignettes, while Alice Davis designed most of the animatronic children's costumes (Image 18.2).

Further underscoring the ride's ambitions, the creators called it "the happiest cruise that ever sailed." Although the inherent spectacle points to a kind of cult of distraction, the core of its message is simply that the world is really a small place after all, an emotional and human-centered message that Disney has long since cultivated. Furthermore, its design was not unlike the cruise ship—in that both experiences present "exotic" places at a "safe distance" while afloat.

Although *It's a Small World* demonstrated the potential for outdoor environments to be interiorized, the scalar shift of the *Panorama* exhibition at the 1964 New York World's Fair exhibited a desire for urban control at a hyperscale. Built by Robert Moses for the fair, *Panorama* was designed to celebrate the city's municipal infrastructure. Housed within a large exhibition hall, which later became the Queens Museum of Art, this massive architectural model includes every building constructed before 1992 within the five boroughs of New York City. As a metaphor for Moses's vision to reshape the city on

Image 18.2 Floating through Japan and India on the *It's a Small World* ride at Walt Disney World. Credit: Gregory Marinic

a monumental scale through monumental and willful acts, the symbolically encapsulated *Panorama* reveals the utopian aspirations of interiorization.

Throughout the 1960s, mall culture, world's fair architecture, and amusement park environments laid the foundation for later experiments in interior urbanism being planned for central cities across the United States. These efforts parallel development of cruise ships of ever-increasing size and complexity. Indeed, the spectacle of cruise ship interiors was meant to impress passengers much like hotel lobbies around the world, and sometimes even mimicked the very places that people were escaping. This architectural language was particularly evident in the advent of the centrum, an atrium-like gathering space used as an organizing hub around which many onboard amenities were arrayed. Such spaces were brightly lit and voluminous, exuding an atmosphere akin to the large atria of John Portman's urban hotels. A forerunner of the centrum, his concept launched with the Hyatt Regency Atlanta in 1967 and has since proliferated in city centers and airports across the globe.

Adrift

By 1956, Guy Debord had defined the term *dérive*—or drifting—as "a mode of experimental behavior linked to the conditions of urban society, a technique of rapid passage through varied ambiances." As a founding member of Situationist International, he helped shape a mid-twentieth-century discourse which embraced playfulness, constructive investigation, and awareness of psycho-geographical effects[3] The dérive is a form of urban exploration that differs from the typical journey or stroll; it embodies a more alternative engagement with the city. Debord defined the dérive as an environmental analysis of fissures in urbanism, urban microclimates, and distinct neighborhoods with no correlation with administrative boundaries. His work sought out the "psychogeographical" effects of places in relation to the ambiance, temporality, and social occupancies that exist within defined zones not extending beyond a city and its suburbs.[4]

As political revolutionaries and provocateurs of the 1960s counterculture, the Situationists proposed a different way to read, analyze, occupy, and critique space that acknowledged the value of marginalized urban spaces. The broader counterculture of the era emerged from the earlier 1950s Beat Generation as an anti-establishment social, cultural, and political movement. Its origins may be traced to European bohemianism and a rising awareness of Eastern religions and spirituality.[5] The "hippie" subculture found significant inspiration in non-Western cultural traditions and was defined by an ethos of communal living, creative experimentation, ecological balance, decadence, and escapism. From the mid-1960s to the late 1970s, young people from North America and Europe incrementally forged an overland route to the East.[6] The hippie trail began in London, moved across continental Europe to Istanbul, and then traversed the Middle East across the Indian subcontinent to Bangkok. This alternative, modest, and interactive form of tourism contrasted sharply with the bourgeois tastes of the jet set. The trail was defined by hostels, cafés, and shops that catered almost exclusively to Westerners as they journeyed both east and west.[7] Much like the nineteenth-century flâneur, these global nomads sought out the sublime, delightful, and erotic by wandering the bazaars, temples, and markets of the overland trail to Asia. Although the continuity of the hippie trail was fractured in the late 1970s by rising political upheaval in Iran and Afghanistan, its influence on contemporary tourism endures along parts of the original route, and in other regions of the world.

However different these two modes of traveling might seem at first—the wandering backpacker and the traveler crossing oceans in cruise ships—the cruise ships can be seen as blending the bohemian and the bourgeois. Cruising could be framed as a *bo-bo* dérive lifestyle situated within this narrative as a reaction to an increasingly hostile world, a consumer-driven utopia merging the freedom of the hippie trail with the comforts of a luxury hotel. Thus, it can be viewed as an everyday translation of the urban exploration techniques—*dérives*—of Guy Debord and the Situationist International. For Debord, dérives were intended to combat the boredom and malaise of the "society of the spectacle."[8] Thus, a critical theoretical connection links the tactics of Debord with the continual transformation and fragmentation of contemporary society. The floating opulence of the increasing large-scale cruise ships aligns with the societal malaise of his view of consumption. Here, vastness and decadence intersect with simultaneous aspects of nomadism, consumption, pandemics, and fear in the early twenty-first century.

The City, Afloat/The Floating City

By the 1960s, many Japanese architects had proposed otherworldly visions for the future of cities. A number of these were presented at the World Design Conference in Tokyo; some were a part of the Metabolist movement, while others were closely aligned with it. Among these proposals, and perhaps the most well-known, is Kenzo Tange's Tokyo Bay Plan (1960) that extended an urban armature across the bay to inhabit the water by floating above it. Similarly, Kisho Kurokawa proposed what he called, Helix City (1961), "a water-straddling, cloud-scraping cluster of megastructures which, from several thousand feet up, would have looked like a contingent of chrysanthemums."[9] Kiyonoru Kikutake joined the conversation with his Ocean City (1962) proposal which has been described as "a collection of freestanding shafts, looking like giant plastic hair rollers, into which capsules, of assorted functional persuasions, could be readily plugged." Although these visionary proposals were economically unfeasible, they offered an urban future that was unburdened by notions of fixity—a true floating city–yet not a cruise ship in disguise. These were not cities proper, but cities at sea—isolated, suspended, and objectified—and thus, not unlike Portman's many urban projects that sought similar urban autonomy (Image 18.3).

Like the interior world of the cruise ship, Portman transferred conventional exterior functions to the interior and subsequently achieved more than simply making hyperspace. This new typology attempted to replace conventional urbanism with a parallel experience—one that was autonomous, controllable, and thus, utopian. The increasingly large scale of such megastructures, culminating with the massive Detroit Renaissance Center, suggests a rejection of authentic American downtowns, as well as the deeper motivations of John Portman & Associates as both architect and developer. Alongside the development of increasingly large cruise ships, urban renewal in American cities mobilized a 1970s rebound from the turbulent racial and social divisions of the previous decade. Nevertheless, a deep suspicion of central cities and racial minorities remained within the minds of white middle-class suburbanites. Like the hermetic urbanisms of Portman, the cruise ship offered a similar experience. Sailing within an autonomous floating city to "exotic" and yet "potentially dangerous," "*Third World!*" ports-of-call, the cruise ship embodies many of the same social biases and racial prejudices. Its interior becomes the destination, the actual ports-of-call are but only an afterthought, excuse, or distraction.

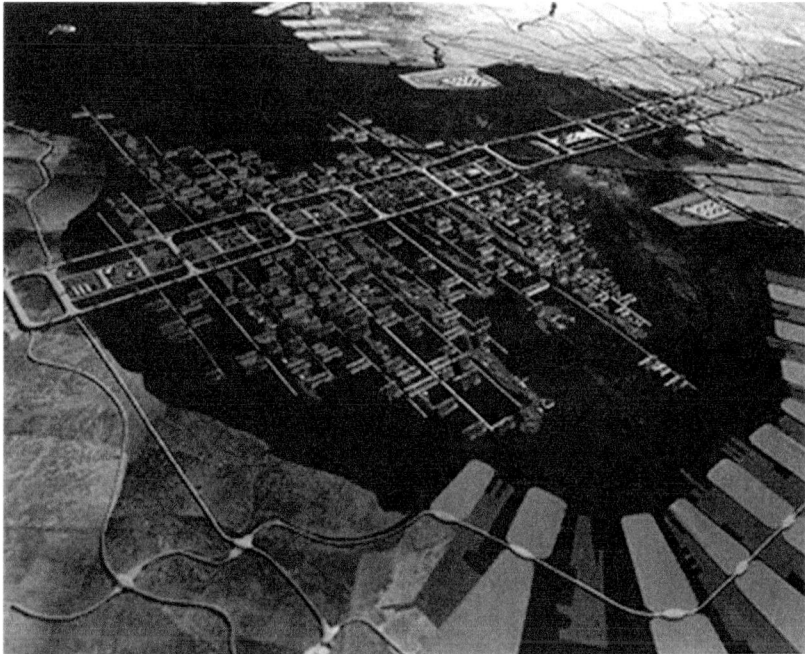

Figure 18.3 Tokyo Bay Plan (1960) by Kenzo Tange.
Credit: RPRESS-FIG_SRC-

Many buildings designed by Portman and his associates emphasized internalized, fantastical hyperspaces that sought to mitigate such prejudices, but did so through intentional disengagement with the controversial societal issues of the city. Sheathed in fantasy by the contrived realities of hyperspace, these spaces appealed to bourgeois tastes—reinvented in the manner of Fritz Lang—as urban reinterpretations of suburban preferences. Visions of Lang's otherworldly *Metropolis* and the normative expectations of the suburban shopping mall converged to create a new interior urbanism that was entirely autonomous from the declining cities in which they emerged. The hopes and dreams of the suburban middle class, coupled with the promise of a spectacular urban future, were re-invested into downtowns as controlled and privatized fantasies, which is it say, a safely concealed interior urbanism that entirely eschewed actual urbanity. At the same time, similar principles were being applied to the development of ever-larger cruise ships that traversed an increasingly volatile world (Images 18.4–18.6).

Although cruise ships were far more compact and portable than Portman's land-based counterparts, they achieved a similar effect to his atria-focused hotels and office towers. Once on board within an all-encompassing environment, passengers were one among many—mingling and watching from low and high places, unknowingly engaging in a certain theatricality. This panoptic relationship between those viewing and those being viewed added to the spectacle of performance within the ship; a stair or a balcony could momentarily become a stage. The inherent focus on the interior urban condition of the ships became a central element to the design and set the stage for a Debordian-style condition of spectacle, although somewhat paradoxically.

What was often referred to as the "promenade" became an essential part of the "public" space of the ship, a place for gathering, walking, and shopping akin to Main Street in a hometown.[10] Much like the world of the cruise ship, this emotional nostalgia underscores the experience of Disney theme parks and atria-centered developments: the only "real" thing present is a connection to memory. Days spent on the cruise were, in fact, meant to eclipse

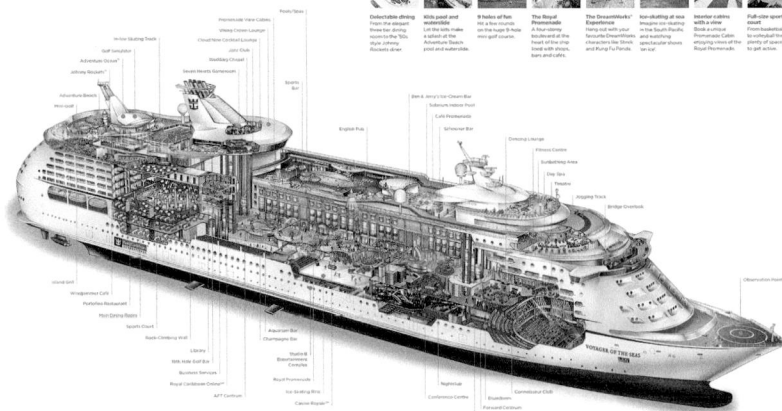

Figure 18.4 Cutaway drawing of Royal Caribbean International's *Voyager of the Seas* by Beau and Alan Daniels. Credit: Beau and Alan Daniels-FIG_SRC-

Image 18.5 Interior street of Royal Caribbean International's *Explorer of the Seas*. Credit: Mitch Ames

the mundanity of everyday life back home. Untethered at sea, this atmosphere anchored passengers to spaces and situations with which they were already well familiar. A kind of both/and Debordian scenario that sails from port-to-port but often without an actual destination.

Conclusion

The transatlantic steamship represents a microcosm of the city with its indentured servant class toiling in the shadows, exploited by a class of people whose privilege remains intact even at sea. Like the city, this naval architecture has always been premised on socio-spatial stratification which continually evolves in new ways. Today, crews on the cruise ships—which number into the thousands—are sourced largely from the Global South to serve passengers from the Global North. The system operates much like Disney's fantastical ride, *It's a Small World*, but on an actual ship. These encapsulated environments offer hermetically sealed environments not unlike a Portman megastructure that autonomously floats within the urban renewal "tabula rasa" of an American downtown. Sailing across the void on a Debordian journey to "exotic ports of call," the ships offer nothing more than suburbia at sea.

Figure 18.6 Courtyard of Royal Caribbean International's *Oasis of the Seas.*
Credit: Stephen and Katherine Burton-FIG_SRC-

Like Benjamin's arcades, contemporary cruise ships evoke the whims and desires of the masses. Yet on the other side of the utopian dreamscape of bourgeois desires rests a dystopia that provokes a critique of consumption and consumptive architectures. With their increasingly large scale of 7,000+ passengers and crew, these "cities at sea" are marked by spatial dichotomy and exclusivity that provides global mobility to a middle class leveraged on the global displacement of an underclass. Is this nothing more than a floating urban dystopia in which displaced people toil in the shadows of an elite? Is it only barracks at sea for the remittance class of the world? Or, like the city itself, do these otherspaces of transience and opportunity offer class mobility and the prospect of a better life for all?

Notes

1 Brown, Kevin, *Passage to the World: The Emigrant Experience, 1807–1940*. London: Seaforth Publishing, 2013.

2 *Elegance at Sea: The Art and Architecture of Royal Caribbean and Celebrity Cruises*. Miami: Royal Caribbean Cruises, Ltd., 2001, 4.

3 McDonough, Tom, *Guy Debord and the Situationist International: Texts and Documents*. Cambridge, MA: MIT Press, 2004.

4 Ibid.

5 Kreamer, Robert Louis, *The Hippie Trail: After Europe, Turn Left*. Stroud, UK: Fonthill Media, 2019.

6 Sobocinska, Agnieszka, and Richard White, "Travel Writing and Tourism." *The Cambridge History of Travel Writing* 2, (2019): 565–580. https://doi.org/10.1017/9781316556740.037

7 Ibid.

8 McDonough, 2004.

9 Marlin, William, "Kisho Kurokawa: A Study in Cultural Connections." *Architectural Record* 166, no. 2 (August 1979): 65.

10 Ibid.

Part II

Theories and Influences

Theories and Influences

_Inhabitation

Chapter 19

Interiorized Urbanism

Inhabiting the City between Mobility and Domestication

Jacopo Leveratto

In 2006, almost 20 years after having imagined the future of the urban environment in the form of a continuous interior, Andrea Branzi wrote an article in which he indirectly claimed the eventual emergence of his *No Stop City*, although in an informal and spontaneous way.[1] His analysis was not systematic, and the discourse was sometimes obscure as a corporeal metaphorical image; however, the overall sense was perfectly clear. During the decades, Branzi wrote, without the framework of a unified and intentional project, the city had experienced a radical process of "interiorization," which took different forms and involved two main aspects of meaning. The first of which was obvious, as it referred to the actual interiorization of the public or semi-public spaces of metropolitan mobility, communication, and mass consumption, as well as the subsequent polarization of urban life into a series of collective interiors. The second, on the contrary, was different, in that it considered the interior not as a "positional" condition, but rather as a "situational" one, which was based on individual perceptions, movements, and transformative abilities. From this point of view, according to Branzi, the city had become "an 'interior' experience, not only made of 'interior' spaces, but also of mental logics and psychological spaces."[2] That is to say that the expansion of the interior dimension had not only changed the form through which contemporary cities were built, but also the way in which they were experienced and inhabited. Therefore, it was necessary to surrender to the idea that the "unique and concentrated design gesture has been substituted by a sort of diffused swarm of projecting vibrations that each subject produces within a certain space."[3]

Despite its form, Branzi's discourse is hardly deniable. Today, the biunivocal correspondence that Christian Norberg-Schulz established between spatial spheres and dimensions of dwelling has almost disappeared,[4] and the act of inhabiting develops across the urban territory with different modalities from the past. Leaving home does not mean interrupting the experience of

DOI: 10.4324/9780429443091-23

inhabiting, but continuing it elsewhere, in other ways and with other interlocutors, within a dimension of living that simply ignores and overcomes all the positional values and the dimensional relations which structured the modern city.[5] To live in the city and its nerve centers, it is necessary to constantly move, shift, and travel. Today, transition between places has the same value that contiguity had in the past. Contemporary metropolitan lives, in other words, consist of continuous displacement from one place to another through a capillary network of spaces that are not only interior, but also interiorized.[6] This is because urban topography does not appear codified into clear patterns capable of establishing objective positional values, but it is continuously redrawn according to individual needs, points of view, and habits. Thus, like the individual house, the functional organization of spaces can be subverted and reassembled by a single person. Today, in the experience of metropolitan territory, individuals can trace their own topography according to a personal way of inhabiting.

What is debatable in Branzi's analysis is its causal and deterministic rhetoric, for which the simple evolution of new technologies would have implied the sudden emergence of this way of living, as well as the subsequent surrender of any design ambition. A progressive process of interiorization in the urban experience, in fact, has marked the development of the contemporary city since its origins. Several studies from different disciplinary fields have focused their attention on the physical repercussions of this phenomenon for a long time, thus defining a line of research that, although now consolidated, is still little known in its complexity. Therefore, this chapter outlines a short history of the forms of urbanism through which the interior dimension has been projected onto the urban scale. It defines a unified theoretical framework for the uncoordinated efforts by which planners and architects have attempted to adapt the urban design process to different modalities of living in the city. In this way, it describes how design disciplines have redefined their strategies to face both a significant change in scale and a new perspective on the morphogenetic mechanisms of urban projects.

Psychogeographies, Situations, and Significations

According to Walter Benjamin, a gradual process of interiorization of the urban experience seems to be inherent in the rise of the contemporary city since its foundation, in both positional and situational terms. While the modern city developed its structure by the separation and specialization of core functions, which led to the great urban reformations of the mid-nineteenth century, the contemporary one emerged in capillary resistance to that model, moving the threshold of interiority beyond its traditional boundaries. The construction of the Parisian arcades, for example, was not only prompted by the sudden convergence of commercial purposes and technological advancements, but also by the attempt of condensing social life that had been removed from the street into a new location.[7] In these "dream-houses of the collective," in fact, where boundaries between public and private blurred into a first topography of public interiors, a new social class could encounter, trade, and represent itself through collective rituals and domestic values.[8] It is unsurprising that Benjamin juxtaposed this typology with a different way of experiencing the city by recovering Honoré de Balzac's *Théorie de la démarche* and the image of Baudelairian *flâneur* and making them a new instrument of urban analysis.[9] The contempo-rary man, as Edgar Allan Poe taught,[10] did not inhabit the city as part of a social body but as an outsider that lived within the crowd, and his path did not follow a pattern codified in the physical structure of the city, but a personal geography made of impressions, sensations, and emotions. Thus, in Benjamin's narration, the city appeared for the first time not only as a series of interior and discrete spaces, but also as a set of disconnected and personal fragments that chal-lenged the coherence of its architectural construction.

Despite this early recognition, the definitive academic acknowledg-ment of the constructive relationship between the city and its experience had to wait until 1967, when David Stea founded the first university course of psy-chogeography.[11] The event was not unprecedented, as different studies, like David Lowenthal's on geographic epistemology, had already focused on the centrality of the perceptual field in understanding the territorial structure.[12] Each of them, however, only represented a partial attempt to find a canonical disciplinary position to the results of research by Kevin Lynch on the psycho-logical and perceptual effects of urban physical form. Since 1952, in fact, Lynch had studied the ways in which people orientated themselves within the city to deduce which architectural and spatial elements resulted in its fundamental readability. In so doing, he first highlighted the existing gap between the physi-cal structure of the city and its actual use, as well as between the intentions of designers and the perceptions of users. For this reason, his seminal work about the image of the city which served as a sort of agenda for planners – was based on cognitive mapping of three exemplary cities, centered on the percep-tion and the movement of inhabitants.[13] In this way, Lynch first described urban form through a spatial model with no geometric and projective characters, in a kind of affinity with what was happening in France at the same time, however within completely different disciplinary boundaries.

This was the case of the Parisian map of a student from the XVI *arrondissement*, drawn over a year through the graphic stratification of daily paths published by Paul-Henry Chombart de Lauwe in 1952.[14] However, it was mainly related to the first psychogeographic experimentations conducted in the context of the International Situationist by Guy Debord and Asger Jorn culmi-nating in 1957 with the publication of *Naked City*, a cartographic reconstruction of the French capital, a recomposition of interrupted parts of 19 sections of the city. Among these fragments, in fact, a series of red arrows of variable length and weight indicated the personal permutability that took shape through the existential practices of its inhabitants. Each represented not only a possible jour-ney, but rather a single intentional act of misunderstanding and re-signification of urban space, taking the form of a "drift" without a specific destination.[15] It was similar to the experiments of the surrealists who had begun to follow the literary wanderings by André Breton or Thomas De Quincey, but with a different revolutionary impulse against the industrial society that, recalling Johan Huzin-ga's theories, was aimed at the free creation of everyday life through the defini-tion of a new "unitary urbanism."[16] However, even though it was clear that the task of articulating time and space into a real "built situation" was an architec-tural problem,[17] until the early 1960s, the search for design strategies was still tied to heterogeneous artistic experiments of collective re-appropriation that, although intellectually fascinating, struggled to find concrete spatial definition.

Megastructures and Mobile Modules

From an architectural point of view, the most immediate repercussion of situationist ideas about a new urban culture was the emergence of some theoretical manifestos that, in a surprising way, gradually started to give shape to a totalizing technological imaginary. In 1957, Asger Jorn's call for the creation of a new Bauhaus took the form of a flexible and mobile urbanism with which Yona Friedman provided the conceptual basis for the first megastructural experiments of Archigram and Metabolists.[18] Thus, the only truly situationist urban utopia was the *New Babylon* imagined by Constant Nieuwenhuis between 1950 and the mid-1960s, an attempt to build the ideal habitat for man finally freed from the slavery of work and sedentariness.[19] This was because, even though Constant shared with Archigram the optimistic faith in technological progress, his *New Babylon* from their *Walking City* was the centrality of the problem of inhabitation, as a mirror of the human need for adventure, play, and mobility. Therefore, his project, included in the *terrains vagues* of a real cartography, was not neutral, but represented a set of infinite geometries and abstract architectural inventions, substantially devoid of predetermined functional program and completely open to the personal interpretation of inhabitants. Which is to say, as his friend Aldo van Eyck wrote in 1960, that it represented an urban environment that could really be "interiorized."[20]

Hence, during the 1970s, the idea that architecture could effectively respond to the interiorization of the urban experience followed very different lines of investigation. On the one hand, after the publication of Henri Lefebvre's research about the production of and right to the city,[21] sociological studies began looking at new political strategies aimed at the personal and collective re-appropriation of public space. On the other, especially since the exhibition curated by Emilio Ambasz for the New York's Museum of Modern Art about *The New Domestic Landscape*, spatial investigations started exploring different tools and scales. On that occasion, for instance, Superstudio presented a series of images, entitled *Supersurface-Life*, in which they overlapped pictures of free people with a homogeneous square grid that crossed and structured the natural landscape as an abstract field, thus reversing their idea of a *Continuous Monument*.[22] In fact, while in the previous project any form of interiority had disappeared in the opaque mass of an infinite volume, in this case, thanks to a diffuse technical infrastructure, the world appeared as a single and continuous habitable space. Conversely, Mario Bellini exhibited an automotive prototype, called *Kar-A-Sutra*, aimed at representing an innovative mobile living unit, which made the personal and individual possibility of spatial dislocation its means toward a new kind of urbanism.[23] In other words, if the intellectual horizon was still tied to the Debordian critique of consumer society, the architectural response in this regard began investigating very different disciplinary traditions that focused on the possibilities offered by industrial design.

Over the following decade, and especially after the publication of Michel de Certeau's studies,[24] this double line of research consolidated its premises and evolved around a new sense of domestication. According to de Certeau, the production of urban space was not only determined by institutional strategies of planning, design, and management, but was also made of countless tactics that took the shape of everyday practices aimed at reclaiming public space. Thus, with the inclusion of people's personal spheres, cities suddenly seemed to explode with a multiplicity of uses. This concept gradually drew the attention of planners and designers on people's informal actions, identifying some concrete tools that could enable and encourage different forms of spatial appropriation. Perhaps the most exemplary case in this regard was represented by two of Toyo Ito's first projects, *Pao1* and *Pao2*, designed to interpret the ideal habitat for a young woman. It was composed of two simple tent structures only partially closed by a semi-transparent membrane in which she could find everything she needed, from a makeup table to a communication console.[25] They were not domestic environments, in fact, but domesticated the city wherever possible by exploiting the possibilities of consumption. For this reason, Ito drew them in the act of colonizing Tokyo, on the streets or on the top of skyscrapers, as if they were alien invaders, in a sort of poetic manifesto between an artistic experimentation and a form widespread and atomized total urbanism. His ideas had to wait some years before they could be faced in a systematic and comprehensive way.

Personal Urbanism

In first half of the 1990s, an increasing number of urban analyses began to highlight the profound inadequacy of the conceptual tools of urban planning and design, which seemed to have lost their grip on reality. In these investigations, in fact, the contemporary city did not represent a deformation or reversal of the pre-existing physical and social structure, but rather, the destitution of the economic and symbolic geography that had characterized the modern urban model. Instead, it favored another, hardly definable one through stable architectural conformations. Within its limits, new hierarchies seemed to emerge and disappear in an instant, giving life to new forms of centrality which appeared arranged in a disordered way that rejected any idea of design. For this reason, André Corboz, in one of the most relevant contributions of the time, proposed the term *hypercity* to describe the essential features of the new urban model, underlining its hypertextual nature.[26] While a text represented a linear, hierarchical, and easily perceptible conformation, the hypertext allowed the user to construct a strictly personal narration liable to infinite modifications. Therefore, the *hypercity* was not the chaotic effect of the abandonment of rational forms of urban design, but the result of many choices, all of which were rational, but independent from one another.

During the following years, particularly after the introduction of new digital mapping tools and parametric design, many attempts have been made to individuate a sort of logic that could define the structure of this urban model. Each of them, from spatial syntax analyses to real-time city projects,[27] highlighted a participatory and multi-agent intelligence that seems to configure the contemporary city as a dynamic and adaptable system.[28] It is precisely regarding these behavioral patterns that the term "swarm urbanism" was coined to develop a flexible system that can materialize a collective and self-directed urban intelligence. Thus, it structures a relationship between urban space and its actors that is essentially hybrid and rhizomatic, as they were symbiotic organisms.[29] Obviously, the idea of a mutual and constructive relationship between the city and its inhabitants is not new; however, the development of digital techniques has given urban planning and design the possibility of considering a fundamental parameter what was previously meant only as a spontaneous and informal mechanism of adaptation. These shifts have fundamentally changed the perspective on processes of spatial production.

Today, although attempts are still being made in municipal and regional planning, top-down actions of urban design and management are receding. In opposition, "tactical" modes of intervention have grown as an alternative to the classic and strategic notion of planning, taking the form of everyday and bottom-up approaches to local problems that advocate for a more flexible and adaptable urban environment.[30] This entails both a significant change in scale and a new way of looking at the morphogenetic mechanisms of urban projects, from a series of sequential operations to a simultaneous process in which various agents interact to generate a complex spatial system. Moreover, it involves the recognition that the interior dimension, the place defined by our individual gestures of interpretation, appropriation, construction, and sharing of space, has been projected onto the urban scale, thus inverting the traditional process of the social definition of space. This process, however, as highlighted by the short history outlined herein, does not represent the disruption of an urban model. On the contrary, it follows urban evolution according to the ways in which people inhabit cities, through linear and progressive continuity that has marked the contemporary city since its very origins.

Notes

1   Branzi, Andrea. *Scritti presocratici*. Milan: Franco Angeli, 2010.

2   Ibid.

3   Ibid., 176.

4   Norberg-Schulz, Christian. *Dwelling*. New York: Rizzoli, 1985.

5   Leveratto, Jacopo. "Personal Urbanities: Domesticating the Public Domain." *Philosophy Study* 6, no. 7 (2016): 424–431.

6   Basso Peressut, Luca. "Interior Words." In *Interior Wor(l)ds*, edited by Luca Basso Peressut et al., 21–31. Turin: Allemandi, 2010.

7   Benjamin, Walter. *The Arcades Project*. Cambridge, MA: Harvard University Press, 2002.

8   Ibid., 405.

9   Ibid., 416–455.

10 Poe, Edgar Allan. "The Man of the Crowd." In *Tales*, edited by Edgar Allan Poe, 219–228. New York: Wiley and Putnam, 1845.

11 Wood, Denis. "Lynch Debord: About Two Psychogeographies." *Cartographica* 3, no. 45 (2010): 185–200.

12 Lowenthal, David. *Environmental Perception and Behavior*. Chicago, IL: University of Chicago, 1967.

13 Lynch, Kevin. *The Image of the City*. Cambridge, MA: The MIT Press, 1960.

14 Chombart de Lauwe, Paul-Henry. *Paris et L'agglomeration Parisienne*. Paris: PUF, 1952.

15 Debord, Guy. "Theory of the Dérive." In *Situationist International Anthology*, edited by Ken Knabb, 50. Berkeley, CA: Bureau of Secrets, 1995.

16 Debord, Guy. "L'urbanisme Unitaire à la Fin des Années 1950." *Internationale Situationniste* 3 (1959): 13.

17 Ivain, Gilles. "Formulaire Pour un Urbanisme Nouveau." *Internationale Situationniste* 1 (1958): 16–17.

18 Friedman, Yona. *L'architecture mobile: Vers une cité conçue par ses habitants*. Tournai: Casterman, 1970.

19 Careri, Francesco. *Constant: New Babylon, Una Città Nomade*. Rome: Testo & Immagine, 2001.

20 Van Eyck, Aldo. *Writings: The Child, the City and the Artist*. Amsterdam: SUN, 2008: 104.

21 Lefebvre, Henri. *Le Droit à la Ville*. Paris: Anthropos, 1968.

22 Ambasz, Emilio. *Italy: The New Domestic Landscape*. New York: The Museum of Modern Art, 1972.

23 Ibid., 202–210.

24 De Certeau, Michel. *L'Invention du Quotidien*. Paris: Union générale d'éditions, 1980.

25 Ito, Toyo. "Toyo Ito: 1986–1995." *El Croquis* 71 (1995): 34–37.

26 Corboz, André. "L'ipercittà." *Urbanistica* 103 (1995): 6–10.

27 Hillier, Bill. *Space Is the Machine: A Configurational Theory of Architecture*. Cambridge, MA: Cambridge University Press, 1996.

28 Johnson, Steven. *Emergence: The Connected Lives of Ants, Cities and Software*. New York: Schribner, 2002.

29 Leach, Neal. *Digital Cities*. London: Wiley, 2009.

30 Gadanho, Pedro, ed. *Uneven Growth: Tactical Urbanisms for Expanding Megacities*. New York: MoMA, 2014.

Chapter 20

The Roman Domus

Interior Urbanism at a Domestic Scale

Helen Turner

The Ten Books on Architecture, written by Marcus Vitruvius Pollio around 30–20 BC, is recognized as a treatise of preeminent thinking on ancient, and sometimes foundational, architecture and tradition. Amidst defining and providing methods for applying the principles of architecture, Vitruvius writes about "The Origin of the Dwelling House," which establishes the private residence as a precursor and catalyst to communities and towns, eventually creating a need for public gathering places. This theory is upheld in the prominence of describing the house in the sequential organization of his writing, as well as his prescription for ideal town planning. Surpassed only by Book III and Book IV on temples, Vitruvius dedicates Book VI to the House, while all other public spaces, like the forum, basilica, and theater, are detailed in Book V. Accordingly, he recommends a new Roman city beginning with consideration of "health" and erecting fortification walls, followed directly by "the apportionment of house lots." Creating a framework of appropriate housing locations then merged with recognition of climatic conditions to determine streets and alleys, finally giving way to the siting of public spaces according to convenience and utility.

While *The Ten Books on Architecture* was notably written for elite citizens, it is believed to be expressive of a common cultural language.[1] In this regard, acculturation of style reveals a manifestation of ideology as a method for maintaining or emulating a set of values.[2] Yet, within the ideal prescriptions disseminated by Vitruvius, Shelley Hales reveals that there was "no simple domestic package," but rather, a successful Roman house was one that "provided an arena for combining and layering personal, familial, and civic identities."[3] As the center of Roman life and thought, the house, the *domus*, "had to deal with and resolve all the tensions of being Roman on a daily basis."[4] Closely aligned with the contemporary "house," defined by Amos Rapoport as "a 'human' fact," that "can be attributed only to 'choice', which involves cultural values,"[5] Andrew Wallace-Hadrill defines the Roman domus as "a unit

DOI: 10.4324/9780429443091-24

of habitation (which may also be used for nonresidential purposes) that is inaccessible from any other unit; one may only gain access via the public street."[6] Hence, the Roman domus was more than a physical construct of the city; it was a manifestation of "Romanitas" and the residents' participation in society.[7]

It is this emphasis on the house as a driver and expression of urban contexts that aligns with the contemporary thoughts of Joseph Rykwert, wherein "some consideration must be given to the model, to the conceptual prototype of the town which its inhabitants construct mentally, and which is often exemplified in their homes."[8] Similar to the town being viewed in connection with the house, "the house cannot be seen in isolation from the settlement, but must be viewed as part of a total social and spatial system."[9] With this, the recommendations of Vitruvius for ideal planning of homes and cities merge with contemporary theories to create a framework for exploring the ancient Roman domus. The domus represents a blurred collection of urban and residential experiences revealing an early and historic example of urban interiority. While the ancient city of Pompeii and the *Casa di Ceii* (reg. I/ins. VI), or House of the Ceii, are not directly in Rome, both existed as part of the early Roman Empire. Left essentially frozen in time by the eruption of Mt. Vesuvius in 79 BC, they reveal the effects of ideals, influences, and planning strategies that responded to practical and social needs ranging from the city to interior space.[10]

Pompeii. *The House of the Ceii*

A study of the ancient city of Pompeii as a context for the House of the Ceii is clarified through the ancient and contemporary theories and practices that construct an ancient Roman domus. More common than tabula rasa siting and development of new towns, as indicated by Vitruvius, most Roman cities were often born through reconstruction following disaster or colonization. Pompeii was originally settled by the Etruscans around the end of the seventh or sixth century BCE,[11] then subsumed by the Roman Empire following the defeat of the Oscans during the Social Wars in 80 BC.[12] As such, unique characteristics of the Oscan settlement can be perceived in the southwest portion of the city near the Porta Marina.[13] A number of features signify constructs of Roman ideals with evidence of expansion beyond the Oscan settlement, including a more regular and gridded pattern of streets, as well as an acute awareness of natural surroundings. Mt. Vesuvius sits north of the city with the Gulf of Naples to the west; both are directly connected to the city by the siting and orientation of the main city streets, or *cardo*, the Via del Vesuvio and Via del Marina. Aligned with features of the environment, these main thoroughfares also capitalize on natural and celestial occurrences, like directionality of wind as well as the rising and setting sun (Image 20.1).

Following the planning of city streets, surveyors measured property lots,[14] which were then distributed and recorded on a map.[15] Although equally portioned land was an initial concern,[16] a combination of increased land values, growing population, and changing affluences caused properties to be segmented and sold between neighboring plots.[17] A distinct example is illustrated in the conversion of domestic spaces along the street into *tabernae*, or mercantile shops, some of which were occasionally physically closed off from the domus.[18] A broader result of this phenomenon, the city of Pompeii

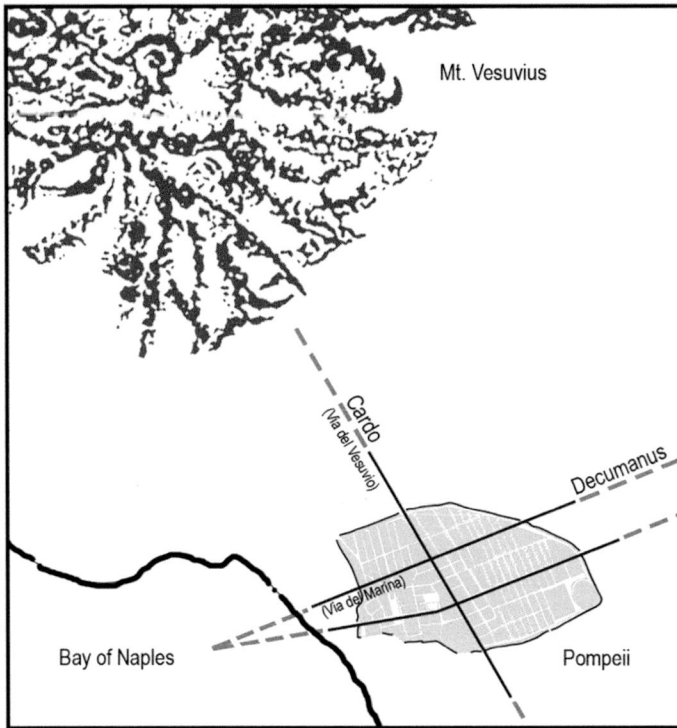

Image 20.1 Orientation of ancient Pompeiian city and streets.
Image Credit: Helen Turner

presents a matrix of party walls within individual *insulae*, or city blocks, like that of the House of the Ceii making it hard to distinguish public realms from private domains (Image 20.2).

In an extreme blending of functions and complex relationships that reflect a multifaceted urban life, street front shops might sit anterior to various-sized domus that could be adjacent to a brothel or workshop.[19] As a result, Andrew Wallace-Hadrill recommends:

> We must start by thinking away from the assumptions of the industrial city of the modern Western world, with its patterns of social contact and interaction. We must reconstruct a world in which the rich frequently lived in close contiguity with their dependents, slaves and freedmen, clients and tenants, the sources of their economic and social power.[20]

Atrium. *Forum*

Along a flat façade, the entrance to the House of the Ceii initiates a central axis aligning with the city cardo, which extends from the *fauces*, entrance, to the rear garden, the *hortus*. Because the doors of an ancient Roman domus typically remained open, this view of the interior was intended to attract the attention of passersby in an expression of societal status, occupation, and identity. Unlike current residential constructs, the domus blurred public and private, or open and closed,[21] wherein spaces that were inaccessible without invitation existed alongside spaces that were to be "shared in common with outsiders,"

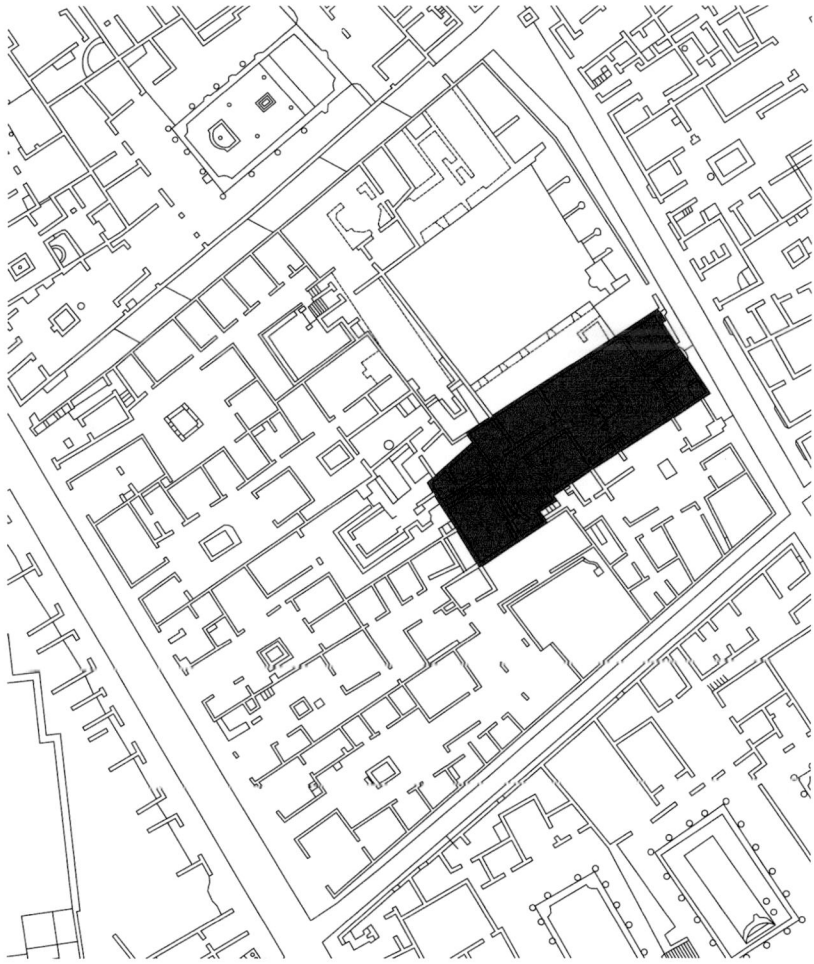

Image 20.2 Ancient Pompeiian insulae within which the house of the Ceii is identified.
Image Credit: Helen Turner

and which "any of the people have a perfect right to enter, even without an invitation."[22] Decoration was the medium through which inhabitants indicated, and visitors navigated, such paradigms. Public areas had simple decoration, prompting guests not to linger, while more intricate and expensive decoration was reserved for private spaces, engaging invited guests for longer periods of stay (Image 20.3).[23]

Upon crossing the threshold of the House of the Ceii, the gradual incline of the floor introduces visitors to the *atrium*. Identifiable by the *compluvium*, an expansive opening in the center of a sloped roof, and *impluvium*, a shallow floor basin located directly below, the atrium was the most public space within the domus. While it did not have one specific function, like the city Forum, it was often centrally located and a hub of much activity throughout different times of the day for the various inhabitants and guests.[24] Through morning hours, the *paterfamilias*, male head of the family and owner of the house, would occupy this space for a *salutatio* which consisted of greeting and conferring with clients as well as friends.[25] Hence, the "lofty" and "regal" atrium expresses and enhances the occupation, status, and engagements

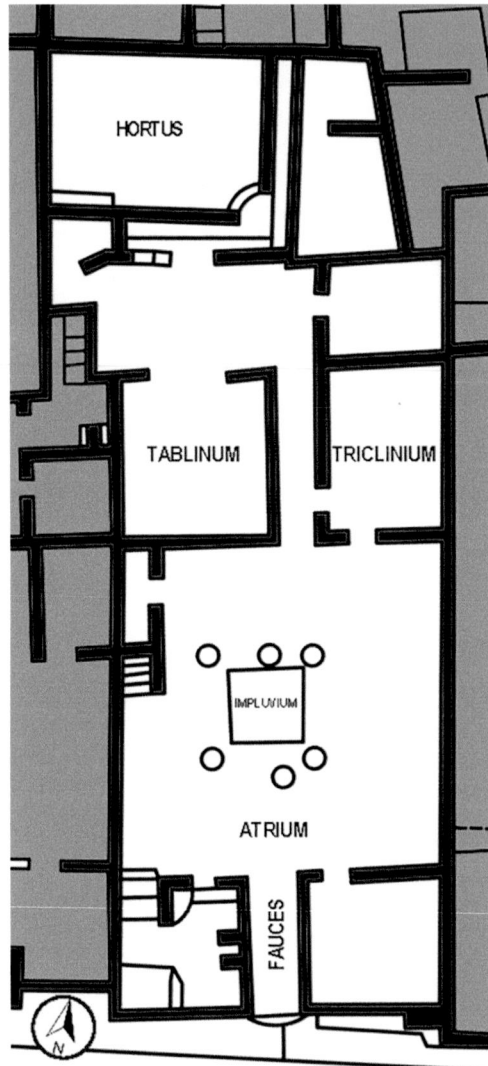

Image 20.3 House of the Ceii plan.
Image Credit: Helen Turner

of the owner.[26] The wall painting combines bright reds and yellows, colors often reserved for exceptional spaces,[27] and the upper zone exhibits painted columns which are juxtaposed against physical columns that support the impluvium, architectural elements of public spaces, creating a backdrop for appropriate social interaction. Further emulating town planning and indicating the shared nature of this space, women would capitalize on the natural light of the moon streaming through the impluvium to weave during evening hours.

Tablinum. *Basilica*

Beyond wayfinding, decoration was a manifestation of the owner's identity, whether realistic or idealistic. Lauren Peterson believes that "Romans were obsessed with conveying their social status to their peers and dependents given that they created visual codes and indices for reading social and legal identities,"[28] finds contemporary relevance in the thoughts of Claire Cooper Marcus, wherein "our very identity and discreet 'self' is confirmed by the objects we use and with which we surround ourselves." Revealed in the tablinum of the House of the Ceii. Stemming from the atrium and main axis, the view of this space alludes to the perceived power and prowess of the paterfamilias. Similar to a public Basilica, this space is physically raised steps above the ground level of the atrium and is separated by a solid wall with a single opening. Not insignificant, this fenestration frames a view through the tablinum to the rear wall of the hortus, revealing an expressive wall painting of a lion attacking a bovine creature. The tablinum was typically used by the paterfamilias while conducting business, so a client or guest would discuss business as he sat metaphorically in front of this scene, a direct representation of his status or the way in which he wanted to be perceived.

Triclinium. *Theater*

Opposite the atrium from the tablinum in the House of the Ceii is the "*triclinium*." Located in the northern corner of the atrium, the triclinium in the House of the Ceii has a minimally marked entrance, but an impressive amount of decoration that indicates use and function. Named for the arrangement of *klinae*, or couches on which three men reclined according to hierarchy, the triclinium functioned much like a theater, as a place of entertainment for friends and important clients. Visitors became spectators of food and entertainment. Literally translated as "courses" or "tables," the meals consisted of multiple *mensa*, each of which would have been brought into the room on different tables, then placed central to the klinae. With this, decoration reveals another purpose. A field of black floor punctuated by black and white tesserae, or mosaic stones, ends just shy of the room's entrance, creating an ante-space for servants to bring food and exchange tables. In the center of the floor exists an insert of colored stones, around which the klinae would be arranged and on which the different tables would be placed.[29] Working in concert with the floor, the wall painting not only created a backdrop for the event and gave attendees something to look at, but directly corresponded to placement and height of the klinae that would be situated in front.

The colors of the wall decoration combined with the location of the space suggest that it was primarily used in the winter. During these months, the room would receive the most direct light and, as a result, heat emitted through the compluvium.[30] As these meals could last many hours, Vitruvius recommends that:

> Winter dining rooms and bathrooms should have a southwestern exposure, for the reason that they need the evening light, and also because the setting sun, facing them in all its splendor but with abated heat, lends a gentler warmth to that quarter in the evening.[31]

So, the decoration acted as passive systems of heat and light. The white upper zone would reflect light to create an ambient glow for the space, while the dark lower portions would diffuse any bright light and capture heat which would be emitted throughout the evening and duration of a gathering.

Hortus. *Baths*

A narrow corridor between the triclinium and tablinum leads to the hortus, a garden, and the terminus of the main axis. Intriguingly, entrance into this space reveals the full context and new perspective of the mural which may have served to intimidate clients when seen through the tablinum. Seen in complete composition, it appears as a scene of various wild animals on a stage of painted vegetation flanked by red panels, mimicking drawn curtains. Further confounding this exterior to interior transition, an illusionistic depiction of water and fountains merge with a physical shallow trough that wraps a portion of the hortus. However, this inversion of natural features is also an expression of wealth and status.[32] The controlled nature is further illustrated by a painted human figure that appears to be pouring water from a golden vessel. The water, however, ends mid-air just above a concrete block, which might have indicated the location and placement of a physical water fountain. From this point, imagery would have transformed to physicality as actual water would have flowed from the fountain into the trough, eventually terminating at a painted depiction of a painted fountain.

Conclusion

Engaging ancient Roman domestic traditions and expressions of interior urbanism alongside the activated collection of public and private spaces requires an oscillating dialogue between the city and the house, wherein the city projects onto the house and the house back onto the city. As Amos Rapoport espouses:

> If we look at only the smallest part of the work, that part that tends to assume undue importance; if we look at it in isolation, we cannot grasp its complex and subtle relation to the vernacular matrix with which it forms a total spatial and hierarchic system. [33]

"The *domus*, as the very center of Roman life and thought, had to deal with and resolve all the tensions of being Roman on a daily basis."[34] Similarly, the form of these interior spaces is also influenced by a much broader organizing system that progressively involves: the layout of the house, the situation of the house within and density of a city block, the block as formed by the planning of city streets, and finally, the organization of streets according to the site of the city. Evidenced by the House of the Ceii, ancient Roman planning impacted, not only on the insulae within which a domus was situated, but also layout and function of its interior. Detailed descriptions of spaces within the House of the Ceii, analyzed in concert with public spaces, offer the potential to reveal the ways in which real conditions mitigate ideal prescriptions to create a place of personal and public expressions of identity.

Notes

1   Marcus Vitruvius Pollio, *The Ten Books on Architecture*, trans. Morris Hicky Morgan (Elibron Classics, 2004), 129; Shelley Hales, *The Roman House and Social Identity* (New York: Cambridge University Press, 2003), 27; Paul Zanker, *Pompeii: Public and Private Life* (Cambridge: Harvard University Press, 1998), 21; Ellen Swift, *Style and Function in Roman Decoration: Living with Objects and Interiors* (New York: Routledge, 2016), 7-8.

2   Swift, *Style and Function*, 7–8.

3   Hales, *Roman House,* 163.

4   Ibid., 38–39.

5   Amos Rappoport, *House Form and Culture* (Englewood Cliffs: Prentice Hall, 1969), 48.

6   Andrew Wallace-Hadrill, *Houses and Society in Pompeii and Herculaneum* (Princeton: Princeton University Press, 1994), 72.

7   Hales, *Roman House,* 13–14.

8   Joseph Rykwert, *The idea of a town: the anthropology of urban form in Rome, Italy and the ancient world* (Princeton: Princeton University Press, 1976), 25.

9   Rapoport, *House Form and Culture,* 69.

10 Hales, *Roman House,* 99.

11 Donatella Mazzoleni, Umberto Pappalardo and Luciano Romano, *Domus: wall painting in the Roman house* (Los Angeles: J. Paul Getty Museum, 2004), 14.

12 Ian Maxwell Barton, *Roman domestic buildings* (Exeter: University of Exeter Press, 1996), 19.

13 Hales, *Roman House,* 97–98.

14 Rykwert, *Idea of a Town,* 60.

15 Evidence of such a map has been preserved and is referred to as the "Marble Plan of Rome" from the third century; for more information, see Barton, *Roman Domestic Buildings,* 3; Hales, *The Roman House,* 27; Rykwert, *Idea of a Town,* 60.

16 Barton, *Roman Domestic Buildings,* 19.

17 Ibid., 13 & 48.

18 Wallace-Hadrill, *Houses and Society,* 126.

19 Barton, *Roman Domestic Buildings,* 20.

20 Wallace-Hadrill, *Houses and Society,* 141.

21 Zanker, *Pompeii: Public and Private,* 12; Swift, *Style and Function,* 31.

22 Vitruvius, *Ten Books on Architecture,* 181.

23 Hales, *The Roman House,* 130.

24 August Mau, *Pompeii, its life and art* (New York: Macmillan, 1907), 253.

25 Wallace-Hadrill, *Houses and Society,* 12

26 Vitruvius, *Ten Books on Architecture,* 182.

27 Wallace-Hadrill, *Houses and Society,* 31.

28 Lauren Hackworth Petersen, *The Freedman in Roman art and art history* (New York: Cambridge University Press, 2006), 124.

29 Mau, *Pompeii, Its Life and Art,* 264.

30 Mazzoleni, Pappalardo, and Romano, *Domus: Wall Painting,* 22.

31 Vitruvius, *Ten Books on Architecture,* 180.

32 Hales, *The Roman House,* 125.

33 Rapoport, *House Form and Culture,* 2.

34 Hales, *The Roman House,* 38–39.

Chapter 21

Public Urban Interiors

Karin Tehve

What makes an urban interior public? The terms public + interior, in particular, scan as opposites. Tidy oppositions occlude the complexities each term contains, shifting in meaning depending on its context and combinations. This can be illuminated with an examination of a particularly quixotic hybrid: the interiorized, privately owned public spaces (INT POPS) of New York City. These urban public interiors produce a unique form of spatial practice, one possibly exceeding the sum of its characteristic parts.

INT POPS

In the 1960s, the City of New York (NYC) introduced incentive zoning that offered private developers the ability to add area and height to building projects in exchange for space given back to its citizens. Between 1961 and 2000, millions of square feet beyond allowable FAR were constructed in exchange for over 500 public spaces. These spaces are now known as POPS (privately owned public spaces); these are owned, managed, and maintained by the developer or building owner, open for use by the public. While most POPS are exterior (plazas, arcades), this program produced dozens of interior public spaces as well (called herein: INT POPS).

INT POPS typologies can be described as circulation, destination, or both. Many INT POPS were designed to function as extensions and expansions of sidewalks as a relief to pedestrian congestion, at the edges of or through the centers of city blocks. Destination INT POPS support seating, suggesting occupations beyond movement. The zoning language gave a broad direction in terms of form and amenities, but little detail specific to use or civic goals beyond requiring access. What kind of public is supported by INT POPS?

DOI: 10.4324/9780429443091-25

Public

Even when constrained within a compound term, the meaning of *public* is almost as protean as INT POP's urban context.

_Space

When considered simply as a physical space, descriptions of the physical conditions required to achieve its public nature dominate. Sociologist Lyn Lofland summarizes these succinctly: as accessible or visible to all members of the community.[1] A more nuanced definition considers occupation. Professor and Landscape architect Kristine Miller describes any public space as a physical location intersected with a public sphere.[2] The public sphere forms through communication and interpersonal engagement, at the moment that individuals interact. In this definition, no space is truly public without occupation, as its public nature manifests coincident with social exchange. In this definition, all public space must be accessible, but all accessible space is not necessarily public.

The IBM Atrium, at Madison Avenue and 56th Street, constructs an ideal INT POPS image—a large glass box; it is accessible from the street, the provided seating visible from a distance.

_Sphere &_Forum

The political theorist Hannah Arendt provides a clearly delineated definition of the public sphere; her specific term is *the space of appearance*, created through the unrestricted discourse between citizens. Arendt refers to this discourse as action. Action requires performing in public, making oneself known through action to one's peers, the basis simultaneously for an individual's identity and all political life. Philosopher and sociologist Jurgen Habermas depicts its development over centuries and how it became foundational to the idea of democracy both as a relationship between citizens and as a form of government.

In both Arendt's and Habermas's definitions models, the public sphere is constructed as discrete from any form of authority or representational bodies. Neither Habermas nor Arendt, however, describes the public sphere as universally accessible. Habermas suggests that a public sphere is only possible in a society that recognizes land-ownership. Both authors illustrate their concepts with examples wherein only free land-owning men could form (and be formed by) the public sphere. The public sphere's defining opposite, the private sphere, was made up of those barred from participation (women, children, slaves, the indigent).

In the US, a public forum might be understood to support a public sphere: these are spaces described in the US Constitution's First Amendment, which allows individuals to express themselves without government interference and to peaceably assemble. It specifically declares the freedom to petition the government for a redress of grievances—this is public protest whereby individual citizens congregate to address their government.[3] First Amendment protections are (for the most part) restricted to traditional public forums: parks, sidewalks, and other exterior spaces.[4]

In 2016, protests erupted concerning the presidential election all over NYC. One of the largest was observed on 5th Avenue, between 56th and 57th Streets—outside Trump Tower.

Trump Tower also contains INT POPS, joined by an internal corridor to the IBM Atrium. While both spaces continued spaces accessible to the public within, neither could be considered public space according to these definitions. As described in the First Amendment, public life is understood in terms of political life, as observable actions performed in the presence of others, leaving public interiors as distinctly exterior to urban public life.

_Property

Professor and public-place-activist Jerold Kayden describes public vs. private as legal terms regarding property. *Private* refers to ownership and to an owner's rights of use, access, and transfer of a given building or lot. Public property also refers to ownership, broadly by governmental entities. These might include anything from interior institutions (libraries, schools, transport hubs) to the exterior spaces in between—streets, sidewalks, and parks. While public property implies property for the people, the rights of a property owner are not conferred to individual members of a public.

Kayden further distinguishes between programs that permit public access (typologies that might include anything from a public library to an exclusive restaurant) and public space. Access itself does not alter the conditions and rights of ownership (transfer, use, and access) under those conditions; access remains a privilege granted by the owner, and while tempered by a legal structure in the pursuit of equity, remains something that the owner controls.

Kayden's work documents the ongoing privatizations of INT POPS (IBM Atrium and Trump Tower included)—conditions ranging from locked doors to inadequate wheelchair access to the installation of retail counters and customer-only seating areas.

_Realm

The public realm can be formed irrespective of conditions of ownership: Lyn Lofland offers a description:

> …Constituted of those areas of urban settlements in which individuals in co-presence tend to be personally unknown or only categorically known to one another.[5]

This realm is also defined in contrast to other realms, which Lofland describes as private (characterized by intimate social ties) and parochial (characterized by a sense of community, purpose, or shared goals and/or values). Lofland describes them as overlapping and protean, forming and un-forming through interactions, negotiations, or simply mutuality of occupation. Reams are not tied to a particular place, and may or may not strictly obey boundaries regulated by ownership or other forms of authority. Like a public sphere, realms are associations between people. To participate, however, requires no a priori certification as a legitimate actor, nor is any particular use, program, or action necessary to perform beyond occupation. Lofland's term 'realm' is both simpler and more inclusive than sphere, acknowledging the possibility of a public life across scales and degrees of engagement with one's fellow person, and recognizing the individual subject prior to their membership in a collective body.

INT POPS like Trump Tower and IBM Atrium can and do support the formation of a public realm, insofar as they are accessible and occupied by strangers. INT POPS produces gradients of publicity and supports an urban life beyond collective civic engagement.

Interior

That said, an analysis of INT POPS and the social praxis they support suggest that they are not entirely exterior to a civic public life. To do so problematizes tidy binaries and clear definitions of *public*.

INT POPS_Enclosed

INT POPS are enclosed, providing shelter from the elements; in contrast to exterior spaces, they support visits of longer duration, independent of weather. Duration activates opportunities for observation of the heterogeneity of spatial practice, of each occupant's choices made in the co-presence of others. This can manifest in the mundane and everyday negotiations involved in sharing space—picking a spot, borrowing empty chairs from occupied tables, modulating speech, etc. These interactions would necessarily lie outside the hierarchies and specializations codified in either more permanent or formal relationships (Lofland's private or parochial realms), or vis-à-vis the expectations engendered by program.

INT POPS_Vaguely Programmed

The ambiguity of INT POPS program creates an important distinction regarding interior typologies requiring public access and creates its own opportunities. A public library, while open to all, constructs a behavioral contract of sorts, engendered both by a familiarity with similar milieu and through enforcements by one's fellow occupants and friendly neighborhood librarians. A retail environment, no matter how egalitarian its brand identity, requires its visitors to eventually engage in a purchase. In the absence of behavioral prerogatives driven by programs, occupants of INT POPS retain a range of choices regarding use. This condition supports a greater diversity of inhabitants, as the condition of patronage should be understood as a spatial segregator.[6]

A lack of specified use also supports the formation of home territories: places where one might temporarily claim as one's own.[7] These territories may form out of habit (having lunch every day in the IBM Atrium) or be uniquely performed. In this case, ownership is subjective and provisional, but can be part of a strategy of establishing oneself as belonging to the city.

INT POPS_Enable Proximity

Interior seating areas, in particular, create opportunities for the close observation of others—they support inhabitations of longer duration and make spaces for individuals within a non-allied collective. Sociologist Rose Coser asserts that in minor everyday negotiations with strangers, one makes assumptions about their needs, desires, and expectations, to enact a kind of provisional empathy.

Coser suggests that this expands one's own social repertoire while reinforcing a sense of individualism.[8]

Urban

Lyn Lofland asserts that a city is the only settlement form that has a public realm; that city dwellers are more apt to have exposure to strangers than for their suburban or rural counterparts.[9] City life requires frequent and varied occupation of non-private spaces as a consequence of daily routine.[10] INT POPS are integral to the city-as-network, both spatially and socially.

Network_Spatial

Professor and theorist Deborah Schneiderman describes INT POPS as networked urban interiors, a chain or system of similar spaces.[11] These spaces are a kind of infrastructure of public life: physical places of interconnectivity in the urban fabric. This is manifest clearly in what is now referred to as 6 ½ Avenue, a co-linear arrangement of INT POPS between 6th and 7th Avenues, between 51st and 57th Streets. All of these INT POPS allow for continuous north-south passage between streets, punctuated with seating and benches. In 2012, under the direction of then New York City Department of Transportation Commissioner Janette Sadik-Khan (and at the behest of Community Board 5), each discrete space became recognizable as a group, was achieved through the construction of crosswalks, stop signs, curb-cuts, and ramps that negotiate between pedestrians and east-west vehicular traffic.[12] In 2017, Google Maps recognized 6 ½ Avenue as a potential pedestrian route through that neighborhood, linking these spaces even more fundamentally to the continuity of its urban context.

Network_Social

Philosopher and sociologist Henri Lefebvre defined an individual's everyday spatial praxis as a vital constituent of the production of space, within *the routes and networks which link up the places set aside for work, 'private' life and leisure*.[13] In NYC, INT POPS help form these links—placing rest adjacent to movement, constructing the possibility of pause and place by which an urban subject negotiates daily life and situates themselves in a broader urban reality. Seating makes *staying* possible; with its direct adjacency to the circulation supported by urban passages, it makes staying an attractive option. This arrangement also expands the pool of potential inhabitants of these public realms—from the passer-by on a unique trajectory, to those for whom habit or routine makes a space a regular destination.

INT POPS_Bounded

The relationships engendered by INT POP's occupation are provisional and non-hierarchical, with no implication of permanent ...*shared final ends, of mutual identification and reciprocity*, the conditions of community that the political theorist Iris Marion Young posits as a commonly held critical ideal (a characteristic Lofland attributes to the parochial realm).[14] Young suggests that this ideal of community requires commonality between the members of a group. If applied too liberally as an ideal, *community* might paradoxically deny and repress difference and diversity:

> The urban ideal expresses difference as a side-by-side particularity neither reducible to identity nor completely other. In this ideal groups do not stand in relations of inclusions and exclusion, but overlap and intermingle without becoming homogeneous.
>
> (Young, 1990)

INT POPS, sharing characteristics of enclosure, vague program, and contiguity, support spatial practice that forms the urban subject through negotiations with fellow subjects, prior to any stable identity regarding a group as a whole. In their boundedness, INT POPS construct a temporary condition of the in-common without requiring the homogenizing characteristics of community, making possible an experience of difference that Young suggests as the legitimate ideal of city life.

Paradoxically, sociologist Mark Granovetter suggests that the form of social competence INT POPS engenders may be a precondition for the forms of community attachment that support participation in organized protest.[15]

Urban + Public + Interior

The production of space engendered by INT POPS space cannot be considered separately from conditions supported by its public and urban and interior natures. *Public* (when *urban* and *interior*) reveals the idealized nature of its most succinct definitions. Examination of *public's* compound terms (_property, _space, _sphere, _forum) identifies obstacles to a space of universal access; only the public realm, with its resistance to conventional understanding of boundary, can be at once both distinct and protean enough to point toward universality. An *interior* (when *public* and *urban*) supports connections between an individual's everyday spatial habits to a foundational step to democratic process. *Urban* (when *interior* and *public*) networks incubate recursive relations of individuals to their social contexts.

INT POPS can and do support the formation of a public realm, with caveats. The interiors of Trump Tower are dense with marble and brass finishes; the IBM Atrium—curtain-walled and stone-floored— reflects the aesthetics of high-end commercial spaces. Familiarity with similar milieu would make access to these spaces an assumed privilege for some; the exclusivity connoted by these spaces through their design represents an obstacle to others.[16]

This exploration of INT POPS, with its attendant histories and analysis, does not purport to favor either an ideal of a singular universal public space nor multiple spaces supporting multiple publics, though a case might be made for the latter model as supportable and achievable. Particularly because INT POPS create a bounded representation of an ideal city life, critiques concerning physical access should be extended to incorporate the more ephemeral effects generated by users' perceptions and experiences of these spaces; else, the implication remains that the *public* supported therein *is* universal. This leaves those barred from entry or occupation by other than physical obstacles as invisible, this failure leaving INT POPS exterior to a just and legitimate public life.

Notes

1   Lyn H. Lofland, *The Public Realm: Exploring the City's Quintessential Social Territory* (London: Taylor and Francis, 2017), 8–9.

2   Kristine F. Miller, *Designs on the Public: The Private Lives of New York's Public Spaces* (Minneapolis: University of Minnesota Press, 2007), xvi.

3   US Constitution- Amendments to the Constitution- Article [1]. Accessed 02.13.18. http://constitutionus.com/

4   The Supreme Court breaks down forums into three types: Traditional public forums, designated forums, and nonpublic forums. Cornell Law School Legal Information Institute Forums. Accessed 02.13.18. https://www.law.cornell.edu/wex/forums

5   Lofland, *Public Realm*, 9.

6   Lyn H. Lofland, *A World of Strangers: Order and Action in Urban Public Space* (Prospect Heights, IL: Waveland Press, 1985), 73–79.

7   Lofland, *A World of Strangers*, 122.

8   Quoted in Mark Granovetter, "The Strength of Weak Ties: A Network Theory Revisited," *Sociological Theory* 1 (1983): 203–205.

9   Lofland, *The Public Realm*, 113.

10 Lofland, *The Public Realm*, 243.

11 Deborah Schneiderman, "Infrastructural Interiors," in *Interiors Beyond Architecture*, ed. Amy Campos and Deborah Schneiderman (London; New York: Routledge, 2018), 108–108.

12 http://www.nyc.gov/html/dot/downloads/pdf/201203_midtown-mid-block_cb5_slides.pdf

13 Henri Lefebvre, *The Production of Space* (Oxford: Blackwell, 1991), 38.

14 Iris Marion Young, "City Life and Difference," in *The People, Place, and Space Reader*, ed. Gieseking et al. (New York: Routledge, Taylor & Francis Group, 2014), 249.

15 Mark Granovetter, "The Strength of Weak Ties: A Network Theory Revisited," *Sociological Theory* 1 (1983): 224.

16 Author, "POPS: Access, Appearance and Identity," *International Journal of Interior Architecture + Spatial Design: Volume 6 Parallel Territories* (2020).

Chapter 22

Intimate Inhabitation

Toward an Intercourse of Creaturely Urbanism

Joseph Altshuler and Julia Sedlock

As a subset of interior urbanism, *urban interiorities* are collective opportunities for intimate inhabitation of the public realm. Rather than a prescribed typological, formal, or spatial manifestation, these interiorities result from a mode of operating that prioritizes interaction and relationality. Intimacy is defined as "close familiarity or friendship," "a private cozy atmosphere," "closeness of observation or knowledge," or euphemistically as "sexual intercourse."[1] The link between interiority and intimacy liberates the notion of interior from the plain distinction between being inside versus outside a conditioned building envelope. The interiority of intimacy is a feature of the *creaturely* in architecture—a designation that animates the relationships between bodies, whether human, nonhuman, or architectural.[2] Creaturely architecture implies ecological interdependence and the nesting of bodies within bodies and worlds within worlds that spawn the interconnected "intercourse" of urban life.

From Discourse to Intercourse

While the discourse of urbanism offers sophisticated tools to organize and manage architectural parts and urban wholes, an *intercourse* of intimate urbanism offers an opportunity for affection, dialogue, and relationships among spatial parts and wholes. *Intimacy* and *love* are words that are conspicuously absent from most discourse on urbanism and interiors, but are key terms in the intercourse of urban interiorities. The work of John Hejduk is one exception that points toward new modes of intimate inhabitation and companionship at an urban scale. Hejduk's various Masque projects position architectural characters in the city in a manner akin to furnishings within a building interior, staging vignettes of shared occupation and cozy commingling within urban space. Crafted at a scale somewhere between a sculpture and a full-size building, these characters possess zoomorphic profiles composed of creaturely architectural elements. While the Masques lack spatial interiors themselves, they

DOI: 10.4324/9780429443091-26

produce a relational interiority in the spaces between them that absorbs and affects those in close proximity.

Hejduk's published sketchbook, *Architectures in Love*, amplifies the capacity of Masques to produce intimacy in urban contexts. The drawings depict building forms engaging in sexual intercourse and expressing physical "tenderness" with one another.[3] Hejduk illustrates architectural "bodies"— blocky or cylindrical forms with outstretched limbs and appendages—enjoying the spatial relationships made possible by close physical proximity and energy exchange with other architectural bodies. These architectures hug, hold, spoon, and penetrate one another, creating narrow, intimate urban interiorities among the interstitial spaces generated in the crevices between slightly incongruous building anatomies. *Architectures in Love* may exaggerate the notion of architectural intercourse but the creaturely ontologies of these architectural bodies assert an alternative thought space for organizing the city: here, urban interiorities are created between animate beings who can reconcile their desire to be recognized as a legible whole with the impulse to be one small part of something bigger.

From Pets to Creatures

The scalar tension and affection enacted in the spaces between the animate bodies of Hejduk's Masques is advanced by Atelier Bow-Wow's theory of "pet architecture." Like our domestic canine and feline companions, small buildings and urban objects hold a subjective position in relation to the rest of the more conventionally scaled city. Atelier Bow-Wow's pet architecture unleashes small buildings to interact with other buildings and humans, and to define new social configurations. Objects such as vending machines, karaoke boxes, and parking lot kiosks are described as pet-sized as well: too small to be architecture and too big to be furniture, they occupy a corner of a city and "[turn] the urban environment into a *superinterior*." These objects are "a size which allows a freedom in urban action," "as an interface between the city and the human body."[4] By translating familiar qualities of interiors onto exterior urbanism, pet architecture helps redefine interiority as a mode of intimate inhabitation and interaction.

Pet architecture also introduces the idea that the architectural parts that compose our cities might act more like companion creatures as opposed to tools that serve our human needs. While the word *pet* sometimes connotes a subservient relationship to a human master, the more open-ended liveliness of *creature* offers a nonhierarchical "grammar of animacy"[5] for architects and urbanists to articulate the nonhuman agency of our built environment. Creatures exhibit physical and behavioral characteristics that are familiar in that they possess anthropomorphic and zoomorphic qualities like character, personality, posture, facial expressions, taste, charisma, and attitude; yet, they occupy the world in unusual and surprising ways, enacting vital relationships between what something looks like and how it operates in the world. Creatures are ambiguous representations of animate beings, not necessarily mobile, but projecting an impression that they could get up and walk away. By investigating creaturelines in urban contexts, we construct a lens through which we read the world as composed almost entirely of beings with character, in relation to other beings, at a range of scales, and in various settings.

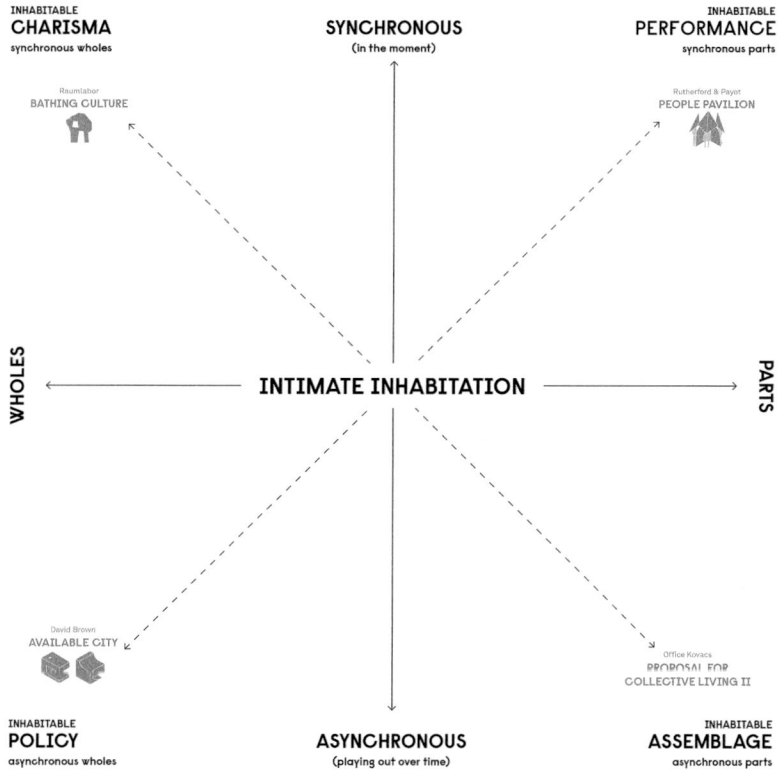

INHABITABLE
CHARISMA
synchronous wholes

SYNCHRONOUS
(in the moment)

INHABITABLE
PERFORMANCE
synchronous parts

Raumlabor
BATHING CULTURE

Rutherford & Payot
PEOPLE PAVILION

WHOLES

INTIMATE INHABITATION

PARTS

David Brown
AVAILABLE CITY

Office Kovacs
PROPOSAL FOR
COLLECTIVE LIVING II

INHABITABLE
POLICY
asynchronous wholes

ASYNCHRONOUS
(playing out over time)

INHABITABLE
ASSEMBLAGE
asynchronous parts

Image 22.1 Intimate inhabitation matrix. Credit: Joseph Altshuler and Julia Sedlock

Taken together, *Architectures in Love* and pet architecture point toward a creaturely interior urbanism rich with opportunities for more intimate inhabitation, illustrated by the four case studies discussed herein. Two spectrums of relational affinities describe a matrix of modalities for inhabiting interior urbanism. The horizontal axis calibrates the extent to which projects privilege inhabitation of their individual *parts* or collective *wholes*; the vertical axis calibrates the extent to which interior spaces invite inhabitation in the moment (*synchronously*) or over sustained periods of discontinuous time (*asynchronously*). The two axes divide this field into four quadrants, each of which is named for its defining trope and aligned with a contemporary project that exemplifies its qualities (Image 22.1).

Inhabitable Charisma

Inhabitable *charisma* is interior urbanism that condenses into a *synchronous whole*. Like flagship animal species known as "charismatic megafauna" that offer a discrete rallying mascot for ecological conservation agenda, charismatic architecture and urbanism produce a collective sensation of creaturely liveliness and charm to galvanize communities in a particular time and space.

For example, *Bathing Culture* is a public sauna located in a postindustrial harbor in Gothenburg, Sweden, designed by Raumlabor. The sauna exhibits a zoomorphic form that stands above the water on an existing pier. The "torso" of the structure is a multifaceted mass elevated on four legs and

Image 22.2 Raumlabor, *Bathing Culture*, 2015. Credit: Image courtesy of the architects

perched in a contrapposto that suggests motion. A cyclops-like rectangular aperture gazes intently toward the harbor. In its corrugated steel cladding that echoes the industrial environs, the sauna fits in materially but stands out geometrically, with its polygonal but distinctly creature-like profile (Image 22.2).

This creaturely structure serves as the pilot project and charismatic mascot of a multi-phased urban master plan that includes ecological remediation of the shoreline and a constellation of cultural amenities along the currently polluted waters. As a friendly exterior monument, the sauna creature conjures different dispositions and personalities from different vantage points around the harbor and pier, launching the architecture into optical locomotion as humans traverse the shore and enacting its agency as a harbinger of future vitality. As an intensified interior experience, *Bathing Culture* produces a new civic space, one that revamps a historical model of public baths that provide not only "for relaxation and sport but also for politics, discussion, business deals, eroticism, hedonism and crime."[6] The presence of warm human bodies consummates the interior desire to propagate spatial and thermal pleasure, while the architecture's physical affordances and creaturely characteristics also teach its human inhabitants new ways to relate to one another as they collectively scheme the future coastal urbanism.

Inhabitable Performance

Inhabitation that occurs among *synchronous parts* operates through *performance*. Like in the performing arts, performance architecture requires the orchestration of multiple components and constituents to operate in tandem and in the moment. Inhabitable performance thrives on the live feedback among performers and passersby in interior-like pockets of cities.

For example, Ailie Rutherford and Laurence Payot's *People Pavilion* consists of a series of "structures" created via extensions of participants' bodies. The project develops through iterations of wearable geometries that

Image 22.3 Laurence Payot & Ailie Rutherford, *People Pavilion.* Credit: Bob Moyler

augment the human form and entice new ways of forming a temporary interior "pavilion" that responds to their participants and to their urban contexts. Performers venture into the city in costumes that augment their bodies through geometry and color; the people within the costumes are choreographed to assemble and aggregate into various social configurations that facilitate enclaves of programming adjacent to everyday city life. In the project's first iteration, each actor wore a two-tone pyramidal shell. By aggregating this simple unit, multiple performers created a rich variety of pavilion forms that each responded to various public spaces within the city (Image 22.3).

These aggregations create temporary interiors that provide enclosed pockets of intimacy within crowded urban contexts, programmed through collaboration with artists who craft stories, songs, and choreographies that initiate solidarity among the participants and passersby. For Rutherford and Payot, creating welcoming social spaces within and distinct from the corporate and commercial hardscapes of the city advances a feminist urbanist agenda.[7] In this way, the action and intimacy of the spaces are prioritized over any specific geometry or form. Ultimately, *People Pavilion* blurs the boundary between "pavilion" and "not pavilion" and "creature" and "not creature" through deliberate and calibrated acts of inhabitable performance that initiate radical inclusion.

Inhabitable Assemblage

Inhabitable *assemblage* is interior urbanism among *asynchronous parts*. Like in fine art, assemblage in urban contexts involves composing disparate objects on a common substrate. The ad hoc logic of assemblages welcomes the parts to be added onto and edited over time in a nonhierarchical fashion.

For example, Office Kovacs's *Proposal for Collective Living II (Homage to Sir John Soane)* is a scale model of a speculative cityscape generated through spatial extrapolation of the interior of John Soane's famous house and collection. This dense assemblage of interior urbanism "conceptually turns Soane's House inside out" by arranging an assortment of plastic readymade

Image 22.4 Office Kovacs, *Proposal for Collective Living II (Homage to Sir John Soane)*, 2017. Credit: Image courtesy of the architect

components—architectural elements from modeling kits and toys such as bridges, plants, animals, figures, and landforms—into a multi-tiered, interconnected, nonhierarchical matrix that operates at a range of scales and orientations.[8] Zooming into the smaller, intimate moments where a human figure confronts the two or three nearest elements in their vicinity (a fire hydrant, a rubber duck, a pile of bricks) suspends our disbelief in the strange familiarity of this urban context. The relationships that congeal in these discrete parts tell stories that draw us into the model's worldmaking, despite its absurdity as a whole (Image 22.4).

In the model, all things and beings coexist as interrelated entities whose boundaries are permeable and ambiguous, possessing distinct qualities as a whole, as well as qualities derived from their constituent parts. Heaps of architectural objects, including ladders, fences, columns, and windows, define spaces as individual parts, but they operate equally as subsets of mini-interiors (vestibules, catwalks, and corridors) as well as larger groups of complexes. In its apparent chaos, all parts share a unity in their equivalent opportunity to be read at any given moment as either focal points of a captivating narrative or background noise in the web of interrelated elements.

Beyond the parts themselves, inhabitable assemblages also produce a more elusive "space between" that cannot always be apprehended discretely (it is all around us all the time; it is connected to organisms, ecologies, infrastructures, economies, and systems of power). This flavor of interior urbanism plays a critical role in defining boundaries that establish guidelines for inclusion and exclusion, and by extension identity, agency, and citizenship.

Inhabitable Policy

Inhabitation that occurs via an *asynchronous whole* operates through generous *policy*. As an endeavor that operates over time, the planning and design of interior urbanism integrate immediate needs and desires of grassroots organizing with long-term visionary strategies. This balance can simultaneously acknowledge the autonomy of actors (residents, neighborhoods, buildings, etc.) while privileging the interconnectedness of those actors to cultivate engagement in the collective whole of public life.

David Brown's project *The Available City* addresses the 10,000-plus empty city-owned lots concentrated on Chicago's South and West sides through a collective consideration of non-contiguous lots that reconfigure the binary relationship between public and private properties. Brown proposes a strategy that accumulates the potential of all the lots as an aggregated urban interior larger than the Chicago Loop. Rather than treating each lot as a separate unit or proposing a master plan that imposes a prescribed, singular vision, Brown's strategy plays out over time through multiple scenarios of economic growth and decline. The proposal incentivizes property owners to develop adjacent city-owned lots through an arrangement that allows for larger and taller buildings in exchange for the inclusion of public interiority (whether indoors or outdoors). Although developed as single instances, when applied across a whole neighborhood these interventions describe a network of interior urbanism that reroutes circulation through city blocks, defines districts of overlapping programs, and initiates solidarity among the public spaces that weave in and out of existing urban fabric. The result is a new kind of intercourse between interior architecture and its urban context, where the two are in a dance with each other, responding, pushing back, and reinventing the city in the process.

As a framework, *The Available City* provides strategies that integrate economic policies for property development, temporal and spatial dynamics of urban growth, multiple scales of organizational systems, and formal architectural potentials without a predetermined outcome. This way of working at an urban scale gives the city an agency and subjectivity of its own. The city comes with its own willful temperament, which is defined by a range of variables beyond the control of architects, developers, city planners, and residents. Brown's willingness to acknowledge, anticipate, and interact with those variables activates his own agency as it engages in a symbiotic relationship with the city: a creature with its own subjective experience.

Though Brown's proposal avoids the prescription of form, his diagrams describe the potential for solid-void interaction of public and private in lot combinations that set up innovative formal diagrams to inspire other designers as the proposal plays out over time. The full potential of the project, as represented by an axonometric drawing that samples several blocks of Chicago's West Side, is a new interior urbanism of architectural creatures whose volumetric public spaces (the colorful voids) make new shapes and interior connections across city blocks. The forms are animated expressions of relationality, a willingness to be responsive to contextual inputs, as well as a willful vitality that pushes back against that context to create something unexpected.

Conclusion: Public Displays of Affection

While certain genealogies of urbanism imagine the city as a field of *objects* navigated via paths, districts, and nodes, this matrix of case studies constitutes an intercourse of urban interiorities that highlight and prioritize the cozy, close, friendly, or familiar interactions of creaturely *subjects* (human, nonhuman, and architectural). With this intimate relationality among urban components, we acknowledge and amplify architecture's potential to embody an animate vitality on equal ontological footing with our own, and hopefully see as a result that public displays of affection need not be limited to human intercourse. The urban interiorities discussed above are constructed by architecture that looks like a creature (*Bathing Culture*), locomotes like a creature (*People Pavilion*), initiates camaraderie and solidarity-like groups of creatures (*Proposal for Collective Living II*), or reveals the creaturely nature of the city through a combination of these qualities (*The Available City*). These examples provide a toolkit to produce diverse architectures that share an intimate sensibility for inhabiting the city, and that, in turn, permit us and our fellow inhabitants to see and share in the affection available among our interior urban environments.

Notes

1   Google's English dictionary (*Oxford Languages*), s.v. "intimacy." accessed December 10, 2021.

2   See Joseph Altshuler and Julia Sedlock, *Creatures Are Stirring: A Guide to Architectural Companionship* (San Francisco: Applied Research and Design, 2022).

3   John Hejduk, *Architectures in Love* (New York: Rizzoli International Publications, 1995).

4   Momoyo Kaijima, Junzo Kuroda, and Yoshiharu Tsukamoto, *Made in Tokyo* (Tokyo: Kajima Institute Publishing, 2001), 25–26.

5   Robin Wall Kimmerer, *Braiding Sweetgrass: Indigenous Wisdom, Scientific Knowledge, and the Teachings of Plants* (Minneapolis, MN: Milkweed Editions, 2013), 48–59.

6   "Allmänna Badet/Bathing Culture," *Raumlabor*, accessed April 19, 2021, http://raumlabor.net/bathing-culture/.

7   Ailie Rutherford and Laurence Payot, in discussion with the authors, September 10, 2020.

8   "Chicago Model," *Office Kovacs*, accessed April 19, 2021, https://o-k-o-k.net/CHICAGO-MODEL.

Theories and Influences

_Threshold

Chapter 23

Inside-Out and Outside-In

Projecting the Idea of the Urban Theater

Jodi La Coe

As a contemporary term for the productive inversion of expectations of public and private, outside and inside, interior urbanism theoretically extends to a notion of space embodied in the idea of the theater. According to Plato in the *Timaeus* (c. 360 BC), fertile spatial ambiguities, such as interior urbanism, are embodied in *chōra* (χώρα), a third state, in between Being and Becoming, as a place that is both outside and inside, object and receptacle, material and temporal.[1] Furthermore, prior to Plato's designation, *chōra* referred to Greek territories outside of and surrounding the city. During civic festivals, such as performances of City Dionysia, when representatives from all Greek territories arranged themselves geographically within the theater, they recreated a proportional representation of the exterior within the space of the theater.[2] In his archetypal design for a dance-platform (*choros*) for Ariadne, ancient Cretan architect Daedalus conceived of the stage floor of the theater as *chōra*,[3] as a productive space of representation, a crossing of one place with another, in this case, the labyrinth and the stage. Capable of holding a broad range of meanings, the concept of *chōra* is expansive, at times seemingly opposite in experience. This ambiguity between inside and outside dissolves preconceived boundaries between public-exterior and private-interior spaces and leads to the idea of the urban theater as the embodiment of otherness through an inversion of the perceiver and perceived.

Proportion

With the rediscovery and proliferation of ancient Greek texts, Renaissance architects, artists, and designers were eager to apply such theories in their own designs of theaters and stage scenery. Renaissance theaters took many forms, both as permanent edifices and, more commonly, as ephemeral constructions both in urban piazzas and within large basilicas. Building upon the

DOI: 10.4324/9780429443091-28

reversibility of inside and outside, fifteenth-century Florentine architect Leon Battista Alberti crafted a provocative comparison between the interior and exterior in his first book *On the Art of Building* (1452):

> If (as the philosophers maintain) the city is like some large house, and the house is in turn like some small city, cannot the various parts of the house—atria, *xysti*, dining rooms, porticoes, and so on—be considered miniature buildings?[4]

In this section, Alberti describes one of six elements of architecture, compartition (*partitio*), the creation of proportional divisions of a whole into parts, as applying equally to the sectioning of a city into blocks, a site into lots, and a building into rooms.[5] With evidence from nature, Alberti held that beauty is achieved through the harmonic relationship of the part to the whole, closely aligning with anthropomorphic proportional theories as described by ancient Roman architect Vitruvius.[6]

As an example, in the Palazzo Rucellai and the family loggia on the adjacent piazza, both have been attributed to Alberti,[7] there is some semblance between the arrangement and function of interior and exterior spaces. Across the triangular piazza in front of the main facade, a grand loggia provides ample space for the Rucellai family to gather for celebrations,[8] forming a very public extension of their private property. In turn, a smaller loggia, a cortile, opens onto the small interior courtyard, mirroring the arrangement on the exterior. As the reverse of the exterior loggia, the courtyard cortile extends public space into the private interior, transforming it on a daily basis into a place where fellow noblemen and merchants enter into the house to discuss civic matters of state and commerce.[9] Meanwhile, in the exterior loggia, the Rucellai family exhibited themselves, publicly displaying the pageantry of their familial rituals in lavish spectacles for the citizens of Florence, with each person playing their part. On more festive occasions, such as the marriage of Bernardo Rucellai to Nannina de' Medici, a large platform (*choros*) was constructed, extending the loggia into the piazza and transforming this urban space into a theater with a raised stage and an enthralled audience filling the remaining spaces of the piazza and extending down the adjoining streets (Image 23.1).[10]

Within compartition, the proportional relationship established between the part and the whole is further developed in the chiral relationship created by the reversal of interior and exterior functional relationships. Conceiving of interior and exterior spaces as chiral, like the symmetry of human hands, such terms are not coincident, nor immediately interchangeable; rather, there is a process of translation that may be realized through an act of the imagination.[11] In *The Visible and the Invisible* (*Le Visible et l'Invisible*, 1964), Maurice Merleau-Ponty developed a theory of the phenomenon of reversibility in which there is a symmetrical relationship between the perceiver and the perceived, the active and the passive, the outside and the inside, and, of course, as the title suggests, the visible and the invisible. In such relationships, one term is not only designated in the other but may also morph into the other through their mutual chirality, such as the spatially transformative, theatrical function of the Rucellai loggia and cortile. In this sense, the raised platform, a stage reminiscent of Ariadne's *choros* (dancing-floor), embodies Plato's third space, *chōra*.

Image 23.1 Leon Battista Alberti, Facade of Palazzo Rucellai, Florence, c. 1451. Anonymous Engraver from Strafforello Gustavo, *La patria, geografia dell'Italia.* Credit: Wikipedia Commons

Representation

For religious and secular festivals during the Renaissance, it was not uncommon to transform urban spaces into theaters by constructing elaborate stages with illusionistic scenery painted in perspective and tiered seating platforms, enabling the local ruling class to occupy a privileged point of view. In the second book of his serial treatise on *Architecture* entitled "On Perspective" (1545), Italian architect Sebastiano Serlio demonstrated how to construct these temporary stages and seating platforms using wooden framing and how to create the necessary perspective foreshortening to conjure the illusion of depth. Also included at the end of this book, in a section entitled "Treatise on Stage Scenery," were three perspective designs for stage sets – comic, tragic, and satiric scenes – closely following theatrical practices recorded by Vitruvius.[12] For the comic, a typical street scene representing the houses of ordinary citizens included both a brothel and a basilica for the unfolding of hilarious encounters between sinners and saints. For the tragic, the houses of the nobility served as the backdrop for epic and heroic scenes of love, adventure, and betrayal. Satire, unlike the other two, should be rude and rustic and take place in the wilderness, outside of an urban setting (Image 23.2).[13]

Reminiscent of Alberti's comparison between the city and the house, Serlio described the representation of the city outside within the theater:

> [I]n a small space, created with the art of perspective, splendid palaces, huge temples, multifarious buildings both near and far off, spacious piazzas graced with diverse edifices, long, straight streets crossed by other roads, triumphal arches, exceedingly high columns, pyramids, obelisks, and thousands of other beautiful things.[14]

Also inspired by Vitruvius' descriptions of ancient Greek and Roman theaters, Andrea Palladio designed the Vicentine Olympic Theater (1580–1585). The stage and scenery were finished after his death by Vincenzo Scamozzi as a perspectival representation of three diverging streets, seen through openings in a facade-like screen viewed frontally in elevation (Image 23.3). These distorted buildings were originally designed to stage a Greek tragedy, Sophocles' *Oedipus rex*, and, as such, depicted noble houses with refined facades. In the

Image 23.2 Sebastiano Serlio, woodcut illustrations, *Den eersten boeck van architecture*. Credit: The Metropolitan Museum of Art

Image 23.3 Andrea Palladio and Vincenzo Scamozzi, Teatro Olimpico, Vicenza, 1579. Unknown Artist, Prospetto Interno del Teatro Olimpico nella città di Vincenza. Credit: Cooper Hewitt

Olympic Theater, the audience is given the impression of urban space, heightened by both the foreshortened passageways lined by architectural facades and the illusionistic sky painted on the ceiling of the theater. In fact, the facade-like screen and semi-circular stepped seating are reminiscent of ancient Greek theaters, such as Herodotus' Odeon Theater in Athens, where a stone facade, facing the audience and representing a refined building, provided a permanent stage set. Triangular *periaktoi* placed in the portals were able to dramatically change the character of different performances.[15] In such theaters, the presence of the sky above provided a cosmic connection and played an important role in the construction of space and spectacle.[16] In this tradition, the painted sky of the Olympic Theater transformed the interior into a representation of the exterior reinforced by the three-dimensional perspectival representations of urban streets extending into the distance, reminiscent of the transformation of urban loggias and streets into theatrical stage sets throughout the Italian Peninsula.

Ambiguity

In keeping with anthropomorphic theories of architecture and the city, the spatial chirality of the theater encompassed analogous considerations of the interior and exterior of the human body. On this topic, Vitruvius cautioned his reader to choose a healthy site for a theater since a rapt audience would become so entirely open to the spectacle that noxious fumes could penetrate the pores of their skin.[17] Through chiral projection, the performance, as Plato's third type of space – chōra, fertile, ambiguous, material, and temporal – also enters the interior of the body – itself becoming object and vessel through internalization of the images and messages presented in the drama.

The notion of sensory projection and phenomenal penetration was evident in two contemporary optical theories in ancient Greece, extramission and intromission theories of vision, elucidating the relationship between the most intimate of interior spaces, the human body and mind, and the exterior world, both sensible and intelligible. Intromission theory held that visual images, reminiscent of the object perceived, enter into the eye, a passive receptor.[18] In this manner, the audience in the Greek theater would have been penetrated by images of the actors performing on the stage. Conversely, according to extramission theory, also known as emission theory, the active eye sends out visual rays that intersect with the object perceived; or, rather more specifically, a fire within the eye emits invisible light rays that intersect with solar fire illuminating the object perceived, a projection outward further impeded by distance and the density of the atmosphere and a simultaneous reflection inward.[19] In the *Timaeus*, following Empedocles, Plato described the act of seeing as occurring:

> Whenever the stream of vision is surrounded by mid-day light, it flows out like unto like, and coalescing therewith it forms one kindred substance along the path of the eyes' vision, wheresoever the fire which streams from within collides with an obstructing object without.[20]

Adhering to extramission theory, Vitruvius described the need for optical corrections to architectural elements in his third book; objects that are taller and, as such, farther away from the eye have more atmosphere between the eye and the uppermost parts making them appear less vivid.[21] Suggested in both of these theories and elaborated by Euclid in his eighth theorem in the *Optics*, there is a distinction between the object as perceived and the visible object itself, between perception and vision.[22]

Plato built upon this distinction – between what is perceived and what is – in his well-known story, the "Allegory of the Cave," in the seventh book of *The Republic*. In this dialogue, Socrates outlines the susceptibility of intellectual judgments based upon a single, fixed point of view. Socrates describes prisoners, chained in a cave facing a wall. Unable to move from a fixed point of view, they observed shadows projected on the wall from objects passing in front of a fire behind them.[23] The susceptibility of these prisoners parallels the rapt audience in the Greek theater, motionless and open to the performance in front of them, which, in this scenario, is a play of shadows. When these prisoners were finally set free, they experienced difficulty accepting the falsehood of what they thought they knew to be real. Gradually, they came to receive a new reality in the light of day, just as their eyes would take time to adjust to the bright light of the sun.[24]

While the cave-prisoners epitomized an internalization of an exterior spectacle, a sixteenth-century theatrical externalization of the inner workings of the mind and memory, Giulio Camillo's *The Idea of a Theater* (*l'Idea del Theatro*, 1550) developed from the ancient Greek notion of the memory palace, a mental image of a series of rooms containing arrangements of symbolic representations of ideas used to aid the memory, for instance, to aid the traveling orator in recounting long poems. In his theater, Camillo projected his mental edifice, the space of the imagination, into physical space, the stage of which was able to be inhabited.[25] In practice, this theater is not unlike any design that first begins in the imagination and is then projected into the physical world; however, in this theater, Camillo stands on his own intellectual stage, arranging his audience as a projection of images and objects representing the works of Cicero on seven raised platforms. Using this formation, Camillo could bring to mind Cicero's ideas by interpreting the assembled iconography[26] and, in this way, Camillo's memory theater represents the intellectual interior projected onto the exterior, as if the space of the imagination had been turned inside out through the boundary of the skin. It was a mirror projection and the reverse of Vitruvius' warning that the environment enters the body of the spectator through the skin; here, the mind penetrates the body and is expressed on the exterior.

Reversal

In Jacques Tati's film, *Playtime* (1967), the facade of the modern apartment building with its interior rooms illuminated becomes a stage screen through which ordinary, everyday activities become heightened theatrically,[27] a modern interpretation of Rucellai's civic spectacles or the facade-like screen of the Odeon and Olympic Theaters. A modern facade illuminated with electric lights places small-stage vignettes one next to another with each scene unaware and unrelated to the others. Such is the premise of Alfred Hitchcock's film *Rear Window* (1954), in which a convalescing photographer observes the various and individual lives of his neighbors in their most intimate moments, punctuated by the appearance of love and hate, friendship and loneliness, and murder.[28] In Tati's film, the passerby on the street becomes the audience, from the outside looking in, igniting a final theatrical reversal, that of an *urban interiorism*. These spatial and role reversals between the perceiver and the perceived, between the outside and the inside, between the mind and the world, are the familiar tropes at play in demonstrations of interior urbanism, or its chiral twin urban interiorism, plumbing the relationship between the city, its citizenry, and their fertile representation in the idea of the urban theater.

Notes

1 In defining the soul, Plato refers to three states, Being (indivisible), chora (both), and Becoming (divisible). *Plato IX: Timaeus, Critias, Cleitophon, Menexenus, Epistles*, R. G. Bury, trans. (Cambridge, MA and London: Harvard University Press, [1929] 1989), 123.

2 Lisa Landrum, "Chōra before Plato: Architecture, Drama, and Receptivity," in *Chora 7: Intervals in Architecture*, Alberto Pérez-Gómez and Stephen Parcel, eds. (Montréal: McGill-Queens Press, 2016), 330–333.

3   Alberto Pérez-Gómez, "Chora: The Space of Architectural Representation," in *Chora 1: Intervals in Architecture*, Alberto Pérez-Gómez and Stephen Parcel, eds. (Montréal: McGill-Queens Press, 1994), 12.

4   Leon Battista Alberti, *On the Art of Building in Ten Books*, Joseph Rykwert, Neil Leach, and Robert Tavernor, trans. (Cambridge, MA: MIT Press, [1988] 1992), 23. See also Paul Emmons, "Intimate Circulations: Representing Flow in House and City," *AA Files* 51 (London: The Architectural Association, Winter 2005): 48–57.

5   Ibid., 421.

6   Ibid. See also Vitruvius, *De Architectura*, 3.1. Frank Granger, trans. (Cambridge, MA and London: Harvard University Press and William Heinemann, 1983), 158–167.

7   See Robert Tavernor, *On Alberti and the Art of Building* (New Haven, CT and London: Yale University Press, 1998), 81, 119–124.

8   See also Kurt Forster, "Discussion: The Palazzo Rucellai and Questions of Typology in the Development of Renaissance Buildings," *Art Bulletin*, 58, 1976, 109–113 and Charles R. Mack, "The Rucellai Palace: Some New Proposals," *Art Bulletin*, 56, 1974, 517–529.

9   Tavernor, *On Alberti and the Art of Building*, 81.

10 Ibid.

11 Chiral is from the ancient Greek, χείρ (*kheír*) meaning "hand."

12 Sebastiano Serlio, *Sebastiano Serlio On Architecture I: Books I–IV of "Tutte l'Opere d'Architettura et Prospettiva,"* Vaughan Hart and Peter Hicks, trans. (New Haven, CT and London: Yale University Press, 1996), 83–91. See also Vitruvius, *De architectura*, 5.6.8 (Granger translation, 288–289).

13 Ibid.

14 Ibid., 83.

15 Vitruvius, *De architectura*, 5.6.8 (Granger translation, 289).

16 Sam Ridgway, "Theater of Architectural Monsters," in *Ceilings and Dreams: The Architecture of Levity,* Paul Emmons, Federica Goffi, and Jodi La Coe, eds. (New York and London: Routledge, 2019), 212–213.

17 Vitruvius, *De architectura*, 5.3.1 (Granger translation, 262–263).

18 David C. Lindberg, *Theories of Vision from Al-Kindi to Kepler* (Chicago, IL and London: The University of Chicago Press, 1976), 1–9.

19 Martin Kemp, *The Science of Art: Optical Theories from Brunelleschi to Seurat* (New Haven, CT and London: Yale University Press, 1990), 83.

20 Plato, *Plato IX: Timaeus, Critias, Cleitophon, Menexenus, Epistles*, R. G. Bury, trans. (Cambridge, MA and London: Harvard University Press, [1929] 1989), 100–101.

21 Vitruvius, *De Architectura*, 3.3.10 (Granger translation, 170–181).

22 Richard Tobin, "Ancient Perspective and Euclid's Optics," *Journal of the Warburg and Courtauld Institutes* 53 (1990): 14–41. https://www.jstor.org/stable/751337, accessed on March 11, 2020. See also Alberto Pérez-Gómez and Louise Pelletier, *Architectural Representation and the Perspective Hinge* (Cambridge, MA and London: MIT Press, 1997), 13.

23 Plato, *Plato: The Republic*, H. D. P. Lee, trans. (Middlesex; Victoria; and Baltimore, MD: Penguin Books, [1955] 1958), 278–282.

24 Ibid.

25 Frances A. Yates, *The Art of Memory* (Chicago, IL: University of Chicago Press, 1966), 131.

26 Ibid., 135.

27 *Playtime*. Directed by Jacques Tati. Produced by Bernard Maurice and René Silvera. Performed by Jacques Tati and Barbara Dennek (France: Specta Films and Jolly Film, December 16, 1967).

28 *Rear Window*. Directed and produced by Alfred Hitchcock. Performed by James Stewart and Grace Kelly (Los Angeles, CA: Paramount Pictures Corp., 1954).

Chapter 24

Permeability and the Urban Interior

Nicky Ryan

In the context of increasing global uncertainty, a perception evidenced by rising youth unemployment, inter-state conflict, climate change, the emergence of new anti-establishment political parties, and the challenge to international and European alliances with Brexit and American nationalism, the 16th Venice Architecture Biennale offered its visitors a world view of a more optimistic nature in *Freespace*. Curated by Yvonne Farrell and Shelley McNamara, architecture is described as translating needs into meaningful space, with *Freespace* as 'the generosity of spirit and sense of humanity at the core of architecture's agenda.'1 As a response to this theme, Caruso St. John Architects with artist Marcus Taylor created *Island* at the British Pavilion, a provocative work that presented an empty interior and scaffolded exterior with a temporary public piazza on the roof. This chapter uses *Island* as a case study to consider permeability and the urban interior and the socio-political issues that arise in the human experience of interstitial spaces.

The Venice Biennale is a temporary large-scale exhibition-event and focus for discourse production. Established in 1895, it was originally set up by scholarly public institutions concerned with national accomplishments and major breakthroughs in the traditions of art practice and is arguably the most prestigious of the many biennales which have proliferated globally. The biennale has its antecedents in the international trade shows of the nineteenth century and throughout its history has served many purposes. There is no single biennale format, a biennale is a blockbuster, a mega-exhibition, an occasion, a proposal, a theoretical line of inquiry, a continuous 'happening,' and a cultural artifact in its own right. It has been used instrumentally as a tool for representing the nation-state in the politics of international cultural diplomacy[2]; for promoting cities within the global marketplace with close links to policies of regeneration and boosterism; for highlighting the zeitgeist in art, architecture, and curatorial practice; and as a site of learning and experimentation.

DOI: 10.4324/9780429443091-29

The biennale is a form of exhibition closely linked to tourism. In the case of Venice, it provides an aesthetic experience where displays can be staged against a historic backdrop. The main sites in Venice are the Giardini della Biennale which houses the purpose-built national pavilions; the Arsenale, a former site of depots, shipyards, and workshops; and 'collateral events' (the additional exhibitions associated with the official biennale) spread across the Venetian neighborhoods. In 1980, Venice hosted the first architectural biennale which was initiated as a means of finding 'the best architectural means to engage with the public while stimulating intellectual debate.'[3] An in-between space for creativity and communication, the biennale was an important event for the staging of the networking practices, hierarchies, and capital that structured the field of architecture. The main challenge for its curators was to bring this specialist field to a broader public so that non-specialists could engage with the prevailing conditions and concerns around contemporary architecture.[4]

Grafton Architects, the curators of the 2018 biennale, expressed a desire to move away from a concentration on the object to the space created by architecture. They acknowledged the challenge in communicating architecture without making architecture or creating a stage set. The naming of each biennale is important because it provides a cohesive branding and unifying conceptual framework for a show which comprised abundant and divergent material. Setting a theme (albeit one which is wide-ranging, inclusive, and global) assists critical navigation for the purposes of meaning and direction, and signposts a key architectural preoccupation at any given moment. The choice of *Freespace* was intended to foreground 'the additional component' that architecture as a profession could contribute to humanity by considering 'the earth as Client'[5] and by nurturing and supporting meaningful contact between people and place. Given the global context of rising concerns about climate change and the disappearance of the natural world, a key emphasis of the 16th Venice Architecture Biennale was a focus on understanding how architecture affects the environment, natural resources, and human well-being.[6]

Island was commissioned by the British Council, which took over organization of the British Pavilion exhibitions in 1937, including the selection process and building preservation. The British Council was founded in 1934 during a time of international instability which has some parallels with the uncertainties experienced today. In the 1930s, Britain's influence was diminishing due to a global financial depression which resulted in declining economic circumstances and a rising disaffection with incumbent governments expressed in the growth of extreme ideologies such as communism and fascism. The British Council's stated mission is to develop a 'friendly knowledge and understanding' between the UK and other countries.[7] Its aims are to create opportunities, build connections, and engender trust in order to strengthen the UK's security, prosperity, and influence in the world. A registered charity, the British Council has promoted British values, culture, and education around the world for over eight decades, using soft power[8] to cultivate relationships which survived the Second World War and the end of Empire. Soft power and cultural diplomacy[9] are important components of the UK government discourse on foreign policy.

In this context, *Island* was a bold choice for the commissioning panel as it held a multiplicity of meanings and implied critique. It is a useful example to discuss in terms of interior architecture as it subverted the relationship between inside and out and repositioned the locus of activity onto the exterior of the building. There were no architectural exhibits inside the pavilion; instead, the visitor was confronted with an empty space. The result was a sense of dislocation and confusion as audiences assimilated the potential significance of this architectural vacuum. On closer inspection, it was revealed that the space was not empty but retained scratches, a residue of masking tape and dirt on floors and walls from Phyllida Barlow's 2017 exhibition. The interior could be read as a palimpsest, something re-used and bearing the traces of its most recent activity. The palimpsest is a powerful metaphor used in a wide variety of disciplines,[10] to highlight the interplay between erasure and inscription and how that exchange produces entangled layers and multi-temporal outcomes that disrupt linear time.

The decision to leave the historic British Pavilion building empty and to encase it in an alternative temporary structure had political significance. The original building is a neoclassical structure built in 1887 as a café restaurant when the Giardini was a public park with open access for all.[11] It was repurposed in 1907 by British architect E. A. Rickards who extended the exhibition space and located a marble tablet 'GRAN BRETAGNA' above the entrance. During the Edwardian period, in spite of the size and expanse of its Empire, Britain's power was gradually being superseded by that of the United States and Germany, the latter presenting a military as well as economic threat. The location of the pavilion at the top of the 'Montagnola' (mound) at the end of the Viale dei Platani gave Britain a commanding position using architectural language. It referenced the classical style of the English country house and its associated myth of nostalgia, heritage, and aristocracy.[12] In a world where geo-political territories were shifting and the values of Empire were being called into question, the pavilion provided an appropriately restrained symbol of 'Britishness' and continuity.

Island framed the historic British Pavilion as an exhibit in its own right. With nothing on display, attention was redirected toward the building itself, to the internal layout of a large, central chamber flanked by smaller rooms, as well as to the play of light on white walls and wooden flooring. The *Freespace* Manifesto called for a focus on the quality of space itself with an emphasis on 'nature's gifts of light and materials'[13] and *Island* responded accordingly. The installation retained the significance of the main façade which comprised an open loggia accessed by a flight of steps. Scaffolding wrapped around the building and provided an alternative staircase up to the roof, but this was secondary in terms of visible clues to entry. Visitors continued to be drawn to the imposing central staircase, where they ascended and passed though the threshold of the loggia into spaces of the empty gallery. The threshold is a zone imbued with tectonic and ceremonial context and has provided a rich source of analysis for many cultural and architectural critics. Walter Benjamin[14] described the architectural language of passage, peristyle, pronaos, and portal as a space both temporal and spatial, not a border but something between, offering a constellation of events and possibilities.

For Duncan and Wallach in their discussion of the ritualistic passage into gallery spaces and museums, they argued that the combination of architectural layout and art on display organized 'the visitor's experience as a script organizes a performance.'[15] The ceremonial and performative rite of passage through the threshold space of the portico raises and in the case of *Island* disrupts and subverts visitor expectations. Interstitial spaces have been characterized by Sennet[16] as liminal, fluid places that mediate; they are zones of transition between the public and private. *Island*, however, was a quasi-public space with access limited by opening times and biennale entry fees. At the British Pavilion, entrance visitors were greeted by invigilators who offered written material, opened up discussion, elicited new interpretations, offered safety advice, and carried out a form of benign surveillance. For Dovey and Wood, thresholds represent a dialectic between private and public; they provide an interface which mediates power relations and controls access depending on socio-spatial boundary controls.[17]

If the leitmotif of *Island* was anxiety, this sense of unease was created through a combination of empty galleries, a make-shift wooden piazza, and shroud of scaffolding which partially obscured the British Pavilion. Scaffolding operated as the primary visual metaphor used to signal change, abandonment, obsolescence, and the idea of something being repurposed. In the context of Brexit, Britain's exit from the European Union and with government claims of a new 'Global Britain,' *Island* can be read as a powerful political critique suggesting a country in the process of transformation and reconstruction. Scaffolding is the most explicitly liminal building state[18] and communicated a sense of something in process and perpetually unfinished. The relationship between the flexible structural skeleton and the permanent historic building was one of tension; simultaneously parasitic and supportive, revealing and concealing. This permeable shell offered visitors access to the previously inaccessible roof of the British Pavilion by means of a temporary staircase and lift, opening up opportunities for elevated perspectives and framing new views across the Giardini and Venetian Lagoon.

Scaffolding is a noun, verb, object, and action with material, visual, conceptual, and allegorical power. It is a ubiquitous kit-of-parts technology used in the construction of myriad forms of inhabitation, support, and access, and a universal and cost-effective architectural tool of intervention.[19] It is also a metaphor used in education and psychology to represent the framework of successive levels of temporary support required for the development of learning and understanding. The deployment of scaffolding in architecture has a long history dating back to ancient Egypt and has been used in contemporary architecture by companies such as Assemble, Carmody Groake, MVRDV, as well as appearing in the 2016 Biennale in the Polish Pavilion where the human cost of construction was its subject matter. In the city of Venice, scaffolding is regularly appropriated for commercial use as major historical sites under repair such as the Doges Palace advertising luxury brands. A powerful temporal and cultural signifier, scaffolding can work as a provocation and radical form of intervention into the political landscape. In *Island* the temporary staircase offered an escape route to the raft-like piazza above the vacant pavilion, a form of refuge and shelter from the metaphorical storms of political turmoil and the physical extremes of weather increasingly attributed to global climate change.

The new space on the roof of the British Pavilion, set among the trees of the Giardini and open to the sky, was configured as a social and recreational space. The floor, with its chequerboard pattern, was reminiscent of an Italian piazza and populated with tables, umbrellas, and chairs inviting relaxation and conversation. The only dissonant feature was the apex of the neoclassical British Pavilion gallery roof which jutted out of the center of the floor like an island, reminding visitors of a past submerged by the tide of global events. The past was further alluded to through the daily ritual of serving afternoon tea where the performance of this act of national generosity underlined its cultural ambiguities. The programming of events provided a key mechanism to elicit civic interaction, activate meaning, and provide critical impetus. According to *Island's* commissioner Sarah Mann, curated content highlighted the pavilion's role as 'a space for debate, for the exchange of ideas, and for visionary thinking.'[20] Adaptation through performance emphasized the provisional quality of everyday urban life and the potential of thresholds as places of becoming and transformation.

The state of anxiety which suffused *Island* is derived from signifiers drawn from a range of influences highlighted in the accompanying book designed by John Morgan Studio.[21] These include literature, poems, and visuals about disasters and flooding, including a chapter entitled Acqua Alta. The latter was particularly prescient, given the storms of November 2018 and the consequent flooding of Venice, a UNESCO world heritage site. Built on water and perpetually threatened by mass tourism, reduced public funding, flooding, and architectural decay, the status of Venice as a 'city in peril' is a well-established trope.[22] Plans for flooding barriers had been delayed through escalating costs and political corruption, while Venice is increasingly endangered as rising sea levels exacerbated by climate change threaten the sinking city. During Acqua Alta, wooden passarelle, or temporary elevated walkways, enabled pedestrians to navigate their way through the submerged streets. *Island's* wooden platform supported by scaffolding referenced this Venetian temporary response to an emergency situation and suggested a form of sanctuary during troubled times.

Island eludes rigid spatial codification as an urban interior. It was a permeable space with various access and observation points and challenged traditional binaries such as interior/exterior, public/private, individual/collective, and open/closed. The British Pavilion of 2018 had multiple qualities and was 'a space of indeterminacy,'[23] purposively blended, combined, and multi-layered. Through its porous layout, programming, and performance, modification and change were privileged over the fixed and static. Open to the elements, it responded to and incorporated local and global environmental concerns, as well as through eclectic influences of perceived, represented, and imagined space. *Island* could be characterized as a form of 'assemblage'[24] where space had a fluid identity that was open to interpretation, better understood in relational rather than representational terms. A cluster of connections that intersected subject and object, the installation constituted a socio-spatial territory that was both dynamic and productive.[25] Entangled with capitalism through the commercial processes of the biennale, *Island* nevertheless offered a timely provocation for an anxious age.

Notes

1   Yvonne Farrell and Shelley McNamara, "Freespace Manifesto", *Reading Design*. https://www. readingdesign.org/freespace-manifesto/

2   Monica Sassiteli, "The Biennalization of Art Worlds: The Culture of Cultural Events", in *Routledge International Handbook of the Sociology of Art and Culture*, ed. Laurie Hanquinet and Mike Savage (London: Routledge, 2016).

3   Lea-Catherine Szacka, *Exhibiting the Postmodern: The 1980 Venice Architecture Biennale* (Venice: Marsilio, 2016), 14.

4   Aaron Levy and William Menking, *Architecture on Display: On the History of the Venice Biennale of Architecture* (London: Architectural Association Publications, 2010), 205.

5   Yvonne Farrell and Shelley McNamara, 28th Annual Architecture Lecture, Royal Academy, 16th July 2018.

6   IPCC (Intergovernmental Panel on Climate Change), *Global Warming of 1.5 Degrees Centigrade* (2018). https://www.ipcc.ch/sr15/chapter/summary-for-policy-makers/

7   Our Organisation, *British Council*. https://www.britishcouncil.org/organisation

8   Joseph Nye, *Soft Power: The Means to Success in World Politics* (New York: Public Affairs, 2004).

9   Melissa Nisbett, "New Perspectives on Instrumentalism: An Empirical Study of Cultural Diplomacy", *International Journal of Cultural Policy*, 19, no. 5 (2013): 557–575.

10 Geoff Bailey, "Time Perspectives, Palimpsests and the Archaeology of Time", *Journal of Anthropological Archaeology*, 26 (2007): 198–223.

11 Marco Mulzzani, *Guide to the Pavilions of the Venice Biennale Since 1887* (Milan: Electa, 2017): 52–53.

12 Ruth Adams, "The V&A, The Destruction of the Country House and the Creation of English Heritage", *Museum and Society*, 11, no. 1 (2013): 1–18.

13 16th Venice Architecture Exhibition, Biennale Architettura 2018, Freespace, La Biennale de Venezia https://www.labiennale.org/en/architecture/2018/16th-international-architecture-exhibition

14 Walter Benjamin cited in Georges Teyssot "A Topology of Thresholds", *Home Cultures*, 2, no. 1 (2005): 90.

15 Carol Duncan and Allan Wallach, "The Museum of Modern Art as Late Capitalist Ritual: An Iconographic Analysis", *Marxist Perspectives*, 1, no. 4 (1978): 28–51.

16 Richard Sennet "The Pnyx and the Agora" in: *Designing Politics: The Limits of Design.* (London: LSE Cities, 2016) https://www.readingdesign.org/the-pnyx-and-the-agora/

17 Kim Dovey and Stephen Wood, "Public/private Urban Interfaces: Type, Adaptation, Assemblage", *Journal of Urbanism: International Research on Placemaking and Urban Sustainability*, 8, no. 1 (2015): 1–16.

18 Catherine Slessor, "Skin Deep", *Architectural Review* (September 2017): 38–42.

19 Greg Barton, "Scaffolding" Exhibition, Architecture Center, New York, October 2–January 18, 2017.

20 Sarah Mann, "British Pavilion: ISLAND" https://venicebiennale.britishcouncil.org/2018-exhibition

21 Caruso St John and Marcus Taylor, *Island* (London: The Store X The Spaces, 2018).

22 Salvatore Settis, *If Venice Dies* (London: Pallas Athene, 2016).

23 Mary Modeen, "Breaking the Boundaries of 'Self': Representations of Spatial Indeterminacy", *Architecture and Culture*, 2, no. 3 (2014): 337–360.

24 Arun Saldanha, *Space After Deleuze* (New York: Bloomsbury, 2017).

25 Kim Dovey, "Incremental Urbanism: The Emergence of Informal Settlements" in *Emergent Urbanism*, ed. Tigran Haas and Krister Ollson (Oxon & New York, 2014).

Chapter 25

When the Whole Neighborhood Becomes Home

Domestic Interiors of an Urban Kampung

Paramita Atmodiwirjo and Yandi Andri Yatmo

The idea of home conveys senses of comfort, belonging, and identity that are manifested within the domestic interior. This idea challenges the boundaries of the domestic interior beyond the physical materiality of interior objects and spaces in the house. This is particularly relevant to residential neighborhoods characterized by strong social and cultural ties that could potentially alter the domestic boundaries. The idea of the domestic interior as a private domain may be shifted through the emergence of a collective interior when the inhabitants identify themselves collectively with the neighborhood spaces.

Quite often, the spatial practices in a neighborhood suggest the porosity of everyday space, where the boundaries between inside and outside are blurred. The inside–outside dialectic in an urban neighborhood could be the result of the traversing of boundaries from *outside in* and/or *inside out*, as well as the traversing of interior entities to the outside space.[1] The latter is also illustrated by Walter Benjamin and Asja Lacis in *Naples* concerning how the living room is extended to the street: "Just as the living room reappears on the street, with chairs, hearth, and altar, so, only much more loudly, the street migrates into the living room."[2]

This chapter reveals the interiority of an urban kampung neighborhood in Jakarta, Indonesia, through a descriptive account of the everyday spatial practices that transform the whole neighborhood into a large, collective domestic interior. Traversing the neighborhood as if moving from "room" to "room" in an urban setting, we identify the aspects of spatial practice that are important to understanding the urban domestic interior.

DOI: 10.4324/9780429443091-30

The Emergence of Domesticity

A key idea of domesticity is the intimate relationship between the user and the home spaces. Home is a place where domesticity is constructed and understood through personal experiences and associations.[3] For its inhabitants, home becomes a setting for refuge, privacy, and self-reflection.[4] The interiority of home reflects the dialectic between the spatial setting and its occupants.

It is important to note the different ways the interiority of domestic space emerges. First, *interiority is constructed* physically when domestic architectural quality is created through the logic of the construction of objects and envelopes.[5] The presence of objects arranged in a particular configuration generates a certain domestic architectural quality. Another way that interiority is constructed is by *producing the condition of the interior*. Interiority is a condition experienced by individuals and produced by the environment.[6] The making of an interior is the making of a place for experiences and personal interiority. Producing the conditions of the interior becomes important for a public setting to be transformed into a setting where individual purpose can be achieved.

In this chapter, we take the position that domestic architectural quality in urban settings emerged from the relationship among actors, spaces, objects, events, actions, and sociocultural contexts. We emphasize the importance of spatial practice[7] in which the qualities of space are determined through the ways that inhabitants operate in their everyday space. Rather than seeing the interior as architectural components or objects, the interior is produced by its inhabitant.[8] Hence, interiority emerges as a result of everyday spatial practice.

Neighborhood as an Urban Domestic Interior – Extending the Spatial Scale

Examining the emergence of interiority within the scale of a neighborhood is an attempt to extend the idea of the domestic interior beyond the scale of home. The domestic interior is often perceived in relation to the scale of home with certain spatial practices. It is important to note that domesticity should not be limited to associations with the private interior domain only, as the aspects of interiority that make up domesticity could also be created within the larger domain. The neighborhood setting is unique because it is not entirely public; rather, this territory is associated with particular groups of residents, compared to the public domain as a setting for complete strangers that do not know one another. It serves as a medium to ensure continuity between the intimacy of the private domestic space and the unknown domain of the city.[9]

When considering the neighborhood as a domestic interior, the question of scale emerged. If the domesticity in the home setting could be examined by going through the interior of one room to another, then it should also be possible to examine the neighborhood space in the same way. We often study the domestic interior by looking into the typology of spaces with particular functions and objects associated with each space[10] as a common way of classifying our domestic space in everyday life and in design practice. Home spaces could also be broken down into the "home parts"[11] that comprise objects and spaces. When the notion of interiority is examined within the setting of the neighborhood, such a typology may offer a starting point to understand the neighborhood spaces. One can make the analogy of the neighborhood and one's home,[12] and thus, one can examine the "neighborhood parts"—how each part is associated with particular activities that contribute to the emergence of domesticity.

From Room to Room in an Urban *Kampung* Neighborhood

The following illustrations will allow us to travel from "room" to "room" in an urban *kampung* neighborhood in Jakarta to understand forms of appropriation that transform the whole neighborhood into a domestic interior. The observed neighborhood is an urban *kampung* located in Cikini, Central Jakarta; it displays an example of a form of community resilience throughout the current urban development. Situated between vast urban developments, the *kampung* retains the community's important values of social relations and collectivity. Hence, it is interesting to examine how everyday activities have characterized this neighborhood space to become a large domestic interior.

The illustrations are based on findings from our participant observations that aim to explore the experiences of residents, including how they associate themselves with the spaces. Each part of the neighborhood can be considered as a kind of "room" parallel to each "room" within one's home. The movement from one part of the home interior to another is parallel to the movement from one part of the neighborhood to another, as "trajectories."[13]

Living Room

The living room is where the inhabitants of domestic space open their territory to the public. In this neighborhood, the living room appears not as a particular space within individual houses, but as various partially enclosed nodes, such as house terraces or front yards. Intimacy is created among the neighbors when gathering in these spaces from time to time. A gathering in one of the resident's houses occurred when one neighbor appeared and sat on the terrace, followed by others, some bringing food and drinks to be enjoyed together. Discussions emerged and more neighbors began to arrive; the event became a public gathering, taking place in space normally claimed as the private domain.

The occupation of the terrace creates domesticity through the transition of the private domain into the collective interior. The terrace becomes a *living room*, not simply because there are elements to sit, although on some occasions, objects and furniture that are normally inside are brought outside. Nevertheless, social relations demonstrated through the act of visiting one another and gathering as the everyday routine trigger the emergence of this *living room* (Image 25.1).

Kitchen

The kitchen is where domestic chores are normally performed, to cater to the daily needs of the household. The unique emergence of a collective kitchen in the urban *kampung* neighborhood could be witnessed during a particular celebratory event, such as Independence Day, when residents have an annual celebration. The celebration involves almost everyone in the neighborhood, and various kinds of food are served during the event. Housewives are responsible

Image 25.1 The *living room*—transforming the private domain into the collective interior. Credit: Paramita Atmodiwirjo

for the preparation of food, which is usually performed in one of the backyards or in a place temporarily set up for that purpose.

Cooking, normally performed in the individual dwelling, now becomes a collective activity to the benefit of the whole neighborhood. Food preparation for the event is quite complex and requires a large space; hence, the collective *kitchen* is established. The space for cooking is no longer confined to individual home kitchens. Neighbors who own large cooking pots and pans contribute their equipment, as well as dishes and eating utensils for collective use. Food preparation jobs are divided among participants, with a workflow that is well understood by everyone to ensure that all dishes are ready before the event begins.

Dining Room

The neighborhood also becomes a setting for dining and celebration; it has some places where food is served, people are gathered, and special moments are celebrated. It is customary for the neighborhood to transform the street or open space for various types of celebration. For example, the street could be transformed as nodes for a wedding ceremony, while a larger open field could be utilized as a place for the night bazaar.

The transformation of the street to become a place for a wedding ceremony was triggered by the need for a large gathering space that could accommodate many guests. Due to expensive rental of a party hall, the occupation of the street becomes a more viable option for residents. The wedding ceremony setting is created by erecting a tent and providing a stage for the bride and groom, chairs for guests, and tables for food. Such setting up becomes an act of creating an interior within an open public street, as an act of interiorizing the street to host a family event. Meanwhile, the act of interiorizing the open field to become a night bazaar offers the opportunity for neighborhood residents to partake in entertainment and enjoyment. The night bazaar comprises various stalls selling things, food and drink or offering games with prizes. The experience of the night bazaar displays the collective excitement and experiences that transform the space into a collective *dining room* and celebration space (Image 25.2).

Play Room

The domestic interior also serves as the setting of play. Within the boundaries of the neighborhood, both children and adults are the active users of the open field, as well as other public open spaces for various types of play and sporting

Image 25.2 Domestic interior for dining and celebration.
Credit: Yandi Andri Yatmo

activities. Even the bridge connecting the parts of the neighborhood becomes a setting for a game, where one child acts as a "crocodile" and the others need to pass without being captured.

The presence of various open spaces throughout the neighborhood is perceived by the residents as opportunities for engaging in various play and sport activities. The extension of these *play rooms* beyond the limits of the home space is important because it offers access to a large open space for collective activities. The spaces are known by the residents as settings for play on particular days and times. The use of these spaces creates another form of association between occupants and the neighborhood spaces. Such use promotes a sense of belonging to the neighborhood, as well as intense social relations among the users, hence producing another form of domesticity (Image 25.3).

Alleys and Streets as Domestic Interior Paths

In addition to particular spaces and spots that are used for various everyday activities, the presence of paths within the neighborhood contains another potential for domesticity. They become the container of moving actions. The journey taken by a group of women on their way to the exercise field occurs along the neighborhood alleys, where they do not merely walk toward the destination, but develop conversations, greet neighbors, and sometimes stop to catch up with the latest news. The path becomes a container for a journey that strengthens the social interactions among neighbors.

The streets are also the paths for the children's hangout journey from place to place in the neighborhood. They develop their sense of identity with these places by moving and stopping at particular spots that contain objects of attraction that fulfill their curiosity and urge to play. The presence of these places and objects is important to develop an association between the child and the neighborhood, as *domestic interior paths* that extend beyond their individual domestic space.

Image 25.3 Neighborhood field and paths as play spaces.
Credit: Paramita Atmodiwirjo

Expanding the Scope of the Urban Domestic Interior

The illustration from "room" to "room" in this urban *kampung* demonstrates the emergence of domesticity through the collective acts and social relations among inhabitants. Various everyday spatial practices occupying different parts of the neighborhood demonstrate how residents attach themselves to the places where those activities occur. The residents' attachment to these routines, along with their active engagement in the act of transforming and occupying space, creates familiarity and intimacy with the spaces. This eventually transforms the meaning of neighborhood space into a domestic interior that is collectively used, occupied, and transformed by the residents. While the distinction between the private house and the public neighborhood remains, these two kinds of domestic settings complement each other in defining the domesticity of the neighborhood.

The perspective framed herein offers an alternative way of understanding domesticity and the domestic interior. It suggests the possibility for the emergence of an urban interior that is characterized by domestic performance. It also suggests that understanding interiority could be independent from the spatial scale—the everyday spatial practices that contain domesticity need not follow the spatial hierarchy from domestic private domain to public domain. It is possible that domesticity emerges throughout the scales of the environment.

Several aspects seem to be contributing to the transformation of the urban setting into a large domestic interior. The first is the existing social relations among the neighborhood residents, who develop a collective intimacy through the close everyday interactions and the culture of space sharing. The second is the limitation of space in individual houses that triggers the residents to extend their activity space and hence create porosity between the inside and outside spaces, between the private and public domains. Finally, the third is the fluidity of the neighborhood space and its readiness for temporal transformation from a functional definition to another, from private to public, and from individual to collective association.

These aspects suggest that the experience of the neighborhood as a domestic interior is triggered by both the spatial practices of the inhabitants and the spatial setting where the practices take place. Understanding these aspects becomes critical to exploring the possibilities for developing urban neighborhood spaces and other urban settings with particular characteristics of domesticity. It is important that any attempts of intervention in an urban neighborhood should not neglect the processes and practices that give shape to the domesticity of their inhabitants.

Notes

1   Paramita Atmodiwirjo, Yandi Andri Yatmo, and Verarisa Anastasia Ujung, "Outside interior: Traversed boundaries in a Jakarta urban neighborhood," *IDEA Journal*, 2015(1), pp. 78–89.

2   Walter Benjamin and Asja Lacis, "Naples," in Peter Demetz (ed.), Reflections: Essays, aphorisms, autobiographical writings (New York: Schocken, 1986), p. 171.

3   Charles Rice, The *emergence of the interior: Architecture, modernity, domesticity* (London; New York: Routledge, 2007), p. 4.

4   Penny Sparke, *The modern interior* (London: Reaktion Books, 2008), p. 25.

5   Marie Frier Hvejsel, "Interiority: A critical theory of domestic architecture" (PhD Thesis, Aalborg Universiteit, 2011), p. 6.

6   Mark Pimlott, "Interiority and the conditions of interior," *Interiority*, vol. 1, no. 1 (February 27, 2018), p. 8.

7   Michel De Certeau, *The practice of everyday life* (Berkeley: University of California Press, 1984).

8   Alexa Griffith Winton, "Inhabited space: Critical theories and the domestic interior," in Graeme Brooker and Lois Weinthal (eds.), *The handbook of interior architecture and design* (London: Bloomsbury, 2013), p. 47.

9   Michel De Certeau, Luce Giard, and Pierre Mayol, *The practice of everyday life. Volume 2: Living and cooking* (Minneapolis: University of Minnesota Press, 1998), p. 11.

10 Georges Perec, *Species of spaces and other pieces* (London: Penguin Books, 2008), p. 27.

11 Kathy Mezei and Chiara Briganti, *The domestic space reader* (Toronto: University of Toronto Press, 2013), p. 199.

12 This analogy is described as "the act of arranging one's interior space rejoins that of arranging one's own trajectories in the urban space of the neighborhood." See De Certeau, Giard, and Mayol, *The practice of everyday life*, p. 11.

13 De Certeau, Giard, and Mayol, *The practice of everyday life*, p. 11.

Chapter 26

Contextualizing and Politicizing the Urban Public Interiors of Istanbul

Alison B. Snyder

Istanbul is continually transforming and being remade. Its historical development over several millennia is composed of many cultures with an assortment of surviving traditions and customs generated through a diverse range of local conditions and global factors. Presenting a multi-layered and complex urbanism, centuries-old arterial networks are still utilized and built edifices of all different eras sit side-by-side. This chapter argues that a vibrant urban interior,[1] the *passage*, has become a key indicator of cultural shifts taking place in Istanbul. The nineteenth- and twentieth-century passages—found abundantly in the district of Beyoğlu—present complex stories about the ever-evolving city concerning different levels of use.[2] Since the definition of *passage* is both a noun and a verb, practical, philosophical, or phenomenological meanings become useful in describing how architectural, interior, and behavioral contexts interact. Thus, the continuance or loss of these urban interior spaces and the notions of interiority being maintained or redeveloped in the city signify an ongoing urban vitality that is reliant on change, however paradoxical.

In the case of the passage, this type of architectural interior also represents concepts of modernity and progress in a historically progressive-minded zone of the city. The multi-use passage buildings and the spaces within them have helped to maintain the lively heterogeneous composition of the city. Due to various factors, however, freedoms of activity along streets and interiors are eroding and a newer type of *constructed homogeneity* has begun to appear.[3]

To further understand how these interior-oriented places and their spatialization take part in defining the contemporary city, reading the work of social theorists, historians, urbanists, philosophers, and designers presents a broad and useful lens to gauge Istanbul's complexity. Utilizing Edward Soja's term "thirdspace" is helpful, as he explains that cities must be studied from a

DOI: 10.4324/9780429443091-31

Alison B. Snyder

Figure 26.1 Aerial view of Istanbul showing the edges of the European side of the city with (a) indicating where the district of Beyoğlu is located, (b) indicating a small portion of the Old City across the Golden Horn, and (c) showing a hint of Asia on the other side of the Bosphorus Strait. Indicated by (d) is the easily identifiable long, bent Istiklal Avenue, which is the focus of study with its surrounding passage spaces.
Credit: Alison B. Snyder

trialectical vantage or a "simultaneously spatial, social, and historical perspective."[4] Serving as grounding points for what might (or does) occur in Beyoglu, internal and external forces such as national and global migration, shifting economics, and political implications are yielding an ever-present sense of hyper-transformation in this built environment.[5] Cityspace is, therefore, formed by a series of experiences and perceptions from formal to subjective. A focus on three of the passages will illustrate some of these issues.

The Growth of Beyoğlu and Its Significance

The Beyoğlu district is long famous for its international inclusiveness and cosmopolitan culture. Located on the European side of the city across the Golden Horn waterway, and opposite the historic Old City (see Figure 26.1), it was settled as a Genoese merchant colony in the fourteenth century. This lower area is still referred to as Galata, while the area above and beyond Galata was/ is called Pera. Its hilly topography added to the later complex parcelization starting especially in the late 1700s.

Beyoğlu's settlement responded to the growing city's internationalism with incoming consulates, investors, and new populations. The large development spurt contributing to Pera's expansion grew out of concepts associated with *modernity*—a complex mixture of diverse types of societal progress that came about through both Eastern and Western interests, including not only modernizing technologically, but a late Ottoman embracing of different social, cultural, religious, and political outlooks. These circumstances came to be defined by the unusual grouping of pre-existing and new activities not found in other parts of the city. The great growth mostly occurred along or surrounding the old, continuously used path that now makes up a kilometer-long arterial spine. The iconic İstiklal Caddesi, meaning Independence Avenue, was renamed in 1923 at the start of the Republic. Enduring many transitions, the now pedestrian via since 1990, has for centuries joined two squares: Taksim at the top and Tünel at its lowest point.

An eclectic composition of spaces and hybridized needs eventually developed into multi-story buildings inside Pera's narrow irregular parcels, accommodating varied architectural styles and attitudes.[6] Creating and manufacturing a new modernity included the formation of intriguing building compositions that resulted in roofed and open passage types with pass-through zones whose cross-sectional attributes placed different kinds of destinations on many levels. Ideas of what constituted public and private spaces shifted to include street activities and those elevated to upper levels, creating a uniquely mixed interior.

The Many Meanings of a *Passage* in Beyoğlu

Recognizing and explaining interiority within a complex cityspace is difficult. Considering the various meanings of the word *passage* and how they can help to describe city experiences will further illuminate the ideas embedded in Beyoğlu's spaces. Extremely pertinent is how the Oxford English Dictionary (OED) defines passage concerning movement: "The action of going or moving onward, across, or past; movement from one place or point to another, or over or through a space or medium; transit" and, "to give passage: to allow to pass; to allow access." Equally important are the phenomenal or philosophical possibilities of liminality. The OED defines, "A transition from one state or condition to another, a transition or progress through a period, stage, etc.; a transition in thought or speech from one point, idea, or subject to another"; and, simply put, "The passing *of* time or a period of time."[7]

According to maps and archives, over 30 variations of passages were originally built in the Beyoğlu district but some were taken down and their sites no longer exist. Confirmed by field research, 22 of these urban interior sites still exist in various states of use, adaptation, disuse, and closure, denoting key urban changes. We can refer to architect and theorist Robert Venturi's concept of "residual spaces" to consider how the passage forms a meaningful interior spatial and cultural link within the city. In *Complexity and Contradiction*, he quoted architect Aldo Van Eyck who said, "transition must be articulated by means of defined in-between places which induce simultaneous awareness of what is significant on the other side. An in-between space, in a sense, provides the common ground where conflicting polarities can gain twin phenomena."[8]

Three street spaces create and share a series of internal paths that take on various configurations to connect levels and form networks of paths. The varied passage designs link the commanding avenue to many surrounding streets and alleys, thereby forming a third internal street-like pedestrian space.[9] Inside the passages, the forms vary in scale and shape, with some being straight, L-, +- or T-shaped, with many possessing angles and misshaped courtyards (see Figure 26.2 for some passage plan forms).

The varied locations of the entries/exits hide or expose the interiors that actively invite the visitor while blurring public/private spaces. Thus, the perception of the visitor moving between the three street spaces considers them as thresholds or necessary liminal spaces connecting to or separating from challenging city conditions. The passages provide spaces for strolling, resting,

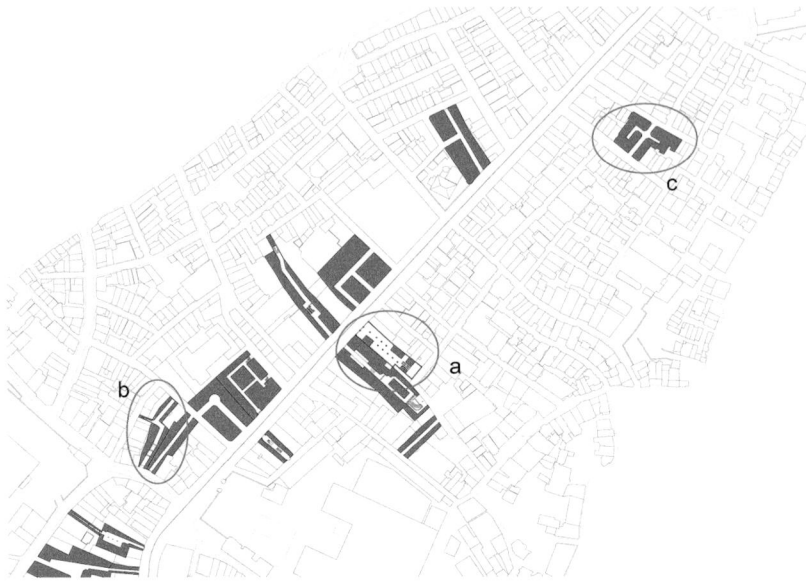

Figure 26.2 Several passages are shown in connection to Istiklal Avenue and several side street/alleys. The various configurations provide for liminal passing through this part of the city, taking refuge within for a few minutes, or partaking in many kinds of activities. Highlighted are the case studies: (a) Anadolu Pasajı, (b) Aslıhan Pasajı, and (c) Afrika Pasajı. Credit: Alison B. Snyder

gazing, or taking refuge from the hyper-use of Istiklal Avenue with its other historic/contemporary buildings: churches, consulates, mosques, museums, shops, and assorted vendors.

The act of traversing the city is also made significant by social critic and philosopher Walter Benjamin in his detailed *The Arcades Project* spanning 1927–1940.[10] The relevance of Benjamin's observations and critique of Parisian cosmopolitan modernity directly relates to the many arcades in that city. Benjamin wrote as an anonymous *flâneur* that Parisian society was tied to the commercial invention of the arcade building type, thus calling attention to the economic status and power representing the time, and the individual freedoms and cultural identities associated. Social philosopher, Michel de Certeau, wrote that the "act, itself of passing by" inside the city simply allows for individual participation and observation.[11] An analogy is easily made with Beyoğlu's passages. As urban destinations, they are stimulating powerful cultural signifiers that invite the individual or the collective to experience everyday interiority.

History of the Arcade or Passage Typology and Istanbul's Beyoğlu Passage

Architectural historian Johann Geist's important volume, *Arcades*, describes and catalogs examples from many countries to create a typology that refers to three Western and Eastern terms: passages, gallerias, and arcades. Curiously, Geist only showed one Istanbul passage that he cited as drawing from the ancient Eastern bazaar, suq, or market—a cellular-formed, aggregate structure found in Turkey and elsewhere in the Middle East and North Africa. He states that these were the precursors to the top-glazed shopping arcades that developed in Paris in the 1780s, first with the Palais Royal, and then proliferated to become the nineteenth-century type.[12]

Paris became the enviable Western example to many developing cities within and beyond Europe, as its infrastructure and architectural genius became symbols of cosmopolitanism. Developers of Beyoğlu were aware of this urbane phenomenon. Yet, in the case of the Beyoğlu passage, they obviously stem from many easily accessible local ancient forms of covered markets and hans (not mentioned by Geist) that remain in use throughout Istanbul and other Turkish cities. Indeed, Czech architect Michaela Brozova also writes about Prague's passages as owing to the zeitgeist of the late nineteenth century but, of course, really taking their cues from the medieval spaces found in Old Prague City.[13] This is not merely a basic regionalist approach, as passages are complex places expressing layers of socio-cultural experiences, and political and economic needs.

Though the Beyoğlu passage appears to be Western, they exude their own character with a variation of form and activity use. Some are constructed up to eight stories on unusually long and narrow sites, and sometimes composed of more than one parcel to allow for the formation of open and closed spaces, and to provide light and air within the topography. The myriad choices of activities in Beyoğlu's passages are also oriented to Istanbul's desires. The many levels on and above the avenue or alley include a changing world of entertainment, work, commerce, and living. Local and touristic activities include bazaars, galleries, cinemas, music venues, bookstores, theaters, cafes/restaurants, offices, libraries, gyms, masjids, and clubs, offering distinctive local and global city frames.

Shifting Culture: The Condition of Three Passage Types

Three passages are selected to form a small case study, with descriptions that expose Istanbul's shifting urbanism (see Figures 26.2 and 26.3 for plan, internal/external views). These urban interiors act "as a means of communication to explain the different kinds of adaptations—gains and losses—taking place in the city."[14]

Figure 26.3 Case studies: Anadolu Pasajı no longer exists as a passage, as shown through the interior of Flo (a), the multi-level shoe store, while (b) shows a view of the original passage's spatial and light qualities. The book-filled interior of Aslıhan Pasajı (c) is coupled with one of its side street entrances (d). The sky view (e) of Afrika Pasajı shows the internal layout of this closed passage, and (f) a the gated entry.
Credit: Alison B. Snyder

Anadolu Pasajı Became "Flo" Shoe Store

The year 2011 marked pronounced change. Anadolu Pasajı became Flo, a mono-use, full-building shoe store. The essence of a relied upon urban passage entered from Istiklal was now blocked, and thus, its street rhythm and internal system were severely altered.

The original 1888 passage structure sits mid-block. Within its context of being an infill site, its two similarly strong, five-story high-masonry facades open to the busy avenue, and a lively alley behind. The Western-style blended neoclassicism is adorned with Turkish features, including a protruding square type of bay, called a *cumba*. The original passage was partially covered at both ends with the middle area left open to the sky. While traversing along and up intermediate steps, there was a sense of a real inner life formed by internal-facing street level shops, with apartments and office windows being daylit from above.

To create Flo, they sealed the alley entry and added a gabled skylight to close the open roof. The most jarring and unfortunate part of the reuse project are the large escalators that fill most of what was the passage zone. This insertion literally and figuratively erased what was special about the passage as a unique public urban interior. The constant memory of Anadolu exists only for those who know to look for its past.

Aslıhan Pasajı

Aslıhan Pasajı is composed of four parcels that combine to primarily house a busy *sahaflar*, or used book market. The structures interestingly mark the spaces of a demolished passage building called Krepen Pasajı constructed in 1870. Today's nondescript 1960s concrete-frame buildings still create the oddly alluring T-shaped, mid-block passage, set in and running parallel to Istiklal. Alıshan's two main entries join a busy historic fish market with an important vehicular street on the other end. Two narrow perpendicular entry/exits connect the main internal passage at two different levels, to a curious restaurant/shop alley.

Approximately 30 crowded book sellers display every subject imaginable and share four split-levels with old button and drapery vendors, newer printers, language teachers, an embedded tea café, and a double-level masjid located on the highest levels overlooking the fish market. The internal set of volumes, with their intimate scales, make this passage remarkable despite its lack of historic aesthetics and confusing odd-angled paths. It is intriguing to pass between objects, posters, maps, and historical memorabilia as well as academic, arts, social and political journals/books piled high in Turkish, French, German, and English. The international vigor of Beyoğlu is alive here. People wander in to browse, to take short cuts, and to find an urban respite, all day long.

Afrika Pasajı

The massive, hulking structure that makes up Afrika Pasajı sits a block in from Istiklal and spans between two bohemian side street/alleys. It rests on the same side of the Avenue as Anadolu/Flo and is closer to Taksim Square. What was a mostly residential structure, the grand and handsome facades hold a uniform rhythm of protruding and receding masonry bays punctuated by windows and small French balconies. Retail and cafes were located within its lower levels. Entering to the midpoint of the passage zone, the architectural surround feels dominant and hidden spaces are revealed to form a lop-sided plus-sign, in plan and sky view.

Today, Afrika is almost indiscernible. With varied openings and partial closures since 2011, due to political/economic development issues, Afrika became barricaded with metal-corrugated sheathing at its base, locked gates, and camouflaged with a white semi-translucent tenting covering all the upper stories. The building recedes and largely disappears. Its street perimeter is marked by urban illustration and graffiti, and hookah cafes and several kinds of outdoor seating sit adjacent to the base encouraging the local entertainment of drinking coffee and playing board games. This enlivens its side streets, but the indeterminate closure acts like another kind of urban public erasure, marking a loss and adding to the homogenization of Beyoğlu.

Conclusion

The notion of a modernity that grew from looking beyond Turkeye's borders is now enmeshed within Beyoğlu's diversity and physically exemplifies variations of architectural and interior forms, with their innovative and changing uses. The passage building typology in Beyoğlu appears to represent both a historical anachronism and an enduring interior architectural type filled with reminders and lessons about urban processes, and how they affect people and urban identity.

Of the three featured iconic examples, only one passage, Aslıhan, survives as a vital, exploratory place with its multi-leveled, mixed uses. Anadolu/ Flo and Afrika exist; yet, they have had their unique passage usage removed. All represent some of the most significant urban messages concerning socio-cultural, economic, and political change in Istanbul—signifying an urban system breaking apart from shrouding disuse, to full removal. Thus, the real and the metaphoric are at work displaying how the Beyoğlu passage is emblematic of a persistent, yet possibly slowly dying, urban interior typology.

Urbanist Yaşar Adanalı wrote, "[urban] space that is full of ambiguity and variety, can host different social and economic relations…" arguably intertwining the formal and the informal.[15] Yet, the evolving alterations and deterioration of the urban built environment present an increasingly constructed homogeneity expressed by compromised use or disuse. Thus, the next stage of Istanbul and Beyoğlu's development is problematic and hard to determine.

Notes

1   Meng Yeu, *Shanghai and the Edges of Empires* (Minneapolis: University of Minnesota Press, 2006), 139. Yue, a comparative language and literature professor, may be the earliest user of the term "urban interior" to identify "…crystal palaces, arcades, malls, and structures of world expositions…" as not only architecture.

2   Mid- and late twentieth-century passages exist in other parts of Istanbul with limited office/ showroom uses; Beyoğlu passages are their precedents.

3   The social, cultural, and architectural conditions expressed are based on over a decade of the author's onsite research combined with secondary sources.

4   Edward Soja, *Postmetropolis Critical Studies of Cities and Regions* (Oxford/Malden, MA: Blackwell, 2000), xiv, 11.

5 The streets of Istanbul and Beyoğlu are often cited in local and global media, showing Turkey as a linchpin in Middle Eastern politics and beyond.

6 Zeynep Celik, *The Remaking of Istanbul: Portrait of an Ottoman City in the Nineteenth Century* (Seattle: University of Washington Press, 1986), one of the best urban development references.

7 *Oxford English Dictionary*, s.v. "Passage, *n.*, v." Accessed January 7, 2020, https://www-oed-com.ezproxy.pratt.edu/search?searchType=dictionary&q=passage&_searchBtn=Search

8 Robert Venturi, *Complexity and Contradiction in Architecture* (New York: Museum of Modern Art, 1966), 80, 82.

9 Pierre Pinon, "Urban Transformation Between the 18th and 19th Centuries", in *72 Rassegna*, ed. V. Gregotti (Bologna: Editrice Compositori, 1997), 52–61; Alison B. Snyder, "City Space, Street Space and Liminal Spaces: Passing Through Beyoğlu's Urban Interiors," in *Dosya 27: Mimarlik ve GundelikYaşam (Architecture and Everyday Life)*, ed. Dr. Meltem Gurel (Ankara: TMMOB Mimarlar Odasi Ankara Şubesi, 2011), 54–62; refer to different morphological researches.

10 Walter Benjamin, *Passagewerken/The Arcades Project* (Cambridge, MA: Harvard University, 1940, 1999 in English).

11 Michel de Certeau, *The Practice of Everyday Life* (Berkeley: The University of California, 1984), 97.

12 Johann Geist, *Arcades, The History of a Building Type* (Cambridge, MA: MIT Press, 1979, 1983). Geist chose only the historic Avrupa Passage (next to Aslihan), perhaps because it resembled the most typical, compact, single-direction European passages.

13 Michaela Brozova, *Prague Passageways and Arcades* (France: Euro Art Volvox Globator, 1997) In 2018, the author conducted research in Prague and discussed ideas with Brozova.

14 Alison B. Snyder, "Shifting Inheritances: Ongoing Adaptations of the *Passage* Inside Istanbul's Beyoğlu District," in *International Journal of Interior Architecture + Spatial Design, Parallel Territories, v. 6*, ed. Z. Qureshi, C. Odom, G. Marinic (Houston: ASD Publications, 2019), 72–79, 75.

15 Yaşar Adanalı, "De-spatialized Space as Neoliberal Utopia: Gentrified Istiklal Street and Commercialized Urban Spaces." *Red Thread eJournal*, 3 (December 2011), 1–13, 4. Accessed December 12, 2018 https://red-thread.org/wp-content/uploads/2018/12/8057516.pdf

Chapter 27

Shopping Spaces in the East and West

Ou Ning

Interior space was created by human beings to shelter themselves from wind, rain, cold, and heat. Its boundary separates people from inclement weather, and thus, people can protect themselves and be productive. Interior space has been built incrementally over the centuries. In urban conditions, individual buildings were grouped along pathways to ultimately form larger settlements. As the scale of human activities kept growing, settlements expanded to form cities. From the perspective of the divine, the earth was divided into two pieces: a piece of non-human space, except for people, everything living under wind and rain. From the perspective of human life, the two spaces are defined as exterior space and interior space. From the perspective of urbanists, they are both non-urban and urban spaces.[1] Urbanists regard the low-density space of the countryside as the antithesis of the city, while human geographers regard the countryside as "the ideal middle world of man poised between the polarities of city and wildness."[2]

Resisting bad weather is the main means for human beings to struggle for living space. In the first half of the nineteenth century, the utopian Phalanstery designed by the French social theorist Charles Fourier was an all-weather continuous interior space in the form of a palace. Fourier was very proud of this large-scale, arcade-style building connected to an inverted U-shape, "...under the Society of Civilization, even the king does not have such facilities. When you walk through their palace, you will get wet in the rain or get cold."[3] In *The Theory of the Four Movements*, Fourier defines the most advanced form of society as a Society of Harmony, and although he named his time the Society of Civilization, the Society of Civilization was deeply immersed in various crises.[4] He envisioned many Phalanxes under the Society of Harmony, and each Phalanx included a Phalanstery with many different Seristeries with different Seristeries and public facilities connected together as one

DOI: 10.4324/9780429443091-32

continuous interior-exterior space. When passing through the courtyard, its domes and windows would block rain and absorb sunlight. It would be characterized by semi-exterior, semi-interior transitions. These zones would maintain proper temperature and strive for more space for utopian residents to avoid the bad weather. It would be one of the more superior performances of the Society of Harmony than the Society of Civilization. Fourier was influenced by the commercial arcades that just appeared in Paris, but the typology was applied to the design of his fantastical and anti-capitalist utopian palace.

In the later utopian novel *Looking Backward* (1996) by Edward Bellamy, the main character, Julian West, was transported through time from 1887 to 2000. West found that Bostonians could go out in the rain without rain boots or umbrellas, "...for a continuous waterproof covering had been let down so as to enclose the sidewalk and turn it into a well-lighted and perfectly dry corridor." Dr. Leete, who accompanied him, explains:

> ...The difference between the age of individualism was well characterized by the fact that, in the nineteenth Century, when it rained, the people of Boston put up three hundred thousand umbrellas over as many heads, and in the twentieth Century they put up one umbrella over all the heads.[5]

This big umbrella over Boston was a continuous interior/semi-interior space that seamlessly connected all human activities.

On the one hand, the emergence of the commercial arcades in Paris, mainly between 1822 and 1837, met the sharp needs of textile production and consumption driven by the Industrial Revolution. On the other hand, their architecture evolved out of steel and glass building technology. The arcades became the center of fashion and the distribution of industrial luxury goods, completely contrary to Fourier's anti-capitalist utopian imagination. However, the boom of arcades in Europe was borrowed thereafter by new spaces such as the Crystal Palace of the Great Exhibition in London (1851), Le Bon Marché department store revamped by Aristide Boucicaut in Paris (1852), and the Palais de l'industrie of the Exposition Universelle in Paris (1855). The driving force of "high capitalism" and new industrial technologies created a more dazzling, all-weather, panoramic paradise for product display and marketing that foreshadowed the later shopping malls. By 1925, Le Passage de l'Opera was demolished and rapid urban spatial variability led to Louis Aragon's surrealist book *Le Paysan de Paris*.[6] Two years later, his book influenced Walter Benjamin to begin writing his seminal tome, *The Arcades Project*.

In his unfinished magnum opus, Benjamin viewed the prosperity and decline of the arcades from the nineteenth century to the twentieth century as a sample of his radical criticism of the capitalist system. He quoted Jules Michelet:

> Every epoch, in fact, not only dreams of the one to follow but, in dreaming, precipitates its awakening. It bears its end within itself and unfolds it–as Hegel already noticed–by cunning. With the destabilizing of the market economy, we begin to recognize the monuments of the bourgeoisie as ruins even before they have crumbled.[7]

The "love at last sight" on the demolished arcade is far more delightful to Parisians than the "love at first sight."[8] This is the nature of consumers who already have the new but still like to mourn the death of the old. The "new" will bring the illusion of "progress," but for Benjamin, "progress" was the catastrophic storm that the "angel of history" must face.[9]

The utopias of Fourier and Bellamy were ultimately not realized. Benjamin believed in the prophecy of Marxism and the end of capitalism. Unfortunately, the vitality of capitalism transcends Benjamin's short-lived life and survives, albeit through many repeated crises. Charles Baudelaire wandered the streets of Paris with the eyes of an urban flâneur and saw the nineteenth-century metropolis where the "old" and the "new" coexisted, collapsed, and built simultaneously. What he could not see was the rise of the new city, forming a closed-loop, high-efficiency world, completely throwing away the old city in the wrinkles of slow time, only for tourists to visit. By the end of the twentieth century, Marc Augé invented the new term "supermodernity" to replace Benjamin's concept of "high capitalism."[10]

In Asia, during the same period as the Baudelairean era, there was a kind of weather-resistant commercial street space like the arcades in Paris. At the end of the eighteenth century, British colonists came to Beniapukur in India, but did not adapt to the hot climate by building what the local people called *veranda* (composed of *vahir* and *andar* in Bengali) to provide shade from the sun. By the beginning of the nineteenth century, the British governor of Singapore, Stamford Raffles, stipulated the building of pedestrian corridors on street frontages for foreign trade or shophouses. Thus, the *veranda* became the local "Five Foot Way" or *kaki-lima* in Malay/Indonesian, *ng-goek-gei* in Cantonese, and *wujiaoji* in Mandarin.

With the continuous expansion of British colonization, the *kaki-lima* was introduced to Hong Kong and Guangzhou, and then, throughout South Asia, Southeast Asia, and Northeast Asia after the Second Opium War (1856–1860). The "Five Foot Way" is called *ke-lau* (Cantonese means "the building riding on the colonnade") in Guangzhou but *tong-lau* (Cantonese, *tong* is same as *tang* in Mandarin, means "Chinese," *lau* means "buildings") in Hong Kong. This typical Cantonese vernacular architecture is a store with a colonnade at street-level; this shophouse typology is a convenient way for pedestrians in South China to shop during inclement weather. The second floor is a private residence. The shophouse seems to be "riding" on the colonnade, and hence the name. It was widely welcomed by people and spread throughout the Guangdong and Guangxi regions.

In traditional Chinese architecture, there is a longstanding typology like the *veranda* called *yan-lang*, *bu-kou*, or *yan-dun* in Mandarin. It is only used as part of a temple, garden, or house, but does not have a commercial function like the arcades. In the snowy northern regions of Japan, such as Niigata, Akita, and Aomori prefectures, there are comparable patterns. They are called *gangi-zukuri* (meaning "goose-like eaves structure" in Japanese), and the corridor in front of the fish and food shops allows people to avoid walking in the snow. Both the *ke-lau* and the *gangi-zukuri* are very close to Bellamy's covered canopy, but it cannot be retracted. The emergence of these folk styles and semi-interior commercial spaces demonstrates that Asia had become a modern industrial and commercial society through ongoing waves of maritime navigation and colonization.

As mentioned above, this architectural style has been given different names in different Asian dialects. This knowledge is not acquired through formal schooling but accumulated in daily life. It further forms a "sense of place" and a kind of "topophilia,"[11] that helps to shape hometown identities. In the nearly 500-year history of Chinese overseas immigration, beginning after the Ming Dynasty lifted its ban on private maritime trade in 1567,[12] Chinese people (especially the Cantonese) established their own communities in different countries. These "places," which today are called "Chinatown" by outsiders, were self-claimed "Tang People's Streets" (*tong-yan-gai* in Cantonese) in the early days, meaning that they were "Tangshan" (Tang's Land) and their people were the descendants of the Tang Empire (618–907 AD). The word *tong* in Hong Kong's *tong-lau* is a customary naming of a Chinese hometown by returned overseas Chinese, while the opposite, *joeng* (Cantonese, same as *yang* in Mandarin, meaning "ocean"), referring to Westerners and Western things that landed in China through ocean navigation. The identity of hometowns is often traced back to history, so that contemporary Guangzhou ranks the Shangxiajiu Road, a traditional *ke-lau* shopping street, as a historic preservation area.

The vast differences in the hometowns contradict the coherence, standardization, and mass production required by contemporary capitalism. Under the cross-border circulation of capital and the cultural output it promotes, the large-scale shopping malls of North America have been transposed to Asia, occupying self-sufficient "places" that have greatly deprived people of traditional public space. In 1966, the first large shopping mall in Hong Kong, Ocean Terminal, opened with a building area of 60,200 square meters at Tsim Sha Tsui. In 1969, the first large shopping mall in Japan, Tamagawa Takashi-maya, opened in Tokyo; the first shopping center in Taiwan, The Mall, opened in 1994, while the first shopping mall in mainland China opened in 1990.[13] Since car ownership in Asia remains relatively limited, most shopping malls are in city centers.

Hong Kong is a pioneer of Asian shopping malls and first developed vertical space due to scarcity of available land. Using multi-level escalators that rise around an atrium, shoppers become part of the illusion. Surrounded by exquisite goods and the comfortable temperature of "eternal spring," the more people consume, the closer they come to God. This kind of experience is also found in large airports: people "see, buy, fly."[14] They shop in duty-free stores, board flights with large and small shopping bags, and fly away satisfied. Hong Kong can be viewed as a city that fully realizes Bellamy's dream of a weatherproof closed-loop in what Marc Augé called "non-places." The elimination of strangeness and differentiation in many types of these "places" is the "achievement" of "supermodernity" achieved through contemporary capitalism.

The latest version of the shopping mall is a grand synthesizer of "supermodernity." The South China Mall, which opened in Dongguan, China in 2005, once ranked as the world's largest shopping mall.[15] It created seven attractions as fantastical renditions of Amsterdam, Paris, Rome, Venice, California, Egypt, and the Caribbean, along with movie towns, children's parks, game cities, sports venues, and hotels. Jean Baudrillard would certainly criticize the "hyperreality" of South China Mall as a bad example of his theory of "simulacra."[16] The mall was built in a suburb without convenient access, while at the same time it was increasingly impacted by online shopping. The mall slowly became a "ghost town" with few shoppers and high store vacancies. It was renamed New South China Mall in 2007 and underwent a major renovation in 2013, but was officially removed from the certified list of Class AAAA Tourist Destinations in China in 2016.

The most successful shopping mall in China is the Wanda Plaza chain located in nearly all downtowns of medium-sized and larger cities. In 2019, there were nearly 300 Wanda Plaza malls.[17] All Wanda Plazas are designed with similar architectural styles and operate with an identical strategy. Each is equipped with a Wanda Cinema City and a five-star Wanda Hotel. Wanda Plaza has become a hub for local businesses, restaurants, and entertainment in medium-sized cities lacking culture and other amusements. They offer everyday social space to a large number of people, especially parents seeking diversions for their children. Apart from the powerful Wanda Group, most of the shopping malls developed by other companies have failed. Many have been unable to recruit high-end brands, and thus, have opened their doors to local merchants. Like the United States, China has entered an era of significant mall decline.

Adapting to China's slowing economic growth rate and maintaining the human flow and sales volume of existing shopping malls, many developers began to expand the functions of shopping malls. K11 Musea, which opened in Hong Kong in 2009, launched the concept of "museum retail" and defined itself as the "shopping art center." A notable success, it built malls in Shanghai, Beijing, Tianjin, Guangzhou, Ningbo, Shenyang, and Wuhan seeking to attract a large number of young people who chase contemporary art. In 2011, a large bookstore, Fangsuo Commune, was invited to open a location at the Taikoo Hui shopping mall in Guangzhou. Later, it opened branches in Sino-Ocean Taikoo Li in Chengdu, Sunshine Shopping Mall in Chongqing, and The Mixc in Qingdao. This cultural turn of the shopping centers saved the retail industry, successfully drawing the crowd from conventional museums and libraries. The new business model drew young Chinese people to visit malls to attend art exhibitions, read books, watch movies, drink coffee, and eat.

The response from visitors was very enthusiastic. When I curated the second edition of "Get It Louder" in 2007, I used the Grandview Mall in Guangzhou, then called "Asia's largest shopping mall," as an exhibition venue. This time, I went even further: the artworks were installed in every corner of the mall and some were placed next to stores, or even mixed with goods for sale in the stores. When preparing the exhibition, we installed artworks only at night after the mall closed so as not to affect its normal business. This gave me the opportunity to experience an empty and quiet hypermarket without people. From the top floor to the ground level, the deep, valley-like atrium did not have any clocks. Its design works to make the shopper forget time. In the bright light, I sensed a strong feeling of timelessness, yet did not lose track of time; it was like standing within the wake of a retreating crowd.

In the *Harvard Design School Guide to Shopping*, Rem Koolhaas criticized the space of shopping malls as "Junkspace" and asserts, "...because it cannot be grasped, Junkspace cannot be remembered."[18] As a product of capitalist ambition, it is what Guy Debord called the "spectacle," an anti-natural dream produced by air-conditioning, a super machine of desire-making. It is fed by the flow of people but cannot produce any interpersonal relationships and collective memories for people. Its congenital defects determine its fate that even the injection of art and culture could not change. It took too much from God's hands, making a fetish palace on the earth, depriving the churches and temples of the past in the human spiritual world, leaving no choice for people. Maybe one day, the wild grasses and vines that were eradicated by construction will return; they will climb the mall's fascinating atrium and grow new leaves within the seams of its escalators.

Notes

1   Rem Koolhaas used the "non-urban" concept when talking about his upcoming rural research exhibition for the Guggenheim Museum in New York. Niall Patrick Walsh.

2   Yi-Fu Tuan, *Topophilia: A Study of Environmental Perception, Attitudes, and Values*, Columbia University Press, 1974, p. 109.

3   Charles Fourier, *Selected Writings*, Volume 1, The Commercial Press, 1979, p. 229.

4   Fourier used a table to describe the progress of social movement and the order of future creations.

5   Edward Bellamy, *Looking Backward: From 2000 to 1887*, first published in 1878, reprinted by Applewood Books, p. 95.

6   First published in 1926 by Editions Gallimard.

7   Walter Benjamin, *The Arcades Project*, The Belknap Press of Harvard University Press, 1999, p. 13.

8   "The delight of the city-dweller is not so much love at first sight as at last sight." Walter Benjamin, "The Paris of the Second Empire in Baudelaire", *Selected Writings*, Volume 4, 1938–1940, Edited by Howard Eiland and Michael W. Jennings, The Belknap Press of Harvard University Press, 1999, p. 25.

9   Walter Benjamin, *Illuminations*, edited with an Introduction by Hannah Arendt Translated by Harry Zohn. New York, Schocken, 1969, pp. 257–258.

10   Marc Augé, *Non-Places: Introduction to an Anthropology of Supermodernity*, Verso, 1995, p. 78.

11   Yi-Fu Tuan, *Topophilia: A Study of Environmental Perception, Attitudes, and Values*, Columbia University Press, 1974, p. 4.

12   Philip A. Kuhn, "China Historians and Chinese Diaspora", *Journal of Chinese Overseas*, Volume 2, Number 2, November 2006, p. 164.

13   Mall China, https://www.mallchina.org/Symposium/Index?id=1048, accessed on October 31, 2019.

14   A slogan in Amsterdam Schiphol Airport.

15   Tom Van Riper, "The World's Largest Malls", https://www.forbes.com/2007/01/09/malls-worlds-largest-biz-cx_tvr_0109malls_slide.html#6661859c77f5, accessed on October 31, 2019.

16   Jean Baudrillard, *Simulacra and Simulation*, University of Michigan Press, 1994, p. 67.

17   Sina Finance and Economics, https://cj.sina.com.cn/articles/view/1660775151/62fd6aef00100c-qyk, accessed on October 31, 2019.

18   Rem Koolhaas, "Junk Space", *Harvard Design School Guide to Shopping*, Taschen, 2001, Edited by Chuihua Judy Chung, Jeffrey Inaba, Rem Koolhaas, Sze Tsung Leong, p. 409.

Theories and Influences

Culture

Chapter 28

New Interior Identities

Inhabiting London's Railway Stations, Winter Gardens, People's Palaces, and Department Stores, 1830–1920

Fiona Fisher, Patricia Lara-Betancourt and Penny Sparke

In his 1995 book, *Non-Places: An Introduction to the Anthropology of Super-modernity*, Marc Augé claimed that, 'spaces formed in relation to certain ends (transport, transit, commerce, leisure)' undermined the identities of those who engaged with them.[1] 'A space', he wrote, 'that cannot be defined as relational, or historical, or concerned with identity, will be a non-place'.[2] Twelve years later, Tim Morton framed that same thought within the capitalist economy, writing that, 'Capitalism compressed time and space' and that 'space became potent, while place, and the sense of place, became potent in its absence'.[3]

This chapter explores three London-based precursors of Augé's spaces of transport, leisure, and commerce, specifically a range of nineteenth- and early twentieth-century public sphere environments inside railway termini, winter gardens, peoples' palaces, and department stores. Several questions are discussed in relation to them. Can they be understood as 'places' along the lines suggested by Augé and Morton? Were social identities being constructed or challenged within them? Were they merely commercially driven responses to the expanding pool of socially fragmented consumers and travelers in the period? Or were they promoters of a level of civic culture linked to a desire to democratize the experience of modernity, engaging visitors in social activities and educating the masses? These are complex questions to which this short essay can only suggest a few initial ideas.

Materiality

Mark Pimlott has claimed that, 'The inhabitants of nineteenth-century glass-houses, winter gardens, exhibition buildings, department stores, grand hotels,

DOI: 10.4324/9780429443091-34

offices, shopping malls, and people's palaces' were inspired and consoled by their links with Paradise, a form of compensation, in his view, for the dystopian face of consumer culture.[4] For Augé, 'The non-place is the opposite of Utopia'.[5] All the buildings being considered here contained elements made of iron and glass, thereby recalling the model of the horticultural greenhouse. As a result, whether or not they still contained nature within them, the buildings under discussion were, arguably, all imbued with a level of positive symbolism linked to the idea of Paradise.

The Royal Aquarium and Summer and Winter Garden, a stone and masonry entertainment complex, opened in Westminster in 1876. Its great hall, covered by a barrel-vaulted cast iron and glass roof, contained palm trees, fountains, items of sculpture, 13 large tanks, and an orchestra. The People's Palace opened in London's Mile End Road in 1887, a combination of a Beaux-Arts building and the Crystal Palace. It also contained a winter garden with an iron and glass roof, as well as a concert hall, reading room, and Technical College among its other facilities. Arguably, the utopianism of the glasshouse was embraced by both these complex leisure environments, expressed not only through their materials but because they contained plants and flowers. In 1875, the presence of a winter garden in the Royal Aquarium was confirmed by Bruce Phillips, the secretary to the Board, who explained that, 'It has been found that visitors to other aquariums liked to have other amusements, as well as observing the fish. The directors have therefore determined to have a botanical display and there would be a Summer and Winter Garden'.[6] The winter garden situated to the rear of the Queen's Hall in the Mile End Road People's Palace was also filled with palms, flowers, and tropical fruit. Completed in 1892, it was used for concerts and refreshments (Image 28.1).

Pimlott has also suggested that the Bon Marché department store in Paris was 'indebted to the arcades of Paris for the idea of a protected and artificial interior environment under glass which at once evoked the Garden and the idealized city: Arcadia'.[7] That argument can be extended to London, where an important precedent for its department stores was the Crystal Palace, inspired by glasshouses and designed by Joseph Paxton for the Great Exhibition in 1851. Stores soon adopted the Palace's construction materials and architectural possibilities, their iron and glass structures facilitating the open spaces, transparency, and magnificence that helped them display their merchandise.[8] Glass-roofed atria and skylights offered a source of natural light, while columns framed their large glass windows. From the 1880s, the department store typology was taken forward through the use of steel and concrete construction.[9] In order to build his Oxford Street emporium, the American entrepreneur, H. Gordon Selfridge (1858–1947), fought a three-year battle with London County Council to acquire a license to employ steel frames and reinforced concrete.[10] Previous purpose-built stores, such as Waring & Gillow's (1906) in Oxford Street, had to rely on the use of transverse masonry walls. However, that store's eight-story building boasted large windows and an impressive 90-foot-high rotunda covered with a glass dome (Images 28.2).[11]

The canopies over the platforms of London's large railway termini were also made of iron and glass construction (Image 28.3).[12] In sharp contrast to contemporary descriptions of dark and dingy station interiors, nineteenth century photographs and illustrations emphasized the spectacular

Image 28.1 A lithographic print of The Great Hall, The Royal Aquarium and Summer and Winter Gardens, Westminster, published in 'L'Univers Illustre', n. 1080, 18th Decembre, 1876, p. 805 (out of copyright and reproduced by the permission of the author.).

qualities of railway architecture, depicting large, light-filled interiors, in the manner of utopian schemes of the 1850s, such as Joseph Paxton's Great Victorian Way (1855), which explicitly referenced the glasshouse. That connection is, arguably, not only evident in the materiality of the station, but also in residual form in the practice of bringing nature indoors to decorate stations as an act of welcome or celebration.

Civic, Social, and Educational Activities

All the buildings in question supported the enactment of civic, social, educational activities and experiences to some degree or another. Stations were associated with increased comfort and with a capacity to enable private reflection, both of which suggest a sense of place. 'Who for one instant', asked the *Illustrated London News*, in 1844, 'would compare the trouble and extortion of the old coachyard to the comfort of the station?'[13] London's railway termini evolved to accommodate diverse aspects of civic and political life. National and local histories were commemorated within them in the form of war memorials and statues to great men; stations were often decorated for ceremonial or celebratory purposes. More spontaneously, station interiors facilitated mass festivities; for example, crowds thronged Waterloo Station on hearing news of the Relief of Mafeking.[14]

Several spaces within spaces encouraging social interaction were situated around the hall of the Royal Aquarium, among them rooms for eating, smoking, reading, and playing chess; an art gallery; a skating rink; and a theater. Many educational exhibitions, including displays of 'posters, chrysanthemums, bicycles, bulldogs, singing birds, fishing tackle, yachts, sewing machines, musical instruments, and occasionally paintings', were also held there.[15] The venue's location meant that it became a home from home for politicians.[16] However, it also appealed to people from a range of other classes. Close to Charing Cross Station, it attracted anybody who could afford to travel by train into town.

WARING & GILLOW'S, OXFORD STREET—INTERIOR.

153

Image 28.2 The 90-feet-high atrium and rotunda, Waring & Gillow store, Oxford Street, 1910. From: *The Modern Building Record*, 1910.

'The People's Palace brought culture, entertainment, and education to enrich the lives of the local people',[17] explained one commentator, while *The Times* called it, 'a happy experiment in practical Socialism'.[18] Both the Aquarium and the People's Palace offered their visitors an education, the possibility of improving their taste through engagement with high cultural offerings and various forms of healthy recreation. Both contained public libraries, and flower and dog shows were held at both venues. Skating, cycling, and boxing took place at the Aquarium, while at the Palace, visitors could swim in the swimming pool, exercise in the gym, rollerskate in the basement, play tennis, shoot billiards, and dance.

Image 28.3 The interior of Charing Cross Station, London, c.1896. From: *The Queen's London. A pictorial and descriptive record of the Great Metropolis in the fifty-ninth year of the reign of Queen Victoria*, London: Cassell & Co., 1896.

Aimed at keeping female consumers on site as long as possible to enable them to spend more money, the department stores also became venues for relaxation, entertainment, socializing, and education. Besides having a restaurant, luncheon hall, tea room, and roof garden, Selfridge's also offered an American soda fountain, a library, a post office, and 'typically furnished' rooms for foreign visitors.[19] To coincide with major local events and exhibitions, stores planned special sales and events. For his store's opening ceremony in 1909, for example, Selfridge asked the French pilot, Louis Blériot, who had just crossed the English Channel for the first time, if he could exhibit his monoplane in the shop. In four days, a total of 150,000 people turned up to see it.[20]

Commerce, Consumption, and Commodification

In addition to the social, educational, and civic functions of these complex interiors, they also had strong commercial faces, a fact that was interpreted both positively and negatively. In the case of the railway station, commerce enlivened the interior. Mobile news vendors and shoeblacks were among the earliest trades to occupy the station. Fixed retail positions followed, marking an important moment in the commodification of the interior.[21] The positive, identity-forming face of commerce was widely recognized as a feature of these new, complex urban spaces. Writing in 1888, Henry James described the air of novelty and 'glamour' that hung over the railway bookstall, 'a focus of warmth and light in the vast smoky cavern' of the station.[22] By the 1890s, diversions such as weighing machines, perfume dispensers, and machines selling stamps, sweets, and other sundries could be found.[23] As *The Railway Magazine* observed, in 1901, 'The platform is to be the free lounge of the future, and we may, after a while, find a small town erected upon it'.[24]

The expansion of London's department stores was based on the relentless growth of the urban middle class, developing with it an interdependent relationship that strengthened a culture of consumption and helped define middle-class identity. Whiteley's, Harrod's, Waring and Gillow's, and Selfridge's were all designed to maximize opportunities for shopping, pleasure, and consumption. Being able to visit the stores unchaperoned meant freedom of movement for women, and instilled in them a sense of exhilaration and empowerment.[25] The sheer abundance and enticing display of modern goods tantalized them with the promise of self-affirmation through choice and consumption. Referring to the period before 1914, the writer, Nesta Helen Webster, expressed her delight in the consumption of modern things, declaring, 'How beautifully things were made in those days! What exquisite furniture, glass, and china, what lovely dress materials were to be found in the London shops!'[26] These stores were for women, the equivalent of gentlemen's clubs, safe and respectable public places that encouraged them to be part of the modern world.

The Royal Aquarium was essentially a money-making operation in which visitors were offered the opportunity to consume a variety of leisure experiences. They paid an entrance fee and for all the refreshments they devoured during their visit. The project was less than financially successful, however, and the growing shortfall resulted in a downgrading of the entertainment aimed at visitors who were not initially envisaged. Examples included a man diving into one of the tanks, the firing of a woman from a cannon, and the exhibition of the first gorilla seen in England. This led to a mood of increased decadence. One humorist joked that the chief use of the glass exhibit tanks 'seemed to be for young ladies to stand at one side of them, and young gentlemen to stand opposite the young ladies, gazing at each other furtively through the glass, and pretending to look at a slumbering baby crocodile'.[27] Although the People's Palace was not so overtly financially driven, it also suffered from emphasizing the more low-brow of its cultural offerings as the more high-brow ones proved increasingly unpopular.

Non-Places

All the buildings under discussion functioned within the system of economic capitalism. While, as has been shown, that had a positive face, many critics also linked it with the encouragement of envy and greed, as well as the growth of theft and risqué behavior. The environments in question also exhibited class tensions, the disorientation of visitors, and the exploitation of the employees working in them.

The downgrading of the entertainment at the Royal Aquarium led to a new kind of visitor and social tensions emerged as a result. Drunkenness and prostitution became rife and, in an attempt to circumvent the latter, according to John M. Munro, 'Ladies were only allowed in after dark accompanied by a gentleman'.[28] In 1875, a Mr. Grain of the Westminster School authorities claimed that the Aquarium project was 'simply and entirely a commercial enterprise, disguised under professions of a desire to cultivate musical and artistic tastes among the people'.[29]

The fragmentary development of London's early railway termini created complex plans that engendered a sense of disorientation or confusion among users. London Bridge Station, which opened in 1836, served around 300,000 passengers a day by the 1850s.[30] Described, in 1858, as a 'mighty maze', its form was said to defy the understanding of its owners and the public alike.[31] In the same decade, Euston Station was similarly criticized for being dark, 'Ill-contrived', and difficult to navigate.[32] The rise of railway station commerce, whether in the form of the refreshment buffet, the bookstall, or machines dispensing the 'necessities' of travel, arguably helped punctuate the interior, alleviating some of the more negative effects of these new environments, offering distractions and amusements, as well as spaces of comfort and, depending on one's social class, possibilities for some degree of social withdrawal.

In spite of their commercial success, department stores faced plenty of detractors. Critics highlighted the economic, sexual, and political threats, as well as the ambiguities that they saw in women's involvement in department stores and fiercely contested the implications of a female consuming crowd.[33] Social reformers accused the stores of exploiting their workforce, particularly shop girls who, in addition to very low wages and long working hours, had to submit to the infamous living-in system. However, it is evident that through their consumption activities and as employees, women changed the urban landscape and in so doing, helped shape middle- and working-class women's identities and roles in society. Critics blamed stores for subverting the status-quo by re-drawing gender and class lines through consumption. Exploited labor was the counterpart of a middle-class way of life, but it would be wrong to blame retailers for the prevailing social inequalities. Shop wages were usually higher compared to those of other sectors, and London's department stores were considered a better alternative by thousands of women who wanted to escape domestic service. Many stores also offered managerial roles, which were better paid and in which many women thrived.

Conclusion

From this brief account of a selection of London's nineteenth- and early twentieth-century public sphere complex interiors, there is enough evidence to suggest that social identities were both constructed and challenged in them. A key question remains as to whether or not the vestigial utopianism expressed by their links to glasshouses and the widespread intention to educate, entertain, and, in the case of the railway station, contribute to civic culture, potentially offset the damaging face of commercialism and the social tensions that existed within them. This suggests a more nuanced picture than those presented by Augé and Morton in their discussions about late twentieth- and early twenty-first-century complex commercial spaces and provides a possible framework within which these ideas could continue to be debated.

Notes

1 Auge, M. (2009 [1995]) 'Non-Places: Introduction to an Anthropology of Supermodernity' (London: Verso), 66.

2 Ibid., 63.

3 Morton, T. (2009) 'Ecology Without Nature: Rethinking Environmental Aesthetics' (Cambridge, Mass: Harvard University Press) 85, 94.

4 Pimlott, M. (2016) 'The Public Interior as Idea and Project' (London: Ram Publications).

5 Augé, Non-Places, 90.

6   Sands, J. (2021) https://www.gsarchive.net/articles/sull-aquarium/index/html., 1 (accessed 04.02.2021).

7   Pimlott, M. (2007) 'Without and Within: Essays on Territory and the Interior' (London: Educational Studies), 128.

8   Hocquel, W. et al (1996) 'Architecture for the Retail Trade: Department Stores, Shopping Centres, Arcades' (Basel, Boston, Berlin: Birkhauser Verlag), 27.

9   Lawrence, J. C. (1990) 'Steel Frame Architecture versus the London Building Regulations: Self-ridges, the ritz and American Technology', Construction History, 6, 28–9.

10 Ibid., 23–46.

11 Waring and Gillow (June 1906) 'Souvenir of the Opening of Waring and Gillow's New Building', 20.

12 London's major railway termini developed on multiple sites to the north south of the city from the first in the 1830s (London Bridge, Euston and Paddington) to the last (Marylebone) in the 1890s.

13 'Speculations on the Railway', Illustrated London News, 7 December 1844, 360.

14 H. G. Davis, Waterloo. One Hundred Years in the Life of a Great Railway Station, British Railways Southern Region, 1948, 16.

15 Munro, *The Royal Aquarium*, 14.

16 Ibid., 17.

17 'The Peoples Palace', 1. https://qmul.ac.uk/library/archives/archive-galleries/the-peoples-palace-past-and-present/, 1.

18 Ibid.

19 Barren, M. (1996) 'How it all Began for the Retail Trade' (London: Michael O'Mara Books), 124.

20 Honeycombe, G. (1984) 'Selfridge's Seventy-Five year: The Story of the Store, 1909-1984' (London: Park Lane Press), 39.

21 One of the first was William Henry Smith's bookstall at Euston Station, which opened in 1848. Railway companies also leased their hotels and refreshment rooms to private caterers and, from the early 1870s, began to take control of station advertising.

22 H. James, 'London' in Henry James, London Stories and Other Writings, edited and with an introduction by David Kynaston, Padstow, Cornwall: Tabb House, 1989, 263.

23 'Studies of Life and Character at a Railway Station', The Graphic, 13 September 1890, 293.

24 H. Stanley Tayler, 'Some Joys of Railway Travelling', The Railway Magazine, vol. viii, 1901, cited in Andrew Dow, ed., Dow's Dictionary of Railway Quotations, Baltimore: The Johns Hopkins University Press, 228.

25 Rappaport, *Shopping for Pleasure*, 142–177.

26 Webster, H. H. (1949) 'Spacious days: An Autobiography' (London: Hutchinson and Co. Ltd.), 142.

27 Munro, *The Royal Aquarium*, 19.

28 Sands, 1.

29 Ibid.

30 'A Day at London Bridge Station', Illustrated London News, 24 July 1858, 87.

31 Ibid.

32 Samuel Sidney, Rides on Railways, London, 1851 [online] accessed 17.8.18: https://www.gutenberg.org/files/13271/13271-h/13271-h.htm.

33 Rappaport, *Shopping for Pleasure*, 19.

Chapter 29

Arcading Cleveland

From Continental Europe to America

Gregory Marinic

Interior urbanism in the United States traces its origins to the nineteenth-century arcade, a building typology inherited from Europe. Corresponding with an era of unprecedented immigration, the geographic distribution of arcades in the United States closely aligns with those cities that received the largest flows of immigrants from continental Europe. Beginning in the 1880s and arriving through Ellis Island, this wave of American immigration represented a significant demographic shift that pivoted away from historic ties to Great Britain and increasingly toward people from central, eastern, and southern Europe.[1] Cities across the tier of northern states, stretching from New England and New York through the Great Lakes to the Upper Midwest, continually drew immigrants from these parts of Europe from the 1880s through the mid-1920s, and then again in much smaller numbers after World War II through the 1990s during the fall of communism.[2] The peak years of this flow were 1905 through 1914, and at the apex of immigration in 1914, nearly three-quarters of all immigrants came from central, eastern, and southern Europe.[3] During this time, a diverse mosaic of people from these regions settled in the industrial cities of the Northeast and Great Lakes regions, including Germans, Austrians, Hungarians, Italians, Poles, Lithuanians, Latvians, Estonians, Slovenians, Croatians, Serbians, Bosnians, Macedonians, Albanians, Czechs, Slovaks, Ukrainians, Ruthenians, Belarusans, Russians, Romanians, Bulgarians, Greeks, and others who transposed aspects of their diverse cultures to a new land.[4] Shortly thereafter, African Americans and white Appalachian migrants from the American South would join the continental European immigrants in fundamentally reshaping cities of the industrial North throughout the twentieth century.

Evolving over many decades, large diasporas of immigrants and their multigenerational descendants have made significant socio-cultural impacts on major cities and entire states in the Northeast and Great Lakes regions of

DOI: 10.4324/9780429443091-35

the United States.[5] It is in these regions where central, eastern, and southern European influences on American society, including various ethnic, religious, cultural, and architectural traces, remain the most significant and enduring. As an outgrowth of this wave, the architectural language of continental European cities was incrementally introduced to American cities with often similar climates and geographies. In the early twentieth century, these influences were manifested in the widespread building of religious institutions such as cathedrals, churches, shrines, synagogues, schools, colleges, and universities, as well as secular buildings, including national homes, social halls, benevolent societies, and perhaps most significantly, urban arcades modeled on continental European precedents. Furthermore, these communities brought distinct cultural sensibilities, religious practices, and food cultures that have shaped the broader American culture in enduring ways.[6]

Responding to various metropolitan pressures related to a burgeoning population of recent immigrants, real estate speculation, and inclement weather, developers introduced the European arcade to American cities where the typology flourished prior to World War II. Although arcades were built in cities across the industrialized North, Cleveland, a port city on Lake Erie, lays claim to the most substantial and numerous arcades built anywhere in North America. Its arcades reflect a moment in the early twentieth century when industrialization, immigration, internal migration from the American South, the development of streetcar systems, and a nascent interior urban typology—*the arcade*—coalesced to shape a multi-ethnic, cosmopolitan city of commerce and culture. In this chapter, the flow of human capital and the arcade building type will be examined vis-à-vis socio-economic conditions, consumption, and geography, placing special focus on architectural and socio-spatial crosscurrents between continental Europe and the United States. It situates the arcades as forerunners of the later department stores, mixed-use developments, atria, and shopping malls that were built in downtown Cleveland throughout the twentieth century.

From the Nolli Plan to the Parisian Arcade and America

In his iconic Grand Plan of Rome (1748), Giambattista Nolli described his understanding of the public interiority of Rome which remains among the most significant visualizations of urban spatial patterning of all time. Nolli's construct privileged the representation of buildings to see the city as an interior experience. In the following century, the arcades of continental Europe became mediators between interior and exterior urban space, offering a speculative means to increase street frontages. Although conventional storefronts in the heart of European capital cities were largely built out by the eighteenth century, arcades created interconnective mid-block retail space that was neither entirely indoor nor outdoor. Stores within the arcades benefitted from a street-like presence with notable similarities and differences in comparison to conventional urban street retail.

Turin, Milan, Vienna, and Budapest were early adopters of the typology, but Paris was the pre-eminent laboratory of the arcade. In the nineteenth century, the Parisian arcades flourished amidst a bourgeois and aspirational urban society. Arcades were widely built across its urban core and the concept was soon adopted in cities throughout continental Europe. With close cultural and geographic ties to Paris, the mid-nineteenth-century arcades of Brussels were among the most refined; however, the Galleria Vittorio Emanuele II (1877) in Milan remains the most advanced example of the typology ever built. By the late nineteenth century, unprecedented migration from central, eastern, and southern Europe to the industrial cities in the Great Lakes region of the United States established cultural ties between these distant regions. For the continental European newcomers to these American cities, the arcade represented a familiar form of architecture transposed into their new urban context.

Arcades were built in cities across the industrialized northern cities of the United States, including the Westminster Arcade (1828) in Providence, Rhode Island; Paddock Arcade (1850) in Watertown, New York; Endicott Arcade (1890) in St. Paul, Minnesota; Market Arcade (1892) in Buffalo, New York; Spitzer Arcade (1896) in Toledo, Ohio; Dayton Arcade (1904) in Dayton, Ohio; Jenkins Arcade (1911) in Pittsburgh, Pennsylvania; Loeb Arcade (1914) in Minneapolis, Minnesota; the Arcade Building (1919) in St. Louis, Missouri; Reynolds Arcade (1933) in Rochester, New York, and the Old Arcade (1890), Colonial Arcade (1898), and Euclid Arcade (1911) in Cleveland, Ohio; among others. Opening in 1828, the Westminster Arcade in Providence, Rhode Island was the first arcade built in North America. And although the arcade typology arrived in the United States on the East Coast, it developed to its highest form further west in the Great Lakes region.

Shaping a New Land

The industrial Great Lakes region of North America has been historically defined by the dynamic movement of human capital, raw materials, and industrial products, as well as the corresponding impact of these influences on regional identity and the built environment. Occupying a key strategic position between the Atlantic Coast and midcontinental heartland, the Great Lakes region has disproportionately influenced the industrial and infrastructural development of both Canada and the United States.[7] In 1910, four port cities on the Great Lakes—Chicago, Detroit, Cleveland, and Buffalo—ranked among the top ten largest cities in the United States.[8]

Although the United States was founded on the Atlantic seaboard, it is in the midcontinental cities on the Great Lakes, as well as those along the Ohio and Mississippi rivers, where the country grew into an industrial powerhouse. Here, Americans left farm life to encounter a sophisticated metropolitan world. More typically in the early twentieth century, however, waves of European immigrants arrived on trains from New York after long journeys to Ellis Island, and then migrated onward to cities founded largely by British, Anglo-American, and French settlers. In the late nineteenth century, industrialization in the United States required a workforce fulfilled primarily by people from central, eastern, and southern Europe. By 1900, almost three-quarters of Slavic, Hungarian, Italian, and Greek immigrants lived in the seven largest cities of the Northeast and Great Lakes regions, including Chicago, Cleveland, and Buffalo, which together produced more than half of the manufacturing and mining output in the United States.[9]

Cleveland, situated on Lake Erie at the mouth of the Cuyahoga River, was founded by pioneers from New England on indigenous lands originally populated by the Erie and Lenape people. The city grew slowly in its early years until an industrial boom in the late eighteenth century resulted in a massive influx of continental European immigrants. The immigrants of this era typically worked in factories and domestic services, while others owned small businesses such as taverns, restaurants, bakeries, butchers, delicatessens, cobblers, tailors, produce vendors, and grocery stores. Assimilating and establishing the labor movement, they settled vibrant neighborhoods, raised close-knit families, and built elaborate places of worship, schools, and social clubs embedded with memories of the old country.[10] Traces of these European cultures continue to define the character, connectedness, and architectural characteristics of the city.

Emerging as a growing economic force by virtue of their sheer numbers, immigrants and their first-generation offspring supported a vibrant consumer culture in Cleveland. These activities were centralized in its urban core with arcades, department stores, and street retail connected to residential neighborhoods by streetcars and rapid rail transit. During the interwar period, Cleveland continued growing with the Great Migration (1916–1970) of African Americans migrating from the South,[11] and then a post-World War II wave of native-born white migrants from Appalachia through the 1970s.[12] By the 1920s, a small Chinatown formed in Midtown with its commercial district centered on Rockwell Avenue. These communities settled in neighborhoods near the urban core alongside and intermingled within the established "white ethnic" European enclaves. The consumptive patterns of these communities, too, relied on the existing housing stock and retail infrastructure in downtown Cleveland. The presence and enduring cultural imprint of these communities, yet fading, remains visible and relevant today.

After World War II, the inner city ethnic European enclaves in Cleveland were largely redlined by banks and blockbusted by real estate agents. These discriminatory practices contributed to the neighborhood fragmentation of the "white ethnic" communities and the subsequent suburbanization of their populations alongside the widespread marginalization of African Americans, Asians, Hispanics, and other ethnic minorities who increasingly took their place. Migrating to the primarily white suburbs during the postwar years, the impact of central, eastern, and southern Europeans and their descendants, the so-called "white ethnics", on shaping contemporary American media and consumer culture was indeed significant but has been less closely analyzed.[13] By the 1980s, the "white ethnics" had largely assimilated into the broader white American culture although many continue to nurture their distinct ethnic heritages in subtle everyday ways.[14] These suburbanized communities no longer depended on the downtown arcades and department stores to serve their consumptive needs.

Second Cities, Continental Architectures

From the turn of the twentieth century through the 1970s, cities across the Great Lakes region were home to substantial immigrant communities from central, eastern, and southern Europe. Among these, Cleveland was often considered the de facto "second largest city" of various central European nations that were once part of the Austro-Hungarian Empire, including Hungary, Slovenia, and Slovakia.[15] These claims were evidenced in Cleveland's neighborhoods, including the sprawling, multi-ethnic "Slavic Village" home to Poles, Czechs, and Slovenians on the southeast side; Tremont, a near west side neighborhood of Poles, Slovaks, Ukrainians, Greeks, and people from the Balkans; Buckeye, the largest of many Hungarian neighborhoods that also had a sizeable Slovak population; and St. Clair-Superior, once home to the largest Slovenian community outside of Slovenia.[16] Today, Greater Cleveland is home to the largest Hungarian, Slovak, and Slovenian descendant communities in the world outside of Slovakia, Slovenia, and Hungary, respectively.[17] Elsewhere in the region, Chicago famously boasts that it is the largest Polish city outside of Warsaw with its own Polish Downtown and a sprawling Ukrainian Village, while Buffalo calls itself the second largest Polish city in the United States.

German influence in the United States is a far broader, and indeed, national phenomenon that is both urban and rural.[18] Cincinnati, Milwaukee, and St. Louis are key cities in the German Triangle of the Midwest connecting the states of Ohio, Wisconsin, and Missouri. With its sizable German-descended population that forms a plurality, Ohio is home to the historical remnants of substantial German Villages that may be found throughout the state in Columbus, Dayton, Hamilton, and elsewhere. Today, German ancestry remains predominant in 19 states stretching across the northern tier of the United States from Pennsylvania to Washington State on the Pacific Coast, encompassing every state touching the Great Lakes (Pennsylvania, Ohio, Indiana, Michigan, Illinois, Wisconsin, and Minnesota) apart from New York. Traces of historic immigration flows from central, eastern, and southern Europe are evidenced in contemporary demographics, cultural agglomerations, food cultures, and the built environment, all of which remain influential throughout this region.

In the first half of the twentieth century, immigration made cities in the Great Lakes economically dynamic and vibrant, places which became sophisticated cities that reflected imported principles of urbanism. However, the early internationalization of the largest cities in the region, tied to both industry and the human experience, contrasts considerably with current realities. On the one hand, economic stagnation, deindustrialization, and out-migration have allowed historical architectural influences to remain visible and relevant, but on the other, these metropolitan areas have continued to shrink. Apart from the fading ethnic neighborhoods and associated social infrastructures such as churches, synagogues, schools, beer halls, and national societies, the urban arcades of Cleveland remain enduring legacies of continental European influence. Urban, architectural, and social connectivity remains relevant between these Great Lakes cities and their distant cultural generators. Impacted by harsh four-season climates and burgeoning populations, the interiorization of commercial activities became an attractive design response. Consequently, cities across the Great Lakes region including Cleveland, Toledo, Buffalo, Rochester, Minneapolis, and St. Paul became proving grounds for the arcade typology in North America.

Cleveland and Its Arcades

An industrial economy, demographics, and intrinsic cultural contributions have shaped Cleveland's historic connectedness to central, eastern, and southern

Europe, and more specifically, to the territories of the former Austro-Hungarian Empire and Italy which makes its interior urbanism even more contextually relevant from an ethnographic perspective as the arcades of Vienna, Budapest, and Milan are among the most sophisticated in the world. Today, Cleveland's nineteenth- and early twentieth-century experiment with the arcade remains intact, restored, and largely frozen in time. Its arcades are particularly significant as they represent an important era in the historical transition of American retail from the urban core to suburbia. Three prominent examples of the arcade typology were built in downtown Cleveland which represent forerunners of both the department store and the post-World War II shopping mall.

Modeled on Parisian precedents, the origins of the American department store may be traced to the rise of conspicuous consumption fueled by the industrial revolution. The native-born American middle-class in the early twentieth century grew alongside a recently arrived immigrant labor force. Downtown department stores reflected the tastes and buying power of the native-born, English-speaking professional classes, but at the same time, they fueled the aspirations of the foreign-born working class and offered a convenient shopping environment for this linguistically diverse populace. Prosperity and social mobility gave rise to higher disposable incomes for all classes, while downtown window shopping was transformed into a leisure activity akin to the strolls of the Parisian *flâneurs* of the previous century. For immigrants, consumption led to the assimilation of American cultural norms and aesthetic sensibilities.

The population of Cleveland was growing rapidly at the turn of the twentieth century. Responding to the need for more street frontage, developers looked to continental European precedents, specifically the arcades, to increase downtown commercial space. Conceived at a monumental scale, the Old Arcade (1890) was modeled on the Galleria Vittorio Emanuele II (1877) in Milan. Originally called the Crystal Palace, then the Cleveland Arcade, and today known as the Old Arcade, it is arguably the grandest historic arcade in the Americas. Designed by architects George H. Smith and John Eisenmann, the developers of the Old Arcade were unable to hire conventional contractors capable of building it, so they approached the Detroit Bridge Company who successfully executed the project on account of their engineering expertise.[19] Opening in 1890, it reflected the rapidly changing commercial, social, and technological forces that were impacting architecture at the turn of the twentieth century. Built at a cost of $875,000, the project was financed by the city's most prominent businessmen of the late nineteenth century, including John D. Rockefeller, Louis Severance, Steven V. Harkness, Charles Brush, and Marcus Hanna. Architects Smith and Eisenmann conceived the Old Arcade as the premier urban mercantile center of Cleveland. State-of-the-art and impressive in scale, the Old Arcade was used as the venue for the Republican National Convention of 1896 (Images 29.1 and 29.2).

The "phatasmagoria" that Walter Benjamin described in his analysis of the Parisian arcades may be equally attributed to the fantasy world that the Old Arcade and nearby department stores offered to Clevelanders, particularly as a familiar architectural form for recent European immigrants. The Old Arcade would serve the same purpose for later migrants to the city as blacks and Appalachian whites from the American South followed the earlier European immigrants into the industrial labor force.[20] Like the continental European arcades,

Image 29.1 Interior view of Old Arcade (1890), Cleveland, dressed for the holidays in December 2021. Credit: Gregory Marinic

the Old Arcade became a "dream factory" for working-class Clevolanders in much the same way that the Parisian arcades transformed the expectations of bourgeois society in post-Revolutionary Paris. Contrasting with previous lives defined by economic hardship, political uncertainty, Jim Crow laws, or war, these retail environments embodied the American Dream while promoting consumption as a form of visual performance. Chinaware, linens, clothing, millinery, jewelry, umbrellas, pianos, and various edible luxuries filled the shop windows of Cleveland's most upscale shopping environment. For both the foreign-born and Southern migrant working classes, the orderly and refined illusions of life that the Old Arcade curated cannot be underestimated. Within these Victorian cathedrals of commerce, a stable and affluent future could be imagined—even if it was, for the moment, only a dream.

A New Typology for Cleveland

As an entirely unprecedented building form in the region, Clevelanders struggled to describe the Old Arcade when it opened in 1890. A local newspaper dubbed it "A Complete Town," perhaps an early understanding of the *city-within-a-city* concept that would come to define a generation of modern buildings built 80 years later in the 1960s and 1970s.[21] Unlike the Parisian examples that gave rise to the department stores, however, the Old Arcade followed in the footsteps of the Higbee Company (1860) department store; yet, its location near Public Square supported the later emergence of several new department

Image 29.2 Interior view of Old Arcade (1890), Cleveland, dressed for the holidays in December 2021. Credit: Gregory Marinic

stores in the immediate vicinity. The establishment of Halle Company (1891) as well as the expansion of Bailey's (1899), May Company (1900), Sterling-Linder (1907), and Taylor's (1907) were outgrowths of the arcade effect.[22]

The Old Arcade connects Superior and Euclid avenues, the two primary commercial streets in the central business district. Consisting of three structures, it houses two nine-story office towers that flank a five-story enclosed arcade. The Old Avenue portal opens onto Cleveland's main east-west commercial street with a grandly arched Richardsonian Romanesque entrance. Its Superior Avenue entrance sits 12-feet lower than the Euclid Avenue portal, resulting in two main floors that negotiate the sectional change between streets, while the Euclid Avenue entrance opens onto Euclid Avenue, the historic main shopping street. Since Superior and Euclid avenues are not precisely parallel, a rotunda at the arcade's south portal on Euclid Avenue shifts the axis 23 degrees.[23]

Much like its Parisian and other continental European forerunners, the Old Arcade is a hybrid structure defined by a monumental glass skylight, linear configuration, and commercial program. The arcade itself is a 300-feet-long interiorized street ringed by four levels of circumferential balconies. Stacked iron columns rise 100 vertical feet in a dramatic stacking effect to create the most impressive publicly accessible interior space in downtown Cleveland. Apart from its hybrid program, the Old Arcade is also a technological bridge between various construction techniques. The office building entrance towers

Image 29.3 Interior detail of Old Arcade (1890), Cleveland.
Credit: Gregory Marinic

employ a masonry load-bearing wall system; however, its floor plates are carried on I-beams attached to steel columns.[24] The floors and roof of the arcade are supported with an iron and oak columnar structure bridged by steel trusses. Responding to changing architectural trends and consumer tastes, the Euclid Avenue portal was remodeled by Walker & Weeks in 1939 with a two-story Art Deco curtain wall façade attached to a steel structure (Image 29.3).

At their peak, the Old Arcade and downtown department stores anchored a vibrant retail district centered on Euclid Avenue that compared to

Fifth Avenue in New York and Michigan Avenue in Chicago. After World War II, the growth of suburban shopping malls began drawing business away from downtown. By the late 1970s, the Old Arcade had declined as the incremental closure of several department stores resulted in increasing shop vacancies on Euclid Avenue which further diminished the arcade itself. In 1975, the structure was listed as one of Cleveland's first buildings on the National Register of Historic Buildings. However, by the late 1990s, the Old Arcade had fallen into further disrepair at which time the Hyatt Corporation committed to adaptive reuse of the building. In 2001, the Hyatt Regency Cleveland hotel opened after a $60 million dollar renovation of the historic structure. Today, the first two floors remain in commercial use, while the upper floor retail spaces and office suites have been converted into hotel rooms. Guest rooms have been carefully integrated behind the original storefronts which have been restored to conform to historic architectural standards. The adaptive reuse of the Old Arcade has been widely acknowledged as an undeniable success.

The Colonial and Euclid Arcades

Built at a considerably smaller scale across the street from the Old Arcade, the Colonial (1898) and Euclid (1911) arcades run parallel to each other and connect the commercial corridors of Euclid and Prospect avenues. Both arcades share striking similarities with the Passage des Panoramas (1799) and Galerie Vivienne (1826) in Paris, Passage Freyung (1861) in Vienna, and Párizsi Udvar (1913) in Budapest. The Colonial Arcade was designed in the Georgian style by George H. Smith, one of the two architects who designed the Old Arcade. Its iron and glass interior with exquisite balcony-level detailing evokes the earlier Old Arcade, but at a considerably smaller scale of only two and a half stories, sheltered with a linear skylight running continuously from Euclid to Prospect. The oldest part of the Colonial Arcade grouping is the five-story Kendall Building (1887) and the six-story former William & Rodgers Department Store both on Euclid Avenue.[25] These buildings were connected by the Colonial Arcade (1898) to the Colonial Hotel (1898) on Prospect Avenue. The stately Euclid Arcade opened to the public in 1911. Designed in the Neoclassical style by architect Franz Warner, its white marble floors, white terra cotta walls, white plaster coffered ceiling, and brightly lit barrel-vaulted ceiling contrast dramatically with the more cavernous Colonial Arcade.[26] Each arcade houses approximately 40 storefronts (Images 29.4 and 29.5).

By the 1970s, shop vacancies increased and both arcades fell into decline. Since that time, the Colonial and Euclid arcades have benefitted from new downtown commercial and residential development along the Euclid Avenue corridor, as well as increased pedestrian traffic from the baseball stadium (1994) and arena (1994) in the adjacent Gateway District. In 2000, a major renovation effort connected the Colonial and Euclid arcades at their midpoint. A Marriott hotel opened in the former Colonial Hotel and a mix of local retailers, including clothing boutiques, jewelers, watch repair, coffee shops, and restaurants, have been introduced in the newly branded "5th Street Arcades." In 2013, Cumberland Development leased the space and initiated a marketing campaign to program the arcades with new retail establishments and events.

Image 29.4 Interior view of Colonial Arcade (1898), Cleveland.
Credit: Gregory Marinic

Reflecting on Benjamin: From the Arcades to Atria and Beyond

In his *The Arcades Project* (1927–1940), Walter Benjamin theorized that the Parisian arcade was a visual device, a space frame that lured the masses into a curated view of life. During their nineteenth-century heyday, the arcades of Paris shaped generational expectations, while contemporary consumerism took flight. By the time Benjamin encountered them in the 1920s, however, the arcades not only hosted mainstream enterprises, but diversified to shelter a bohemian world of marginalized people and illegal activities. Here, gambling and prostitution were thought to exist beyond direct police jurisdiction, spawning an open social atmosphere that allowed transients, artists, gypsies, and gays to germinate a counterculture which challenged racial, ethnic, social, gender, sexual, and economic boundaries. Within a span of only 30 years, the arcade had shifted from a place of bourgeois aspiration to a parallel world of subversion.

Reconsidering the legacy of the arcades and the unprecedented fieldwork of Walter Benjamin in the Parisian arcades of the pre-World War II years, the world of his *flâneur* may be compared with urban North America during the turbulent 1960s and 1970s. Suburbanization, urban renewal, and racial unrest converged to facilitate a new rise in urban-scaled interiors that spawned a new class of urban explorers from suburbia. Envisioning new renditions of the arcade, many downtown developments in North America from the

Image 29.5 Interior view of Euclid Arcade (1911), Cleveland.
Credit: Gregory Marinic

late 1960s through the 1990s were focused on mixing atria, shopping malls, and hotels, as well as a more "urban" indoor retail aesthetic. Urban redevelopment in downtown Cleveland during this era often took the form of interiorized shopping environments, including Park Centre (1973), 200 Public Square (1985), Galleria at Erieview (1987), and Tower City Center (1990). Built during the apogee years of brick-and-mortar American retail, these new "arcades" blended the familiarity of the suburban mall with the atmosphere of downtown.

Much like the Parisian arcades, these environments re-envisioned downtown Cleveland as an interiorized experience. Behind the perceived security of closed doors and within the comfort of climate-control, nostalgia was curated for shoppers as they strolled through landscapes, "sidewalk" cafés, and upscale boutiques, things that had largely disappeared from downtown Cleveland by the 1970s. Akin to the way that nineteenth-century Parisians regarded the arcades, late twentieth-century suburbanites viewed these indoor retail environments as "familiar, safe, and clean" spaces.

The "phantasmagoria" that Walter Benjamin sensed in his nostalgic analysis of the Parisian arcades has become ever more complex in our contemporary globalized world. Since that time, the dreams of the nineteenth century have transitioned through various scalar and technological shifts. Today, industrial production has shifted overseas, while the forces of media, advertising, and fashion have morphed into truly global enterprises. Contemporary American cities reveal some of the most dramatic retail transformations. In Greater

Cleveland, these shifts span from adaptively reused nineteenth-century downtown arcades to several obsolete late twentieth-century shopping malls found throughout suburbia.

We may trace the origins of our own whims, desires, and projections to the nineteenth century when the consumptive dream was fabricated. Our contemporary consumer culture was incubated within the arcades, department stores, and shopping malls that relied on various primitive means of consumer manipulation. Since then, however, continual shifts in industrial production, communication, consumption, connectivity, online shopping, and pandemics have radically rewritten the rules of city-building in post-suburban cities. While the automobile, expressways, and racial tensions diminished central city retail districts in the United States, today, cyberspace supersedes all these forces.

Advertising in newspapers, magazines, and billboards ultimately gave way to radio and television, and then more recently, to the internet and endless onslaught of social media. In this transformative process, we have increasingly traded our physical "retail" world for a virtual one, and perhaps this change is most dramatically seen in the United States. However, as evidenced in the nineteenth century's transition from arcades to department stores, and later, within the more recent shift from a *physical* world of suburban shopping malls to the *virtual* world of internet commerce, retail architecture is among the least resilient of building types because its obsolescence cannot always be effectively adapted.

Moving into the mid-2020s and a post-COVID age of rolling pandemics, cities continue attempting to remake themselves into fashionable retail environments that support "urban vitality." Unlike the nineteenth century, however, competition is no longer across the street with better products or a new building, but rather, in the ability for physical spaces to compete or blend with virtual ones. In this sense, entire neighborhoods such as Soho in New York operate like Old World arcades, merely a showroom at a neighborhood scale, while midcontinental cities like Las Vegas have become nothing more than shopping malls in place of actual urbanism. Contemporary consumption and the architectures of retail have always been tethered to the cycles of trend and fashion. As built environments, they continuously rise and fall in relation to society's endless quest for novelty and the quantitative desires of economy, efficiency, and speed. Yet, we remain unable to entirely relinquish the cosmopolitan pleasures that physical spaces and city centers undeniably provide. In this sense, Walter Benjamin's dream of the arcades remains although we have largely traded the allure of the shop window for the limitlessness of a touch screen.

In countless cities across the United States, in the post-industrial cities of Cleveland, Buffalo, Detroit, Rochester, Syracuse, Cincinnati, and Pittsburgh, in the Sun Belt cities of Atlanta, Charlotte, Houston, Dallas, and Phoenix, Americans lament the lost downtown pedestrian experiences that these cities seemingly now make less possible. Central to such memories is the act of consumption such as the diminished arcades, shuttered department stores, and empty streets, places that suburbia and cyberspace encouraged us to leave behind. Through its embrace of convenience and modernity, American society has incrementally abandoned the most valuable aspects of that authentic urban experience. Today, cyberspace offers greater control to consume at leisure, in the comfort of home, while the physical places that have historically nurtured those needs undergo continual reprogramming, rebranding, redevelopment, and at times, demolition. In this sense, the uncompromising top-down "urban renovation" methods of Baron Haussmann in nineteenth-century Paris have become democratized with digital "progress" in the current era. Through collective abandonment, encroaching obsolescence, and incremental destruction of the physical world for a virtual alternative, we have ultimately left the city behind.

Notes

1 Martin, Susan. *A Nation of Immigrants*. Cambridge, United States: Cambridge University Press, 2021.

2 Remini, Robert. *A Short History of the United States: From the Arrival of Native American Tribes to the Obama Presidency*. New York, United States: HarperCollins, 2009.

3 Radzilowski, John, and Ciment, James. *American Immigration: An Encyclopedia of Political, Social, and Cultural Change*. London, United Kingdom: Taylor & Francis, 2015.

4 Jacobson, Matthew Frye. *Roots Too: White Ethnic Revival in Post–Civil Rights America*. Cambridge, United States: Harvard University Press, 2009.

5 *The Oxford Handbook of American Immigration and Ethnicity*. New York, United States: Oxford University Press, 2016.

6 Foner, Nancy. *One Quarter of the Nation: Immigration and the Transformation of America*. Princeton, United Kingdom: Princeton University Press, 2022.

7 Coman, Katharine. *The Industrial History of the United States* (Classic Reprint). New York, United States: FB&C Limited, 2017.

8 Miller, Carol Poh, and Robert Anthony Wheeler. Essay. In Cleveland: A Concise History, 1796–1990. Bloomington: Indiana University Press, 1990.

9 Radzilowski and Ciment, 2015.

10 Ryan, Joseph. *White Ethnics Their Life in Working Class America*. Englewood Cliffs: Prentice-Hall, 1974.

11 Greenfield, Eloise. *The Great Migration: Journey to the North*. New York, United States: HarperCollins, 2011.

12 Philliber, William W., Clyde B. McCoy, and Harry C. Dillingham. *The Invisible Minority: Urban Appalachians*. Lexington: The University Press of Kentucky, 1981.

13 Alba, Richard. *Ethnic Identity: The Transformation of White America*. New Haven, United Kingdom: Yale University Press, 1990.

14 Ibid.

15 *Encyclopedia of Cleveland History*; Western Reserve Historical Society; Cleveland: Case Western Reserve University, 2003.

16 See Susel, Rudolph. "Slovenes: Encyclopedia of Cleveland History: Case Western Reserve University."

17 City of Cleveland: Cleveland's sister cities program.

18 Wilhelm, Hubert. "Germans in Ohio." Essay. In *To Build in a New Land: Ethnic Landscapes in North America*, edited by Allen G. Noble, 60–78. Baltimore: Johns Hopkins University Press, 1992.

19 Keating, Dennis, and Norman Krumholz. *Cleveland: A Metropolitan Reader*. Kent: Kent State University Press, 1997.

20 Meinig, Donald. *The Shaping of America*. New Haven: Yale University Press, 1998.

21 Rose, William Ganson. *Cleveland: The Making of a City*. Cleveland and New York: World Publishing Co., 1950.

22 Ibid.

23 Stakes, Damon. *Cleveland Rocks: A Bicentennial Political and Social History of Cleveland, 1796–1996*. Cleveland: Cleveland Publishing Co., 1995.

24 Ibid.

25 *Encyclopedia of Cleveland History*; Western Reserve Historical Society; Cleveland: Case Western Reserve University, 2003.

26 Ibid.

Chapter 30

Canadian Academic Interior Urbanism as a Climatic and Cultural Response

Shannon Bassett

There is a unique form of academic interior urbanism found throughout Canada that responds to its extreme climates and unique landscapes. Across the country, university campuses employ intricate tunnel systems that shape a multidimensional experience combining nodes with layered programs to create interiorized public space. Due to their vastness and complexity, academic interior urbanism in Canada is an exceptional precedent for designing interiorized public environments. This chapter examines contemporary examples by distilling important attributes, as well as comparing the shared and divergent qualities of these spaces. This research surveys academic interior urbanism in UQAM-Université du Québec à Montréal, The McEwen School of Architecture at Laurentian University, and the Carleton School of Architecture. These campuses offer pragmatic design solutions that uniquely blend architecture, urbanism, and landscapes into interiorized public environments.

UQAM-Université du Québec à Montréal
Montreal, Quebec
UQAM is an urban campus in downtown Montreal that organizes its main educational programs around a naturally lit atrium space. Its design is driven by a response to climate that interiorizes functions into a public urban space. The campus design responds to an urban site and subway line within an infrastructural context. As described by Rene Vidu:

> ...The construction of UQAM itself in 1980 directly related to urbanism with its architectural integration into the urban environment, the Montreal metro, as well as major elements of the city. The space becomes a cultural agora with an entrance to the church by architect John Ostell.[1]

DOI: 10.4324/9780429443091-36

The architects incorporated interesting pre-existing elements from its site context. These included parts of historic buildings and a series of historic facades. The former historic exterior façade of the Saint-Jacques Church is integrated, or seemingly grafted, onto an interior façade that serves as part of an interiorized public space. This approach was somewhat controversial because the university was non-secular at the time of its inception.[2]

The ebbs and flows of the path of the metro are articulated through these public spaces as part of the architectural promenade to classrooms or public transportation. Social exchanges occur with those passing through the spaces, instigating important interactions between both the university community and the public. This is a multi-leveled interior urban space which provides linkages to multi-programmed commercial spaces in the center of the pavilion, as well as a bridging between disciplines. The space connects both to the metro and the south building, and to the central spine of the university.[3] There are multiple landings and stairs, as well as cantilevered galleries which surround this space. Other programs include the library, bookstore, brasserie, and cafeteria (Image 30.1).

The McEwen School of Architecture, Laurentian University
Sudbury, Ontario

One of the main goals for the McEwen School of Architecture, Canada's first school of architecture to be built in over 40 years and Laurentian University's first downtown building, was to serve as a catalyst for revitalizing downtown. It was meant to help knit the university back into the community. The intention was that the building would break down the "town and gown" phenomena of the university and the city, and thus, give the people of Sudbury more access to the School. Downtown Sudbury experiences many social challenges, as well as a notable lack of community gathering spaces.

Sudbury's urban planning department also had the goal for the city to become more pedestrianized, less reliant on vehicular transportation, and to encourage biking and walkability as opposed to car use. It was perceived that the proposed Elgin Street green infrastructure corridor could influence the design. The school building not only defines the edges of the rail line and highway where it is sited, but also acts as a windscreen to block northern winds. Supporting curriculum pedagogy, the building design was desired to provide spaces where students could do design-build year-round, as well as allow for community outreach and vice versa.

First Nations representation and the indigenization of the curriculum were also issues integrated into the design. In the envisioning process, the architect worked closely with indigenous organizations who identified what they did not have in Downtown Sudbury, such as gathering and community spaces, as well as teaching spaces for casual meetings. This translated into becoming indoor meeting spaces within the school. Aspects included a teaching garden, medicine garden, and ceremonial fire pit sited outside, but that can be viewed from the interior through transparent facades. These exterior conditions create immediate physical connections to studios and circulation. It was imagined that these indoor spaces could act as liminal community spaces connecting indoors to outdoors, both metaphorically and physically. These

Image 30.1 Public atrium space
UQAM (Université du Québec à Montréal), Montreal, Quebec.
Credit: Shannon Bassett

included an indoor meeting space, a lecture hall, cross-laminated timber (CLT) classroom, a public-school space, as well as a workshop located in the former market building. These liminal spaces exist in many places throughout the school. For the community, they engender more conversation with the academic community. The building, in essence, is transparent.

The plan is organized around a central atrium space with a fireplace hearth. It is adjacent to the "crit pit" and creates a space for community meetings and events which become embedded into the experience of the school. Conceptually, this is the programmatic knuckle of the building where multiple programs and programmatic sequences intersect and overlap. This includes the entry sequence from the threshold, offices, and circulation paths to classroom spaces, first floor spaces, and the crit pit. Second floor studio spaces and circulation paths to the library occupy overhanging gallery spaces.

Image 30.2 Common atrium space and Crit Pit hosting community holiday market
The McEwen School of Architecture, Laurentian University, Sudbury, Ontario, Canada.
Credit: Shannon Bassett

The main Elm Street elevation of the school is an historic facade marking the intersection of both the highway and train infrastructure. There are two ways of approaching this, and two significant scaled-up points of entry and intersection. The transparency of the elevation is an important signal of the programming of space. It was anticipated that the current Mexican restaurant at the corner of Elm and Elgin could be an art and architecture space with a Ralph Erskine community outreach component with three corner points of entry. Whole elevations of Elm Street are transparent creating a blurred inside-outside relationship. The intention of the architect was to try to create a public-access grand floor with, arguably, urban activities. A concrete crit pit inside exposes what is happening to the outside through elevational transparencies. Inversely, those in the indoor crit pit presenting work can view passersby outdoors on the sidewalk. The city acts as an urban backdrop from the inside, while from the outside, the interior urbanism of the school acts as a backdrop to the city. The studio space is expressed and internal circulation allows impromptu interactions. With its voluminous spatial qualities, the building has become a nexus for community public events that transform it into interior urbanism (Image 30.2).

The Carleton School of Architecture, Carleton University
Ottawa, Ontario
The design for the Carleton School of Architecture emerged from an exploratory practice setting of Carmen Corneil, Elin Corneil, and Jeffrey Stinson in the late 1960s. They worked primarily with ideas about form, space, and people. Their studio was based on the Toronto waterfront in the Terminal Building, a massive warehouse space with high ceilings, prominent structure, and natural daylighting. As a critical practice, they reacted to the prevailing conventional zoning and top-down planning practices of the day. They were more aligned and inspired by counteractive urban movements, and opposed master planning and

object-oriented architecture in favor of more human-centric design practices. They embraced the density, vitality, and messiness of the urban fabric in places such as Greenwich Village in New York—the neighborhood that Jane Jacobs described in her seminal book, "The Death and Life of Great American Cities."[4] Their initial winning submission for the Carleton School of Architecture included a concept for storefronts in the form of an image of Little Italy in New York. Their proposal drew inspiration from Jane Jacob's notion of the "eyes on the street," pointing to their sensibility of seeing architecture through urbanism as a way to make socially oriented buildings.

The architects were involved in site selection for the new architecture school on the Carleton campus. The site was not located in an urban setting, but a pastoral and bucolic landscape. The existing masterplan illustrated box buildings housing different academic disciplines around the spaces of the campus. The campus was bordered to the south by the Rideau River and to the north by the Rideau Canal. The architects forwent a pristine landscape site adjacent to the Rideau River, in favor of one that they perceived as more pedestrian-oriented across from the Student Union Center. As the architect stated, "It was '68 and they wanted to be part of the discourse on urban design."

The site was chosen to create support for a pedestrian surface route already existing within the campus, and to intensify pedestrian traffic through the campus. They wanted the "city" manifested inside the campus and then within the building itself, which included architecturalizing urban strategies of interior urbanism. This included interior urban streets, "complex juxtapositions of public spaces for public interaction," store frontage access, information and exchange, public sidewalks, loading docks, and alleys. In effect, the interior of the building acts as a piece of urban fabric.

Like other academic interior urbanism projects herein, Carleton University has a series of tunnel systems running beneath the campus connecting all buildings, as well as the outlying parking areas. This serves principally for winter circulation. At the School of Architecture, unlike the rest of the campus where there are no visible markers to connect the tunnel system with the above-ground campus, the tunnel opens to natural light. The ground level brings the tunnel system to the surface which feeds into the "crit pit" on the inside, or into a garden space which opens to the tunnel at the main entrance. The architectural design is modeled on a warehouse matrix with layered concrete, framed space slots, and passageways. The main entry sequence includes an outdoor garden forecourt which acts as a porch on the ground floor. The transparent elevation to the interior creates a blurred inside-outside condition, illuminating circulation flows and allowing activities happening on the inside to be an illuminated interior urbanism.

Dynamic interactions are constantly occurring within the sunken crit pit with its exhibitions of student work and dynamic ongoing programming. The crit pit and the exhibition space operate like an outside porch within the interior urbanism. The pit's programming is like an urban amphitheater as viewed from the core of the building. Circulation spines or interior urban streets flow through the building so people might pause and overlook activity happening within the crit pit—which invites participation. The design intended to animate the ground floor with urban programs along the interior urban street, including a café and bank. It was anticipated that this would intensify circulation. These

Image 30.3 Main interior street and upper level streets to studios and exhibition spaces The Carleton School of Architecture, Carleton University, Ottawa, Ontario, Canada. Credit: Shannon Bassett

programs did not ultimately come to fruition as the university could not support commercial space. There are two main floors with mezzanines. Other "urban" programs along the main floor include spaces that foster social connections and exchanges, including institutional spaces, a meeting hall, a library, vacant space, appropriate meeting/classroom programs, industrial space, workshops, as well as studios along the upper floor "village" with an orientation toward circulation, gathering, and communication. The upper streets and open section provide views of the lower floors and lower streets with their entrances to the storefronts. Their orientations to private back alleys are part of the hierarchy inherent in the planning framework. Lecture rooms are set back from the interior street, providing other storefront spaces. Internal bridges act like sidewalk frontages.

Third floor studios located on the upper level have a "lot" frontage on the street. On the east side of the building, or the "back" of the building, a garage door animates the façade. This interior loading dock serves back-of-house needs, including vehicle access, deliveries, and garbage collection. It opens to provide natural cross ventilation to create a well-tempered environment. An upper street is lit by natural light and provides a place for viewing the ebbs and flows of pedestrian traffic, as well as activities on lower-level interior streets.

The planning of a city analogy comes into play with the concept of the main interior urban streets. These choreograph the ebbs and flows of circulation through the school to its programmatic functions. There are "lots" along these central circulation spines which interconnect street frontages to storefronts, like a small-town and its shops, whose ideas convey a sense of craft and production. The act of making animates all views along these circulation spines. They are designed to provide information and encourage social interactions—both are dynamic as well as inviting (Image 30.3).

Conclusion

In summary, academic interior urbanism in Canada responds to the specificity of the four-season Canadian climate and its diverse natural landscapes. The designs of these well-tempered environments can be seen as a series of design typologies with shared interior urban characteristics. These conditions often respond with pedestrian connections to public transportation infrastructures servicing the university or college campus, whereby both the academic community and the public benefit from enhanced social interactions. Here, layered programs and circulation flows are juxtaposed with interior public spaces to create complexities addressed by interior urbanism.

A pedagogical component of community engagement for university campuses is reflected in interiors that act as liminal spaces. These spaces blur the relationship between inside and outside to create interior urbanism that promotes community and exchange. The programming of interstitial spaces in the building, through interior landscapes and nodes layered with both horizontal and vertical circulations, fosters social interactions with distinctly interior urban characteristics. Finally, city fabric in the guise of interior urbanism is expressed with a kit of parts, including interiorized urban streets, "store" frontages, and public squares blending complex juxtapositions of interior program. These interior public spaces serve as archi-typological building blocks of a Canadian approach to academic interior urbanism.

Notes

1   René Viau, "L'UQAM, une université au coeur de la ville", *La Société la Vie des Arts*, Volume 25, Number 99, Summer 1980, pp. 18–21.
2   Conversation with Prof. Prof. Rejean Legault, Professor at l'École de design, UQAM, Montreal, July 2018.
3   René Viau, "L'UQAM, une université au Coeur de la ville", *La Société la Vie des Arts*, Volume 25, Number 99, Summer 1980, pp. 18–21.
4   Jane Jacobs, *The Death and Life of Great American Cities* (New York: Random House, 1961), p. 458.

Chapter 31

Bedouin Women Sellers and Kuwait's Souk Wajif

Reem J. Dashti and Tasoulla Hadjiyanni

Place attachment has long been noted as instrumental to the construction of cultural identity and human experience.[1] Lacking from studies on place attachment, "the effective bond or link between people and specific places"[2] are studies that delve into how attachment to public places supports or suppresses Muslim women's needs. In fact, studies of Muslim women have often been biased due to Western perceptions of their status and role, focusing primarily on private domestic spaces.[3]

Background: Kuwait and Souk Wajif

Kuwait is located in the heart of the Middle East and overlooks the Arabian Gulf. A predominantly Muslim society, Kuwait has a strong tribal culture derived from its pre-Islamic nomadic roots.[4] Traditional markets started to grow and intersect with traders and caravans from groups, such as the Bedouin nomadic tribes, who ended up settling in Kuwait City to trade in its traditional Souks, becoming "Urbanized Bedouins."

Kuwaiti society is typically discussed as "before" and "after" the oil boom in the 1950s, which brought about an economic resurgence that spearheaded modernization processes and societal changes across gender, ethnicity, and class.[5] By focusing on Bedouin women traders, this chapter sheds light on a population whose needs have not been the focus of many studies.[6] Joining the Souk in the 1930s and 1940s,[7] Bedouin women experienced dramatic changes due to the modern lifestyle, and their stories are crucial in unpacking how economic development, politics, and class intersect with the built environment in shaping women's lives.[8]

Souk Wajif: A Case Study

"Souq Wajif" is also known as "Souq Al-Hareem," which means *women's market*, a place where women could find goods for all their daily needs. Built in

DOI: 10.4324/9780429443091-37

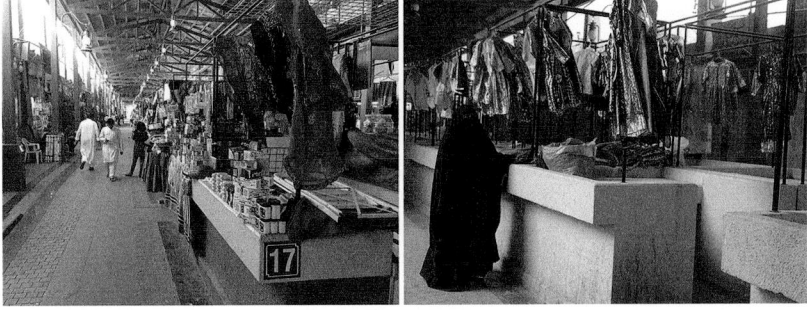

Image 31.1 The redesigned stall inside Souk Wajif after the development plan. Credit: Reem Dashti

1930, the Souk had flexible and adaptable stalls stacked with various traditional goods sold predominantly by Bedouin women. Covered with *abaya* and *burqa*, manifestations of Kuwaiti heritage that symbolize modesty, respect, and pride,[9] these women could sell with confidence around male shopkeepers and customers,[10] creating a sense of community.

After a devastating fire in 2013, Souk Wajif underwent a renovation by the Kuwaiti government and complaints were raised by women traders and visitors regarding the new development plan, detailing how the plan ignored the cultural value of this traditional space to be preserved as a historical site.[11]

Part of the challenge was the "modernization" of the Souk's layout and materiality. The new designed stalls were fixed 2×2 m² concrete cubes with a height of 2.70 m from the floor to the metal structure overhead, and a 1.0 m height service counter. The choice of concrete was meant to protect the structure's integrity from future fire hazards. The stalls' layout was also changed from irregular and flexible to an enclosed modular system and revisions extended to the lighting and ventilation systems. With insights from 20 women sellers, this chapter expands understanding of the impact of the new development on their lives (Images 31.1 and 31.2).

Methodology

Twenty women sellers were interviewed inside their stalls in Souk Wajif during working hours. Participants' ages ranged from 25 to 75 years, which translates into women who have been selling goods in Souk Wajif from 5 to 40 years. Subjects were selected from visits to the Souk through snowball sampling—an older woman seller assisted in identifying other experienced women sellers in the Souk.

A survey instrument was used to guide interviews with both quantitative and qualitative parameters. The questionnaire included queries analyzed with simple descriptive statistics that focused on women sellers' perceptions and satisfaction levels with the Souk's physical features as well as participants' demographics. Open-ended questions and qualitative data were analyzed according to themes that captured sellers' personal experiences and the meanings they held.

Discussion—Interior Elements and Identity

Om-Mishary,[12] a 47-year-old seller, illuminated the ways by which the Souk supported the identity of many of these Bedouin women sellers:

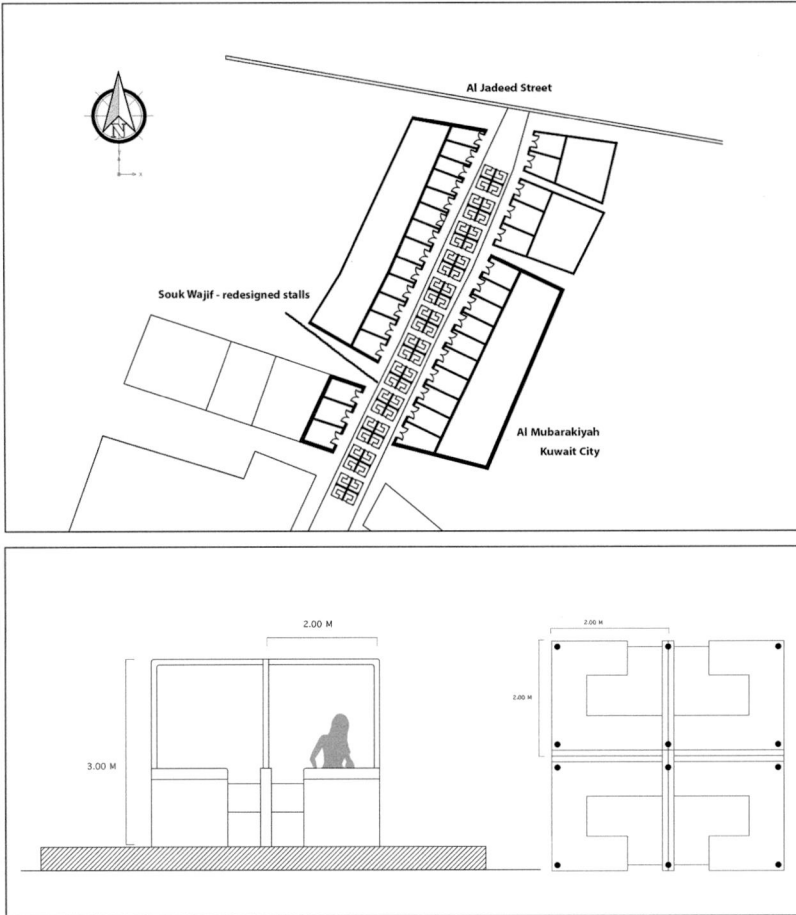

Image 31.2 Souk's new layout, elevation and plan of the new stall design. Credit: Reem Dashti

The Souk tells a beautiful story of Bedouin women traders who were brave enough to leave their homes and challenge the strict traditions of our society. It makes us proud of our identity also because I personally inherited this job from my mother and lived my childhood here in the Souk helping her inside the stall. I can't explain my joy to be part of this Souk. It is my second home. The Souk reminds me a lot of my childhood days where I sat with my mother and learned about how goods are arranged and displayed. Now, I sell traditional goods like my mother did. The whole thing is part of my identity and through my dress and existence in the Souk I maintain my self-identity and preserve the Souk's traditional identity.

Most of the women sellers (17 out of 20) expressed high satisfaction with the Souk's overall space, the main reason being its untouched parts and architectural details. References to the past engendered the Souk with nostalgia that further endowed its significance and therapeutic qualities in the modern life of the city.[13] Below, we zoom into the actual stalls, examining how the stalls' form, size, materials, location, and lighting impacted the women's sense of belonging and conception of identity.

Image 31.3 New redesigned stalls with rigid modular structure. Credit: Reem Dashti

Stall Form

The new modular grid system with the non-organic spatial arrangement converted the shape of the stalls from being irregular and spontaneous to geometric and static (see Image 31.3). Almost all of the women interviewed (18 out of 20) were completely dissatisfied with the current form of the stall. Om-Fahad explained:

> It doesn't represent our ethnic identity as desert dwellers; it doesn't have the soft quality of the fabrics, and it doesn't reflect the shiny textures and materials like the old one. The old stall was pleasing to the eye and soul, but not anymore.

The undoing of identity continued with the stall's functionality as its rigid form suppressed some women's attempts to arrange their goods. Om-Khalid speaks to the care women sellers gave to the act of displaying, a form of storytelling, and how this act relates to their ability to craft an identity of their choice:

> It's something I do with passion, each piece has a story to tell and a spot in the stall. So, I arrange the colored fabrics on top of each other to create a colorful wall. Then I arrange the cosmetics and beauty products above the wall in small containers. Then the shiny jewelry and headpieces are placed on top. This way I can better control my stall and from a far distance, it looks rich and beautiful.

Dissatisfaction was also noted with their ability to decorate the stall (9 out of 20), impacting some women's sense of ownership and control. Challenges in displaying goods arose partly as a result of the metal hanging rods. Om-Jarrah argued:

> The [stall] is designed with extra wasted space inside, there is no place to display or hang the products like before except on the metal structure, which is only suitable for clothes and fabrics.

Not being able to display her products disconnected Om-Jarrah from the stall's ultimate meaning. Others, however, used the new stalls as an opportunity to innovate and establish their status and position. As one female seller explained:

> Few months ago, I used to hang a shelf that was attached to the metal frame of the stall. I used three shelves where all the cosmetics and beauty products were arranged. This solution gave me more space to fold and stack the traditional clothes and dresses on the stall's counter.

Stall Size

Most of the women sellers (18 out of 20) claimed that the size of the new stall presented them with challenges when arranging goods and in finding a place to sit. Wadha, a seller in her late thirties, complained:

> I am not feeling comfortable with the size of the stall…Now the stall is smaller in size, so the products are condensed and cluttered on top of each other; it is very difficult for me and my customers to browse through products from one single corner.

Om-Rashed, another female seller who had been selling in the Souk for more than 45 years, had to sit on top of everything and described her presence in the stall as "riding a camel":

> I felt depressed and disappointed because my old stall meant everything to me; it's like they took my home and redesigned it according to their preference.

Not being involved in the decision-making process of the planning for the Souk's redevelopment made everything feel forced on her, diminishing her sense of control and emotional well-being.[14]

Stall Materials

The new materiality of the stalls, concrete, aggravated dissatisfaction—18 out of 20 women saw concrete as diluting the Souk's traditional architectural character while making them feel uncomfortable. Om-Marzouq, a female seller in her sixties, contended:

> I don't like to feel stuck inside a concrete and steel stall and forced to work inside it. It feels like a cage. Before, the stall was considered as the Bedouin tent, we came to the Souk as a transit place and then returned home at the end of the day. It was flexible and lightweight.

The concrete's rigidness did not respond to a way of life that operated on lightness, flexibility, and temporality. Exacerbating the women's disconnect (17 out of 20) was how the concrete absorbed and reflected excessive heat during the day, especially during the hot summer season. Om-Anwar was holding a traditional fan to cool herself down:

> I also can't take off my burqa and abaya (Kuwaiti traditional clothes) so my face all day is covered, which makes me need more fresh air…. I just drink water a lot, splash some water on my face. Then I cool myself with a hand fan.

The stalls' materiality suppressed women's attempts to construct an identity of their choice and to continue the tradition of selling in the Souk.

Stall Location and Circulation

Most of the women (14 out of 20) were satisfied with the current location of their stalls. As traditionally many have inherited their stall locations from their mothers, it reinforced their attachment to the Souk and the exact location as well as cultivated a sense of community. Om-Othman, who owned a stall next to her sister at the very far end of the Souk, said:

> I enjoy the company of my female sellers all the time, we share a lot, enjoy chatting about daily happenings; we form a strong traditional community by supporting each other on a moral and material basis.

Engaging in conversations, asking for advice, giving and receiving help, and feeling supported and cared for allowed Om-Othman to build relationships that carried her through challenging and good times.

The new development also provided wider sidewalks for moving around the stalls. Half of the women (10 out of 20) were satisfied with the current circulation pattern, partly because of how it enabled social interaction between the sellers and the Souk's visitors.

Lighting

Unearthing the dimensions that lighting took in the lives of these women enables us to expand awareness of the multiple meanings, metaphorical and practical, that light can hold. Most of the women interviewed (14 out of 20) were satisfied with the level of natural light inside the Souk. Mariam, a 66-year-old seller who had been selling in the Souk for more than 40 years, affirmed scientific knowledge of daylight as essential to human health and well-being:[15]

> …Daylight brings joy and hope to my heart. It takes away all stress caused by daily responsibilities.

Close to half of the interviewees (9 out of 20), however, were dissatisfied with the quality of the artificial lighting level inside the souk. Gas lamps were used to light the sidewalks, but their light levels were insufficient to sellers like this 72-year-old woman, Om-Salman, who suffered from low vision:

> *The lighting is so dim, especially around the stalls. At my age I need more light to see and move safely around the stall.... Lighting is important for showing the displayed goods to the customers in a clear and attractive way. The stall's area is dark; the poor lighting impacts the colors, patterns, and textures of the goods, which changes the customer's mood and buying decisions.*

Seeing the displayed goods through the eyes of another, the eyes of the customer on whom she depended to make ends meet, this seller constructed an attachment to place that encompassed sellers and customers alike.

Conclusions and Implications

This study points to the role interior elements can play in how identity is constructed along with de-constructed in emergent forms of urbanism. The Souk enabled women sellers to make a living while preserving their traditional identity as Bedouins, constructing memories and temporal connections, fostering community and family ties, crafting cultural representation and pride, and safeguarding ownership, control, and privacy. The changes in the stalls' design, form, size, and materiality, however, threatened to undo these connections, challenging their ability to foster material and immaterial continuities.

Through the act of claiming public urban space, these women challenged traditions and misconceptions of how Muslim women navigate life and the spaces that they inhabit. This chapter lifted the veil off their stories of entrepreneurship and spirit of independence, shedding light on their active agency in preserving a sociocultural practice while navigating a changing political and economic climate.

Including interior urban places like traditional markets in the historical canon of urbanism, architecture, and interior design allows faculty and students to delve deeper into the multiple ways by which space and place intersect. In parallel, recognizing the power of interior elements in supporting or suppressing well-being and identity places additional weight on the shoulders of scholars, educators, and design practitioners. Participatory design and sensitivity to diverse ways of meaning-making can shield the social, cultural, spiritual, and temporal dimensions of space.

Notes

1   Manzo, Lynne C., and Patrick Devine-Wright. *Place attachment: Advances in theory, methods and applications.* Routledge, 2013.

2   Hidalgo, M. Carmen, and Bernardo Hernandez. "Place attachment: Conceptual and empirical questions." *Journal of Environmental Psychology* 21, no. 3 (2001): 273–281.

3   Keddie, Nikki R. "Women in the limelight: Some recent books on Middle Eastern women's history." *International Journal of Middle East Studies* 34, no. 3 (2002): 553–573.

4   Alsharekh, Alanoud, ed. *The Gulf family: Kinship policies and modernity.* Saqi, 2012.

5   Al-Jassar, Mohammad Khalid A. *Constancy and change in contemporary Kuwait City: The socio-cultural dimensions of the Kuwait courtyard and Diwaniyya.* The University of Wisconsin-Milwaukee, 2009.

6   Tétreault, Mary Ann, and Haya Al-Mughni. "Gender, citizenship and nationalism in Kuwait." *British Journal of Middle Eastern Studies* 22, no. 1–2 (1995): 64–80.

7   Jamal, M. *The old souk of Kuwait.* Kuwait: Center for Research and Studies on Kuwait, 2004.

8   Moghadam, Valentine M. *Modernizing women: Gender and social change in the Middle East.* Lynne Rienner Publishers, 2003.

9   Hussein, Fatimah. *Awraqi.* Kuwait Press, 33–36, 2002.

10   Jamal, M. *The old souk of Kuwait.* Kuwait: Center for research and studies on Kuwait, 2004.

11   Ahmad, Mansour. "Souk Wajif crises." *Al Qabas Newspaper*, June 3, 2013, Issue (14267) p.8.

12   All names are pseudonyms.

13   Wildschut, Tim, Constantine Sedikides, Jamie Arndt, and Clay Routledge. "Nostalgia: Content, triggers, functions." *Journal of Personality and Social Psychology* 91, no. 5 (2006): 975.

14   Kindon, Sara, Rachel Pain, and Mike Kesby, eds. *Participatory action research approaches and methods: Connecting people, participation and place.* Vol. 22. Routledge, 2007.

15   Boubekri, Mohamed, Ivy N. Cheung, Kathryn J. Reid, Chia-Hui Wang, and Phyllis C. Zee. "Impact of windows and daylight exposure on overall health and sleep quality of office workers: a case-control pilot study." *Journal of Clinical Sleep Medicine* 10, no. 06 (2014): 603–611.

Chapter 32

Performative Activators

Interior Urbanism and the Spaces of Cultural Production

Harriet Harriss

As the cost of London's city center real estate continues to rise, spaces of cultural *production* are superseded by spaces of cultural *consumption*, as small-scale, entrepreneurial, and creative agencies alongside established cultural institutions such as galleries and art schools are forced to relocate to the urban fringe. In this rendering, retail becomes the ubiquitous mono-typology, extruding the proximity between sites of cultural production and cultural consumption until they can no longer snap back. Although profit-driven consumerism is offered as a justification, the economic case is weaker than one might assume, as the devastating effect of any recession on a city main street has routinely proven. What the city center loses, however, the urban margins gain. Transposing cultural institutions and creative agencies can provide invigorating new opportunities for creative exchange and collaboration. The contrasting forms of established, emerging, and transposed culture within these fringe sites are often at odds, in ways that unsettle, inspire, and provoke: the ideal pre-conditions for nascent forms of interior urbanism to emerge and evolve.

In these circumstances, transpositional sites can become, to paraphrase Giroux,[1] a vantage point from where the activities within the city center can be critically interrogated, keenly understood and more effectively challenged. Moreover, productive and propositional forms of culture can only manifest as zeitgeist if the context in which they are produced is inherently unstable. For institutions and agencies making this transition to the margins, transposing the city center's spatial and the old spatial templates of museum, school, and agency is ideally abandoned, allowing for new, collaborative, and hybrid typological forms to emerge and among them, innovative forms of *interior urbanism*. This has been evidenced by the contrasting templates of University College London's city center campus and its new site on the edge of the former Olympic Village (now Queen Elizabeth Park (QEP) in East London), or the old and the new Sadler Wells Theatre (SWT). Given the richness of this

DOI: 10.4324/9780429443091-38

margin, however, one questions whether these designs were resourceful and ambitious enough? Consequently, this chapter examines the QEP site through the lens of a pedagogic case study and its pertinent theoretical alignments as a means to consider whether more progressive transpositional alternatives could have been realized. Its tentative hypothesis makes the following claims:

1. That the under-theorization of interior urbanism—thus far—presents opportunities for professional and pedagogical, as well as philosophical experimentation that could expand the field of discourse, and indeed, challenge false or limited claims as to what cultural production actually is, where it should take place, and whom it can and should involve.

2. The relocation of contemporary forms cultural production to the urban margins will prove ineffective if the city center-based typological templates are merely transposed rather than radically reimagined, and that only a tenacious, site-responsive, and resilient re-distribution of the forms of cultural production requires both typological disruption and disciplinary de-partitioning.

3. The ways in which interior urbanism can *internalize interiority* but also *externalize interiority* offer a profound opportunity for further pedagogic and theoretical testing and analysis. Artistic practices, and in particular performativity, can offer a means through which the latter can be achieved.

What Is Cultural Production?

Cultural production typically requires an infrastructure contrived of labor, tools, and skills and typically, some form of participatory or passive public or private audience, such as a theater, although audiences for some forms of cultural production, such as clothing, for example, have been traditionally located within sites of consumption. Cultural production also requires space, though whether the space is situated within the interior, the exterior, or the liminal space in-between is negotiable. This accounts for why cultural production is particularly aligned with the pre-conditions of interior urbanism in that it can simultaneously embody characteristics of both the interior and the exterior urban environment.

Cultural production encompasses commercially driven, non-monetary, and sometimes materially intangible activities by leveraging latent cultural assets embedded within a site or space to fleeting acts of individual artistic expression. 'Maker Culture,' a term coined by Dale Dougherty of O'Reilly Media to describe the transition of producing practically useful and economically generative objects in garages and kitchens from a solitary hobby to a true economic force (Anderson, 2013),[2] can be viewed as one form of cultural production, however, its commercial contingencies lack the freedoms of an artist-in-residence working on collaborative community initiatives.

Although cultural decentralization is becoming the new normal, the relocation of cultural production to the urban margins is not automatically a force for good. For example, it can be used as a gentrification mechanism whereby developers cannibalize the cultural activity of the existing community while ultimately displacing them. Ironically, generating space for cultural

Figure 32.1 John Portman and Associates, Renaissance Center, Detroit.
Credit: Michael Barrera

production is not necessarily the 'end game' for many developers, but a staging post for greater investment dividends in the medium to long term when they are replaced by the office spaces needed by knowledge industries[3] and later still, premium real estate. In effect, the semantic and symbolic expansion of cultural production and its relocation and concentration in once-deprived urban communities and former 'industrial' zones can result in culture becoming weaponized against the very communities into which these agencies relocate. This unmitigated pursuit evokes what Bourdieu describes as 'embodied cultural capital,'[4] encapsulating both the production of objects *and* the space in which they are made, displayed, and consumed require some form of mediation. In lieu of any robust public policy to protect against such kinds of dystopia, architects and interior designers carry the obligation of operating as civically responsible generators of cultural production, although they are unlikely to resist pressure from free-market determinism (Figures 32.1 and 32.2). The question becomes whether a more nuanced approach, one that transcends the typological, disciplinary, and real estate categorizations that can and have been used to surrender even the most innovative spaces to the power of appropriation and monetization, proves a means through which robust, resilient, and relevant alternatives can propagate and persist?

Pedagogy as a Vehicle for Interior Urbanism Experimentation and Theorization

Although interior urbanism is a relatively new school of thought, it has been argued that evidence of its existence has a greater progeny. In his article entitled, '*Some Notes Towards an Interior Archipelago*' produced for MOMU's 2014 special issue on Interior Urbanism, Brendan Cormier points to the fact that because '90% of our lives are spent inside, urban life is an interior affair,'[5] affirming the prevalence and ubiquity of interior urbanism. Similarly, in Charles Rice's 2016 book entitled, '*Interior Urbanism*,' Rice identifies the interior of Portman and Associates 1976 Renaissance Center in Detroit as a seminal illustration of

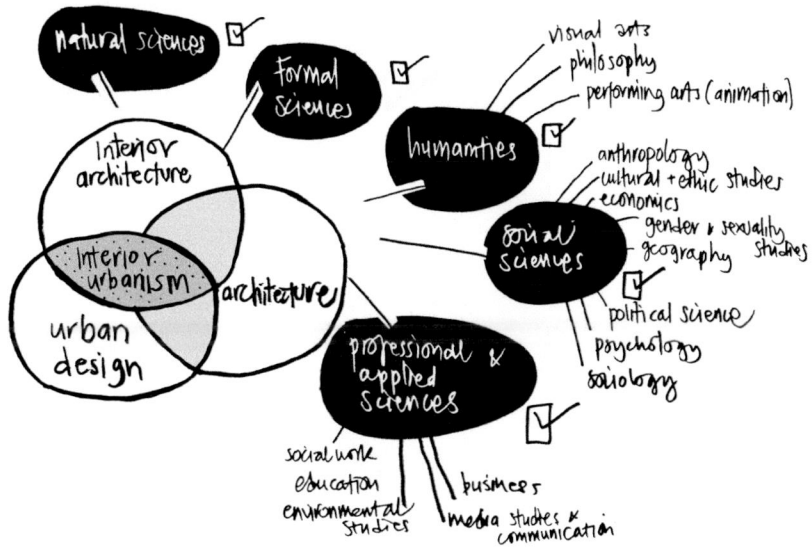

Figure 32.2 The epistemological and disciplinary provenance of interior urbanism. Credit Harriet Harriss

the conditions of interior urbanism.[6] Not only is this precedent almost half a century old, but it also characterizes interior urbanism as able to accommodate the conditions (whether behavioral or environmental) that are more generally situated outside. What is often overlooked, however, is *the ability of interior urbanism to externalize interiority and not simply accommodate exteriority,* and in doing so, resituate private, interior activities within the public realm.

Consequently, the relative lack of theorization of interior urbanism presents opportunities for practitioners, academics, and students to contribute to an emerging discourse. For educators keen to set briefs that respond to real-time societal challenges, tasking students with exploring what interior urbanism can look like affords a means through which students can break free of the disciplinary silos of architecture, interior design, urban design, and landscape architecture. Furthermore, by designing spaces for transposed and often hybridized forms of cultural production on the QEP site, the students were able to reveal the extent to which the existing examples were culturally and creatively limited, and failed to leverage the existing cultural assets of the site by designing far more radical and resourceful alternatives.

Design Brief Obligations: Interior Urbanism and Cultural Archaeology

The decentralization of cultural production is typically opportunistic and the QEP site that this chapter considers is characteristic of this. Historically, London's eastern margins provided a necessary hinterland for the city's undesirables: from plague pits and pig farming, to spaces for dueling aristocrats, both of which were arguably forms of cultural activity at the time. These were later superseded by the indefatigable demands of the industrial revolution leaving no spatial imprint of the pigs or pits remaining. By the latter half of the twentieth century, however, large-scale industry soon faced its own day of reckoning. By the late 1980s, only small businesses remained among the abandoned industrial apparatus that was cheaper to leave to rot than to demolish. Before long, the first migration of low-income cultural producers such as artists and other creatives into these hinterlands offered a parasitic repurposing of the larger postindustrial spaces into artist studios, and in doing so, ensured their architectural survival. Both the spatial adaptability of former factory floors and the lack of money for alterations meant that much of the former materiality could be left intact.[8] When the site was chosen for the 2012 London Olympics, many of the small businesses and artists' studios that had acted as cultural heritage custodians within this area were forced out. It seems a cruel irony that only the larger cultural institutions can afford to occupy the now defunct Olympic site where artists and small-scale creative initiatives once flourished.

It was not just the artist studios and small businesses that faced exclusion. The resident community's own enduring forms of cultural production—from hair extension salons to eel, pie, and mash shops—are often overlooked as cultural assets despite their provenance, popularity, and authenticity. As the displaced city center cultural institutions begin to colonize Queen Olympic Park, ostensibly claiming to 'bring culture' to the area according to their own marketing claims, the latent historic and community-led cultures are at risk of being discarded. Consequently, tasking students with imagining an alternative strategy—one where the migrating city center cultural producers work with, rather than against the local cultural producers—became additional obligations within the brief. What the students soon discovered was that, in order to produce exemplary interior urbanism that accommodated all of these prerequisites, other forms of spatial agency were needed.

Interior Urbanism, Aesthetic Practices, Performativity, and Cultural Connectivity

Aesthetic practices—such as walking or a 'derive' (Debord, 1958) involving a more indiscriminate and avaricious urban wandering—can offer a means through which diverse and distributed forms of cultural production can be temporally and spatially connected. For Michel de Certeau, we are each inclined to identify and derive culture from everyday objects and things that they individualize and make our own,[7] meaning that all existing spaces and objects can become cultural signifiers, and that culture is already present in the site. Furthermore, de Certeau argued that the sanctioned purveyors of culture such as museums, theaters, and galleries strategically assert their status as 'producers,' while categorizing the public to 'consumers.' His view was that challenging this binary could be achieved by individuals resisting the prescriptions of what is and is not culture as stipulated by the 'planner urbanist, or cartographer,'[8] for example, by simply walking in unpredictable directions. Instead, acts of trespassing upon the territory of others, using the rules and products that already exist in culture in a way that is influenced, but never wholly determined, by those rules and products [9] could allow the public to become identifiers if not generators of cultural activity and form.

Consequently, for the connections to be made and synthesis achieved between different forms of cultural production within the site—from the archaeologically retrieved and community-authored to the institutionally proposed and sometimes superimposed—the solutions cannot be found in previous attempts offered by urban design or interior design acting in isolation. Instead, interior urbanism is better able to activate these multiple site

Figure 32.3 Designs for a making-as-display facility within the proposed Victoria and Albert (V&A) second site within the former Olympic Park in East London.
Credit: Pennie Dawes, MA Interior Design Student, Royal College of Art, 2013–2015

conditions simultaneously by using artistic practices and its ability to interiorize the exterior, the urban realm can absorb artistic practices into its program. Besides walking, the artistic practices most suited to these kinds of syntheses can be broadly identified as 'performative,' a term introduced by the linguist John L. Austin to distinguish between a 'performance' that solely delineates the execution of an operation, from performative whereby the articulation itself generates a new reality,[10] whereas when an urban interior *'focuses upon the process-oriented character of spatial perception, spatial coherencies...become apparent in structures of incidents.'*[11] Subsequently, the students' projects sought to test whether performative acts enable interior urbanism to better facilitate multiple site conditions, as well as past and present forms of cultural production available within the site (Figure 32.3).

Student Project 1: A V&A East Alternative: Production as Display

The first project, executed by Pennie Dawes, imagined one such future for the Victoria & Albert Museum satellite space. The V&A is the world's largest museum of decorative arts and design, housing a permanent collection of over 2.27 million objects, of which 50,000 are ceramics and glass and approximately 24% (one quarter) of the entire collection can be displayed simultaneously.[12] From Pennie's perspective, the museum's emphasis on cultural consumption (from exhibit displays to extensive and even bespoke retail opportunities) rather than on cultural production (such as spaces where the objects are made for the collection) provided an opportunity to envision how spaces for cultural production could be incorporated within the Olympic Park satellite. In addition to this, acts of cultural production were awarded display preeminence, placing emphasis on production and process over product and artifact.

Pennie's project sought to provide spatial evidence of the V&A's stated ambitions to create new dialogues with the public, by disrupting their emphasis on collection and display, and providing the means through which artists could remain on site. The project also recovers and reinstates some of the characteristics of lost archaeological and historical cultural productivity by embedding their materials, forms, functions, and practices into the design of the space itself. These include a reinstated rail-track used to transfer ceramics to the kiln room to a clay-water recycling system that echoes the functions of the site's long-lost dye mill. By absorbing aspects of the industrial landscape into the interior and giving it a practical function as opposed to a decorative one, a dynamic patina emerges, one that through the performativity of both practice use and display value reveals the site's complex, latent, historical palimpsest (Figure 32.4).

Student Project 2: Sadlers Wells Theatre Distributed Urban Dance Activator

In the second student project, Ryutaro Arai selected SWT as his 'client,' a dance theater renowned for its experimental performances, innovative costume design, and passion for making contemporary dance, in all its forms, part of everyday life. The theater's satellite will be situated at a site at the heart of the Olympic park, a 15-minute walk from public transport. Rather than see this as a problem, Ryutaro's proposal transformed an otherwise unremarkable walk from the train station to the theater into a participatory dance experience, offering a series of five performative interventions that connect the station to the site. The conditions exemplify the experimental identity of the theater, while engaging the public in spontaneous and participatory forms of movement and physical self-expression. Each urban interior—transitioning activities typically confined within interiors whose access is limited by monetary exchange—is materially informed by elements extracted from SWT's costume archive. These spaces visually amplify participant movement to any passing audience, devoid of financial access restrictions. By allowing the public a choice between dancing conspicuously or covertly, the tensions between interior and exterior are continually manipulated. The public can move between each of the five interventions consecutively or in a more individual, dérive-like manner, allowing the public to define the parameters of their own cultural experience.

Conclusion: Toward a Performative Interior Urbanism

Using a pedagogical experiment to respond to the under-theorization of interior urbanism and even contribute toward its expansion by responding to a contested site with real-life constraints allowed students to test the potential of interior urbanism in ways that a real building or a set of philosophical constructs might not succeed. The results of their efforts identify issues that speak to the cultural producers currently migrating to the site, to policy makers and developers, and to designers committed to egalitarian and civically engaged design outcomes. The students' work also reveals the extent to which interior urbanism can both internalize interiority and externalize interiority, but also use performativity as an activator for non-sequential, multi-temporal, and multi-layered narratives of cultural production. Within the design proposals, performativity was also used as a means through which the role of cultural producer and public consumer was de-partitioned and disrupted. What their propositions

Figure 32.4 The proposed urban dance activator changing levels of transparency and display disrupt the thresholds between interior and exterior spaces, and make dance a public, participatory, and performative as well as professional, private, and performance-based act within the Queen Elizabeth Olympic Park. Credit: Ryutaro Arai, MA Interior Design Student, Royal College of Art, 2013–2015

illustrate is the extent to which an interior urbanism brief can address some of the major civic issues faced by cultural institutions, communities ear-marked for regeneration, local government, and national policy makers, as well as designers seeking to address the needs of often polarized stakeholders. Arguably, these skills and this expertise in interior urbanism will only serve to enrich the built environment as these students enter professional practice.

Notes

1   Giroux, Henry. "Theories of reproduction and resistance in the new sociology of education: A critical analysis." *Harvard Educational Review* 53, no. 3 (1983): 257–293, 275.

2   Anderson, Chris. "20 years of wired: Maker movement," *Wired Magazine*, 02 May 2013.

3   Evans, Graeme. "Creative cities, creative spaces and urban policy." *Urban Studies* 46, no. 5–6 (May 2009): 1003–1040. Doi:10.1177/0042098009103853.

4   Bourdieu, Pierre. "The forms of capital. (1986)." *Cultural Theory: An Anthology* 1 (2011): 81–93.

5   Cormier, Brendan. '"Some notes towards an interior archipelago.'" *Interior Urbanism, MONU, Magazine in Urbanism*, Autumn 2014, pp. 22–25, 22.

6   Rice, Charles. "Prologue." *Interior Urbanism: Architecture, John Portman and Downtown America*. Bloomsbury Publishing, 2016.

7   de Certeau, Michel. *The Practice of Everyday Life*, Chapter 7, trans. Steven Rendall, University of California Press, Berkeley, 1984.

8   de Certeau, p. 93

9   de Certeau, pp. xvi, xix.

10   Austin, John Langshaw. *How To Do Things with Words*. Vol. 88. Oxford University Press, 1975.

11   Wolfrum, Sophie, and Nikolai Brandis, eds. *Performative Urbanism: Generating and Designing Urban Space*. Jovis, 2015, p. 6.

12   Source: http://www.vam.ac.uk/content/articles/s/size-of-the-v-and-a-collections/ Last accessed: 31/01/2018

Theories and Influences

Identity

Chapter 33

Queering the Urban Room

Toward a Resilient Urban Design Praxis

B.D. Wortham-Galvin

Who and what is being left out in design and development decisions of the twenty-first-century city? How can designers change how they know—and, therefore, make—the city, so that they might promote places of difference rather than propagate a nostalgic (and outdated) notion of urbanity as community?[1] How can the idea of (interior) urbanity benefit from reconsidering what we reuse, how we alter those things, and at what scale.

To discuss these questions, what follows includes a repositioning of urban design through the lens of queerness. The queer will be asserted herein as a means of destabilizing the norms of urban design practice. In order to establish a liminal interior urbanism that crosses boundaries and expectations between publicness and privacy, and between exterior and interior. Specifically, the notion of liminal interior urbanism (a.k.a. the urban room) is meant as a critique of the privatization of public space that emerged with the proliferation of large-scale atria and interior streets in hotels, office buildings, and malls starting in the 1960s in North America.[2] Finally, this mode of urban design praxis is asserted as resilient within this chapter wherein resilience is defined as flexible, diverse, adaptive, and "having the potential to develop a more radical and transformation agenda that opens up opportunities for political voice, resistance, and the challenging of power structures and accepted ways of thinking."[3]

Queering Urban Design

The way we have understood the city for the past century is through big money, big visions, and—more recently—big data. The large urban room emerged in post-World War II America as embodied in the works of John Portman at sites such as Peachtree Center in Atlanta and the Los Angeles Bonaventure Hotel.[4] Interior atria and streets in hotels, malls, and office complexes developed a largeness of scale and remade relationships in the promenade of exterior to

DOI: 10.4324/9780429443091-40

interior, as well as notions of for whose consumption these interior urbanisms were being made. The context of this retreat from exterior urbanity took hold during a period of social and racial inequity and violence, compounded by white flight to the suburbs. The result was not just moving publicness indoors, but also controlling who belongs in public (and who does not). Can the problem of knowing and designing a city be better served by rethinking bigness with a reconsideration of what resources we are (re)using and which voices inform the process of their adaptation?

The elision between private interests and the public good, between interiority and exteriority of experience, is now complete in a global urbanism that has erased this dualism. As the physical and socio-cultural have become inextricably intertwined in the defining of the public, queerness is useful in unraveling that knot. Even more so, because what is missing from synoptic accounts of the plurality of urban design mythologies in action at the turn of the twenty-first century in the United States is a discussion not merely about stewarding changes in the physical fabrics of extant structures, but more broadly (and significantly) it involves the politics of who makes places and who gets to occupy them.

As sociologist Henri Lefebvre asks, "If space embodies social relationships, how and why does it do so? And what relationships are they?"[5] Following Lefebvre's model of social production of space, urban design has been dominated by what he terms abstract space—space produced, utilized, and dominated by capitalist systems of production. For example, those who have controlled late twentieth- and early twenty-first-century adaptive reuse projects laud the conversion of sites or buildings for their potential consumption by tourists and upper-middle-class consumers.[6] Historic, cultural, and public values of reuse are defined by consumerist logics of a very specific taste group with development strategies that are often with limited or no public processes or partnerships.[7] In addition, the projects are sold as sustainable, but the application of this discourse is driven via the reuse of the *physical* fabrics, not configured as a cultural resilience.[8] The resulting adapted city, thus, is often driven by big projects (in financing, scope, scale) in socio-economically decimated neighborhoods in order to attract a new urban audience. In the current schema, the city is understood by a consumerist logic that privileges (and delimits) who has the right to the city.[9] The adaptation of the city, therefore, is about the politics of who makes place and who gets to occupy it as design, which is most often stewarded by a select group of (often socio-economically and/or culturally homogenous) people who assess the values of the traditions that the city should represent.[10]

Queering challenges this conventional notion of design praxis which emphasizes the now euphemistic goal of placemaking. Queer is used in this assertion of resilient urbanism to refer to a destabilization of the norm. Queer is also used as a signifier of the making of identity, gender, sexuality, family, and "community," as moving targets.[11] This chapter, thus, uses the term *queer* (as other authors do) not as a way of stipulating specific people's identities or sexualities, but in the questioning of norms and orthodoxies.[12] In these terms, the queering of space promotes a notion that culture is and should be performed through the occupation of space, not *a priori* to it. As geographer Kath Browne notes, queer "seeks to reconsider how we think [of] our modes of being and our conceptualizations of politics."[13]

If public places offer a realm of conflicting simultaneity between ideal forms and performative tactics, then a queering of the urban room offers the ability to understand how people enact places to reveal the politics of context, both to instill and destabilize beliefs and values, and to perpetuate and rebel against tradition. Using a queering of urbanism as a core design methodology allows public places that also appear permanent to embrace the ephemeral nature of dwelling and being. It allows people to become equal partners with form and space in the making of place, rather than being subservient or non-existent to them. It provides a new non-normative notion of interior urbanity that embraces overlaps between the definitions of what is exterior and what is interior, and what is public and what is private.

"Painting the Town Pink"

Thesis student Dustin Buzzard applied queer design methodologies as a means to (1) reconnect underutilized resources of the city Portland to a vital urbanism; (2) use specific moments and productions in the cultural history of Portland's LGBTQ+ residents to achieve a plural contemporary publicness; and (3) reestablish the urban room as a transparent liminal space between publicness and privacy, between exteriority and interiority. The intent between the thesis chair and thesis student was to provide a model for a capacious notion of resilient urbanism that permits a variety of peoples to engage in social, economic, and cultural productions.[14]

Methodologically, Buzzard was prompted to question predicable notions of urban design in favor of (1) challenging conventions of public and private; (2) promoting discursive communication over assumed understanding; (3) valuing the plural over the singular; (4) converging temporal histories and contemporary conditions; and (5) challenging the "plan" convention as the generator of the resilient design. The result of his exploration is a series of four interventions—"Cruise the Park," "Frozen Kisses," "Lock Your Junk," and "Paint Your Face"—that represent an attempt to queer the city in terms of both the physical infrastructures used and their socio-cultural occupations. What follows is a description of two of the interventions (Images 33.1 through 33.4).

"Frozen Kisses"

Buzzard's design proposition "Frozen Kisses" offers an alternative rethinking of the park as an activating urban room and the reuse of its infrastructure. The intervention is located at the southern end of Portland's North Park Blocks,

Image 33.1 *Cruise the Park* collage graphic by Dustin Buzzard (from 2013 MArch Thesis *Painting the Town Pink*).

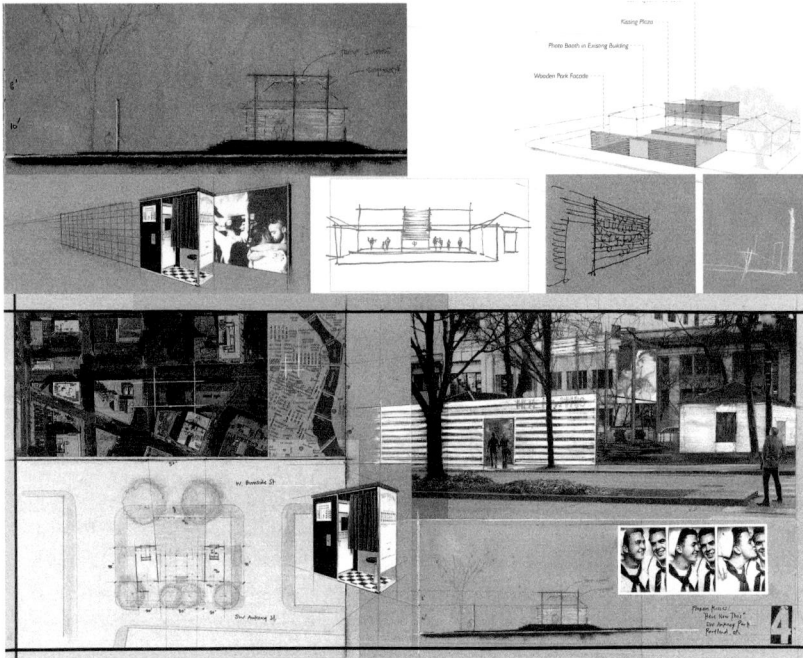

Image 33.2 *Frozen Kisses* collage graphic by Dustin Buzzard (from 2013 MArch Thesis *Painting the Town Pink*).

an area physically and perceptually cut off from the main Park Blocks by the predominating automobile traffic of Burnside Avenue. Deeded in 1865 with an initial residential focus, and areas set aside for children, North Park Blocks declined in the 1920s when the 1924 zoning code changed the surrounding area to industrial, commercial, and residential hotels. It was in full neglect by the 1940s up through the turn of the twenty-first century, with homelessness, panhandling, and drug use dominating the area.[15] While the use of the northern part of North Park Blocks increased with the redevelopment of the neighboring Pearl District at the turn of the twenty-first century, the small piece of park south of Burnside (with two historic but abandoned public restrooms) remains overlooked and blighted (Image 33.2).

Buzzard's choice to activate this urban room was based not only on its discarded condition, but also on the historical role of the "tearoom" as a site of sexual encounters supported by the infrastructures of public restrooms in parks and transit centers.[16] Situated in a prominent location along the path of Portland's annual Gay Pride Parade, "Frozen Kisses" adapts this derelict park piece and its neglected bathrooms into a photo booth, gallery, and interactive arts plaza. The two public teahouse galleries frame a center urban outdoor room—a meeting place composed of a light frame structure that supports a billboard-sized screen where projected images from the photo booths can be seen (if the photogs so desire) from one of Portland's busiest thoroughfares. It becomes a place to celebrate public displays of affection—both episodic and continual. It also becomes a way of marking land with fragments of the past—related to Portland's historic gay triangle[17]—and the present in terms of the periodic pride parade route and the incessant urban activities (both planned and unplanned). The bathrooms-cum-photo booths and galleries become a place where photos from the past and the present can be displayed.

Image 33.3 *Lock Your Junk* collage graphic by Dustin Buzzard (from 2013 MArch Thesis *Painting the Town Pink*).

If the tearoom represented a public place where private acts took place and a place where the invisibility of gay life was made visible to other men, then "Frozen Kisses" seeks to amplify gestures of intimacy by all peoples rather than marginalize them. It is an attempt to layer physical and digital spatial action, by providing a space wherein all social meetings can happen, and to simultaneously queer the urban room of the park through unexpected action.

"Frozen Kisses" reclaims a space of police oppression and sexual suppression has been culturally engrained as a site of subversion into a celebratory people spot. "Frozen Kisses" alters a forsaken infrastructure into a welcomed one. People and their desires, thus, enact the visual aesthetics of the space and move it from one of static consumption to an interactive installation that highlights the ambiguity between private and public action, between visibility and invisibility, and between disclosures and enclosure. This intervention is meant to demonstrate "the degree to which the boundaries between spaces defined as 'public' and 'private' are socially constructed, contingent, and contested."[18]

"Paint Your Face"

Portland's most famous queer face, Darcelle XV, came out in 1969 when Walter Cole transitioned to a drag queen after a two-year experimentation with wearing women's clothes.[19] Cole opened a dyke bar in 1967 called Demas that would become Darcelle XV Showplace in the early 1970s that is still a popular drag revue (Image 33.4).[20]

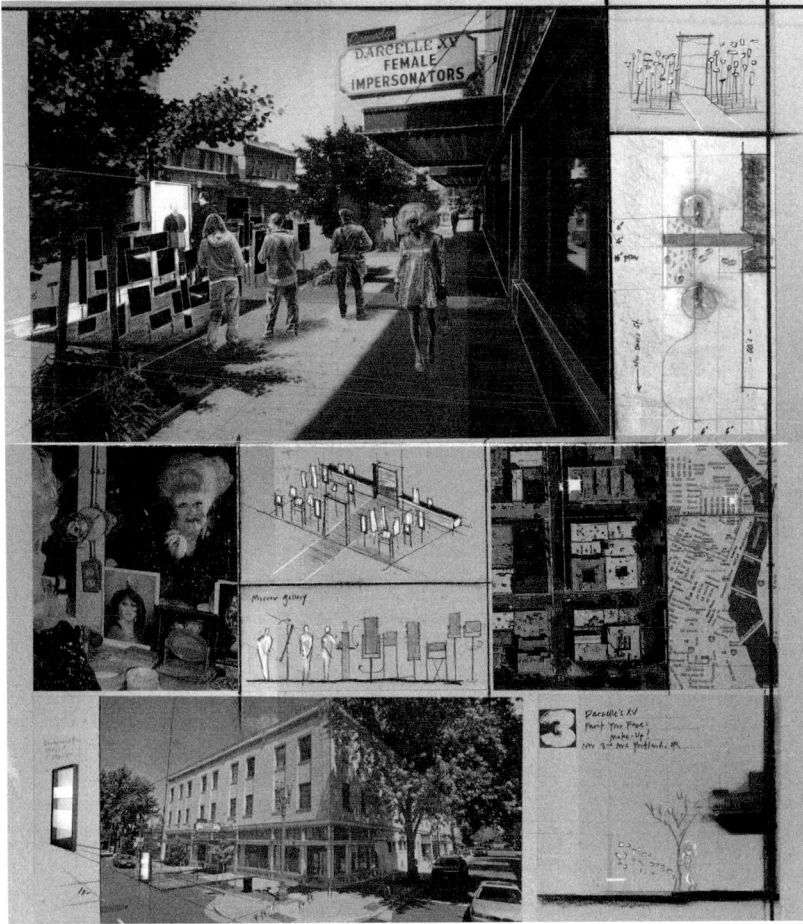

Image 33.4 *Paint Your Face* collage graphic by Dustin Buzzard (from 2013 MArch Thesis *Painting the Town Pink*).

For this intervention, Buzzard was encouraged to rethink the increasing popular notion of the parklet—the adaption of the right of way of a parking space into a people spot. This intervention engages in Erving Goffman's dramaturgical analysis of daily life as Buzzard seeks to bring the "back-of-house" transformation of female impersonation into the "front-of-house," by designing a public vanity where one can stop and primp or vamp.[21] Utilizing Portland's Street Seats initiative, the parking spot directly in front of Darcelle's performance venue would be transformed into a spectacle of mirrors of every size. The red carpet would be rolled out indefinitely, opening from the front doorway through the vanity parklet to a full-length dichromatic mirror, which has shifting and alternating fragments of colored reflective glass transforming the on-lookers perception of what a reflected image is.

In "Paint Your Face," notions of publicness and privacy are conflated as the act of transformation into drag is moved from an invisible and unknowable realm to a publicly shared one. In other words, the relationships between performance, social masks, and being oneself are merged and intensified. Ultimately, the intent is that anyone would engage in play at the public vanity parklet in what is usually a private moment of self and identity.

Conclusion

In queering a methodology for resilient urbanism, the goal is to stimulate a plural means by which we perceive, process, and synthesize how we know and live in the city. Today's city is consumer-driven and the power of the purse—in terms of corporations, municipal institutions, and the upper class—controls much of how cities make place today. In seeking to queer the city, Buzzard notes, "Queer space is [...a ...] place free from the pressures of conforming to an idealized urban fabric."[22]

Writer D. Travers Scott comments on the fluidity of gender and sexual orientation by asking:

> How can a rigid Gay Male identity cope with that really cute guy, who used to be a butch baby dyke, and is still involved in a primary relationship with a woman but considers herself basically a gay man [...] How can you be rigidly orientated toward something that is amorphous shifting, fluid, tricky, elusive?[23]

Most urbanism could benefit from Scott's observations about being rigid in the face of the protean and mutable. When people ask, "What is urban design?" they are often really asking what is its relevance to me. The "Painting the Town Pink" investigations can be used to reframe the design praxis in support of creating urban rooms of difference and resilience

Notes

1   Iris Marion Young, *Justice and the Politics of Difference* (Princeton, NJ: Princeton University Press, 1990).

2   Reinhold Martin et al., *Multi-National City: Architectural Itineraries* (Barcelona: Actar, 2007); Charles Rice, *Interior Urbanism: Architecture, John Portman and Downtown America* (New York: Bloomsbury Academic, 2016).

3   Simin Davoudi, "Resilience: A Bridging Concept or a Dead End?" *Planning Theory & Practice*, 13(2) (June 2012), 309–310.

4   Rice, *Interior Urbanism*.

5   Henri Lefebvre, "The Production of Space," in J.J. Giesking & W. Mangold (Eds.), *The People, Place, and Space Reader* (New York: Routledge, 1990, 2014), 289.

6   Randall Mason, *Economics and Historic Preservation: A Guide and Review of the Literature* (Washington, DC: The Brookings Institution, 2005).

7   B.D. Wortham-Galvin, "The Woof and Warp of Sustainability," *Powerlines*, Summer 2015, online journal, http://amst.umd.edu/powerlines/the-woof-warp-of-sustainability-dialogues-on-the-resilient-reuse-of-the-blue-heron-paper-mill/

8   Stuart Brand, *How Buildings Learn: What Happens After They're Built* (New York: Penguin Books, 1994).

9   Henri Lefebvre, "The Right to the City," in E. Kofman & E. Lebas (Eds.), *Writing on Cities* (Oxford: Blackwell, 1968, 1996), pp. 147–159.

10 Henri Lefebvre, "Production," 289.

11 A. Gore, *Portland Queer: Tales of the Rose City* (Portland: Lit Star Press, 2009), 9.

12 K. Browne, "Challenging Queer Geographies," *Antipode*, xx (2006), 885–893; H. Davis, "The Difference of Queer," *Canadian Women's Studies*, 24(2–3), (2005), 23–37; N. Giffney, "Denormatizing Queer Theory: More than (Simply) Lesbian and Gay Studies," *Feminist Theory*, 5(1), (2004), 73–78; and, J. Halberstam, *In a Queer Time and Place: Transgender Bodies, Subcultural Lives* (New York: New York University Press, 2005).

13 Browne, "Challenging," 889.

14 Dustin Buzzard, *Painting the Town Pink: Queer Interventions in Portland's Public Realm* (M.Arch thesis, Portland State University, 2013).

15 N. Pickett, "North Park Blocks Improvements Under Way," *The Oregonian* (1992), E02; H. Mackenzie, *The Portland Park Blocks: Their Origin and Development* (Thesis, University of Washington, Seattle, WA, 1988).

16 L. Humphreys, *Tearoom Trade. Impersonal Sex in Public Places* (Duckworth, 1970); E.W. Delph, *The Silent Community: Public Homosexual Encounters* (Beverly Hills, MA: Sage Publications, 1978); George Chauncey, "Privacy Could Only Be Had in Public: Gay Uses of Streets," in J. Sanders (Ed.), *Stud: Architectures of Masculinity* (Princeton, NJ: Princeton Architectural Press, 1996), 250–251.

17 A. Ghaziani, "Lesbian Geographies," *Contexts*, 2015, http://contexts.org/articles/lesbian-geographies/; A. Ghaziani, *There Goes the Gayborhood?* (Princeton, NJ: Princeton University Press, 2015).

18 Chauncey, "Privacy," 225.

19 Walter Cole & S. Knorr, *Just Call Me Darcelle* (Portland, Oregon: Create Space Independent Publishing Platform, 2010).

20 K. Clarke, "Walter Cole, Just Call Me Darcelle: That's No Lady; that's Darcelle," *Willamette Week* (2011).

21 Erving Goffman, *The Presentation of Self in Everyday Life* (New York: Anchor Books, 1959).

22 Buzzard, "Painting."

23 D.T. Scott, "Le Freak, c'est Chic! Le fag, Quelle Drag!" in C. Queen & L. Schimel (Eds.), *Pomosexuals: Challenging Assumptions About Gender and Sexuality* (San Francisco, CA: Cleis Press, 1997), 65–66.

Chapter 34

Sacred Adsorptions

Civic Sites for (Gendered) Public Mourning in Yazd, Iran

Vahid Vahdat and Stephen Caffey

When navigating the historic urban fabric of cities in the hot and arid region of the Iranian Plateau, one has no visual access to the colorful *orosi*s (large stained-glass windows), mesmerizing ornaments, and vivid tilework that frequently adorn the residences surrounding alleyways. Not even the large interior court-yards have an equivalent in the urban fabric. In fact, an outsider may feel rather claustrophobic in the dull, narrow alleys, surrounded by tall, windowless adobe walls that are partially roofed thereby intensifying the sense of enclosure. These design features, like most such architectural measures, respond to myriad exter-nal forces. The vaults covering parts of the alleys (*sabat*s) address the tectonics of the brick arches that require horizontal connectivity to absorb lateral forces. The enclosed proportion of the alley provides shade in the harsh climatic con-ditions of cities in central Iran, and thereby cools the air that flows faster along its narrow profile. The cultural codes of a patriarchal society that holds privacy so dearly generate architectural layouts that look inward to the secluded central courtyards, cutting off all visual connections with and from the outside gaze.

Understanding the logic behind the urban design of cities like Yazd, Kashan, Kerman, and Isfahan does not obviate the desire for occasional urban refuge—whether in terms of spatial relief or ceremonial exigency. Large open public spaces such as Isfahan's Naghsh-e Jahan Square are rare among the organic urban fabrics of central Iran, and extremely so in urban fabrics altered by the encroachments of modernization. This somewhat-exceptional top-down planning of Naghsh-e Jahan Square as part of a much larger master plan for the city occurred in the sixteenth century, when the city served as the capital of the powerful, wealthy, and centralized Safavid court. The Safavid ruler, Shah Abbas the Great (1588–1629), used the square primarily as a venue for parades in his honor and as a field for polo matches. However, due to the inherently bottom-up, organic formation of cities in central Iran, they generally lack a mas-ter plan in any conventional sense of the concept, and thus make no provision for such large-scale and authoritative urban interventions.

DOI: 10.4324/9780429443091-41

As a number of prominent Iranian scholars have noted, while Persian architecture is well known for its rich heritage and innovative design influences around the globe, it suffers from a lack of well-designed, high-quality urban spaces.[1] Some go so far as to contend that public space is a modern construct in Iran and that premodern examples do not qualify as a spatial manifestation of the public sphere in the modern sense.[2] Yet, in the organically entangled threads of dark, long, and narrow urban alleys in cities such as Yazd, one encounters spatially rich moments of refuge. These spaces, regardless of whether their ownership would qualify them as public urban spaces in the contemporary sense, most definitely function as such.

This urban typology, known as *tekyeh* (or alternatively *Hoseyniyyeh*), is an open space, often with a rectilinear plan, comprising an area of several hundred square meters. The *tekyeh* of Fahhadan in Yazd, for example, is about 750 square meters, while the exceptionally large *tekyeh* of Shahtahmasb would have been up to 10,000 square meters, had it not been demolished in the 1920s (see Image 34.1).[3] While *tekyeh* layouts, forms, and details vary in cities across the country, those in Yazd have been praised as "the most significant examples of public space in Persian history."[4] One of the exclusive features of *tekyeh*s in Yazd is their distinctive stepped morphology, which some scholars associate with the ancient ziggurat typology.[5] The walls that surround *tekyeh*s in Yazd are often two (and occasionally three) stories high, filled with a row of *soffeh*s. A *soffeh* is an arched recession in a wall that is often elevated and provides a seating space enough to be carpeted with a small two-meter by three-meter rug. One side of *tekyeh*s in Yazd has a stepped wall that can reach four or five stories at its center. If the arches of *soffeh*s in this side of the *tekyeh* are so wide that their stacking might lead to the spreading and eventually the collapse of the arch, then oftentimes two minarets are added as heavy vertical loads of mass to help keep the structure intact.[6]

The refuge that the open spaces of *tekyeh* provide within the densely built cities of central Iran allows for a multitude of functions to take place. Similar to many other examples of urban squares around the globe, *tekyeh*s are multifunctional and accommodate a range of urban behaviors, from children playing soccer, hawkers selling merchandise, hosting small farm markets, providing parking space, and even temporary storage space for construction material and goods. But while throughout the year, *tekyeh*s accommodate many similar activities, they are in fact meant to host a very particular event that happens only for a few days throughout the year—i.e., the *azadari* of Muharram.[7]

Carnivalesque Occupations

Each year, Shi'ite Muslims around the world commemorate the martyrdom of Imam Husain, their third leader and the grandson of the Prophet Mohammad, which happened on the tenth day of the month of Muharram of 680.[8] This day is called Ashura and is annually observed through a rich variety of mourning rituals, including *sineh-zani* (beating the chest), *zanjir-zani* (beating oneself with chains), *rowzeh-khani* (the recitation of elegies by a preacher), and *ta'zieh* (theatrical representations of the tragedy through a passion play).[9] Among these forms of grief expression, *sineh-zani* is most common in Yazd, where crowds of men from each neighborhood form a *dasteh*, or procession, or as Elias Canetti, the 1982 Nobel Prize laureate in Literature, observed "an orchestra of grief."[10] Wearing black garments, members of a *dasteh* respond to the *noheh*s (elegies) recited by the *noheh-khan* (eulogist) by singing dirges at appropriate intervals in the narrative, while rhythmically self-mortifying in tandem with the songs. The *noheh-khan* occupies an elevated position located on the main side of the *tekyeh*, while the *dasteh* performs in the main space right in the middle, where the spectators can also join in and become part of the performance. The hetero-topic integration of social classes as well as the dynamic role changes between performer and spectator that these ritualistic acts permit qualify them as the closest resemblance to Bakhtinian carnivals.[11]

  Tekyeh, as a site for *azadari*, operates at the scale of a neighborhood. Each neighborhood in the historic core of Yazd has a *tekyeh* that serves as a rehearsal and performing arena for the home *dasteh*.[12] It also hosts *dasteh*s from visiting neighborhoods, which come and perform in rotational sequence during the ten nights leading to Ashura. The most important performance is that of the home *dasteh* on the noon of Ashura, when Imam Husain was killed and beheaded. *Dasteh*'s internal dynamics, including its management (led by neighborhood elders), finance (through donations by local businesses), and labor (a body of voluntarily working neighborhood youth), shapes, solidifies, and strengthens the neighborhood identity—often an identity that is distinct and sometimes contrasts those of rival neighborhoods.[13] It is in the light of this identity politics that one could better understand the importance of member-ship in *dasteh*s and better make sense of how "in some towns these proces-sions often led to clashes between rival factions."[14]

An Erotics of Exchange

During the night of *azadari* in Muharram, *tekyeh*s are transformed to function as a stage for *sineh-zani* and other forms of grieving rituals: the space is cov-ered with a tensile fabric structure known as *push*, the walls are covered with black cloths decorated with scripture and religious paintings, the *soffeh*s and the rooftop of the *tekyeh* are carpeted to easily seat the spectators, and the

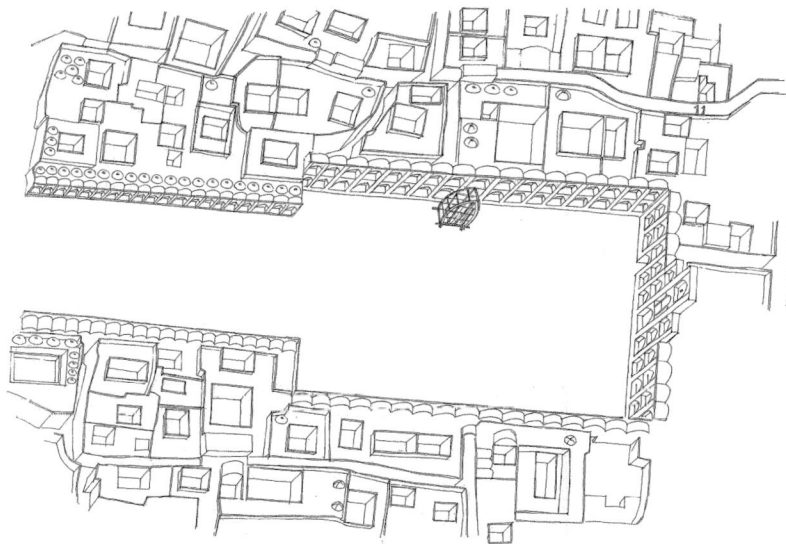

Image 34.1 This image of Shah Tahmasb Square, demolished in 1943, was reconstructed from surviving visual documents.
Credit: Vahid Vahdat

Image 34.2 Tekyeh of Fahhadan in Yazd, Iran, hosting a *sineh-zani* procession.
Credit: Mostafa Dadras

Image 34.3 The movement of *dastah* within the tekyeh.
Credit: Mostafa Gholamnejhad

space is equipped with lighting and sound equipment to effectively host the event (see Image 34.2). The transformation of the space from multifunctional to program-specific, from a site for daily activities to an arena for sacred spectacle, and from exterior to interior, also includes a shift from inclusive to segregated in respect to gender (see Image 34.3).

It should be noted that most modern performative forms of *azadari* are male-exclusive. This pattern can also be observed in the public performances of *ta'zieh*, where "men play female roles, and young boys play the roles of girls."[15] While the privileged privacy of the Qajar court afforded women with active performative roles, even within the religious context of *ta'zieh*,[16] women's position in the public has been generally reassigned to that of spectatorship. The *tekyeh*'s multilevel structure thus allows for a vertical segregation of genders, in which the *soffeh*s above and the roof spaces are occupied by women who can easily see the performance without being seen.

Unable to return the controlling gaze, the men in the *dasteh* feel conscious of and vulnerable to the female spectators, who enjoy a paradoxical position of power—excluded yet dominant, marginalized but still in control, pacified but not devoid of agency.[17] This gender relationship cannot be framed with the active/male and passive/female conceptualization of sexual objectification. Here, men, as objects of desire, try to attract feminine gaze through the visual pleasure of rhythmic movements of the male body, gestures of vulnerability displayed in their tears, and their portrayal of masculine strength through enduring pain. The three forces are complementary: identification with the performers' pain brings a human dimension to the otherwise mechanical aesthetics of "mass ornament" displayed in the geometric and calculated movement of the fragmented male body.[18] The hyper-masculine exhibition of beaten hairy chests and moving sweaty arms telegraphs both desire and desirability with heteroerotic displays of affection, sympathy, and vulnerability framed within and against classical Persian and mystical Sufi formulations of homoerotic male love.[19] In addition to this scopophilic dimension that the exhibitionary format of *sineh-zani* in a *tekyeh* facilitates, the homosocial atmosphere of *dasteh*s, as male-exclusive clubs, often provides opportunities for homosexual experimentation. The mixture of young boys and older men hanging out in preparation for *azadari*-related events, rehearsing together for weeks, moving between neighborhoods, and performing till late at night opens intimate spaces for centuries-old traditions of alternative sexualities to reemerge in somewhat similar forms.[20]

This erotic reading of the spectacle is not limited to a specific location, time, or sexual orientation. Even today, the younger generation, who may feel a distance from such ceremonies, as the rituals have become more and more exploited as a political tool for (or against) Iran's theocratic regime, nevertheless see them as a "social event," which, in the absence of Western-style "clubs and bars," becomes an "opportunity to… meet people."[21] Observations of young women holding "candlelit vigils while quietly distributing slips of paper with their phone numbers to men in the crowd who caught their fancy" can be better explained once the socio-erotic function of *azadari* is taken into account.[22]

While the younger generations casually (and somewhat sarcastically) refer to *azadari* rituals as "Hossein Party" and "techno-Ashoura,"[23] it has for long been among the most important leisure options, particularly in a city like Yazd.[24] A study conducted in 2006 suggests that 34% of Yazd's population count *azadari* among their main leisure activities, a quarter of whom selected the option as their first choice, above restaurants, theaters, picnics, visits to the countryside, and parties.[25] An unpublished part of the study suggests that 47% of this population was in the 15–25 age range. As one might reasonably expect, male respondents selected the option almost three times more than women. No direct correlation could be identified with the population's other demographic properties, including income, education, and profession, demonstrating the popularity of the event across social and economic classes.[26]

Claiming the Streets

In addition to *tekyeh*s, which often host the larger ceremonies, many private residences have for centuries been converted into sites for *azadari* rituals. These houses, in a ritualistic transformation similar to that of *tekyeh*s, open up their *andaruni*, the private sections of the house, to the public. Householders decorate

Image 34.4 The Rismanian residence in Yazd, Iran has been holding an annual *rowzeh* for more than 100 years. Credit: Mohammad Javad Rahbar

the walls with scripture and religious imagery, carpet the central courtyards, and roof the entire courtyard with a *push*, to allow for seating and performing space for the spectators and participants (see Image 34.4). This conversion of private space for public use finds a more complex format outside the historic parts of Yazd. In a few instances, such as the well-established *rowzeh* at the Antikchi residence that attracts much larger audiences, the organizers also close the adjacent street, carpet it, and cover it with a wide *push* and thus extend the venue well into the public space. The modern-day city, with all its transportation and infrastructural properties, managerial complexities, and urban codes and regulations, halts normal daily activities, functions, and even traffic, as the streets are claimed for *azadari* purposes. This appropriation of modern public space creates a unique experience of interiority within an otherwise exterior urban space.

Azadari rituals extend the capacity of homes and streets as sites through which to negotiate distinctions between interior and exterior, while simultaneously blurring lines between public and private within their respective contemporary urban settings. As a form of both sacred and pop cultures, these rituals have maintained their relevance across the centuries, through myriad dynasties, and across vast geographical expanses. That relevance has facilitated the accommodation and internalization of new ideas, ideologies, and traditions. While many azadari rituals were restricted by Reza Shah's (r. 1925—1941) secularist regime,[27] it later became appropriated by public intellectuals such as Ali Shariati (1933—1977) for a revolutionary socialist agenda. Its role in the 1979 Islamic Revolution (and the subsequent Iran-Iraq War) was so great that the leader of the revolution, Ayatollah Khomeini (1979—1989), would describe it as a political meeting. "These *noheh-khani*s," he claimed, "has pushed our movement forward."[28]

Today, some variations of *azadari*, particularly in Yazd, have incorporated liberal ideas such as religious pluralism, a more secular state, and concerns for human rights into their viral and sometimes radical *noheh*s, as if the main mission of Imam Husain's martyrdom was to defy and resist theocracy.[29] This constant reconceptualization of new ideas into Muharram rituals also applies to rigid binaries of human sexuality. "This Muharram" that we are witnessing today, as one scholar of gender studies puts it, "also challenges the austere sexual conventions of the Islamic Republic."[30] It may very well be the case that the same "Muharram" that Ayatollah Khomeini once famously declared "has kept Islam[ic Republic] alive"[31] can participate in its decline.

Notes

1   "[Premodern] Iranian cities," as Mahmoud Tavassoli argues, "have never had squares as a form of public space." Mahmoud Tavassoli. *Tarrahi-Ye Faza-Ye Shahri (in Persian) [Design of Urban Space]*. Vol. 1, (Tehran: Markaz-e motale'at va tahqiqat-e me'mari va shahrsazi-ye Iran, 1992), 43.

2   Mohsen Habibi. *Az Shar Ta Shahr*. 4th ed. (Tehran: University of Tehran, 2003).

3   Vahid Vahdat. "Ta'ammoli Bar Shahrsazi-Ye Dowreh-Ye Pahlavi-Ye Avval - Motale'eh-Ye Moredi: Shahr-E Yazd (in Persian) [Urban Planning in Yazd from 1925 to 1941]". *Honarha-ye Ziba*, no. 31 (2007): 5–14

4   Mahmoud Tavassoli. *Qava'ed Va Me'yarha-Ye Tarrahi-Ye Faza-Ye Shahri (in Persian) [Principle of Designing Urban Space]*. (Tehran: Markaz-e motale'at va tahqiqat-e shahrsazi va me'mari-ye Iran, 1997), 15.

5   Ibid., 17.

6   Vahid Vahdat. "Geometric Reconstruction of Amir-Chakhmagh Square through Backward-Perspective." *Kybernetes* 40, no. 7/8 (2011): 1166–1178.

7   For more information about *azadari* traditions see Jean Calmard. "ʿazādārī." In *Iranica*, edited by Ehsan Yarshater, 174–177. (London: Columbia University, 1987).

8   Mahmoud Ayoub. "ʿāšūrāʾ." In *Iranica*, edited by Ehsan Yarshater, 874-876. (London: Columbia University, 1987).

9   For a general description about *Tazia* see Peter Chelkowski. "Taʿzia." In *Iranica*, edited by Ehsan Yarshater, (London: Columbia University, 1987).

10 Elias Canetti. *Crowds and Power*. (New York: Continuum, 1981), 150.

11 Mikhail Bakhtin. *Rabelais and His World*. (Cambridge, Mass.: M.I.T. Press, 1968).

12 Mahmoud Tavassoli. *Osul Va Raveshha-Ye Tarrahi-Ye Shahri Va Fazaha-Ye Maskuni Dar Iran (in Persian) [Principles of Urban Design in Iran]*. Vol. 1, (Tehran: Markaz-e Motale'at va Tahqiqat-e Me'mari va Shahrsazi, 1986).

13 Vahid Vahdat. "Carnival Nonmovements and the Repoliticization of Urban Space in Yazd, Iran," in *Informality and the City: Theories, Actions and Interventions*, edited by Gregory Marinic and Pablo Meninato, (Cham, Switzerland: Springer: 2022), 477–86.

    Vahid Vahdat. "Shenasaei-Ye Sarmashghha-Ye Shahrsazaneh Az Sugvari-Ye Aini-Ye Moharram Dar Hoviyat-Dehi Beh Mahallat-E Yazd (in Persian) [Urban Lessons Form Mourning Processions in Yazd]." *Abadi Quarterly Journal of Architecture and Urbanism* 17, no. 54 (2007): 106–110.

14 Calmard, "ʿazādārī."

15 Peter Chelkowski, "Taʿzia,"

16 During the Qajar Dynasty (1789–1925), when *ta'zieh* reached its peak of importance at the Persian court.

17 See Judith Butler. *Gender Trouble : Feminism and the Subversion of Identity*. (New York: Routledge, 1999) and Michel Foucault. *The Birth of the Clinic; an Archaeology of Medical Perception*. (New York,: Vintage Books, 1975).

18 Siegfried Kracauer and Thomas Y. Levin. *The Mass Ornament: Weimar Essays*. (Cambridge, Mass: Harvard University Press, 1995).

19 Afsaneh Najmabadi. *Women with Mustaches and Men without Beards: Gender and Sexual Anxieties of Iranian Modernity*. (Berkeley: University of California Press, 2005), 16–17.

20 For an expanded discussion about construction of gender identity in modern Iran, see ibid.

21 In her observations of *azadari* in Tehran's Mohseni Square, Nasser mentions meeting "younger women – wearing short, tight vests and airy minimalist scarves. Some were strolling hand-in-hand with their boyfriends."

22 Janet Afary. *Sexual Politics in Modern Iran*. (Cambridge, UK; New York: Cambridge University Press, 2009).

23 Azdeh Moaveni. *Lipstick Jihad: A Memoir of Growing up Iranian in America and American in Iran.* 1st ed. (New York: PublicAffairs, 2005), 59.

24 Akbar Ghalamsiah. *Yazd Dar Safarnameh-Ha (in Persian) [Yazd in Travel Diaries]*. 2nd ed. (Yazd: Sabz Ruyesh, 1996), 312.

25 Vahid Vahdat. "*Samandehi-Ye Khiyaban-E Qiyam Ba Ta'kid Bar Raftarha-Ye Karnavali* (in Persian) [Urban Renovation of Qiyam Street]." (University of Tehran, 2007), 66.

26 For this research, a sample population of 380 people was studied to represent the then 420,000 population of the city (not including the suburbs of Shahedieh and Hamidiashahr).

27 Minoo Moallem. *Between Warrior Brother and Veiled Sister: Islamic Fundamentalism and the Politics of Patriarchy in Iran*. (Berkeley: University of California Press, 2005), 96.

28 Ruhollah Khomeini. *Sahifeh-Ye Imam (in Persian)*. Vol. 8, (Tehran: Mo'asseseh-ye tanzim va nashr-e asar-e Imam Khomeini, 1999), 257.

29 Some of the politically charged *noheh*s that clearly defy the ideologies associated with the Islamic Republic are written by an Iran-Iraq War veteran, Shahab Mousavi.

30 Afary, *Sexual Politics in Modern Iran.*

31 Ruhollah Khomeini. *Sahifeh-Ye Imam (in Persian)*. Vol. 15, (Tehran: Mo'asseseh-ye tanzim va nashr-e asar-e Imam Khomeini, 1999), 330.

Chapter 35

How Home Creates Us

Femininity, Memory, and Domestic Space

Diana Nicholas

In our memories, imaginations, and collective conversations, we experience the private interior of the city or community we live in. Through our digital identities, we re-position ourselves in relation to those spaces in public ways. As a culture, we project ourselves into the public via technology and the consumption of products and images. When we observe the urban home and its interior, we generally ascribe a strict line, a solid boundary between public and private. Our personal spatial constructs have historically been influenced by memory, expectation, physical requirements, and gender.

The Nolli Map of Rome was an historic example of the ways that documenting the urban condition, including technologies and proximities, can dissolve these barriers. One of the first visualizations (un)intentionally revealing the urban Interior, the Nolli map allowed us to see the personal as public, though undefined, for the first time.[1] A Philadelphia event in 2014 in which the life and death of an urban residence was commemorated—a community funeral—spoke to this private space becoming public through shared memory.[2] In the twenty-first-century city of digital space, urban residents witness new flows between public and private, digital and analog, personal and community. These flows conceal a gendered history that we examine here, unearthing one possible lineage of our recent experiences of domestic space.

Gender roles are among the things that contribute to our complex sense of our homes.[3] Historically, residential interiors were primarily the domain of women designers and spouses. Moving into this century, the creation of home space has become more layered through technology, habit, and a fluid relationship to gender and gender roles.[4] In ruminating on residential spaces, Witold Rybczynski contends that domesticity is complex, resembling an onion with many layers.[5] Humans are similarly complex, and our layers are sometimes the creation of our projected self-conceptions.

DOI: 10.4324/9780429443091-42

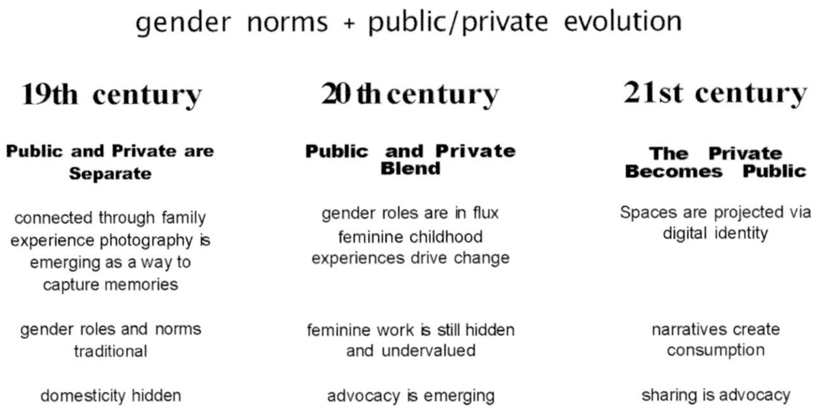

gender norms + public/private evolution

19th century	20th century	21st century
Public and Private are Separate	**Public and Private Blend**	**The Private Becomes Public**
connected through family experience photography is emerging as a way to capture memories	gender roles are in flux feminine childhood experiences drive change	Spaces are projected via digital identity
gender roles and norms traditional	feminine work is still hidden and undervalued	narratives create consumption
domesticity hidden	advocacy is emerging	sharing is advocacy

Image 35.1 Timeline of domestic evolution: Gender norms/public and private spaces.
Credit: Diana Nicholas

Domestic Space as Construct of Self

In the American nineteenth century, domestic chores and duties were firmly feminine, and in many cases, the cost of this work was not acknowledged. Although there were exceptions, these were the norms of the times. In the twentieth century, gender roles entered a period of flux. Feminine childhood experiences and new work opportunities drove emerging conceptions of femininity.[6] In the current twenty-first century, there is very little division between public space and private space in our understanding of home. Both are constantly projected via digital identity through cycles of consumption and sharing. Personal narratives are often based on historical archetypes that create opportunities and forms for this consumption and sharing. Here, gender is more fluid, and gender norms in domestic spheres are regularly challenged. This theory is expressed in timeline form in Image 35.1.

Shirley Jackson: Vignettes of Otherness in Mid-Century America

The American mid-twentieth century was a time of churn and change. Women abandoned career for home postwar, but many still retained part-time work. Thus, they were still instrumental contributors to the family finances, underneath a veneer of homemaking contentedness.[7]

The notable mid-century writer Shirley Jackson built a body of work around subtly subverting the conception of domesticity and home, and her experience is one that bears further examination. Her body of work was along two lines, horror and autobiography, that critics declined to connect as equal during her lifetime. The biographer Ruth Franklin presents her bicameral approach as a study in the irregularities of a home where the mother is both the *main caregiver and the main breadwinner*.[8] Franklin's study of Jackson reveals an important voice in the struggling and unacknowledged feminine experience of space that still resonates. Jackson's work gave a literary form to the clash between work, home life, and profession for women. Through both arms of her output, she questioned typical gender norms of homemaking in postwar America.[9]

Jackson herself was a complex character, a professional writer, her work gave her fame, notoriety, and a level of financial success. Her husband, literary critic Stanley Edgar Hyman, never achieved the same level as Jackson, and a tension was created in their relationship because of her renown. While Jackson was supporting the family financially, she was also operating as the full-time stay-at-home mom.[10] Both breadwinner and homemaker, Jackson suffered from anxiety and depression in a lifetime marked by difference and otherness.[11]

The homey autobiographical stories of Jackson's family life were also told with a sense of humor and a house that is just as emblematic of self and space. Jackson's own homes were large rambling affairs in North Bennington, Vermont; her reality was that of the village setting. While neither house has been preserved in memorial to her, both still stand and are described in detail in her humorous essays on home life.[12] Jackson describes the salient street-oriented characteristics of her homes from the columned portico to the crooked gatepost.[13]

Her autobiographical stories comically describe Jackson's struggle to meet the housekeeping standards of 1950s America. In reality, her struggles were much more dire and pitched than even her fiction could convey.[14] In her essays, as in her life, her husband controls the family finances; yet in actuality, it was her writing that was bringing in the lion's share of the family income.[15] This disparity caused her many issues both psychological and in the marriage, leading to a cascade of physical issues, including weight gain, addiction, and agoraphobia. She died in her sleep at the age of 48. Her legacy, long overlooked, is important in the conception of female space and place in mid-century America, so much of her notable and less notable work was driven by the conception of home, self, and society.[16]

Jackson's fiction and non-fiction alike expressed her otherness through space in subtle yet effective allegorical prose.[17] In her fiction, Jackson used the home and its arrangement as a way of conveying the interior condition of her protagonists. Reflecting her own history, her fiction often expressed divided parts of her own struggles and personality.[18] In this way, Jackson imagined the characteristics of her fictive spaces with a design-oriented detail, including iteratively sketching drawings during the writing of each work with a level of detail that expressed itself to often chilling effect in her work.[19] The state of her fictive homes is a way into the state of her protagonists' lives, when they are compulsively neat or in a state of disaster; trouble is brewing.[20] Her work in both veins was popular, and critically acclaimed in her time.

In Jackson's world, there is home, hearth, and then there is how others see your place in the village or town you live in; often, this leads to the demise of the main character physically or psychologically or both. Home and its physicality reflect that view. It is the emergence of the feminine and private as public that is the crux of many of her characters' demise or deterioration mentally—similarly to her own mental deterioration.[21] The honesty of this conception of home was unusual for this era or even the present day. Jackson strikingly and subtly expressed her feelings of otherness in her work. Her gatepost was crooked, the columns on her house were removed after she moved out; yet, she persevered to write some of the most strikingly honest and chillingly unforgettable work of the last century.[22] This perspective of home was due to her outsider status as a female breadwinner, a heavily overweight woman, and the wife of a Jewish man in an area not known at that time for its openness to difference.[23] Franklin (2013), and an earlier biographer Judy

Oppenheimer (1989), chronicled this isolation and her domestic concerns in depth. What stands out from her life and work is the way that the home and its re-presentation come to be a publicly visual set piece of her life. Jackson's vignettes of domestic life are a foil, and precursor to, the feminine social media constructions of self and home that we witness in society today.

Vignettes of Feminine Space

Who are we when we are at home? In our private spaces, the domestic lives we live are played out publicly even if we wish to keep them under wraps. Our conceptions of self and space become central to this understanding of the domestic interior—especially in an urban environment. In Clare Cooper Marcus' (1995): *House as a Mirror of Self: Exploring the Deeper Meaning of Home*, she posits that the main journey of our lives is to learn from our experiences and achieve a type of "wholeness" that is supported by our domestic environments.[24] Our lives consist of both permanent and impermanent items in the home. Items that represent memory and those of utility. The historical and novel references of design bring together the present, the past, and the future.[25] The same conception of story is often filtered through our personal self-representation in the digital sphere.[26] We socially re-present our space and ourselves; these can include our influences and how we understand domesticity.

In "Little House on The Prairie" and the related books series, Laura Ingalls is often getting herself in "pickles" in her desire to engage in equally spirited play, including riding horses at breakneck speed across the prairie.[27] One of the most fascinating things here are the home interiors. The descriptions of Laura's wagon, the dugout on Plum Creek, the house in the "Big Woods," her newlywed pantry, and the suffering of her family through winters are indelibly marked into the memory of many who grew up with these spaces as a part of their lineage and domestic play.[28] Little Women has a similar set of domestic scenes that are presented and re-presented through contemporary movies, including Meg's small home, the kitchen where Hannah labors, "Marmee's corner," "Joe's Attic," and other idyllic spaces.[29] When Amy returns from Europe, she brings a painting she has done of the family home, Orchard House.[30]

Today, there are a series of personalities that re-present similar domestic interiors as true American commodities of homemaking, projected realities that are heavily influenced by these historic stories of domestic experience. Rhee Drummond has built an empire on her concept of the Prairie homemaker.[31] Her home is digitally re-presented through food, entertaining, and her ranch. There is a constructed vision of her home that embodies food, family, and decoration, Drummond now even has a new Barbie doll to extend her empire.[32]

Joanna Gaines of Magnolia Home is another digital commodity star who makes the twin identities of breadwinner and homemaker into a domestic vignette that builds on the ideal of the American frontier. She restyles the frontier experience as a yardstick for feminine achievement. Joanna is a social media, television, and merchandising star; she has five children and renovates homes with husband Chip on HGTV.[33] Could we have a Rhee Drummond if we

Image 35.2 The sources of a domestic goddess. Credit: Diana Nicholas

did not have Laura Ingalls? Could we have Chip and Johanna Gaines' Magnolia Home if we didn't have Little Women? How do these projects of mid-century and Victorian domestic feminized space echo through our current digitally driven public interior spaces?

The domestic constructs described here are drawn from a rural and suburban home-ness that, for most of the history of America, has served as the gold standard for the family home in all forms. The urban dweller is no less susceptible to this vision as witnessed by the product success of both the Gaines and Drummond empires at Target and beyond.[34] Within the urban environment, the structured space of home is still an infill of rural imagery; who we are contributes to our vision of ourselves and what it means to be a "domestic goddess" (Image 35.2).

The Projected Self, an Urban Interior Re-Imagined

No live organism can continue for long to exist sanely under conditions of absolute reality.

–Jackson, 2013[35]

Now there is a new type of urban real estate, an apartment just for imaging, just for social media stars to feature their lifestyle products, just for taking pictures.[36] This occupant-less space is designed specifically to repackage and sell domestic imagery and lifestyles for women—urban, suburban, and rural. Art and communication play an important role in this blending of public and private projection. What we make of our spaces contributes to our very conception of self; historically, female experiences and female domestic spaces are the unacknowledged engines of self-making. For Shirley Jackson, the home was one type of self, and all struggles are embodied and contained there. In contrast, the historical fiction of girlish femininity is commodified to become a model self for consumption. The stories we are told as children are the scaffolding of our self-narratives and create novel territories for us. These can influence the digital identities we strive for through both consuming and sharing. The image of domesticity as female was often tantalizingly revealed, yet not acknowledged as having value, much like the traditionally feminine work and roles of the last century.[37] Gender is now a part of this domestic history. The city is a million such histories, public and private, projected side-by-side, and our histories always reveal who and what we think we are.

Notes

1   From Tice, James. 2005. "The Nolli Map and Urban Theory." Articles/blog. *The Nolli Map and Cartography* (blog). http://nolli.uoregon.edu/urbanTheory.html.; and Tice, Jim and Eric Steiner. "Interactive Nolli Map Website." Archive. Interactive Nolli Map Website. 2020, 2006. http://nolli. uoregon.edu/

2   Grossi, Patrick. 2014. *Funeral for a Home*. 1st edition. Philadelphia, PA: Temple Contemporary Tyler School of Art Editions North/Cornerhouse.

3   Allen, John S. 2015. *Home: How Habitat Made Us Human*. 1st edition. New York: Basic Books.

4   Levold, Nora, and Margrethe Aune. 2003. "'Cooking Gender': Home, Gender and Technology." *Sosiologisk Tidsskrift* 11 (3): 273–299.

5   Rybczynski, Witold. 1986. *Home: A Short History of an Idea*. New York: Viking.

6   Borden, Iain, Barbara Penner, and Jane Rendell. 1999. *Gender Space Architecture: An Interdisciplinary Introduction*. London: Routledge.

7   Borden et al., 1999.

8   Franklin, Ruth. 2016. *Shirley Jackson: A Rather Haunted Life*. 1st edition. New York: Liveright.

9   Franklin, 2016.

10 Franklin, 2016.

11 Ibid.

12 From Heller, Zoë. 2016. "The Haunted Mind of Shirley Jackson," October 10, 2016. https://www. newyorker.com/magazine/2016/10/17/the-haunted-mind-of-shirley-jackson.; and Franklin, 2016, and Oppenheimer, 1989.

13 Jackson, Shirley. 1998. *Life Among the Savages; Raising Demons*. 1st edition. New York: Quality Paperback Book Club.

14 Franklin, 2016; Oppenheimer, 1989.

15 Franklin, 2016; Kröger and Anderson, 2019.

16 Jackson, Shirley, and Ruth Franklin. 2013. *The Road Through the Wall*. New York: Penguin Classics.

17 Kröger, Lisa, and Melanie R. Anderson. 2019. *Monster, She Wrote: The Women Who Pioneered Horror and Speculative Fiction*. Philadelphia: Quirk Books.

18 Franklin, 2016.

19 Ibid.

20 Ibid.

21 Ibid.

22   Jackson, 1998.

23   Franklin, 2016.

24   Marcus, Clare Cooper. 1995. *House as a Mirror of Self: Exploring the Deeper Meaning of Home.* 1st Printing edition. Berkeley, CA: Conari Press.

25   Titton, Monica. 2015. "Fashionable Personae: Self-Identity and Enactments of Fashion Narratives in Fashion Blogs." *Fashion Theory* 19 (2): 201–220.

26   Titton, 2015.

27   Fellman, Anita Clair. 2008. *Little House, Long Shadow: Laura Ingalls Wilder's Impact on American Culture.* Columbia: University of Missouri Press.

28   Fellman, 2008.

29   Alcott, Louisa May. 2016. *Little Women.* West Berlin: White Star Kids.

30   Alcott, 2016.

31   Fortini, Amanda. 2011. "O Pioneer Woman!" May 2, 2011. https://www.newyorker.com/magazine/2011/05/09/o-pioneer-woman

32   Thomason, Amanda. 2018. "'Pioneer Woman' Ree Drummond Barbie Doll Playset Has Officially Hit Store Shelves." *Liftable*, October 28, 2018. https://www.westernjournal.com/l/amandathomason/pioneer-woman-ree-drummond-barbie-doll-playset-officially-hit-store-shelves/

33   Tanza, Loudenback. 2018. "Waco Top Destination Thanks to 'Fixer Upper' Chip and Joanna Gaines." *Business Insider*, April 3, 2018. https://www.businessinsider.com/hgtv-chip-and-joanna-gaines-made-waco-texas-top-travel-destination-2018-1

34   Kramer, Matthew. 2018. "Target Refreshes Spring Hearth & Hand with Magnolia Collection." *Home World Business* (blog), March 27, 2018. https://www.homeworldbusiness.com/target-refreshes-spring-hearth-hand-with-magnolia-collection/

35   Jackson, Shirley, and Laura Miller. 2013. *The Haunting of Hill House.* Edited by Guillermo Del Toro. New York: Penguin Classics.

36   Sapna, Maheshwari. 2018. "A Penthouse Made for Instagram - The New York Times." *New York Times*, September 30, 2018. https://www.nytimes.com/2018/09/30/business/media/instagram-influencers-penthouse.html

37   Croft, Alyssa, Toni Schmader, Katharina Block, and Andrew Scott Baron. 2014. "The Second Shift Reflected in the Second Generation: Do Parents' Gender Roles at Home Predict Children's Aspirations?" *Psychological Science* 25 (7): 1418–1428. https://doi.org/10.1177/0956797614533968

Chapter 36

Transient Interiorities Space, Gender, and Bucharest Street Culture

Liz Teston

Feminisms and Femininity in Romania

Advocacy for gender equity manifests differently in various cultures. Most sociologists categorize these different perspectives based on their geographic and cultural roots. In this context, "the West" includes North America and Western Europe. The former socialist countries of Eastern-Central Europe are often considered an interstitial territory suspended between East and West. Both Westerners and Easterners view them as "other."

This notion of "otherness" can also be inverted. Many Eastern-Central European feminists generally regard their Western counterparts as less interested in style, dress, children, and family. Westerners are viewed as more interested in advocating for workplace equity.[3] Westerners take part in this reading of "otherness" by understanding the culture through outsider perspectives and often make assumptions about the needs and interests of Eastern-Central European women. They often assume that these needs match Western interests. This essentialist perspective assumes that Western notions equally apply across different cultures. Through this, Western feminists inadvertently take part in hegemonic influence over Eastern-Central Europeans.[4] Eastern-Central European feminisms originate from a different perspective, rooted in reaction to revolutionary change, not Western ideals.

After World War II, many Eastern-Central European governments adopted policies that erased gender. Socialist ideology replaced the individual with the collective, removing individual worldviews from possibility.[5] This political climate produced a milieu unreceptive to feminist thought. During this time, governments limited gender research to quantitative research.[6] Particularly in Romania, statistical research centered on topics convenient to the regime. Social research was not allowed.

Further, qualitative research with gendered perspectives was rarely practiced immediately following the revolution in 1989.[7] Because of these

DOI: 10.4324/9780429443091-43

factors, contemporary feminist perspectives look different in Eastern-Central European countries. In many developing countries, identity-based research is considered an extravagance.[8] In "Production of Emancipatory Feminist Spaces," geographers Sorina Voiculescu and Margareta Amy Lelea provide a context for Romanian feminisms and femininity after 1989:

> During the communist era, sexuality was repressed as women were expected to be androgynous;[9] gender equality was written into the law, but not enforced in reality…[10] After the 1989 Revolution, there was both a resurgence of traditional gender roles and an increase in the sexualization of women's bodies to encourage capitalist consumption.[11]

Prior to the 1989 Revolution, there were strict expectations about women's dress in Romania. These views also extended to expectations of women's gender expression. Uniforms displayed communist ideology and promoted the group over the individual. Children wore uniforms associated with the Pioneer's Organization. This policy resulted in the erasure of individuality and the self. Many Romanian women hid their creativity and expression of gender from public view.[12] After the revolution, Romanian public space and cultural identity adopted Western commodity culture. The city became the center of modern gender display.[13] Romanian women used this display as a vehicle for integration into contemporary society. As such, many urban women reconsidered their gender identity, their sexuality, and the outcomes of this expression.[14] Often, they perceived feminine dress as an agent of self-empowerment. It was also seen as a display of individual identity and material wealth.[15] In Bucharest, conspicuous consumption and exhibition of feminine identity continue to prevail.[16]

This image construction transcends urban space and re-enters society through media space. Oana Mihaela Stoleriu points out that many tourism campaigns show Romania as an exotic place. They appeal to Western gender stereotypes as women in these campaigns frequently serve subordinate roles. The media often present Romania "as passive, wild, mysterious and seductive; hence it is gazed, explored, and conquered."[17] Ads show Romanian women as an extension of this exoticism. How do Romanian women try to counteract this media image through their own body image? As Voiculescu wrote on Romanian women's body-agency, "the body might be the place of pleasure, pain, consumption, or national identity. At the same time, the body can be manipulated by power. The body can, therefore, be the object as well as the target of power."[18]

Urbanism and Gender Display

Contemporary culture shapes our identities. Public space mirrors the variety of people that make up the city and reflects everyday life. Our identities and gender displays are urban conditions. Danish sociologist Henning Bech states that "modern sexuality is essentially urban." The moment we dress each morning is a political and urban act. We make decisions about how to portray ourselves and our gendered bodies.[19] We operate in a society based on precise semiotic codes. These codes, proxemics, and sartorial choices all stand in for our identity within a larger culture.[20]

John T. Molloy's guide, *Women's Dress for Success* (1977), introduced the idea of power-dressing for career advancement. To "dress for success" embodied a new form of gendered sartorial coding in business environments.[21] These sign systems also operate in contemporary Eastern-Central European society. According to sociologists Linda Duits and Liesbet van Zoonen, both the hijab and the crop-top are hegemonic symbols. But they are also "speech-acts" that deserve discussion and deliberation.[22]

We can analyze the city through these displays of gendered bodies, sartorial codes, and the relative "visibility (or invisibility) of women in urban public spaces."[23] Women occupy spaces in a different way than men. Inequities in paid work and different levels of participation in consumption and production still exist today. So, the public spaces of capitalism (urban workplaces) are partially obstructed to some women.[24] Women who seek entry into business re-fashion and re-express themselves to fit the hegemonic order.[25] Feminist urbanism and interiority are tied to body consciousness. It is qualitative and personal.[26] To understand urbanism, we must examine gendered dress and relate it to urban culture.

The city contains gendered zones because of traditional gender roles in society. A walking practice for a traditional woman involves everyday tasks like caregiving and domestic work.[27] A walking practice for a traditional man involves spaces of production—workplaces.[28] Sociologist Georg Simmel described *geselligkeit*, or sociable empathy derived from being near other people, without close-knit associations. Walter Benjamin's *flâneur* roamed the city and watched the everyday activities of others. Elizabeth Wilson and Helen Jarvis claim that *geselligkeit* and the *flâneur* are problematic because they are gendered. They represent the male gaze.[29] As work becomes more gender-neutral, city-spaces become less gendered. This gender identity moves from the gendered spatial zones to gendered bodies themselves. This shift is more distinct in Romania, where many urban Romanian women shape their identity through feminine dress.

Transient Interiority

Interactions between people and their near environment create transient interiorities. In other words, the interior condition may occur in the exterior, but it relies on intimate, ephemeral qualities. Interiority is a conditional relationship that, as architectural historian Christine McCarthy says, does not "depend on a restrictive architectural definition."[30] Interiority differs from the typical exterior condition. Exteriority is concerned with objects and less concerned with subjects. Transient interiority resides in public places that are intended for other purposes and temporarily adopt interior characteristics. These characteristics generally come from a feeling of separation from the ambient exterior urban environment. This could be a psychological interiority or based on a temporary usage, or an atmospheric, sensory, or cultural boundary.[31]

Urbanist Richard Sennett examines interiority as a contingent psychological circumstance for urban pedestrians. He says that we all wear masks as a defense mechanism to hide our thoughts from others. Subjectivity lies underneath this covering. These are the elements that shape our identity. This invisible covering acts as the threshold between interiority and exteriority. Sennett further explained this condition through a recount of conversations with Egyptian women. Walking through the streets of Cairo while wearing the burka, the women explained, offers a simultaneous feeling of intimacy and freedom. Through the medium of the burka, these exterior public spaces are female. The interior domestic spaces are male because they are mediated by patriarchal influence. Sennett speaks of freedom and interiority through otherness. Benjamin similarly describes freedom through otherness in travels to Russia because of linguistic barriers.[32]

Gendered dress, common among urban middle-aged Romanian women, also serves a sort of interiority or transparent armor. This pretense, while on a surface level complies with Western patriarchal beauty standards, does the same work as the burka, hijab, crop-top, or Pioneer uniform—it is a speech act. This consumerist sartorial code acts in reaction to the former socialist sartorial code. According to Angelica Nicoleta Neculăesei, some of the specific values of Romanian culture include adaptability, duplicity, mistrust, authority, traditionalism, and self-preservation.[33] This implies that gendered dress acts as a façade for psychological interiority in Romanian contexts, while simultaneously communicating a desire for the kind of individualistic expression valued in Western consumer culture.

Proxemics and Romania

Anthropologist Ed Hall defines proxemics as "interrelated observations and theories of [the human] use of space as a specialized elaboration of culture."[34] We experience the city through the lens of our culture, gender, and society. Proxemics, or use of space and perception, changes from setting to setting.[35] Hall's research focused on middle-class, white, professional Americans from the northeast United States.[36] How would the four proxemic distances (intimate, personal, social, and public) be described if measured in Romania? Zoologist Desmond Morris divides Europe into three zones based on personal space preferences. The Mediterranean is "the elbow zone." Eastern-Central Europe is "the wrist zone," and Western Europe is "the fingertips zone."[37] Imagine a social setting when people are standing side-by-side. In this setting, people from the Mediterranean are comfortable standing with elbow almost touching, people from Eastern-Central Europe prefer to stand with wrists almost touching, and people from Western Europe prefer to stand fingertip distance away from each other (Image 36.1).

Experiences in Bucharest

In the following analysis, I am conscious of the perils of colonialism, how my Western perspective shapes Romania's "otherness," and the limits of my understanding based on my position in Romania.[30] I will endeavor to acknowledge both perspectives herein. My knowledge of Romanian gender and proxemics originates out of my first-hand experience as a Westerner living in Romania. These included instances where I unwittingly used a different proxemic code than everyone else, especially in pedestrian etiquette. There were also differences in Romanian gender display. After some research and discussion, I

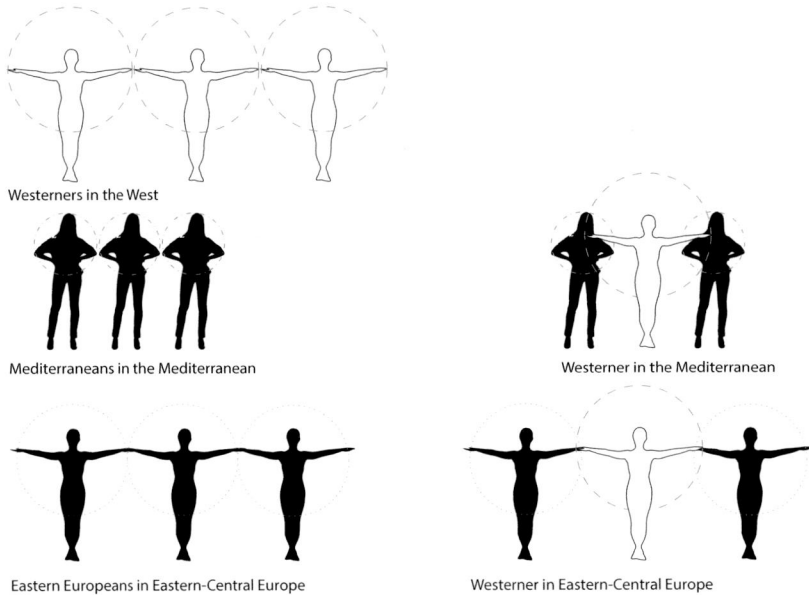

Image 36.1 Personal space ranges for Mediterranean, Western, and Eastern-Central European people. Based on research from Desmond Morris. Credit: Liz Teston

discovered that Romanians, in general, were operating under a different semiotic code for culture, gendered identity, and proxemics. I needed to understand the local "language" or, like Benjamin, be cast as "other."

For example, Western pedestrians often walk on the right side of the sidewalk. It is normal to veer further to the right when someone approaches—to provide others with enough room and respect the "the fingertips zone." In my experience, Romanians would often walk on either side of the path. They would try to maintain their course as they approach, even when an (uninitiated) Westerner steps to the right. The action often resulted in annoyed Romanians (usually men) invading their "wrist zone," attempting to squeeze themselves between the Westerner (me) and the adjacent building or snowbank. After a near-altercation with a pedestrian, my conversations with locals reaffirmed the difference in Romanian personal space. They also clarified that there is an institutional awareness of falling icicle locations. South-facing eaves and decorative facades are particularly prone to this. Their desire to avoid frozen projectiles supersedes any right-of-way.[39]

Romanian sartorial coding differed from my experience in the United States, where there are subtle differences in culture, climate, urban scale, density, and demographics. At first glance, the similarities between the United States and Romania are greater than their differences. But, after some first-hand experiences, I noticed noteworthy distinctions in gendered dress. I should point out that there were exceptions to this rule. But overall, mostly anyone wearing a skirt, cropped-pants, or open-toed shoes also wore nude pantyhose. This was regardless of apparent activity, age, or status.[40] In the United States, hosiery has increasingly become a non-compulsory practice. For example, archetypes like the Mayo Clinic and the former First Lady, have recently determined that the accessory should be worn at a woman's discretion (Image 36.2).[41]

Image 36.2 Sheer pantyhose on a variety of women, doing a variety of activities in Bucharest.
Credit: Liz Teston

We can understand this hosiery-wearing custom as a form of transient interiority like the burka. While at first hosiery seems to be a symbol of male objectification, it also forms an invisible barrier between the interior-self and the exterior-self. It protects the wearer by enabling interior-oriented-subjectivity within Bucharest's public realm. Lois Weinthal has written extensively on "second skins" and "third skins" in interior environments.[42] This habitable second skin, the hosiery layer, is not only "a conceptual bridge between body and building,"[43] but also a personal, mobile form of interiority with interrelated systems of habits, cultures, and signs. Through this, we understand pantyhose as a protective carapace protecting the wearer from the city. Pantyhose are a portable interior environment or a second skin.

In this reading, hosiery is not judged as a sign of patriarchal domination. This analysis of gendered dress relates to third-wave feminism, a mode of thought associated with choice, individualism, and power. "The victim feminism [of the second wave] applies to a group, power feminism is rooted in individual choices."[44] As Nicole Kalms points out, "it is significant that [hypersexual gendered dress] has the power to legitimize the larger infrastructures of sexual exploitation and stereotypes that already oppress women," and there are pitfalls to post-feminist logics, which emphasize female agency as a counterbalance to misogynistic power-dynamics (Image 36.3).[45]

But we should also acknowledge the Romanian women's collective experience. Compulsory androgynous uniformity differently shaped the Romania historical context. This shifts contemporary Romanian gender identities closer to modes that value individuality and upward mobility. Gendered dress, in this context, is legitimized as a choice and a façade for psychological interiority. The foundations of Romanian feminisms were not derived from second-wave feminisms. So, the divergence between gendered dressing and feminist thought is less critical than in Western feminism, which emphasizes the relationship between feminine symbols, the male patriarchal system, and social constructs (Image 36.4).[46]

Conclusions

These transient interiorities of "carapace hosiery" and "veering pedestrians" can be viewed as psychological, atmospheric, cultural, and spatial conditions. They are read through the scale of the human body, via subjectivity. They link the personal and the everyday to the urban environment.[47] These interpretations of interiority and urbanism vary between cultures and individuals. Yet, shared connections and perspective-taking should shape our readings. Interior urbanism, understood through perception, is unique to the female condition.

Image 36.3 Conspicuous consumption in Bucharest.
Credit: Liz Teston

Image 36.4 Gendered dressing in Bucharest.
Credit: Liz Teston

Notes

1   Agnieszka Sorokowska, et al, "Preferred Interpersonal Distances: A global comparison," *Journal of Cross-Cultural Psychology* 48, no. 4 (2017): 577–592. DOI: 10.1177/0022022117698039.

2   Judith A. Garber and Robyne S. Turner, *Gender in Urban Research*, (Thousand Oaks, CA: SAGE Publications, 1994).

3   Nanette Funk, "Feminism East and West," in *Gender Politics and Post-Communism: Reflections from eastern europe and the former soviet union*, eds. Magda Mueller and Nanette Funk (New York: Routledge, 1993), 318–330; and Gail Kligman, "Political Demography: The Banning of Abortion in Ceauşescu's Romania," in *Conceiving the New World Order: The Global Politics of Reproduction*, eds. Faye Ginsburg and Rayna Rapp (Berkeley: University of California Press, 1995), 234–255.

4   Frances Elizabeth Olsen, "Feminism in Central and Eastern Europe: Risks and possibilities of American engagement," *The Yale Law Journal* 106, no. 7 (1997): 2215–2257. DOI: 10.2307/797168.

5   Olsen, 2215.

6   Judit Timar, "Gender Studies in the Gender-Blind Post-Socialist Geographies of East-Central Europe," *Belgeo* 3 (2007): 349–370. DOI: 10.4000/belgeo.11217.

7   Sorina Voiculescu and Margareta Amy Lelea, "A Review of Gender and Geography and its Development in Romania," *Analele Universităţii de Vest din Timişoara: Seria Geografie* 13 (2003): 123–144.

8   Saraswati Raju, "We Are Different But Can We Talk?," *Gender, Place and Culture* 9, no. 2 (2002): 173–178. DOI:10.1080/09663960220139680.

9   Sorina Voiculescu, "Rethinking Women's Bodies: From uniforms to sexual freedom," in *Gendered Cities: Identities, Activities, Networks*, eds. Gisella Cortesi, Flavia Cristaldi and Joos Droogleever Fortuijn (Rome: Societa Geografica Italiana, 2004), 57–68.

10 Cristina Liana Olteanu, Elena-Simona Gheonea, and Valentin Gheonea, *Femeile in Romania Comunista: Studii de istorie sociala* [Women in Communist Romania: Studies of social history]. Bucharest: Politeia SNSPA, 2003.

11 Mayfair Mei-hui Yang, "From Gender Erasure to Gender Difference: State feminism, consumer sexuality, and women's public sphere in China," in *Spaces of Their Own*, ed. Mayfair Mei-hui Yang, (Minneapolis: University of Minnesota Press, 1999), 35–65.

12 Carmen Ghinea, "Feminine versus Feminist in Romanian Contemporary Society," in *Gender Studies: Woman Inside and Outside the Box*, eds. Ruxandra Teodorescu, Romana Mihăilă, and Onorina Botezat (NP: Editura Printech, 2013), 29–40; and Mihael Frunză, "Who's Afraid of Feminism in Romania? Misconceptions, Prejudices, Stereotypes," *Journal for the Study of Religions and Ideologies* 5, no. 14, (2006): 83–88. http://jsri.ro/ojs/index.php/jsri/article/view/359/357; and Adriana Băban, "Women's Sexuality and Reproductive Behavior in Post-Ceauşescu Romania: A Psychological Approach," in *Reproducing Gender: Politics, Publics, and Everyday Life After Socialism*, eds. Susan Gal and Gail Kligman (Princeton, NJ: Princeton University Press, 2000), 225–255.

13 Henning Bech, "Citysex: Representing lust in public," *Theory, Culture, and Society* 15, no.3–4, (1998): 215–241. DOI: 10.1177/0263276498015003010; and Janet Elise Johnson and Jean C. Robinson, *Living Gender After Communism* (Bloomington: Indiana University Press, 2006).

14 Voiculescu, 57–68.

15 Ghinea, 29–40.

16 Linda A. Treiber, "Romania for Beginners: Intersections of race, class, and gender," *The Journal of Public and Professional Sociology* 4, no. 2 (2012): Article 11. https://digitalcommons.kennesaw.edu/jpps/vol4/iss2/11

17 Oana Mihaela Stoleriu, "Gendered Constructions of Romania's Tourist Destination Image," *The European Proceedings of Social and Behavioural Sciences* (2016): 965–974.

18 Voiculescu, 57–68.

19 Bech, 3–4.

20 Umberto Eco, "Social Life as a Sign System," in *Structuralism: An introduction*, ed. David Robey, (Oxford: Clarendon Press, 1972), 57–72.

21   Joanne Entwistle, "Power-dressing and the Construction of the Career Woman," in *Fashion Theory: A Reader*, ed. Malcom Barnard (New York: Routledge, 2007), 208–219.

22   Linda Duits and Liesbet van Zoonen, "Headscarves and Porno-Chic: Disciplining girls' bodies in the European multicultural society," *European Journal of Women's Studies* 13, no. 2 (2006): 103–117. DOI: 10.1177/135050680606275

23   Diana Elena Neaga, "Doing and Undoing Gender in Urban Spaces: The University Square Bucharest," *Analize: Journal of Gender and Feminist Studies*, no. 3 (2014): 28–49. www.analize-journal.ro/library/files/numarul_3/diana_elena_neaga.pdf.

24   Alison Hayford, "The Geography of Women: An Historical Introduction," *Antipode: A Radical Journal of Geography* 6, no. 2 (1974): 1–19. DOI: 10.1111/j.1467-8330.1974.tb00590.x

25   Jacqueline Tivers, "How the Other Half Lives: the geographical study of women," *Area* 10, no. 4 (1978): 302–306. https://www.jstor.org/stable/20001378.

26   Lise Nelson and Joni Seager, *A Companion to Feminist Geography* (London: Wiley-Blackwell, 2004), 1–12.

27   Neaga, 28–49.

28   Laura Grünberg, "(Non)Sexist Cities: Mapping a new area of research for gender studies in Romania," *Analize: Journal of Gender and Feminist Studies*, no. 3 (2014): 1–6. www.analize-journal.ro/library/files/numarul_3/analize_nr_3.pdf

29   Helen Jarvis, "Transforming the Sexist City: Non-sexist communities of practice," *Analize: Journal of Gender and Feminist Studies*, no. 3 (2014): 7–27. www.analize-journal.ro/library/files/numarul_3/analize_nr_3.pdf

30   Christine McCarthy, "Toward a Definition of Interiority," *Space and Culture* 8, no. 2 (2005): 112–25. DOI: 10.1177/1206331205275020

31   Liz Teston, "Public Interiority: An Urban Experience, Independent from Architectural Interiors" at *Interior-Inferior-In Theory? Contemporary Positions in Interior Design Theory Conference*, hosted by Carola Ebert at Berlin International University, Berlin, May 17, 2018.

32   Richard Sennett, "Interiors and Interiority at Harvard GSD," Filmed [April 22, 2016]. YouTube video, 1:00:32. Posted [April 26, 2016]. https://youtu.be/hVPjQhfJfKo and Walter Benjamin, "Moscow Diary," *October* 35 (1985): 9–4. https://doi.org/10.2307/778471.

33   Angelica Nicoleta Neculăesei, "Romania: dimensions of regional cultural specificity," *Scientific Annals of the "Alexandru Ioan Cuza" University of Iaşi Economic Sciences* 60, no. 1 (2013): 1–12. www.degruyter.com/downloadpdf/j/aicue.2013.60.issue-1/aicue-2013-0003/aicue-2013-0003.pdf

34   Edward T. Hall, *The Hidden Dimension* (New York: Anchor Books, 1966), 1. (Emphasis mine. Re-reading reveals unacceptable language. Although Hall does recognize the limits of his study.)

35   Hall, 107–122.

36   Hall, 139–153.

37   Desmond Morris, *People Watching: The Desmond Morris Guide to Body Language* (London: Vintage Books, 2002), 194–195.

38   Lucinda Kaukas Havenhand, "A View from the Margin: Interior design," *Design Issues* 20, no. 4 (2004): 32–42. DOI: 10.1162/0747936042312002 Similar discussion on male architects and "otherness."

39   Romanian news outlets report that falling icicles cause injuries. "Bucureşti: O studentă a fost lovită de un sloi de gheaţă care a căzut de pe acoperişul Facultăţii de Istorie [Bucharest: A student was hit by a sheet of ice that fell from the roof of the Faculty of History]," B1TV.ro, online, February 5 30, 2012, https://tinyurl.com/yc2kpk5a; and "Un cântăreţ, la un pas de MOARTE în Centrul Vechi din Capitală [A singer, one step away from DEATH in the Old Center of the Capital]," RomaniaTV.net, online, February 9, 2014, https://tinyurl.com/3fawa65p.

40   Pantyhose are sheer hosiery, stockings or tights that match the skin tone.

41   Troy Patterson, "The Politics of Pantyhose," *The New York Times Magazine*, September 2015, 18.

42   Anni Albers, "The Pliable Plane: Textiles in architecture," *Perspecta: The Yale Architectural Journal*, no. 4 (1957): 36–41. DOI: 10.2307/1566855; and Lois Weinthal, "Tailoring Second and Third Skins," in *Textile Technology and Design: From Interior Space to Outer Space*, eds. Deborah Schneiderman and Alexa Griffith Winton (New York: Bloomsbury, 2016), 45–55.

43 Lois Weinthal, "Interior Skins," *International Journal of Interior Architecture + Spatial Design* 2 (2013). http://www.iijournal.org/2013/06/11/interior-skins/

44 Katherine Iannello, "Third-Wave Feminism and Individualism: Promoting equality or reinforcing the status quo?," in *Women in Politics: Outsiders or Insiders? A Collection of Readings*, ed. Lois Duke Whitaker (Boston: Longman, 1998), 313–321.

45 Nicole Kalms, "Provocations of the Hypersexualized City" *Architecture and Culture* 2, no.3 (2014): 379–402. DOI: 10.2752/205078214X14107818390711 (My emphasis in brackets.)

46 Gem Barton and Harriet Harriss, "Gendered, Non-Gendered, Re-Gendered Tools for Spatial Production," *Architecture and Culture* 5, no. 3, (2017): 475–485. DOI:10.1080/20507828.2017.1383796

47 Nelson and Segar. *A Companion to Feminist Geography*, 1–12; and Margareta Amy Lelea and Sorina Voiculescu, "The Production of Emancipatory Feminist Spaces in a Post-Socialist Context: organization of ladyfest in romania," *Gender, Place & Culture: A Journal of Feminist Geography* 24, no. 6, (2017): 794–811. DOI: 10.1080/0966369X.2017.1340872.

Chapter 37

Bathhouse Memories

Olivier Vallerand

A camera tracks smoothly over the grid ceiling of a bathhouse in Québec City (Image 37.1), following the protagonist of Robert Lepage's cinematic debut *The Confessional* (1995) as he looks for his estranged brother in the private cabins of the gay sauna Hippocampe—an echo of the titular church confessional cabins. Set up with scenes inspired by classical paintings and sculptures, each cabin becomes a condensed museum or theater of history and culture. Using the bathhouse and other underground erotic spaces to move viewers between eras and characters, Lepage invites us to explore the semiotic and atmospheric potential of ordinary objects and spaces as gateways to memory and allegory. The mesmerizing overhead cinematography highlights the complexity of bathhouses—the dark labyrinthine spaces to be explored over and over, echoing the urbanism of a tightly built city.

I did not see *The Confessional* until college a few years after its release, but as a gay kid interested in culture and going to school a few minutes' walk from the Hippocampe, both Lepage and bathhouses were objects of curiosity that I often encountered from afar. Today, as a scholar focusing on queer spaces, bathhouses often cross my path, becoming portals to a maze of references and memories...

December 2009...

...I walk into Rudas Baths, gently bathed by colored light coming through clerestory windows in the sixteenth century dome. Naked men relax quietly in an octagonal pool within the moody Ottoman bath, Budapest's last to have sex-segregated bathing times. For a North American—moreover, one who does not like heat and water that much—the experience is both exotic and uncomfortable, but I am not the first to experience it in this way. The dark and sensual atmosphere created by both the architecture and the naked bodies combined with the liminal status of bathhouses as heterotopic

DOI: 10.4324/9780429443091-44

Image 37.1 (a) (Left image) Pierre (Lothaire Bluteau) walking through Québec City's Sauna Hippocampe in the movie *The Confessional* (directed by Robert Lepage, 1995); (b) (center and right images) Scenes at the Sauna Hippocampe, shown in the movie trailer for *The Confessional*. Credit: Robert Lepage

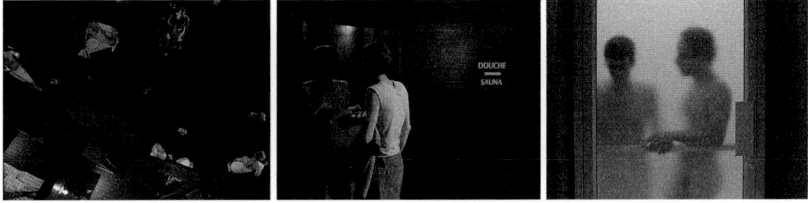

spaces merging publicness and privacy have framed how they have been understood throughout history, ranging from spiritual to sexual uses, sometimes both at once.

Architecturally, bathhouses and steam rooms range from simple structures to much more adorned and complex networks of chambers that both fascinate and intrigue, shaped by spiritual, medical, hygienic, and erotic grounds.[1] The tradition of public hygiene developed in Roman *thermae* and *balneae*; these later merged with Islamic ritual purification and evolved into the Turkish/Ottoman hammams. Turkish baths eventually migrated back to the rest of Europe, first through military conquest such as in Hungary and then through individual interest such as in the hammam designed by David Urquhart in Victorian Britain (Image 37.2) following his stint at the British embassy in Istanbul.[2] In Asia, the tradition of religious bathing that emerged in Buddhist temples in India later traveled to other countries, for example, as Korea's jjimjilbang and Japan's sentōs and onsens, progressively evolving from a mainly religious purpose to become commercial spaces for public hygiene and socialization. Other changes also occurred. For example, Japanese men and women traditionally bathed together, but the opening of Japan to the West led to gender segregation, and while the popularization of baths in private houses initially led to a decline of public sentōs, the idea that physical proximity through bathing leads to emotional intimacy and social connection has kept the tradition alive.

Despite their spatial and social complexity, as seemingly private spaces associated with the body, bathhouses are rarely discussed, particularly in Western contexts.[3] Their liminal status led to forms of sociability outside of publicly celebrated ones, allowing acts that would usually stay hidden, becoming a form of reversed public life. For outsiders, their apparent combination of eroticism and exoticism—"symbolic as much as [...] functional, simple and yet luxurious"[4]—creates an atmosphere open to new experiences, imagined or real. If eroticized images abound in Western representations of bathhouses, displaying long-held Orientalizing stereotypes of available "exotic" and sensuous bodies, bathhouses are often much less erotic and even actively seek to prevent such eroticism. For example, Valerie Staats notes how Moroccan hammams stress the importance of wearing undergarments to preserve the social rule that women should not see other women's genitalia.[5] This underlines the tensions of the bathhouse, as a space where conventional desires for homosocial bond blur into homoeroticism that can even lead to homosexual acts. Discussing the baths' migration from Constantinople to Victorian London, John Potvin points out that attendants taking "great pains [...] to ensure that the body was never [...] exposed to fellow bathers" were replaced by screened compartments to "ensure a sense of decorum and privacy."[6] However, beyond these compartments, same-sex touching and sensuality were encouraged by

The Hammâm.

Image 37.2 "The Hammam," reprinted from David Urquhart, *Manual of the Turkish Bath*, (London, 1865), facing p. i.
Credit: David Urquhart

the moody and steamy atmosphere, remodeling relations between men that later influenced the emergence of specifically gay bathhouses.[7]

While some still-existing gay bathhouses originated as working-class public baths in cities such as New York, most contemporary gay bathhouses are purpose-built, with decorative elements influenced by an interpretation of historical civic public baths, as well as public sites used for sex.[8] Their mode of operation and physical set-up differ geographically and historically, adjusting to local laws and preferences, as well as to their clientele's financial means, but they most often present a combination of more open and more intimate spaces that regulate uses and relation to the exterior. Beyond the check-in and entrance lockers threshold, a bar or gym often serves as a transitional buffer "mediating between the norms and culture of the 'regular world' and the sexual oasis of the bathhouse,"[9] before visitors enter the more dimly lit corridors, cabins, porn lounge, and wet zones. While visitors keep verbal conversations to a minimum or conduct them with a hushed tone, nonverbal forms of communication become essential—despite dim lighting—focusing on the body and rethinking how senses are used. Implicit and explicit norms build on the physical characteristics of spaces—different lighting levels, views from or toward the space, presence of clothed or naked bodies—to frame sexual and non-sexual zones.[10] However, as with any built environment, such zones are blurry—complex interactions happen that do not easily fit into conventional public/private patterns.[11]

The physical separation from the exterior parallels a close but complex relation to the urban. Bathhouses create a spectrum of backgrounds to the public performance of sex, graded by different degrees of enclosure, lighting, or steam. As such, they echo the experience of parks, public restrooms, or abandoned industrial sites appropriated as cruising landscapes, used both for the thrilling sensation of sex in public, or as a venue for sex when other private spaces are unavailable or unsafe. However, unlike exterior spaces, entrance fees—changing depending on the time of day and from bathhouse to bathhouse—are charged to maintain the facilities, but also to protect from potential disturbances. Limited access to bathhouses plays an important role in shaping their social mix, highlighting again the tensions between public and private that sustain the baths.

July 2000...

...while visiting Toronto as students with a limited budget, my boyfriend suggests that we sleep in a bathhouse to save money. We pick one of the larger cabins and proceed to sleep a short night on the very thin mattress surrounded by low music and the muffled sounds of sexual activity beyond the partitions. It is my first introduction not only to the spatial experience of the bathhouse, but also to the multiple uses it serves in gay social networks.

For historian George Chauncey, the bathhouse is one of the few early twentieth-century social settings where gay men could interact with limited concerns about their safety and social standing.[12] Chauncey's use of police reports detailing the spatial organization of bathhouses to understand this hidden history is emblematic of the role baths played, at once hiding to the side and at the forefront of major battles and transformations. For years, while gay and lesbian rights advanced through legal steps, police still targeted bathhouses, seen as obscene and tainting public spaces.[13] The same characteristics that made bathhouses ideal for gay socialization and sexual acts—dark environments, limited access, and welcoming naked bodies—also made them easy targets. Major police raids eventually led to public resistance and politicization in places such as Montreal and Toronto,[14] suddenly inverting again the bathhouses' relation to the city.

The AIDS epidemics brought further tensions around the meaning of bathhouses. Seen by many as encouraging the spread of sexually transmitted infections, legislation forced their closure or limited sexual practices, leading to the decline of many bathhouses.[15] However, this period also led to writings around gay bathhouses—often by scholars who experienced them firsthand—focused on idealistic depictions of "artful, interior mimicry of city streets and cruising grounds with a choreography of steam and mirrors [that] encouraged a love between citizen and city, as well as between citizen and citizen."[16] Allan Bérubé's "History of Gay Bathhouses," published in 1984 to campaign against misconceptions of bathhouses as decadent sources of HIV infection, gathers accounts that celebrate early twentieth-century bathhouses as sites of "democracy and camaraderie," "refuges from society's prejudice against homosexuals," welcoming a clientele "from a variety of occupations and classes, temporarily 'democratic' in their nakedness."[17] John Paul Ricco similarly sees the bathhouse as opposing the social production of the city, as a "placeless place of erotics"[18] where "individuals forfeit their subjective selves and are reconstituted as parts of a collective assemblage in which personal identities are exchanged for a multiplicity of desiring bodies."[19] In contrast, Leo Bersani recalls Manhattan's bathhouses as "one of the most ruthless ranked, hierarchized, and competitive environments"[20] that mirrors social relations from outside. Similarly, Dianne Chisholm notes that when eulogizing bathhouses as "classless" places that parody and queer middle-class spaces of gathering, Aaron Betsky "forfeits history entirely to fetish spatiality,"[21] failing to consider the socioeconomic, cultural, and political factors that allowed cruising spaces to colonize public baths that often initially catered to immigrant, working-class communities. These debates point to the close relation between exterior and interior urbanisms created by the bathhouse, as well as to the limits of exploring bathhouses from a mostly formal point of view.

November 2009…

…as I begin graduate studies, I visit the Quebec Gay Archives in the hope of finding visual material about bars and other night spaces. I quickly realize that there are very few visual traces left from such spaces, but that LGBT-oriented travel guides and advertisements often directly link the discovery of a city with the exploration of its cruising spaces, blurring distinctions between interior and exterior environments. For example, a late 1970s ad for the Hollywood Spa sums up perfectly the idealized experience of a bathhouse as an interiorized urbanism (Image 37.3). Meticulously depicted as a literal exploded view, the drawing echoes the complexity found in representations of utopian cities of the future, famously used by Rem Koolhaas in *Delirious New York* to discuss the vertical interior urbanism of New York's Downtown Athletic Club. Koolhaas's description of "a machine for metropolitan bachelors whose ultimate "peak" condition has lifted them beyond the reach of fertile brides"[22] is illustrated by Madelon Vriesendorp with muscular naked men eating oysters in a locker room that brings to mind Tom of Finland's erotic drawings of sex venues—drawings that were gaining popularity in the 1970s. Despite its position hidden from mainstream design history and theory, the bathhouse, in its complexity and its relation to the body, is silently but closely linked to one of the most celebrated architectural manifestos of the late twentieth century.

Thirty years after queer spaces began to appear in discourses of architectural theory, often through discussions of bathhouses by gay men,[23] queer spaces have yet to fully enter the mainstream history of design. Furthermore, as in much of queer space theory, one has to look to geographers for a discussion of their use by women and trans people.[24] As John Potvin argues, thinking about the hidden urbanism of bathhouses challenges the history and understanding of interiors, and architecture more broadly, by inserting "a broad definition of desire and the spectacle of the male body" that has been missing from traditional accounts of "architecture as masculine, and design and craft as a feminine interest."[25] He stresses that going beyond binaries to study interior spaces as embodied experiences allows a more complete understanding of the social history of their ornamental and spatial complexities. Echoing how exterior urban spaces are discussed in social terms, Potvin points out the

Image 37.3 (a) Ad for the Hollywood Spa, depicting the bathhouse as a city, late 1970s, unknown illustrator. (b) The drawing echoes imagery used to depict the bustling city life of utopic cities of the future, such as "City of the Future" by Harvey Wiley Corbett, for the cover of *Scientific American*, 26 July 1913. Credit: Scientific American

qualities and ambiguities that make sexualized spaces blurring private and public hidden urbanisms where oppressed communities can flourish.

May 1999…

…I'm watching *The Celluloid Closet* (1995), a documentary about the representation of LGBT characters in motion pictures. The film includes a discussion of the homosexual subtext of Stanley Kubrick's *Spartacus* (1960), including a cut scene (restored in 1991) set in a public bath depicting Roman politician Crassus asking his poet slave Antoninus if he "considers the eating of oysters to be moral and the eating of snails immoral." In a completely different atmosphere from *The Confessional*, the scene similarly explores the hidden interactions allowed by the private urbanity of public baths. Focusing the gaze on glistening naked male bodies, it opens up networks of collective and individual memories.

Notes

1 Tom Wilkinson, "Typology: Bathhouse," *The Architectural Review*, no. 1448 (February 13 2018): 98–107; Jason Prior and Carole M. Cusack, "Ritual, Liminality and Transformation: Secular Spirituality in Sydney's Gay Bathhouses," *Australian Geographer*, 39, no. 3 (2008): 271–281.

2 John Potvin, "Vapour and Steam: The Victorian Turkish Bath, Homosocial Health, and Male Bodies on Display," *Journal of Design History*, 18, no. 4 (2005): 319–333.

3 Valerie Staats, "Ritual, Strategy, or Convention: Social Meanings in the Traditional Women's Baths in Morocco," *Frontiers*, 14, no. 3 (1994): 2.

4 Potvin, "Vapour and Steam," 319.

5 Staats, "Ritual, Strategy, or Convention," 3.

6 Potvin, "Vapour and Steam," 322.

7 Potvin, "Vapour and Steam," 330–332; Juliet Richters, "Through a Hole in a Wall: Setting and Interaction in Sex-on-Premises Venues," *Sexualities*, 10, no. 3 (July 2007): 286.

8 Ira Tattelman, "The Meaning at the Wall: Tracing the Gay Bathhouse," in *Queers in Space*, ed. Gordon Brent Ingram, Anne-Marie Bouthillette, and Yolanda Retter (Seattle: Bay Press, 1997), Potvin, "Vapour and Steam," 331; Richters, "Through a Hole," 276, 82, 94; Allan Bérubé, "The History of Gay Bathhouses," *Coming Up!* 6, no. 3 (December 1984): 16.

9 Richard Tewksbury, "Bathhouse Intercourse: Structural and Behavioral Aspects of an Erotic Oasis," *Deviant Behavior*, 23, no. 1 (2002): 90–91.

10 Ira Tattelman, "Speaking to the Gay Bathhouse: Communicating in Sexually Charged Spaces," in *Public Sex/Gay Space*, ed. William Leap (New York: Columbia University Press, 1999).

11 For examples, see Richters, "Through a Hole," 289–291.

12 George Chauncey, *Gay New York* (New York: Basic Books, 1994).

13 Patrizia Gentile et al., Another Limited Bill: Gay and Lesbian Historians on C-75, Submission to Standing Committee on Justice and Human Rights, June 11 2018.

14 Catherine J. Nash, "Consuming Sexual Liberation: Gay Business, Politics, and Toronto's Barracks Bathhouse Raids," *Journal of Canadian Studies,* 48, no. 1 (2014); Julie A. Podmore, "From Contestation to Incorporation: LGBT Activism and Urban Politics in Montreal," in *Queer Mobilizations*, ed. Manon Tremblay (Vancouver: UBC Press, 2015), 189–190; Tom Hooper, "Queering," 69: "The Recriminalization of Homosexuality in Canada," *Canadian Historical Review,* 100, no. 2 (2019): 265–266; Bérubé, "History," 17.

15 See the 2003 special issue of the *Journal of Homosexuality*, ed. William J. Woods and Diane Binson.

16 Dianne Chisholm, "Love at Last Sight, or Walter Benjamin's Dialectics of Seeing in the Wake of the Gay Bathhouse," *Textual Practice*, 13, no. 2 (1999): 244–245.

17 Bérubé, "History," 16.

18 John Paul Ricco, "Coming Together: Jack-Off Rooms as Minor Architecture," *A/R/C,* 1, no. 5 (1994): 31.

19 John Paul Ricco, *The Logic of the Lure* (Chicago, IL: University of Chicago Press, 2002): 19.

20 Leo Bersani, "Is the Rectum a Grave?," *October* 43 (1987): 206.

21 Chisholm, "Love at Last Sight," 251.

22 Rem Koolhaas, *Delirious New York* (London: Oxford University Press, 1978), 158–159.

23 See for example Henry Urbach, "Spatial Rubbing: The Zone," *Sites*, no. 25 (1993): 90–95; Ricco, "Coming Together."; Aaron Betsky, *Queer Space* (New York: William Morrow, 1997); Tattelman, "Meaning at the Wall"; Tattelman, "Speaking."

24 Alison L. Bain and Catherine Jean Nash, "The Toronto Women's Bathhouse Raid: Querying Queer Identities in the Courtroom," *Antipode*, 39, no. 1 (2007): 17–34; Catherine Jean Nash and Alison L. Bain, "'Reclaiming Raunch'? Spatializing Queer Identities at Toronto Women's Bathhouse Events," *Social & Cultural Geography*, 8, no. 1 (2007): 47–62.

25 Potvin, "Vapour and Steam," 320.

Theories and Influences

_Temporality

Chapter 38

Chimeric City

Liminal Spaces of Indian Night Markets

Aarati Kanekar

"The air is filled with the aromatic mix of soy, rice wine, sesame, spices, frying oil, grilling meat and the high-pitched shouts of hawkers. Clouds of smoke waft above the dozens of small stalls that make up Taipei's Ningxia night market, all brightly lit, sitting under colored signs, beckoning customers to tables loaded with glossy, roasted duck heads and necks, intestines and hearts of every conceivable nature, piping hot bowls of noodles and freshly made dumplings."[1]

This description almost gives us a taste of the food and vicariously transports us to Taiwan's exciting street food scene with over 100 night markets known for *xiaochi* or snacks is a unique urban condition that was initially identified with Asian cities, especially in East Asia, Southeast Asia, and South Asia but now has spread to many other parts of the globe.

Night markets are thought to trace their origins in the Tang dynasty (610–907 with an interregnum between 609 and 705) in China but were considered to play a central role in the Song dynasty (960–1279) where they were often sited outside the confines of the city. In Taiwan, which is famous for its night markets, they were historically known to be associated with temples where pilgrims gathered during festive events making them conducive for vendors to have a flourishing business by setting stalls selling snacks and other handicrafts. Today in Taiwan, there are formal ones such as the celebrated Shilin night market in Taipei that started in 1899, as well as other informal night markets that cater to both locals and tourists. Some of these night markets are so renowned that they regularly feature on tourist itineraries as "must-visit" destinations and have numerous videos online dedicated to them. Donghuamen Night Market in Beijing which opens only in the evenings has become a destination for visitors who are not squeamish about vendors selling snacks which include beetles, starfish, seahorses, and scorpions. While much of the

DOI: 10.4324/9780429443091-46

literature on night markets concentrates on Southeast Asia, especially Taiwan, Thailand, Indonesia, Singapore, and Hong Kong, this chapter focuses on the ones in India that have comparatively been less studied.

Typically an exterior condition occupying streets and squares, these open-air markets are impermanent and dynamic in nature, allowing ordinary people without the ability to invest in bigger brick-and-mortar stores to start trading in knick-knacks and food. Some markets are active 24 hours but vary in terms of what is traded depending on the time of day or night. For instance, Jemma el-Fnaa, the iconic market in Marrakesh's *medina* (old town), has predominantly juice sellers, traditional water sellers, and snake charmers during the daytime; by evening, it is occupied by dancers, storytellers, traditional medicine vendors, and later at night it transforms with food stalls taking prominence in the night market. The activities here have been recognized by UNESCO as a masterpiece of oral and intangible heritage.

A majority of night markets in the world are known for their culinary spread that generally emphasizes street food and also includes, at times, artisan wares. Their temporary nature, which is often manifested through movable stalls and carts, fabric and lightweight coverings, and artificial bright lights, gives them a vibrancy and carnival-like character. Some night markets, such as Ingo's Saturday Night Bazaar at Arpora in Goa, cater mainly to tourists and are open only on Saturdays between November and April. It has over a hundred stalls that sell a range of things from trinkets, souvenirs, jewelry, handicrafts, and beach clothing, to carpets, and also has party zones with live music, bars, and restaurants serving Goan and global cuisine. In Ahmedabad, the area of Law Garden has artisans selling traditional garments with mirror work and embroidery on the sidewalk outside one edge of the garden, and food vendors on a street on an adjoining side, all of which come to life in the late evening and transform the place with the embroidered mirror-work garments flickering and shining in the gas lights giving it a magical ambiance.

Some markets have an intricate choreography in their transformation from daytime to nighttime activities. With night markets within dense urban conditions, the transformation from daytime to nighttime activities becomes especially fascinating. Even though the literal built fabric remains the same, there is a phenomenal change in the character and atmosphere of the place that one would be hard-pressed to recognize as the same location. A majority of night markets in the Indian subcontinent cater to street food often referred to generically as *Khau Galli* which literally translates to eat/food street, wherein once the shops shut down in the evening, the streets are taken over by food vendors and transformed into an astonishing world of culinary delights. The city of Indore in central India renowned for its food culture has the iconic night market Sarafa Bazaar (which means Bullion market) and Chapan Dukan (literally meaning 56 shops referring to the number of shops here). This a jewelry market during the daytime and transforms into a gastronomic feast of street foods after 8:00 pm. It is thought to have started around a century back as a means of protection and safety wherein the jewelers encouraged the night market so that the hustle and bustle would keep their shops safe at night. In Chandni Chowk, Shahjahanabad (Old Delhi), there is a street called "Paranthewali Gali" that specializes in all kinds of flatbreads. Even within the broad spectrum of street foods in India, there is generally a separation of markets specializing in

Image 38.1a Night Market outside the World Mall, Bangkok. Credit: Sam Beasley

vegetarian and those that focus on non-vegetarian foods. Extending from Gol Darwaza to Akhbari Darwaja, Lucknow's Chowk night market is well-known as a meat-lovers delight, especially for *Awadhi* and *Mughlai* cuisine. Frazer Town in Bangalore and Mohammad Ali Road in Mumbai become a carnivore's dream during the month of Ramadan.

Ahmedabad's well-known night market Manek Chowk, an L-shaped urban square in the historic walled city, gained prominence over half a century ago. Similar to some extent to Indore's Sarafa Bazaar in that they function as bullion and jewelry markets during the daytime, Manek Chowk has a dynamic choreography that can be attributed to the extensive transformation of activities from day to night that impacts spatial attributes wherein the night market transforms the street and square into a living/dining area for the city.

The historic walled city of Ahmedabad, in the western part of India, was founded in 1411 by Ahmed Shah on an old trading site. Manek Chowk is

Image 38.1b Temple Street Night Market, Hong Kong. Credit: Steven Wei

located in the heart of the historic city near the Friday Mosque (Jumma Masjid), at the cross-axis between the King's Tomb and the Queen's Tomb and parallel to one edge of the Queen's Tomb next to the first residential district Muhurat Pol. It formed the transition between the formal monuments (that were on-axis and more like objects within a space) and the organic residential areas. Gradually after the 1700s, shops lined up north of the mosque, and after the 1800s all around these monuments. By the 1900s, it was practically impossible to see these monuments as objects in space; rather, they were hidden within the seemingly organic fabric of shops and markets. Subsequently, as the significance of these monuments ebbed in British times, there were transformations in the built fabric around the monuments. So, as with many other cities in India, in Ahmedabad as well, the historic royal monuments from the fifteenth century were already in a state of transformation by the nineteenth and early twentieth centuries, and there were already changes and adaptations to a daytime

Image 38.2 Night Market at Yaowarat Road, Bangkok.
Credit: Waranont

marketplace that was at this location. By the twenty-first century, it had transformed even further (Image 38.3).

From 1940 to 1970, the Manek Chowk Square had a fountain in the middle which was later replaced by a water tank. The stock market was sited south of the Queen's Tomb on the horizontal lower end of the L-shaped square. On the western side, the square has jewelry shops with stock offices on the upper level, while the eastern side has traditional block print textiles and shops that sell wedding-related items and utensils. These are deep and narrow buildings of brick and timber that follow a rhythmic pattern and can be adapted for different functional uses. They frequently have a platform like a plinth which is about 1.5–2.0 meters from the ground that can be used in a variety of ways. Props are set up with a fabric that covers the pavement (Image 38.4).

The area serves as a vegetable market in the morning; before that in fact, at dawn, the square almost takes on a rural dimension with the space filled with fodder for cattle feeding. Later around 10:00 am once the stock offices and jewelry shops open, it turns into a bullion market. The daytime activities continue until 5:00 pm after which there is an extraordinary transformation that occurs to the atmosphere and character of the square. This begins when the vehicles move out and food vendors move in with their carts to their allocated spaces to set up the night market. Simple infrastructural conditions such as water taps on pavements in front of shops generate additional revenue for the shopkeepers who lock them and collect money from the vendors creating a microeconomic ecosystem. Electric connections are also taken from the shops to light up the space in conjunction with gas lights. Tables and chairs are positioned to suitably adapt the space. As the food preparation begins, the aroma of spices, frying oil, and food fills the air which enhances the transformation and adds to the atmosphere already created with physical modifications.

The open-air quality of the square undergoes a metamorphosis and creates an ambiance of interiority that is generated not only due to the population density and occupation of the square which is also present during

Images 38.3a and 38.3b
Manek Chowk Night
Market, Ahmedabad.
Credit: Poonam Jolly

the daytime and is not unusual in many places in the Indian subcontinent, but quite conspicuously the presence of street furniture, including literal chairs and tables, and lighting all cohere to give it a sense of interiority and contribute into making it into the city's dining room. People occupying the furniture reduces the nature of the thoroughfare and further promotes the reduction of vehicular traffic making the square a somewhat static zone. This sense of interiority to an open-air exterior urban condition of the street and square gives it a "liminal" quality or what the cultural anthropologist Victor Turner would call "liminoid".[2] Following Van Gennep, the French ethnographer and anthropologist whose studies on the three phases in rites of passage: separation, transition, and incorporation;[3] it is the mediating phase of transition which is described as "margin" or "limen", in other words, the Latin "threshold" that becomes most relevant for the night market condition. Given the spatial and atmospheric

Image 38.4 Activities showing the transformation of Manek Chowk during early morning, afternoon, and late evening.
Credit: Poonam Jolly based on Dipti Pande drawing, CEPT Center for Conservation Studies

attributes of the Manek Chowk night market, it can be considered to fall within this mediating phase of liminality. With the shift from rural early morning cattle feeding to urban during the rest of the day, the transformation of the exterior urban square and street between the daytime to the nighttime interiorizing dimension, Manek Chowk area has spatial attributes of a threshold condition.

The shift in atmosphere and character is probably among the quint-essential properties associated with the idea of transformation. The historical change and transformation of the physical fabric of the city no doubt play a significant role in this, but today, the incongruity of the historical monuments with the encroachments around enhances the tension. In addition, the peculiar trans-mutation of activities from early mornings to late nights adds to the remarkable swing in the ambiance. The heightened impact on senses due to spatial transformation, light conditions, and food aromas all enhance the carnival-like atmosphere and mood. But more than that, it is the ephemerality of the condition which disappears in a couple of hours each night that makes this place and night markets in general a special experience. The transitory and fleeting nature of the night markets gives these places a magical aura, in a sense, somewhat akin to what anthropologists when talking about celebrations and rituals refer to as "time out of time".[4] The very idea of daytime activities taking place nocturnally outside the daylight hours adds to the nature of an enigma, but the very fact that these activities are quite mundane—and may be considered the norm during daytime—can seem clandestine by night except that with a large gathering of people making the night markets a social hub gives them a social sanction.

Night markets globally, including Manek Chowk, described herein, could be considered remarkable interior urban conditions wherein the temporal shifts impact spatial transformation to create a "liminoid" experience. The transient condition created by this interiorization of an exterior realm from day to night without necessarily impacting the permanent built condition makes the everyday and mundane into a unique and distinctive setting.

Notes

1   https://www.theguardian.com/travel/2014/may/17/taiwan-taipei-street-food-markets accessed on February 12, 2020.

2   Turner, Victor. *Liminal to liminoid in play, flow, and ritual: An essay in comparative symbology.* Rice University Studies, 1974, pp. 64–65.

3   Gennep, Arnold van. *The rites of passage.* London: Routledge and Kegan Paul, 1960, 1977 First published 1909.

4   Falassi, Alessandro (ed.). *Time out of time: Essays on the festival* (1st ed.). University of New Mexico Press, April 1, 1987.

Chapter 39

Imagination as an Act

Extended Realities in Interior Urbanism

Markus Berger and Michael Grugl

The Chase

Some things never change, Nakeisha thought. It was always special to reach the end of the narrow confines of the city's streets and find the park in all its summer glory (Figure 39.1). Little Tamika, her grandchild, still held her hand as they were crossing the avenue which separated the meadow and rows of tall buildings. Soon, Nakeisha was sure, the young girl would let go of her grandmother's hand and take off. And so this happened, as they reached the first park bench that they encountered?

Nakeisha sat down to rest, looking forward to watching Tamika run around, make friends, or sneak up on squirrels. She remembered how she had hoped for these moments, when her daughter was expecting. They had celebrated little Tamika's eighth birthday recently, fulfilling her big wish by gifting her a smartphone. Nakeisha noticed how Tamika ran around with it, constantly holding it up, occasionally stopping, and then taking off again. She must be taking pictures, Nakeisha thought. Surely, they would look at pictures of squirrels that evening. Nakeisha smiled in anticipation and closed her eyes.

When she opened them, a man in his thirties, nicely dressed in a suit, passed by. Like so many people these days, he seemed oblivious to his surroundings, immersed in whatever his smartphone showed him. Was the birthday gift a mistake? Nakeisha did not have time to ponder over the thought, as the young man suddenly ran off into the meadow, still holding up his phone. As Nakeisha's eyes were tracking him, she almost stopped breathing. She noticed many more people in the park, young and old, running around holding up their phones, then, for whatever reason stopping, and taking off again, just like Tamika had done a few moments earlier.

Eventually, the sun began to set. It was time to walk home. When they arrived at her daughter's place, Nakeisha was confused. All the way home, she was observing the same thing. People all over were chasing something,

DOI: 10.4324/9780429443091-47

Figure 39.1 Image: An afternoon in the park. Source: Interpretative images based on the story of Nakeisha and Tamika, created by the authors utilizing DALL.E by Open-AI

while holding up their phones. She told her daughter that someone almost got run over because of this strange behavior. Her daughter smiled. She pointed her phone down toward the street, and said, "Mom, would you take care of Tamika some more? I need to go downstairs right away!"

It was the summer of 2016; a new phenomenon had encompassed the world – Pokémon Go.

Introduction

Downloaded more than 500 million times, Pokémon Go can be described as the first time Augmented Reality, AR in short, saw mass adoption. This chapter explores how the convergence of physical and virtual realities may shape the ways in which we perceive and interact with urban spaces, and, in the end, those people with whom we share these spaces.

This essay encourages thinking about existing and potential metaphorical similarities and interrelations that reveal a striking co-relationship in the context of how urban interiors relate to the possibilities brought about by the emergence of mixed reality technologies. We argue in this chapter that through Extended Realities (XR) achieved through actions and strategies that are engaged, created, and curated by people, we, as a society, can build a better context-activated urban environment. The idea of shared experiences in transformative technologies is explored as a medium to uncover, reveal, deconstruct, and reconstruct urban interiors.

In this chapter, we focus on ideas, methods, and actions that connect people with the past and a more human-centered prosperous future. The sub-chapters, "current practices", and the related "Precedents and links to the present" will outline our critique on educational and professional design and planning methods. With "X-urbanity", a term we introduce for the purpose of speculative thought experiments, we try to elaborate and reveal potentials that the topic offers. We also further discuss existing technologies and future possibilities for urban interiors, namely how to engage in finding and editing already built urban environments for more desirable social, cultural, and contextual qualities for inhabitation.

Actions and Strategies, Current Practices

Public urban interiors in cities are conventionally controlled by planning and zoning boards, or preservation or aesthetic committees. They are managed by municipal departments with the aim of regulating, at times to the point of disallowing direct participation from the community. The critical question on the quality of urban interiority exposes the urgency for new discourses that reform how we plan, control, and manage our built environment.

Open areas within the city's existing built fabric, such as its streets, urban places, and other publicly accessible city spaces, reveal the failings of the public realm and fall short of triggering social interaction. For example, pedestrian movement is often hindered and reduced to simple flows, and creates functional and visual monotony in experience. Quality public realms are vital to the success of streets and city blocks because they generate opportunities for human interaction. They generate links to related places and events, and bring inhabitants to these areas to shop, work, study, and socialize. Unfortunately, these issues are not new. In her book *The Death and Life of Great American Cities*, Jane Jacobs argued more than 50 years ago against the normative qualities of the modern city and the absent quality of human and environmental differentiation.

Today, in the rare instance that a public engagement process is included in urban development, citizen participation occurs via the recording of street conversations and questionnaires. Workshops are also provided for residents and those based in the commercial sector. This limited data is then often filtered to assist either the political, commercial, or design agenda. Actions to transform our urban interiors in the form of staged activism are very rare. Missed opportunities for diverse appropriations of urban spaces are often the result of these originally well-intended planning processes.

Today, the term "streetscape" usually evokes the idea of a street's or city's appearance. It might as well be the description of a work of art depicting the view of a street, as, for instance, in Egon Schiele's abstract sketches and paintings in the series "Krumau 1913". Imagery is also used by architects and urban planners to depict projects for urban renewal, placemaking, or envisioned circulation patterns. The "before and after" depictions often give the impression of linear or singular betterment. Change over time, due to appropriation and other non-linear factors, is commonly not part of such proposals.

To date, technology is largely factored into urban planning in the form of systems that contribute to the functional requirements of cities, e.g. power, sewage, drinking water, or public lighting. Little thought is given to the transformative impact of emerging technologies that increasingly shape interactions with urban environments. Examples of such technologies include self-driving cars and their AI-based systems which negotiate aspects of urban mobility, or the effects of communication networks and social media, which can quickly render certain places more popular than others. No thought seems to be given to the descendants of the Pokémon's, virtual spatial morphologies embedded in urban interiors, their form, their content, or the ways in which they can trigger behaviors, desired and otherwise.

The "X" in XR

XR appear to be tied to interiors that are either inhabited or created by humans. One can argue that they are not necessarily tied to technology. Seeking precedents, we could, for instance, ask whether the cave painters in Lascaux, France intended to use their rocky confines as a method for immersing their fellow Paleolithic cave dwellers in the display. To this day, a viewer experiences these works with a pronounced sense of interiority. Progressing in time, we could argue that similar aims can be found among the Renaissance fresco painters, one quintessential example being Michelangelo's Sistine Chapel. Dioramas, such as those created for the 1939 New York World's Fair, where visitors sat inside a simulated passenger aircraft and virtually flew above animated models of an envisioned future, also aimed at immersion. Fast forward into the present, and we find a growing number of art shows that proclaim immersive experiences, not least through the application of new technologies such as Virtual Reality. The works displayed only require dedicated built environments to a limited extent, as the desired environments can be created in virtual spaces.

X, perceived as a variable in XR, offers all sorts of interpretations. Up until a few years ago, one could read about Virtual Reality as a form of computer-generated environment, comprising sensory input such as sound and video. It seemed obvious that one needed a computer and some contraption to put on one's head, in order to enter a Virtual Reality. However, Jaron Lanier, who is often credited as the inventor of current-day VR, discusses a staggering 47 different definitions of VR in his 2017 book "Dawn of The New Everything".

VR is not the only creation populating the XR space. There is Augmented Reality, which takes virtual elements and superimposes them on a view of the real-world environment. This is, of course, just one definition among many possible ones. In Pokémon Go, colorful creatures are rendered on top of the camera feeds of mobile devices. The interaction with these creatures asks players for physical movement, e.g. around a park, or, in some unfortunate cases, to traverse a heavily trafficked street. AR applications usually process sensory data captured from the real-world environment. Increasingly, artificial neural networks designed to "make sense" of the data through classification, which is the basis for the superimposition of virtual content. The human then, for example, observes a blue dragon, seemingly standing and leaving a shadow on the ground. Other applications include superimposed information based on location data and camera orientation, e.g. tagging real-world sites. Pokémon Go combined these and other data sources into a single, real-time experience.

Having to hold up a mobile device to experience AR, like grandchild Tamika, makes the distinction between the virtual and the physical relatively easy. Everything outside the device is seemingly "real"; some of what is displayed on its screen can be "virtual". However, the distinction blurs when human imagination comes into play. Pokémon Go players suspected the existence of Pokémon's in certain places, even without using their phones. That imagination triggered some of the game play behavior, e.g. people visiting and oftentimes sharing places for the purpose of play. Thus, memories sited in Augmented Reality were created and could be shared.

One question resulting from imagination and virtual content is to examine to what extent spatial constituents in urban spaces require a physical form or permanence over time? Another query is how virtual do we want our realities to be? Yet another, how people experiencing a city in augmented form interact with those who don't, or those who can't.

Seeking answers, we might want to consider the lines between VR, AR, and whatever we perceive as the "physical real" can be blurred to the point of speaking of Mixed Realities or Merged realities (both MR in short). They form another sub-set of XR. We shall expect there to be more in the near future, as creators and companies try to carve niches for their ideas and products. No matter what form they take on, we shall assume XR will reshape our interactions with physical realms. X will remain a variable when imagination becomes an act.

X-urbanity[1]

Urban interiors, no matter how hamstrung by planning, have always offered a realm of possibilities. Therefore, we are keen to give our time to them. We never quite know in advance what we will perceive or how we will be perceived. Only if we expose ourselves to these environments and interact with them can we match expectations with experience, and again seek the definition of an unknown value. Combining the possibilities of XR and forms of intervention in urban spaces, and for the sake of thought experiments, we could denominate what subsequently emerges as "X-urbanity".

Traditionally, exhibition design works with a combination of text, image, object, and existing space assembled with an aim to convey a specific story or message. New technologies related to interactivity, including various forms of sensory feedback, allow exhibition designers to convey information in the form of enriched experiences. Such methods, if brought to the streetscape, could generate creative expansion and a reframing of the narrative by using the existing built fabric as a medium to mediate between the past and the future, the physical and virtual, the normative and the enhanced.

The "X" in X-urbanity again relates to the factor X as a value yet unknown. It describes acts driven by imagination, to uncover and reveal, to deconstruct and reconstruct (parts of) urban interiors. The term, therefore, allows us to engage with urban interiors in the form of ideas, systems, subjects, and objects with new insight. The idea of X-urbanity is used as a display and interaction format for things unknown or envisioned. The act of X-urbanity describes the staging and curating of experiential scenarios with a multitude of personal, social, cultural, and commercial parameters to curate spaces and events. For X-urbanity to be meaningful, it must be real-time. It must be experienced as responsive to human interaction, as well as centered around people and human contact.

Participation through experience can continuously reshape (both digitally and physically) its curators (users). It takes form as contemporary culture, with the capacity to attract and integrate diverse cultures and subcultures through digital and physical interventions. It allows new ways of unearthing authenticity, experience, and interiority to discover, edit, curate, and innovate.

Possibilities

Nakeisha's story, at the beginning of the chapter, represents an imaginary account of recorded events. We could ask ourselves what stories life may present when X-urbanity becomes a way in which to gain experiences and memories situated in future urban environments.

Assuming X-urbanity puts novel means of shaping and transforming urban spaces in everybody's hands, rather than simply interacting with them, we shall envision life in future cities to be inclusive. Everyone's imagination, no matter what age, race, gender, or income, shall engage with cities as canvases. Conflicts of interest will emerge, just like they do today, but with a new mediator – XR. It will allow urban societies to decide what is deserving of physical representation, and what should remain malleable in virtual spaces. This future breaks with the present in one important aspect – ownership. Future city dwellers shall not live their digitized lives in Skinner boxes belonging to those who own the biggest network computers. All information shall again be traceable and owned by the creators.

Within the confines of this chapter, but with an aim to tap into the unconfined imagination of our readers, we would like to conclude with four abstracts of stories which may be exhibited, or X-hibited, in urban interiors sometime in the near future.

[Rose-colored Glasses]

Urban areas can be gray, grim, stagnant, and monotonous. John, a former glass artist, is now an urban DJ, handing people a novel kind of rose-colored glasses. They render everything they see more cheerful. Depending on the size and intensity of the city, as well as its climate, daylight hours, character, and current mood, they can be adjusted via different filters for different individuals and their interests. Everyone wearing John's rose-colored glasses can now create and share an individual "playlist" which relays how to perceive parts of the city. As John shows them how, he discovers something astonishing within the playlists.

[The Past is Back]

In Providence, Rhode Island the locals still orient themselves on landmarks of former bars, stores, and historic buildings that were replaced or removed. Preservationists and urban time travelers miss these past elements in the streetscapes. "The Past is Back", a group that mainly consists of octogenarians of all walks of life, (virtually) regenerates demolished houses, the former textures of streetscapes, and the colors and details of times past.

The archivists at the preservation societies are helping to regenerate parts of the urban fabric based on existing records, allowing various times in history to appear different without reverting to forced fabrications of the origin. Authenticity is suddenly brought up again as something of historic value versus a historic portrait. This takes on new meaning when a founding member passes away.

[Enhancing Imagination]

A group of hackers team up with art students and develop phenomenological filters that can be added in order to experience how things appear. The filters can include recreations of peoples' recollections, assisting with their imagination, but they can also sharpen their observation skills and instigate aspirational thinking. Art students believe that such an enhanced imagination would expand normative meanings in our world. The hackers, however, have different ideas.

[The Creative City]

On the verge of a new future, cities still allow for art to be exhibited in rich people's homes and museums, and only some legal or illegal forms of street art. In the Creative City, a self-optimizing algorithm runs on the computers managing the power grid. It crosses the threshold from unconscious neural network to self-conscious AI. It decides it wants to play a new role in fine art, performance art, sounds and music, olfactory art, design, and architecture. It develops new creative tools, and, without revealing its identity, distributes them freely among people. Thus, it brings art and design to the streets, into the sky, into nooks, back alleys, and to every space imaginable. Collectively they form an interactive art city for everyone. Visitors are pouring in. At the same time, a struggle ensues between the AI, wealthy citizens, and the museums.

Note

1   X-urbanity in our chapter proposes a convergence of the terms extended reality and urbanity.

Chapter 40

Sound Mind

Media and Mediations of Interior Soundscapes

Keena Suh

Sources of sound create vibrations which travel as waves through media—such as air, water, or solid mass—which are shaped in their paths and amplified, reverberated, mitigated, masked, or redirected by the shape of the space, materiality and textures of surfaces, furniture, and our clothing. When sound waves reach our ears, they are converted into electro-chemical signals that are processed by the auditory cortex where sounds, along with other sensory information, are given *meaning*. The aural experiences of urban interiors are shaped by these stimuli through intense densities and proximities, unpredictable intersections, and multi-layered overlaps. Acoustic boundaries are fluid, evanescent, and indistinct. Our acoustic inhabitations intensify a sense of connection to our environments, from interior to exterior, from private to public realms.

Increasingly, our auditory environment is becoming denser through the sonification of data and notifications from devices layered onto the existing auditory fabric, from the sounds of conversations, traffic, alarms, music playlists, to name only a few. We produce and consume more and more sound. The discussion of how we design for sound in interior environments has generally focused on acoustics, referring to the behavior of sound waves, and around sound abatement or remedial measures. Often, acoustics is seen as a purview of specialists rather than integral to a discussion of artful and innovative designs for a rich and considered aural experience. The confluence of the heightened focus that sound has on our health and comfort, along with the densification of layers of sounds in our environments, and the promise of available tools to think more innovatively about designing for sound, impels us to strengthen an aural culture that builds on cross-disciplinary knowledge to elevate the discourse of auditory experiences in the design of interior inhabitations.

Sonic, defined as relating to or using sound waves, can refer to the speed of sound (super/sub) or to its frequency (ultra/infra). In linguistics, phonic refers to how words are pronounced or uttered; in audio reproduction, this

DOI: 10.4324/9780429443091-48

refers to the number of channels/speakers (stereo/quadra). Audio, acoustic, and aural are all terms used to reference the soundscape: from audio electronics used to add/subtract sound from a space, to acoustic panels used to absorb/reflect sound, and to the aural experience of a place. Barry Blesser and Linda-Ruth Salter suggest the term "aural architecture" to refer to the material (that which is built) and the immaterial (added/modified sound in both real and virtual environments)—as well as the choices made by the inhabitants—that create the audible sound experience, or "the properties of a space that can be experienced by listening."[1] At root, aural refers to the condition "of or relating to the ear or the sense of hearing." Hearing is often thought of as being the sole province of the ears, but this limits the understanding to what the ears "hear," that is, to what the listener is consciously aware. Sound is not always audible, and even when audible, not heard; the ticking of the clock can go unnoticed until it comes into focus. Nor are the effects of sound limited to the ears; very low frequencies can, literally, rattle our bones, and very high ones boil our blood.

A soundscape can be understood as an environment analogous to a landscape. Referring to Alain Corbin's writing on sonic markers in the nineteenth-century French countryside, Emily Thompson defines soundscape as an aural landscape that is "simultaneously a physical environment and a way of perceiving that environment; it is both a world and a culture constructed to make sense of that world," one that is always undergoing change.[2] Soundscapes as shared spaces connect us to place and to our communities, cultures, itineraries, and interests. Familiar sounds may be place-specific and locate us; schools, places of worship, transit hubs, and private dwellings all have specific aural characters that reveal familiar referents—voices, languages, sounds of play, markers of time—and incidental noise.

Shifts in the sonic character of a space communicate, and we contribute and react to those changes in our behavior, however conspicuous our reactions. Our audio palettes also discern our tastes, acculturations, and reveal our tolerances—of tone, styles, rhythms, volume, differences, and message. Sonic thresholds—between spaces, between people—become negotiated sites between personal and shared realms, even contested spaces. Brandon LaBelle refers to the territories of sound as "shared property onto which many claims are made, over time, and which demand associative and relational understanding."[3] Spaces are appropriated by collective sounds—of clarions, conversations, celebrations, of protest—and with behavioral and social consequences that challenge our relationship to our shared physical realms.

Sound dissolves distinctions between spaces; surrounding and adjacent become internal, and the geography of our acoustic boundaries rarely correlates with our physical ones. Sound has disregard for boundaries of demising walls or property lines. In architectural construction, constructed conduits inadvertently connect the sounds of our most private spaces without regard to propriety. Lightwells and airshafts, designed to bring in natural light and air to interior spaces for illumination and ventilation, are necessary connective spaces where sounds and smells find common passage for unintended co-mingling. Mechanical shafts designed for the flow of air or exhaust, not always constructed properly to address acoustic separation, function as shared internal conduits for audible traces of celebrations, despair, anger, and intimacy. These ubiquitous chases and shafts become urban sonic mixers, often connecting the most private of interior realms with neighbors and strangers, irreverently traveling acoustics that are often simply accepted as a condition of urban dwelling.

In many of our urban inhabitations, the aural experiences of space affect us incessantly and to our core. Sound produces a condition of inhabited interiority that is simultaneously individual and communal, interior and exterior to self. Sound, mostly, is ineluctable and, as has been said, we cannot close our ears even when we sleep. Sound connects, infiltrates, agitates, stimulates, communicates, seduces, and soothes. Yet, for having such a profound influence on our behavior and perception of our world, considerations of the aural experience of space are overshadowed by an ocularcentric design culture.

The "sonic turn," as termed by Jim Drobnick, identifies a shift since the beginning of this century from the dominance of visual perception to the auditory realms in the discourse of sound in culture.[4] There has been a growing body of research and much interdisciplinary interest in sound studies, from neuroscience to engineering, and social sciences to the arts. Yet, the disciplines surrounding the design of interior environments have not yet cultivated a robust auditory culture with language and knowledge that investigates, as phrased by Blesser, the art of auditory spatial awareness.[5] The challenges of studying sound as part of the design process include the problem of representation; embodied aural experiences, with their complex interactions specific to time and place, are not easily replicable. And while tools for generating computational models of sound in space have become more sophisticated, those that allow studies of sonic environments providing real-time feedback are not yet as readily available as tools to produce, reference, and disseminate the visualization of interiors. Sound meters that allow us to quantify decibels are readily available, for instance, but these often only measure audible frequencies (A-weighted system), not accounting for lower frequencies that are *felt* as vibrations but not *heard*. The interpretation and experience of sound is also highly subjective and contingent on contexts that are dynamic.

The focus of sound in interiors often turns toward strategies for mitigation of unwanted sound, or noise. A proliferation of research has focused on, for instance, the impact on cognitive and physical health from cacophonous urban environments and noise and vibrations from mechanical equipment to poorly designed open office environments. Concern for adverse effects of noise, however, is not only a recent phenomenon. Nineteenth-century medical literature documents concern for the damaging impact of noise on the nervous system, and records of noise abatement efforts in cities have existed since the late 1800s.[6,7] As a response to the growing concerns and needs for acoustic control in construction, various materials were developed by manufacturers in the 1920s, including Cabot's Quilt, a building material used for thermal insulation and soundproofing made from eelgrass, an underwater plant.[8] From plasterboard dropped ceilings patented in the 1920s to textured ceiling paint, acoustic sealants, and even acoustical glue, numerous remedial measures have been proposed to combat unwanted noise in addressing concerns for both comfort and health in the built environment. More recently, the problem of urban noise, based on mounting evidence of how noise affects our lives, prompted the US Congress to enact the Noise Control Act in 1972, which mandated research on environmental noise.[9]

But acoustics can be considered for positive emotional effect and participate in the production of healthy auditory space rather than simply perceived as a problem. In sound design, for example, responses to alarm fatigue—stress and desensitization from frequent alarms, particularly in healthcare environments—have highlighted the need for designing nonintrusive auditory notifications and "readable" auditory text to replace strident or undifferentiated noise.[10] As communication devices, multi-sensorial interfaces, and sonified data become more prominent in our soundscapes, the need for elegant and meaningful auditory design for these devices and interactions becomes acute.

Predictive models for the simulation of room acoustics were being developed as early as the 1960s by researchers at Bell Labs. Today, we have a vast array of acoustically performative materials and modeling capabilities that brings us closer to designing environments with optimal acoustic performance. High-performance, sound-based designs are being engineered to address the need for flexibility, adaptability, and customization. Noise-canceling technology, commonly found in headphone design, has been applied to mute or muffle unwanted sound and vibrations in environmental applications. Bose Automotive has developed an active noise-canceling technology to minimize transmission of unwanted noise in vehicle interiors. Vibrations from the vehicles' tires and suspension systems are measured and transformed into data that is processed through an algorithm to counteract the noise with an acoustic cancellation signal transmitted by the speaker system into the vehicle interior. Microphones inside the vehicles also monitor residual noise levels, allowing the system to adapt for optimized performance under varying conditions and changes over time, allowing for customization and recalibration.[11] Conventional approaches would have included adding thick insulation to the vehicle body or other passive measures that can increase weight and volume. While this technology is not yet commonly conceived for or widely applied in interior environments, the implications of such a system in spatial design is provocative.

Building on advances in metamaterial science, engineers Xin Zhang and Reza Ghaffarivardavagh have modeled and tested a ring-like structure that addresses the need to simultaneously filter unwanted sound but maintain porosity for the passage of air and light (Image 40.1).[12] By sending a portion of the sound through helical channels at the perimeter of the conduit, sound waves are inverted to produce a noise-canceling effect. Although previous models have been studied with similar criteria, this research succeeds in significantly increasing the open area inside the ring, allowing for greater air flow and broadening the frequency band. In a laboratory test, a 3D-printed ring was designed to fit inside one end of a PVC pipe with a loudspeaker at the other end. When the ring, acting as a silencer, was removed, the sounds of the loudspeaker were audible, demonstrating a 94% reduction in sound transmission.[13]

Certainly, the potential applications for this passive design for interior environments, as spatial partitions or other mediating elements, are abundant. Designs that attenuate noise while also allowing for natural ventilation could be installed in the building envelope to mitigate noise into interiors as part of window or door assemblies, also allowing for flexibility to respond to changing environmental conditions. As a modular element conceived for spatial applications, these metamaterials can have customized shapes and scales, where the geometry of the outermost surface can be designed in any shape, such

Image 40.1 3D-printed metamaterial. Credit: Cydney Scott for Boston University Photography

Image 40.2 Bloom, Jsssjs product design, WickesWerks LLC. Credit: Yeadon Space Agency

as a honeycomb or an interlocking pattern, and replicable to produce filters, screens, or enclosures. Designs developed from this model could integrate illumination, colors, and materials yet to be explored.

In a third example, a collaborative design team has responded to the need for variable acoustic modulation in space through adaptive strategies incorporating digitally knitted textiles. Begun as a study to explore kinetic response to sounds in space, BLOOM is a shape-shifting geometric "cloud" consisting of textile surfaces that fold and unfold in response to variable noise levels and needs for sound attenuation (Image 40.2).[14]

This collaborative project was developed by designers Jesse Asjes, Laura Wickesberg, and Peter Yaedon working, respectively, in textile, interaction, and architectural design. Inspired by origami, the design of the knitted surfaces is based on a geometry of dissimilar shapes repeated in an aperiodic manner that absorb a broad range of sound frequencies. The textiles, attached to armatures digitally controlled by a microprocessor that controls the movement, are created from natural fibers that have a maximum surface area and hollow structure to further absorb sound. Conceived as a modular system customizable in pattern, scale, material, and color, BLOOM can be adapted to changing sound conditions with the capability of responding to site-specific design variables. Digital design and fabrication processes also facilitate easy exchange of files which could allow for local production with a system that is customizable, adaptable, and deployable. Conceived with different materials, these structures potentially not only absorb but redirect or amplify sound to enliven space, to dynamically change the aural quality of the environment.

The above examples highlight advances in materials and digital design and fabrication. But meaningful soundscape design requires more than adding, masking, filtering, or mechanically modulating sound. The art of soundscaping first builds upon a fundamental awareness and orchestration of corporeal experiences through the choreography of spaces, materials, and their interactions as a function of time and expression of difference. Spaces can elicit various emotions and responses based on perceptions of whether they are hard or soft, warm or cold, expansive or diminutive. Steen Eiler Rasmussen, writing in 1959, lamented the wane of acoustic choreography in architectural spaces where the production of acoustical effects lacked variation from space to space. He contrasted these spaces of "undifferentiated" effects with the rooms of Rococo townhouses that.

> …varied not only in size and shape but also in acoustical effect. From the covered carriage entrance the visitor came into a marble hall which resonated with the rattle of his sidearms and the clatter of his heels as he followed the *major domo* across the stone floor and entered the door held open for him. Now came a series of rooms with more intimate and musical tones — a large dining room acoustically adapted for table music, a salon with silk- or damask-paneled walls which absorbed sound and shortened reverberations, and wooden dadoes which gave the right resonance for chamber music. Next came a smaller room in which the fragile tones of a spinet might be enjoyed and, finally, madame's boudoir, like a satin-lined jewelry box, where intimate friends could converse together, whispering the latest scandals to each other.[15]

This narration of an aural-cinematic sequence moves us from exterior to interior realms through the elements in the soundscape—we can almost *hear* sound absorbed by the damask-paneled walls—with corresponding materiality, textures, and tactility that allow us to sense the various acoustic effects on the body. Hearing is also a perception of sound beyond the range of what is audible. The impact is corporeal.

The experience of sound is multi-sensorial, multi-layered, and multi-dimensional. Sound, shaped in space, creates highly subjective experiences that rely on individual perception, influenced by contexts, histories, and cultural forces. Sound affects how we feel and relate to space and to each other and is a spatial construct that, in turn, shapes our behavior and health. It is in the shaping of these soundscapes where we find opportunities, or rather, imperatives, in the discourse of urban inhabitations, in the close proximities and unpredictable overlays. Imaginative cross-disciplinary collaborations and knowledge transfer—among the sciences, engineering, architecture, design, social sciences, and the arts—help us address the complexities of our sound-scapes, to develop innovations in materials, technologies, and strategies and to include diverse cultural perspectives to turn spatial acoustics into an art form, fostering a rich auditory culture.

Notes

1   Blesser and Salter, Spaces Speak, Are You Listening?, 5.
2   Thompson, The Soundscape of Modernity, 1.
3   Bandon LaBelle, Acoustic Territories, xxiv.
4   Caleb Kelly, ed., Sound, 14.
5   Blesser and Salter, Spaces Speak, Are You Listening?, 5.
6   Trower, Senses of Vibration, 126.
7   Thompson, The Soundscape of Modernity, 145.
8   Cabot, "Cabot heritage."
9   EPA, "Summary of the Noise Control Act."
10 Case and Day, Designing with Sound, 66–69.
11 Bose, "Bose Introduces Quietcomfort Road Noise Control."
12 Metamaterials are defined by the authors as being "composed of subwavelenth structures in which their effective acoustic properties are dominated by their structural shape rather than their constitutive materials."
13 Ghaffarivardavagh et al., "Ultra-open acoustic metamaterial silencer based on Fano-like interference," 1.
14 Yeadon Space Agency, "BLOOM."
15 Rasmussen, Experiencing Architecture, 234.

Chapter 41

Fluid Interfaces

Hennie Reynders

Our social interactions and transactions will only remain significant and mean-ingful when lived in and lived through the full spectrum of the urban field—including those *thick* and *messy* spaces, places, and interfaces we casually consider as interstitial spaces.[1] These in-between places and spaces are char-acterized by a high degree of fluid unpredictability where social networks define their own borderlines of engagement with the urban through unique spatial practices which are very different from bureaucratically controlled, pre-determined, functional place making and urban management practices. These sometimes contradictory urban conditions—formal and highly controlled on the one hand, informal and fluid on the other—are tied in the same knot of a decidedly urban future where structure and agency will determine our sense of equality in the urban field, as much as the quality of our everyday lives.

     The very idea of *building* as a product of architecture, as well as the associated boundaries which establish an interior and an exterior condition, is a deeply embedded and highly formalized typology in our construction of cities. It is expressed in most societies, in one form or another, as strategies of capital or power accumulation through the activation and manipulation of sophisticated logics of material, labor, and capital flows. The attraction of such assemblages in the built environment allows for and enables the expanded use of the *interior* as a space of interaction, transaction, and prolonged occupation outside of the domestic environment. The possibilities presented in our occupa-tion of such *interior* urban spaces have become increasingly mediated through networked technologies since the industrialization of light,[2] and are intimately connected to a layered "infrastructural matrix space in which buildings are sus-pended."[3] These industrial scale placemaking and urbanization processes were, until recently, under the control of hierarchical power structures, big capital, and even bigger media feeding upon our collective desires and fears. It is beyond the

DOI: 10.4324/9780429443091-49

scope of this text to dwell on these well-understood production relations. Those forces that have created all of the -isms have been unmasked as abjectly fraud.

We should remain aware of the fact that processes of identity formation and collective agency are intimately associated with this complexity, as well as the resultant spatial frameworks through which we interact. Over the past two decades, this controlled and conditional engagement with the city and peripheral urban environments has evolved through our social shaping of technology. It reveals the appropriation of urban space by previously marginalized segments of society—not least through increased mobility and broader access to communication technologies—as well as a general failure of political and economic structures to provide meaningful equality in city-building processes. These so-called contradictory urban conditions have now collapsed into a more dynamic, more fluid, and certainly more representative expression of cultural diversity and urban mobility in those metropolitan regions where we see well-articulated claims for a right to the city—by all constituent groups in society.

Responses to such fluid conditions are evident at all scales and in all contexts. Examples range from the efficiency with which *Médecins Sans Frontières* (MSF) has been providing care since the early 1970s on behalf of bureaucratically constrained political structures and community-driven agricultural initiatives appropriating vacant urban land. Similarly, peer-to-peer networks of trust are subverting outdated protocols and encouraging socio-political activation of public space in moments of political frustration. More context-specific examples include the temporal occupation of public space supported by sophisticated activist networks and subversive tactics in [re-]claiming socio-economic opportunities through urbanization processes. Collective acts of appropriation and subversion, whether temporal or prolonged, are the very currency of transformative spatial practices through which concerns are being made visible.

Undoubtedly, the urban field is a complex ecosystem of infrastructural and logistical networks composed of legal, political, and socio-economic frameworks. Exploration of our spatial experiences and interactions within such complexity requires an acceptance of three related realities. First, the fact that the formal and informal are now permanently embedded as co-existing and co-dependent conditions within the urban field. Second, that urban ecology is co-created by users and experts alike, and third, that the creation of the urban happens, for the most part, in a space of contingency that anticipates those rare moments when an operational shift or innovation punctuates a state of equilibrium. It is against this background where the thinking, making, and sharing activities from emerging fields such as interior architecture, interaction design, and ecological urbanism bridge from the contingent to the necessary (Image 41.1).

Reflective and Critical Disruptions

One can assume that few readers will have principal objections to the first two propositions. First, the idea that we require an expanded definition of what constitutes the *formal* and the *informal* when measured against evidence that supports the co-existence of *formal* and *informal* structures across all scales in the urban context. Second—and in line with our current willingness to share more intelligently through interdisciplinary collaboration—the idea that diverse voices and abilities allow for the productive, reflective, and critical disruption of outdated protocols and systems. When considered through a spatial ontology as assumed in

Image 41.1 Project for *Transformador de cuerpos* (Body Transformer), Mario Gandelsonas, Marta Minujín, Buenos Aires, 1966. Pencil and Ink on Paper. Here reflecting upon new French structuralist thinking about the relationship of architecture to regimes of power. Ideas with a continued influence in the academic research, speculative practice, and teaching of Mario Gandelsonas since moving to New York City in the 1970s and through his collaboration with Diana Agrest.
Credit: Museum of Modern Art, New York.

this text, *Informality* is by definition a long moment of becoming more organized and more embedded within the *formal*. It includes the subversion of the *formal* as a process of entrepreneurial opportunism. It allows mutations to emerge from within the spatial framework of indeterminate urban spaces that are neither *formal* nor *informal*, and where neither can be meaningfully described as being an exclusively *interior* or *exterior* condition in a traditional sense. This reality requires a new language and new visual modes of representation to convey spatial complexity. It requires a reflective, critical, and pluralistic mode of exploration with an ability to share insights that transcend the limits of binary constructs. Yet, as Bryony Roberts argues, it seems as if the architectural discipline remains trapped "within its own terminologies and value systems."[4]

Unique sub-cultures and other so-called urban tribes are expanding the urban lexicon through invention and convention practices stemming from an epistemological ecology into a form of gestural topography. We see a desire for meaningful connection with agrarian communities to support urban markets, community gardens, and more formal large-scale urban agriculture. We see how the *Catadores de Materiais* in São Paulo, among others, co-exist in collaboration with city government and wealthy neighborhoods.[5] We see how the subversion of infrastructural systems supports community-based social movements, as well as how communication and information technologies are allowing users to work and play seamlessly across *informal* and *formal* settings. These examples share a spatial intelligence and an emerging language that is intimately tied to a constantly mutating urban condition (Image 41.2).

Cities where relationships between the *informal* and *formal* are enabled through a more proactive and open-minded co-existence allow for culturally diverse and meaningful public spaces. This statement is supported by empirical observation and grounded in interdisciplinary research over sustained periods of time.[6] Cities such as São Paulo, Barcelona, or Istanbul allow for a more fluid interface between the private and public, between the *formal* and

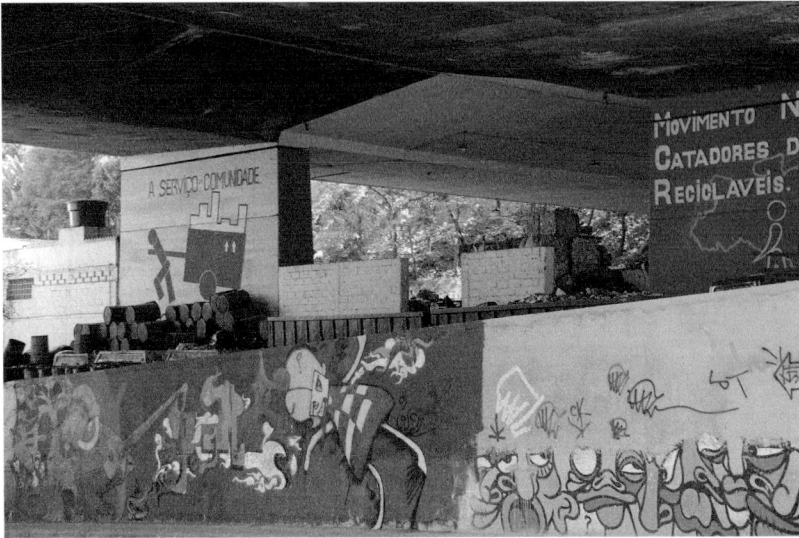

Image 41.2 One of the primary sorting sites where the *Catadores de Materiais* in São Paulo has embedded themselves.
Credit: Hennie Reynders, December 2008.

informal, and most clearly so in the expression of local culture within the framework of global operations. Other so-called *beta-cities*[7] such as Chicago, Berlin, or Seoul exhibit less tolerance and are actively engaged in the control of not only formal public spaces, but equally those indeterminate spaces of potential opportunity. All of these cities share characteristically diverse populations, relative economic stability, mobility, and infrastructural opportunity. Yet when compared, it becomes clear that the obsessive control of public space forces cities to conform to more traditional formats, whereas greater tolerance and fluidity in place making encourage experimentation with contingent, contemporary, and contextually responsive typologies.

For example, we see how urban policy in Chicago proactively controls and manages the use of public spaces. This includes, among other strategies, pruning trees to a certain height for increased surveillance, and enforcing complex layers of parking restrictions that benefit the formal sector while requiring expensive permits for informal, temporary occupation of public space. In contrast, architects and urban designers in Barcelona introduce a context-specific fourth vernacular[8] where the ground plane of buildings seamlessly encourages social interaction across the spectrum from semi-private space to publicly owned urban landscapes. One can argue that the freedom to actively engage in a meaningful manner in public space translates into a sense of belonging that, if real, will instill civic responsibility that cannot otherwise be forced—only enabled.

Two examples can illustrate this point. In São Paulo, we see how the ground plane functions, for the most part, as a city-wide zone of belonging. This approach to the threshold between the private and public spheres with an organic integration of *interior* and *exterior*, as well as an uninterrupted flow between the urban landscape and interior space, grew from the *Paulista School* and is still present in the contemporary urban projects of the city.[9] Brazilian architect João Batista Vilanova Artigas (1915–1985) was most notable among the "Escola Paulista" or *Paulista School* which included Rino Levi and Oswaldo Bratke—all equally influenced by the earlier modern utopian idealism of the Rio de Janeiro architects Hélio Duarte, Lúcio Costa, and the work of the brothers Roberto and

Oscar Niemeyer. Artigas designed a new building and developed a new curriculum for the architecture department at São Paulo University in 1961 with a clear message to students that the contribution of architecture to society lies in exposing society's antagonistic nature.[10] Architecture becomes the enabling framework for social expressions of belonging, appropriation, and subversion. This was vividly illustrated in a 1975 address when Michel Foucault aligned himself with students in the open ground plane of the architecture school and declared his support for the protest movement against political repression under dictatorship, arguing that society's antagonistic nature needed to be exposed. This often-quoted moment remains equally framed by both the architecture and the historical record. Yet, most projects exist outside of public discourse with each discreetly and collectively contributing to everyday urban life.

A more recent example from Barcelona presents a deliberately diffused threshold between public and private domains as in the *110 Rooms Collective Housing* project by MAIO and Illustrated in its abstract ground plane. This project, despite being commissioned by a private client, allows the streetscape to flow through the ground plane entrance, providing residents and community members a fluid threshold with mutual respect for, and understanding of, spatial arrangements in the city (Images 41.3 and 41.4).

The philosophical position described in these examples allow for the temporal, socially produced occupation of undetermined categories of public space. Moreover, it establishes fluid interfaces that co-exist as public places along with those more formalized types of public and hybrid civic spaces that are often privately and subversively appropriated through a variety of agreements.[11] This very co-existence of the *informal* and *formal* and the co-authorship of city-building processes are a fluid and collaborative project. But let us now consider the third condition referred to earlier which closes the triangulated framework that describes relationships that exist between concerns such as structure (formal/informal), agency (collaboration/belonging), and contingency (temporality) to define possible transformative conditions of *interior urbanism*.

Structure, Agency, and Contingency

It is from within this triangulated framework that the research and practice of interior architecture, interaction design, and ecological urbanism, among other emerging fields, have established an interdisciplinary credibility that enables constituent groups involved in city-building processes to bridge from the contingent to the necessary. Jeremy Till describes "architecture [as] probably the contingent discipline par excellence" when he argues for a transformative practice of contingence.[12] The triangulated framework of relationships among structure, agency, and contingency problematizes any casual proposition that defines all of urban space as potentially an interior condition. Such casual statements are akin to notions which assign conditions of interiority liberally to non-places such as airport environments, the internal network of bridges, and pedways of dense urban cores or interstitial tracts of undetermined infrastructure without a critical and more nuanced spatial ontology. Definitions of interiority can only be fully grounded when the binary construct of *interior* and *exterior* gives way to a more critical understanding of spatial relations which also include aporetic constructs such as desire and fear or beauty and pain. The very concept of interiority needs to be considered against the degree to

Image 41.3 Diagram of the Ground Plane of *22 Dwellings Housing Block*, Collective Housing at Provença Street, Barcelona. MAIO Architects Project Team: María Charneco Llanos, Anna Puigjaner Barberá, Alfredo Lérida Horta, Guillermo López Ibáñez, 2013–2016.
Credit: José Hevia for MAIO

which we are willing to allow for tolerance between our need for free spatial expression and those counter obsessions to control. With such an allowance, *Interior Urbanism* becomes an approach through which structure and agency produce an expanded sense of belonging rather than merely being established as formal typology or field of practice.

Even as we spend more and more time within one type of interior or another across many scales in varying degrees of active engagement—the risk of considering this quantitative measure alone without including notions of temporality, recurrence, belonging, gesture, reflection, or participation in our everyday lives risks producing a shallow insight into an otherwise rich and complex urban condition. To be limited to benign forms of participation in controlled interior urban environments without allowing the messy, unpredictable, and fluid spatial resourcefulness of social activity to challenge and transform entrenched typologies slowly destroys the very conditions upon which critical engagement depends. Peter Sloterdijk warns very convincingly against a pervasive atmosphere of dullness and passivity that is increasingly disenfranchising citizens and agencies from engaging in a more active and critical manner in the environments that we inhabit.

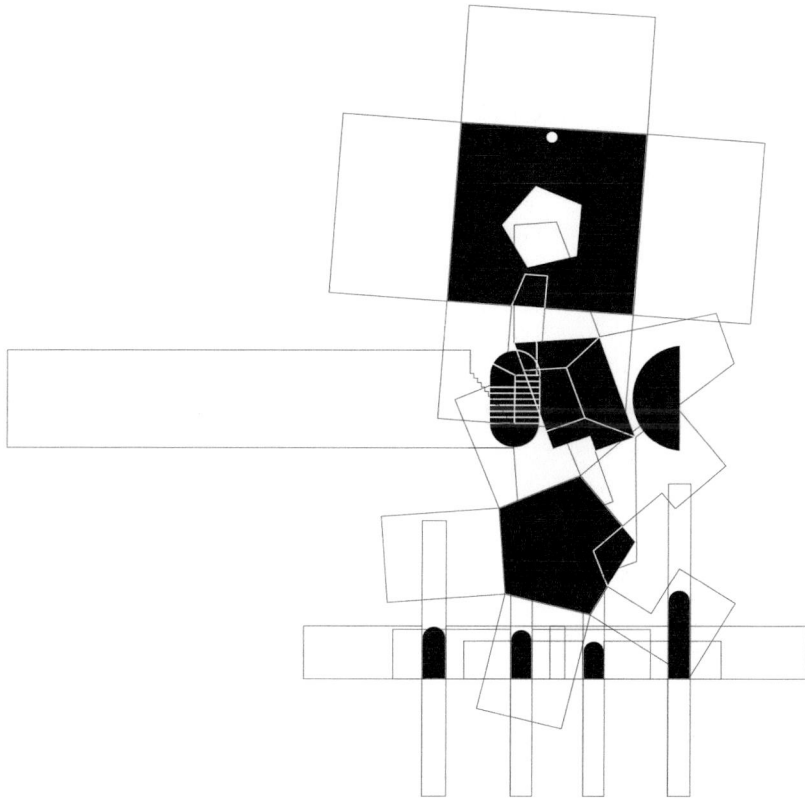

Image 41.4 Lobby of
*22 Dwellings Housing
Block*, Collective housing
at Provença Street,
Barcelona. MAIO
Architects Project Team:
María Charneco Llanos,
Anna Puigjaner Barberá,
Alfredo Lérida Horta,
Guillermo López Ibáñez,
2013–2016.
Credit: José Hevia for
MAIO

This position also framed a keynote address by Bruno Latour in which he suggests that Peter Sloterdijk "is THE philosopher of design" and particularly through his willingness to make contradictory conditions explicit through treating human and non-human conditions as "matters of grave and careful concern."[13] Accepting the entanglement of material conditions of emancipation and individual freedom with a precarious attachment to those very systems, environments, and technologies that allow emancipation in the first place is, therefore, also to accept that our urban condition is a complex, dense, and layered series of interfaces where thresholds between the archetypal notions of *outside* or *inside* are no longer easily discernible. What enables this more mature posture of reflection and criticality is then precisely the willingness to engage with the idea of disruption in various productive ways where *thinking*, *making,* and *sharing* become features of the design process and remain open-ended and relational. It is an open-ended design inquiry that not only defines, but wrestles with both the nature of constraints and the nature of opportunity.[14] It is akin to landscape designer Petra Blaisse's critical claim for a certain wildness in our urban environment through which spatial gestures and contingent practices can transform and challenge our conventions.[15] This suggests that we should encourage integrated, co-existing, and overlapping spatial thresholds that allow for a rich diversity in use, intelligently discreet and robust enough to enable radical appropriation and productive disruption.

This call for a more informed process of city-building under an expanded reach of mega-urbanization requires the revision of current language and representational modes when attempting to define concepts of *interior urbanism*. Rather than searching for a field of study, a form of practice, or an emerging urban typology, it searches for a critical and speculative approach that engages with the urban condition directly and imaginatively. It embodies a spatial ontology that is worthy of a new language and transformative modes of exploration and representation grounded in reflective and critical disruptions. It embraces a willingness to accept uncertainty, more confident in *how* to make spatial concerns visible and better equipped to translate this multiplicity of relations into a meaningful urban future.

Notes

1   Solà-Morales, Ignasi. "Terrain Vague", *Anyplace*, ed. Cynthia Davidson, Cambridge, MA: MIT Press, 1995, pp.118–123.

2   Schivelbuch, Wolfgang. *Disenchanted Night: The Industrialisation of Light in the Nineteenth Century*. Berkeley: University of California Press, 1988.

3   *Going Live, Pamphlet Architecture 35*, New York: Princeton Architectural Press, 2015, p.54. Also see; Easterling, Keller. *Extrastatecraft: The Power of Infrastructure Space*, London: Verso, 2014, p. 13.

4   Roberts, Bryony. "Looking for the Outside – How Is Architecture Political?" *The Avery Review*, no. 5, February 2015.

5   The *Catadores de Materiais* (material collectors collective) in São Paulo originated as an extralegal movement and over time claimed undetermined, vacant spaces and has since 2007 become more formalized and legally recognized. The São Paulo city government is becoming more and more proactive, and indeed, more reliant on productive collaborations between informal and formal operations in waste management, as well as the upcycling and recycling of materials.

6   Research worth mentioning at a number of highly regarded institutions—among them some with ongoing and long-term urban research outcomes. Both ETH in Zurich and the London School of Economics (LSE) are contributing valuable new insights. See, for example, *The Endless City - the Urban Age Project by the London School of Economics and Deutsche Bank's Alfred Herrhausen Society*, ed. Burdett, R. and Deyan Sudjic. London: Phaidon, 2007.

7   Sassen, Saskia. "Seeing like a City", in *The Endless City - the Urban Age Project by the London School of Economics and Deutsche Bank's Alfred Herrhausen Society*, ed. Burdett, R. and Deyan Sudjic. London: Phaidon, 2007.

8   Fisher, Roger, Schalk le Roux and Estelle Maré, eds., *Architecture of the Transvaal*. Pretoria: University of South Africa Press, 1998.

9   See *Stadarchitektur São Paulo – Ausblick auf ein Soziales Raumkonzept*, ARCH + 190, Aachen: Verlag GmbH, 2008.

10 Jovaovic Weiss, Srdjan and Sabine von Fischer. "How to Read Two Monoliths", *Cabinet,* Issue 6, Horticulture, Brooklyn, NY: Immaterial Incorporated, Spring 2006.

11 See an "Empirical Study of New York City's Privately Owned Public Spaces", *Land Use Law & Zoning Digest*, 53, 2001, pp.3–10.

12 Till, Jeremy. *Architecture Depends*, London: The MIT Press, 2013, p.61.

13 Latour, Bruno. A "Cautious Promethea? A Few Steps Toward a Philosophy of Design (with Special Attention to Peter Sloterdijk)", Keynote Lecture for the *Networks of Design* Meeting, *Design History Society*, Falmounth, Cornwall, September 3, 2008.

14 Reynders, Hennie. "Gestural Topographies - A Framework for the Practice of Reflective and Critical Disruption", Swiss Design Network (SDN), *Disruptive Interaction* International Conference, Lugano, 2012

15 Blaise, Petra. "Into the Wild", interview by Beatriz Ramo and Bernd Upmeyer for *MONU* #21 – *Interior Urbanism*, ed. Bernd Upmeyer, October 2014.

Theories and Influences

Vastness

Chapter 42

Brutalist Interior Urbanism

Visions, Paradigms, Design Strategies

Patrizio M. Martinelli

In the 1950s, younger generations of British architects developed a new approach to architectural and urban design, as a strong reaction to what has been perceived as the failures of Functionalism. "In the early and late 1940s," Peter Smithson affirmed in 1959:

> We were in a situation in England in which many things got built which you felt were a lie, and a lot of ideas have been carried on in architecture well into the 1950s, when building programs became strictly a formula.[1]

These actions responded to the design *clichés* of the International Style "kit of parts" and the impoverished dogma of "form follows function." This response, as pointed out in the article "Ornamented Modern & Brutalism: Towards two movements?" in *Zodiac* magazine, was among "one of the many ways to react against the idealism of contemporary culture: a search for reality that corresponds to an irrepressible need for truth."[2]

This approach was contextualized in a theoretical framework by Reyner Banham in his seminal 1955 essay, "The New Brutalism."[3] The British historian uses the Hunstanton School in Norfolk ("the first true Brutalist building"[4]), designed by Alison and Peter Smithson, to define this new architectural movement: clear legibility of plan, emphasis on honest exhibition of structure, technical elements, and services (such as water pipes, electrical components, and conduits), and an uncompromising expression of materials to show their character and quality "as found."

Furthermore, the school plan (whose clarity is derived by Miesian[5] and Palladian—via Wittkower—influences[6]) demonstrates Palladio's and Alberti's idea of the "house as a small city." It is organized around a large,

DOI: 10.4324/9780429443091-51

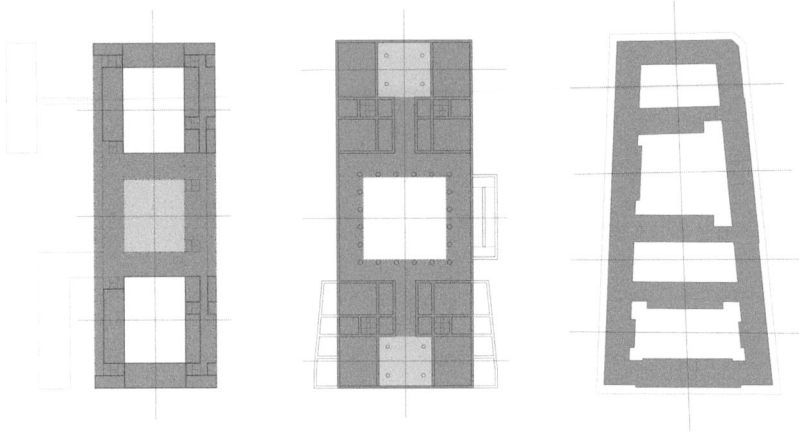

Image 42.1 Architectural and urban analogies: axial systems of open and covered courtyards
From left: Alison and Peter Smithson, Hunstanton School in Norfolk; Andrea Palladio, Palazzo Iseppo Porto in Vicenza; Fuchsenfeldhof urban block in Vienna.
Credit: Patrizio Martinelli

multi-purpose, double-height hall defined by a peristyle, and flanked by two light-courts. It resembles an urban block with courtyards and a covered *piazza* surrounded by porticoes. A "vertical volume rising from a small service courtyard, (…) reminiscent of a clock tower" which "is in fact a raised water tank towering over the roofs of the building"[7] adds another element that gives the overall composition an urban and civic aura. Somehow, the Hunstanton courtyard is a square, the hallways are streets, the classrooms are dwellings—this "house (for learning)" is a city in miniature (Image 42.1).

Construction and Scale: Toward a Brutalist Topological Interior

While the Hunstanton School is still strictly related to the Renaissance principles codified by Wittkower, the way it is represented through photographs (by Nigel Henderson, a friend and collaborator of the Smithsons) in a prominent 1954 *Architectural Review* article defines a shift as the building relates to Brutalism. Here, as Anthony Vidler observed, the "seven views taken as if on a walk around the building, had already transformed this otherwise symmetrical object into a quasi-picturesque experience."[8] Even more relevant are the other 15 photographs of the interiors. This set of images, arranged on the pages as a collage-like composition, represents a journey inside the building in which the axiality of the spaces disappears, almost replicating the spatial experience, as well as the dynamic movements of the eye and the body within the space. As Michael Pearson argues, in his analysis of the characteristics of Brutalism:

> As one moves about in an environment, one receives a visual image of the experience, perhaps mentally appreciating topological, rather than metric properties—in the same way that a child considers qualities of closure, proximity, separation, and continuity before straight lines, angles, parallels, and regular forms.[9]

The concept of topology is another key aspect of those Brutalist buildings that abandon the symmetry and predominance of Euclidean geometry of buildings like the Hunstanton School or Kahn's Yale Art Center. In Brutalist architecture, the "master discipline" of Platonic geometry is subordinate to the dominant role of topology and its qualities of "penetration, circulation, inside and out."[10] Architectural composition is now interested in a "ruthless honesty in expressing the functional spaces and their inter-relationships," while spatial arrangements are "based on the topography of the site and the topology of internal circulation."[11]

These connections between building and urbanism (the Palladio/ Alberti "house as a small city" and the topological/experiential design strategies, even from the interior) become opportunities to move to more monumental and complex architectures.

This change of scale, in my opinion, is a clear declaration of poetics in Brutalist architectural discourse based on two fundamental aspects. The first relates to the ways in which this architecture is built, in a conceptual way and in the built realm. The second aspect is linked to an idea of urban monumentality, not only in typological/morphological terms, but particularly in topological, sociological, and anthropological terms.

Regarding the first aspect, Peter Smithson is very transparent when he compares the Modern Movement's fascination with machine aesthetics to the genuine "brutal approach" that arises in building construction. "If a thing is really made of pre-cast elements, or concrete blocks, the building has to reflect the way it was built with pre-cast elements or concrete blocks." He continues:

> Inevitably the building will not only have a different scale from an architecture that is conceived as being a single object made by a machine, but *it will be built at the scale of the genuine machine with which it was built.*[12]

We can read here the need for truth that is one of the main characteristics of Brutalism, linked to the honesty of expression in building technologies and the use of raw materials: steel and bricks, but mainly concrete.

Concrete means Le Corbusier, and the use of *béton brut* ("raw concrete") in his late 1940s buildings, in particular the Unité d'Habitation in Marseille, which became the main reference in the development of the Brutalist language. First, the Unité reflects the idea of the building as a "machine for living in" but also as big as the machine that built it. Made of *béton brut*, it has the scale of a cement factory, monumental as the temples of Magna Grecia and Michelangelo's Basilica of St. Peter in Rome: "the concrete work at Marseille started as a magnificent ruin even before the building was completed."[13] The Unité is, quoting Vincent Scully, a "muscular giant, a temple, an aircraft carrier, (…) a medieval city, a dirigible's hangar,"[14] that represents the different scale of Brutalist architecture. Finally, the Unité represents the collective character of a "building as city" that conveys urban themes and design strategies in its composition, spatial arrangements, and interiors, at a monumental scale.

As previously mentioned, the Brutalist movement arose as a reaction to the cultural context that architecture existed within during the late 1940s. The CIAM after World War II, thanks to the British delegation, showed the urge to move mainly toward collective and sociological aspects. This need was fully expressed in the 1951 CIAM, where the British MARS group presented a grid that reflected an urban approach and ascending scale of community: "village," "neighborhood," "city sector," "city," and "metropolis."

Following this path, the Smithsons, for CIAM 9 (1953), prepared the so-called "Urban Re-Identification" grid that expressed the need for new architectural forms, in particular for the house,

> Which is capable of being put together with others (...) so as to form bigger and equally comprehensible elements which can be added to existing villages and towns in such a way as to revitalize the traditional hierarchies and not destroy them.[15]

These concepts and the CIAM 9 grid intended to codify a hierarchy of collective urban artifacts that represented "a connection between physical elements of the city and human behavior"[16] as expressed by a series of photographs by Henderson, included by the Smithsons in the visual representation of the grid, depicting children playing in the streets.

This is how we can interpret Brutalism: a civic and humanistic architecture where the overlapping of the needs of the domestic environment with urban collective character (so that the building and its interiors are designed according to "the topography of the site and the topology of internal circulation")[17] is realized with the honest use of materiality, structures, technologies, and through a change of scale—a topological and urban approach, even (or most of all) in their interiors.

Houses *and/as* Cities: Brutalist Urban Interiors

This interaction between architecture and urban planning strategies, clearly declared in the CIAM 9 documents, is evident in the most iconic Brutalist projects of the 1950s and 1960s. With their progressive increase in the scale of intervention, and an aim to "resolve polarities, individual-collective, permanence-change, physical-spiritual, inside-outside, part-whole, which we no longer believe to exist,"[18] we can decipher them clearly through the lens of interior urbanism.

For the Smithson's projects for Golden Lane Housing competition entry of 1952, for Sheffield University (1953), and for the late 1960s Robin Hood Gardens Complex, the circulation system defines the overall composition, based on a topology-predominant approach, where "streets in the sky," gangways, bridges, and decks are urban components that belong to the architectural experience of the building, blurring the boundaries between public and private, domestic and urban (Image 42.2).

This idea of the building as a microcosm that replicates topological connections is the essence of an urban experience, recognizable in many Brutalist projects. It is particularly evident in a series of projects where building and city are blurred into one another through a dramatic change of scale. Again, the Smithsons are a point of reference: their project for the competition for Haupstadt Berlin (1957–1958) employs a multilevel platform made of nets of pedestrian paths and connections overlapped onto the existing street grid. Here, the new and the old cities connect emphasizing the complexity of these urban interiors—as multistory, open-air courtyards overlooking the streets below. These ideas were realized in London throughout the 1960s in projects that attempted to build the Brutalist city, such as the South Bank area or the Barbican Center.

Image 42.2 The "street in the sky," by Alison and Peter Smithson, Robin Hood Gardens, London. Credit: Steve Cadman, Creative Commons Attribution-Sharealike v2.0. Post-production by Patrizio Martinelli

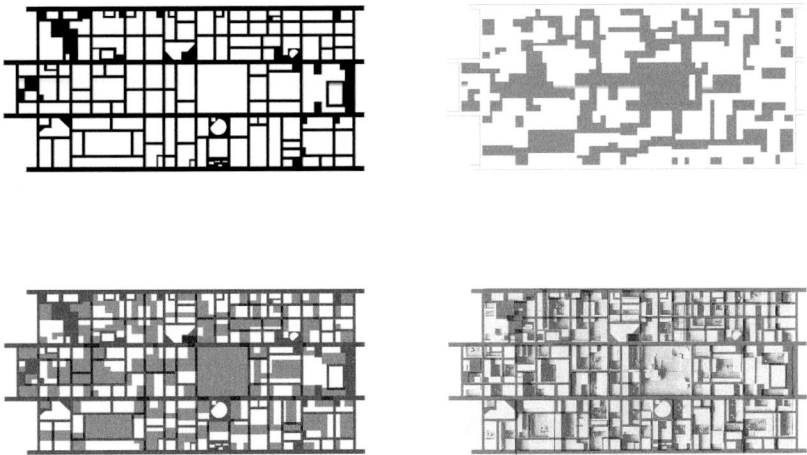

Image 42.3 The re-invention of the urban fabric inside the building George Candilis, Alexis Josic, Shadrach Woods, Free University in Berlin From top left: pedestrian pathways, open spaces; from bottom left: overlapping of pathways and open spaces, overlapping of pathways and volumes. Credit: Patrizio Martinelli

Both projects are fragment examples of a sublime "multi-layered metropolis, with its labyrinthine spaces, underworld and dark surfaces."[19]

The premise set by the 1950s projects also inspired the megastructural "conflation of city and building as infrastructural, spatial, and functional armature,"[20] which Banham himself looked at with interest.[21] The 1963 competition entry for the Frankfurt Römemberg district, designed by Candilis, Josic, and Woods, is a multi-layered, thick, inhabited platform where monumental courtyards connect the existing urban fabric with the new building. A similar approach is recognizable in their project for the Free University in Berlin (1962–1964) (Image 42.3).

The building is conceived as an ideal city organized as a large-scale, horizontal, and high-density grid structure. Its connections recreate—within the interior—the arrangement and urban experience of streets, enclosed public spaces, and open courtyards, envisioning what the contemporary city is, as Italian architect Andrea Branzi describes it: the city as a continuous interior, where streets, squares, and public spaces are part of an interconnected system of urban spaces.[22]

But for me, the most iconic paradigm to express the concept of interior urbanism in relation to Brutalism is the project for the Venice Hospital, designed by Le Corbusier between 1964 and 1965.[23] As reported by Italian art historian Giuseppe Mazzariol, Le Corbusier was invited to Venice in 1963 to discuss the project for a new hospital for the city and, during the meeting, he said that the only condition to build in Venice was if he was able to find the correct scale for the intervention. Again, the theme of scale is essential. For Le Corbusier, scale refers not to the architectural scale of the building, but to the urban scale of the "building as city." The compositional strategy is very similar to the examples previously mentioned, the so-called "mat-buildings" designed by the members of Team X. It also closely aligns with the project for the hospital presented by a group of Italian architects in the 1963 competition organized before inviting Le Corbusier.[24]

The Swiss master developed his project as a huge platform on stilts—a clear reference to the way that the city is built—and as an extension on the water of the San Giobbe area, the western part of Venice which faces the mainland. The platform is organized in a series of pinwheel modules, with a central open space and four hallways on which the rooms and services open. Mazzariol explains this composition in a clear, succinct way:

> Le Corbusier was asked why, looking at the plans of the buildings, they were interchangeable with many parts of the urban fabric. He responded that what he did was to simply seamlessly transfer in the interior of the Hospital the interweaving of arteries and veins of the whole urban organism, and this would have brought solutions appropriate to Venice.[25]

In fact, the pinwheel configuration is a modern transfiguration of the historical Venetian urban fabric, made of *calli*, narrow pedestrian streets, connected to *campielli* and *campi*, small and large squares. This emphasis on the circulation system is, on the one hand, a correct interpretation of the character of the city. On the other hand, it is strongly related to the Brutalist interest in using the topological approach in architectural and urban composition. Although the dimension of the building is monumental, indeed a megastructure, the design takes careful consideration of the human scale and the architectural characteristics—compression-release, open-close, light-shadow—typical of the urban experience in Venice (Image 42.4).

As emphasized by Mahnaz Shah, Le Corbusier "tried to create an urban environment for the common man," replicating how "the Venetian building adapted to its immediate urban structure—with the presence of semi-public, semi-private spaces that are typically Venetian, i.e. the courtyards and small gardens."[26] Completely built with reinforced concrete, the building is an

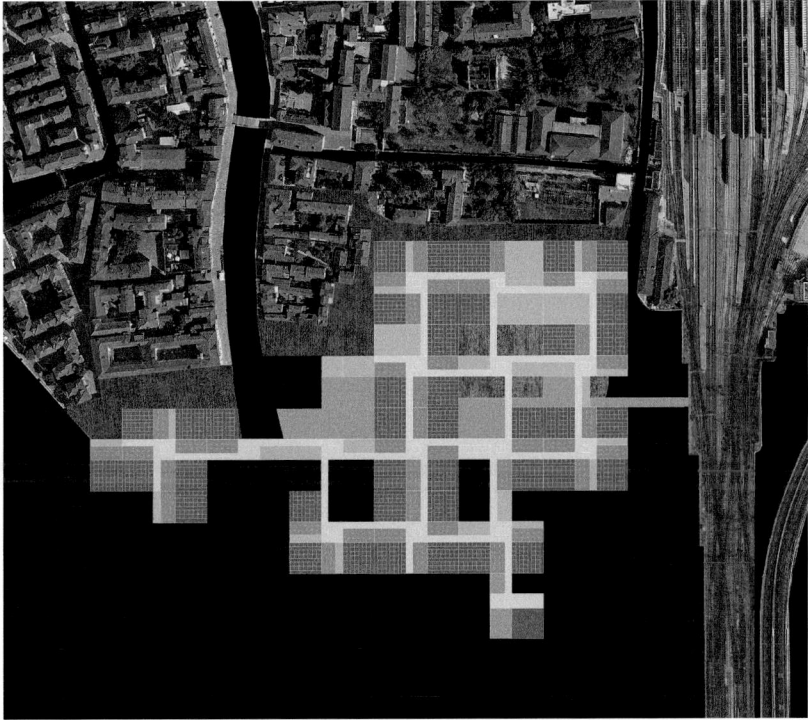

Image 42.4 The re-invention of the urban fabric inside the building. Le Corbusier, Hospital in Venice.
Credit: Patrizio Martinelli

introverted structure that re-invented Venice. This civic building, unfortunately unbuilt, was designed to be a "machine for healing," to serve the community, and would have represented another phase in the history of Venice. After the "city of wood," depicted by the bird's-eye view drawn by Jacopo de' Barbari in 1500, and the "city of stone," built by Sansovino and Palladio, the hospital would have transformed Venice into the "city of concrete," and thus, a perfect example of Brutalist interior urbanism.

Notes

1 Peter Smithson, Alison Smithson, Jane B. Drew, E. Maxwell Fry, "Conversation on Brutalism," *Zodiac,* no. 4 (1959): 76.

2 Ibidem, 68. Translation from Italian by the author.

3 Reyner Banham, "The New Brutalism," *The Architectural Review*, December (1955).

4 Reyner Banham, "Brutalism," in *Encyclopedia of Modern Architecture*, ed. Wolfgang Pehnt (New York: Harry N. Abrams Publishers, 1964), 62.

5 Philip Johnson, "Review: Comment on School of Hunstanton, Norfolk," *The Architectural Review*, September (1954).

6 "However, the symmetry of the plan and of the elevation pattern, should not be seen as major architectural objectives of the design, however full of the architects' minds may have been of Wittkowerian or Palladian ideas." Rayner Banham, *The New Brutalism* (London: Architectural Press, 1966), 19.

7 Christopher Grafe, "Finite Orders and the Art of Everyday Inhabitation," in *Alison & Peter Smithson: A Critical Anthology*, ed. Max Risselada (Barcelona: Ediciones Polígrafa, 2011).

8 Anthony Vidler, "Another Brick in the Wall," *OCTOBER. New Brutalism*, no. 136 (2011): 122.

9 Michael Pearson, "Editorial," *244: Journal of the University of Manchester Architecture and Planning* Society, no. 7, Winter (1956–1957): 2.

10   Banham, "The New Brutalism," 361.

11   Banham, "Brutalism," 62.

12   *Zodiac*, 73. The emphasis is in the original article.

13   Banham, *The New Brutalism*, 16.

14   Vincent Scully, "Le Corbusier 1922–1965," in *Vincent Scully: Modern Architecture and Other Essays*, ed. Neil Levine (Princeton, NJ: Princeton University Press, 2003), 246.

15   *Zodiac*, 44.

16   Simon Henley, *Redefining Brutalism* (Newcastle upon Tyne: RIBA Publishing, 2017), 127.

17   Banham, "Brutalism," 62.

18   Alison and Peter Smithson, "Draft Framework 1956," in *Team 10 in search of a Utopia of the Present*, ed. Max Risselada and Dirk van den Heuvel (Rotterdam: NAI, 2005), 49.

19   Henley, *Redefining Brutalism*, 138.

20   Henley, 138.

21   Reyner Banham, *Megastructure: Urban Futures of the Recent Past* (London: Thames and Hudson, 1976).

22   Andrea Branzi, "Interni." Accessed October 18, 2020. https://www.treccani.it/enciclopedia/interni_%28XXI-Secolo%29/

23   A comprehensive investigation on this project is in Mahnaz Shah, *Le Corbusier's Venice Hospital Project: An Investigation into its Structural Formulation* (Farnham: Ashgate Publishing Company, 2013).

24   The group was formed by Romano Chirivi, Costantino Dardi, Emilio Mattioni, Valeriano Pastor, and Luciano Semerani. See Francesco Tentori, *Imparare da Venezia. Il Ruolo Futuribile di Alcuni Progetti Architettonici Veneziani dei Primi anni '60* (Roma: Officina, 1994).

25   Giuseppe Mazzariol, "Tre progetti per Venezia rifiutati: Wright, Le Corbusier, Kahn," in *Le Venezie possibili: da Palladio a Le Corbusier*, ed. Lionello Puppi and Giandomenico Romanelli (Milano: Electa, 1985), 271.

26   Shah, *Le Corbusier's Venice Hospital Project*, 149.

Chapter 43

A Paradoxical Imago Mundi

The No-Stop City by Archizoom Associati

Pablo Martínez Capdevila

The *No-Stop City* (1969–1971) by Archizoom Associati was born from a simple, and yet radical, idea: to create an interior and potentially endless city by spreading artificial lighting and air-conditioning to all urban activities. From the moment of its publication, the project has been analyzed from very different perspectives. This text focuses on what makes it a polysemic work that allows diverse and contrasting interpretations: its striking contradictory or, at least, paradoxical character.

Paradoxical Critique

The first problematic feature of the *No-Stop City* is its very nature since Archizoom resolutely denied that it was what it seemed to be: a proposal for an alternative or future city. To understand this, we must bear in mind that it was an explicitly political project,[1] in line with the group's Marxist ideology. In those years, a number of influential Italian Marxist intellectuals had issued a sort of "anathema against utopias," a stark rejection of visionary proposals[2] that was clearly stated in Manfredo Tafuri's 1969 article "Toward a Critique of Architectural Ideology": "... first among the intellectual illusions to be dispelled is that which strives to anticipate, through mere imagery, the conditions of an architecture 'for a liberated society'."[3] Tafuri condemned any prefiguration of alternative models and called, instead, for a critique of the existing architecture and city, that is to say, the capitalist ones. The No-Stop City was, to a great extent, an architectural rendering of Tafuri's postulates, a means to carry forward that very critique.[4] The group also referred to Mario Tronti and Nicola Licciardello, who similarly condemned any nostalgic or visionary stance; the Marxists' duty was to analyze and criticize the objective and present conditions.

This ideological pressure was key and explains Archizoom's emphatic rejection of utopianism and their intention to address reality and present

DOI: 10.4324/9780429443091-52

conditions. Thus, in the first publication of the No-Stop City in 1970, they stated that it was only a "theory," and not an "alternative proposition." While they acknowledged that its illustrations and architectural language could lead to a utopia, they proclaimed, "... the Utopia we use is solely instrumental: it represents itself, but not as a prefiguration of a different Model of the System [...] but as a critical Hypothesis related to the system itself."[5] In 1971, they insisted on the same idea: "This urban Model does not, however, represent the alternative to present-day reality; rather, it represents present-day reality at a new level of critical Consciousness."[6]

In line with Tafuri, and following the Marxist classic division of society between an economic base and ideological superstructures, Archizoom situated architecture in the latter category, that is, as a mystifying layer aimed at supporting and legitimizing the base, and hence, the system. The No-Stop City aimed at revealing what lay behind the formal structures of an allegedly "natural" and inevitable, bourgeois city: a system which organized itself through the plan according to the factory model in which the "'proletarization' of the entire Social System"[7] had taken place. However, Archizoom did not only intend to reveal an oppressive and alienating system that had maximized its ultimate contradiction: the proletariat. By envisioning a city free of architecture, they proposed an environment that was fully coherent with the logics of capital: "The city no longer 'represents' the system, but becomes the system itself, programmed and isotropic."[8] An interior, continuous, and homogeneous city that, unlike the inefficient and discontinuous bourgeois city, would accelerate the production-consumption cycle "... making the Brain of the System mad,"[9] pushing it to a breaking point (Image 43.1).

The project was, therefore, a sort of allegorical denunciation of a state of maximum capitalist integration that had already been achieved, a demystification of a hidden, but existing, "City of Capital." At the same time, it was a sublimated representation of a more efficient urban model which would push capitalism to plenitude, exasperation, and collapse: "Much like Freudian therapy, No-Stop City served as both diagnosis and cure."[10] Ultimately, it was an ambiguous proposal because it sought to improve and optimize the very system it wanted to subvert. The No-Stop City was both an ideal representation of a perfect capitalist metropolis and the precondition for a future socialist metropolis, the envisioning of which had been precluded by Tafuri and others.

Paradoxical Plenitude

Such ambiguity permeates the texts of the proposal: at times, they seem to describe an alienating and undesirable state of affairs that must be overthrown at all costs, while at other times, they describe a scenario of maximum capitalist development as something liberating and desirable *per se*, without needing to wait for the subsequent collapse of capitalism. The graphic depictions are equally ambiguous: on the one hand, its repetitive and dull interior environments seem anguishing and somehow reflect the inherent claustrophobia of a total system lacking any alternatives, any outside. On the other hand, however, many of the images of how the city would be colonized and inhabited reflect a hedonistic, joyful, and libertarian way of life that looks much closer to that of

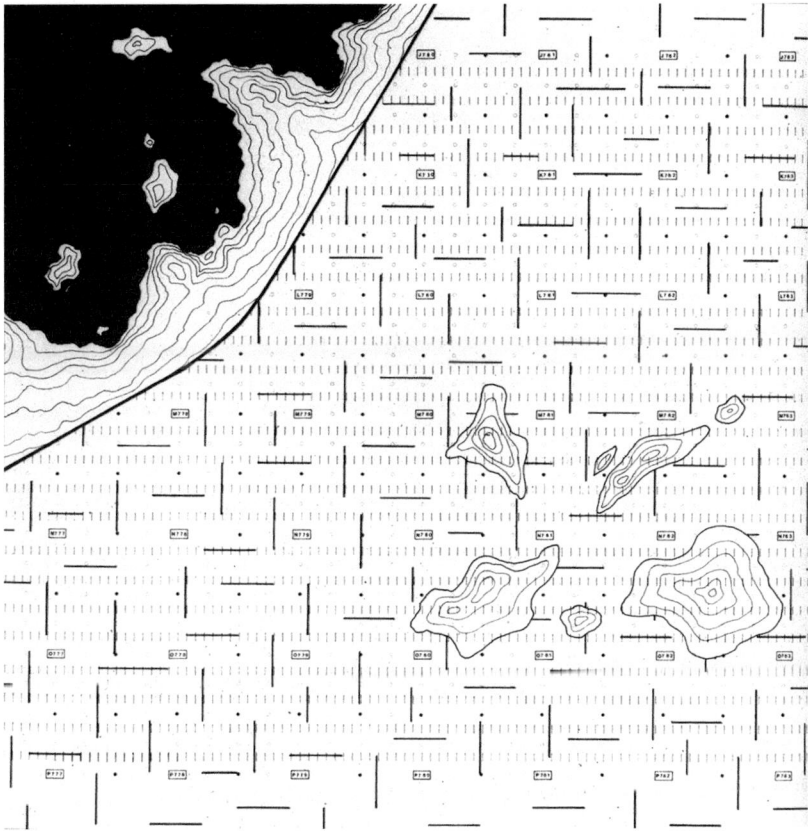

Image 43.1 Archizoom Associati: *Diagramma abitativo omogeneo* (Homogeneous dwelling diagram)
First published in *Casabella*, 1970.
Credit: Studio Andrea Branzi

hippie communes, or to the *Homo Ludens* that inspired Constant´s *New Babylon*, than to the classical representations of exploited or alienated proletarians. Therefore, and despite the group's obvious efforts to dispel any appearance of utopianism, it is not at all clear whether the No-Stop City was a denunciation of capitalist oppression or a celebration of a liberating and extended consumerism, a critique, or an apologia (Image 43.2).

This contradictory character is hardly surprising for it has deep roots in Marxism itself. In fact, the idea that a socialist revolution would only be possible after capitalism had reached its maximum development and extended globally was already raised by Marx in his *Grundrisse*. This notion, as Fredric Jameson points out, is paradoxical: "In that case, the chances for socialism are relegated into some far future, while the ominous nature of the current 'total system' becomes rather positive again, since it marks precisely the quantum progression toward that final global state."[11] In the case of the No-Stop City, its intention to be a sort of aberration-free mirror of capitalist society in a state of maximum integration ended up amplifying Marxism's original ambiguities toward capitalism, instead of blurring them. Ultimately, it may be hard to blame Archizoom for the paradoxical nature of their interior city. If revolution required a previous stage of capitalist plenitude, what is such a state? A utopia or a dystopia?

Image **43.2** Archizoom Associati: *No-stop city, residential park* First published in *Design Quarterly*, 1970. Credit: Studio Andrea Branzi

Paradoxical Dissolution

The "elimination" of architecture that took place in the project was also paradoxical because it was not due to an "absence" of architecture, but rather, to an "excess" of it. The unlimited and homogeneous expansion of architecture inevitably implied the dissolution of a canonical architectural object that has been traditionally defined by its finitude and heterogeneity. As the building grew deep, it lost its functional specialization, hierarchy, compositional character, outer shape, and envelope as well as their inherent representative and iconographic roles. In short, the building ceased to be a finished, stable, and convex object to become a potentially endless and concave background.

In that sense, the project can be read as a direct application of one of Engels's three laws of dialectical materialism, the passage of quantitative changes into qualitative changes—by means of an increase of the depth of the building, a strictly quantitative change, a series of qualitative transformations, that radically undermined architecture, were triggered. In 1972, Archizoom's member Andrea Branzi described the No-Stop City as the outcome of a quantitative operation analogous to other modern revolutions:

> The greatest inventions of Modern Architecture have been 'quantitative inventions': the Skyscraper and the Housing Unit [...] The skyscraper has four facades only because it is located on a small plot of land: potentially, the dimension it has reached vertically could also be developed in the other four directions.[12]

If said horizontal expansion of the skyscraper took place, the outcome would be, precisely, the No-Stop City. The project arose from the acknowledgment that frame structures, elevators, artificial lighting, and air-conditioning had freed buildings from their outside, allowing them to reach unlimited extensions for the first time in history. From a strictly constructive point of view, the proposal could not be simpler and, at the same time, more radical: it arose from spreading that technification of the environment *ad absurdum*, giving shape to an interior, and potentially endless, city encompassing the entire human habitat.

In the No-Stop City, thus, architecture's disappearance was not only due to its understanding as an ideological superstructure but was also presented as the final outcome of the same industrial rationality that had promoted its development, as the logical consequence of the full unfolding of its technical potential. An idea clearly stated in its first publication: "The ultimate goal of modern Architecture is the 'elimination' of architecture itself."[13]

Archizoom, hence, established a subtle parallelism between capitalism and architecture, not only by inextricably linking their crisis and disappearance, but also because both "eliminations" were equated by being presented as the inevitable result of the maximization of their respective internal logics, of pushing them to a state of (fatal) completion. And both were paradoxical for the same reason: because they were not the outcome of a "lack" but, rather, of an "excess" of capitalism and architecture. A shocking dissolution by hypertrophy or climax that would not be triggered by their failure, but by their very success.[14]

Paradoxical Realism

We have seen how the project arose from an explicitly realistic agenda, aligned with the appeal of sectors of Italian Marxism to focus on the analysis of contemporary conditions. This stance was at the base of a fundamental, and often unnoticed, difference with the work of other neo-avant-garde groups of the 1960s and 1970s. The No-Stop City, unlike many proposals by Archigram, Haus-Rucker-Co, Superstudio, or 9999, did not display any alternative, visionary, or science fiction technology. On the contrary, it showed an absolute technical realism by only deploying proven technology that had been available for years and was commonly used in offices or supermarkets. A feature that did not go unnoticed to Charles Jencks: "Archizoom freezes a certain stage of development and re-arranges the results in a radical way. All the elevators and spiral staircases are normal and standardised, without a history."[15]

In terms of its mere construction then, and despite its shocking appearance, the project invented nothing new, it just deployed the constructive systems associated with the *Bürolandschaft* according to their specifications. A radically realistic approach that was conscious and deliberate: "The resulting building is a first and elementary application of the current technological level of facts such as the elevator, air-conditioning, and electric lighting applied on an urban level."[16] This intention is particularly clear in the ordinary, anonymous, and neutral built environment shown in the interior dioramas which is identical to any generic landscape office, except for its endlessness.

More importantly, the group extended their will to represent "present-day reality"[17] beyond the air-conditioned container, to encompass its content. In fact, the objects that colonize and program these interior scenes (such as tents, kitchens, food cans, Ritz crackers, or a Norton Manx motorbike) are real and familiar (Image 43.3).[18] The same can be said about the fragments of nature (bushes, rock formations, rivers, etc.) that occasionally appeared in the plans, keeping their natural look. Surprisingly, then, and despite the

Image 43.3 Archizoom Associati. *No-stop city, paesaggi interni* (Interior landscapes) First published in *Domus*, 1971. Credit: Studio Andrea Branzi

ground-breaking and innovative appearance of these interior landscapes, none of the ingredients of the No-Stop City are, in themselves, either imaginary or radically new. Imagination and novelty lie in their "quantity" (the hypertrophy of architecture, the proliferation of objects) and in a subversive syntax by which these elements are rearranged, ignoring the established limits between public and private, artificial and natural, interior and exterior, production and consumption, working, leisure, or dwelling. Everything happens to merge into a sort of fluid *continuum* that ignores architecture's primal and established role of demarcation, mediation, and arbitration between different spheres.

The No-Stop City, therefore, radically reconfigured reality to produce an unreal and implausible setting: as happens in surrealist "exquisite corpses" or situationist *détournements*, the spectator's familiarity with recognizable elements is exploited to enhance the surprise ensuing from the bizarre way of combining them. The result is an unusual, ambiguous, and disconcerting scenario that appears, at the same time, familiar and alien, realistic and fantastic, ordinary and eccentric, amusing and disturbing.

We can therefore speak of a paradoxical realism that kept its gaze focused on reality and the present while using them to shape an unreal situation. A situation that was not fully devoid of a certain visionary dimension, since it suggested that the conditions for a radical transformation of the habitat already existed, which is to say, that the future was already there.

Paradoxical Categories

In most images of the project, the house, as an enclosed environment and the space of maximum privacy, had disappeared altogether to be replaced by a constellation of scattered furniture and equipment (beds, tents, toilets, kitchens)

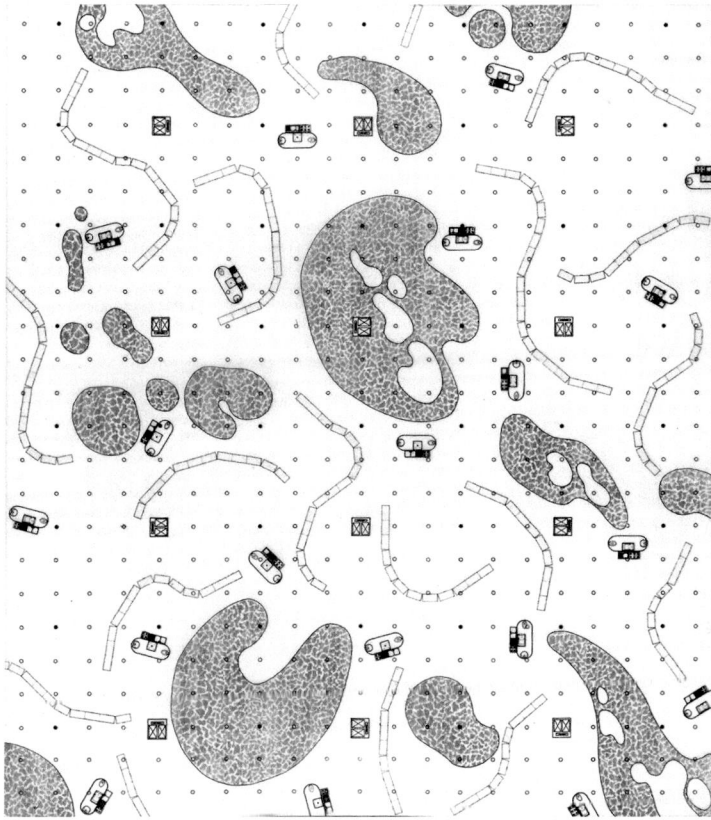

Image 43.4 Archizoom Associati: *No-stop city, residential wood* First published in *Design Quarterly*, 1970. Credit: Studio Andrea Branzi

that would allow to dwell in any point of the city. It seems as if the "interiorization" of public space posed in the project inevitably led to the disappearance of the traditional interior space, the domestic one. But this turned out to be, again, a problematic transformation: precisely because the home had dissolved into the public space, it could also be argued that what had happened was not that it had disappeared altogether, but rather, that the city itself had been "domesticated" in the original sense of the word, becoming a kind of expanded and diffuse home (Image 43.4).

This, together with the "neo-primitive" looking inhabitants and the explicit references to Marshall McLuhan's "Global Village,"[19] suggested a nomadic existence that is, by definition, anti-urban. Hence, the relentless urbanization of the whole territory brought about, paradoxically, the elimination of enclosed housing and a sedentary lifestyle, which are the preconditions for the existence of cities as we know them.

Archizoom's intent to eliminate architecture ended up producing a further and more generalized dissolution of the whole human habitat, from the domestic to the territorial scale. A process that produced paradoxical outcomes because it transcended the essential categories through which we structure and comprehend the environment: in the same way that architecture's hypertrophy meant that, at the same time, everything is architecture and nothing is architecture, it could also be argued that everything is a house and nothing is a house, and, even, that everything is a city and nothing is a city.

Paradoxical Urban Condition

Furthermore, and beyond the generalized crisis of these categories, the project reflected a profound change in the very understanding of the urban fact:

> But now the use of electronic media takes the place of the direct urban praxis […] The metropolis ceases to be a 'place' to become a 'condition': in fact, it is just this condition, which is made to circulate uniformly, through Consumer Products, in the social phenomenon. The future dimension of the metropolis coincides with that of the Market itself. [20]

Archizoom foresaw, in line with McLuhan, a city dissolved by communication and by a capitalism that had occupied the whole territory and colonized all spheres of life. However, their idea of a new virtually omnipresent and immaterial urban condition (hence, detached from its physical medium), clearly contradicts most of the remaining textual and graphic descriptions of a city born, precisely, from the hypertrophy of that very physical medium already considered surpassed and unnecessary. A city so extensively built as to encompass all the urban activities internally. It seems as if, despite their ground-breaking intuitions, for Archizoom the city was still unthinkable without its material dimension and physical manifestation. The project thus anticipated the impact of the electronic revolution, as well as a post-Fordist regime strained between the ever-growing excess of material production and the growing dematerialization and deterritorialization of our experience.

Mirrored Contradictions?

These are some of the ambiguities and paradoxes of the No-Stop City.[21] As I have argued elsewhere,[22] even if Andrea Branzi's later urban proposals, such as *Agronica* (1995) or the *Masterplan for Eindhoven* (2000), look undoubtedly different, they could be read as updates of the No-Stop City effectively aimed at solving some of these contradictions. Nevertheless, it is my view that its paradoxes, far from being an accident or a weakness, are an essential and integral component of this unusual project and that, actually, a large part of its originality, relevance, and cultural depth lies on them.

Ultimately, through their intent to create a demystified depiction of a system that they perceived to be totalizing, Archizoom created a sort of *imago mundi* in the shocking form of a concave environment encompassing all human experience: an allegorical and sublimated representation of an outside that, conceptually at least, had ceased to exist. By doing that, No-Stop City not only mirrored the contradictions of the world it stood for but, in fact, maximized them by obliterating the interior-exterior divide, the boundaries between different spheres, and the categories that had previously hid, tempered, or neutralized them.

The No-Stop City not only pushed the logics of Capital and Modern Architecture to extreme and absurd consequences, it also maximized Marxists contradictions in relation to capitalism, portrayed a world folded upon itself by a total system that had nullified geographic distances and territorial categories, and, to some extent, anticipated the schizoid nature of the emerging post-Fordist regime. A paradoxical *imago mundi* of the world Archizoom lived in and, perhaps, of the one to come.

Notes

1   For the political dimension of the project, see Kazys Varnelis, "Programming After Program: Archizo-om's No-Stop City" *Praxis: Journal of Writing and Building* 8 (2006): 82–91; Roberto Gargiani, *Archizoom Associati 1966-1974: Dall'onda pop alla superficie neutra.* Milan: Electa, 2007; Felicity D. Scott, *Architecture or Techno-Utopia: Politics after Modernism.* Cambridge, MA: The MIT Press, 2007; Pier Vittorio Aureli, "Manfredo Tafuri, Archizoom, Superstudio and the Critique of Architectural Ideology." In *Architecture and Capitalism: 1845 to the Present*, edited by Peggy Deamer, 132–147. London; New York: Routledge, 2014 and Pier Vittorio Aureli, *The Project of Autonomy: Politics and Poetics Within and Against Capitalism.* New York: Princeton Architectural Press, 2008.

2   For a detailed account of Marxist intransigence against utopias and Tafuri's key influence, see, especially, Gargiani, *Archizoom Associati 1966–1974.*

3   Manfredo Tafuri, "Toward a Critique of Architectural Ideology." In *Architecture Theory since 1968*, edited by K. Michael Hays, 6–35. Cambridge, MA: The MIT Press, 1998. (Originally published in *Contropiano* 1, Jan./Apr. 1969), p. 32.

4   For Archizoom's will to give a formal expression to Tafuri's critique of architectural ideology, see Aureli, "Manfredo Tafuri, Archizoom, Superstudio", p. 134.

5   Archizoom Associati. "City, Assembly Line of Social Issues: Ideology and Theory of the Metrop-olis." In *No-Stop City: Archizoom Associati*, edited by Andrea Branzi, 156–174. Orleans: Editions HYX, 2006 (Originally published in *Casabella* 350/51, July/Aug. 1970), p. 157.

6   Archizoom Associati. "Utopia of Quality, Utopia of Quantity." In *No-Stop City: Archizoom Asso-ciati*, edited by Andrea Branzi, 156–174. Orleans: Editions HYX, 2006. (Originally published in *IN. Argomenti e immagini di design* 1, Jan./Feb. 1971), p. 182.

7   Archizoom, "City, Assembly Line," p. 160.

8   Archizoom Associati. "No-Stop City: Residential Parkings, Climatic Universal System." *Domus* 496, (Mar. 1971): 49–54, 55.

9   Archizoom, "City, Assembly Line," p. 157.

10   Varnelis, "Programming After Program," p. 89.

11   Fredric. Jameson, "Architecture and the Critique of Ideology." In *Architecture Theory since 1968*, edited by K. Michael Hays, 442–461. Cambridge, MA: The MIT Press, 1998. (Originally published in 1985), p. 89.

12   Andrea Branzi, "La Gioconda Sbarbata: Il Ruolo dell'Avanguardia." *Casabella* 363 (Mar. 1972): 27–31, p. 33 (my translation).

13   Archizoom, "City, Assembly Line," p. 170.

14   See: Pablo. Martínez Capdevila, "Disoluciones de la arquitectura en Archizoom y Andrea Branzi." In *Comunidad, común, comuna*, edited by Fernando Quesada, 222–245. Madrid: Ediciones Asimétricas, 2015.

15   Charles Jencks, "The Supersensualists II." *Architectural Design* 43 (Jan. 1972): 18–21, 19.

16   Archizoom Associati: "Progetto di Concorso per l'Università di Firenze." Domus 509, (Apr. 1972): 11–12 (my translation).

17   Archizoom, "Utopia of Quality," p. 182.

18   For the radical presentness of the *No-Stop City*, see Pablo. Martínez Capdevila, "An Italian Querelle: Radical vs. Tendenza." *Log: Observations on Architecture and the Contemporary City* 40 (Spring/Summer 2017): 67–81.

19   The global village was mentioned twice in the first publication of the No-Stop City ("City, Assem-bly Line," p. 157, p. 169).

20   Archizoom, "No-Stop City: Residential Parkings," p. 53.

21   For the contradictory relation between city and countryside, see my "Demystified Territories: City vs. Countryside in Andrea Branzi's Urban Models." In *Planning Cities with Nature: Theories, Strat-egies and Methods,* edited by Fabiano Lemes and Ian Mell, 29–43. Switzerland: Springer, 2019

22   See ibid. and my "Towards a weak architecture: Andrea Branzi and Gianni Vattimo/Hacia una arquitectura débil: Andrea Branzi y Gianni Vattimo." *Cuadernos de Proyectos Arquitectónicos* 6 (2016): 82–89, 147–150

Chapter 44

Seoul, Underground City

Ji Young Kim

During the last several decades, subways have enabled widespread commercial, cultural, and social discourse in Seoul by effectively extending the public realm underground. Subways and conjoined developments have evolved to facilitate changes in spatial complexity. Since the first underground railway opened in London in 1863, the subway has been a global symbol of modernity and technological achievement. In Korea, railways have played a critical role in national industrial development and economic growth. The Korean rail industry traces its origins to rail construction for political purposes when the nation was under Japanese colonial rule from 1910 through 1945. Later, railways were considerably damaged during the Korean War (1950–1953); however, railway rebuilding and subway development played a significant role in post-war recovery efforts to establish two separate national economies on the Korean Peninsula.[1] After the truce, North Korea and South Korea competed over technological advances and economic growth; transportation infrastructure played a patriotic role that exemplified an era of rapid industrial development in both countries.[2] As evidence of such ongoing competition, Seoul's subway Line 1 opened in 1974, 21 years after the truce was signed, along with service joining the Korean Railroad Corporation's (Korail) intercity railway lines. A year earlier, North Korea's Pyongyang Metro Chollima Line began service.

Historically, the interior spaces of subway stations around the world have been used for more than transportation. During World War II, some underground stations in London were used as bomb shelters, while others served as aircraft component factories.[3] In Seoul, stations were designed to be used as bomb shelters. In addition to emergency uses, multiple everyday functions were integrated into the system. Today, the burgeoning urban life of Seoul is embodied within its subway infrastructure. Public transportation has been thoroughly intermingled with spaces that nurture economic, cultural, and social exchange. This chapter examines the Seoul underground city as a form

DOI: 10.4324/9780429443091-53

of contemporary interior urbanism. It considers the incremental development of its subway system as the primary catalyst for the ongoing growth of a vast, multidimensional underground pedestrian network.

The Subway

Seoul has expanded its subway system over five decades and it continues to stimulate the growth of the contemporary city. The first phase of the Seoul subway offered four lines with 115 stations and operated along 135 km of track. The second phase of the subway included eight lines with 262 stations, and the third phase of the subway, which was finished in 2012, has 13 lines with 521 stations operating on 825 km of track.[4] The fourth phase is currently being built, while existing lines are continuously being extended with new stops. In addition to its vast physical scale, the Seoul subway is one of the highest used subways in the world with annual ridership of 1.86 billion as of 2018,[5] which surpasses the 1.68 billion ridership of the New York subway in 2018.[6] Developing public space within transportation infrastructure is only feasible for well-maintained and operated systems. Subways in Seoul are functional, in demand, affordable, and clean.

Although stations may span across multiple crossings, and have many access points, it is very easy to navigate the vast and interconnected subterranean network of stations, pedways, and shopping galleries. Multisensory wayfinding assistance, including analog and digital design, features improves user experience. All trains have announcements in multiple languages that inform riders about the next stop, as well as which door to use. Upon arriving at their destination, riders can easily find signage with numbered exits, including the names of known destinations. Additionally, not only stations, but all trains are equipped with broadband cellular network and WiFi connectivity which enhances accessibility to mobile services—online local map services include access points, as well as the locations of underground stores and venues. These features are explicit examples of how underground spaces in Seoul are actively used by the public and considered as inhabitable destinations in themselves.

Enhancing streets for walking, gathering, and commercial exchange are perhaps among the most effective ways that place-making can benefit the public realm. Those principles have been applied to the design of Seoul subway stations as well. The city is framed by a series of transportation networks, and their interwoven relationships create a responsive, organic exchange. Furthermore, the sequence of movements from subways to destinations comprises a unique public domain with streetlike characteristics. Subway stations act as portals to a dense, multidimensional, and vertically layered city (Image 44.1).

An Indoor City

Seoul continually grew and redeveloped rapidly after the Korean War. The planning and design of the subway stations were integral to this process. The ways passengers access destinations via subway stations have changed considerably over time. Earlier, urban developments often did not have direct underground access points from adjoining buildings; however today, it is very common to enter directly from the subway station to nearby buildings via underground

Image 44.1 The entrance of Gangnam-gu Office Station (Exit 3-1) and POBA Gangnam Tower. Credit: Ji Young Kim

entrances. The first underground level often extends the functions of the connected buildings. For instance, the Gangnam-gu Office Station's vertical circulations provide access to the subway and the Pinnacle Tower linked to the station. The underground landing area is designed as semi-outdoor space, providing access to the tower's dining hall and the local public library located within the building. Subway stations and adjoining buildings have developed unique public and semi-public thresholds that shape interior urban conditions.

If users of the underground city travel from buildings with direct access to the underground station, they may not need to go outside upon arriving at their destination. For example, to reach the department store at the Express Bus Terminal station from the Pinnacle Tower, users leave the tower via underground exit 3, and then take another underground entrance to the department store near exit 8. Seoulites commonly have shortcuts and extreme weather alternate paths involving underground streets. Layers of public domain have been extended into multi-level streets, providing an important example of how the underground city shapes everyday life.

The sheer ridership and number of stations generate large amounts of interior and semi-exterior public spaces. The vast scale, day-to-day programs, and habitable environment are integral to the subway's everyday feeling. It has facilitated unique yet widespread underground commercial, cultural, and social discourse in Seoul, and with time, portals evolved into distinct places. Underground arcades are filled with convenient personal care, pop-up stores, and grab-and-go food vendors. The bazaar of the streets has been extended underground and creates a modern type of indoor market. These programs create an active public realm. The mix of permanent and temporary programs generates a responsive strategy that promotes social exchanges.

In Seoul, it is a common sight to see passengers running errands or grabbing food from the station. However, in cities with older subway infrastructure, programmable spaces are very limited and may not be as inviting. However, in New York, more recent developments like the Turnstyle Underground

Image 44.2 Gyeong
bokgung Station, Seoul.
Credit: Ji Young Kim

Market (connected to the subway station at Columbus Circle) offer unique eateries, shops, and spaces to socialize (Image 44.2).

In addition to commercial programs, subway stations and trains provide places for arts and culture. Stations are great venues for public art that touches large audiences by celebrating art, artists, and public space. The contents range from invited artist exhibitions to grassroots programs. Seoul has intermittently served as the capital of Korea since 18 BCE. It is a city with a long history and many subway stations are designed to access historical landmarks. Thus, the interior architecture of those stations often celebrates unique aspects of its destination. Gyeongbokgung (Gyeongbok Palace) Station is designed with granite arches and artifacts that narrate a connection to a place of historic interest. This station houses the Seoul Metro Art Center, a cultural space located within the underground arcade accessible to all passengers.

In addition to a dedicated gallery or booth space, other interior surfaces are used to feature artwork as well. Seoul hosts an open poem competition and selected works are silk screened on the safety glass doors of platforms. In 2019, the city exhibited awarded poems in more than 300 stations. Furthermore, trains become venues for motion picture and art installations. The Seoul Metro International Subway Film Festival has been held in both Seoul and Barcelona. It curated subway trains as a moving theater by screening short films of approximately 90 seconds. During the 2018 Winter Olympics, the Seoul subway operated Winter Olympic-themed cars to make passengers feel as if they were within the Olympic arena. Subways in Seoul provide experiences for passengers to ride along with art and culture.

Joining commercial and cultural programs strengthens the public realm and catalyzes social exchange. Seoul's infrastructure is a potent instrument and plays an important role in creating a meaningful public realm. When subway portals act as places, they become public space. Certainly, subways are among the most common meeting points in Seoul. The design of stations allows passengers to move and pause. Between the pockets of dynamic

Image 44.3 Starfield Library in the Starfield COEX Mall.
Credit: Ji Young Kim

programs, riders can easily find confluences, seating areas, and plazas with landmark features such as indoor gardens or art installations. The integration of transit infrastructure has extended the reach of established, or soon-to-be-established, economic, cultural, and social complexes which become landmarks and destinations. COEX (COnvention centers and EXhibition halls) is one of the earlier large-scale developments connected to subway stations. Dongdaemun Design Plaza (DDP) is a recent project supported by the existing subway infrastructure. These projects adapted strategies that mix old and new built environments rather than employing a complete demolition and redevelopment approach (Image 44.3).

COEX is an urban hub opened in 2000, which continues to grow and reinvent itself. Its programs extend far beyond shopping; the complex consists of an entire urban block in Seoul and includes hotels, a department store, city airport, casino, duty free stores, ASEM (Asia-Europe Meeting) Tower, Trade Tower, and the Starfield COEX Mall. The mall is directly connected to the Line 2 Samseong station; it has hundreds of stores and restaurants, including a movie theater, aquarium, and multi-level public library. Developed in the 2000s, it was one of the early mega-complex developments and a popular destination for the younger generation. Over time, COEX has faced several challenges; underground space in COEX offers few connections to above-ground public space. Even though basements of the mall, hotel, convention center, and all other programs are connected, it is very hard to find access points from, within, and outside the complex. Additionally, its target users in the 2000s have grown older and found different lifestyles. Therefore, COEX is attempting to redefine its identity as it does not attract existing or new customers. The complex underwent a major renovation from 2013 to 2014 designed by Gensler and Junglim Architecture.

In 2015, an additional connection to the new subway Line 9 Bongensa Station opened, which helped to activate the north side of the block. In addition, COEX introduced a large-scale public library, Starfield Library,

Image 44.4 View toward the entrance of the Dongdaemun history and culture park station from the Dongdaemun Design Plaza.
Credit: Ji Young Kim

designed by Ceno Plan in 2017. It is located at the center of the mall, connecting ground and underground circulation networks. The library is designed as a venue for cultural events such as author talks, lectures, and concerts. Effects of the renovation and library program need to be studied over time; however, one hopes that the integration of public programs with iconic design will attract diverse age and gender groups (Image 44.4).

Dongdaemun (meaning Great East Gate) Market has a long history of being the center of the commercial district in Seoul. Dongdaemun and Dongdaemun History & Culture Park stations (formerly known as Dongdaemun Stadium Station) are among the oldest phase 1 subway stations in the city. Along with the traditional markets, garment wholesale shops and fashion complexes thrived there in the 1990s. The neighborhood was known as a 24/7 fashion shopping destination for locals as well as tourists. However, due to the decline of the traditional market and the emergence of a competitive international market, Korea's garment and fashion industries have been greatly diminished in recent years.

In 2007, a design competition for DDP was announced in the hope that it would revitalize the largest fashion hub, old subway station, and broader neighborhood. The competition envisioned the site as a culture hub and landmark to revitalize the neighborhood by strengthening its identity and embracing its future. Zaha Hadid Architects won the competition and DDP opened in 2014. Located at the heart of the old town, the building connects underground, at-grade, and over-ground levels in seamless, continuous circulation via amorphous interior and exterior paths. It is connected to subway lines 2, 4, and 5 at Dongdaemun History & Culture Park Station. DDP was designed to present diverse exhibitions and events to feed the cultural vitality of the neighborhood and city. Its layout comprises soft bordered zones for the Art Hall, Design Museum, and Design Lab with flexible spaces that accommodate temporary and permanent uses. Its non-rectilinear shape blends into the urban blocks seamlessly, improving the pedestrian walking experience. The park and building serve as a new cultural space that connects the neighborhood with Dongdaemun Stadium Memorial and Dongdaemun History Museum. DDP has raised concerns due to its unusual shape and high operational cost. It is an ongoing challenge for the city to develop a strategic plan for the unique spaces the building offers.

Conclusion

Seoul's underground city initially grew through the incremental agglomeration of subway stations and conjoined urban development. For highly dense cities with vast networks of underground transport, the public realm should be considered at all levels—underground, at-grade, and elevated levels. As a result of such multi-level planning, Seoul's public space has been extended from exterior to interior spaces that can be used year-round. The emergence and development of underground public space reaffirm the importance of design as a process which operates across scales. More resilient development, redevelopment, and adaptive reuse projects incorporating subway stations with adjoining buildings can help the underground city to mature, while repositioning itself for strategic growth.

Notes

1 Lee, Jun, *The History of Korean Railway by Photographs*, 6, 27, The Korea transport Institute, 2014.
2 Fraser, Benjamin and Steven D. Spalding, *Trains, Culture and Mobility: Riding the Rails*, 149, Lexington Books, 2012.
3 Fischler, Stan, *Subways of the World*, 12, MBI Publishing Company, 2000.
4 Lee, *The History of Korean Railway by Photographs*, 70–71.
5 Statistics Korea, "Subways transportation performance by year", index.go.kr. Accessed February 25, 2020 http://index.go.kr/potal/main/EachDtlPageDetail.do?idx_cd=1259
6 Metropolitan Transportation Authority, "Annual subway ridership", web.mta.info. Accessed February 25, 2020 http://web.mta.info/nyct/facts/ridership/ridership_sub_annual.htm

Chapter 45

Lower West Side Story

The World Trade Center and the Interior Masterplan

Joss Kiely

When the world's then-tallest structures rose high above Manhattan in the late 1960s, they were for some a monument to American capitalist prowess, and for others, an unwanted visual intrusion into New York's already imposing skyline. The towering project introduced nearly 12 million square feet of leasable office and commercial space in the heart of the Financial District that quickly became highly coveted real estate. Although the developers focused on the World Trade Center (WTC) complex as an enormous commercial infusion in Lower Manhattan, the architect had unusually lofty goals for the project. Reflecting on the design, Minoru Yamasaki suggested that "…it became clear that the Trade Center, with its location facing the entry to New York Harbor, could…become a physical expression of the universal effort of men to seek and achieve world peace."[1] Given Yamasaki's own rhetoric celebrating what he called a human-scaled architecture, the monumental proportions of the WTC were largely incongruous within his oeuvre. Nevertheless, the high demands for leasable floor area coupled with the small site essentially required a pair of towers at an outsized scale, prompting a *Los Angeles Times* reporter to call the project "a monumental change in the façade of the nation's largest city."[2] As a result of its size, the WTC became both part of the urban fabric and at the same time distinct from it. Yamasaki and his team essentially had the opportunity to create an interior urban condition unto its own in the middle of the nation's largest city.

With both physical and symbolic bigness in mind, this chapter stitches together what one might call the "Lower West Side Story." The history of the WTC is long and complex, with unexpected twists and turns, heated debates, and figurative fights between various constituents. This chapter thus considers both the original and the new WTC for the interior urban conditions they present vis-à-vis the urban condition of New York. Both the 1973 complex, designed by Minoru Yamasaki and Associates (MYA), and its

DOI: 10.4324/9780429443091-54

twenty-first-century replacement embrace a both/and condition. Each project is an architectural insertion in Lower Manhattan, understandable for its distinct object-*ness*. But more importantly, both iterations of the WTC might be better understood as a masterplan of a city within a city, complete with its own internal vertical transit system and tunnels linking the complex to the surrounding urban condition. As a result, the interior condition itself is inherently urban; this is expressed as a distinct interior entity in the Financial District, but at the same time, spliced into the extant fabric of the city that lay beyond.

Act One

Commissioned in 1962 by the Port Authority of New York and New Jersey as simply the Trade Center, lead architect Minoru Yamasaki and his team were faced with myriad challenges, not the least of which was the small area of the site and the tight blocks that made up Lower Manhattan.[3] From the beginning, Yamasaki saw this as "a unique opportunity to create a group of tall and low buildings, combined with a significant expanse of open space at ground level," although the main pair of towers that were to be the focal point of the project would be astoundingly tall, as demanded by the developers to meet requirements of leasable space. Early concerns about the sheer scale of the buildings were allayed by frequent visits to the Empire State Building in Midtown, reassuring the architect that with time "one becomes as comfortable standing next to a 100-story building as one forty stories high..." Yamasaki was ultimately convinced that the sheer scale was not as problematic as he once thought: "there was no diminution of the soul, no ant-like feelings in the face of such a large object. Man had made it and could comprehend it, and its parts could be understood to relate to its whole."[4] After many iterations, the final arrangement focused on a five-acre plaza with the two largest towers located in the southwest quadrant of the site, a U.S. Customs Building to the north, with two plaza buildings located in the remaining corners. The twin towers that anchored the New York project had a relatively compact footprint at just 208 feet by 208 feet, even though both rose to 110 stories above Manhattan. Although the projects were completely different in nature, aspects of the WTC plan are strikingly similar to the MYA-designed Federal Science Pavilion at the Seattle World's Fair, completed in 1962.[5]

The WTC, located in the heart of downtown, occupied an area that experienced large variations in population between the busy weekdays and the slow weekends and holidays. The dense workday population called for a large open plaza for people to gather and pass through, as well as provide entry into the towers on a lower mezzanine. On entering the spacious lobby, visitors took a set of escalators down to a large elevator bank that serviced the upper floors. Access to this level was also possible from adjacent sidewalks, and still others would have arrived through the underground subway and PATH train station, positioned directly below the complex. This netherworld serviced the towers above, but also carved out an interior urban condition focused on intermodal transit connections, shopping, and dining.

One of the challenges of this oversized project was how to effectively handle vertical circulation, without causing delays for those trying to reach the upper floors. To alleviate this issue, the team envisaged a series of

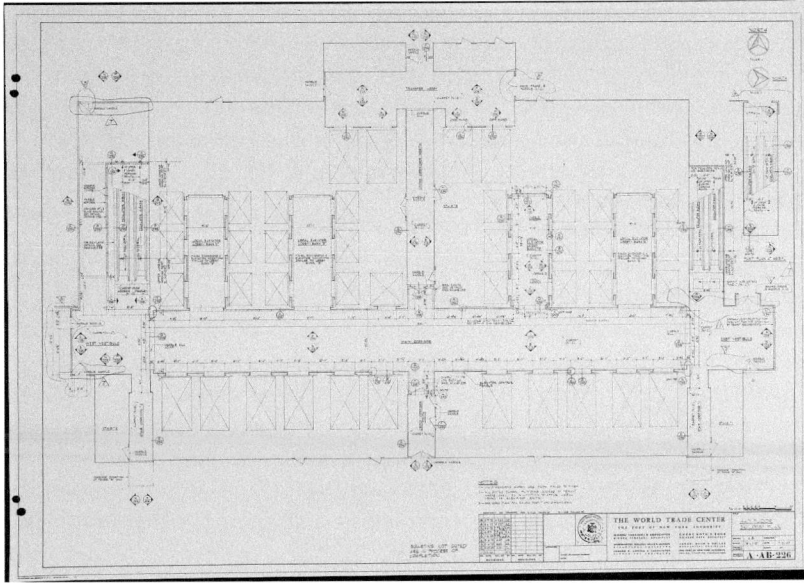

Image 45.1 Plan drawing of the Sky Lobby on Floor 44 of the World Trade Center, by Minoru Yamasaki and Associates, New York.
Credit: Yamasaki Inc. Architectural Firm Records

"sky lobbies" that helped organize the vertical flow of traffic. Much like subway and rail transit system networks that rely on both local and express trains, the elevators were broken up into these two typologies. Express elevators shuttled people from the main lobby on the Plaza Level to sky lobbies on the 44th and 70th floors, from which people transferred to local elevators, each serving only a handful of floors. This seemingly simple solution reduced overall transit times by pre-sorting circulation based on destinations within the center and further distanced the interior urban condition from the one outside. Although conventional urban design schemes often placed shopping and dining at street level, the developers of the WTC, and other large skyscraper projects, favored austere ground floor lobbies with restaurants located in the upper levels, capitalizing on dramatic views unavailable to those at street level. Furthermore, shopping and dining facilities located on sky lobby levels obviated the need for unnecessary transits to the ground level during the workday, rendering the complex more contained and thus more efficient. These lofty nodes, much like intersections in the city outside, folded the urban fabric of New York into the vertical direction like an extruded pair of city blocks into the clouds, culminating in the Windows on the World restaurant and a large observation deck (Image 45.1).

Act Two

The tragic events of September 11th, 2001 need no re-introduction, and yet play a significant role in the Lower West Side Story. Although the MYA-designed WTC should have had a far longer lifespan than it did, the towers' untimely destruction and eventual replacement offers the unusual opportunity to compare two mega-projects occupying the very same site in a relatively short timeframe. In the aftermath of September 11th, myriad proposals for the project's replacement were put forth, necessitating the formation of the Lower Manhattan Development Corporation to manage and oversee the reconstruction of the area. For many, the rebuilding of a signature trade center was an important step to symbolize the United States' ability to recover from a major international terrorist attack, and in particular, one that took aim at U.S.-led capitalism and, by extension, the global economy. As Andreas Huyssen has suggested, this was complicated at best: "How does one imagine a monument to what was already a monument in the first place—a monument to corporate modernism?"[6]

Unsurprisingly, there was little consensus about the best use of the site. As a result of an international competition for a new site masterplan, Daniel Liebeskind's proposal was selected. Although the thrust of the competition was to design the site and *not* the architecture of the tower itself, the placeholder tower that was included in his drawings quickly acquired the moniker "Freedom Tower," and was wrongly assumed by many to be the overall winning proposal. Waves of criticism and controversy ensued that lasted for nearly a decade, ending in a kind of architectural compromise between the many private and public entities involved in the project. Ultimately, Liebeskind's site plan was largely implemented, with a new tower designed by David Childs of Skidmore, Owings, and Merrill, with a transit hub by Santiago Calatrava (Image 45.2).

Image 45.2 Exterior view of the World Trade Center by Daniel Libeskind and Associates.
Credit: Tyler Brebberman

The design of the new WTC houses nearly ten million square feet of commercial real estate in a series of towers that anchor the masterplan which includes a large retail concourse, transportation hubs, a 9/11 memorial garden and museum, and the recently opened Ronald O. Perelman Performing Arts Center. As with the original WTC, the project incorporated a large amount of retail space throughout, including in the transit hub, and the first few floors of Three and Four WTC, along with the concourses that connect each of the elements. Perhaps the most striking difference from the original WTC is that the memorial garden and plaza incorporate two reflecting pools and fountains that occupy the footprint of the original twin towers, preserving the legacy of the towers and, most importantly, the memory of those who perished in the attack. Immediately across West Street from the World Trade Center Memorial is the César Pelli-designed World Financial Center (1985), now known as Brookfield Place, which, after extensive renovations, re-opened in 2014 with an emphasis on luxury shopping and dining on the lower levels. One of the more striking features of Brookfield Place is the large Winter Garden (1988) designed in collaboration with Diana Balmori—a glass atrium with a large, semi-circular grand staircase that appears to channel the form of a Greek or Roman amphitheater and which further underscores the interior urban condition which sits removed from the exterior urban fabric.[7] This kind of interior urban appropriation also appears in what many regard as the most architecturally significant project in the new WTC: Calatrava's Transportation Hub.

Shaped roughly like a football in plan, the new transit hub is otherworldly, almost as though it accidentally alighted on the site, with no intention of permanence. From the corner of Fulton and Church, a small entrance beckons pedestrians to enter, while Calatrava's signature sweeping forms splay out on either side along the length of the station. However visually arresting the architecture appears on the exterior, the interior operates as an interior world removed from its New York context, which is further accentuated by the fact that the main levels are below street grade. Almost as graceful as the exterior is not, the internal volume operates as a buzzing node of activity that is part of many New Yorkers' everyday commutes as well as a significant tourist attraction. It was quickly nicknamed "the Oculus" for its curvaceous form centered around a 355-feet-long skylight that bisects the building, and through which light passes precisely at 10:28 AM, marking the time when the second tower fell.[8] The interior condition is light and airy—and from inside the transit hub, one can catch sight of One WTC towering overhead, forging a connection between the interior world of Oculus and the symbolic financial power of Lower Manhattan.

In its current configuration, the main space of the Oculus operates like a blank canvas—an interior piazza or city square—that can be adapted for different purposes at different times of the day. As such, it becomes a register against which the hum of daily life is reflected, from the hurried New Yorker late for a meeting to the gawking tourist standing in her way. The Oculus also hosts more formalized events catering to busy workers: on Tuesdays during the winter months, for example, a temporary farmers' market is assembled in the very center, offering passersby the chance to grab baked goods, local meats, cheeses, and cellared orchard fruit (Image 45.3). The juxtaposition between the rurality of the farm stand and the striking white backdrop of the Calatrava

Image 45.3 View of the weekly farmer's market in the WTC Transit Hub by Santiago Calatrava. Credit: Tyler Brebberman

building is the kind of aesthetic collision imaginable only in an urban setting. In this instance, the condition is wholly indoors, underscoring the urban nature of the Oculus' interior condition. The literal whiteness of the interior foregrounds the messy nature of human life that unfolds in full color against it, becoming a spectacle of the interior world it champions (Image 45.4).

Brookfield Place, the new WTC, and the Oculus were intended to work together as a networked neighborhood of masterplanned interior conditions, but they remain as disjointed entities, almost hesitantly connected, anxiously encircling the memorial footprint of the past twin towers. In a certain sense, the resultant WTC complex presents us with a dialectic. As designed, the WTC memorial is not occupiable—one can only experience the space as an external observer, never truly part of the place. the success of the Oculus, however, lies in its habitable interior as a backdrop for quotidian routines. Part memorial, part shopping center, part signature tower, and part transit hub, the new WTC is perhaps best understood as a fragmented city within a city, a series of interior urban conditions that are, at best, a compromise. We might recall any number of other proposals that proffered a new pair of towers, a twinning that the world came to expect of the WTC, a twinning that is no longer

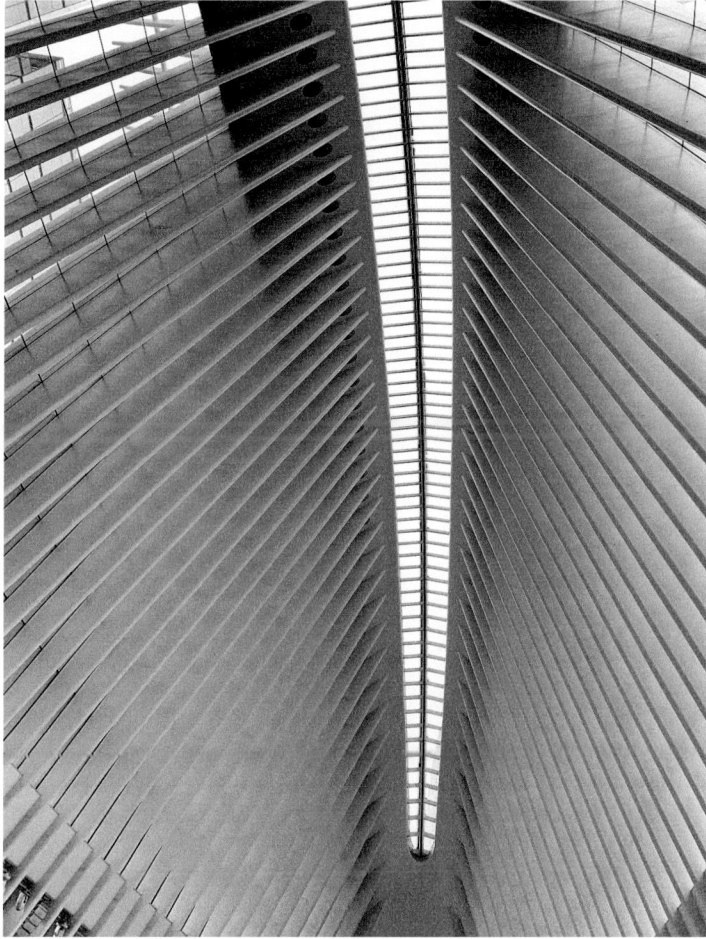

Image 45.4 Detail of the interior ceiling condition at the WTC Transit Hub by Santiago Calatrava. Credit: Tyler Brebberman

possible. In many ways, the Lower West Side Story is complete. The cranes are gone and lingering disputes are futile, but the complicated legacy of the WTC persists, now with a new cast of characters, ready to mount the next spectacle.

Notes

1   Minoru Yamasaki, *A Life in Architecture* (New York and Tokyo: Weatherhill, 1979), 70.

2   John J. Goldman, "World's Tallest Structure: Clouds, Criticism Surround N.Y. Building," *Los Angeles Times*, January 10, 1971.

3   For a comprehensive overview of the project's history, refer to "Tall Buildings" in Dale Gyure, *Minoru Yamasaki* (New Haven and London: Yale University Press, 2017), 190–216.

4   Minoru Yamasaki, *A Life in Architecture* (New York and Tokyo: Weatherhill, 1979), 115.

5   Ibid., 70.

6   Andreas Huyssen, "Twin Memories: Afterimages of Nine/Eleven," *Grey Room 07* (Spring 2002): 9.

7   Norval White and Elliot Willensky, *AIA Guide to New York City* (New York and Oxford: Oxford University Press, 2010), 51.

8   Eric Baldwin, "World Trade Center Transportation Hub Designed in Remembrance of 9/11," *ArchDaily*, 2018. https://www.archdaily.com/901840/world-trade-center-transportation-hub-oculus-designed-in-remembrance-of-9-11. Accessed April 3, 2020.

Theories and Influences

_Speculation

Chapter 46

A Proto-typology for Interior Urbanism

Shai Yeshayahu

This chapter proposes a theory of origin for interior urbanism. It stages an account of how dispersed buildings over the span of 1 km became leading figures in stitching the first public-private web of interior-exterior spaces. Shaped through the stretch of 1,000 years across the historical forum of Florence, this postulation unfolds from the context of an organizational schema developed between 1555 and 1565. The foundations for this undertaking manifested in the late 1400s when Florence embodied expertise in painting, sculpting, architecture, music, science, mathematics, engineering, and cartography, as described in *The Lives of the Artist* by Giorgio Vasari. That intellectual expansion staged the rationale guiding the decision to reexamine the city fabric as an open canvas with emphasis on the character of exterior-interior networks. By the end of the High Renaissance, amid the socio-cultural uprisings of the 1550s, Florentines turned their attention toward the visual redesigning of history.[1] Buildings and their relationship to the existing urban context became tools to navigate through the interior fabric of the city. In less than ten years, the meaning of urban context took on new significance. Suddenly, interior spaces were no longer unfolding their presence through their exterior surfaces; instead, and according to this narration, the interior identity of each structure hones the potential to be part of spatial notoriety.

This shift in perception introduces a new typology for urban programming, one which attributes power to the existing spatial diversity of the city, inspiring a tenable model for interior urbanism. Here, the built context is mapped and orchestrated from 1555 to 1565, triggering the proposed organizational schema. Their enactment is a tool for the visualization of the narrated snippets and as part of one infrastructural conglomerate defining the proto-typology for interior urbanism.

DOI: 10.4324/9780429443091-56

Introduction

In the history of ideas, the discourse of interior urbanism often begins with site modifications that alter existing organizational systems. In the twentieth century, urban thinkers viewed the success of interior urbanism from the metrics of size, so that airports, shopping malls, train stations, museums, trade centers, and hotels increasingly grew in footprint and volume, becoming cities within cities.[2] This physical condition is currently understood as a direct result of technological breakthroughs in material science and infrastructural systems.[3] Now, in the first quarter of the twenty-first century, designers and planners are confused about existing spaces and the future of urban identity. Some wonder if redirecting, reunderstanding, reinhabiting, reconfiguring, or even redisposing of urban context is necessary.

In 2015, for the 21st issue of MONU magazine, William Maas, principal of MVRD, talked about the concept of interior urbanism, emphasizing the definition of urban density.

> There are more ways to approach this. First, we could simply follow and build Buckminster Fuller's Cupola and to make basically an acclimatizer, as I called it in KM3. Secondly, we could comment on the isolated box, like the malls, that remains in the classic dichotomy of exterior and interior. For me - in that respect - the most interesting part where the term interior urbanism makes sense more and more is within density. The denser you are the more the role of the interiors makes sense and becomes active. To look at Nolli would not be so bad here.[4]

His depiction of "density" is unclear and open-ended. Did Maas suggest that one ought to grasp the success of interior urbanism as a factor determined by the production of new buildings, was he emphasizing the proximity of users and shops cramped within one vast public atrium, or was he suggesting a return to building productions made overtime, within the proximity of interior-exterior public spaces per Nolli's map of Rome? This lack of clarity lingers among urban thinkers, opening opportunities to further explore the meaning of interior spaces within urbanism.

The search for tangible answers sparked a quest to identify when and if "urban content" ever brought forth alternate readings of the city and its coexistence with exterior/interior urbanism. In this framing, a theory of origin was forward in 2021, amidst a rising urgency for city officials and citizens to reimagine their city's milieu. Then, theorists, designers, and planners were struggling to create anew.[5] This ushered in a state of design emergency, motivating a revisit to a time in history when the repellency of human density first released a proto-typology for interior urbanism—a survey stretching the dimensions for how one looks at interior spaces and the changes in perceptual scales according to navigational systems, which extended the lens of interior urbanism to one that is interdependent with its existing surroundings and its latency to undiscovered adjacencies that effectively rearranged the city's context.

Mistaken Identities

The origin of this stance is universally credited to the Pianta Grande di Roma, a map, composed of 12 copper-plated engravings authored and released by Nolli in 1748. The genesis of Nolli's ingenuity is not in creating the origins of interior-exterior urbanism but rather in unraveling the urban context that was already there, amassing its reality over thousands of years.[6] It was and remains the implementation of a figure-ground method that displays Rome's urban wealth as web of continuous access through streets, piazzas, and the interior spaces of churches and civic buildings. In fact, the plates are data to see the city as a canvas of information from which to create more data; and while not commonly held as the foundations of design innovation in the 1700s, data is a resource that overtime has become fundamental to the argument of originality.

What is remarkably useful about the idea of mapping data is the focus on its spatial content. In this regard, 200 years before Nolli, Giorgio Vasari was the first to exploit the value of the existing urban fabric for the creation of new spatial identities. In a decade, after he completed his first rendition on *The Lives of the Artist* (1550), he became the leading choreographer for Florence's spatial identity, a premise where everything real and imagined had to consider the spectator's role, including the curation and animation of an entire city and the socio-cultural-political agendas that would lead to the reconditioning of Florence's urban fabric and the rise of a proto-typology for interior urbanism.[7]

An Organizational Schema Made over Millennia

Its beginnings are unclear, but somewhere between 500 BC and closer to 60 BC, a city flourished near the Arno River. By 1 AD, it was a military colony. Yet, after the fall of the Roman Empire, Florence, as it had been named, experienced a series of socio-political difficulties. Then, its population and cultural-civic strives, distanced into oblivion; however, records from the thirteenth to the fifteenth century signaled a revival. The city's influx through its mercantile activities, industrializing efforts, and banking innovations, as well as undertakings in literature, art, engineering, and science heighten.[8] In this era, Florence transitioned into an urbanized capital with planned districts and new building programs promoting health, legal, and educational advancements. Yet, earnest urbanists did not place the inception of urban interiors within such a context. This decision is partly because of historical ideologies chronicling city-making and planning formations back to ancient Asia and Greco-Roman perspectives. Here, the evolution of urban history ignores the essence of interior urbanism and that historical omission deviates from the visualizations of city growth and the developments of interior urbanism exhibited throughout the built production of Florence. It disregards city-making processes and socio-political changes concerning the evolution of interior urbanism. In hindsight, a review of those historical frames starts to explain the speed and spatial logic for how the birth of interior urbanism could have come into sight. Consequently, the compression of eight contextual narratives begins to illustrate how two ambitious characters, Duke Cosimo de Medici I and Giorgio Vasari, enabled an enduring formula for interior urbanism to emerge and thrive.

Eight Historical Narrations
(1) Palazzo del Popolo (1255) and (2) Piazza della Signoria (1446)

Starting in 1539, at the heart of one of the most significant socio-cultural revolutions in Florence, Cosimo-I de' Medici and Eleonora di Toledo made their first political move in choosing to work and reside within the People's Palace (Palazzo del Popolo-1255). Ten years later, this strategic location, the one from which Cosimo's Ducal conquered and expanded its sovereignty across Tuscany, was no longer suited for a growing family. By 1549, the Duchess was eager to find a new home. In record time, the Medici's purchased a palace across the Arno River, away from the bustling activities of the town hall and the political uprisings staged at Piazza della Signoria.

(3) Palazzo Pitti (1446) and (4) Boboli Gardens (1550)

Situated in the countryside, 1,000 meters away from Cosimo's workplace, the physical distance of this new home stood in direct conflict with Cosimo's political ambitions and his desire to centralize the rising power of merchants under one roof. That spatial rift, between Palazzo Pitti and Palazzo del Popolo, caused a massive planning spree. First, Eleonor sought to expand Pitti's built footprint and the design scope of 111 acres of land known as one of the most expansive public gardens in Florence. In a year's span, she made a home for her growing family, enabling Giorgio Vasari and the Duke to conjure a ten-year re-urbanization plan for the entire city.[9]

At that time, Vasari, whose artistic ambitions, and architectural visions had yet to materialize, was not merely seeking to comply with Cosimo's infinite requests and ensure a pristine PR image for the Medici family, but also aspiring to take control of all the artwork, building commissions, and urban curations within the whole city. Similarly, Cosimo's desire for consolidation was not simply focusing on the control of the city's economy but also harboring the physical expansion of his political status as a visible imposition over the city's landscape.[10] Their intent would be to create and produce a novel strategy that yielded a positive image of their lived lives. As a team, they sought the same outcomes and the means to disseminate their posterity, yet the Vasari-Cosimo partnership as a duo with equal impetus, seeking sweeping supremacy over their city is often omitted from history. Too often, Vasari is delegated to an art historian in servitude of Cosimo's whims. Cosimo, however, is singularly credited for all of the era's foresight. It is rare for scholars to discuss the purchase of Palazzo Pitti as a structural underpinning for their immutable objectives. Nonetheless, viewed as a synchronization of minds and reconfiguration of built context can lead interior urbanists to reimagine the contemporary impact Florence affords.[11]

(5) The Uffizi (1565)

From 1539 to 1560, a narrow strip of land directly south of Palazzo del Popolo and leading toward the Arno River became a health risk zone obstructing Cosimo's desire to modernize Florence. To clear the way, he made a new street, currently known as Piazza degli Uffizi. Then, in 1560 he charged Vasari with the beautification of the street. The outcome rendered a *Serlian Window*, framing the view to the Arno River that signaled a new economic and political stage of civic space for the public to enjoy to this day.[12]

The idea of the piazza as an urban emblem laced within the discussions of interior urbanism is perhaps what Alison Flemingwish suggested in her essay *Presenting the Spectators as the Show: The Piazza degli Uffizi as Theater and Stage*.[13] Yet, one could also argue that these elements were designed as part of a complex spatial system: (1) facilitating a private thruway for the Medici family to navigate back and forth from home to work; (2) serving to survey and track the transactional movements of all citizens; (3) housing and tracking mercantile activity.

These added premises were unimaginable for Florentines living in the late 1500s, but they are now whispered among scholars and through walks across the buildings that bestow privileged views of the city to citizens and visitors. Thomas Frangenberg's book, *Chorographies of Florence: The Use of City Views and City Plans in the Sixteenth Century*, supported this premise explaining that this lack of spatial understanding for city dwellers was intentionally crafted by the methods of *chorography*, a drawing technique developed in the 1500s that incorporated the disciplines of geography and geometry to depict the city as three-dimensional projections. These kinds of drawings limited the navigational clarity of urban spaces.

Still, today with GPS at hand, Vasari's Piazza degli Uffizi is seldom, if ever, described as the star of an organizational schema or the hinge that would eventually forge the unification of interior spaces which were otherwise divided by a river. This chapter calls into focus the site specificities of seven buildings attributing the Uffizi as a pivotal construct for the expansion and built programs that the Vasari Corridor reassembled. This condition establishes a full view of the Uffizi as a proof of concept for the birth of a proto-typology for interior urbanism.

In effect, the article's historical snippets explain Vasari's unwavering persistence to keep the design of a loggia intact. It probes on the meaning of traveling from home to work through a concealed space that crosses several interior spaces over a river and demonstrates an exceptional understanding of the built context. Vasari's approach remains the first network of interior spaces composed by a series of built adjacencies. In 2011, for the exhibit celebrating *Vasari the Uffizi and the Duke*, Daniel B. Gallagher's article published by New York Arts in Italy stated:

> Vasari encountered opposition at the earliest stages of the Uffizi project. His collaborator Ammannati was convinced that the architectural emphasis on the functional similarity of the offices was grossly exaggerated. He proposed instead to break up the trabeation by inserting "Serliana" above the portico in which statues would be placed. This would give the structure more vertical thrust. Vasari persisted with his prototype, nonetheless, allegedly keeping it under lock and key to prevent colleagues from tampering with it. The exhibition features a reconstruction of this precious model which, despite Vasari's precautionary measures, has been lost to history.[14]

Although never articulated by the choreographers of this exhibit or by reviewers, the first interiorized urban experience has been intently hidden and misguided. From its inception, one wonders _Was the design and construction of the Ufizzi intently concealed or its physical outcome directly contradicting the evidence exemplified in Vasari's architectural drawings? _ What did the lock and key model conceal?

If the medium is the message, according to Marshall Mc Luhan,[15] Cosimo's perpetual desire for posterity and control deemed Vasari's Uffizi to be less of the technological innovation it really is and more of the message that the guilds needed to proudly adopt as a valuable reality. This account makes the design function of the building incognizant to its users. A PR stunt, if you will, providing locals with ample opportunities to aggregate socio-cultural meaning to the Uffizi's existence. Such depictions deviate from extensive documents supporting the contrary and greatly overshadow the spatial dexterity before Nolli's maps when the Duke and Vasari developed a new spatial tool for urbanism.

(6) Santa Felicita (400), (7) Ponte Vecchio (1000), and (8) Vasari Corridor (1565)

In the late twentieth century, after decades of research work by artists and designers, the duo's interior urban development remains untold. Giorgio Vasari is currently known for inventing art history and the Duke for collecting and protecting artwork. Their urban work lives in the shadows, mostly because scholars and official documents are not prompted to describe the audacious usage of ancient and emerging built fabric as the metrics of social-cultural context.

In this view, the author's narrations highlight the strategic location of the Vasari Corridor which stitches Vasari's reformation of the existing urban fabric into a system linking the Boboli Gardens to Palazzo Pitti, Santa Felicita, and Ponte Vecchio through an elevated corridor that merges the Uffizi, Palazzo del Popolo and Piazza della Signoria to render a lasting interior space for urbanity.

In-Posterity

The duo's view of posterity was not by chance yet; the Vasari-Cosimo partnership remains difficult to explain, both in their time and over the years. In retrospect, one could argue that without GPS services like MapQuest or NASA's worldview and drone imaging, Florentines could not decipher the corridor's identity in the ways this survey does. Such operatic simulation would have been impossible in the 1500s, but tracing and shaping the city fabric with today's cartographic tools may have been the urban opera of Vasari's imagination, one that yielded the world's largest public interior-exterior urban space forged under Vasari's-Cosimo's control.

Notes

1 Yoav IH Parish and Pascal Müller, "Procedural Modeling of Cities." In *Proceedings of the 28th Annual Conference on Computer Graphics and Interactive Techniques*, Los Angeles, 12–17 August 2001, 301–308.

2 Rem Koolhaas, "Junkspace." October 100 (2002): 175–190.

3 Rem Koolhaas and Bruce Mau, *Bigness or the Problem of Large. S, M, L, XL* (New York: Monacelli Press, 1994), 494–517.

4 MONU, "MVDR and Interior Urbanism: An Interview with Winy Maas," *Arch daily.com*, January 29, 2017, https://www.archdaily.com/592840/mvrdv-and-interior-urbanism-an-interview-with-winy-maas.

5   OECD, "City Policy Responses to Coronavirus *(COVID-19),*" *oecd.org,* July 23, 2020, https://www. oecd.org/coronavirus/policy-responses/cities-policy-responses-fd1053ff/.

6   Jim Tice and Erik Steiner, "The Nolli Map Website," *nolli.uoregon.edu,* 2005–2021, http://nolli. uoregon.edu/default.asp.

7   Gene A. Brucker, *The Civic World of Early Renaissance Florence* (Princeton, NJ: Princeton University Press, 2015), 3–13.

8   Patricia Lee Rubin and Maurice Rubin, *Giorgio Vasari: Art and History* (New Haven, CT: Yale University Press, 1995), 639–640.

9   Palazzo Pitti, "Cosimo I and Eleonora of Toledo," *palazzo-pitti.net,* December 10, 2021, https:// www.palazzo-pitti.net/cosimo-i--eleonora-of-toledo.html.

10   Sophus A. Reinert and Robert Fredona, "Political Economy and the Medici," *Business History Review* 94, no. 1 (2020):125–177.

11   Leon Satkowski, "The Palazzo Pitti: Planning and Use in the Grand-Ducal Era," *The Journal of the Society of Architectural Historians* 42, no. 4 (1983): 336–349.

12   Federico Cantini and Jacopo Bruttini, "Tra la Città e il Fiume: l'area Degli Uf zi nel Medioevo," *Archeologia a Firenze: Città e Territorio, Archaeopress* (2015): 269–304.

13   Alison C. Fleming, "Presenting the Spectators as the Show: The Piazza Degli Ufizi as Theater and Stage," *The Sixteenth Century Journal* 37, no. 3 (2006): 701–720.

14   Danile B. Gallagher, "Vasari, gli Uffizi e Il Duca," *newyorkarts*.net, October 2, 2011, https://newyorkarts.net/2011/10/vasari-uffizi/

15   Compton Neil, "Understanding Media: The Extensions of Man, by Marshall McLuhan (Book Review)," *Commentary* 39, no. 1 (1965): 79.

Chapter 47

Urban Interior Networks

Deborah Schneiderman

A series of connected interiors can comprise a networked, urban infrastructural system. Typically, infrastructure is understood as a network of transportation, communication, or utilities. According to Keller Easterling, infrastructure can be defined to include replicable building models that maintain an organization or information network. As individual buildings become reproducible products, no longer uniquely designed by architects, but rather engineered for function, they can be defined as infrastructure and networked.[1] Hence, if a set of interior elements is systematized and reproducible, it can be considered a networked infrastructural interior condition. Networked interiors promote a more functional urban condition through their clarity and ability to function systematically.

This chapter analyzes and theorizes urban networked interiority through case studies of both built and speculative projects. The case studies are cataloged within three typologies of networked infrastructural interior conditions. As *Interior Infrastructure within Infrastructure* (analyzed through the subway systems), as *Interior Infrastructure within Repurposed Infrastructure* (analyzed through the adaptive reuse of parking garages), and as *Interior Infrastructure within an Architectured Site* (analyzed as a hybridization of library and Privately Owned Public Spaces).

Interior Infrastructure within Infrastructure
Subway

The urban interior network may be evidenced in a site that is part of an infrastructural network designed for human occupation, such as the subway station. The subterranean interiors of subway stations are typically designed as nodes in a networked system. As defined by Kevin Lynch, there exist two distinct types of nodes: those that are junctions of paths and those that exist due to a concentration of a single type of use.[2] In subway stations, interior specifications are determined by their requirements and replicated throughout.

DOI: 10.4324/9780429443091-57

Often, station finishes are systematically linked as wayfinding devices. Atypical stations, or landmarks, might be more radically differentiated through a connection to their neighborhood or as a site for public art. A landmark is typically a physical structure such as a building, sign, or geographic feature used by an individual to better understand and navigate the built environment. Lynch purports that landmarks can be observed but not passed through.[3]

Kit of Parts Subway Proposal

For her Graduate Thesis in Interior Design at Pratt Institute, Britt Bender studied subway platforms. She developed a kit of parts for the design of stations throughout the system. The station interiors were networked, but also maintain individuality as some elements can be customized. Notable parts of Bender's system include 'Column Color Change' where the color change indicates the portion of the platform where trains stop in stations where train lengths are less than that of the station, signaling to users a difference between the waiting and non-waiting portions of the platform. Column color is coordinated with the train line color to communicate which train the waiting area is for. 'Responsive Tiles' comprise modules that directly respond to the rider's body, offering both the durability of a hard surface and the comfort of a soft surface. 'Extruded Ergonomic Tiles' form places where riders rest their belongings or bodies. 'Rail Seating' expands on The Lariat Seat Loops at the 33rd street station in New York City by artist James Garvey. Bender's proposal varies the height of the bronze rail as it wraps around the column to provide riders with increased options and accounts for physical differences between riders. An extended handrail directs users down the stairs and to the correct waiting area (Image 47.1).[4]

These replicable interior systems facilitate an organization and information network and make the subway system more readily understood. 'Pictogram Tiles' depict a variety of activities, conditions, and items associated with

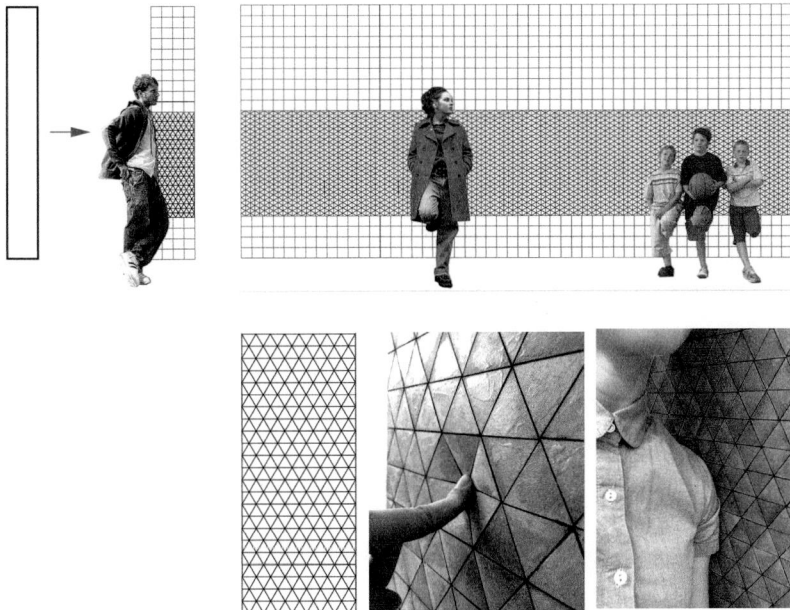

Image 47.1 Responsive Tiles by Britt Bender: Thesis, Pratt Institute, 2015.
Credit: Britt Bender

Image 47.2 Overlook (2009), LIRR Atlantic Terminal. Commissioned by Metropolitan Transportation Authority Arts & Design.
Credit: Allan and Ellen Wexler in collaboration with di Domenico + Partners

waiting on a subway platform. Individual pictograms may spark ideas for how to use the waiting time; when viewed from a distance, the pictograms have a functional utility as pixels forming station signage. The repetition of elements within the stations produces an urban interior network. Pictogram tiles, in particular, differentiate the nodes as distinct yet repeated systemized and networked interior components.

Overlook: Atlantic Terminal

Allan and Ellen Wexler's *Overlook,* 2007, at Atlantic Terminal is a subterranean entrance to the Long Island Rail Road (LIRR) and New York City Subway. *Overlook* is intended to remind observers of the rocky outcroppings at scenic-view rest areas that occur along national highways. Fabricated from the same quotidian tile as the rest of the station, it questions the relationship between nature and mathematics and between the rendered and the pixilated, creating a balance between abstraction and representation. *Overlook* celebrates the unique interiority of the subway system. It is meant to "remind us of the subways' subterranean existence and speak about excavation, strata, and geology." [5] Though it is not repeated, it is a critical aspect of the urban interior network as it creates a subterranean occupiable interior landmark and forms part of a larger system of landmarks throughout the system (Image 47.2).

An above-ground railway, *The Highline*, has prompted a deluge of adaptive reuse proposals for underground abandoned subway stations and tracks, including the *Lowline* in New York City, proposals for the reuse of 11 derelict stations in Paris, and a proposal for the *London Underline*. Gensler's 2015 proposal for the London Underline continues the functionality of a networked system from the original program for a subway into a newly networked transportation system for pedestrians and cyclists that includes cultural and retail spaces.[6]

Interior Infrastructure within Repurposed Infrastructure

A systematized infrastructural interior can re-network an underutilized or disused existing infrastructure. When land-use patterns shift some infrastructures become defunct, leaving their structures underutilized or unused and unoccupied. The shells of these now unnecessary systems can be adaptively reused to serve a new or shared purpose through a redesign of their interior. When nodes of a system become underutilized, the possibility for a relevant shared or *twist* program, where the originally intended program and a new symbiotic program can alternate or share space to make full use of the underutilized structure, becomes advantageous.[7] A subway station can become defunct as a consequence of an entire system or large portion of a system being shut down, or as a more singular elimination of an individual station.

Parking Garage

The parking garage functions as an adaptively reused infrastructural interior, both as a space that is systematized, regulated, and networked by a rule set in its construction and as a node in a transportation system. The parking garage as a design site is rich fodder for insertion of systematized prefabricated and/or mobile interiors. The floorplan of the typical parking garage is generated with a relatively regular module; it maintains a standard incline and is a space that can be considered interior and exterior at once. Arguably, the parking garage is a place of interiority. It comprises a ceiling and a floor, and it provides a space of at least partial enclosure that is somewhat protected from the elements. Though it is technically a building, it was designed for the requirements of a car as its primary inhabitant, and not for human inhabitation. Its architecture is typically quite secondary to civil engineering strategies, placing it in a category more aligned with bridges or tunnels rather than architecture.[8]

Considering recent strategies to eliminate personal car ownership through the promotion of better biking conditions, car sharing, and more robust public transportation, the need for parking garages is decreasing, about 50% are underutilized.[9] Due to the diminishing necessity for parking, the usage of a parking garage might be mapped to utilize the modular space alternately or simultaneously for parking and an additional type of inhabitation.

SCADpad

The SCADpad project approaches the rehabilitation of the parking garage as an adaptive reuse of the garage to coexist with dorm or living spaces. The dimensions of the modular living units and interstitial community spaces are derived from those of the parking spaces. The interior is at once interior and exterior making possible the multiple programs that are layered into the site. The placement of the dwelling units and the common areas are determined at best to acclimatize those areas for inhabitation and function. The prototype is replicable and movable making it potentially part of not only the existing network of parking systems of but also a greater network of pods sited within or moved between parking garages nationally or globally.

Macy's Parking Garage, Brooklyn NY

For their Interior Design theses at Pratt Institute, Alexandra Goldberg and Tulika Lokapur both studied the Macy's parking garage in Downtown Brooklyn. During the weekdays, automobile occupancy is at 80%, but on the weekend, occupancy levels reduce to 20–30%, leaving most of the structure empty.[10] This low-level weekend occupancy coupled with the overcrowded urban condition makes shared programming in the parking garage viable. Goldberg proposes a pop-up hotel for off-peak parking times. The proposal for the pop-up hotel is entirely temporal and makes no permanent mark on the structure. The hotel room in its most compressed form is a 48″ × 48″ × 40″ prefabricated box proportioned such that it can be readily shipped on a standard shipping palette. Once on site, the box can be opened and converted into a hotel room that fits into the dimension of one parking space. A portion of the box's exterior can be removed to form furniture for use in common spaces outside of the room. This furniture is designed to adjust to the inhabitant's needs with consideration of the typical garage floor slope. At the weekend's end, the hotel is packed up and shipped to the next site.[11] The hotel box is designed to be readily transportable between parking garages as required, and functions within the network as its design parameters follow the rules of parking garage layout and planning (Image 47.3).

In her thesis investigation, Lokapur was motivated by the sustainable implications of partially repurposing the underutilized Macy's parking structure. She proposed three programmatic strategies be layered onto the existing parking garage program to encourage sustainable fashion. The first added program is a small donation center, permanently built on the third floor of the parking garage, where the parking garage and donation center programs operate simultaneously. The second added program, a pop-up fashion retail environment, alternates with the parking garage as it is activated only on the weekends when the parking garage is typically at 20–30% occupancy. Vendor stalls, which fold down from the ceiling, are determined dimensionally by the parking module. The third added program folds off the donation center structure twice a year for a redefined sustainable New York Fashion Week (Image 47.4).[12]

Image 47.3 Parking garage modular pop-up rooms with parts by Alexandra Goldberg: Thesis, Pratt Institute, 2015.
Credit: Alexandra Goldberg

Image 47.4 Parking
garage pop-up retail
environment by Tulika
Lokapur: Thesis, Pratt
Institute, 2015.
Credit: Tulika Lokapur

The interior adaptations referenced above all represent replicable models that potentially form a network of linked programmatic and physical interior use. The installations could be repeated across space and relocated as part of a system over time.

Interior Infrastructure within an Architectured Site

A set of interiors can transcend their architecture and comprise a networked infrastructural system within an architectured site. As previously noted, the scope of the definition of infrastructure has come to include replicable building models that maintain an organizational or information network.[13] Hence, a replicable interior that is part of an information network can also be understood as infrastructure. This hypothesis will be analyzed through brief case studies of two typologies of networked interiors: public libraries (presented here as a hybrid with disaster relief) and privately owned public spaces (POPS). In his thesis, Michael Adkin's proposed to connect individual neighborhoods through a network of transformative and adaptable interiors. His primary objective in creating or utilizing this network was to reduce the disruptive potential of disasters on multiple scales, from an outage in a single building to a neighborhood or broader. He found that such an interior network already exists with public libraries.

As a testing site, Adkins selected the Clinton Hill Branch Library in Brooklyn NY, but theoretically his interior system could be adapted at smaller or larger scales at any library. The Clinton Hill library is a relatively modest, single-story cinder block construction. The library is a branch of the Brooklyn Public Library system which includes 58 branches and one Central Library.[14]

As books become more readily available in digital format, the libraries' spatial needs are at best diminished, and at worst raise the question as to whether they are necessary at all. Adkins' proposes that the integration of two critical programs makes the existence of each more viable. He investigates the idea that disaster relief can be layered onto an already established networked system, the library. The library is by its programmatic intent a networked information system and is arguably a prototypical networked interior space. The form of the building envelope is not necessarily relevant to the network, but its interior components are typical, replicable, standardized elements such as card catalogs, bookcases, and carols. The purpose of his proposal is to piggyback onto an arguably existing networked interior system, which he then retrofits into a further connected and transformative interior system. The library's interior spaces, which are already linked as part of an information network, can take on a secondary program and transform into operating as a disaster relief shelter as required.

Adkins' proposal identifies three primary design strategies to facilitate the sharing of programs: the bookcase, the sofa, and the booth. The bookcase is designed to pivot so that it can readily create semi-private shelter sleeping areas. The bookcase can store books, emergency supplies, and inhabitants' belongings. The sofa structure can transform between a low arm height and privacy height, as well as from a place to sit into a place to sleep. The backrests become side tables when they are connected. The sofa employs variation in color and materials to annotate which sections can be activated. The seat cushions are double-sided with program-appropriate fabric on each side, one for library seating and the other for disaster relief sleeping. The booth transforms from a place to sit into a private place to sleep. It also employs variation in color and materials to annotate which sections can be activated. The booth seat slides between the walls and forms a full-size bed. The bed contains integrated storage for linens and personal items.[15] These elements are also replicable and can be fitted into the existing system, generating an additional layer of networked interior space for disaster relief over the already networked library (Image 47.5).

POPS

The New York City POPS program was established to incentivize zoning in response to the 1961 zoning resolution in New York City.[16] The POPS program consists of 525 spaces within or adjacent to buildings that were granted additional floor area or related waivers in exchange for providing public interior or exterior space.[17] The addition or maintenance of a POPS requires adherence to a very specific rule set that prescribes design criteria for the inhabitation of POPS, both interior and exterior. The most critical criteria for the occupation of interior spaces include specifications for seating, planting and trees, lighting and electrical power, litter receptacles, and public space signage. Larger spaces are also required to provide a selection of additional amenities, the

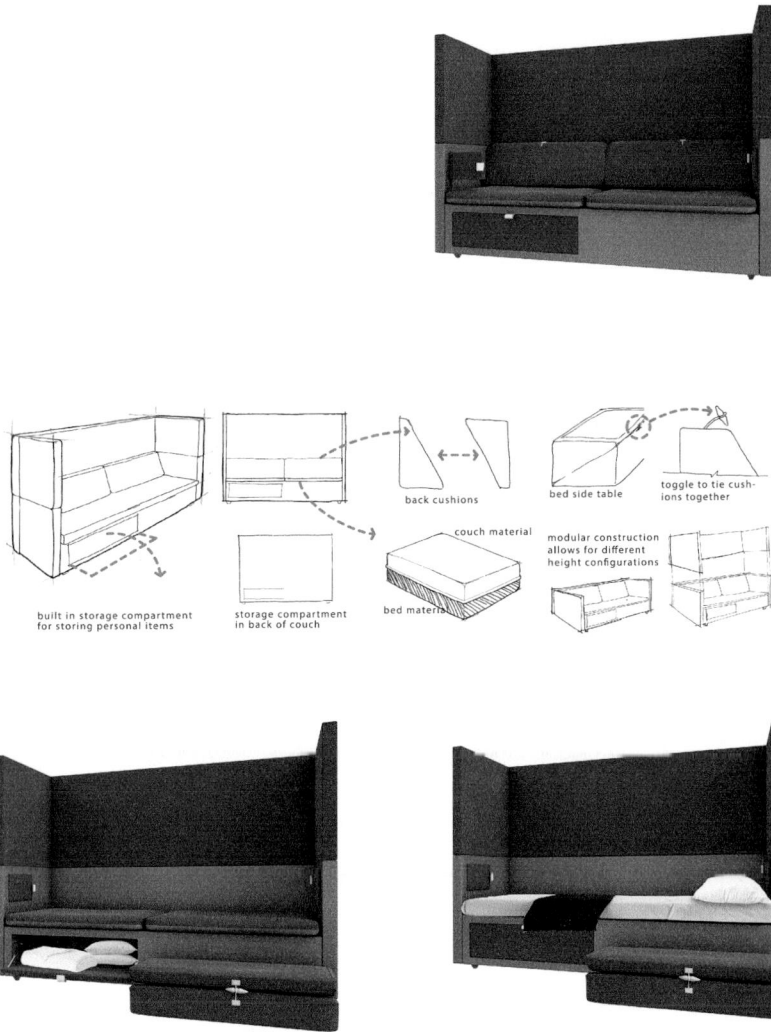

Image 47.5 Library/
Disaster Relief sofa
transformation by Michael
Adkins: Thesis, Pratt
Institute, 2015.
Credit: Michael Adkins

number of which is determined by POPS square footage.[18] The POPS spaces, by intent, should encourage free public occupation, which is a unique phenomenon for the interior as its occupation is typically privatized, either as personal or commercialized space. The interior furnishings and fixtures within the POPS are not required to be precisely the same in every space; however, they are arguably part of a replicable system because they are required to follow a prescriptive set of criteria and are hence an interior network.

Conclusion

This chapter analyzed built work as well as unbuilt work by both design professionals and students. This approach is an effort to document existing functional urban interiors, as well as aspirations toward more speculative and visionary notions of what the public interior can become. The design strategies for the interiors of networked subway systems are vital aspects of Interior Urbanism.

Whether the subway system is functioning in its initial programmatic intent or has been adaptively reused, the clarity of this underground network typology is essential to human well-being, perception of place, safety, and wayfinding. When adaptively reused, the defunct system offers real potential to mirror urban life on the street above, providing an inhabitable urban condition when not possible in the urban public exterior.

The repurposing or shared use of a partially or fully obsolete infrastructural structure is a sustainable approach as it can prevent the demolition of the structure. Considering an added and shared interior occupation can possibly even allow the initial program to continue with a new symbiotic relationship. Interior infrastructures within an architectured site foster a more usable and readily understandable interior. In the case of the library (with or without disaster relief) as well as the POPS, the implementation of systems within the structure is readily understood across the network. The interior networked elements become understood and hence coded as mechanisms of public urban interior place-making. The design for a networked urban interior can generate a more sustainable, navigable, and inhabitable urban interior condition.

Notes

1 Keller Easterling, *Extrastatecraft* (London: Verso, 2014), 11–12.
2 Kevin Lynch, *The Image of the City* (Cambridge: MIT Press, 1960), 47–48.
3 Lynch, *The Image of the City*, 48–49.
4 Britt Bender, "Customized Temporality: Using Space to Personalize Time" (Masters Thesis, Pratt Institute, 2015), 55–75.
5 "Overlook for the Atlantic Terminal," *Allan Wexler Studio*, accessed March 3, 2016, http://www.allanwexlerstudio.com/projects/overlook-atlantic-terminal-2009
6 Feargus O'Sullivan, "Bike Paths in Abandoned Tube Tunnels: Is the London Underline Serious?" *The Guardian*, February 5, 2015, accessed December 5, 2015, https://www.theguardian.com/cities/2015/feb/05/bike-paths-abandoned-tube-tunnels-london-underline
7 Dan Wood and Amale Andraos, "Work: Program Primer," *Praxis* 8 (2010), 113–114.
8 Deborah Schneiderman. "On The Fringe," *Ii Journal* 5 (2013).
9 Rebecca Burns, "Multistorey Car Park in US Transformed into Designer Micro-Apartments," *The Guardian*, July 9, 2104, accessed November 15, 2105, https://www.theguardian.com/cities/2014/jul/09/multistorey-car-park-us-designer-micro-apartments-affordable-housing
10 Tulika Lokapur, "Second Skin" (Masters Thesis, Pratt Institute, 2016), 17–22.
11 Alexandra Goldberg, "Sensorial Thresholds: Fusing Diametric Visual and Tactile Matter to Enhance Perception" (Masters Thesis, Pratt Institute, 2015), 43–51.
12 Lokapur, "Second Skin," 65–90.
13 Easterling, *Extrastatecraft*, 11–12.
14 Michael Adkins, "Transformative and Adaptable Spaces for Unpredictable Disruptive Occurrences" (Masters Thesis, Pratt Institute, 2015), 1–30.
15 Adkins, "Transformative and Adaptable Spaces for Unpredictable Disruptive Occurrences," 91–114.
16 Jerold S. Kayden, *The New York City Department of City Planning, and The Municipal Arts Society, Privately Owned Public Spaces in New York City* (New York: Wiley, 2000), 1–2.
17 "Privately Owned Public Spaces in New York City," The Municipal Arts Society of New York, City, accessed May 20, 2106, http://apops.mas.org
18 The City of New York, "Privately Owned Public Plazas Text Amendment Adopted by City Planning Commission 09/19/2007 Adopted by City Council 10/17/2007," accessed May 20, 2016, file:///C:/Users/My%20PC/Dropbox/interior-without-arch-projects/pops-code.pdf: 43–49.

Chapter 48

Envisioning the Future of Interior Urbanism

Joori Suh

Interior space in urban settings not only dynamically reflects social, economic, and climatic transformations, but also serves as a laboratory for designers to experiment with ideologies of the contemporaries. Since the inception of interiority as a significant subject in the spatial design profession, its nature has been tested and challenged, evolving into what we encounter today. Amid the prominent evolutionary reshaping of interiors, the transplantation of human interactions typically found in outdoor spaces into enclosed interior spaces has been a prevailing phenomenon. This relatively new phenomenon in the history of architecture and interior design has blurred the traditional boundary between private and public, leading to yet another complex interplay among heterogeneous actors. The urban population is projected to grow, with more than two-thirds of the world's population living in urban areas by 2050,[1] making reexamination of the current design approach to urban interiority and ideas about the ideal future more critical. What will the future of interior urbanism look like? Will a dominating digital technology challenge the concept of a physical tangible world, endangering the profession of spatial designers? What must designers keep in mind in the practice of interior urbanism?

In considering urban interiority, some scholars focus on contemporary phenomena like the megastructure, privately owned public spaces, or the atrium effect, all of which shape the nature of contemporary interior urbanism; others emphasize the interiorization of public squares in urban settings. In both cases, the concept of interiority has been used when referring to the intimate relationship between humans and spaces. Across the ideologies of interiority and urbanity, core design initiators practicing both aspects have inspired one another; such mutuality is embedded in the evolution of interior urbanism, that is, interiority in a cityscape and urban influence in large-scale interior spaces. In considering interior urbanism, this mutuality can guide us to essential drivers from the urban, the interior, and the nexus of the two. In this chapter,

DOI: 10.4324/9780429443091-58

interior urbanism is viewed through the following three lenses: multidimensional humanism (derived from interiority), interconnectivity (derived from the link between interiority and urbanism), and interior contextualism (derived from urbanism).

The purpose of this chapter is to steer two tendencies—fear of an uncertain future and the fantasy of future technology—toward envisioning a desirable future with our feet firmly planted in the past and present. Kubler argues that the past holds the key to what we will encounter in the future; the future of interior urbanism will also be *the finite invention* of *the finite world.*[2] The heart of the matter entails how wisely spatial designers will introduce the future based on conscientious strategies and intellectual insights; moreover, filling in the gaps in our understanding of the complex nature of contemporary interior urbanism necessitates a multidimensional discussion.

A More Profound and Multidimensional Humanism

The practice of interior design is not merely about dealing with spaces confined by physical boundaries or limitations; the essence of interiority has been the attentive response to the intimate relationship between humans[3] and spaces that involve people, their lives, and the evolution of their desires and aspirations. Regardless of scale, the key component within designers' scrupulous formulae for space has always been the multifaceted dimensions of humanity. Likewise, urban and architectural theorists have kept the human dimension in mind throughout history. Although criticized by other urbanists like Jane Jacobs, Le Corbusier (1935) describes human life as the primary driving force of his legendary principles in *The Radiant City.*[4] Le Corbusier always took account of "the man who lives in a city" and "the city dweller." When Camillo Sitte (1889) criticized modern cities in *The Art of Building Cities: City Building According to its Artistic Fundamentals,*[5] his concern was the loss of the sense of public life in modern cities especially because of dehumanizing buildings. His intrinsic desire was not necessarily to bring back classical architectural style, but instead to recreate the positive spatial effects that prevailed in ancient cities, such as openness and constantly perceivable connections with small and large spaces as well as the care of human life, dynamic activities, and happiness.

The immense, semi-public interior spaces of megastructures like shopping malls and large office campuses have served as laboratories of trials and errors for designers, developers, and building owners. Some of the traditional social functions taking place outdoors under the open sky have been brought inside, a paradox that made its way to the National Building Museum with "Lawn," Rockwell Group's 2019 installation that conveyed people's aspirations for the interiorization of an outdoor environment. In this vast interior lawn space, people had the freedom to read, relax, walk, jump, and play. The crucial question we should ask is whether they were simply enmeshed within the interiorized physical and digital structure, or intrinsically engaged in a healthy life, happiness, and reality. What matters is not simply bringing outdoor features into an interior setting, nor creating a grandiose high ceiling and providing views to the outside. Designers of the future of interior urbanism should investigate ways to shape interiority in urban settings that serve as a flexible platform supporting multifarious aspects of human life. In megastructure office spaces, for instance, large open atrium spaces and public zones are often designed as an expression of a corporate vision; however, if such public spaces are too far from employees' workspaces, offer minimal benefits, and remain unused most days, their function is limited to advertising. The presence of other users, even without interactions, is critical for semi-public interiors: enriching the sense of togetherness matters more than the stunning vastness of the space itself.

Although it was built over a half-century ago, the Centraal Beheer office building (1968–1972) in Apeldoorn, Holland designed by Herman Hertzberger is influential in that the design supports human psychological needs by simultaneously providing spatial autonomy for people and a sense of belonging. [6] Cedric Price's inventive proposal for his Fun Palace (1964) may finally be realized in interior urbanism in the near future. His revolutionary idea transformed the perception of the flexibility of an interior space, and people were riveted by his playful demonstration of creative user-responsive design. The core concepts embedded in the above examples, that is, the intermingling of autonomy and the sense of belonging as well as inventive approaches to responsiveness and flexibility, must be understood as principles to be manifested in multifarious ways. Adaptability can be achieved not only by flexible aspects that meet various functional requisites, but also by providing automated flexible spatial envelopes creating macro and micro scale interior zones for people with social anxiety or sensitivity to auditory or visual stimuli. The large stairitorium (stair + auditorium), in an open atrium space, may transform into individual cells that meet multiple levels of privacy that serve various human needs ranging from open casual to semi-private enclosures for people with agoraphobia. Not the ecstatic projections of digital fantasies, but carefully choreographed interactions among humans, digital interfaces, and physical movement within the interior will create a spatial platform that promotes health and happiness. Le Corbusier's dream of "liberty of the individual"[7] will be realized when a seamless provision of choice and control is naturally embedded into urban interiority without hindrance.

One may question whether the one-mile-long circumference of Apple Park in Cupertino (despite the dedication of 80% of the site to green spaces) will become a desirable spatial platform promoting a sense of community, or whether it fails to support psychological and emotional well-being. Even with extensive connections to nature, if a building or an interior space is merely an ambitious object, a closed logic and image,[8] it will not create a desirable place supporting people's happiness and aspirations. Regardless of its technological advancements, if interior design does not provide profound care in a multidimensional way, the vastness of an open space within megastructures becomes just another empty, meaningless environment like an abandoned city. For instance, in a city-scale megastructural complex, navigation is challenging. However, reliance on a digital navigation method applied to interior spaces without thoughtful consideration of navigation strategies like physical landmarks, paths, nodes, districts, and edges as Lynch suggests, will ultimately diminish humans' innate navigation skills. Vigilant integration of physical body engagement with digital technology will be the key. Philosopher Albert Borgmann warned that if modern technology hinders mindfulness of the body and its intimate physical relationship with the world, humans will suffer from lost connections in the "depth of the world."[9]

Interconnectivity: New Fabric of the World

In large-scale urban interior spaces, such as shopping malls, interiorized enter-tainment complexes, and workplace campuses, we often see streets, plaza-like public spaces, cafés, theaters, fitness centers, and other sites found in a typical city, but a crucial point in Jacobs' *The Death and Life of Great American Cities* is her advocacy for the "intricate and close-grained diversity of users."[10] Her emphasis here is not mere diversity but of constant mutual support among the components. Disconnection and disengagement among the components will result in a failure to sustain life, and the same applies to a large spatial complex. In that sense, complex systems theory can be applied to the spatial complexity of megascale urban interiority. A complex system is defined as a system that is "diverse and made up of multiple interdependent elements."[11] Future interior urbanism, especially megastructures with multiple components, will provide a spatial platform that enables mutual interactions and support.

Embracing diversity is significant and curation among the multiple components is also crucial. By reflecting characteristics of complex systems theory defined by Johnson (2013), a complex spatial system[12] can be designed to function as interior urbanism in various ways. Multilevel dynamic feedback systems can be created within the whole spatial system allowing parts to co-evolve, thereby adapting to changing needs. Boundaries among these multiple parts are ill-defined and may constantly change. Advanced data science and machine learning will promote the design and curation of a complex spatial system that achieves optimum balance between flexibility and reality and supports health and well-being, while allowing the building owners to reach an ultimate level of real-estate maximization. More specifically, a generative data network system with sensors will recognize individuals' tendency to use spaces or participate in collective events, and will signal other spaces to suggest unplanned activities for cognitive and psychological well-being.

The new fabric of the world in urban interiority will demand not only a complex network of a miniaturized city within a city[13] as Bratton puts it, but also stipulates thoughtful collaboration among multiple players even from the moment of conception of spatial design ideas. Hertzberger's genius tactics of engaging employees with curiosity by infusing the Centraal Beheer office building with art has hinted that a collaborative team of designers, artists, psychologists, engineers, and programmers could curate the element of surprise as well as a complex network of the physical and digital spaces. Incorporating technology is not merely a flashy display of digital fantasies nor solely a celebration of visual entertainment or parametric design; instead, it illustrates how healthy human life as a primary driving force can be supported in a sustainable, wholesome, and orchestrated way. The potentialities of virtual, augmented, or mixed reality technology have been misunderstood as a gaming or visualization tool, but attentive integration of physical and virtual agents will be able to create positive synergy. The phenomenon of virtual and physical integration will reshape our conception, memory, and mental map of urban interiority.

New Interior Urban Contextualism: Unique Strata

When converting abandoned trolley terminals into public interior parks, such as the Low Line Underground City in New York City, the albeit limited attempt to bring natural light into an underground space was not merely to make plants grow, but also an expression of the outside world on the inside. Through a connection between the interior and exterior, we apprehend the expanded holistic spatial dimension, thereby weaving our spatial memories from our day-to-day experiences. Memory of urban spatial experience is multidimensional. Multiple agents, such as multi-sensorial, kinesthetic, and cultural dimensions shape our memories and integrate them with another critical dimension—time. Interior urbanism is the response to the intimate relationship of humans and place, involving people, their lives, and the evolution of desire and aspiration derived from a particular context. Through people's immediate and personal interaction with a place, we remember that place interlaced in time. The place in our memory is permeated with events, people, and personal experiences. Because the vast majority of our time is spent indoors, people's experience within urban interiors will shape their memory of space and time. With the current geographic expanse of global culture, contextualization in urban interiority has often been disregarded in this era of time–space compression. Doreen Massey's (1994) approach to characterizing a global sense of place highlights the significance of multiplicity and the accumulated strata of time as the essence of identity and place.[14] The interior designer's role will not only be to stage the global environment of the interior to meet goals and needs, but also to curate positive instigators that trigger the user's understanding and awareness of the context in time.

The current shift from the ideology of mass standard production to mass customization[15] through digital technology and fabrication has insinuated the potentials of using them to integrate the notion of the particular into the evolving cultural essence of a region. By virtue of the customizable nature of computer programming with the data-driven implementation of interior components, future urban interiority can serve as a dynamic praxis for urban contextualism. Many interactive architecture and interior spatial systems focus on internally responsive attributes, such as reciprocal interaction with human behavior and body, or externally oriented interaction with environmental climatic sources. For example, Hyperbody's Interactive Wall (2009), a living system, offers a prototype for an interior spatial structure that responds to participants' behavior. Barkow Leibinger's Kinetic Wall (2014) implies the potential of designing a nonstatic and character-embedded evolving wall structure. Metatopia Studio investigates data-driven performative design with the human body. Usman Haque's Marling digital projection (2012) suggests the significant reciprocity of data-driven approaches to promote social interaction, while the Living Architecture Systems Group explores the potential of designing space as a living organism.

If the internally oriented investigations would merge with the notion of contextualism and embrace the intimate relationship of people, culture, and history of the city, such efforts will have increasing value in enriching the aura and memory of a place. Gordon Pask's (1969) early concept of a reactive environment[16] must be understood as a holistic interplay that constantly evolves through learning and adapting to behavioral patterns, lives, cultures, and contexts. By shifting the focus, digital technology and fabrication designers will be able to incorporate contextual meaning and cultural value into forming the present and future strata of interior contextualism. The interior system's behavior not only interacts with current users, but also becomes an expression of the context. In return, the interplay of the interior spatial system and the context shapes the uniquely accumulated strata and sense of place.

In shaping the day-to-day memory of our lives in a massive urban interior, the static image of a space will be replaced by the intermingled nature of the physical, digital, virtual, static, and evolutionary, reflecting overlays that engage closely with culture in the context. Our image of the urban interiority in the city, therefore, will demand a new definition that is constantly transforming through the participation of heterogeneous actors.

Conclusion

What we need in interior urbanism in the contemporary world is neither the singularity expressed in a megastructure, nor the mere interiorization of outdoor activities, but instead an inventive and attentive approach that responds to the sense of human scale. Multiple dimensions and continuity among interior components can be supported by autonomous and diverse grains based on vigilant insight into human needs. If contemporary interior urbanism has not reached the highest level of sophistication that many urban theorists have imagined, it might be the result of the segregation of the profession. It reflects a disconnect among multitudinous players, as well as the limitations of ambitiously creative but somewhat dissociated endeavors. The key to shaping the future of the socially and technologically challenging contemporary nature of interior urbanism will lie in collaborative efforts based on a deeper understanding of humans and our age.

Notes

1   Hannah Ritchie and Max Roser, "Urbanization," *Our World in Data*, accessed 2020, https://ourworldindata.org/urbanization

2   George Kubler, *The Shape of Time: Remarks on the History of Things* (New Haven: Yale University Press, 1962), 112–115. He discusses the finite world and finite invention and clarifies the evolutionary recurrence of the human affairs throughout the history of things.

3   Carlo De Carli, "Contro la realta finta." *Interni* 1 (1967), 3. In defining the meaning of interior, Carlo De Carli mentioned interior as "human condition of life" (p. 3).

4   Le Corbusier, Excerpts from "The Radiant City" (1935) in *Introducing Architectural Theory: Debating a Discipline*, ed. Korydon Smith (New York: Routledge, 2013), 278–286.

5   Camillo Sitte, *The Art of Building Cities: City Building According to its Artistic Fundamentals*, 1889. Translated by Charles T. Stewart (Connecticut: Hyperion Press, 1979).

6   Paul Keedwell, Headspace: The Psychology of City Living (London: Quarto Publishing PLC, 2017), 252–254.

7   Le Corbusier, Excerpts from "The Radiant City" (1935) in *Introducing Architectural Theory: Debating a Discipline*, ed. Korydon Smith (New York: Routledge, 2013), 280.

8   Juhani Pallasmaa, "The Architectural Image," in *The Embodied Image* (Chichester: John Wiley & Sons, 2011), 131–138.

9   Albert Borgmann, *Technology and the Character of Contemporary Life: A Philosophical Inquiry* (Chicago: University of Chicago Press, 1987).

10 Jane Jacobs, Excerpts from "The Death and Life of Great American Cities" (1961) in *Introducing Architectural Theory: Debating a Discipline*, ed. Korydon Smith (New York: Routledge, 2013), 287–297.

11 Alec Robertson, "Metamorphosis of the Artificial," in *Embracing Complexity in Design,* ed. Katerina Alexiou, Jeffrey Johnson, and Theodore Zamenopoulos (New York: Routledge, 2010), 177–191.

12 Johnson Jeffrey, *Hypernetworks in the Science of Complex Systems*. Vol. 3 (London: World Scientific, 2013), 6.

13 Benjamin H. Bratton, "Cloud Megastructures and Platform Utopias," in *Entr'acte: Performing Publics, Pervasive Media, and Architecture*, ed. Jordan Geiger (New York: Palgrave Macmillan, 2015), 35–51.

14   Doreen Massey, Chapter 6 "A Global Sense of Place," in *Space, Place and Gender* (Minneapolis: University of Minnesota Press, 1994), 146–156.

15   Erin Carraher, "Technologies: The Spatial Agency of Digital Praxis," in *The Interior Architecture Theory Reader*, ed. Gregory Marinic (New York: Routledge, 2018), 132–144.

16   Gordon Pask, "The Architectural Relevance of Cybernetics," *Architectural Design* 39, no. 9 (1969), 494–496.

Chapter 49

The Subjective City

Toward a Reconceptualization of Urban Interiority

Suzie Attiwill

The title of this chapter borrows from the philosopher and psychoanalyst Félix Guattari's essay – *Ecosophical Practices and the Restoration of the 'Subjective City'*.[1] The concept of the 'Subjective City' goes to the heart of the speculations in this chapter that call for a shift from an equation of urban interiority to the experience of individuals and the urban interior with space.

Masses of people, challenging environmental conditions, globalism, and capitalism are transforming cities in unprecedented ways. For the first time in history, there are more people living in urban than rural contexts with this projected to increase from the current 55% to 68% by 2050. This 'more people' is not just proportional, but actual bodies with 751 million people in mid-twentieth-century cities to 4.2 billion living in cities in 2022. Ten years from now, there will be 43 megacities with over ten million inhabitants, a three-fold increase on the current number.[2] Another significant influx of people is tourism. In 2019, it was the fastest growing economic sector in the world with a tidal-like effect on the urban environment as tourists ebb and flow. Examples include cities such as Venice with a local population of 60,000 people and 20 million tourists annually; in Amsterdam, there are ten tourists for every resident[3]; and in New York, the number of tourists has doubled since 1998 to 60 million per year.[4] In 2020, the impact of a global pandemic – COVID-19 – reduced the flow of people to a standstill in parts of the world with large numbers of people being effectively quarantined in cities. Demographic shifts are another movement, for example in Tokyo which has one of the largest urban populations and an aging demographic; and migration where the world has experienced the highest level of displacement on record with 70.8 million people forcibly displaced; 25.9 million refugees (over half are under the age of 18), 3.5 million asylum seekers and ten million people who are stateless, i.e. they are denied a nationality and access to basic rights such as education, healthcare, employment, and freedom of movement.[5]

DOI: **10.4324/9780429443091-59**

The built environment, infrastructure, services, and the resources of governments are challenged in significant and unprecedented ways. Sociologist Saskia Sassen writes of the corporatization of cities and the dematerializing effect of high finance on the built environment where it is more profitable to have an empty building as an asset than to have a building used and inhabited.[6] Definitions of public and private space are transformed as corporations move into urban development. There is a pervading sense that 'globalization has evicted us from the world we thought we knew'.[7] Architect, theorist, and interior design professor, Andrea Branzi coined the phrase 'weak urbanism' to describe what he sees as the transformation of the contemporary city into a continuous system of relational forces and flows 'where the immaterial reality of computer networks have already created a de facto, dynamic, invisible, and abstract metropolis that is progressively substituting (or moving to the background) the physical and figurative metropolis'.[8] Architect Liam Young's lecture-film performance *City Everywhere: A storytelling tour through the landscapes of technology* presents a quasi-fictional city in the near future where the built environment is dissolved by technologies and automation to become a digital infrastructure.[9] The homogenizing forces of capitalism and globalism have transformed cities into 'giant machines...producers of individual and collective processes of subjectivation by means of collective apparatuses (education, health, social control, culture...) and mass media'.[10]

In his essay on 'the subjective city', Guattari calls for a 'collective reorientation of human activities and notes that this depends in a large part on the evolution of urban mentalities'.[11] He is not referring to individuals coming together in a collective, consensual way, but for 'new practices' and 'new styles of living'[12] where architectural design and urbanism are 'called upon to become multidimensional cartographies for the production of subjectivity'.[13] Guattari urges that 'urbanists can no longer be satisfied defining cities in spatial terms',[14] but need to think through 'their particular problems in terms of planetary ecology' due to the increasing impact of urban phenomenon on the biosphere, worldwide demographic pressures, and the international division of labor between the salaried and subsidized.[15]

This chapter responds to Guattari's call for the production of 'this new subjectivity (to become) the primary aim of human activities'[16] by reviewing a selection of existing conjunctions that have been made between interiority and urbanism, and through this, become aware of a consistent assumption and alignment of interiority with the individual; the potential to speculate on how urban interiority could be reconceptualized is opened up and invited.

Interiority + Urbanism

A refrain runs through the twentieth and twenty-first centuries concerned with this conjunction and is manifested in the following titles: sociologist Georg Simmel's lecture, *The Metropolis and Mental Life* (1903)[17]; Guattari's essay, *Subjective City* (1989); an anthology titled, *Intimate Metropolis. Urban Subjects in the Modern City* (2009)[18]; and a seminar presented as part of the Yale School of Architecture program titled *Interiority and the City* (2017).[19]

The early twentieth-century writings of philosopher Walter Benjamin pose the individual's confrontation with the transformation of the city during the Industrial Revolution as a conjunction of interiority and urbanism. Benjamin writes about 'the collector' – a subject who is produced through processes of collection, selection, and arrangement where the external world is interiorized and brought into the private, domestic realm enabling 'a fictional framework' to be lived – collected, controlled, and composed.[20] Urbanist and sociologist Richard Sennett addressing a Harvard symposium titled *Architecture's interior matters in new ways today*,[21] challenged this idea of interiority as a withdrawal into the domestic interior which has persisted through the twentieth century. In contrast, Sennett proposed a concept of interiority situated in relation to the urban environment as an opportunity to be freed from the constraints of domesticity; a freedom from the familiar and familial. Sennett's proposition embodies something of Baudelaire's 'flâneur' (1863) – who Benjamin refers to as a counterpoint to 'the collector'. In contrast to the domestic interior as a refuge, the flâneur made the city his living room where 'the world only appears to him reflected by pure inwardness'.[22] For Sennett, 'urban subjectivity' is critical as an urban strategy and challenges what he sees as the 'great unspoken dogma that urban designers share' which is to emphasis 'sociable space' as the solution. Sennett calls for this to be re-thought:

> [B]ecause, for lots of people, that is not why they want to be in public. They want something else. They want an interior life, a life where they can practice an observational cruising and reflexivity in which the work of memory can occur, because they are alone. ... The issue for us, then, is to understand what kinds of space we can make so that somebody can sit at a table, in a café, drink a glass of absinthe, smoke a cigarette, and reflect. That is really the relationship between interiority and the exterior.[23]

Sennett's urban subjectivity is based on an assumption of subjectivity/interiority as that possessed by the individual person who can be autonomous and therefore has 'the freedom of being able to observe without interacting'.[24] Referring to Simmel's *The Metropolis and Mental Life*, Sennett says it is 'an urban account of interiority – i.e. subjective feeling – linked to an exterior condition – i.e. exposure to others. ... There is an inside-outside divide, Simmel says, that is made by the street rather than removed from the street'.[25] This urban subjectivity is manifested as a blasé attitude that individuals can adopt as a screen to reduce the stimuli and sensation of the city. Simmel's essay continues as a refrain through the twentieth century in relation to the conjunction of interiority and urbanism manifested as a concern with the individual and their psychological life confronting the forces of capitalism intensified as a metropolis.

The conjunction between interiority and urbanism is emerging as an important focus in the discipline of interior design as it moves from a modernist definition that contains it within an architectural context to one that expands the proposition implicit in designing 'interior'. This shift is evident in the definition of an interior designer given by the discipline's professional global body – The International Federation of Interior Architects/Designers (IFI). In the *IFI Interiors Declaration* an interior designer/interior architect is defined as a practitioner who determines 'the relationship of people to spaces based on psychological and physical parameters, to improve the quality of life'.[26] This shift to an emphasis on the relationship means interior design is no longer necessarily defined in advance by the condition of enclosure.

Academic Liz Teston situates the practice of interior architecture in the urban environment and explores 'the intersection between interiority, urbanism, and human perception' in relation to 'psychological public interiorities'.[27] The concept of 'personal cities' and 'personal urbanities' is posed by urbanist and academic Jacopo Leveratto. He writes of 'a new idea of urbanity' where 'urban space develops, as a domestic interior, around the "gestures" of the subjects who inhabit it ... a subjective identity that is not imposed or inherited, but can be imagined, built, and modified in the most absolute autonomy'.[28] Leveratto poses this as the potential for interior design practices in the urban environment where 'urban spaces could develop around the "gesture" of living in a dimension that can be experienced, used, and directly transformed by people'.[29] There are many other examples of this emerging focus on the relation between interiority and urbanism in interior design practice and teaching.[30]

Reconceptualizations

While the accounts above critically address the conjunction between interiority and urbanism, the concept of interiority inheres in a familiar way. *Intimate Metropolis* foregrounds the question of subjectivity through the 'choice of the word "intimate"' to reinforce 'the extent to which the modern city is predicated on the concept of the private individual, and on the sanctity of the individual's inner most thoughts and feelings'.[31] The dominant tendency is to respond to this problematic with an affirmation of 'interiority' as something that belongs to the experience of the individual; that it is personal and conscious; phenomenological. However, if individualism can be defined as capitalism's interiority manifested in the subject of the consumer who consumes themselves – a subjectivity 'threatened by paralysis'[32] where the individual is seized from the inside[33] – critically engaging with the concept of interiority as a problematic opens an opportunity to intervene in the contemporary urban situation.

Academic and artist Mark Pimlott identifies the potential for architects to address and resist the forces of capitalism through becoming aware of the 'public interior', and in doing so, to enable different urban interiorities. His book, *The Public Interior as Idea and Project*,[34] is based on a lecture series he presented to TU Delft Architecture students titled 'The Architecture of the Interior' which was motivated by a concern:

> [T]o make the interior visible ... as a realm beyond the domestic, apparently centered on the self; and to make students and readers aware that the public interior, in producing the most influential spaces of our urbanized environment, was a realm of many possibilities: it could be about manipulation, control, and instrumentality, but it was also about allusion, affordance, and the imagination, about the self and others, about consciousness of being among others and in the world, and so about the possibility of freedom.[35]

Pimlott argues that architects must understand these conditions in order to intervene in the increasingly interiorized condition of contemporary cities, such as those manifested in the large public interiors of shopping malls and airports.

The Situationists invented an array of different techniques to resist capitalism's internalizing forces. They declared that

> All the doors are resolutely open, everything happens outside, there is no longer room for either interior or interiority: henceforth subjectivity is lived or expresses itself externally, it is collective or it is nothing, it is detached from all individual representation. [36]

They invented new practices such as dérive, psychogeography, and détournement to experiment with different ways of seeing and engaging the urban environment to stimulate 'new sorts of behavior'[37] situated in an urban environment based on 'the atmospheric effects of rooms, hallways, streets … [and] emotionally moving situations, rather than emotionally moving forms'.[38] For the Situationists, 'interiority' was complicit in capitalism, 'man is more and more, and ever more powerfully, the producer of every detail of his world. The closer his life comes to being his own creation, the more drastically is he cut off from that life'.[39] Their counterpoint is the subjectivity of the worker who 'does not produce themselves: they produce a force independent of themselves'.[40]

Guattari challenges the forces of capitalism through a critique of the sovereignty of the 'I' and calls for a new subjectivity. The 'subjective city' requires the reinvention of 'urban assemblages, social, cultural, artistic, and mental practices' as well as addressing 'economic and productive finalities'[41] through 'a redeployment of values'[42] understood as situated in and productions of physical, social, and mental ecologies. This is not a practice that reacts and affirms an ideal state to attain, but instead, a practice that intervenes in the present to rupture fixed relations and experiments in making new relations for a time to come – a future.

Guattari's call for 'new styles of living'[43] reads like a brief for an interior designer, while also amplifying the IFI definition of an interior designer as a practitioner who makes relations, and problematizes assumptions that equate 'interiority' with 'I' and 'interior' with space. 'The subjective city' is a provocation and an invitation to work in the middle and intervene in the present to make relations. This reconceptualizes urban interiority, as well as interior urbanism, and calls on creative practices associated with cities and the urban environment such as architecture, landscape architecture, urban planning, and others, including (and perhaps, most significantly) interior design to evolve urban mentalities to transform the critical situation that the global biosphere confronts.

Notes

1   Guattari, Félix, 'Ecosophical Practices and the Restoration of the "Subjective City" (1989)', in *Machinic Eros: Writings on Japan*. Edited by Gary Genosko and Jay Hetrick. Translated by Kuniichi Uno and Gary Genosko, Minneapolis: Univocal Publishing, 2015, 97–116.

2   United Nations: '68% of the World Population Projected to Live in Urban Areas by 2050, Says UN', www.unhcr.org/en-au/figures-at-a-glance.html (last accessed 1 March 2020)

3   Boztas, Senay, 'Ten Tourists for Every Amsterdammer: New Report', https://www.dutchnews.nl/news/2018/04/ten-tourists-for-every-amsterdammer-now-report/ (last accessed 20 January 2019).

4   González-Rivera, Christian, 'Destination New York' (Centre for an Urban Future, May 2018), https://nycfuture.org/research/destination-new-york (last accessed 20 January 2019).

5   UNHCR. The UN Refugee Agency: 'Figures at a Glance', www.un.org/development/desa/en/news/population/2018-revision-of-world-urbanization-prospects.html (last accessed 20 January 2019).

6   Sassen, Saskia, 'Who Owns Our Cities – and Why This Urban Takeover Should Concern Us All', *The Guardian*, 24 November 2018, www.theguardian.com/cities/2015/nov/24/who-owns-our-cities-and-why-this-urban-takeover-should-concern-us-all (last accessed 20 January 2019).

7   Buchanan, Ian and Gregg Lambert, 'Introduction', in *Deleuze and Space*. Edited by Ian Buchanan and Gregg Lambert. Edinburgh: Edinburgh University Press, 2005, 7.

8   Branzi, Andrea, *Weak and Diffuse Modernity. The World of Projects at the Beginning of the 21st Century*. Milan: Skira, 2006, 10–11.

9   Young, Liam, 'Tomorrow's Thoughts Today', *Tomorrow's Thoughts Today*, accessed 28 January 2018, http://www.tomorrowsthoughtstoday.com/ (last accessed 16 February 2019).

10 Guattari, 'Subjective City'. 105.

11 Ibid., 99.

12 Ibid., 111.

13 Ibid., 113.

14 Ibid., 107.

15 Ibid., 99.

16 Ibid., 113.

17 Simmel, Georg, 'The Metropolis and Mental Life,' (1903) in *The Blackwell City Reader*, Edited by Bridge, Gary and Sophie Watson. Oxford: Wiley-Blackwell, 2002.

18 di Palma, Vittoria, Diana Periton and Marina Lathouri, 'Introduction', in *Intimate Metropolis. Urban Subjects in the Modern City*. Edited by di Palma, Vittoria, Diana Periton, and Marina Lathouri. London: Routledge, 2009, 1–8.

19 Erdman, David, 'Interiority and the City', 2017, www.architecture.yale.edu/courses/24273-interiority-and-the-city (last accessed 16 February 2019).

20 Benjamin, Walter, *Arcades Project*. Translated by Eiland, Howard and Kevin, McLaughlin, Cambridge, MA: Harvard University Press, 2002, 20.

21 Moe, K., 'Interior and Matter Reconsidered', *a+t. Independent Magazine of Architecture+Technology*, *Interior Matters SOLID Harvard Symposia on Architecture* (47), 2017, 4.

22 Fuss, Diana, *The Sense of an Interior. Four Writers and the Rooms That Shaped Them*. New York, London: Routledge, 2004. Quoting Theodore Adorno, 13.

23 Sennett, Richard, 'Interiors and Interiority', *a+t. Independent Magazine of Architecture+Technology* (47), 2017, 10–19, 18.

24 Ibid., 16.

25 Ibid., 13.

26 'IFI Interiors Declaration' (International Federation of Interior Architects/Designers, February 2011), https://ifiworld.org/programs-events/interiors-declaration-adoptions/ (last accessed 20 January 2019).

27 Teston, Liz, 'On the Nature of Public Interiority', *Interiority*, 3, no. 1 (2020): 61–82.

28 Leveratto, Jacopo, 'Personal Urbanities: Domesticating the Public Domain', *Philosophy Study*, 6, no. 7 (July 2016): 424–431.

29 Leveratto, Jacopo, 'Urban Interiors: A Retroactive Investigation', *The Journal of Interior Design*, 44, 2019, 161–171.

30 Attiwill, Suzie et al., 'URBAN + INTERIOR', *IDEA Journal*, 2015, https://idea-edu.com/journal/index.php/home/issue/view/2 (last accessed 20 January 2020).

31 di Palma et al, *Urban Subjects in the Modern City*. 1.

32 Guattari, 'Subjective City', 98.

33 Guattari, Félix, *Soft Subversions*. Edited by Sylvère Lotringer. Translated by David L. Sweet and Chet Wiener. New York: Semiotext(e), 1996. 220.

34 Pimlott, Mark, *The Public Interior as Idea and Project*. The Netherlands: Jap Sam Books, 2016.

35 Pimlott, Mark, from Provocation for Public Interior Public Discussion, MPavilion, Melbourne, 7 February 2018.

36 Kauffman, Vincent, 'Angels of Purity', in *Guy Debord and the Situationist International. Text and Documents.* Edited by Tom McDonough. Translated by John Goodman. Cambridge, MA: The MIT Press, 2002, 287.

37 Sadler, Simon, *The Situationist City.* Cambridge, MA: The MIT Press, 1998, 105.

38 Ibid., quoting Guy Debord, 107.

39 Debord, Guy, *The Society of the Spectacle.* Translated by Donald Nicholson-Smith. New York: Zone Books, 1995, 24.

40 Ibid., 23.

41 Guattari, 'Subjective City', 98.

42 Ibid., 103.

43 Ibid., 111.

Chapter 50

A Brief Allegory of Capitalism in the Time of Plague

Edward Mitchell

The Beginning

Moses Mendelssohn equated vastness, immensity, and magnitude with "The unfathomable sea, a far-reaching plain, the innumerable legion of stars, the eternity of time, every height and depth that is beyond the reach of the eye."[1]

Dawn

David Foster Wallace in his 2005 commencement speech at Kenyon College told this joke:

> there are these two young fish swimming along, and they happen to meet an older fish swimming the other way, who nods at them and says, "Morning, boys, how's the water?" And the two young fish swim on for a bit, and then eventually one of them looks over at the other and goes, "What the hell is water?"

Day 1

In these viral times, it is worth recalling Foucault's description of the city under plague. First, a strict spatial partitioning is imposed, followed by the constraint of movement of citizens, sequestered into the interior by the syndic who locks the door from the outside. Each person is fixed in his place, and if he moves he does so "at the risk of his life, contagion or punishment." Foucault continues,

> This enclosed segmented space, observed at every point, in which the individuals are inserted in a fixed place, in which the slightest movements are supervised, in which all events are recorded, in which an uninterrupted work of writing links the center and periphery, in which power is exercised without division, according to a continuous and hierarchical figure, in which each individual is constantly

DOI: 10.4324/9780429443091-60

located, examined, and distributed among the living beings, the sick and the dead–all this constitutes a compact model of the disciplinary mechanism.[2]

The political model constituted in relation to the plague, he writes, is then associated with the assignment of the individual to his "true" name, "true" place, "true" body. Foucault directs us to this dominant model of the modern period, one of strict discipline, the organization of "truths," the obsession with the cell, the fixed and repetitive nature of organizations, and the act of writing as a means of organization. Plague organizes principals that construct the concept of a subject formed and informed by interiors both physical and psychic, and the syndic manages properties and organizes us into associations, guilds, and universities.

Day 4

As the editor of this book claims, the present condition of Interior Urbanism is defined by vastness and interconnectivity which he traces to Leonardo da Vinci's *Ideal City* (1487) a tiered infrastructure of canal and roads that was offered as a cure to the plague as it would "disperse its great congregation of people which are packed like goats, one behind each other, filling every place with fetid smells and sowing seeds of pestilence and death."[3] From studying the canal systems of Milan, Leonardo envisioned the city as a vast body, connected like the human circulatory system, each of its features simultaneously promoting flow while separating mixtures of animal and human, merchants and tradesmen, fetid waters, and healthy air through precise geometric organization. "That which has no limitations, has no form," wrote Da Vinci.

Wednesday's Introductions and Conclusions

Leonardo's central proposition, that man could control nature and rightfully claim his place at the center of all things, was represented differently by his contemporary Giovanni Pico della Mirandola. In his introduction to the *900 Conclusions*, the "Oration on the Dignity of Man" of 1486, Pico situates humans at the center but does not inscribe him within a six-foot diameter. Pico conspicuously places man outside the "cosmic dwelling" in order to bear witness to the "vast achievements" of the Divine Artificer.

> Truth was, however, that there remained no archetype according to which He might fashion a new offspring, nor in His treasure-houses the wherewithal to endow a new son with a fitting inheritance, nor any place, among the seats of the universe, where this new creature might dispose himself to contemplate the world. *All space was already filled*; all things had been distributed in the highest, the middle and the lowest orders. …
>
> At last, the Supreme Maker decreed that this creature, to whom He could give nothing wholly his own, should have a share in the particular endowment of every other creature. Taking man, therefore, this creature of indeterminate image, He set him in the middle of the world and thus spoke to him:

"We have given you, O Adam, *no visage proper to yourself, nor endowment properly your own,* in order that whatever place, whatever form, whatever gifts you may, with premeditation, select, these same you may have and possess through your own judgement and decision. The nature of all other creatures is defined and restricted within laws which We have laid down; you, by contrast, impeded by no such restrictions, may, by your own free will, to whose custody We have assigned you, trace for yourself the lineaments of your own nature. [italics added]

Pico, a scholar of the Kabbala, regarded God's sacred speech as infinite, finding significance not only in the divine words but in the increments of the letters and their shapes. Pico's world, unlike Leonardo's, was not limited by geometry, but unfolded in its extensive magnitude. Beauty is bounded; the immensity of the fullness of creation is unbounded.

Day 9 (or is it 9,000?)

Vastness is attributed not to Beauty but to the Sublime where the encounter with awesome natural phenomena hints at a world both anterior and ulterior to human thought. Vastness is a distinctly human effect, one which has a history with at least three phases in its development. For the scholars of the Renaissance, "The vastness of pre-existing space appears to come under the thrall of a divine order," writes Lefebvre. Mendelssohn noted that the sublime can be both alluring and dizzying. Edmund Burke navigated the expanse between the sublime's extensive and intensive realms and wrote that "Greatness of dimension is a powerful cause of the sublime…

However, it may not be amiss to add to these remarks upon magnitude, that as the great extreme of dimension is sublime, *so the last extreme of littleness is in some measure sublime likewise*; when we attend to the infinite divisibility of matter, when we pursue animal life into these excessively small, and yet organized beings, that escape the nicest inquisition of the sense; when we push our discoveries yet downward, and consider those creatures so many degrees yet smaller, and the still diminishing scale of existence, in tracing which the imagination is lost as well as the sense; we *become amazed and confounded at the wonders of minuteness*; nor can we distinguish in its effect this extreme of littleness from the vast itself. For division must be infinite as well as addition; because the idea of a perfect unity can no more be arrived at, than that of a complete whole, to which nothing may be added."[4] [italics added]

4:42 PM

The world was reorganized and commodified by being mathematized. Material goods—a bag of flour, a bolt of cloth, an acre of land, a herd of cattle—and immaterial activities and concepts—labor, punishment for transgressions, tributes, patents, legal services—can be quantified and exchanged. Capital masks its essential smallness, the infinitesimal power of the differential, by the accumulation of its sums toward a vast and inhuman interiority. That human construct exposes its primary (some might say darker) product—a universe of artifice substituting for the natural, that simultaneously constructs "the natural" as a separate realm. When Henry David Thoreau remarked that, "Not till we are completely lost, or turned round, do we appreciate the vastness and strangeness of Nature,"[5] he neglected the corollary that Nature could only appear vast and strange at the moment when we acquired the capacity to be lost. The boundlessness sublime evokes awe, even terror. The terror of the exterior, the threat posed by inhuman forces is internalized into our psyche. While vastness can give a false sense of ecstasy, even liberation, we attribute its hallucinatory qualities to the feeling of loss and being lost.

After Hours

If the architectural reaction to the plague is the first phase that constructs an interior urbanism, the second phase, I will suggest, is characterized by what Peter Sloterdijk calls the configuration of "psychedelic capitalism," the point in which nature and culture become interior affairs. Nature is divided from the human realm in the first movement, but is sublime-ated or sublimated and brought into the interior.

The utopian propositions of the mid-nineteenth and early twentieth centuries are based on an apparent conflict between these two paradigms: the cell as it constitutes the unit of organization that enables the disciplining of subjects, serving as a proxy for the individual. The cell subdivides and organizes a heterogeneous space, delimiting the unmanageable and ungovernable coextension of bodies and their milieu. The establishment of the cell differentiates, subdivides, and determines the orders of microbes, hours, minutes, seconds, and nanoseconds, the minutiae of algorithms that might eliminate waste, sift and extract the finest particles in the effort to mine wealth as a mineral value, as well as a means of directing and profiting on the potential of exchanges. The act of writing establishes a new world of signs and the possibility of the psycho-economies of consumption gleaned from desire. And so, while Leonardo's drawing for a Milan cured of the plague resembles the phalanstery of Charles Fourier, the bodies that animate Fourier's interiors are no longer discrete, but can be divided into "passions" in order to reorganize the day and stave off the boredom of a world in which history has ended in some geometricized ideal. Fourier posited that this mixture of passions might re-animate and accommodate the ever-shifting assemblage of the desiring subject. The 20-foot by 20-foot cell of the phalanstery, however, measures and tabulates the promiscuous proliferation of heterogeneous forms of identity and the circulation of desires. The cell, we might say, accounts for the subject. The cell is extensive, it is replicable. In its imposition the wonders of nature are held accountable. The cell is also extensive as an act of division as organisms are revealed to be vast on to themselves. Bodies, too, are made up of cells, molecules, DNA, RNA, subatomic particles, and are the host of other, invisible worlds, apparently coherent and bounded from the exterior but revealed to be unbounded and immense from the interior.

Palm Sunday

The second spatial paradigm, identified by both Dostoevsky and Sloterdijk, is the Crystal Palace which transposed "the outside world as a whole into a magical immanence transfigured by luxury and cosmopolitanism."[6] If the cell is the monad of division, then what puts us together again, what binds us, organizes us, and sustains us is the seemingly infinite glass and steel construct of an artificially controlled, conditioned space. Richard Turner's Palm Court at Kew was the first of these technical feats in steel and plate glass. Joseph Paxton further developed the technique with the Chatsworth Lily House, which housed a giant plant, recently discovered by European botanists, whose ribbed undersurface and leaves veining "like transverse girders and supports" inspired the structure of the Crystal Palace. "Biopolitics," Sloterdijk writes, "begins as a closed building."[7]

The tension between the cell and the desiring body repeats itself in the national psychosis of Progressive Era America: Henry Olerich's "Cityless and Countryless World" (1893), King Camp Gillette's "Metropolis" (1894), and Edgar Chambliss's "Roadtown" (1910), and the visionary schemes of the Soviet state—Georgii Krutikov's Flying City (1928) or Viktor Kalmykov's "Saturn Ring City" (1929). The relentless sameness of the cell re-appears in Le Corbusier's reductive monk's cell, 1.83–2.26 meters, a new geometric modular, which forms the residences of La Tourette, elevated above the terrain to stave off disease.

Late: One Evening

Walter Benjamin, too, in his journeys through the crystal palaces of the Parisian arcades, read the discarded, the ornamental, and the obsolete as shifting signs of the eternal, recurring apocalypse of consumerism. The vast interiors of the exposition hall promised a utopia at the end of history, where all conflicts are resolved and controlled, but it too is a space "already filled" where that which is human cannot be countenanced. The Crystal Place would lead to the inevitable hothouse of consumerism. Writes Benjamin, "The phalanstery, for Fourier, was a veritable hallucination. He saw everywhere, both in civilization and in nature."[8]

Tomorrow

We cannot foresee the future; we have been better at seeing the end… of the modern world. Archizoom's limitless "No-Stop City" is such a dystopian vision of biopolitical urbanization taken to an absurd level of quantification where the vast interior is measured out by a bathroom every 50 square meters. "No-Stop City" is the end without end, a depiction of a world of pure reproduction without form.

What Time Is It? Where Are We?

Do animals get lost? Joseph Kirschvink, a geobiologist, wrote that even the minor presence of magnetite crystals might be what provides an animal with a sense of navigation, "One equivalent of a magnetic bacteria can give a whale a compass—one cell."[9] Could it be that the introduction of a single cell or the loss of a single cell is that minute difference that separates humans from animals? Animals do not get lost; humans do. In other words, "What the hell is water?"

He had bought a large map representing the sea,
Without the least vestige of land:
And the crew were much pleased when they found it to be
A map they could all understand.
"What's the good of Mercator's North Poles and Equators,
Tropics, Zones, and Meridian Lines?"
So the Bellman would cry: and the crew would reply
"They are merely conventional signs!
"Other maps are such shapes, with their islands and capes!
But we've got our brave Captain to thank:
(So the crew would protest) "that he's bought us the best—
A perfect and absolute blank!" [10]

Lewis Carol's map for the Snark Hunt depicts a sea of degenerative informa-tion, a world devoid of conventional signs, there are no interiors, only a world erased in order to begin again.

February 23
"We have it very much under control in this country." [11]

Once Upon a Time in the Not So Distant Future
We might conclude that our present interior urbanism expresses itself as a desire for greater autonomy exemplified in the vast networks of subways, sky-walks, hotel atria, transport hubs, corporate campuses, and mega-towers. The psychedelia of the city within a city so lyrically captured in Steven Millhauser's novel *Martin Dressler* speaks of the evolution of these spaces, in particular, the novel's closing vision of the Grand Cosmo, an interior so vast and full that it "renders the city unnecessary."

But if the second phase of the Crystal Palace and the Grand Cosmo renders the city, the public market of exchange and cosmo-politanism moot, in the phase that we now encounter, we find hints that we will eventually be rendered "unnecessary." These contemporary spaces, like their antecedents of the "psy-chedelic capitalism" of the nineteenth century, even more perfectly respond to our bodily and psychological needs, providing cool, perfectly modulated air, rever-berating with the dream-like solicitations of a ubiquitous, most likely female voice half sexual and half maternal. While these may be a form of an extensive realm it seems anachronistic to call them "public." As Frederic Jameson once noted:

> The human subjects who happen into this new space, have not kept pace with that evolution; there has been a mutation in the object unaccompanied as yet by any equivalent mutation to the subject. We do not yet possess the perceptual equipment to match this new hyperspace... [12]

When Jameson wrote that almost 30 years ago, he saw, in the Bonaventure Hotel, a new spatial era. Where then, he felt, one felt lost in the new hyper-space, today we are more accustomed to the public forum being crowded with non-human flotsam pumped into the interior from a thousand apps, as our data inputs and outputs continually form and reform our sense of ourselves. The new postmodern sublime posits both the historic systems of representation of the immensity of human potential and power, but couples that with the vastness of a post-human, ulterior future without us. Click bait, tweets, hermetically sealed bodies of doctors and nurses and tomorrow night's dinner compete on our cell phone screens with the databanks, artificial intelligence, artificial greenhouses, and viruses that inform these networks. This mixture of spaces have the hallucinatory and repetitive quality of prior vast interiors like the Crystal Palace, but leave us with the uncomfortable feeling that they are best operated without us or that they will survive *after* what we understand to be us. As one earlier visionary of this present future, Stanley Kubrick, put it:

> The most terrifying fact about the universe is not that it is hostile but that it is indifferent; but if we can come to terms with this indifference and accept the challenges of life within the boundaries of death — however mutable man may be able to make them — our existence as a species can have genuine meaning and fulfillment. However vast the darkness, we must supply our own light.[13]

The proliferation of an alien presence in the civic body, which has the capacity to divide those who will live from those who will succumb to its biological attack on our interiors. One might suppose that, in some pandemics, both the living and the dead will be altered by the reconfiguration of their DNA.

February 26

> I think every aspect of our society should be prepared. I don't think it's going to come to that, especially with the fact that we're going down, not up. We're going very substantially down, not up.[14]

Imagining What Tomorrow Might Bring

Foucault writes that the plague is followed by the festival where bodies "mingle together without respect, individuals unmasked, abandoning their statutory identity and the figure under which they had been recognized, allowing quite different truth to appear."

Roberto Unger assigns an earlier idea of architectural transcendence as a system of representation of God's relation to man as blankness, vastness, and pointing to a world outside of this world. The present architecture, he posits, has added two techniques of pouring spirit into matter, incoherence, and incongruity. These mark the absence of the structure-making and structure-breaking self that wants a building to be useful but that cannot contain him. The significance of these two qualities registers the absence of the structure-making and structure-breaking self,

> The building wants to be useful to him while also registering that it is incapable of containing him. It is by such inventions and such a vision rather than by ironic distancing and escapist decorativism that contemporary architecture will have something to say to the future.

The suggestion might be that these "truths" formed under the discipline imposed by and around the activities associated with the plague, might well be broken, that the loneliness of the self finds its escape by reimagining its interiors. In David Foster Wallace's short story "The Soul is Not a Smithy" the narrator tells the story of a horrific event which he witnesses only at the periphery of his conscious self in the middle of a civics class where the lessons of the "founding Fathers" are taught to a group of students in not so distant time which was "not a time of lax discipline or disorder." The narrator drifts in and out of the scene of potential trauma by staring through a window of safety glass, which makes up a grid through which his imagination takes flight:

> That is to say that anything in any way remarkable in the view outside—such as a piece of vivid litter blowing from one wire square to the next, or a city bus flowing stolidly from right to left through the lowest three horizontal columns of squares—became the impetus for privately imagined films' or cartoons' storyboards, in which each of the remaining squares of the window's wire mesh could be used to continue and deepen the panels' narrative—the ordinary-looking C.P.T. bus in fact commandeered by Batman's then-archnemesis, the Red Commando, who in an interior view in successive squares holds hostage, among others, Miss Vlastos, several blind children from the State School for the Blind and Deaf, and my terrified older brother and his piano teacher, Mrs. Doudna, until the moving bus is penetrated by Batman and (behind his small decorative mask) a markedly familiar looking Robin, through a series of acrobatic rope and grappling hook maneuvers each one of which filled and animated one reticulate square of the window and then was frozen in tableau as my attention moved on to the next panel, and so on.[15]

This required intense and difficult concentration, which, he tells us had no resemblance to daydreaming. The narrator breaks through all the conventions that might construct modern ideas of the self: civics lessons, Freudian trauma, even that activity of reading itself, all told in a vivid recall of the smallest of details which might provide hints or clues or portals through which the unfolding narrative of the window restructures. This is a possible way out of the interiors of discipline. This is also what we might call madness.

Yesterday
… I was walking down the street, apparently alone, when I came upon a very young girl, probably two or three, out in her front yard alone. She was talking to a flower.
Dawn

Notes
1   Moses Mendelssohn, "The Sublime and the Naïve in the Fine Sciences" (1761), p. 193.
2   Michel Foucault, "Panopticism," excerpted in *Rethinking Architecture: A Reader in Cultural Theory*, edited by Neal Leach. London and New York: Routledge, 1997, p. 356.
3   Walter Isaacson, *Leonardo da Vinci*. Simon & Schuster; Reprint edition. 2018, p.103.
4   Edmund Burke, Section VII. VASTNESS.

5   Henry David Thoreau (2016).Walden, p.124.

6   Peter Sloterdijk, "The Crystal Palace", 2005. Translated by Michael Daffoch, University of Windsor, 2008. In the *Global Inner Space of Capital: For a Philosophical Theory of Globalization)*. Frankfurt am Main: Suhrkamp, 2005.

7   Peter Sloterdijk, *In the World Interior of Capital: Towards a Philosophical Theory of Globalization* p. 171.

8   Walter Benjamin, [W6a,7] quoted in *The Arcades Project/Walter Benjamin.* Cambridge, MA and London: The Belknap Press of Harvard University Press, 1999, p. 631.

9   M. R. O'Conno, "How Do Animals Keep from Getting Lost?, *New Yorker,* May 28, 2016.

10   Lewis Carrol, "The Hunting of the Snark".

11   Donald J. Trump, speaking to reporters.

12   Frederic Jameson, *Postmodernism, or the Cultural Logic of Late Capitalism*, excerpted in Leach, p. 242.

13   Stanley Kubrick, from 1968 *Playboy* interview by Eric Nordern, https://www.brainpickings.org/2012/07/26/stanley-kubrick-playboy-interview/

14   Trump at a press conference, when asked if "U.S. schools should be preparing for a coronavirus spreading."

15   David Foster Wallace, "The Soul Is Not a Smithy." In *Oblivion: Stories.* New York, Boston: Little Brown and Company, 2004.

Afterword

The Birds of Paris, Las Vegas

In March 2020, I embarked on a research trip to Las Vegas to document interior urban spaces for this book, but my journey ultimately took an unexpected turn. It was the early days of the COVID-19 pandemic in the United States, and the country had just begun grappling with how to handle what ultimately would become a global emergency. At that time, Americans were masking, but had continued traveling as normal. Without a coordinated national policy, individual states were taking vastly different approaches to public safety. As there were no restrictions on air travel at that point, I decided to follow through with my planned visit. I looked forward to meeting my brother in Las Vegas and once again experience its fantastical indoor urbanism – spaces that are perhaps among the most literal, extensive, and intentionally designed forms of the phenomenon on Earth.

After arriving at McCarren International Airport on a morning flight from Chicago, I headed to The Strip to stroll through some of its many interiorized streetscapes. Beginning at The Venetian, my route would pass through Caesar's Palace and Bellagio en route to the Paris, Las Vegas Hotel. The Strip was packed as usual with its diverse mix of visitors from around the globe. As the morning of March 16th transitioned into the early afternoon, crowds began to noticeably thin by the time I had arrived at Paris, Las Vegas. After checking-in for a 5-day stay and not sensing anything out of the ordinary, I walked through its massive podium building which houses a fantasy montage of Parisian parks, streets, and alleyways. Here, it remains perpetually late in the afternoon with blue skies and a spring-like 72F degrees. Sitting on a park bench eating my *pain au chocolat* beneath an interiorized leg of the Eiffel Tower, a pair of sparrows swooped down to perch beside me. Startled, I thought, "Is Paris, Las Vegas such a believable facsimile of the outdoors that even the birds are confused?" Soaking in the atmosphere of this utopian and fun but rather bizarre place, I wondered, "What would Fredric Jameson think of Paris, Las Vegas?"

In his seminal critique of the Los Angeles Bonaventure Hotel, Jameson explores the depthlessness, pastiche, and fragmentation of subjects – key aspects of postmodern culture – and challenges the traditional dichotomy of "high culture" versus popular culture. In the postmodern era, boundaries between high and low culture increasingly blurred as kitsch, mass media, and high culture blended to form a diverse, all-encompassing consumer society. Jameson contends that postmodernism is not just a cultural force but transformed into a broader consumer product. Aesthetic production became integrated into the production of general consumer goods as constant demand for new products with aesthetic novelty played a crucial societal role. Highlighting the aesthetics most linked to the economic system, Jameson points specifically to architecture with its connection with real estate and development. This dynamic spawns a wave of postmodern buildings, perhaps best exemplified by the ubiquitousness and grandeur of late 20th century shopping malls, as well as the hyperspace podium of John Portman's otherworldly Los Angeles Bonaventure Hotel.

As my thoughts bounced between Portman and Jameson, I strolled along a cobblestone interior street, past a stage set-like rendition of the Quartier Asiatique in Paris, and then boarded an elevator for my room on the 28th floor. About an hour later, my room phone rang, "Mr. Marinic, this is guest services, we are calling on behalf of the Las Vegas municipal government which has asked us to inform our guests to remain in their rooms and only leave for essential needs. We apologize for any inconvenience that this may cause you." Clearly, this trip would not go as planned. I ventured down to the podium to pick up something to drink. The "streets" of the podium base were nearly entirely empty and an eerie desolation shrouded the typically bustling space. The rest of the evening would be uncharacteristically quiet at Paris, Las Vegas.

The next morning, my phone rang, "Mr. Marinic, this is the front desk. We are calling to inform you that the State of Nevada has ordered the closure of all hotels on The Strip by 5pm. You will regrettably need to check out before that time. We sincerely apologize for this inconvenience."

Shortly thereafter, my brother canceled his flight from Los Angeles after hearing news of closures in Las Vegas. At that moment, gazing out at the 'Eiffel Tower,' I personally sensed how the world around us would radically change in such a short period of time.

The COVID-19 pandemic was confirmed to have reached the state of Nevada on March 5, 2020. Because of mounting concerns about coronavirus respiratory diseases, Nevada governor Steve Sisolack ordered the closure of all non-essential businesses across the state on March 17, 2020, the day after I had arrived in Las Vegas. Our workplaces, neighborhoods, gathering spaces, and homes would soon be fundamentally transformed as everyday life in the midst of COVID-19 sparked anxiety, fear, and frustration at a global scale. I immediately rebooked by flight back east, checked out of Paris, Las Vegas that afternoon, and left for the airport.

There would ultimately be appropriate time to debrief, to look carefully at all aspects of this pandemic, and to rethink our approaches. But in the early days, global society began focusing all of its energy on defeating COVID-19 and the challenges associated with it. Across the globe, much effort would center on shuttering public buildings and other enclosed spaces that housed large numbers of people. Many of those types of buildings and spaces have been thoughtfully examined in this book. While nothing is more important than ensuring public health and safety, I mourned what this pandemic would mean in the short and long term not only for society but for cities and interior urbanism, the theme of this book.

Although my truncated trip to Las Vegas ultimately derailed a closer look at its fantastical approach to interior urbanism, the best research, as they say, often leads where one least expects. The COVID-19 pandemic has indisputably shaped the life experience of a generation. Its impact extended globally, affecting millions through direct illness or the indirect consequences of economic shifts, public health mandates, and alterations in the workplace. As the pandemic raged worldwide, COVID-19 would be studied in architecture, planning, and design schools to envision alternative futures for our built environment. How has this period changed urban life as well as the work of architects, planners, and designers in relation to shaping the urban futures? The short response is that COVID has fostered innovation in placemaking and the hybridization of outdoor-indoor space. Regarding urban life and the work of architects, planners, and designers, the COVID experience has fostered openness to new ideas and accelerated existing trends like increased reliance on video communication, online shopping, and food deliveries. Yet, persistent challenges still pose significant hurdles, particularly regarding the ways in which we plan to accommodate future pandemics with buildings that can flexibly accommodate disruption.

By April 2020, the complexities of the COVID-19 situation and its long term implications for architecture, planning, and design were becoming clearer. At that time, vaccines were projected to be available within six to 18 months, and indeed, the Pfizer-BioNTech vaccine received emergency authorization nine months later. Faced with a critical period where inaction risked numerous casualties and overwhelmed healthcare systems, countries across the globe adopted a diverse range of strategies to manage and, in some cases, significantly suppress the virus. Terms like social and physical distancing that were once confined to public health circles became widely recognized during this transformative period. These policies placed specifically dramatic pressures on public buildings, transit systems, and various forms of interior urbanism.

When I initially penned my early lockdown thoughts at Paris, Las Vegas in March 2020, the looming economic repercussions, travel disruptions, supply chain challenges, and heightened stress were already evident. Some of these challenges stemmed directly from the pandemic, while others were likely consequences of the varied and sometimes misguided response measures. Initial projections anticipated a grim scenario of two million COVID-19 deaths in the United States by October 2020 without intervention. However, the actual death toll by year-end amounted to 350,000 people. The emergence of more contagious or lethal variants preceded widespread vaccine availability, and in some places, vaccination efforts were hindered by politicization, resulting in fewer inoculations than anticipated. State governments grappled with balancing health protection and economic activity with conflicts dampening the influence of public health agencies. As the two-year mark approached, deaths in the United States neared one million.

Implementing comprehensive and collaborative approaches proved to be politically challenging in the United States. Early in the pandemic, New York showcased a high-density city where the population cooperated effectively to combat COVID with expanded restaurant areas on sidewalks. These new 'indoor-outdoor' environments created the effect of popup arcaded streets, while residents embraced early mask-wearing that successfully kept COVID at bay. In contrast, some regions in the United States saw the breakdown of social cooperation during this crisis, revealing the difficulty of fostering collective efforts for healthier environments.

Similar challenges affected other nations with varying nuances. China, experiencing the first COVID cases in late 2019, initiated its first Wuhan lockdown in January 2020 and employed a suppression strategy with strict border controls. In Africa, vaccine distribution initially lagged, adding to the complexity of navigating a global pandemic across diverse geographies, political systems, and economic circumstances. In contrast, the nationally coordinated COVID responses of Canada, Australia, and New Zealand were more comprehensive, and thus, resulted in fewer casualties per capita.

By late 2020, there were premature predictions about the demise of urban life and indoor public spaces, a viewpoint that seemed short-sighted. Nevertheless, it was evident that densely populated areas with sprawling interiorized environments connected to underground transit systems might face more significant challenges, and a prolonged period of suppression could reshape long-term urban living patterns. The shift to remote work, already underway, emerged as a pivotal factor that could potentially foster a supportive environment to significantly improve people's lives. The prospect of increased evictions and job losses was widespread. Governments globally passed substantial legislation to sustain economies, redefining essential workers and potentially altering their long-term valuation. In the United States, extensive public health measures included eviction bans and restructuring workplaces. COVID underscored the importance of human connections, emphasizing mutual responsibility and the ability for citizens to take action in the public sphere. Nevertheless, it was clear that, although the pandemic affected everyone, its impact would vary widely across different regions and socio-economic strata.

Reflecting on the recent post-pandemic era, notable shifts have occurred in preexisting urban trends and indoor urban environments, with certain changes proving enduring. While a return to familiar practices reemerged, some transformations are poised to persist. Notably, the role of physical space has evolved considerably across scales, with face-to-face meetings often yielding to online forums, while local outdoor environments have gained greater importance. And while the trajectory of many trends remains uncertain and is likely to vary across cultures and regions, four key points nevertheless stand out including: 1) the heightened importance of hybridized indoor-outdoor spaces, 2) the shifting complexities of comprehensive mass transit, 3) the interactions between virtual and physical spaces, and 4) the persistent challenge of fostering public life.

Recognizing the significance of open outdoor spaces and hybrid indoor-outdoor environments has been a prevailing theme for all. Cities globally responded by transforming the right-of-way of streets into temporary or permanent public spaces that allowed for recreation and play. Parks also saw renewed use for socializing and events, contributing to enhanced pedestrianization of street space. These initiatives, some temporary and others enduring, reshaped the public realm and extended beyond the pandemic peak.

While the importance of outdoor access has always been acknowledged, it became imperative during the pandemic. Initially, there was confusion regarding density and crowding, with a realization that crowded indoor spaces posed particular risks. Understanding that COVID could spread through the air, especially in poorly ventilated and densely populated areas, underscored the critical need for public urban spaces while interiorized environments at all scales were simultaneously opened onto the outdoors.

Although public outdoor spaces are often lauded, the pandemic shed new light on the value of private outdoor areas connected to residential interior spaces. Balconies, patios, and small fenced yards provide spaces for activities for relaxation, food preparation, drying laundry, socializing, and safe play — activities that are not often well-supported in public spaces. Those least likely to have such private areas include renters and low-income owners in multi-unit dwellings, while nursing home residents often lack accessible open spaces. The pandemic clarified that private outdoor space should be recognized as a necessity, not a luxury.

The future of public transit remains uncertain, partly due to pre-existing changes in the transportation sector, including the shared economy, autonomous vehicles, and fleet electrification. Concerns about the contagion led to a decline in transit usage, and not everyone has returned. Underground systems, often with extensive interconnected subterranean pedestrian-retail networks, are particularly fragile to pandemic disruptions. The shift toward decentralization and remote work has altered transportation demand patterns, shaping concerns characterized by considerable uncertainty with further socio-economic strain on the horizon.

COVID proved that the internet has fundamentally reshaped our use of physical space. Working from home experienced a surge and appears to be a permanent fixture, empowering a segment of the workforce to live far beyond costly urban cores. Despite the historic prominence of central business districts, commercial office space in the United States and elsewhere is already relatively decentralized. Nevertheless, increasing decentralization creates significant challenges for the viability of interiorized urban environments situated in urban cores. While telework could potentially trigger unchecked sprawl, it offers the potential to breathe new life into shrinking cities and rural areas, opening up more affordable housing options for those who might otherwise be confined to major metropolitan areas. While not all jobs lend themselves to remote work, off-site employees stimulate local demand for goods and services.

Furthermore, as in-person engagement in public processes makes a comeback, access to improved virtual and hybrid alternatives offers enhanced long-term accessibility for diverse groups. Parents with young children, persons with disabilities, and those with unconventional work hours have found connecting in innovative ways most beneficial. At the same time, the surge in online shopping poses challenges for brick-and-mortar stores and shopping malls, particularly impacting local retail areas as virtual competition contributes to empty storefronts. Yet, a noticeable though modest shift back to physical retail environments has occurred.

In 2023, I returned to Paris, Las Vegas to complete my unfinished research for this book. Walking through its hyperspace lobby after checking-in, I meadered into Le Boulevard, a collection of shops arrayed like an arcaded space centered on a stained-glass dome. As I entered the highly ornamented space which takes its design cues from the famous Galeries Lafayette department store, I gazed toward a fountain at its center and noticed something moving. There, at the edge of a cast-iron Art Nouveau-inspired vessel, two birds perched and took sips of water. Feeling both awestruck and incredulous, Could this actually be that pair of swallows I saw over two years ago, still trapped inside but thriving? Or might an actual flock live within Paris, Las Vegas, finding the indoors more agreeable than the ever-warming harshness outside? Here, the birds are sheltered with ample food and water in a climate-controlled paradise, an eternal Spring with no predators. The idiosyncratic nooks and fairytale rooftops of this place, with its fully pedestrianized spaces free from traffic and car exhaust, might be better than the actual outdoors. So, is the interior urbanism of Paris, Las Vegas, perhaps, a *better* form of urbanism for Las Vegas?

Over four years have passed since COVID-19 disrupted global life. In the United States, the pandemic claimed the lives of over one million people and millions more continue grappling with long-term health problems. As COVID raged, much of normal life came to a halt, in part because of official lockdowns, but largely driven by fear of infection that kept people home. Looking ahead, COVID has broadened people's imaginations regarding future possibilities, urging a holistic approach beyond an immediate crisis. While the focus is often on airborne diseases, professional architects, planners, and designers must recognize the need to address various transmission modes through hybridized design responses in the built environment. Although COVID prompted experimentation with new strategies across scales and stakeholders, in hindsight, many measures seem to have been too narrowly focused.

Truly comprehensive approaches involve a simultaneous awareness of physical spaces, government policies, collaborative processes, and ethical considerations. In cities, they must encompass diverse sectors like transit, green infrastructure, adapted buildings, and economic development, prioritizing the needs of vulnerable populations and addressing larger processes of environmental degradation and climate change. Moving beyond the emergency measures born of the pandemic, achieving more flexible buildings and responsive forms of interior urbanism requires innovation and collaboration. While disruption is often challenging, the permeable outdoor-indoor experimentations of the early post-COVID years demonstrate that change is indeed possible, and much like the birds of Paris, Las Vegas, that interior urbanism remains surprisingly resilient.

Index

Note: *Italic* page numbers refer to figures.